The Modern Prince and The Modern Sage

The Modern Prince and The Modern Sage

Transforming Power and Freedom

Edited by

Ananta Kumar Giri

SAGE www.sagepublications.com
Los Angeles • London • New Delhi • Singapore • Washington DC

First published in 2009 by

SAGE Publications India Pvt Ltd
B 1/I-1, Mohan Cooperative Industrial Area
Mathura Road, New Delhi 110 044, India
www.sagepub.in

SAGE Publications Inc
2455 Teller Road
Thousand Oaks, California 91320, USA

SAGE Publications Ltd
1 Oliver's Yard, 55 City Road
London EC1Y 1SP, United Kingdom

SAGE Publications Asia-Pacific Pte Ltd
33 Pekin Street
#02-01 Far East Square
Singapore 048763

Published by Vivek Mehra for SAGE Publications India Pvt Ltd, typeset in 10/12pt Aldine401 BT by Star Compugraphics Private Limited, Delhi and printed at Chaman Enterprises, New Delhi.

Library of Congress Cataloging-in-Publication Data

The modern prince and the modern sage: transforming power and freedom / edited by Ananta Kumar Giri; with a foreword by Johan Galtung.
    p. cm.
Includes bibliographical references and index.
1. Power (Social sciences) 2. Freedom. 3. Social change. I. Giri, Ananta Kumar.

| HN49.P6M63 | 303.3—dc22 | 2009 | 2008048174 |

ISBN: 978-81-7829-827-6 (Hb)

The SAGE Team: Sugata Ghosh, Vikas Jain, Anju Saxena and Trinankur Banerjee

For
Gaura Devi, Lech Walesa, Aung San Suu Kyi,
Nelson Mandela, Mikhail Gorbachev, Thich Nhat Hahn,
and millions of children, women and men struggling for
freedom, dignity, peace and soulful togetherness in our times of
war and terror.

Contents

PART I
RECONSTITUTING POWER AND FREEDOM:
MODERNITY AND BEYOND

PART III
Transforming Power and Freedom:
New Horizons

List of Tables

List of Figures

Foreword
On the Political: An Introduction

Ananta Kumar Giri has edited a fascinating book about power and politics around two key figures, the Modern Prince and the Modern Sage. How modern and how timeless can be discussed, but they are easily conjured up for our inner eyes, dressed in the garbs of their age. A third one is missing, the Modern Merchant, for instance in Venice. Sad for him that he did not make it to the book. But he can draw some comfort from the present era, no doubt that of the merchant in Sarkar's sense, of the *vaisya*, not the *brahmin* sage, nor the *kshatriya* prince. Like the others he is now dressed in a grey flannel suit with white shirt and blue tie, if not in jeans and checkered shirt. Their public persona have converged, but their keys to power and politics have remained the same, the power of bullets for the Prince, of ideas for the Sage and of money for the Merchant.

Like most intellectuals, or so I presume, I prefer the Sage because that is where my own ambitions are located. In this short introduction I would like to sketch why I hold the Sage approach to the political to be at a higher level than the other two. They have their roles to play. But that is also all they have; theirs not to change reality unless we are dealing with a rare combination, the Prince, or Merchant, who is also a Sage.

Let me illustrate building on the fable known to all Italian school children, *Il lupo di Gubbio*, The Wolf from Gubbio (a little village in the Apennines, close to Assisi)—but sadly distant from what passes for princes and sages in Italian politics. The winter was atrocious. So was the wolf, starving, and then descending on a village, eating one of the villagers.

Enters the Sage, Saint Francis, Francesco d'Assisi. Brother Wolf he says, 'what's the matter. 'I am starving', the wolf says. 'But why did you eat that nice person in the village?' 'The only thing there was', the wolf says, 'what else is there?' 'Let me see', Francesco says, leaving the wolf, entering the village.

'Sisters and brothers', he addresses them, 'what's the matter?' 'That terrible wolf', they answer in unison, 'he just ate one of us'. 'Very bad', Francesco says, 'but let me ask you a question: he is hungry and you always have some leftovers from your meals, could you imagine putting them in a bowl and place the bowl at night at the outskirts of the village?' 'OK', they say, 'but only once, to see whether it works. We really want to kill him!'

Francesco goes back to the wolf, tells what happened and asks the wolf whether he could imagine helping himself from that bowl? 'OK', he answers, but only once, to see whether it works.

So bowl and wolf meet, the content passes from the village bowl to the wolf's bowels, a happy, contented wolf. The experiment is repeated, and repeated, and the villagers find in the wolf an impeccable garbage dump, and the wolf in the village a bottomless source of leftovers. The wolf gradually conquers space and time by venturing further into the village, even at dusk and dawn, testing the waters. In the end the wolf is seated at the table, helping himself to his new favourites, occasionally donating an animal or two from his meager winter catch. And at the very end they are all dancing, brothers and sisters, with Francesco.

However, when using this story to inspire a workshop of general staff Italian officers to solve the Iraq problem they said: 'we are not Francesco'. And there were even two wolves, Bush and Saddam. Dear Reader, solve that one; be a Sage, not a Prince!

Francesco, the Sage set the tone by humanizing both parties, the killer as well as those out to kill, as brothers and sisters. Using shuttle diplomacy he emphatically explores their goals, food and survival, both legitimate, and uses his Sage creativity to bridge that apparent incompatibility. He transcended, into a new reality of conviviality, and even helped solving an environmental problem.

What would the Prince have done? Depending on whom he considers the most valuable future ally, the villagers or the wolves (assuming there are more wolves where he comes from), he would have given the green light, even the order, Kill the wolf!, or Go ahead, serve yourself from the villagers! But that is not politics defined as the art of the impossible, a Francesco making the incompatible compatible. This is merely politicking, creeping on the belly, licking some crumbs from the table of the Sage.

What would the Merchant have done? Bargaining, and then a deal, some kind of compromise. How much is the wolf willing to pay for not being killed and what is the commission fee for a merchant who brokers that deal? Or, how much are the villagers willing to pay for not being killed? Killing is sweet, but money is also sweet and more lasting, and the merchant might become quite rich if he brokers both deals at the same time.

The Prince injects orders as his approach to social order, the Merchant greases the system with money, and the Sage lifts the system to a higher level through the power of ideas. As everybody says, if it had not been impossible, then where is the art? Art is by definition to transcend, to create a new artistic reality. If it is just repetition then it is merely decorating, which is to art what politicking is to politics.

The political is transcendence. And for transcendence a Sage is needed. To prevail a Prince suffices, for compromise a Merchant.

Let us take on another example, another piece of Christianity, the Passion of the Christ, Matthew 27, to show the Prince rather than the Sage at work. We see the Passion as a drama with six roles, ala Pirandello, with well-known actors and well-known goals:

- **The Father:** the Lord out to prove his love of humanity by sacrificing his Son and to prove that His will is the Law;
- **The Son:** Jesus, the Christ, whose kingdom is not of this world but within and in the afterlife, wanting to be released from his fate, crying his *Eli, Eli, lama sabachtani*—my God, my God, why have you forsaken me (Matthew 27:46)—possibly hoping for an angel to intercede like the Angel of God did when Abraham was about to sacrifice Isaac (Genesis 22:17, in the *Akedah*);
- **Barabbas:** the notorious criminal whose goal is to be set free;
- **Pontius Pilate:** the governor of that Roman Empire province whose goal is to govern, with the consent of the people;
- **Caiaphas:** the High Priest, whose goal, like for his people, is a kingdom of this world, an Israel, a Zion;
- **The Roman Empire**, embodied in the Emperor whose goal is expansion and eternal life for the empire.

Let us let loose as mediators the two Marias, the Mother and the Magdalena, with the task of the art of the impossible. But let us first take note of what in fact happened: Jesus is sacrificed, Barabbas is released, Pilate continues as governor, Caiaphas gets rid of a charismatic competitor. And in the background are the two columns of princely power, the power over life and death, the Lord and the Roman Empire, both untouched by the Golgata drama. Drama unfolds, but the sources of so many massacres ordered by God and of so much deprivation of freedom and subsistence built into the Roman Empire survive. Who said that the message is only in what changes, not (also) in what remains constant—like in John 3:16:

> For God loved the world so much that he gave his only Son so that anyone who believes in him shall not perish but have eternal life.

A latter day version, there are many between Golgata and Iraq:

> For Bush loved the world so much that he gave his only soldiers so that anyone who believes in Bush shall not perish but have eternal empire.

A highly unacceptable story thus interpreted. We are dealing with ultimate level politics, so let us see what the two Marias might get out of this seemingly impossible situation.

A conflict with six actors cannot be reduced to 15 bilateral conflicts, like that between wolf and villagers. There is something holistic about it. But let us assume that the Father is persuaded by the shouting of his son at about three o'clock to send the Angel of God. Jesus is released by the will of God, Barabbas by the will of the people, and Pilate is washing his hands. Building on the differences between their kingdoms Caiaphas may be persuaded to accept Jesus as a Minister of interior and posterior religious affairs not meddling too much into the here and now. There is a job prospect for the brawny Barabbas: as the Minister's bodyguard. Matthew 26–27 gives ample testimony to the need for some security.

And Pilate is easily persuaded to continue as governor of an ever more autonomous province, in close cooperation with Caiaphas and his people, in a marriage of interest rather than love.

With all four relatively content time then comes to turn to those two pillars of princely power. 'I'll talk to my Father', Jesus says, and 'I'll talk to the Emperor', Pilate says. And the Marias have some ideas: tell your Father that he is better off with his son alive than dead for the colossal task soon to be written up in Matthew 28:19-20, and tell the Emperor that more true strength can be derived from humane flexibility than from rigidity.

As a conclusion God inspires humanity by compassion rather than doctrine. And the Roman Empire becomes a community of equals.

Let us conclude after these exercises in the soft Christianity of the Sage, and the hard Christianity of the Princes, with an all time favourite, evidently more Muslim:

> Once upon a time a mullah was on his way on a camel to Mecca.
>
> Coming to an oasis he saw three men standing there, crying. So he stopped the camel, and asked, My children, what is the matter? And they

answered, Our father just passed away, and we loved him so much. But, said the mullah, I am sure he loved you too, and no doubt he has left something behind for you?

The three men answered: Yes, he did indeed, he left behind camels. And in his will it is stated 1/2 to the eldest son, 1/3 to the second and 1/9 to the youngest. We love camels, we agree with the parts to each. But there is a problem: he left behind 17 camels and we have been to school, we know that 17 is a prime number. Loving camels, we cannot divide them.

The mullah thought for a while, and then said, I give you my camel, then you have 18. And they cried, No, you cannot do that, you are on your way to something important. The mullah interrupted them, My children, take the camel, go ahead.

So they divided 18 by 2 and the eldest son got 9 camels, 18 by 3 and the second son got 6 camels, 18 by 9 and the youngest son got 2 camels: a total of $9 + 6 + 2 = 17$ camels. One camel was standing there, alone: the mullah's camel. The mullah said: Are you happy? Well, then, maybe I can get my camel back?

And the three men, full of gratitude, said, of course, not quite understanding what had happened. The mullah blessed them, mounted his camel, and the last they saw was a tiny cloud of dust, quickly settling in the glowing evening sun.

That mullah was a Sage, like Francesco and the two Marias as here portrayed. There are many of them, probably many more than there are princes and merchants, and probably most of them less famous, mainly found close to the grassroots and maybe more often female than male, at least in the spirit.

The reader will find this book a treasure trove of wisdom, leaving a Thucydides, a Macchicavelli and a Hobbes with all their tricky, violent advice for the Princes behind—granted that there may be some jewels also in that slam. Long live the Sage!

Alfaz del Pi   **Johan Galtung**

Preface

All people are children when they sleep
There's no war in them then
They open their hands and breathe
In that quiet rhythm heaven has given them.
They pucker their lips like small children
And open their hands halfway
Soldiers and statesmen, servants and masters
The stars stand guard
And haze veils the sky
A few hours when no one will do anybody harm
If only we could speak to another then
When our hearts are half-open flowers
Words like golden bees
Would drift in
God, teach them the language of sleep

Jacobsen (2007: 45).

No mere modification of our existing world view and the manner of human life that results from it can save us; what is required is a critical evaluation of the very foundations of modern culture and a new openness and honesty concerning the repressed fears that fuel beliefs and actions that are driving us to the edge of catastrophe.

Smith (2007: 73).

Life is self-fulfilment which moves upon a ground of mutuality; it involves a mutual use of one by the other, in the end of all by all. The whole question is whether this shall be done on the lower basis of the ego attended by strife, friction and collision with whatever checks and controls, or whether it can be done by a higher law of our being which shall discover a means of reconciliation, free reciprocity and unity.

Aurobindo (1919: 603).

This book has been a long journey beginning with an initial conversation I had in the fall of 1997 with Professor Ashok Vohra, then Member Secretary, Indian Council of Philosophical Research, at a very interesting and creative Gurudwara, Gurudwar Gyan Prakash, Ludhiana. Sant Baba Sucha Singh who is no more with us physically had created new spaces of dialogue in the Gurudwara and we were there to discuss the issue of concept of mind. It is in this radiating Gurudwara and in the community of seeking souls that the seeds of this book were sown and it came to a provisional blossoming when some of the contributors of the book assembled at TMAM Research and Orientation Center in Kottayam in April 1999. Since then this seed has taken roots with the flow of love and life and my journey around the world in the last ten years has been blessed by my meeting with many kind and enriching souls who then have very graciously agreed to join us in this journey.

The idea of this book grew in a Gurudwara and it is a joy on our part now to humbly present this flower to seeking humanity on Baisakhi day. Power and freedom are perennial human questions but at this moment of growing violence and ecological disaster, there is an epochal need to foundationally reconstitute these categories and be engaged with new modes of relationships of power and freedom which embody beauty, dignity, solidarity and responsibility. We hope that this flower is a humble contribution to this epochal search for new ways of thinking and being together.

It is now our joy to humbly dedicate this flower to humanity and to the immortal work and loving spirit of Gaura Devi, Lech Walesa, Aung San Suu Kyi, Nelson Mandela, Mikhail Gorbachev, Thich Nhat Hanh and millions of children, women and men who are striving and struggling for dignity, peace and soulful togetherness in this troubled time of ours. Four decades ago Gaura Devi had inspired the birth of Chipko movement in Uttarakhand which then had a world-wide influence in shaping the emerging environmental awareness around the world. When powerful axe men arrived to cut down trees from her village, Reni Gaura Devi told her fellow women: 'My dear sisters! Now we can realize why our men folk have been taken away to the court on a false case. But even though our men folk are not here are we so helpless? Let us hug our trees and let the axe men fell us first.' The axe men returned but this courageous act of resistance by putting one's body and soul on the front together inspired new modes of resistance and realization of consciousness around the world. I recall warmly the night I had spent with Gaura Devi, her son and his family in Reni in the summer of 1987. More than two decades have passed by now and Gaura Devi is not here physically to see this flower. Let us pay our tribute to her immortal spirit.

Gaura Devi is probably little known in the world but it is these little known people who are fighting against tyranny of many kinds in myriad ways and helping us realize that there is a larger purpose in life beyond acquisition of money and power. Lech Walesa was also little known outside Gdansk before the emergence of Solidarity in 1980. But he and Solidarity contributed to peaceful overthrow of communist dictatorship in Poland, Eastern Europe and the Soviet Union and realization of dignity of people. As Walesa tells us in his autobiography *A Way of Hope*:

> Though we are caught in the vise of a fossilized system, a product of an outdated partition of our planet, in August 1980 we overthrew an all-powerful political taboo and proclaimed the dawning of a new era. The Polish nation achieved this as a force before the eyes of the world without threats, without violence or a drop of the opponents blood shed; no ideology was advanced, no economic or institutional theory: we were simply seeking human dignity. In both camps, free and unfree, this episode has been regarded as a revolutionary act. But we saw nothing revolutionary in what happened. We merely felt that after so many years of living upside down, we were at last beginning to walk on our feet (Walesa 1987: 2).

Walesa and his co-workers' peaceful struggle in Solidarity is inspiring though one wishes that he and Solidarity should have continued this struggle now especially when Poland has made an uncritical turn to capitalism and European and American geopolitical interest. At the same time what he writes challenges us not to despair:

> I do my best to look on political events in the same light as my personal problems, and try to resolve them similarly. I never take a tragic view of life. Even if nothing in this world really depends upon us, that shouldn't excuse us from putting all our efforts in a dignified way, into finding the best possible solutions, and the most honest ones (ibid.: 3–4).

The struggles of Gaura Devi and Lech Walesa resonate with the exemplary struggles of Aung San Suu Kyi, Nelson Mandela, Mikhail Gorbachev and Thich Nhat Hanh. Aung San Suu Kyi is still struggling for freedom of her people in Burma where nothing has much changed even after the recent non-violent protest and martyrdom of many monks and people. But for me reading her *Freedom from Fear* nearly fifteen years ago was a deep experience which in a way had made me reflect upon the challenge of freedom politically and philosophically. My approach to freedom was also shaped by the exemplary struggle of Nelson Mandela whose *Long Walk to Freedom* was also an enriching experience to be with. Like Suu Kyi and Mandela almost around the same time Mikhail Gorbachev was and continues to be an inspiring presence. Two decades ago while doing graduate work in the States reading his *Perestroika* was a lesson in thinking and imagining beyond the settled. Gorbachev gave voice to millions of people struggling for freedom and in this struggle though he lost politically he has not forgotten his native spirit of festivity and cosmopolitanism. Gorbachev (2005: 9) tells us in his dialogue with Daisaku Ikeda *Moral Lessons of Twentieth Century*: 'Probably the wisdom of life consists in being able to enjoy a festival, even when everything else looks dark.' This native wisdom of Gorbachev finds a resonance in the native wisdom of Thich Nhat Hanh, who, as a remarkable teacher of peace from a village in Vietnam, reminds people that when everything else looks dark, they cannot forget to take steps towards peace where peace is the way; as suggested by one of his many books, *Peace is Every Step*. In his recent *The Art of Power* Thich Nhat Hanh (2007: 1) invites us to explore another dimension of power which is in tune with the spirit of the book.

> Our society is founded on a very limited description of power, namely wealth, professional success, fear, physical strength, military might and political control. My dear friends, there is another kind of power: the power to be happy right in the present moment, freedom from addiction, fear, despair, discrimination, anger and ignorance. This power is the birth right of any human being, whether celebrated or unknown, rich or poor, strong or weak. Let us explore this extraordinary kind of power.

I have not yet had the blessing to meet this remarkable teacher of humanity but during my journey I have had the blessing of fellowship of many of his co-walkers notably Helena Tagesson who is one of our contributors in this book.

I now thank from the bottom of my heart to all those who have made this co-journey and blossoming possible. They are innumerable and one cannot thank these kind souls enough and one can only share one's silent gratitude. I thank Rev. Sunny George, then director of TMAM Orientation and Research Center, Kottayam, who so graciously offered to host us when at the last minute we had nowhere to go and to Professor Paul Appasamy, then director of Madras Institute of Development Studies, who so generously made some resources possible which facilitated our meeting. I also thank colleagues and staff at Appalachian Center, University of Kentucky; Department of International Relations,

Aalborg University, Denmark; and Institute of Sociology, Albert Ludwig University, Germany where I have spent time as a visiting scholar and visiting professor in the last years which have contributed to the shaping of the book in our hands. I also thank each of our contributors for their generosity and patience. I especially thank Professor Johan Galtung, an inspiring teacher and tireless seeker of peace, for his foreword and Professor Chitta Ranjan Das, an exemplary experimenter in education and human creativity, for his afterword to the book.

We most cordially invite you to join us in this journey and hope this work contributes to our ongoing evolutionary striving to transform power and freedom and create worlds of beauty and dignity.

Baisakhi Day   **Ananta Kumar Giri**
April, 2008   Madras Institute of Development Studies

References

Gorbachev, Mikhail and Daisaku Ikeda. 2005. *Moral Lessons of The Twentieth Century: Gorbachev and Ikeda on Buddhism and Communism.* London: I.B. Tauris.

Hahn, Thich Nhat. 1991. *Peace is Every Step: The Mindfulness of Everyday Life.* NY: Bantam.

———. 2007. *The Art of Power.* NY: Harper Collins.

Jacobsen, Rolf. 2001. *The Roads Have Come to An End Now: Selected and Last Poems of Rolf Jacobsen.* Washington DC: Copper Canyon Press.

Smith, David. 2007. *Moving Towards Emmaus: Hope in a Time of Uncertainty.* London: SCPK.

Sri Aurobindo. 1962 [1919]. *The Ideal of Human Unity: War and Self-Determination.* Pondicherry: Sri Aurobindo Ashram.

Walesa, Lech. 1987. *A Way of Hope: An Autobiography.* NY: Herry Holt & Company.

Acknowledgements

Some of the contributions of the book were published in two special issues on 'Transforming Power and Freedom' in the *Asian Journal of Social Sciences*, Volume 33 (1), 2005 and Volume 34 (1), 2006. I thank its editor Dr. Syed Farid Alatas for his encouragement and its publisher Brill for permission to print the following chapters:

1. Jan Nederveen Pieterse, 'Metamorphoses of Power: From Coercion to Cooperation?'
2. Helena Tagesson, 'A Yearning of the Heart: Spirituality and Politics'.
3. Fred R. Dallmayr, 'A War Against the Turks? Erasmus on War and Peace'.
4. Ananta Kumar Giri, 'Power and Self-Cultivation: Aesthetics, Development Ethics and the Calling of Poverty'.
5. John Clammer, 'Beyond Power: Alternative Conceptions of Being and Reconstitution of Social Theory'.

And also to :

1. S.N. Eisenstadt for contributing an extract from his much larger work on democracy and political theory, *Political Theory in Search of the Political*;
2. Fred R. Dallmayr whose contribution in the volume also forms part of his *Peace Talks* from University of Notre Dame Press;
3. Indian Institute of Advanced Studies, particularly its public relations officer, Mr. A.K. Sharma for helping with a copy of Mrinal Miri's article, 'Gandhi and Empowerment,' originally published in the Institute's IIAS Summer Hill Review;
4. Dietmar Mieth for his contrbution which also appeared in *Towards a New Heaven and a New Earth: Essays in Honor of Elisabeth Schlusser Fiorenza*, New York: Orbis Books, 2003;
5. Abdullahi Ahmed An-Naim for his contribution which is adapted from his essay in Ahmed An-Naim et al. (eds), *Human Rights and Religious Values: An Uneasy Relationship?* Grand Rapids, MI: W.B. Erdmans, 1995.

Introduction

Transforming Power and Freedom

ANANTA KUMAR GIRI

The entire tradition of political theory seems to agree on one basic principle: only 'the one' can rule, whether that one be conceived as the monarch, the state, the nation, the people, or the party. The three traditional forms of government that form the basis of ancient and modern political thought—monarchy, aristocracy, and democracy—reduce, from this perspective, to one single form. Aristocracy may be the rule of the few, but only in so far as these few are united in one single body or voice. Democracy, similarly, can be conceived as the rule of the many or all, but only insofar as they are unified as 'the people' or some such single subject. It should be clear, however, that this mandate of political thought that only the one can rule undermines and negates the concept of democracy. *Democracy, along with aristocracy in this respect, is merely a façade because power is de facto monarchical.*

Hardt & Antonio Negri (2004: 328-329); emphases added.

When my powers clash with the powers of another man they are reduced to nothing; and this is due to the fact the other is, as it were, another me—a creature belonging to the same species that I do and thus endowed with capacities and means that are essentially equal to my own.

Hoffman (1996: 5).

In human life, Suffering is the antitheses of Power, and it is also a more characteristic, and more fundamental element in Life than Power is. [...] Suffering is the essence of Life, because it is the inevitable product of an unresolvable tension between a living creature's essential impulse to try to make itself into the center of the Universe and its essential dependence on the rest of creation and on the Absolute Reality on which all creatures live and move and have their being. On the other hand, human power, in all its forms is limited and, in the last resort, illusory. Therefore any attitude towards Life that idolizes human power is bound to be a wrong attitude towards Suffering and, in consequence, a wrong attitude towards Life itself.

Toynbee (1956: 74).

I

The prince has been the dominant archetypal model of being and becoming in modernity and despite the supposed beheading of the kings in the modern world, as Machiavelli (1981) and Antonio Gramsci (1957), among many others, tell us it is the values of the prince, namely his will to power, that guide us in the modern world rather than the values of an unconditional ethical obligation of the self to the other. Power, politics and empowerment have provided determinant frames of self-constitution and social emancipation in the modern world and they have provided the singular definition of freedom as well. Modernity has been characterized by the ascendancy of politics and a power-model of the human condition over all other modes of being and values of life such as those of virtue, *shraddha* (reverence and love) and *tapashya* (loving meditation for transformation). There, of course, has been a shift in the locus of power in the evolution of modern society. If earlier, power was embodied in the prince as an individual, in the course of history this locus has shifted to institutions and systems of society. But the institutionalization of power in the modern and late-modern world does not mean that it has ushered in more freedom for the subjects since in both the cases, i.e., in the case of the prince and in case of the modern prince—the modern institutionalized locus of power, not only Gramsci's political party—it is power as domination, or in Max Weber's phrase, 'the ability to carry over will against the will of others,' which has guided our thought, practice and conduct.

In fact, the modernist preoccupation with politics and power has been accompanied by very little realization of transformation beyond the capture of power despite thinkers such as Gramsci challenging us: 'An important part of the Modern Prince will have to be devoted to the question of intellectual and moral reform [...]' (Gramsci 1957: 139). Those savants in the modern world such as Erasmus who have provided us with an alternative challenge of being and becoming and who have urged us to strive for freedom and radical reflection without the capture of power and authority and through 'faith in man' have been totally sidetracked by other leaders in religion and politics whose main objective has been capture of power and through this to ensure human emancipation.[1] It is the *weltanschauung* and the will-to-power of these leaders which is noticeable in all movements of emancipation in the modern world whether it is the movement of the liberals or the communists. But after one hundred and fifty years of experience and experiments with such power models of emancipation, freedom and the human condition, we are slowly realizing that capture of power is neither the end all or be all of life and it is certainly not a guarantee for the attainment of a dignified life and the establishment of a 'good society.' It is perhaps for this reason that commentators such as Anthony Giddens (1991) urge us to make a distinction between power politics and life politics where life politics is a politics of self-actualization and is concerned with the question: 'how we should live our lives in emancipated social circumstances.'

But even Giddens cannot explore the logic of self-actualization without the addendum of politics as is the case with another commentator such as Seyla Benhabib (1987) who cannot proceed even a step further in her meditation on norm and utopia without the adjective and the noun—political and politics, without the words such as 'politics of fulfilment' and 'politics of self-transfiguration.' This shows the hegemony of the power-model of the human condition and the prince's will to power in our current thought and practice. This hegemony of a power-perspective on the human condition has recently received a new lease of life from a contemporary master interlocutor such as Michel Foucault whose disciples assert that there is no escape from the circle of power and counter-power and any project of a 'good life' which is determined to put power in its place and strives to actualize an unconditional ethical obligation of the self to the other is doomed to failure to begin with. But in Foucault himself, we also find a realization of the limitation of power in ensuring human emancipation as he himself writes: 'In fact, I have especially wanted to question politics—the questions I am trying to ask are not determined by a pre-established political outlook and do not tend to the realisation of some definite political project' (Foucault 1984: 376). For Foucault,

> In short, it is a matter of starting out search of a different critical philosophy: a philosophy that does not determine the conditions and limits of a knowledge of the object, but the conditions and undefined possibilities of the subject's transformation (Foucault 2005: 526).

In his posthumously published work, *The Hermeneutics of the Subject*, Foucault urges us to realize:

The political, ethical, social, philosophical problem of our day is not try to liberate the individual from the state and its institutions but to liberate us both from the state and the type of individualisation linked to the state. We have to promote new forms of subjectivity [...] (ibid.: 544).

Our present book is concerned with the questions of rethinking and transforming power as a theme in itself and in the light of contemporary transformations in discourse and society. It is born out of a realization that interrogating the modernist faith in politics and power as sole guarantors of human well-being and freedom constitutes an epochal challenge before us in this new century and in our new millennium. It seeks to explore how we can transform power in the late-modern condition of the systematization and institutionalization of power. For example, one key question now is whether only either the route of individual asceticism or democratic transformation of institutions is enough to transform power or does it call for simultaneous work on self-transformation and structural transformation. The book also seeks to explore how we can rethink power and realize its transformative meaning. It seeks to explore the resources it can derive from many different sources—traditional philosophies, religions, spiritual movements, and alternative quests within modernity—in this task of rethinking and reconstruction. For example, when an interlocutor such as Hannah Arendt (quoted in Cohen and Arato 1992: 178) writes that to have power is 'acting in concert, on the basis of making and keeping promises, mutually binding one another, covenanting,' it provides us another mode of being vis-à-vis power— one of 'power with' rather than 'power over.' In the book, we shall have dialogues with such other conceptions of power, for example power as inner liberation as suggested in Dietmar Mieth's essay on Meiker Eckhart in the volume.

But while exploring the transformative contours of power, the book does not propose a simple polarity between power and virtue, the prince and the sage, power as 'evil' and the goodness of wisdom and explores transformation in the context of the complex multidimensional reality and possibility of power. As Stellan Vinthagen echoes the spirit of nuanced transformative engagement with power on the part of many contributors in the volume, 'power is many-faceted and [...] even the will, body and the mind of the resistance fighter is not free from power.' This points to our implication in a field of power. For Judith Butler, power shapes the formation of subjectivity: 'Power not only *acts on* a subject but, in a transitive sense, enacts the subject into being' (Butler 1997: 13).

Though the indispensable force of power in the shaping of subjectivity in many conditions (which make Butler write: 'No individual becomes a subject without first becoming subjected to or undergoing subjection') cannot be summarily dismissed in the name of any *apriori* spiritual enthusiasm, at the same time it does not exhaust all the possibilities of the subject, including her transformational and transcendental dimension. Our implication in the field of power does not lead only to the double subjectivity that Butler talks about: our subjugated subjectivity and our emergent subjectivity shaped by power. Our implication in the field of power is also the very field for transforming the logic of power and working towards a transformational self and society where the goal is realizing what Dallmayr, building on Heidegger, calls a 'power-free' existence (cf. Dallmayr 2001). Butler's view of the subject even in her double subjectivity does not give enough attention to the transcendental dimension of the subject which while being subjugated by power still refuses to surrender and strives for transformation. But here instead of proceeding with a polarity between subjugated and transformative view of self and power, an acknowledgment of our complex implication in the field of power is an indispensable and helpful companion to our political and moral struggles to transform power. In this context the insights of Foucault can be brought transformationally together with insights of experimenters such as Erasmus, Eckhart, Gandhi and Subcommandate Marcos of Zapatista movement who challenge us to go beyond the trappings of power and counter-power.

An important challenge here is also to transform power into what Antonio Negri (1991), building upon Spinoza, calls 'constituent power' in which it is freely constituted by the multitude. Constituent power is not 'power over' but 'power with' as 'power over' obstructs the unfoldment of potential of not only the dominated but also the dominating.[2] The idea of the multitude is neither just the mass nor the people, it is a web of existence which is characterized by the simultaneous work of singularity as well as the emergent commonality among singularities self-awareness of one's common condition as well as the need for transformation. Constituent power is linked to ongoing democratic transformations of society in which the sovereign power which rules in the name of One is subjected to the power of the Multitude going beyond the polarity and dualism of the One and Many. As Michael Hardt writes about Negri's interpretation of the very significant transformative reconstitution of power in the hands of Spinoza:

[For Spinoza] Democracy is to be the absolute, unlimited form of government, because in it the Supreme Power is fully constituted by the power of the multitude. Spinoza's democracy is to be animated by a constituent Power, a dynamic form of popular authority [...] In effect democracy is a return to a plane of the *Ethics*: Power (*potentia*) does not exist in Spinoza's democracy except to the extent that it is a constituent Power completely and freely constituted by the power of the multitude [...] If *Ethics* reduces the distinction and subordinates Power [Sovereign Power, for example] to power in the idealistic terms of its utopian vision, the *Political Treatise* poses the real tendency toward a future reduction of the distinction, when a democratic power would be completely constituted by the power of the multitude

(Hardt 1991: xvi).

But is this process of democratic transformation only political or it is at the same time a multidimensional work on self-transformation and collective transformation?[3] As Ramashroy Roy poses this problem in a provocative way in his *Beyond Ego's Domain: Being and Order in the Vedas*:

[Public order is threatened by the split between] man's concern for his own good and that for the good of others. But can this threat to the public order be mitigated, if not completely eliminated, by the installation of the Polis? [...] For Aristotle, transcendence of self-interest is consequent upon participation in public affairs [but] the shortcomings associated with personal character cannot be expected to be rectified by the public realm, if it lacks necessary support from individuals reborn as citizens. To be reborn as a person who, rising above his self-interest, becomes attentive to and actively seeks to pursue collective good, is, then, to willingly accept a life dedicated to the cultivation of *dharma*.

(Roy 1999: 5).

For fuller democratic realization, Roy here points to the need for being reborn as persons and citizens and cultivating *dharma* which here can be understood as nurturing a mode of dutiful and compassionate engagement which helps self, society, the commons and cosmos to blossom. Negri's interpretation of constituent power lacks this simultaneous engagement with political and spiritual transformation of self, society and polity and the present book seeks to carry out such a connected inquiry, interrogation and transformation.

As the book strives to transform power, it is also animated by a desire to transform freedom, here again as a theme in itself and in the light of contemporary transformations in discourse and society. The current discourse of freedom, like the discourse of power, is at a dead end. It is certainly nice to hear from a thinker such as Ernesto Laclau:

> We are today coming to terms with our own finitude and with the political possibility that it opens. This is the point from which the potentially liberatory discourses of our post-modern age have to start. We can perhaps say that *we are at the end of emancipation and at the beginning of freedom* (Laclau 1992: 137).

But Laclau does not tell us how we can rethink freedom today and have an integral realization of it, a realization which transcends the familiar dichotomies in thinking about and striving towards freedom: economic and political, food and freedom, and political and spiritual. Our task of transformation is made enormously difficult by the fact that in the current euphoria about global democratization and civil society, we proceed with a narrow view of freedom, where we are primarily concerned with freedom from authoritarian structures and the individual's freedom of choice. The works of Isaiah Berlin (1958) and Amartya Sen (1999) as they make a distinction between negative freedom and positive freedom promises a step forward in the current impasse, especially out of the current libertarian capture of the calling of freedom but the promise of recovery even in this agenda is an illusory one as neither Berlin nor Sen tells us how we can transcend the dualism between negative and positive freedom. They are silent about the ontological and aesthetic preparation we need to have at the level of self and society so that the devotion to freedom becomes an integral one and the individual in her own life is able to ensure liberty for herself and at the same time becomes an agent of well-being in the life of others. Though Sen's challenge of linking food and freedom is important, the lack of ontological preparation in such rethinking of freedom is still a crucial gap for us to overcome.

To put it succinctly, the current reflection on freedom again reflects the modernist preoccupation with power and political freedom and has not given enough attention to the challenge of spiritual freedom as an ideal and practice at the level of both self and society nor has it given enough attention to the aesthetic dimension of freedom. By having a view of freedom as a spiritual and aesthetic[4] process of transformation and the agent of freedom as a transformative self, which begins with self-control of one's lower self and cultivation of one's higher self, we can go beyond good and evil, positive and negative. It is crucial here to realize that despite our use of words such as 'lower' and 'higher' which is a reflection of our inescapable human finitude, especially the finitude of language, lower and higher self here, as it is in many spiritual traditions of the world, do not point to a hierarchical fixation. Lower self, for example, is not the self which just wants to have sex, and higher self salvation meditating under the bush. Rather, lower self points to a self which is bound to itself, its ego understood in a narrow way, and with maximization of one's pleasure even when it involves slitting the throats and spilling the blood of others while the higher self points to a seeking for relationship[5] and transformation transforming the quality of our desire no matter whether the desire is for flesh or for God.[6] Transforming freedom is thus confronted with task of transformation of self from lower to higher (understood in a non-dual and non-hierarchical way) and embodiment of responsibility (cf. Levinas 1974; 1990). For instance, Sri Aurobindo (1962) argues that standards of conduct and the practice of freedom must be anchored in a spiritual plane where the goal of freedom is not only to have the freedom to choose but also to transform our needs and desire. A spiritual seeking also helps us to discover the emergent universal ground within us where the social distinction between individual and collective, negative and positive freedom gets a new frame of reference for criticism and transcendence even if it does not get out rightly dissolved.

An aesthetic and spiritual engagement with freedom helps us transform our dominant conceptions of governmentality where self-governance becomes the foundation and model of governance. This is the spirit of Gandhi's striving for *Swaraj* and Foucault's later engagement with self-government. The key issue here is: for self-governance the very machinery and telos of governance has to be changed, rule in self-rule is not the same as we know in familiar machineries of rule. It calls for more persuasion and transformation rather than just repression and the application of force.[7]

II

The book seeks to transform power and freedom by exploring contours of a new politics and spirituality emerging in our times which contribute to self-transformation, world transformation and cosmic transformation. The first part of the book, 'Reconstituting Power and Freedom: Modernity and Beyond,' begins with a foundational essay on the reconstitution of the political in modernity by S.N. Eisenstadt. For Eisenstadt, modernity began with an emphasis on autonomy of man and this new ontological conception not only led to the breakdown of traditional legitimation but loss of traditional markers of certainty. Social movements of various kinds played an important role in the reconstitution of the political in modernity. Social movements became bearers of utopian visions carrying the 'roots of modern political program in the heterodox Gnostic traditions of medieval Europe.' For Eisenstadt, 'The Great Revolutions [of modernity] can indeed be seen as the first or at least the most dramatic, and most successful attempt in the history of mankind to implement on a macro-societal scale utopian visions with strong Gnostic components.' Furthermore, 'Such visions became closely connected with the second major component or orientation of the political programme of modernity—namely the recognition of the multiple interests and of multiple conceptions of the common good, slowly extending also to the realm of (religious) beliefs.' But this reconstitution of the political in modernity along with the axes of pluralism had its limits in authoritarian regimes which 'tended to espouse a very restricted, limited conception of citizenship and a highly regulated access of civil society to the state.'

But in the very formative moment of European modernity there was a deep contestation of authoritarianism in religion and politics and striving for a new mode of relationship and Erasmus emdodied this. As Felix Wilfred writes in the second chapter of the book: 'Erasmus positive vision of the humankind marked a significant departure from the medieval Christian tradition insisting on human sinfulness and frailty—a tendency Luther carried to the extreme. The modernity was a rejection of such a conception, which it replaced with a more trusting attitude in the human and its ability'.

French Revolution was the paradigmatic act of breaking away from authoritarian foundationalism and in his contribution, 'Political Symbolism: Or How to Stay on the Surface,' historian and philosopher Frank R. Ankersmit helps us in understanding the significance of anti-foundationalism for the sake of continued political reconstitution and representative democracy. For Ankersmit, 'The French Revolution was *not* such a decisive social and political *caesura* because it had discovered the absolutely sound foundation for a wholly new political order—it could only be such a revolutionary event, because it did away with the very notion of *foundations* in general [...] Both French Revolution and representative democracy presuppose the rejection of political foundationalism.' In this creative anti-foundational strivings, political symbolism plays an important role but for this politics should not be left reduced only to issues of management. Ankersmit makes a distinction between politicians and political managers and urges us to continue to nurture anti-foundational political symbolism especially at the contemporary juncture as politics is increasingly being reduced soleley to problems of management.

But French Revolution was only a beginning in the direction of needed multidimensional transformation. While its slogans of equality and liberty became orthodoxies in the political movements of liberalism and socialism, fraternity is still crying in the streets around the world. Of course, today fraternity means both brotherhood and sisterhood, a part of what Binod Kumar Agarwala in his subsequent contribution on Kant calls belonging. Agarwala critically interrogates as well as interprets Kant in a novel way as concerned with the calling of belonging. For Agarwala, the 'Kantian ruler is as absolute as the Hobbesian sovereign but Kant succeeds in evading this from the readers by claiming that the sovereign is not the head of the state' 'but a public law, act of a public will.' But in his *Critique of Judgment*, Kant was fascinated with the calling of belonging to community where authority is based on 'knowledge— knowledge as virtue, not power.' For Agarwala, we can overcome this antinomy between power and liberty by belonging to nation and state. But given the complicity of both nation and state in a violent project of homogenization and exclusion, it is helpful to transform Agarwala's proposal into a community of virtues which also celebrates colours of pluralism.

Agarwala's contribution points to the limits of power and liberty in modernity and the subsequent contribution of Philip Quarles van Ufford, 'The Power of Modernity and the Tail of the Devil,' explores these limits in a very foundational way in both the European home and outside the colonized world. In European home, modernity has asserted its power by banishing the devil from the world but Quarles van Ufford, taking cues from Goethe's *Faust*, urges us to realize that the devil has performed a disappearing act himself. In this context, for Quarles van Ufford, '..we may discern the tail of the devil in everyday life in the form of exaggerated forms of optimism and overly facile promises of social order.' Violence becomes indispensable in such a project of abolition of evil and establishment of order, as Quarles van Ufford shows remarkably with examples of Dostoevsky's Grand Inquisitor and Arthur Koestler's party executioner. With colonialism this project of killing is let loose globally but the fire that burns other's homes finally comes back and engulfs the home of European modernity as well (see Uberoi 2002).

With the help of Conrad's *Heart of Darkness* Quarles van Ufford shows us how this devastation comes home.

In this context, a great challenge of dealing with power of modernity and modernistic power is confronting violence and coercion and the subsequent contributions of a philosopher and a sociologist are highly instructive. In her contribution, 'Rethinking Power: Aesthetics, Dialogue, Hegemony,' Kanchana Mahadevan discusses insightfully the seminal works of Hannah Arendt, Michel Foucault and Antonio Gramsci. For Mahadevan, '[...]violence is an indifference to the point of view of the other' but building on Arendt, Mahadevan argues that power cannot be equated with violence. Rather, 'Arendt's notion of power promises to be a constructive endeavour towards evolving new forms of solidarity.' Mahadevan ties this notion of power as the 'art of public dwelling' from Arendt with conceptions of struggles building on Foucault, Habermas and Gramsci argues that 'politics is the struggle for public discourse.' But is this struggle only political? Doesn't it involve self-transformation and ethico-moral and spiritual transformation of societies? Giri explores the challenge of self-cultivation that power is confronted with in the third section of the book but before this sociologist and cultural theorist Jan Nederveen Pieterse presents us the empirically as well as normatively challenging issue of metamorphoses of power. One important aspect of metamorphoses of power in society and history is a very fragile shift from coercion to cooperation. Nederveen Pieterse challenges us to go beyond the reversals in contemporary real *politik* and to acknowledge both cooperation and coercion in the working and trajectories of power. Nederveen Pieterse discusses several trends towards a democratic and cooperative regulation of power over time, such as, among others:

1. Over time the exercise of power is increasingly *normatively regulated*. Political and military power generally since the era of the French Revolution and the 'age of democratic revolution' have been increasingly subject to constitutional and legal structures;
2. In most countries there is a shift from government to governance and towards interactive decision-making and decentralization in public administration....

But Nederveen Pieterse himself urges us to realize that this is by no means a generalized trend: 'A countertrend is the growing global and domestic inequality and concentration of income and power at the top, which in the United States increasingly takes the form of plutocracy.'

For Nederveen Pieterse, 'Nevertheless the empirical circumstances that underlie these trends—growing demographic densities, global inter-dependence and growing human capacities—are structurally significant. This makes greater cooperation likely.'

But the likelihood of this realization is dependent upon varieties of transformative struggles and the part two of the book, *Beyond the Modern Prince: Varieties of Struggles and New Intimations*, presents some of these. It begins with Stellan Vinthagen's discussion of non-violent movements and the challenge of transformation of power. As has been already discussed, through exploring non-violent resistance Vinthagen goes beyond a simplistic view of power and resistance and urges us to understand their complex constitution as well as differentiation by presenting power as subordination and resistance as disobedience. Power as subordination is not totally subjection: it is dependent upon the wilful participation of those who are part of it, including their act and potential of disobedience. Power does not create subjects in automatic processes, but through the constant participation and modification by the very subjects themselves. For Vinthagen, 'Power as subordination is integrally linked to resistance as disobedience. Thus, non-violent movements are significant examples of resistance to power as well as transformation of it.' While explicating non-violent resistance with example from Gandhi, Vinthagen urges us to realize: that Gandhian non-violence 'involves a simultaneous resistance against the oppressive system role of the counterpart and a *cooperation* with the same counter-part as a human being and part of a unity of humanity.'

Vinthagen's explorations are followed by Bernard Adeney-Risakotta who in his essay, 'Origins and Sources of Power: Indonesian Paradigms and Beyond,' also discusses the issue of non-violent resistance to power. Beginning with a discussion of the issue of the similarity and differences between Javanese and Western approaches to power, Adeney-Risakotta also challenges us to understand the distinction between power and violence. Building on the non-violent struggles to overthrow the autocratic regime of Soeharto and other such movements in society and history, especially the non-violent struggle for freedom led by Gandhi, Adeney-Risakotta writes: '[...] the classic, almost universal paradigm of power as domination based on violence, generates more misunderstanding than clarity. Power is very diverse and distributed in different ways among the people. Power is not primarily the possession of a small elite but rather is located in the people. Power is the ability of the people to act together to achieve their aims. Powerlessness is the inability to initiate real change in human social reality.' (We can relate this to Spinoza's constituent power that we discussed before). He also challenges us to understand that power is not just reducible to social immanence or social practice, there is a mystical dimension to the work of power as well as in the resistance towards its tyrannical and dictatorial manifestations in societies and histories.

Adeney-Risakotta's reconstitution of power is carried forward to new height and depth in the subsequent contributions in the section. Sang-Jin Han describes democratic transformation in contemporary Korea in which 'middling grassroots' play an important role: '[...] the middling grassroots are those who are part of the middle class objectively, yet distinctive in that their identity as part of 'people,' not the 'power-bloc.' Jose Jowel Canuday helps us understand the creative potency of humans even in the most difficult situations of war and devastation. Canuday tells us how people caught in between armed conflicts in Mindanow, Philippines and subjected to evacuations 'carry themselves with dignity as they struggle and initiate ways to survive and recover.' The displaced people come back to their lands and villages and cultivate it. The issue of land is a crucial issue for people all over the world and in his contribution in this section Piet Strydom tells us about search for structures of cooperation in the land reform dispute in the post-apartheid South Africa. Mateo Mier y Terán G.C. tells us about the walking rebellion of the Zapatistas in Mexico which challenges the taken-for-granted foundations of economy, polity and society by striving for autonomy and radical democracy. At the core of this is a project to transform power in a foundational way through its principle of 'commanding by obeying' which has enkindled creative and radical imagination world-wide.[8]

Commanding by obeying involves an aesthetic transformation of the modernist cult of mastery to an ethics and aesthetics of servanthood where we relate to each other not as masters but as servants (cf. Giri 2002; Ruskin 2004).[9] In their contribution in this section, 'Ecological Ontology and Landscapes of Democratic Struggle in Globalization Politics: Residual, Emergent and Transformative Dimensions,' Herbert Reid and Betsy Taylor urge us to realize the significance of place and ecological ontology in our very constitution of self and the public, and in the work of democratic struggles and global justice movements. They urge us to understand how sensibility in creative social movements such as global justice movements 'discloses ways in which *place experience* nestles both ecological and historical horizons that open towards what the late

Raymond Williams called resources of hope.'[10] Reid and Taylor present us a feast of ideas and practices for nurturing what they call body-place-commons and present forums such as World Social Forums as emergent global public spheres. They also invite us to walk together with thinkers such as John Dewey, Maurice Merleau-Ponty, and Raymond Williams in going beyond dualism and fighting against domination of capital and expert knowledge in our lives and the world at large.

For Reid and Taylor, Williams and Dewey help us realize a 'democratic professionalism' which 'cultivates a cultural memory of an experimental knowledge that hones itself in the living landscapes where participatory reason serves sustainable life.' They both urge us to go beyond debilitating dualisms of many kinds and 'cages of institutional cynicism and transnational elitism.' An important part of the challenge of transforming power and freedom, for Reid and Taylor, is to nurture a participatory logic and to overcome the 'logic of fungibility' 'which reduce beings to an assemblage of predefined traits.' For Reid and Taylor, 'Fundamentalism of all sorts operate by locking individuals to pre-given categories that are fetishized as immanent to their substantive being, rather than emergent from relational processes of co-creation between individual and matrix' (Reid and Taylor 2006). Participatory logic helps us to 'reclaim democratic politics' from space-based logics of fungibility to place-based logics of democratic public inquiry': 'Particpatory reason moves scientists from the laboratory into the field, moves citizens from media-spectatorship into place-based inquiry, moves pedagogy and professionalism from class-rooms into civic engagement and public debate, moves art from commodified fashionable reactions to risky and original encounters within history and life-world' (ibid).

Reid and Taylor especially present us many gifts from Dewey for transforming power and freedom such as what they call 'an aesthetic ecology of public intelligence.' Going beyond corporate power, elitism and various divides Dewey pleads for a vibrant democratic participation nurtured by an aesthetic ecology and an ecological ontology. Dewey also brings a new emergent dimension to the work of self and society which goes beyond conventional pragmatism: '[...] Dewey does not mean an Aristotelian notion of potentiality as the emergence of a *fixed* end which the individual actualizes. Rather, he means an *emergent* quality of co-creation between individual and world [...]'

In their essay, Reid and Taylor tell us of new global social movements for generating global commons and we are fortunate to have in our midst reflections from Helena Tagesson, a participant in one such movement, namely Attac (Association for the Taxation of Financial Transactions for the Aid of Citizens), a movement for global justice. Tagesson shows us from example of her own participation in Attac how such movements embody a yearning of the heart for a new politics and spirituality. Tagesson also discusses the issue of disappointment in working with liberatory struggles and different possible ways of working with it. This resonates with Mateo's discussion of difficulties of social change in the communities in which Zapatista works.

Contributions in the third section of the volume, 'Transforming Power and Freedom: New Horizons,' continue this exploration of new horizons of politics and spirituality in transforming power and freedom. It begins with the insightful contribution of Akop P. Nazaretyan on power and wisdom in the history of social behaviour. For Nazaretyan, 'While weapon's killing power and people's concentration have been successfully growing for millennia, war victim's ratio has not.' For Nazaretyan, this is a fragile suggestion of work of wisdom in history vis-à-vis the power to annihilate. Nazaretyan calls it 'technohumanitarian balance' which states that 'the higher production and war technologies' power, the more refined the behaviour-regulation means that is required for self-preservation of society.' This balance, like Nederveen Pieterse's discussion of metamorphoses of power, is tenuous and calls for continued work on inner liberation on the part of both self and society. Theologian Dietmar Mieth presents us glimpses of this calling of power and inner liberation from the inspiring life and works of mystic Meister Eckhart from Europe. With a radical interpretation of the meaning of Christ as well as the vocation of being a Christian, Eckhart challenges us to understand the power of inner liberation: 'Christ reveals both the compassion of God as the inner structure of the world and solidarity as the inner structure of the human being.' Eckhart's power of inner liberation was accompanied by continued striving for justice or 'ardour for justice.' Eckhart preached in the vernacular and was inspired by as well as supported the feminine spirituality of the Beguines: 'The Beguines were free groups of women who, often following deaths of their husbands, in times of war or in times of surplus in general, or perhaps in times of a new emancipation of women, joined together to lead a simple religious life in poverty.' Probably this feminine spirituality inspired Eckhart to envision each human being as a mother. For Eckhart we are continuously called upon to give birth to God at each moment of our lives.

Eckhart's critique of power as domination and continued search for multidimensional inner liberation in self and society finds a parallel in the life and thoughts of Erasmus. Erasmus explored new dimensions of human and social transformation beyond the dominant logic of power. It is in this context, philosopher and transformative thinker Fred Dallmayr's subsequent contribution on Erasmus, 'War Against the Turks? Erasmus on War and Peace,' helps us address the challenge of war and peace as an integral part of transforming power and freedom (see Hardt and Negri 2004). Dallmayr begins his essay: 'Today, democracy is joined by another fugitive: everywhere peace seems to be in retreat or on the defensive [...] In such grim surroundings, Erasmus continues to offer inspiration and solace—a solace nurtured by his close familiarity with the perennial follies of humanity.' For Erasmus, 'we are betrayed by our lust for power.' Machievelli, a contemporary of Erasmus, had described this lust for power in *Prince* and in his contribution Sapir Handelman challenges us to go beyond the prince and understand the crucial significance of leadership responsibility. For Handelman, holders of power have to embody responsibility especially in situations of intractable conflicts such as Israel and Palestine. But this calls for bathing in streams of wisdom and not only drinking from the cups of lust of power and in his subsequent contribution Christian Bartolf presents us gifts of wisdom from Tolstoy's last major work, *A Calendar of Wisdom: Daily Thoughts to Nourish the Soul*. Bartolf concludes with Etiene de la Boétie's seminal contribution, '*Discourse on Voluntary Servitude*' in which la Boétie, a contemporary of Machievelli, had challenged us to first acknowledge our voluntary servitude[11] and then strive to transform this. Boétie had written way back in 1548: 'Obviously there is no need of fighting to overcome this single tyrant, for he is automatically defeated if the country refuses consent to its own enslavement' (de la Boétie 1548: 22). This is also spirit of Gandhi's refusal in one's own enslavement though Gandhi here emphasizes the need for non-violent resistance. Gandhi also challenges us to go beyond the trappings of power as determined destiny. As Mrinal Miri interprets the Gandhian pathway in his subsequent contribution: 'What we must strive for is not a tenuous, uneasy equilibrium of power, an equilibrium which is always on the brink of being upset. Gandhi's preferred word here is "fellowship"—fellowship between communities and individuals.'

Gandhi speaks about fellowship beyond the logic of power and this finds a correspondence in our mutual implication as suggested in Robert Bernasconi's subsequent elaboration of Sartre's ontology of freedom as 'None is free until all are free.' Sartre ties freedom to responsibility. As Bernasconi tells us, 'Freedom is ultimately for Sartre not freedom over other man or woman: the meaning of freedom for Sartre is responsibility, or, more specifically, it is for each of us *my* responsibility. My ontological freedom is responsibility for everything, except my responsibility itself, which is given.' In his *Notebooks for An Ethics*, Sartre tells us: '..if one had a full intuition of one's own freedom, one would see it as requiring universal freedom and one would not be able to destroy the freedom of others.' Mark Lindley discusses this calling of responsibility in an urgent field of our times namely our planetary ecology. He also discusses the challenge of rethinking freedom in the face of ecological crises.

This mutual implication and imperative of responsibility is taken up in the subsequent contribution of Ananta Kumar Giri, 'Power and Self-Cultivation: Aesthetics, Development Ethics and the Calling of Poverty,' who joins the discussion of transformation of power and freedom by exploring the challenge of self-cultivation that confront both. In exploring the challenge of self-cultivation that the logic and holders of power face, Giri discusses the other Foucault who talks of care of self. Giri also explores several alternative traditions, namely the Indian tradition of sharing food, the European tradition of *Bildung* and the Confucian tradition of self-formation. Giri carries out this exploration of power and self-cultivation with specific reference to the field of development and discusses the issue of aesthetics, ethics and poverty, pleading for how all these transgress boundaries and call for a new politics and aesthetic ethics of sharing.

Giri discusses the challenge of development ethics and poverty and the subsequent contribution of Thanh-Dam Truong explores this through a discussion of human security from a Buddhist perspective. Truong's explorations of security and peace and quest to 'open the space for inter-paradigmatic learning' resonates with the earlier contribution of Dallmayr. For Truong, 'the human security project cannot succeed if based on neo-liberal individualism'; it calls for 'the search for a communicative non-identitarian subject with a heart.' Like Clammer's concluding reflections to follow, Truong challenges us to understand the connection between dualism and violence and the significance of non-dualism for transforming power and freedom. At the same time, Truong self-critically acknowledges that Buddhism does not offer a theory of social power and has not addressed the issues of social and gender hierarchies. Nevertheless its epistemology of connectedness and wisdom is crucial towards transforming power and freedom: '[...] One conceptual error, if not corrected, leads to imbalanced action, causing imbalanced responses leading to other conceptual errors, and the chains of error and imbalanced action continues. The will of mind (determination) in Buddhist thought is not geared towards power and control but towards understanding through meditative techniques to develop a wholesome mind. A wholesome mind is the key to the release of compassion and non-violence. In this regard, ontological security is not derived from the notion of fixed stable self (socially or morally defined). It is derived from the ethical ideal to perceive oneself in relation to others and as others.'

If Truong presents us with a Buddhist perspective on human security, Abdullahi Ahmed An-Naim presents us an Islamic perspective on human rights. This is followed by the provocative essay, 'Beyond Power: Alternative Conceptions of Being and the Reconstitution of Social Theory,' by John Clammer who, building upon Buddhism as well as Gandhi, challenges us: 'The key to understanding models of power/anti-power is a question of ontology. Anti-power that is simply a struggle against power can never succeed: what is necessary is to deconstruct the notion and necessity of power itself and the impoverished conception of humankind upon which power theories are based, one that suggests in fact that humans cannot act ethically or outside of a framework of pure interest.' Clammer makes clear: 'The issue here, as for Gandhi, is not the abnegation of power, but its transformation from a means of domination and mechanism of violence to a force for the positive remaking of human and natural life, the harnessing of the energy (in Japanese *ki*) that flows throughout the universe but which can be focused, concentrated and utilized for healing and never for destruction.' This calls for personal revolution in self and science, along with structural transformation, a point stressed by Chitta Ranjan Das-a heart-touching critic and transformative experimenter of our times—in his *Afterword*. For Das, '[...] to be and not merely to know is the real thing, the real catalyser.'

III

Clammer challenges us never to use power for destruction but for healing but in major traditions of thought and practice, power has been instrumentally used to inflict suffering on self, other and society. Much of this has been inflicted not only on humanity but also on the non-human world in the name of sovereignty: the cult of sovereignty which wants to control all in the name of the Sovereign One—the Lord, the

Man, Self and the nation-state. In this context there is an epochal challenge now to transform sovereignty which is based upon bare life and violated bodies and souls into shared sovereignties animated by a multi-valued logic of autonomy and interpenetration (cf. Agamben 1998; Giri 2005). Practice of shared sovereignties has the potential to help us overcome the violence of sovereignty which we see in intractable battles over ego and territories at the level of both self and nation-state. Shared sovereignty is facilitated by post-national transformations of nation-states and post-egotistic transformations at the level of self. This is also facilitated by the work of what Dallmayr (2005) calls 'sacred non-sovereignty' where a sovereign self or society is not preoccupied with power and mastery but with an ethics and spirituality of servanthood. This transforms the *Prince* in religion, politics and now in many domains of our lives into little princes and princesses where we are able to laugh at those who just want to sit on the thrones and those who spend their whole life in counting coins.[12] Practice of shared sovereignty and 'sacred non-sovereignty' also transform our Gods into small gods helping us co-walk in the evolutionary tryst of this fragile cosmos of ours.

Shared sovereignty and sacred non-sovereignty call for shared suffering for realization of our potential—self as well as collective, societal as well as cosmic.[13] But apart from democratic transformation this also calls for the need to undertake suffering on the part of the self to touch the heart and soul of the other including that of sovereign power. Transforming power and freedom thus calls for preparation to undertake and embody suffering as a mode of being and relationship including political struggle which is neither sadistic nor masochistic but a participation in the joys of transformation and for building a collective and ontological foundation of dignity and for multidimensional human, societal and cosmic flourishing.

Undertaking suffering here is an act of love as exemplified in the life of martyrs[14] in visions and history from Antigone to Ken Saro-Wiwa to Chhattisgarh Mukti Morcha,[15] Socrates to Gandhi but love here is neither a reduction of the self and other but discovery of each other's mystery. Transforming power and freedom thus brings us back as well as forward to our originary and ever-present constitutive poetics and politics of love. It is no wonder then that two critical thinkers of our times conclude their fascinating political treatises on our times with love. Write Michael Hardt and Antonio Negri in their *Multitude*: 'The new movements demanding global democracy not only value the singularity of each as a fundamental organizing principle but they also pose it as a process of self-transformation, hybridisation, and miscegenation. The multiplicity of the multitude is not just a matter of being different but also becoming different. Become different than you are! These singularities act in common and thus form a new race, that is, a politically coordinated subjectivity that the multitude produces. The primary decision made by the multitude is really the decision to create a new race or, rather, a new humanity. When love is conceived politically, then, the creation of a new humanity is the ultimate act of love' (Hardt and Negri 2004: 358).

But the creation of a new humanity is not only a matter of 'biopolitical production' as Hardt and Negri would suggest but also of spiritual generation. Transforming power and freedom through the poetics and politics of love challenges us to overcome modernist primacy of both the productive and the political and be engaged with love and politics in infinitely generative ways beginning with love as a mystery of communion rather than just production. As Luc Irigaray (2002: 115–117) would challenge us:

> Carnal sharing becomes then a spiritual path, a poetic and also a mystical path [...] Love takes place in the opening to self that is the place of welcoming the transcendence of the other. [...] The path of such an accomplishment of the flesh does not correspond to a solipsistic dream [...] nor to a fin-de-siecle utopia, but to a new stage to be realized by humanity. [...] Nature is then no longer subdued but it is adapted, in its rhythms and necessities, to the path of its becoming, of its growth.[16] Caressing loses the sense of capturing, bewitching, appropriating [...] The caress becomes a means of growing together toward a human maturity that is not confused with an intellectual competence, with the possession of property [...] nor with the domination of the world..

Notes

1. Here we can think of Martin Luther who after the success of his Protestant revolt sided with the kings in suppressing the peasant revolts in Germany. He even did not mind sending one of his co-Protestant fighters, Thomas Munster, to the gallows for supporting the peasant revolt. See Chitta Ranjan Das' (1989) essay on Luther and Erasmus. Also see Chapter 2, by Felix Wilfred, in the present volume.
2. As Arne Naess (1999: 49) interprets Spinoza (ibid.: 48), 'Power over others tends in the direction of limiting others' right to unfold their nature.' According to Spinoza, 'The more we unfold the manifold (or many-side)

of our nature, the more we are in ourselves (in suo esse), and the higher degree of freedom we achieve. This kind of development is experienced by joy, one's world is colored by joy, or more precisely is more joyful.'

3. Spinoza calls for a simultaneous spiritual and political transformation. In his unpublished theses on Spinoza submitted to Visvabharati, Shantiniketan, India in 1948, Chitta Ranjan Das explores both the spiritual and political dimensions of Spinoza's work and struggles. Fortunately this insightful work has just come out after sixty years as *Benedict-Spinoza: An Appreciation* from Shipra Publications, Delhi.

4. Here the following lines of Frederik Schiller are significant: *Es die schoonheit ist durch, welche Man zu der Freihieit* (It is beauty through which man makes his way to freedom).

5. It is helpful here to read the following fascinating interpretation of Freud that Reisner (2003: 234) presents, '[In his fourth chapter of Beyond the Pleasure Principle, Freud talks about binding and unbinding]. We can take binding and unbinding as a dynamic way of describing the transformation of id into ego. This is an internal acquiring of culture, the development of the civilization of the self. Binding is achieving a certain internal form, putting drives into coherent patterns, making them accessible and controllable. Fastening the neurobiological to the psychological and, ultimately, to the ethical dimension of existence, Freud addresses himself to dreams and says that we return to the unbound in order to bind; it is for this purpose that we obsessively, fanatically return to the area of the unbound. In one of his last works, *An Outline of Psychoanalysis*, Freud returns to the question of binding and unbinding on a metapsychological scale. Then on, he finds desire to be the final binding force, the aim of Eros to 'establish ever greater unities and preserve them ... to bind together. The same essay finds that "destructive instincts" work to undo connections and so to destroy things.'

6. It is interesting here to remember solitary points of illuminations of scholars such as Claus Offe (1991), himself a political sociologist, challenging us to realize that democracy confronts us with the challenge of distinguishing between our 'more desirable desire' and 'less desirable desire'.

7. As Foucault (2005: 544) writes: 'It is not a matter of governing oneself as one governs others, seeking models in military command or the domination of slaves, but when I have to govern others, I can only do so on the model of the first, only decisive, essential, and effective government: the government of myself.'

8. As Subcommandante Marcos (1996: 69) tells us: 'We thought that we needed to reformulate the question of power. We will not repeat the formula that to change the world you need to seize power, and once in power you will organize it the way it is the best for the world, that is, what is the best for me because I am in power. We thought that if we conceived a change in the premise of the question of power, arguing that we did not want to

take it, this would produce a different form of politics, another kind of politicians, other human beings who could make politics very different to the one practised by the politicians we suffer today along the whole political spectrum.'

9. Consider here what John Ruskin (2004: 17) wrote more than a century ago: 'I know not if a day is ever to come when the nature of right freedom will be understood, and when men will see that to obey another man, to labour for him, yield reverence to him or to his place, is not slavery.'

10. This nurturance of hope finds a resonance in the works of creative pioneers such as M.S. Swaminathan who also talks about 'ecology of hope'. Swaminathan strives towards a generation of 'eco-technology' which 'involves the integration of the best of traditional local community knowledge with frontier science and technology like renewable energy' (cf Swaminathan and Ikeda 2005: 62). He also talks about the need to cultivate spiritual globalization as part of an ecology of hope:

> The movement towards multilateralism and globalization must be not merely economic, but also spiritual. What we need most is spiritual globalization [...] By spiritual globalization, I do not mean that every one should belong to the same religion. I am speaking of building security in the wider sense of human dignity and gender equity. (Swaminathan and Ikeda 2005: 135).

11. What de la Boétie (1548: 7) writes deserves our careful consideration: 'But

> o Good Lord! What strange phenomenon is this? What name shall we give to it?.... To see an endless multitude of people not merely obeying, but driven to servility? Not ruled, but tyrannized over? These wretches have no wealth, no kin, nor wife nor children, not even life itself they can call their own. They suffer plundering, wantonness, cruelty, not from an army, not from a barbarian horde, but from a single man.... Too frequently this same little man is the most cowardly and effeminate in the nation, a stranger to the power of battle and hesitant on the sands of tournament; not only without energy to direct men by force but with hardly enough virility to bed with a common woman!' He concludes his treatise as: 'There is nothing so contrary to a generous and loving God as dictatorship' (ibid.: 22).

12. We can hear recall the heart-touching journey of the little prince in Antoine de Saint Exupery's Little Prince. But we have to co-walk in this journey as both little princes and princesses. A foundational question to this project of ours on Modern Prince and Modern Sage was raised by Yale Handelman, a singer and dreamer of life, and wife of Sapir Handelman, a contributor in the present volume. During a conversation in Freiburg, Germany, Yale asked like a little princess of de Saint Exupery: 'What about the modern princess?' I agree with her that in our book we could have done

more on recording the contribution of women's movement in transforming power and freedom, and the significance of creative feminine politics and spirituality. But at the same time, we have to ask whether the feminist movement embodied values of the Princess and her will-to-power, and whether this needs to be now transformed into a simultaneous will for dignity and solidarity.

13. For realizing the significance for potential, especially my existence in the context of yours, my and our potentiality, note the following thoughts of a Nobel prize winning novelist and a philosopher. Writes Imre Kertesz (2002: 12) in his novel, A Kaddish for a Child Not Born: 'Yes, my existence in the context of your potentiality…. Now I no longer have doubts—it is in the clouds where I make my bed. And this question—my life in the context of the potentiality of your existence—proved to be a good guide.' And writes philosopher Georgio Agamben (1993: 44) in his Coming Community: 'The recognition of evil is older and more original than any blameworthy act, it rests solely on the fact that, being and having to be only its possibility or potentiality, humankind fails itself in a certain sense and has to appropriate this failing—it has to exist as potentiality. [The only ethical experience is] the experience of being (one's own potentiality). The only evil consists, instead, in the decision to remain in a deficit of existence, to appropriate the power to not-be as a substance and a foundation beyond existence; or rather (and this is the destiny of morality), to regard potentiality itself, which is the most proper mode of human existence as a fault that must always be repressed.'

14. Here J.P.S. Uberoi's thoughts about the loving self-sacrifice of the martyrs of the world are noteworthy. For Uberoi (1996: 130), the elementary structure of martyrdom is 'manifestly the non-dualism of loving self-sacrifice … but equally it is the responsibility of "arising to bear witness" on the duality of the true and false, religion and irreligion, liberation and bondage.' Furthermore, 'The martyr is one who must love his enemy in some sense since he or she is the perfect witness (saheed-ul-kamil) that God, who at this time takes an interest in history and politics, does not want his servant to suppose, as the dualist would, that Satanism has any true independent existence, and so dharmayudhya, the righteous war, can be transformed into satyagraha' (ibid.: 124). What Uberoi (ibid.: 88) writes about Antigone, the first martyr of the world, deserves our careful attention as it is linked with the project of martyrdom in both Gandhism and Sikhism: 'I think that perhaps the world's first martyr of truth and non-violence was a Greek, Antigone, a European and a woman, best known to us as depicted by Sophocles, c.500 BC Antigone, who preceded both Socrates and Jesus, wanted the integration of religion and society to be upheld by her freedom of conscience and immemorial usage, the custom of civil society, while Creon, the King, wished his reasons of state to be separate from, and to override, both religion and society. I will not attempt to decide which of

the two points of view is modern for Europe, but it is Antigone's that is closest to Sikhism and Indian modernity. She had established the truth that no power on earth can make the self do anything against its nature, except indirectly confer martyrdom on it, which is also the basis of Gandhism in politics.'

15. Ken Saro-Wiwa is the martyr from the Ogoni tribe of Nigeria who was executed on false charges for his struggle against the multinational Shell and the dictatorship of the Nigerian nation-state (see Saro-Wiwa 1995). The martyrdom of Shankar Guha Niyogi, the founder of the Chhattisgarh Mukti Morcha (CMM), fighting for the dignity of workers and people, is also exemplary here. Niyogi was gunned down by hired goons of the industrialists while he was asleep. What is striking is that even now in the face of murder and much violence, the CMM continues on the path of non-violent struggle. As Chandhoke (2003: 206) writes: 'Despite the fact that [the] CMM used only non-violent means of protest, such as peaceful demonstrations, dharnas, strikes, morchas and petitions—all of which are permissible in civil society—their protests were savagely put down. During a conversation with one of the CMM's leaders, I wondered whether it was not legitimate to use violence in a society where the regime virtually used violence against its own people. His answer was an emphatic no; violence, he argued, would impoverish the movement and denude it of any spirit of commitment.'

16. Such a transformational relationship with Nature is crucially significant as much of modernist emancipatory politics, including the so-called post-modern emancipatory project of Hardt and Negri under the rubric of 'biopolitical production', does not involve a foundational interrogation and transformation of anthropocentrism. Though we have not been able to engage ourselves fully with this issue in the present volume, overcoming and transcending anthropocentrism is an important part of the political and spiritual struggle to transform power and freedom.

References

Agamben, Georgio. 1993. *The Coming Community*. Minneapolis: University of Minnesota Press.

———. 1998. Homo Sacer: Sovereign Power and Bare Life. Stanford: Stanford University Press.

Benhabib, Seyla. 1987. *Critique, Norm and Utopia*. New York: Columbia University Press.

Berlin, Isaiah. 1958. 'Two Concepts of Liberty', in Isaish Berlin 1969, *Four Essays of Liberty*, pp. 118–72. Oxford: Oxford University Press.

Butler, Judith. 1997. *The Psychic Life of Power: Theories in Subjection*. Stanford: Stanford University Press.

Chandhoke, Neera. 2003. 'When the Voiceless Speak: A Case Study of the Chatisgarh Mukti Morcha.', in *Does Civil Society Matter? Governance in Contemporary India*, Rajesh Tandon and Ranjita Mohanty (eds), pp. 198–242. New Delhi: Sage Publications.

Cohen, Jean and Andrew Arato. 1992. *Civil Society and Political Theory*. Cambridge: The MIT Press.

Dallmayr, Fred. 2001. 'Resisting Totalizing Uniformity: Martin Heidegger on *Macht* and *Machenshaft'*, in idem, *Achieving Our World: Toward a Global and Plural Democracy*, pp. 189-209. Lanham, MD: Rowman and Littlefield,

———. 2005. 'Empire and Faith: Sacred Non-Sovereignty', in idem, *Small Wonder: Global Power and Its Discontents*, pp. 199-206. Lanham, MD: Rowman and Littlefield.

Das, Chitta Ranjan. 1989. *Shukara o Socrates* [The Pig and Socrates]. Berhampur, Orissa, India: Pustak Bhandar.

———. 1948. Spinoza. Unpublished theses. Shantiniketan: Biswavarati.

de la Boétie, Etienne. 1548. Discourse on Voluntary Servitude. Published under the title Anti-Dictator. NY: Columbia University Press. Downloaded from http://www.constitution.org/la-boétie/serve_vol.htm on May 23, 06.

Foucault, Michel. 1984. 'Politics and Ethics: An Interview', in Paul Rabinow (ed.), *The Foucault Reader*. New York: Pantheon.

———. 2005. *The Hermeneutics of the Subject: Lectures at the College de France, 1981–82*. New York: Palgrave.

Gramsci, Antonio. 1957. *The Modern Prince and Other Writings*. London: Lawrence and Wishat Ltd.

Giddens, Anthony. 1994. *Beyond Left and Right: The Future of Radical Politics*. Cambridge: Polity Press.

———. 1991. *Modernity and Self-Identity: Self and Society in the Late Modern Age*. Cambridge: Polity Press.

Giri, Ananta Kumar. 2002. *Conversations and Transformations: Towards a New Ethics of Self and Society*. Lanham, MD: Lexington Books.

———. 2005 Creative Social Research: Rethinking Theories and Methods and the Calling of an Ontological Epistemology of Participation. Madras Institute of Development Studies: Working Paper.

Hardt, Michael. 1991. 'Translator's Foreword' to Negri 1991.

Hardt, Michael and Antonio Negri. 2004. *Multitude: War and Democracy in the Age of Empire*. New York: The Penguin Press.

Hoffman, Piotr. 1996. *The Quest for Power: Hobbes, Descartes and the Emergence of Modernity*. Atlantic Highlands, New Jersey: Humanities Press.

Irigaray, Luc. 2002. *Between East and West: From Singularity to Community*. New York: Columbia University Press.

Kertesz, Imre. 2002. *A Kaddish for a Child Not Born*. Evanston, IL: Northwestern University Press.

Laclau, Ernesto. 1992. 'Beyond Emancipation', in *Emancipations, Modern and Postmodern*, edited by Jan Nederveen Pieterse. London: Sage Publications.

Levinas, Emmanuel. 1974. *Otherwise Than Being or Beyond Essence*. Dordrecht: Kluwer Academic Publishers.

———. 1990. *Difficult Freedom*. London: Athlone.

Machiavelli, Niccolo. 1981 [1520]. *The Prince and Other Political Writings*. Selected and Translated with introduction and notes by Bruce Perman. London: Dent Everyman's Library.

Marcos. 1996. Quoted in Gustavo Esteva, 'Celebrating Zapatiemo', manuscript.

Naess, Arne. 1999. Det frie menneske (The Free Human Being). Oslo: Kagge Forlag.

Negri, Antonio. 1991. *The Savage Anomaly: The Power of Spinoza's Metaphysics and Politics*. Minneapolis: University of Minnesota Press.

Offe, Claus. 1991. 'Democratic Institutions and Moral Resources', in David Held (ed.), *Political Theory Today*. Cambridge: Polity Press.

Reid, Herbert and Betsy Taylor. 2006. 'Globalization, Democracy and the Aesthetic Ecology of Emergent Publics for a Sustainable World: Working from John Dewey', *Asian Journal of Social Sciences*, 34(1): 22–46.

Reisner, Gavriel (Ben-Ephraim). 2003. *The Death-Ego and the Vital Self: Romance and Desire in Literature and Psychoanalysis*. Crarbury, New Jersey, USA: Associated University Presses.

Roy, Ramashroy. 1999. *Beyond Ego's Domain: Being and Order in the Vedas*. Delhi: Shipra Publications.

Ruskin, John. 2004. *On Art and Life*. London: Penguin.

Saro-Wiwa, Ken. 1995. *A Month and a Day: A Detention Diary*. London: Penguin Books.

Sen, Amartya. 1999. *Development as Freedom*. Oxford: Oxford University Press.

Sri Aurobindo. 1962. *Human Cycles*. Pondicherry: Sri Aurobindo Ashram.

Swaminathan, M.S. and Daisaku Ikeda. 2005. *Revolutions To Green the Environment, To Grow the Human Heart: A Dialogue between M.S. Swaminathan and Daisaku Ikeda*. Chennai: East-West Books.

Toynbee, Arnold J. 1956. *A Historian's Approach to Religion*. New York: Oxford University Press.

Uberoi, JPS. 2002. *European Modernity: Truth, Science and Method*. Delhi: Oxford University Press.

———. 1996. *Religion, Civil Society and State: A Study of Sikhism*. Delhi: Oxford University Press.

PART I

Reconstituting Power and Freedom: Modernity and Beyond

Modernity and the Reconstitution of the Realm of the Political

1

S.N. Eisenstadt

The modern project, the cultural and political programme of modernity as it developed first in the West, in Western and Central Europe, and expanded from its inception through the world—initially encompassing most of the world—entailed distinct ontological as well as institutional premises. On the ontological level, it implied some very distinct shifts in the conception of human agency, of its autonomy and of its place in the flow of time. Its conception of the future was one in which various possibilities that can be realized by autonomous human agency—or by the march of history—are open. The core of this programme has been that the premises and legitimation of the social, ontological and political order were no longer taken for granted.

The central core of this cultural programme has been possibly most successfully formulated by Weber. To follow Faubion's (1993: 113–15) exposition of Weber's conception of modernity:

> Weber finds the existential threshold of modernity in a certain deconstruction: of what he speaks of as the 'ethical postulate that the world is a God-ordained, and hence somehow meaningfully and ethically oriented cosmos....
>
> What he asserts—what in any event might be extrapolated from his assertions—is that the threshold of modernity has its epiphany precisely as the legitimacy of the postulate of a divinely preordained and fated cosmos has its decline; that modernity emerges, that one or another modernity can emerge, only as the legitimacy of the postulated cosmos ceases to be taken for granted and beyond reproach. Countermoderns reject that reproach, believe in spite of it....
>
> One can extract two theses: Whatever else they may be, modernities in all their variety are responses to the same existential problematic.

The second: whatever else they may be, modernities in all their variety are precisely those responses that leave the problematic in question intact, that formulate visions of life and practice neither beyond nor in denial of it but rather within it, even in deference to it.

Concomitantly, there developed a very intensive reflexivity around the basic ontological premises as well as around the bases of social and political order of authority of society—a reflexivity that was shared even by the most radical critics of this programme, who in principle denied the legitimacy of such reflexivity. The reflexivity that developed in the programme of modernity went—because all such responses leave this existential problematic intact—beyond that which crystallized in the Axial Civilizations (Eisenstadt 1952: 294–314, 1986). This critical reflexivity focussed not only on the possibility of different interpretations of the transcendental visions and of the basic ontological conceptions prevalent in a society or civilization, but came to question the very givenness of such visions and of the institutional patterns related to them. In contrast to Axial Civilizations, it focussed not only on the religious or social sphere but also on the political. It gave rise to an awareness of the existence of a multiplicity of such visions and patterns, and of the possibility that those visions and conceptions could, in a sense, have to be contested. In Lefort's (1988: 215) words:

It entailed the loss of the 'nuances of certainty' in the face of a dissolution of the ultimate markers of certainty, under the effect of which an adventure inaugurates itself in which the foundations of power, the foundations of law and the foundations of knowledge are called into question.

This 'new indeterminacy' (Lefort 1988: 215) generates, as Peter Wagner, pointed out, an openness of a space of interpretation and the great variety of new—and always temporary and never final—answers (Eisenstadt 2001: 320–40, 2002a; Wagner 1994).

The awareness of such multiple possibilities of interpretations has been closely connected with some of the core characteristics of two central components of the modern project, emphasized in the early studies of modernization by Dan Lerner (1958), and later by Inkeles and Smith (1974). The first such component is, as illustrated by the famous story in Lerner's book about the grocer and the shepherd, the recognition, among those becoming and being modern, of the possibility of undertaking a great variety of roles beyond any fixed or ascriptive ones, and restricted ones; and, second, the concomitant possibility of belonging to wider translocal, possibly changing, communities and the closely related receptivity to different communications and messages which promulgate such open possibilities and visions.

Closely related to such awareness and central to this cultural programme was the emphasis on the autonomy of man—his or hers, but in the initial formulation of this programme certainly 'his'—emancipation from the fetters of traditional political and cultural authority, and the continuous expansion of the realm of personal and institutional freedom and activity, and of human ones. Parallelly, this programme entailed a very strong emphasis on autonomous participation of members of the society in the constitution of the social and political order, and its constitution; on autonomous access of all members of the society to these orders and their centres.

The modern programme also entailed a radical transformation, which developed—even if slowly and intermittently, though continually—first of all in Europe and then in what would become the United States of America, and, above all, in the Great Revolutions and their aftermaths, of the conceptions and premises of the political order, of the constitution of the political arena, and of the characteristics of the political process, the major characteristics of which was, indeed, also its openness (Eisenstadt 1978).[1]

At the core of the new conceptions of the political order was the breakdown of traditional legitimation thereof, the resultant opening-up of different possibilities of constitution of such order and the consequent contestation about the ways in which political order was to be constituted by human actors.

As with respect to the general cultural programme of modernity, it was the breakdown of traditional legitimization of the political order; the perception of this order as not preordained by some divine or transcendental force, and one that could be constituted by activities of people and the concomitant opening-up of different possibilities of legitimation, that constituted the core of this political programme. This has been recognized by Montesquieu, and more fully in the Federalist papers and in the work of Alexis de Tocqueville, and almost in all of the political discourse that developed after the American and French revolutions. Thus, the modern political programme entailed a continual tension between, on one hand—to use Claude Lefort's words—the loss of 'markers of certainty' inherent in the breakdown of traditional legitimation and, on the other hand, the continual attempts to regain such certainty manifest in the continual attempts to reconstitute the political order (Lefort 1988: 215).

Such attempts at the reconstitution of the political order could develop, above all, in two—sometimes complementary and sometimes opposing—directions. One such direction, is reflected in the view that it is possible to bridge, through political action, the gap between transcendental and mundane orders, and to realize in the mundane orders, in social life, some of the utopian, eschatological visions. And the possibility that the transformation of society through political action guided by a distinctive vision with strong utopian orientations could be implemented was rooted in some of the aspects of the Great Revolutions. These constituted the culmination of the sectarian, heterodox potentialities that developed in the Axial Civilizations, especially where political space was defined as at least one of the arenas of implementation of the transcendental vision which was predominant in them. Such transformation involved turning upside-down—even if ultimately in secular terms—the hegemony of the Augustinian vision, which promulgated the separation of the City of God from the City of Man, and the resultant attempt to implement the heterodox and the sectarian visions, often imbued with strong gnostic elements that wanted to bring the City of God to the City of Man. The Great Revolutions can indeed be seen as the first—or at least the most dramatic and the most successful—attempts in the history of mankind to implement on a macrosocietal scale, utopian visions with strong gnostic components. It was Eric Voegelin's (1952, 1954, 1978) great insight—though he possibly presented it in a rather exaggerated way—to point out the roots of the modern political programme in the heterodox and gnostic traditions of medieval Europe.

Since then the search for the ways in which the concrete social order, as it crystallized in the Great Revolutions, could become the embodiment of an ideal order became a central component of the modern political discourse and tradition. It was closely connected with the charismatization of the centre as the area in which such visions could and should be implemented through the full and active participation of members of society (Eisenstadt 1978).

Such visions became closely connected with the second major component or orientation of the political programme of modernity, namely, the recognition of the legitimacy of multiple interests and of multiple conception of common good, slowly extending to the realm of (religious) beliefs also. This emphasis was at least implicit in theories of natural rights, especially those that emphasized the right to property, with the transformation of the attitude towards property from the republican view.

This stressed the importance of freeing citizens for responsible participation in the political community, to the view of property as embodying 'natural rights', almost a precondition of political community, making the political community the guardian of property.

The continual tensions between such visions and the recognition of the legitimacy of multiple interests and conceptions of the common good and tensions between them constituted the background for the continual attempts to combine different conceptions of *volonté du tous* with those of *volonté générale*, that constitute, as we have seen, the crux of the realm of the political in modern societies.

In close relation to these characteristics of the political order, there developed in modern societies some distinctive characteristic of their centres and peripheries, and of the relations between them. First was the development of very strong tendencies to permeate the peripheries by the centres and of the impingement of the peripheries on the centres, with continual attempts by the periphery to impinge on the centres and to participate in the constitution of their charismatic attributes, thereby blurring the distinctions between the centre and the periphery. Second, there developed a strong emphasis on, at least, the potential active participation of the periphery(s) of 'society', of all its members, in the political arena. Third, in close relation to the development of these new centre–periphery relations was the crystallization of relatively widespread autonomous public sphere(s). In these, different sectors of the peripheries organized themselves in order to explore publicly the open ways in which they could exert their influence on these matters and gain a relatively autonomous way of access to the centre or centres. Fourth was the combination of the charismatization of the centre(s) with the incorporation of themes and symbols of protest, which became components of the modern transcendental visions as basic and legitimate components of the premises of these centres. Themes and symbols of protest—equality and freedom, justice and autonomy, solidarity and identity—became central components of the modern project of the emancipation of man. It was indeed the incorporation of such themes of protest into the centre which heralded the radical transformation of various sectarian utopian visions into central components of the political and cultural programme, combining orientations of rebellion and intellectual anti-nomianism, together with strong orientations to centre formation and institution building. This gave rise to social movements: movements of protest as a continual component of the political process.

The quest of the periphery(s) for participation in the social, political and cultural orders, and the concomitant demands for the incorporation of themes of protest into the centre, and for the concomitant possible transformation of the centre was often guided by the various attempts to reconstitute the makers of certainty the political arena grounded in utopian visions, visions promulgated, above all, by the major social movements that developed as an inherent component of the modern political process.

Out of the combination of the transformation of incorporating the symbols and demands of protest into the central symbolic repertoire of society, and of reconfirming the legitimacy of multiple interests, the continuous restructuring of centre–periphery relations has become a central focus of political process and dynamics in modern societies and of the demands for the reconstitution of the realm of the political within them. The various processes of structural change and dislocation that took place continually as a result of the development of capitalism, economic changes, urbanization, changes in the process of communication and new political formations have led in modern societies not only to the promulgation by different groups of various concrete grievances and demands, but also to a growing quest for participation in the broader social and political order and in the central arenas thereof—indeed in its reconstitution—that is, of the realm of the political.

These demands for participation in the centre were closely connected with the crystallization of the basic characteristics of the modern political processes—the common denominator of which was first the openness. While these characteristics naturally are most visible in open, democratic or pluralistic regimes, they are also inherent in autocratic and totalitarian regimes, even if the latter attempt to regulate and control them in such a way as seemingly to 'close' them. The first of these aspects of the political process in modern societies, attesting to such openness, has been the emergence of a new type of 'political class' or 'classes' and of new types of political activists—a non-ascriptive class, the recruitment to which was, in principle if not in fact, open to everybody. The second is the continual attempts of these class(es) and activists to mobilize political support through open public contestations. The third is the fact that such attempts at the mobilization of such support and governance are closely related to the promulgation of policies and their implementation. The fourth is the very strong tendencies—unparalleled in any other regime, again with the possible partial, but very partial, exception of some of the city-states of antiquity—of potential politicization of many problems and demands of various sectors of the society and of conflicts between them.

It was the combination of these processes with the incorporation of themes of protest and within the continual reconstruction of centre–periphery relations that provided the dynamics of the quests for the reconstitution of the realm of the political in modern societies.

The cultural and political programme of modernity also entailed a very distinctive mode of constitution of the boundaries of collectivities and collective identities. In some, even if certainly not total contrast to the situation in the Axial Civilizations, collective identities were not taken as given or as preordained by some transcendental vision and authority, or by perennial customs (Eisenstadt 2003). Very much in line with the general core characteristics of modernity, the most distinct characteristic of the construction of modern collectivities was that such construction was continually problematized in reflexive ways and constituted a focus of continual struggles and contestations, indeed, one of the major foci of struggle about the reconstitution of the realm of the political in modern societies.

Such continual contestations were borne by distinct social actors—be they political activists, politically active intellectuals or distinct social movements and, above all, national or nationalistic movements—oriented towards the construction of such new collectivities. One of the most distinctive characteristics of the continual process of reconstruction of modern collective identities was the centrality in this process of special social and political activists bearing distinct visions of collective identities and ideologies, and mobilizing wide sectors of the population.

It was these activists and movements that were among the most important bearers of contestations and struggles, often couched in highly ideological terms, around the far-reaching transformation in comparison with the preceding Axial periods, of the basic components of collective identity and of the relation between them, as well as of demands for the incorporation of themes of protest into the centres of the society and of the reconstitution of centre–periphery relations (Eisenstadt 2002a). Among the most important of such transformations of the themes of collective identity attendant on the development of modernity, and which first emerged in Europe, was the development of new—mainly secular—definitions; yet, often couched in highly ideological and absolute terms, of each of the components of collective identity—the civil, primordial, and universalistic and transcendental 'sacred' ones; the growing importance of the civil and procedural components thereof; of a continual tension among these components; and a very strong emphasis on the construction and institutionalization of collective identities in territorial boundaries. There was also the establishment of a very strong connection between the construction of the boundaries of political orders and that of the major 'encompassing' collectivities, a connection that later became epitomized in the model of the modern nation-state.

The major foci of the reconstitution of the realm of the political in modern societies: The major issues of political struggle

The general tendency to the continual redefinition of the scope of the realm of the political, that of the loss of the markers of certainty and the search to attain them again, and to the concomitant continual contestation of the boundaries of what is considered as the appropriate scope of political action, of the boundaries of the political, of the legitimate, open political arena and action, has indeed been rooted in the basic characteristics of the modern political process in combination with the radical transformation of the parameters and premises of the political order, of its legitimation, and of the basic orientations to tradition and to authority.

But the concrete contents of these demands for the reconstitution of the political as they have crystallized in different modern societies and in different periods of their histories developed out of the confrontations and contradictions between the premises of the cultural and political programme of modernity, on one hand, and the developments in the various institutional arenas, on the other, especially the economic and political ones, and the constitution of collective identities, and of boundaries of political units, that is, the modern states.

The initial framework of these developments were several distinct historical processes that developed from the sixteenth century onwards in all Western, Northern and Central European countries, the relative tempo and concrete constellations of which varied. The most important of these processes are the formations of the modern states—the absolutist states or patrician/republican ones that were later transformed in the wake of the Great Revolutions into modern constitutional—often into nation-states. Also important were the development of new state–society relations, most fully manifest in the emergence of a distinct type or types of civil society, the crystallization and constitution of new types of collectivities, and last but certainly not the least, the development of capitalist, later industrial-capitalist, types of political economy. It was the problems generated by these processes—by the construction of the new political formations and of new collectivities by the development of new economic forces and of new types of political economy, above all, of course, of capitalism, later on of industrial capitalism—and the continual tendencies to democratization that gave rise to the most important political demands and struggles that developed in modern polities in modern political regimes for the reconstitution of the realm of the political. Among the most important of such demands were the specification and definition of the basic components of collective identity, of the boundaries of the major collectivities, especially of the states and/or of nations; the demands of various sectors of society for full membership in the political community, for access to the centres and to political power, and for the accountability of rulers; and demands for definition of the public sphere(s) and regulation of economic process.

Or, in greater detail, the major concrete issues of political struggle that developed first in Europe, and which in a way became prototypical for the development of all modern regimes, were first the definitions of the symbols and boundaries of these collectives. This was true especially of the relative importance in their constitution of primordial, territorial, civil and transcendental, religious or secular revolutionary components; the definitions of the territorial scope of such collectivities and the autonomy of different groups within them.

Second, closely related to the problems of constitution of the symbols and boundaries of collectivities were those bearing on the mode of legitimization of the new regimes. In this context, the major problems or demands first focussed on the bases of legitimation of the political regimes, especially on the very establishment of constitutional government, and on the specification of details of the constitutional arrangements, such as the types of electoral systems, usually closely interwoven with the juggling of different groups for relative power positions. Also, in this context was the specification of the right of access of various sectors of the population, be it classes or primordially defined groups or categories of people, especially those defined according to gender or age, race, ethnic origin or religious affiliation, to the centre. That is, the definition of the scope of citizenship, and of the nature and scope of the entitlements that go with citizenship, such as, first of all, suffrage, but also various 'social' or economic entitlements.

The third major pole or focus of political contestations or struggle in modern societies and of the concomitant demands for the reconstruction of the realm of the political have been those related to the development of modern capitalism and industrialism, and their major social repercussions. In this context, the major foci of contention and the major issues of political struggle developed around different types of economic problems and policies, especially those related to the scope and limits of regulation of the economic life, of industrial relations, the constitutionalization of public goods, and of distributive allocation to be undertaken by the state.

While these issues developed in all modern societies, their relative importance and timing varied greatly in different societies and periods. They developed, first, in a certain sequence in modern European societies; and in Europe itself, they developed in different constellations. The way in which these issues have developed in Europe have been greatly influenced by the particular historical experience of modern Europe and were not necessarily to be 'repeated' in other European societies, and even more so beyond Europe.

It was these issues as they became articulated in the political arena—both as multiple concrete demands borne by numerous groups that provided the mill of routine politics as well as demands for entitlements, connected with broader conceptions of the common good—that constituted the crux of the demands for the reconstitution of the realm of the political in modern societies. All of these were rooted in the cultural and political programme of modernity and of the institutional contours thereof, the continual propensity to the reconstitution of the realm of the political that developed in modern societies.

Social movements, political parties and the reconstitution of the realm of the political in modern societies

The demands for the reconstitution of the realm of the political was promulgated in modern societies by many political actors and activists. Of special importance, among them, have been relatively autonomous intellectual and political activists, representatives of different interest groups and leaders of political groups—and perhaps, above all, the distinctively modern forms of political organization—and social movements, movements of protest and political parties, within which such activists usually played an important role, albeit always in close relation to other social and political actors (Tarrow 1994).

Such openly politically active social movements constituted transformations in the modern setting, first of the various heterodoxies of the Axial Civilization—above all of those heterodoxies that sought to bring about, by political action, the realization and the reconstruction of the centre of the Kingdom of God on earth. Second were popular movements—movements of protest and subaltern rebellions—and they constituted distinctive modern phenomena. Many of these movements epitomized the search for the ways in which the concrete social and political order could become the embodiment of an ideal order and that such a search constituted a central component, if certainly not the only one, of the modern political discourse and process. It was such different movements that constituted in modern societies one of the main bearers, perhaps the main bearer, of different utopian visions. At the same time, many of these movements became the channels through which subaltern protests were articulated in different confrontational situations. These activists and movements of protest were among the most important bearers of the symbols of protest that moved, as we have seen, in modern societies from the margins to the central political arenas of their respective societies, becoming parts of that arena and process, being of central importance in the continual reconstruction of centre–periphery relations and of the concomitant reconstitution of the realm of the political.

The concrete institutionalization of the demands for the reconstitution of the realm of the political was always contingent on some cooperation between such movements and other political actors, especially, although not only, of the political parties and organizations, and different, continually changing 'publics'. Such parties and publics constituted yet another distinct modern type of political process, rooted in its very openness and, above all, in the necessity of the would-be groups and individuals competing for power to mobilize openly and continually gain wider political support. The concrete relations, cooperative and contestual, between social movements and political parties, as well as other types of political organizations, social associations and publics, differed greatly between different societies and in different periods of their respective histories, but in all of them, they entailed the interweaving of conceptions of the common good, of *volonte generale* with different constellations of *volonte du tous*, attesting to the continual interweaving of these components in the modern political processes.

Whatever the differences between them, these movements constituted a continual component of the modern political scene, of the modern political processes. One very important type of such movements were the centre-oriented ones that aimed at the reconstruction of the centres and boundaries of their respective societies and tended to be closely connected to the charismatization of the centre as the major arena in which such visions could and should be implemented.

The major aim of such movements was the reconstruction of the centres of their respective societies. Among such movements were those that aimed to change the distribution of power and its bases within a given society. The most important of them in modern times were, first, those that aimed at the inclusion of a wider strata into the central political framework (through the extension of suffrage); and second, the socialist and communist movements that added the demand for the reconstruction of the patterns of the political economy. This latter goal was to be effected by reconstructing economic relations and abolishing the more hierarchical premises of their respective centres. A second type of centre-oriented movement aimed at the reconstruction of the boundaries of political collectivities, mainly national or ethnic ones.[2]

Alongside such centre-oriented movements, there also developed religious reform movements, cooperative or syndicalist movements aimed at reorganizing aspects of life in different sectors of society, anarchist movements that opposed the state in principle and popular movements emphasizing autonomous participation in the political process against bureaucratic or centre domination. Many of these movements promulgated a total denial of the basic premise of modernity and its major institutional implications, and some of these movements, including earlier religious-reformist, syndicalist and many post-modern ones, seemingly rejected any orientation towards the centre. They tended, instead, to emphasize the construction of new spaces seemingly independent of the centre, though in many cases impinging on it. In practice, most movements always promulgated some overlap between orientation towards the centre and the construction of new spaces, and the concrete themes proclaimed by them would often, in later periods, become transposed into centre-oriented ones. Lately, many of the 'new' types of social movements, such as women's movements, various minority movements and many fundamentalist movements, and in the later decades of the twentieth century, religious communal movements initially demanded changes in the principles of allocations of resources (Johnston and Klandermans 1995; MacAdam et al. 1996; Melucci 1985; Offe 1985; Zald and McCarthy 1987).

These numerous, continually changing movements developed first in Europe, then in the Americas, and later throughout the world, in close relation to the problems arising out of the contradictions between the basic premises of the cultural and political programme of modernity, and the actual processes of its institutionalization in multiple concrete historical settings in Western Europe and beyond it. These movements arose foremost in close relation to the processes and problems arising from industrialization and development, and the expansion of capitalism; from the construction of new modern political regimes and formations, and international systems; and of the concomitant new types of collectivities—nations and nation-states. Beyond Western Europe, these movements arose in relation to the expansion of modernity throughout the world through imperialist, military, economic and ideological channels, and to the confrontation between Western hegemony and the Central Eastern European, and Asian and African traditions, civilizations and societies, and between such hegemonies and the search of the new societies of an autonomous standing in the new international systems. All these movements continually intermeshed with more 'traditional' types of rebellion as well as popular movements of resistance to the constitution of the modern state, industrialism and market economy.

The relative importance of these different perpetually changing social movements varied greatly in different societies and in different periods. There developed great differences in different modern societies and periods with respect to the extent and ways in which these movements became interwoven with the other major actors on the political scene, especially with political parties and interest groups.

While their aims and the concrete problems to which these movements, organizations and parties were oriented were continually changing, the ideologies promulgated by these movements were always focussed on some of the major components of the modern cultural and political order, its antinomies and tensions. And it was these movements that were among the most important actors promulgating the central demands for the changes in the realm of the political.

These movements were international even if their bases or roots were in specific countries. Their activities were not confined to the limits or frameworks of any 'single' society or nation-state, even if it was such societies or states that constituted the major arenas of implementation of the programmes and goals of such activities. The more successful among such movements have always crystallized in distinct ideological and institutional patterns that became often identified with specific countries, as was the case, for instance, first with revolutionary France and later with Soviet Russia, but whose reach went far beyond them (Furet 1970, 1982; Nahirny 1983).

These various continually changing movements developed side by side, being often mutually complementary, but also competing and being in conflict with one another. They were complementary as they were rooted in the common cultural and political programme of modernity and in the historical experience of their societies. But different movements developed in conjunction with the different aspects or dimensions of this experience, and emphasized different problems and contradictions between the premises of this programme and to its institutionalization that developed in conjunction with this experience.

Most—possibly all—of these movements addressed themselves critically to different components or dimensions of the political and cultural programme of modernity, and to the basic tensions and antimonies inherent in this programme and in its institutionalization in the different historical settings and contexts. It was the abolition or overcoming of some of these tensions and contradictions that usually constituted an important component in the ideologies and programmes of these movements.

Thus, for instance, the criticisms of the existing order of modernity promulgated by the socialist movements were mostly couched in terms of the non-completion of this programme and were oriented towards its fuller implementation. National movements built on those components of the revolutionary heritage that emphasized the right of self-determination of a collectivity. They aimed, above all, at the reconstruction of the boundaries of newly crystallizing collectivities, promulgating usually highly particularistic primordial terms. They entailed the confrontation between the universalistic and more particularistic or ascriptive components of legitimization of the modern regimes. Their criticism of the existing order could develop in the direction of a more extreme negation of the universalistic components of the cultural programme of modernity. The extreme nationalist movements denied the universal and universalistic orientations of these regimes and espoused primordial racial orientations in an extreme ideological way. Unlike the conservative movements that were predominant throughout most of the nineteenth century on the 'right' wing of the political spectrum, these 'new' extreme nationalist fascist movements evinced strong Jacobin mobilizing tendencies. Later on, on the contemporary scene, the fundamentalist movements promulgated extreme anti-Enlightenment ideologies.

The different movements promulgated different visions of modern life, of modern social and political order, of modernity. Accordingly, they could also, under some conditions, oppose and contradict one another, and come into intensive ideological and political conflicts with one another, as was the case in the fierce ideological and political struggle between communist and fascist movements in the 1930s or between communist and liberal democratic ideologies during the Cold War. The contestations between these movements and the visions they bore, and between them and other political actors, took place in all modern states, first in Europe and later in the Americas and throughout the world.

It was these contestations that promulgated different directions for the reconstitution of the realm of the political. These were of crucial importance in shaping the different patterns of modern societies, first of all of territorial and nation-states, in generating within them different definitions of the premises of political order; of accountability of authority relations between state and civil society; of patterns of collective identity or self-perceptions of societies, or in other words, of the basic contours of multiple modernities.

The demands for the reconstruction of the realm of the political as promulgated previously, all by such movements, and the institutionalization of such demands as effected in cooperation with political parties or other political organizations, usually brought out or highlighted the tensions between the Jacobin and pluralistic components in the political programme of modernity, and the confrontation between the autonomy of civil society and the power of the state, and between the self-legitimacy of the rules of the constitutional game and legitimization in terms of some other, often 'ultimate' visions, couched in primordial and/or some sacred—religious or secular—terms as well as between the 'routine' and the 'revolutionary' aspects of politics.

The ubiquity of these movements and the demands for the reconstruction of the realm of the political and the concomitant challenge of the contradiction between an encompassing, totalistic, potentially totalitarian vision and/or a commitment to the pluralistic premises constituted an inherent element of everything modern, including constitutional regimes and a basic component of the political dynamics of the modern era. None of the modern constitutional and/or liberal democracies has entirely done away with a Jacobin component, especially with its utopian dimension, with orientations to some primordial or 'sacred' religious components in collective identity, and of the legitimization of the political order (Eisenstadt 1999a; Sternhell 1996).

The demands for the redefinition of the boundaries of the political as promulgated by various social movements interacting with and implemented in cooperation and contestation with other political actors develop and become most visible in periods of extensive change. And it is in such periods and situations that promulgation of protest usually comes forward as a major component of the political process. However—and this is of great importance for our discussion—the various demands for the reconstitution of the realm of the political, as borne by social movements, and the attempts at their institutionalization in cooperation with other political activists and organizations, especially political parties, were usually of great importance also in less dramatic situations, constituting a continual component of the modern political process.

A central component of the reconstitution of the realm of the political and of specification of the attributes of citizenship has been the constitution of public spaces, but not the homogenizing spaces as implied in the Habermasian conception thereof, but as shown from different points of view by Margaret Sommers and Nancy Fraser, in multiple and continually changeable public spaces (Elias 1978–82; Foucault 1965, 1973, 1975, 1988). The constitution of such public spaces, attendant on the reconstitution of the realm of the political, could indeed develop in several directions, in line with its different demands, namely, demands for the redefinition of at least some of the premises and of the patterns of legitimization of regimes; implementation of policies aiming at the redistribution of resources and of public entitlements; and the construction of social spaces in which different groups could develop distinct patterns of social, cultural or economic activities, and promulgate their distinct identities, up to the possibility of the establishment of new distinct political collectivities.

As indicated earlier, the demands for political reconstitution could first entail the reconstruction of the symbols of collective identity and develop in several directions. This multiplicity of possible directions in modern societies attests to the prevalence of multiple, plural ways in which the constitution of political spaces could develop. But these have worked out in different ways in different modern regimes.

Reconstruction of the realm of the political and of the variability of patterns of citizenship: Pluralistic and totalistic tendencies

The ways in which these potentially pluralistic dimensions of the constitution of the political domain, of the relations between state and society, and the constitution of public space has worked out in different ways in different modern regimes are very much according to their different patterns analyzed earlier.

First of all, they developed in different ways in pluralistic, autocratic and totalitarian ones. The crux of the differences is best manifest in their respective approaches to the reconstitution of the political and in the concomitant directions of the relations between state and civil society, which are characteristic of each of them. In pluralistic regimes, there developed the continuous expansion, growth, diversification and reconstruction of civil society and its relation to the state. In these regimes, autonomous access of different sectors of society to the centre was fully admitted or continually extended, and was closely connected to the possibility of development of responsible citizenry and leadership through an open political process, giving rise to a multiple, continually changing political arena in different directions, entailing different conceptions of positive liberty. This did not necessarily involve the diminution of the power or scope of activities of the state; rather, it involved a continuously greater participation of different sectors of the society in the political arena.

As against this, in totalitarian and authoritarian regimes, access to the realm of the political has become monopolized by the state and the party, denying the possibility of its reconstitution in different, pluralistic ways, potentially inherent in the modern political system, without, however, being able to entirely do away with it.

The authoritarian regimes tended to espouse a very restricted, limited conception of citizenship and a highly regulated access of civil society to the state—restricted to select groups and limited with respect to its reach and impact on the centre. In the totalitarian regimes, the legitimacy of the right of access to all sectors of society to the centre was seemingly fully acknowledged, but these regimes regulated such access through a highly controlled mobilization of the population. The control of access to political arenas was regulated by the hegemonic party, which was presented as the sole bearer of the common good and the regulator of the expression, of the will of all, and of various discrete interests that were, in principle at least, totally submerged in the centre and the party.

Here we encounter a very interesting and important paradox from the point of view to the bracketing out of the concern with the reconstitution of the political from the mainstream of political theory. The crux of this paradox lies in the fact that all such attempts can be seen, as indicated by Katznelson in his critical remarks about Berlin's attitude to the New Deal of attempts to constitute some modes of positive liberty (Berlin 1975; Katznelson 1999), as cases or manifestations of 'positive liberty', but not of the totalitarian kind. Such attempts are, of course, radically different from the totalitarian conceptions and implementations of 'positive' liberty. Paradoxical, indeed, it was in the totalitarian regimes with their totalistic conception of positive liberty that possible reconstruction of the realm of the political in different directions is not officially allowed and suppressed, as against the recognition of the pluralistic heterogeneous and potentially contentious directions of such reconstruction, in the pluralistic constitutional regimes—including also, of course, the 'liberal' or 'European' ones, but also in regimes such as India and Japan.

The second mode of variations was the relative importance of the different components of collective identity, that is, of the primordial and civil and sacred (religious or secular) ones and the different combinations thereof. It also focussed on the modes of their interweaving, as we have seen earlier, especially the extent to which there developed totalistic, as against multifaceted, visions of those basic collective identities, and ways to which the basic themes of constitution—primordial-national, civil and universalistic orientations—were interwoven in them. In all modern European societies, there developed a continual tension or confrontation between the primordial components of such an identity, reconstructed in such modern terms as nationalism and ethnicity, and the modern as well as more traditional religious, universalistic and civil components, as well as among the latter ones, and the mode of interweaving of these different components of collective identity varied greatly among different modern societies.

While the relative importance of the different components of collective identity varied greatly within each group or category of regimes, in the pluralistic, authoritarian and totalitarian ones, there developed a very close elective affinity between the multifaceted interweaving of such components and pluralistic regimes, and between totalistic modes of such interweaving, and authoritarian and totalitarian regimes. The extent to which, in the historical experience of those societies, none of these dimensions has been totally absolutized by their respective carriers against the other dimensions, or organized in a clear hierarchical way, or contrariwise the extent to which there developed rather multifaceted and relatively flexible patterns of collective identity, greatly influenced the way in which the tension between pluralistic and totalistic tendencies inherent in the cultural and political programme of modernity was played out.[3]

The constitution of different modes of collective identity and the concomitant struggles about the reconstitution of the realm of the political has been connected in Europe—and beyond Europe—with specific institutional conditions, the most important among them being the flexibility of the centres and of the major, newly constructed elite, the mutual openness between them, and their relations to broader social strata. There developed in Europe, and later in other societies, a close elective affinity between the absolutizing types of collective identity and various types of absolutist regimes and rigid centres, and between the multifaceted pattern of collective identity, in which the primordial, civil and sacred components were continually interwoven with the development of relatively open and flexible centres and of mutual openings between the various strata (Eisenstadt 2002b). It was the concomitant development of relatively strong but flexible and open centres, multifaceted modes of collective identity and autonomous access of the major strata to the centre that was of crucial importance in the development of a distinct type of civil society, a society that was to a large extent autonomous *from* the state, but at the same time, autonomous *in* the state, and had an autonomous access to the state and participated in formulating the rules of the political game. It was such conditions that made possible the minimization of the tendencies to barbarism and exclusion (Eisenstadt 1992a, 1992b; Arnason 1993; see also Eisenstadt 2002a).

Notes

1. On the Revolutions and modernity, see, for instance, the special issue of *Social Research* (1989). On the role of groups of heterodox intellectuals in some of the revolutions and in the antecedent periods, see Baechler (1979), Cochin (1924, 1979) and Furet (1982).

2. On socialist movements see, for example, Bell (1968). On nationalism and movements see, for instance, Eley and Suny (1996), and Guibernau and Hutchinson (2001).
3. For a fuller account, see Eisenstadt (1999b).

References

Arnason, Johann P. 1993. *The Future that Failed: Origins and Destinies of the Soviet Union*. London: Routledge.

Baechler, J. 1979. 'Preface', in A. Cochin, *L'esprit du Jocobinisme*. Paris: Universitaires de France.

Bell, Daniel. 1968. 'Socialism', in David L. Sills (ed.), *International Encyclopedia of the Social Sciences*, Vol. 14, pp. 506–34. New York: The Macmillan Company and the Free Press.

Berlin, Isaiah. 1975. 'Two Concepts of Liberty', in Isaiah Berlin, *Four Essays on Liberty*, pp. 118–72. London: Oxford University press.

Cochin, A. 1924. *La Revolution et la Libre Pensee*. Paris: Plon Nourrit.

———. 1979. *L'esprit du Jocobinisme*. Paris: Universitaires de France.

Eisenstadt, S.N. 1952. 'The Axial Age: The Emergence of Transcendental Visions and the Rise of Clerics', *European Journal of Sociology*, 23(2): 294–314.

———. 1978. *Revolution and the Transformation of Societies*. New York: Free Press.

——— (ed.). 1986. *The Origins and Diversity of Axial Age Civilizations*. Albany, NY: SUNY Press.

———. 1992a. 'Center and Periphery Relations in the Soviet Empire: Some Interpretative Observations', in Alexander J. Motyl (ed.), *Thinking Theoretically about Soviet Nationalities*, pp. 205–23. New York: Columbia University Press.

———. 1992b. 'The Breakdown of Communist Regimes and the Vicissitudes of Modernity', *Daedalus*, 121(2): 21–42.

———. 1999a. *Fundamentalism, Sectarianism and Revolution: The Jacobin Dimension of Modernity*. Cambridge: Cambridge University Press.

———. 1999b. *Paradoxes of Democracy: Fragility, Continuity and Change*. Washington, DC: Woodrow Wilson Center Press.

———. 2001. 'The Civilizational Dimension of Modernity: Modernity as a Distinct Civilization', *International Sociology*, 16(3): 320–40.

——— (ed.). 2002a. *Multiple Modernities*. New Brunswick: Transaction Publications.

———. 2002b. 'Barbarism and Modernity: The Destructive Components of Modernity—The Perennial Challenge', in Ernest Krausz and Gitta Tulea (eds), *Starting the Twenty-first Century: Sociological Reflections and Challenges*, pp. 25–36. New Brunswick: Transaction Publishers.

Eisenstadt, S.N. 2003. 'Cultural Programs, the Construction of Collective Identity and the Continual Reconstruction of Primordiality', in *Comparative Civilizations and Multiple Modernities*, Part I, pp. 75–134. Leiden/Boston: Brill.

Eley, Geoff and Ronald Grigor Suny (eds). 1996. *Becoming National: A Reader*. Oxford: Oxford University Press.

Elias, Norbert. 1978–82. *The Civilizing Process*. New York: Urizen Books.

Faubion, James D. 1993. *Modern Greek Lessons: A Primer in Historical Constructivism*. Princeton: Princeton University Press.

Foucault, Michel. 1965. *Madness and Civilization: A History of Insanity in the Age of Reason*. New York: Pantheon Books.

———. 1973. *The Birth of the Clinic: An Archaeology of Medical Perception*. New York: Vintage Books.

———. 1975. *Surveiller et Punir: Naissance de la Prison* [Discipline and Punish: The Birth of the Prison, trans. Alan Sheridan]. Paris: Gallimard/New York: Vintage Books.

———. 1988. *Technologies of the Self: A Seminar with Michel Foucault*. Amherst: University of Massachusetts Press.

Furet, F. 1970. *The French Revolution*. New York: Macmillan.

———. 1982. *Rethinking the French Revolution*. Chicago: University of Chicago Press.

Guibernau, Montserrat and John Hutchinson (eds). 2001. *Understanding Nationalism*. Cambridge: Polity Press.

Inkeles, A. and D.H. Smith. 1974. *Becoming Modern: Individual Change in Six Developing Countries*. Cambridge, Massachusetts: Harvard University Press.

Johnston, H. and B. Klandermans (eds). 1995. *Social Movements and Culture*. Minneapolis: University of Minnesota Press.

Katznelson, Ira. 1999. 'Isaiah Berlin's Modernity', *Social Research*, 66(4): 1079–1101.

Lefort, C. 1988. *Democracy and Political Theory*. Cambridge: Polity Press.

Lerner, D. 1958. *The Passing of Traditional Society: Modernizing the Middle East*. Glencoe: Free Press.

MacAdam, Doug, John D. McCarthy and Mayer N. Zald (eds). 1996. *Comparative Perspectives on Social Movements: Political Opportunities, Mobilizing Structures and Cultural Framings*. New York: Cambridge University Press.

Melucci, A. 1985. The Symbolic Challenge of Contemporary Movements. *Social Research*, 52(4): 790–816.

Nahirny, Vladimir, C. 1983. *The Russian Intelligentsia: From Torment to Silence*. New Brunswick: Transaction Publications.

Offe, C. 1985. 'New Social Movements: Challenging the Boundaries of Institutional Politics', *Social Research*, 52(4): 817–68.

Social Research. 1989. Special issue on 'The French Revolution and the Birth of Modernity', 56(1[Spring]).

Sternhell, Zeev (ed.). 1996. *The Intellectual Revolt Against Liberal Democracy, 1870–1945: International Conference in Memory of Jacob L. Talmon.* Jerusalem: Israel Academy of Sciences and Humanities.

Tarrow, Sidney. 1994. *Power in Movement: Social Movements, Collective Action and Politics.* Cambridge: Cambridge University Press.

Voegelin, E. 1952. *The New Science of Politics: An Introduction.* Chicago: University of Chicago Press.

———. 1954. *Order and History.* Baton Rouge, LA: Louisiana State University.

———. 1978. *Anamnesis.* Notre Dame: University of Notre Dame Press.

Wagner, P. 1994. *A Sociology of Modernity: Liberty and Discipline.* London: Routledge.

Zald, Mayer N. and John D. McCarthy (eds). 1987. *Social Movements in an Organizational Society: Collected Essays.* New Brunswick: Transaction Books.

Play of Power and Struggle for Freedom in Renaissance Humanism

2

Erasmus between Scylla and Charybdis

FELIX WILFRED

I observe that it is my fate, that while I strive to be of service to both parties, I am stoned from both sides.

— *Erasmus of Rotterdam*

Luther hatched the egg Erasmus laid.

(*A sixteenth-century saying*)

At the turn of the sixteenth century, Erasmus of Rotterdam (1469–1536) stood on the European landscape like a colossus towering far above all the Renaissance humanists of his day. He was the embodiment of scholarship and a trailblazer in many respects. His innumerable works published in many translations and their immense popularity are evidence of the influence he wielded at a critical time when Europe was moving from the old medieval world into a new one. In his own lifetime, some of Erasmus works saw over thirty editions—an amazing fact, considering the infancy of printing at the time. Emperors, kings and popes eagerly awaited the honour of one or the other book by Erasmus dedicated to them. The cities of Europe looked forward to having the privilege of Erasmus visit. He has even been the official councillor to Emperor Charles V, and the popes in Rome corresponded with him and wanted to get closer to him. As Zweig (1956: 98) says:

To pronounce the name of Erasmus was, in the early decades of the sixteenth century, to call up the perfect image of the wise man, the

optimum et maximum, the best that brain could conceive of and the most
sublime—as Melanchton writes in his Latin panegyric—the unsurpassed
authority in matters concerning the scientific, the poetical, the mundane
and the spiritual achievements of his epoch.

And yet, this man, in the evening of his life, was deserted and died a lonely
death. History has also been unfair to him. One reason is that he was
not a sanguine hero like his contemporary Luther who could stir up the
whole of Europe with his religious passion; nor was he a man like his
other contemporary Machiavelli, who favoured the unscrupulous pursuit of power, no matter by what means. The ideal of Erasmus was one
difficult to practise; his praxis was one that refused to take sides. Such an
ideal and praxis had their own costs to pay. A pacifist by temperament
and choice—though a revolutionary in thought—Erasmus was dragged,
against his will, into the vicissitudes and controversies of his time on
the eve of modernity. He was far from being a spectator of events taking
place around him. Amidst the pulls from every direction, he stood for
freedom and independence, for democratic ways and peace. Today, no
history of power and freedom could be written without reference to
Erasmus and his vision.

The radicality of his views and the force of his critique on the prevailing order of the day, both in the political and religious realm, were
cloaked in his ingenious literary devices. A consummate master in
the literary arts—*bellae litterae*—he expended his literary genius for the
cause of transformation in political and religious fields. Erasmus was
considered as the one who laid the egg of revolution; others hatched it.
The revolution took a direction with which, ironically, Erasmus could
never agree. He was caught in the dilemma of power and freedom. In
this respect, he was far ahead of his own times. In the battle cries of the
time, Erasmus voice of sanity was drowned, and finally he himself was
deserted. History moved on to the path of what Machiavelli prescribed
to wielders of power. Machiavelli's—and not Erasmus—prescriptions
have found ardent supporters among rulers and princes till our day.
Little wonder that Machiavelli has found most numerous followers
than Erasmus in the course of history.

Erasmus generally kept away from the centres of power and yet he was
sought after. For, where Erasmus stood, mattered. What he wrote about
his close friend, Thomas More, is but a reflection of his own attitude:

> Formerly he [More] disliked court life and the company of princes, for
> the reason that he has always had a peculiar loathing for tyranny, just

as he has always loved equality.... He is by nature somewhat greedy of independence.... No man ever worked so assiduously to gain admission to the court as he studied to escape it. But when the king decided to fill his household with men of weight, learning, sagacity and integrity, More was one of the first among many summoned by him.[1]

While acknowledging the honours that came his way, Erasmus studiously avoided any compromise with the powers, lest his freedom and independence should be in any way affected and compromised. Freedom, for him, was a value that mattered most. In the thought of Erasmus and the vicissitudes of his life, we can observe the dialectic between power and freedom. To highlight this, I have chosen, in the first part of this chapter, to discuss the views and vision of Erasmus over against the thought of Machiavelli relating to power. In the second part, Erasmian vision of freedom is studied over against the bitter controversies roused by Luther and the Reformation.

Play of power and vision of peace

In terms of age, there was, if at all, one or two years of difference between Erasmus and Machiavelli.[2] We do not have evidence of any interaction between these two Renaissance personalities. Nor do we find any mutual reference in their works. Striking, however, are the two poles of thought that these two men represent in the field of politics. Interestingly, both Erasmus and Machiavelli wrote short treatises for the purpose of instructing princes. The rulers depended for their education in governance on such manuals and guides produced by seasoned statesmen. Erasmus wrote *The Education of Christian Prince*, which was meant for a 16-year-old prince, the would-be Emperor Charles V. Machiavelli, on his part, wrote *The Prince* for instructing Lorenzo the Magnificent, son of Piero Di Medici of Florence, in whose court Machiavelli was the chief political architect until he fell in disfavour (Mukherjee and Ramaswamy 1993; *Routledge Encyclopedia of Philosophy* 1998: 17–22).

Ultimately, the difference between Erasmus and Machiavelli can be traced back to the conception of the human nature underlying their writings. No one can fault Erasmus of being naïve when it comes to realities of life, institutions, governance, and so on. He proved himself to be the fiercest critique of the order of the day. Anyone leafing through the pages of his *In Praise of Folly* will be convinced of this fact. Be it secular or religious powers, he never shunned from voicing his critique. What is remarkable is that, in spite of the many things he denounced, he had basically a positive outlook on human nature; he thought in terms of general peace, concord and harmony. In this, he is very close to his lifelong friend Thomas More. Both, *Utopia* of More and the treatise of Erasmus on political governance, are inspired by a general vision of humanity and the ideal of peace with a strikingly positive note. Let us observe how Erasmus instructs Charles in the way of peace (Halkin 1994: 102):

> But your noble prince Charles, are more blessed than Alexander, and will, we hope, surpass him equally in wisdom, too. He for his part had seized an immense empire, but not without bloodshed, nor was it destined to endure. You were born to a splendid empire and destined to inherit one still greater, so that, while he had to expend great efforts in invasion, you will have perhaps to work to ensure that you can voluntarily hand over part of your dominions rather than seize more. You owe it to Heaven that your empire came to you without shedding of blood, and no one suffered for it; your wisdom must now ensure that you preserve it without bloodshed and at peace.

We are struck by Erasmus ideal of peace, particularly when placed against the backdrop of his times. It was the age of warfare, political rivalries and court intrigues, and what counted most to the princes and rulers was the military and political triumphs over rivals and enemies. Much like More's own vision, Erasmian appeal to peace sounded utopian. The peace project of Erasmus also needs to be placed over and against the times in which the seeds of nationalism were beginning to sprout. It is an accepted fact that Reformation made a decisive contribution to the emergence of European nationalism. Though manifestly a religious reform, it, in fact, symbolized the protest of the Germanic peoples against the dictates of the Romans power. The Erasmian goal, on the other hand, was not nationalistic; he projected, instead, the ideal of the 'citizen of the world' with a sense of universal belonging. In fact, he was constantly on the move through many European nations establishing wide contacts among intellectuals, scholars, nobility, and such others.

While Erasmus visualizes the shape of the things to come, Machiavelli embraces the *zeitgeist*, and wants the princes and powers to act successfully. For him, it was not a matter of ethics or ideals, but to know and describe how 'things really are' (*la verità effecttuale della cosa*) and to play one's best game in the given situation. As Zweig (1956: 240–42) observes:

While Erasmus demanded that princes and peoples should freely ... subordinate their personal, their egoistic, their imperialistic claims to a fraternal commonwealth of the whole of mankind, Machiavelli belauded the will to power of every prince. Erasmus ... held ... that politics should be placed in the same category as ethics; a prince, as the leader of the state, should, first of all, be ... the exponent of the ethical ideal. Machiavelli, with the practical experience of a diplomatist, made politics an amoral and independent science, saying that they had as little to do with ethics as had astronomy and geometry. In the material realm of history, the principle of power has achieved a predominant position. Not so Erasmus ideal of politics based upon conciliation and the unity of mankind.

Underlying the Machiavellian pragmatism is basically a negative conception of the human with all its egoistic and base inclinations. Given human perversity, how should a ruler act so as to succeed? This is the concern that runs through the work *The Prince*. In fact, addressing the question whether it is good for a prince to be loved or feared, he notes, how men are 'ungrateful, voluble, dissemblers, anxious to avoid danger and covetous of gain' (Machiavelli 1950: 61).

If, on one hand, Erasmus and More are united by a kindered spirit, there is, on the other hand, a certain point of convergence between Machiavelli and Luther. Like Machiavelli, Luther was conscious of human depravity and its inclination to evil. But the perspective from which they responded to this human situation was different. For Luther, the answer to human evil—radical sinfulness—is to have recourse to God and allow him to rule over us, since human will is incapable of overcoming this perversity. In short, Luther's answer was a religious and theological one. Machiavelli, on the other hand, departing from the same premise of human depravity, perfidy and corruption, proposes that the prince should act in such a way that these are controlled and held in check through his political stratagem and statecraft. In other words, human corruption cannot be cured by laws but by the dexterous use of power, which is politics in its dynamic reality.

Though Luther's vision was theoretically motivated, in actual practice, it appears to me that, at times, he followed the ways of Machiavelli. A clear example is his stance in the case of the German peasant war (1524–25). Fearing that the peasant uprising may endanger his own programme of Reformation and it may invite reprisal from the ruling powers, Luther incited the prince to suppress with force the peasants who were then slaughtered in thousands. He even published a booklet with a fiery title: *Against the Murdering, Thieving Herds of Peasants*. The concrete history of the following centuries went the way of Machiavelli and Luther. Europe became a battleground for religious and political wars, to the eclipse of the Erasmian ideal of peace.

Erasmus positive vision of the human marked a significant departure from the medieval Christian tradition insisting on human sinfulness and frailty—a tendency that Luther carried to the extreme. The modernity was a rejection of such a conception, which it replaced with a more trusting attitude in the human and in its abilities. Erasmus was the pioneer of this alternative conception, which he drew from his study of the classical Greek and Roman authors of the ancient period. Very different from the Machiavellian approach, Erasmus is of the view that a ruler needs to be a philosopher. In this he is closer to Plato, Aristotle and the classical tradition. But Erasmus hastens to add what is meant by philosophy (Augustijn 1991: 73):

> Not that philosophy, I mean, which argues about elements and primal matter and motion and the infinite, but that which frees the mind from the false opinions of the multitude and from wrong desires, and demonstrates the principle of right government by reference to example set by the eternal powers.

Was Erasmus an impractical visionary? That would be an unfair judgement. His knowledge of realpolitik, however, did not hold him back from pursuing the ideals that are indispensable for the survival of humanity. Aware of conflictual situations among powers—whether political or religious—he proposed the need for peace and conciliation. In his view, an impartial arbitration in cases of conflicts among the princes could avoid wars and bring about peace. This was also, as we shall see shortly, the solution he proposed in the thick of the crises unleashed by Luther. The realism of Erasmus and his keen observation of the courts of the day can also be gleaned from his advice to the prince. He knew that flattery is a temptation to which princes could easily succumb and it can ill-dispose them towards fulfilling their duty. Hence, he advises the prince on how to guard oneself against flatterers.

Whereas authority was seen as identified with ancestry and the qualities of the prince with those proposed by Machiavelli, Erasmus sets forth a different set of criteria. At the very beginning of the pedagogical work meant for princes, he observes (McConica 1991: 84):

> On board ship we do not give the helm to the one who has the noblest ancestry of the company, the greatest wealth, or the best looks, but to him

who is most skilled in steering, most alert, and most reliable. Similarly, a kingdom is best entrusted to someone who is better endowed than the rest with the qualities of a king namely wisdom, a sense of justice, personal restraint, foresight, and concern for the public well-being.

Another innovative contribution of Erasmus was his challenge to the widespread theory of a 'just' war. He has a very striking title for one of his works: *Dulce Bellum Inexpertis* (War is Sweet to the Inexperienced). War cannot be the path of wisdom and sanity. It is in this spirit that he appeals to the prince in his instruction (Halkin 1994: 102–3):

> I have no doubt, most illustrious prince, that you are of one mind with me, by your birth and by your upbringing at the hands of the best and most upright of men. For the rest, I pray that Christ, perfect and supreme will continue to favour your noble enterprises…. He rejoices to be called the Prince of Peace; may he do the same for you, that *your goodness and wisdom may al last give us relief from these insane wars* [emphasis added].

Living still in the age of Christendom, in which the political, social and the religious realms mingled and merged, Erasmus has no hesitation to take recourse to noble religious motivations in his instructions to the ideal prince. At the time of Erasmus, monkhood or the clerical state was considered as the superior form of Christian life. With an inborn democratic spirit, Erasmus maintained that the practice of Christian ideals was not the preserve of a privileged clerical state, but that every Christian is called to follow the Gospel in the vicissitudes of daily life. In this respect, for him the whole world is a monastery where noble ideals are pursued. It is the same spirit that inspires the instruction of Erasmus to the princes and rulers. The rulers ought to consider their position as one of service and they ought to be aware of this call and fulfil their duties.

This was certainly a very revolutionary thought ahead of his times. These were the times that upheld the so-called theory of the 'divine right of kings who were not answerable to anyone'.[3] The general climate was one in which political absolutism of monarchs was taking shape; Europe was at war with the Ottoman Empire; the princes and rulers were in relentless strife among themselves; and the national spirit and conflicts were beginning to manifest themselves. In such a climate of thought and praxis, the projection of power and governance as service that should follow ethical standards was certainly very unusual and innovative. In the atmosphere where war on the Turks was justified in the name of religion and the security of Europe, Erasmus candidly opposed it. It is true that the appeals of Erasmus for peace were not heeded and were not followed in practice. On the other hand, ironically, his ideals found great resonance, confirmation of which is the fact that his occasional piece *Querela Pacis* (Complaint of Peace)[4] was reprinted twenty-six times during his lifetime. Could it be that Erasmus expressed the deep longings of the people of his epoch, which they were not yet ready to practise?

Erasmus critique of war expresses itself when he directs his attention to the soldiers. His attitude towards them is one of pity as well as of indignation. He pities them because they are simply mercenaries who were deluded into serving the cause of the prince. His indignation towards them is for their culture of murder, killing and plunder, not only during war but also during times of peace.

It is interesting to note that Erasmus put forward his vision of peace, power and freedom in a very ingenious literary form. It is something similar to his other renowned work *In Praise of Folly*. Here folly is personified. She addresses everyone and praises herself. She feels victorious because without her the world does not seem to work! The personified Peace, on the other hand, feels as someone wounded and neglected, and she makes her passionate appeal to rulers, monks and the general populace. But, unlike Folly, she is not listened to. Swathed in this fine piece of work is the Erasmian radical critique of society bent on war and conflict (Agustijin 1991: 81).

We understand better the pacifism of Erasmus in the context of his attitude to all kinds of institutions. Be they the nations, the political powers or the Church-institutions, his is an attempt to transcend these externals and move in search of much wider and broader ideals. He was against all kinds of passionate attachments to institutions that could cloud the mind and work against the true welfare of the people. In this sense, in Erasmus we have a trasnational and cosmopolitan figure at a time when nationalism was beginning to show its ugly visage in the European history. This history was to culminate in the two horrendous World Wars of the twentieth century. This transnationalism is the result of his deep humanism. As we see in Halkin (1994: 280):

> His homeland was where he felt most at ease. It was indeed everywhere he was loved as long as he was loved. *Ubi bene ibi patria* [where well-being, there homeland]… The attachment to human beings and relative indifference to institution was very Erasmian. Nations quarreled over Erasmus, but he gave himself to all and belonged to none.

The Renaissance humanism in the case of Erasmus did not simply mean a return to the sources of the ancient world. Of course, he was unsurpassed in his scholarship of the ancient Latin and Greek writers and thinkers, and was extremely dexterous in critically handling the texts. These were then the general part of the Renaissance culture. What distinguished Erasmus from the rest of Renaissance figures was his reach, out to the whole of humanity, which he considered as one, and his relativization of all conventional borders. In the appeal to the general public, Erasmus let the personified Peace say this (*Querela Pacis*, as cited in McConica 1991: 83):

> Here you must show how the combined will of the people can prevail against the tyranny of the powerful; here must be the focal point of all endeavours. Eternal concord should unite those whom nature has made one in many things … and all should join in a united effort to bring about what concerns the happiness of one and all.

Erasmus struggle for freedom

The issue of freedom, which later the Enlightenment tradition would develop, is already anticipated in Erasmus. Quite contrary to the general mood of his epoch, Erasmus emphasized that powers—whether political or ecclesiastical—should respect freedom. He believed in the fundamental freedom with which every human being is endowed and, therefore, any relationship of the rulers to the subjects should be such that freedom is not compromised. No prince may consider his subjects as his property. Erasmus went even to the point of maintaining that it is the 'consent of the People' that made the prince really what he is, foreshadowing the later development of democratic thought.[5]

Erasmus, who was critical of powers and kept a distance from the rulers, had to struggle hard to maintain his own personal freedom and independence of thought. Nothing illustrates this more than his attitude towards Luther and Reformation. Erasmus was caught in a storm of controversies but he refused to be identified with any of the contending parties in the battlefield of Reformation. To be able to understand the dilemmas of this great humanist, we should take note of the fact that in the first decades of the sixteenth century, Reformation was not simply a religious event but a serious crisis and turning point in the political and social history of Europe. It ripped open the seamless garment of a homogeneous Christendom, challenged tradition as criterion of truth, and introduced the spirit of individualism; it brought to the fore for the first time, the question of religious pluralism (Protestantism and Catholicism) in a society that had enjoyed religious unity for over a thousand years. And this new situation had its political, social and cultural consequences.

Obviously, Luther was the standard-bearer of Reformation. And yet, Luther is not understandable without the seeds of revolution Erasmus sowed. In fact, in the early years of his Reformation programme, Luther showed great deference towards Erasmus and acknowledged his seminal thoughts and their effects on the much-needed change in the religious life of the times. Even before Luther rose in protest, Erasmus in his own inimitable way (through satiric writings), launched a virulent critique on the abuses within the Church, the superstitious practices of the gullible people, which were exploited by the monks and the clergy. He reserved his most stringent critique for theologians of the decadent scholasticism who indulged themselves in arid discussions far removed from the lives of the people and their issues. He refused to concede that monastic and clerical way of life represented the Christian ideals in its highest form.

If Erasmus criticism of the existing system was expressed through satire in works like *In Praise of Folly* and *Colloquies*, his positive vision of Christian life came out in his work, *Handbook of Militant Christian* (Erasmus 1962). The significance of this work can be appreciated only when we take note of the importance attached to external rituals, to veneration of saints and their relics, pilgrimages, and so on. The vision of Erasmus was one that radically relativized the exterior manifestations of all kinds, while delved incessantly into the depths in search of authentic Christian message and its spirit. Luther received no small impetus and no few insights from this Erasmian vision for his practical programmes. Finally, the method Erasmus employed for the Reformation was to rid the Church of all those traditions and practices through a critical reading of the Scriptures. His critical reconstruction of the New Testament text gave a solid empirical basis for a much-needed reform in the Church. Against this background, Luther felt himself close to Erasmus. Naturally, Luther expected Erasmus to come out in the open in support of his anti-papal and anti-tradition programmes. It is here that Erasmus and Luther parted company in spite of many things that united them. Erasmus showed himself to be a man of freedom and independence but at no small cost.

On the other side, Erasmus was singled out by the orthodox forces as the root cause of all the upheaval the reformation was causing. And, therefore, those in authority and the conservative academic world associated with different universities of Europe began to turn their guns on Erasmus for not condemning Luther. Pope Adrian IV even wrote a personal letter to him to engage his expertise to counter Luther and his programmes, saying (McConica 1991: 73):

> The affection which we feel for you and the concern we have for your reputation and true glory prompt us to urge you to employ in an attack on these new heresies; the literary skill with which a generous providence has endowed you so effectually, for there are many reasons why you ought properly to believe that this task has been reserved by God especially for you.

Erasmus was caught in the cross-fire. The pope and other higher authorities of the Church entreated his support, which he declined to give.[6] On the other side of the battlelines were Luther and the reformers (some of whom were Erasmus earlier admirers) who now saw in Erasmus a coward who betrayed them, even though he held views very similar to theirs. In the initial stage, Erasmus showed sympathy towards the intentions of Luther in reforming the Church, which coincided with his own concerns, but distanced himself from the ways in which Luther went about it concretely. When Luther continued to hurl accusations, Erasmus did not fail to respond with a sting (Johnson 1976: 278):

> How do your scurrilous charges that I am an atheist, an Epieurean and a skeptic, help your argument? It upsets me dreadfully that your arrogant, insolent and rebellious nature should have put the world in arms. I would wish you a better disposition, were you not marvelously satisfied with the one you have already. Wish me anything you will—except your temper.

In spite of all this, Erasmus never condemned Luther. Nor did he support the orthodox party. In fact, when Emperor Charles V asked for Erasmus counsel to resolve the issue of Luther, Erasmus is reported to have told the Emperor in an ambiguous way that the trouble with Luther was that 'he hit the monks in their bellies and the pope in his crown' (Todd 1972: 225). Consistent with his outlook, Erasmus proposed an arbitration committee to end the crisis. Apart from his proposal for arbitration, in the spirit of reconciliation, he set to himself the task of preparing a book of dialogue between a Lutheran, an Orthodox Catholic and an impartial arbitrator. The book, unfortunately, did not see the light of the day.

The approach of Erasmus was intellectual and could not move the masses as the passions and emotions of Luther could.[7] Nor did Erasmus care to cultivate any discipleship. Unlike a guru whose personality is invariably associated with a band of disciples, Erasmus remained a *rishi*, someone who offered a vision for the welfare of society, without himself becoming the centre of attention as a leader with a following. Another thing about Erasmus that strikes us is that, in spite of the enormous influence he wielded with the powers of the time, he never tried to manipulate it to his cause. Luther, on the other hand, knew where the powers lay and was able to steer it to his cause and goals. He also wrote to the princes (*To the Christian Nobility of German Nations*), calling on them to take up the reform of the Church. With a tinge of nationalism, Luther was able to turn the princes against the traditional Church and its ways, which, according to him, exploited the German nation. He knew that his survival and programme crucially depended on the support of the princes and rulers. Without it, he could end up on the stake, like the Bohemian Huss and the English Wycliffe, and many others. Getting the princes on his side also meant compromises. In all this, Luther proved himself a follower of Machiavelli rather than of Erasmus. This was most evident in the case of the peasant war. Though the discontent of the peasants was triggered under the influence of the egalitarian ideas of Reformation, to result in an open rebellion against the princes, in Luther's political calculation he would gain more by placing himself on the side of the princes than that of the peasants.[8]

None of all this politicking is to be seen in Erasmus for whom freedom and independence reigned as supreme values and guiding principles. Given his orientation to peace, concord and harmony, he could not subscribe to the convulsion, which, in his view, the impetuosity of Luther had brought about. The stance of freedom and independence of Erasmus are not difficult to explain. It was not a mere question of religious disputes; the life and limb of many people were at stake. That is one reason why Erasmus refused to accept the repeated invitations from Luther and his followers, including Duke Hutten, to extend his hand of support to Reformation. Erasmus remained true to his motto *concedo nulli* (I yield to no one). To the Duke's *Expostulatio cum Erasmo* (Entreaties with Erasmus) of 1523, in which he said that it was the ambition of Erasmus and his fear of losing his reputation that prevented him (Erasmus) from supporting Luther and the Reformation, Erasmus responded (Iserloth et al. 1980: 145):

I remain on the outside ... I am not a party to any side.... By taking sides, I mean total adherence to all that Luther has written. But I have complete freedom and will not and cannot ever serve on one side.

From the theological angle, in spite of many points of convergences between Erasmus and Luther, there was one thing that pulled them apart. Whereas Luther was taken up by the transcendence of God and his revelation to the contempt of human wisdom (which he considered foolishness), Erasmus believed in no such anti-thesis between human wisdom and God's ways in revelation. His immersion into the world of the classical led him to see human wisdom and Christianity in a harmonious relationship. All the classical learning and wisdom that mattered most to Erasmus were reviled by Luther and was held in very low esteem. Luther could not pardon Erasmus for this and he wrote to him (Todd 1972: 229):

My heart went out to you as having defiled your lovely brilliant flow of language with such vile stuff. I thought it outrageous to convey materials of so low a quality in the trapping of such rare eloquence.

A man of infinite passion, incurable acerbity and unrestrained impetuosity, Luther never heeded the voice of moderation that came to him through the letters of Erasmus.[9] Instead, he fulminated against what he perceived as elusiveness of Erasmus and his refusal to take sides; he ridiculed Erasmus for what he saw as inconsistency and contradiction (Todd 1972: 258):

A man who does not treat the question seriously and has no interest in the issues, whose mind is not on it and who finds it a ... chilling and a distasteful business cannot help uttering absurdities and follies and contradictions all along the time; he argues his case like a man drunk or asleep blurting out between snores 'Yes', 'No' as different voices sound upon his ears.

Though Erasmus did not allow himself to be dragged into a conflict through the provocation of Luther, nevertheless, at an intellectual level, he dared to challenge some of Luther's views. One such renowned issue concerned the freedom of human will, which Luther denied. The response of Erasmus took the form of a book: *De Libero Arbitrio* (On Free Will) in which he examines dispassionately the views of Luther.

Erasmus struggle for freedom and independence had to do not only with Luther and Reformation. The test of freedom came also from the

opposite quarters: for the representatives of orthodoxy—both ecclesiastical leaders as well as theologians—Erasmus was the arch-heretic.[10]
Therefore, their programme, from attempts to win him over, was directed towards condemning him for his heresies. We need to remember
that in that epoch, to be condemned for heresy was not simply a matter
of orthodoxy and heterodoxy; it was a matter of deadly seriousness—
a matter of life and death. We need to only recall the lot of Savanorola of
Florence, Huss of Bohemia, and in the following century the tribulations
of Galileo. Erasmus was not someone, according to his own admission,
made for martyrdom. There may be people who want to give up their life
for some doctrine or other. This, for Erasmus, was no appealing ideal.
Apart from maintaining his freedom and independence, he preferred to
'stay away from all controversy, if possible, in order to be the more useful for the revival of scholarship' (Jedin and Dolan 1980: 144). He writes
(Augustijin 1991: 125):

> Mine was never the spirit to risk my life for the truth. Not everyone has
> the strength needed for martyrdom. When popes and emperors make the
> right decision I follow, which is godly; if they decide wrongly, I tolerate
> them, which is safe. I believe that even for men of good will this is legit-
> imate, if there is no hope of better things.

The attacks on Erasmus came especially from some of the most influential universities of the times. In the set-up of the sixteenth century,
these academic institutions had an important role to play in maintaining orthodoxy. Their views were crucial in identifying the heretics to be
condemned and punished. The University of Sorbonne in Paris pronounced censures against Erasmus thrice, and his work *Colloquies* was
condemned in 1526. Similarly, in Spain the monks attacked him at the
conference of Valladoli. From Louvain came the challenges of Maarten
van Dorp to the methods of Erasmus. In all these attacks from the side
of orthodoxy, Erasmus outlook of peace and freedom was such that he
did not allow himself to be entangled with the theologians of the times
for whom he had, anyway, scant respect. He had already migrated into
a world of freedom with which his detractors could not catch up.

Conclusion

In a world marked by serious conflicts, Erasmus stood as a *rishi*, refusing
to scale the heights of power. He extricated himself from the realpolitik

and the vicissitudes of his times to be able to inspire society with a broad vision of humanity and remind it of such noble ideals as peace and concord. He drew much of his inspiration from the classics, which he tried to relate harmoniously with the core of the Christian message. In his own personal history, caught in the midst of a raging storm, he stood for freedom and independence, and did not allow himself to be swept off by any group or current.

How come that Erasmus, inspired with such a noble vision, gave the impression of being someone not daring to stand for his ideals and to suffer the consequences of his convictions like a prophet? It is here that we find the real Erasmus who defies any easy categorization. He fits into no frame—certainly not that of a prophet who dies in testimony of his beliefs. As a matter of fact, it is his close friend Thomas More who chose martyrdom. For More, martyrdom was the way to freedom in the serious confrontation with the regal powers of Henry VIII. Erasmus approach to power and freedom is such that while one can offer a vision like *rishi*, one could still retain freedom by refusing to get submerged within power conflicts and controversies. In short, *distancing* was the way to freedom in the vision of Erasmus. This is a point on which the assessment of the personality and works of Erasmus will differ.

Erasmian vision of power was much ahead of his time, so much so that he can be viewed as a European Enlightenment figure even before the age of Enlightenment dawned. We can find in his thought certain seminal ideas that will have their full fruition in the subsequent periods. One such idea of Erasmus was that *the authority of the rulers rests on the consensus of the people*. In Erasmus, this view, however, coexisted with another theologically inspired view: he saw the rulers as the image of God in his caring and providing aspects. Erasmus never arrived at any synthesis nor did he try to reconcile these two different views of power, which may appear as contradictory.

In any case, his vision was far removed from the model of a self-justifying and despotic power in whose service Machiavelli wrote *The Prince*. On the contrary, a relentless critique of powers was truly the spirit of Erasmus. Undogmatic in his attitude, he stood for the freedom of all Christians in the face of ecclesiastical powers that reserved all authority to themselves. He relativized the institutions that supported such power concentrations and pointed towards those realities that transcend the externals. His critique of rulers and princes flew in the face of the prevailing aristocratic conceptions of power. Luther, his contemporary, too, was critical of power but it was limited to the ecclesiastical sphere.

Actually, the religiously anti-authoritarian posture of Luther went to strengthen the hands of the princes who exploited the situation, and all this paved the way for absolutist monarchies.

What Locke in his *Letter on Toleration and Kant on Perpetual Peace* had to say cannot but remind us what Erasmus, as a pioneer, contributed to the important question of peace and tolerance long before these authors. He was, in a way, the precursor. To this we should also add the significance of Erasmus in relating ethics with the issue of power. When the statecraft and manipulation of power (to which even the religious reformer Luther succumbed) in the Machiavellian style mattered, Erasmus stood for an ethical outlook on power. He was too wary of the dangers that lurk in any exercise of power bereft of ethical values and ideals. When power disentangles itself from ethics, it runs amok, victimizing people all along. For him, any political act, therefore, is necessarily an ethical act. A sign of this ethical vision is his opposition to the conventional view of a 'just' war. Ethics remains the catharsis of any power. For his views on the nature of power as resulting from the consensus of the people, his faith in conciliation and arbitration in matters of conflict, his ethical and humanistic vision and ideals, his anti-war posture and his advocacy of peace and tolerance, Erasmus remains highly relevant to illumine the contemporary situation of humanity and to delineate its future trajectory.

Notes

1. This is what Erasmus wrote when the German Knight and humanist Ulrich Hutten asked for a portrait of More ('Selection from Letters of Erasmus', in Huizinga 1957: 233, 237).
2. There is some uncertainty regarding the exact year of Erasmus birth, as to whether it was 1466 or 1467. Machiavelli was born in 1469.
3. The divine right of kings was further developed by the French theorist Jacques-Benigne Bossuet (1627–1704) and in England by Sir Robert Filmer in his work *Patriarcha* (1680). Such views were countered by John Locke in his *Civil Government* (1987).
4. This piece of writing was done, at the behest of the chancellor of Burgundy and in support of a planned treaty of peace among rulers in Europe, which, however did not materialize. See Augustijin (1991: 73).
5. But, as Augustijin (1991: 82) points out, Erasmus did not raise a question which is consequent upon this, namely, the right to resistance by the people.
6. In his inimitable and non-confrontational style, Erasmus responded to the pope for not being able to go over to Rome, citing his old age and health (!). See Bouyer (1969: 130).

7. In this context, it is interesting to note that St. Ignatius of Loyola, the founder of the Society of Jesus, attests having read the *Enchiridion* (a popular work of Erasmus) and 'observed that the reading of the book chilled the spirit of God in him and gradually extinguished the ardour of devotion', (Olin 1969: 116).

8. Erasmus was not unaware of these developments. As Oberman (1986: 164) observes, 'for him [Erasmus], the history of Reformation until 1525 is a drama in three acts. The first is the campaign of humanism; the second is the battle around Luther; and the third and final act is the armed clash between the princes an the peasants.... For the humanist from Rotterdam, however, this is not merely a chronological succession of three acts, but rather a spiritual descent in the direction of catastrophe.'

9. In one of his letters, Erasmus writes to Luther: 'How I could wish that you always kept an escape route open, especially when you are attached in discussion' (Augustijin 1991: 120).

10. Erasmus works would be subsequently placed by the church authorities in the index of prohibited books.

References

Augustijin, Cornelius. 1991. *Erasmus: His Life, Works and Influence*. Toronto: University of Toronto Press.

Bouyer, Louis. 1969. *Erasmus and His Times*. Westminister: Newman Press.

Erasmus. 1962. *Handbook of the Militant Christian* (translated with an introductory essay by John P. Dolan). Notre Dame: Fides Publishers.

Filmer, Robert. 1680. *Patriarcha or the Natural Power of Kings*. London: Weftmirfter Hall.

Halkin, Leon-Ernest. 1994. *Erasmus: A Critical Biography*. Oxford: Blackwell.

Iserloth, Erwin et al. 1980. 'Reformation and Counter Reformation', in H. Jedin and J. Dolan (eds), *History of the Church*, vol. V. London: Burns & Oates.

Jedin, H. and J. Dolan (eds). 1980. *History of the Church*, vol. V. London: Burns & Oates.

Johan Huizinga. 1957. *Erasmus and the Age of Reformation with a Selection from the Letters of Erasmus*. New York: Harpe.

Johnson, Paul. 1976. *A History of Christianity*. New York: Athenaeum.

Locke, John. 1987. *Two Treatises on Government*. Boston: Unwin Hyman.

Machiavelli, Niccolo. 1950. *The Prince and the Discourses*. New York: The Modern Library.

McConica, James. 1991. *Erasmus* Oxford and New York: Oxford University Press.

Mukherjee, Subrata and Sushila Ramaswamy (eds). 1993. *Great Western Political Thinkers*, vol. 3: *Niccolo Machiavelli*. Delhi: Deep and Deep Publications.

Obermann, Heiko Augustinus. 1986. *The Dawn of the Reformation: Essays in Late Medieval and Early Reformation Thought*. Edinburgh: T & T Clark.

Olin, John C. 1969. 'Erasmus and St. Ignatius Loyola', in John Olin et al. (eds), *Luther, Erasmus and the Reformation: A Catholic and Protestant Appraisal*. New York: Fordham University Press.

Routledge Encyclopedia of Philosophy. 1998. Machiavelli Niccolo. vol. 6. London and New York: Routledge.

Todd, John M. 1972. *Reformation*. London: Darton, Longman & Todd.

Zweig, Stefan. 1956. *Erasmus of Rotterdam*. New York: Viking Press, New York.

Political Symbolism or How to Stay on the Surface

3

FRANK R. ANKERSMIT

Introduction: The French Revolution's anti-foundationalism

The French Revolution destroyed a thousand-year-old monarchy, institutions and traditions so secure that they almost seemed to have become part of human nature, and a political order apparently sanctioned by the Christian God himself. Never before—and never since—has humanity been prepared for such a total and irrevocable rupture with its past and with all that the political wisdom of the ages had left us. It must seem that the people so eager to engage in this sublime act of destruction should have had no doubts about the justification of their brutal declaration of war on History and on the wisdom of the ages. For, the person who destroys must think himself to be in possession of a higher and more comprehensive wisdom than the person who is content merely to rebuild or to repair.

If one asks the historian about the nature of this supreme wisdom legitimizing the destruction of all that the past had created and the introduction of a wholly new secular dispensation, his answer is not difficult to predict. He will point out that the natural law philosophy inspiring most of the seventeenth- and eighteenth-century political philosophy was inherently a- or anti-historical and that, therefore, natural law philosophy has been the *foundation* of this unsparing attack on the legacies of the past. Surely he would admit that natural law philosophy was not always revolutionary in content and in its implications. On the contrary, he would recognize that it had often been used to defend the cause of absolutism or that of enlightened despotism—think of Thomas Hobbes or of Christian Wolff. The decisive fact is, however, that natural law philosophy sees in the state of Nature, the criterion of political truth, and the very idea of a primordial state of Nature is *sui generis* inimical to the practical wisdom that has been gathered all through the ages. Moreover, the historian would point out that the origins of modern natural law philosophy must be traced back to the sixteenth-century monarchical tradition establishing under what circumstances the rejection of an un-just monarch is permitted. The revolutionary potential of natural law philosophy is, therefore, no less obvious than that of Marxism. And he would conclude his argument by saying that this may explain why the Rousseaus, the Mablys, the Morellys, and so on, should have so much captured the imagination of the French revolutionaries.

I will question here this so-familiar type of argument not by placing question marks behind its individual components (though I am sure that this would be advisable, too), but rather by turning the whole argument upside down. To put it into one sentence, I will argue that the French Revolution could be such an unparalleled revolutionary event *not* because it had its theoretical foundations in a system of political thought (whether historist or anti-historist), but precisely by robbing any existing system of political thought of any relevance. The French Revolution was *not* such a decisive social and political *caesura* because it had discovered the absolutely sound foundation for a wholly new political order; it was such a revolutionary event, nay, it *could* only be such a revolutionary event, because it did away with the very notion of *foundations in general*. It really created itself *ex nihilo*, and was not dependent on anything outside itself for its emergence and for its continuation. It is in this little observed fact about the Great Revolution that we should discern the condition of its sublime pretensions and of its so unique role in the history of the Western world. Moreover—as will become clear in the second part of my argument—this is exactly what the Revolution shares with representative democracy and why we are well advised to pay a little more attention to this hitherto ignored aspect of the Great Revolution. Both, the French Revolution and the representative democracy, presuppose the rejection of political foundationalism.

Lynn Hunt on the French Revolution

When presenting my case of the anti-foundationalism of the French Revo-lution, my main witness will be Lynn Hunt. In two studies—*Politics,*

Culture and Class in the French Revolution (1984) and *The Family Romance of the French Revolution* (1992)—Hunt presented a new and fascinating account of the political culture of the French Revolution. According to this account, it was the political symbolism created by the French revolutionaries as the Revolution followed its course, and not some foundationalist argument that determined the logic of the Great Revolution. The revolutionaries saw themselves compelled to develop such a political symbolism and to adapt it at each time to unexpected new circumstances, and it was this political symbolism that made the French Revolution into the wholly unprecedented historical event that it has been.

Hunt's main thesis in *Politics, Culture, and Class in the French Revolution* is that the Revolution has been revolutionary in *two* relevant aspects. It was a revolutionary rupture with the Ancient Regime insofar as the Revolution was the *coup de grâce* to the few remaining remnants of feudalism, to Bourbon monarchy, to the political role of the clergy, to class society, and so on. All this was revolutionary enough already, of course. But apart from, and beyond this, the Revolution was also a revolutionary metamorphosis of the *very idea of revolution itself*. For the first time in its history, humanity decided to radically break with its past, to take its fate into its own hands and to create *ex nihilo* its own world, and its own new social and political reality. This was an enterprise not having its equal in all of history; moreover, all thinking people at the time were aware of this and of the time-transcending promises implied by it. Nobody ever expressed this more aptly and eloquently than Hegel (1976: 926), who, when looking back from the perspective of 1830 at this announcement of a new dawn in mankind's history, says:

> *Solange die Sonne am Firmamente steht und die Planeten um sie herumkreisen, war das nicht gesehen worden, dass der Mensch sich auf den Kopf, das ist, auf den Gedanken stellt und die Wirklichkeit nach diesem erbaut. Anaxagoras hatte zuerst gesagt dass der nous die Welt regiert; nun aber ist der Mensch dazu gekommen, zu erkennen, dass der Gedanke die geistige Wirklichkeit regieren sollte. Es war dieses somit ein herrlicher Sonnenaufgang. Alle denkende Wesen haben diese Epoche mitgefeiert ... als sei es zur wirklichen Versöhnung des Göttlichen mit der Welt nun erst gekommen.*

...for as long as the sun stands high on the firmament and for as long as the planets circle around it, it has never been seen that that mankind takes mind or thought as its perspective and organizes the world accordingly. Anaxagoras had once said already that 'nous' (i.e. thought) rules this world; but now mankind came to recognize that thought should rule spiritual reality. Hence, it was a magnificent new dawn. All rational people rejoiced in what happened (...) as if a real reconciliation between God and the world had been brought sbout' [my translation]

In continuation with Hegel's suggestion, Hunt emphasizes that what the French revolutionaries attempted to do was wholly without percedent and, moreover, that they were not only well aware of this but even saw here precisely the sublimity and the legitimization of their enterprise. For, they realized that there were no models or examples that could be used as guides in their enterprise; they knew that at each moment and that in the case of each crucial dilemma, they had to invent the revolution, *their* revolution, anew. This is where the French Revolution differed not only from its Greek and Roman precedents, and in terms of which the French revolutionaries so much liked to metaphorize their dilemmas, but also from more recent revolutions such as the Puritan Revolution of 1641, the Glorious Revolution of 1688 or the American Revolution of 1776.

Moreover, this is also where it differed from all the later revolutions insofar these revolutions always modelled themselves on their so singularly unique French predecessor. As for its uniqueness, one may well say that a truly naïve and honest revolution can only be made once in the history of mankind and that this explains the supreme importance of the French Revolution, whereas later revolutions could never be more than its dishonest and disloyal simulacra. For, as soon as the political logic of revolution had once manifested itself, later revolutions could not possibly ignore this logic. As a result, these later revolutions could at best only be applications of this logic to new historical circumstances. And it will require little intellectual effort to see that such an application of a logic already known, could never be revolutionary in the true sense of the word. In this way, one might well say that there has been in Western history *just one real* revolution—the French Revolution—and that the event could, by its very nature, never be repeated.

One is reminded here of von Schiller's (undated: 110) very useful distinction between naive and sentimental poetry.[1] The distinction comes down to this: naive poetry is natural, it is a natural expression of poetic genius, it requires no thought, no reflection; it is wholly free and spontaneous. Opposite to this highest form of poetry—that von Schiller associated primarily with Shakespeare or Goethe—we will find sentimental poetry. Sentimental poetry arises from an awareness of the greatness of naive poetry; it recognizes this greatness and then tries to emulate and imitate it, but it will never be successful in this because it necessarily lacks spontaneity, which is the condition of true poetic genius. One may say that the French Revolution was naive in the Schillerian sense of the word, whereas all later revolutions have merely been its sentimentalist simulacra.

And this brings us to the heart of the matter. For, as soon as we have recognized with Hunt the radical and inimitable newness of the French Revolution, we will become sensitive to its singular anti-foundationalism. It did not materialize in actual political reality the dreams of Rousseauistic natural law philosophy; it was not the implementation of some political programme or ideology that had already been defined before the emergence of the revolution—as should be clear to anybody who has ever taken the trouble to read the speeches and the addresses of the main revolutionary readers. For, these philosophical pipe-dreams are most conspicuously absent in them. Revolutionary speeches, the revolutionary idiom, always came into being on the spur of the moment, they were always speech acts with the help of which one tried to conjure an unexpected calamity or to exploit an unforeseen windfall. The French Revolution was a continuous makeshift affair, a continuous desperate attempt to live up to the circumstances and, more specifically, to find the most appropriate language and symbolism to meet the challenges of these new circumstances and to make sense of them. During all of the French Revolution, one never actually arrived at the situation that one could quietly contemplate the application of revolutionary political ideals to existing circumstances; on the contrary, the Revolution was a continuous improvization, a continuous attempt to stave off the worst and to adapt oneself as well as one could to a never-ending series of calamities. And, as the revolutionaries found out in due time, the only instrument they had for doing so was political language and political symbolism. Language was their only weapon in their struggle with all these unforeseen and unforeseeable disasters. As Hunt puts it (1984: 54, 55):

> The French Revolution brought the process of symbol making into sharp relief, because revolutionaries found themselves in the midst of revolution before they had the opportunity to reflect on their situation.... They invented their symbols and rituals as they went along.... Thus the revolutionaries' passion for the allegorical, the theatrical, the stylized was not simply a bizarre aberration, but rather an essential element in their effort to mold free men.

And since it has pleased History to place the fate of the Revolution into the hands of the person who possessed an almost uncanny capacity for grasping its logic, we are well advised to listen to de Robespierre (1965: 190) himself:

> *La théorie du gouvernement révolutionnaire est aussi neuve que la Révolution qui l'a amené. Il ne faut pas la chercher dans les livres des écrivains politiques qui n'ont point prévu cette Révolution, ni dans les lois des tyrants, qui, contents d'abuser de leur puissance, s'occupent peu d'en rechercher la légitimité; aussi ce mot n'est-il pour l'aristocratie qu'un sujet de terreur our un texte de calomnie; pour les tyrants qu'un scandale; pour bien des gens, qu'une énigme; il faut l'expliquer à tous pour rallier au moins les bons citoyens aux principes de l'intérêt publique.*

The theory of the revolutionary government is as new as the Revolution that had produced it. One would look for it in vain in the books of the political writers who foresaw this Revolution or in the laws of the tyrants who, content to abuse their power, did care little about legitimacy. Moreover, the term revolutionary government will provoke terror and calumny in the circles of the aristocracy; for the tyrants it is a scandal, for many people an enigma; and it needs to be explained to everybody in order to convince at least the good citizens of the principles of public interest' [my translation]

One might put it as follows. The French revolutionaries had thrown themselves into a kind of political vacuum where nothing could offer them any independent support anymore. So the only support one still had and could still trust were the realities that one created by the means of the revolutionary discourse and of revolutionary symbolism. More specifically, under these wholly unknown and exceptional circumstances, revolutionary language and symbolism were the only instruments one possessed for making sense of events, for obtaining a grasp, however precarious, of them, and for recognizing and understanding what oneself and others were doing and aiming for.[2] So this is why words and political symbols could assume such an unprecedented important place in politics; and one feels tempted to paraphrase here the Gospel of St. John by saying that *in the beginning was the revolutionary logo, and this logo constituted political reality.* If, then, the Austinian notion of the performative use of language ever made any sense at all, this was during the heady days of revolutionary France, when the word was political reality and, at times, as effective as an army and as lethal as the guillotine.

We can now also understand why de Robespierre (1965: 21) fought a continuous war on calumny and was so characteristically explicit about its extreme importance within the logic of revolutionary government:

Citoyens!

Je veux vous entretenir aujourd'hui d'un sujet qui n'a point été traité, que je sache, par aucun écrivain politique. Je parle du pouvoir de la calomnie. Il fallait une Révolution comme la nôtre, pour la déployer dans toute son étendue.

Citizens!

I want to talk to you today about a topic that has, as far as I know, never been dealt with by any political writer before. I have in mind the power of calumny. It needed a Revolution like ours in order to realize all its potentials. [my translation]

He then goes on to explain that all that went wrong during the Revolution and all that might discredit it in the eyes of the well intentioned, has grown out of the insidious seeds of calumny. And in his marvelously eloquent speech he then asks his audience (Robespierre 1965: 24ff):

Quel est ce pouvoir magique de changer la vertu en vice, et le vice en vertu! De donner à la sottise, à la corruption et à la lâcheté le droit d'accuser hautement le courage, l'intégrité et la raison?

what is this magic power trying to tranform virtue into vice, and vice into virtue! To grant to foolishness, to corruption and cowardice the right to accuse courage, integrity and reason? [my translation]

And the answer is:

C'est la calomnie qui fonda ces clubs antipopulaires, destinés à assurer l'empire de la faction, en dégradant l'opinion publique…. C'est la calomnie qui fit absoudre la tyrannie et la trahison dans la personne du dernier de nos rois…. C'est la calomnie qui, alors, éleva le monstrueux ouvrage de la révision de l'acte constitutionnel. C'est elle qui, avant cette époque, avait assassiné à Nancy les plus zélés défenseurs de la liberté.

it was calumny that founded these anti-revolutionary clubs, aiming at the victory of factionalism by degrading public opinion (…) It was calumny which blinded people to the tyranny and treason of the last of our kings. (…) It was calumny that gave rise to the monstruous enterprise of the revision of our constitutional act. It was calumny which, before this took place, had assassinated in Nancy the most devoted defenders of liberty etc. [my translation]

And calumny could do all these things so successfully, since there is neither objective political reality nor an indisputable *foundation* for political speculation that would mercilessly expose calumny as such.

There is only opinion, there is only revolutionary language and symbolism, and this is why the Revolution is so peculiarly helpless against calumny and, hence, why calumny must be the Revolution's worst enemy.

This is also why revolutionary rhetoric—as Arendt (1990) has so brilliantly argued—was mainly a war on hypocrisy and why hypocrisy was considered to be the worst crime one could make oneself guilty of. Addressing the French Revolution, Arendt (ibid.: 101) comments:

> It must seem strange that hypocrisy—one of the minor vices, we are inclined to think—should have been hated more than all the other vices taken together? Was not hypocrisy, since it paid its compliments to virtue, almost the vice to undo the vices, at least to prevent them from appearing and to shame them into hiding? Why should the vice that covered up vices become the vice of vices?

But as Arendt (1990: 107–8) then goes on to point out, this was precisely why hypocrisy was feared and hated so much by the revolutionaries:

> What made the hypocrite so odious was that he claimed not only sincerity but naturalness, and what made him so dangerous outside the social realm whose corruption he represented and, as it were, enacted, was that he instinctively could help himself to every 'mask' in the political theatre, that he could assume every role amongst its dramatis personae, and that he would not use this mask, as the rules of the political game demand, as a sounding board for truth but, on the contrary, as a contraption for deception.

Or to put it in terms of the present argument, the hypocrite was much like an uncontrollable meaning and symbol maker; he could, therefore, at all times throw sand in the revolutionary meaning-making machine. Nobody would then be able to sort out what the lubricating oil and what the sand in the machine was, with the inevitable result that the revolutionary machine would come grinding to a halt. One is reminded of a love affair in which the non-feasibility of the sexual act itself (and of the indubitable truth that this always brings) will endow the words that these lovers speak to each other with an unexpected importance. For now on, these words are no longer merely the discourse of love—*they are love themselves*—and any deception must then irrevocably mean the end of it. There simply is nothing *beyond* these words and if they are false and hypocritical, an odd situation will arise in that the love affair will have come to an end while one could not possibly be aware of this.

We can now also understand two more features of the Great Revolution. In the first place, revolutionary language and symbolism could only be effective—and thus succeed in anchoring the Revolution in the citizen's mind—to the extent that the citizen's mind is truly susceptible to them. So one had to transform the citizen into a political being and drag him out of his pre-political consciousness. Political education, thus, had to become one of the Revolution's main targets, or as Hunt (1984: 73) puts it:

> As a consequence, revolutionaries had to place great faith in their ability to reshape society and the individual in a very short time. To this end, they mobilized enormous pedagogical energies and politicized every possible aspect of daily life. Transparancy could only work if didacticism prepared the way.

Once again, the message is that the Revolution was by no means this utterance of a political magical formula inspired by an insight into the foundations of the political order. On the contrary, it was the entry into a wholly new world, full of unpleasant surprises, and that demanded of the revolutionaries a continuous and quasi-sleepless effort to keep on the right side of the course of events. In this way, it was a return to the world of Machiavellian fortune, requiring above all political *virtù*. Thus, the Revolution was wholly at odds with this aspiration of a reduction of everything to the place natural law philosophy assigned to it, that traditional accounts of the Revolution have always read in it. This may also make us recognize the amazing Machiavellianism of the otherwise so ethically minded revolutionaries.

This brings me to a second feature of the Revolution, identified by Hunt. If one had now entered a new world devoid of any familiar political structures or signposts, the only *brute datum* left was human nature. Robbed of traditional and inherited patterns of power, and of social and political hierarchy, human nature was now very much left to its own devices—and this may explain why so many peculiarities of the Revolution invite so much an explanation in terms of social psychology. This is what Hunt has tried to do in her *The Family Romance of the French Revolution*. In the preface to this book, Hunt elucidates its title as, 'by *family romance* Freud meant the neurotic's fantasy of 'getting free from the parents of whom he now has a low opinion and of replacing them by others, who, as a rule, are of a higher social standing.' And a moment later she (1992: xiii) adds, 'by *family romance*, I mean the collective, unconscious images of the familial order that underlie revolutionary politics.

I will be arguing that the French had a kind of collective political un-conscious that was structured by narratives of family relations.'

The obvious link between the Freudian notion of the *family romance* and the French Revolution is, of course, that we may see the latter as a variation on the venerable Freudian theme of the attack on and, the murder of, the Father (that is, the King). Elaborating this theme, Hunt demonstrates that the execution of Louis XVI was, indeed, experienced as a parricide in the political subconscious of the French. On the eve of the execution, an awed silence gripped the capital, as if some terrible and unspeakable crime had been committed (Hunt 1992: 60): 'the decapitation was supposed to serve as a warning to other kings, but it also had a resonance of murder of the father, cannibalism, and potential anarchy.' And just as the murder of the primeval Father in Freud's *Totem und Tabu* resulted in the ban of brothers tortured by a common sense of guilt, so was the execution of Louis XVI: an irremovable burden on the revolutionary enterprise. In her book, Hunt investigates the fascinating socio-psychological and sexual mechanisms that were thus put into motion. And she concludes that the main difference between the French Revolution and others, such as the American Revolution, is that the latter always succeeded in hitting somehow upon some substitute father-figure—such as George Washington, the Pantheon of the Founding Fathers, or even more abstractly, the Constitution. Strangely enough, the French Revolution never proposed such a substitute in order to satisfy the citizen's natural Oedipal needs. This proves once again that unlike previous and later revolutions, the French Revolution entered wholly unknown political territory and, thus, always had to invent and reinvent itself. This brings us back to Hunt's claim that the French Revolution owed both its grandeur and its miseries, both its successes and its disasters, in short, its *sublimity*, to the fact that it knew no basis and legitimacy outside itself and was, in this way, the embodiment of the politics of anti-foundationalism.

Political symbolism in representative democracy

Now I come to the second part of my argument—that much the same story can be told for representative democracy and, in this way, representative democracy can be seen as the true heir to the French Revolution.

Elaborating this point may make clear a few things about representative democracy that we might all too easily forget when ignoring to what extent the French Revolution has been the precursor of the political system that we so eagerly and rightly embrace.

In order to get to grips with the anti-foundationalism of representative democracy, it would be best to start with what is arguably Rorty's (1991) most valuable contribution to political theory: his essay titled 'The Priority of Democracy to Philosophy'. Rorty develops his position here in the form of a commentary on Rawls' later writings, where according to Rorty, Rawls successfully distances himself from the foundationalism that one might still discern in his *A Theory of Justice*. Rorty follows Rawls when the latter argues that 'philosophy as the search for truth about an independent metaphysical and moral order cannot ... provide a workable and shared basis for a political conception of justice in a democratic society.' We should, therefore, confine ourselves to collecting 'such settled convictions as the belief in religious toleration and the rejection of slavery' and then try to 'organize' the moral intuitions 'implicit in these convictions into a coherent conception of justice' (ibid.: 180). The crucial idea is that politics and political justice need not, and even should not, pronounce on the philosophical and metaphysical foundations of our moral and political convictions, but be content to accept them for what they are and then organize them into a more or less coherent conception of justice that is more or less acceptable to all of us. The suggestion is, hence, that in politics we should avoid getting entangled in foundationalist philosophical debate, but be content to discuss political issues with our fellow citizens and then see how far this discussion may get us. Put differently, we should stop searching for the *depth* of ethical and political *foundations*, and restrict ourselves to the *surface* of the give-and-take kind of discussion that one would find in a decent and well-functioning democracy. Democracy is not academia: we are not so much interested in the philosophical soundness of the opinions of others, as much in how we can live together in a decent and well-ordered way with people holding these different opinions. Hence, this 'priority of democracy to philosophy'.

In order to correctly perceive the signficance of Rorty's argument, we should recognize what is good and what is bad in it.[3] What is bad in it can be discerned already in the kind of examples of democratic discussion Rorty takes over from Rawls.[4] These examples were, as one will recall, religious toleration and the issue of slavery. Now, I do not think that issues like these could ever be the stake in the kind of give-and-take discussion we have in our representative democracies. These are the kind of issues that may occasion—and have—occasioned civil wars; and the explanation is that they really determine the heart of the body politic and, next, that they tend to be all-or-nothing issues. You cannot have a little more or a little less of slavery or of religious toleration. You have it or you don't have it; it is as simple as that. So these things really have to be settled once and for all before something like a workable democracy could come into being at all; and as history shows, it may well take a lengthy and bloody civil war before the dispute has been settled either way. These issues truly *are* foundationalist, and decisions binding all citizens and all political parties must be taken about them and be codified, for example, in the constitution. They are unfit for democratic discussion and democracy would be helpless if it had to deal with them—and if it tried to do so, it would, in practice, effect the continuation of the conflict rather than its solution.

So, what is wrong with Rorty's and Rawls's argument is that it fails to distinguish between what are the constitutional and/or foundationalist conditions of a well-functioning democracy, and what is achieved in a democracy after these conditions have been satisfied. Making this distinction will render us sensitive to the lessons we may learn from the French Revolution. For, as my account of the French Revolution may suggest, the exceptional situation obtained during the French Revolution is normalized into daily practice in a well-ordered democracy; in the sense that every problem is typically 'new', that no foundations can be called upon in order to deal with them and that it will require each time a *creatio ex nihilo* in order to find a solution that works. In this way, the Revolution has been encapsulated into our contemporary, representative democracies; encapsulated in the sense that 'foundationalist' constitutions have defined the limits within which the 'permanent revolution' of democratic government may take place. To which one may add that those romantic revolutionaries of the 1960s have been so naïve not to see that the 'permanent revolution' so hotly demanded by them had already been granted them with democracy.

But within the constitutionally defined arena, the political game is played much in the way as was indicated by Rorty and Rawls. This is definitely good news about Rorty's claim about democracy's priority to philosophy. Hunt's argument about the French Revolution explains as to why an appeal to foundations makes no sense here, since what is being built in a democracy is essentially 'new' and not a structure to be erected on already existing foundations. Most of the legislation in a modern democracy is not a matter of either an application of the constitution to new circumstances and emphatically not an effort to deduce new legislation from the constitution. This Cartesian model of democratic politics is as useless as it is nonsensical.

This does not entail, however, that there would be no system in the apparent madness of democratic decision making. And, once again, Hunt's argument about the French Revolution suggests what the nature of the system in question is. We should recall here, above all, her claim about revolutionary language and revolutionary symbolism, and her claim that there was nothing outside this language and this symbolism to keep the body politic together. Only in terms of this language and in terms of these symbols could politicians and citizens recognize each other, make sense of each other's intentions and actions, and succeed in conveying political meaning to each other. The world of democratic politics is a world of words, of speech acts, of meaning; it is an elusive reality having no foundations outside itself and consisting exclusively in this continuous, immensely complex interplay of words. Political decision making comes into being when in the appropriate gremia, this interplay tends to freeze or fossilize into fixed forms. And, as this meta-phor suggests, the more complex and variegated the interplay of words has been, the more all permutations of words have been experimented with and tried out, the more successful decision making will be, and the more it may expect to have and to deserve the support of the citizen. This is why we need the media so much: the newspapers, TV, participation of the electorate, and so on. Hence, participation of everything that may hinder the politician and be obnoxious to him, since they are the most powerful generators of new political words and of new meaning, and the most powerful stirrers for mixing old words and meanings into new permutations.

From democracy to nemocracy

If we are willing to learn this lesson from the French Revolution, we will also see what may endanger the functioning of a democracy. As soon as the discourse of foundationalism gets the upper hand in political discourse, democracy is in danger. As soon as the results of the (social) sciences, as soon as statistics, as soon as the data of bureaus for political planning come to dominate political decision making, democracy dies a partial death. Democratic discussion and democratic decision making should always stay on the surface. It must avoid, at all costs, depth, foundations and the pseudo certainty that the social sciences seem to provide the politician with; a *pseudo* certainty, since political truth is not to be found in the kind of data that the social sciences so abundantly—and often so vacuously—produce.[5] Not because these data should be unreliable—though this also will often be the case—but because political truth only announces itself in political interaction. Similarly, for a woodcarver 'the truth' about wood is not to be found in physical data about wood, such as about its specific gravity or its chemical properties, but in how it may react to and resist the woodcarver's efforts to make what he has in mind. The political foundationalist is like somebody believing that the woodcarver would truly be helped with this kind of data—and this surely is one of the profoundly worrying aspects of contemporary political culture that we seem to have lost sight of it and have begun to believe that statistics and such others ought to be the politician's guide.

But political truth and political knowledge are an essentially *experiential* form of truth and knowledge, and both announce themselves only and exclusively in the politician's *interaction* with political reality. They lie on the surface—on the interface between the self and the political world—and are not hidden in some 'foundationalist' depth. The politician should, therefore, *always seek to stay at the surface*—and the more *superficial* he is, the more he succeeds in expanding this surface over all of political reality, the more successful he will be, and certainly *deserve* to be. For, the surface is where political meaning and political symbolism come into being, and the politician yielding to the scientistic temptation will only destroy them.[6] This is, once again, the lesson about democratic politics that we must learn from the French Revolution.

In this context, it will be useful to distinguish between the *political manager*, or administrator, on one hand, and the *politician* in the true sense of the word, on the other. The political manager believes in a quasi-scientific truth. He will believe that politics consists of the identification of the crucial social and political problems, and that these will, at all times, permit a technocratic solution. He will see his discussions with his fellow politicians as the political version of scientific debate—and no less—as the only path to truth. He will, therefore, much prefer the debate with other politicians to that with the so dreadfully ignorant public—in the same way that the scientist will dislike discussing his scientific research with the first man he meets. He will distrust or even hate the media and the unstable chaos of ordinarily ill-informed opinion in the electorate;

he will have his doubts about democratic procedures since these will ever so often frustrate a direct and efficient solution of political problems. He will resent the fact that the electorate tends to get in the way between himself and the political problems requiring a solution—much in the way that a scientist would resent the obligation to continuously popularize what he is doing. Indeed, science will always be his model and ideal.

And it is precisely the reverse with the politician: the true politician dealing with a political problem knows that everybody—in fact, the whole nation—stands between him and the problem he wishes to solve. He will recognize that the continuous interference of the public with his activities is not a regrettable jamming station, but an asset to be used and to be played with, to be exploited as fully as possible for his own purposes. He does not put the public at a distance, as the scientist will typically do, but he will *dance* with the public, and in agreement with the old saying 'who can tell apart the dancer from the dance', he will recognize that he can only be a politician in this dance of his. He will rejoice in all the complexities, the ironies, all the contradictions and even in all the absurdities of the modern media, since he knows that these are for him an inexhaustible goldmine for meaning and for symbol making. Just as great literature differs from a shilling shocker by its ambiguity, by its giving room to ever new readings, so do the paradoxes of the media present the politician with an unprecedented wealth of new opportunities. He will, therefore, love the media precisely because of their obstruction of transparency and their capacity to create complicated and unforeseen dust clouds of meaning. He will welcome in all this a challenge to his talents as a politician, much as the skier will welcome all the difficulties of the terrain as the appropriate challenge to his skills.

Finally, what should our *moral* assessment be of this difference between the political manager and the politician? Admittedly, much is to be said in favour of the political manager: for, is not the search for truth and, hence, for political truth as well, our highest destination as human beings? And are not the political manager's often clumsy dealings with the media the unmistakable sign of his intellectual and political honesty? Should we not automatically distrust a person, like the politician, functioning so well in the doubtful company of the enemies of truth? Have not the horrors of the previous century made us all too painfully aware of the disasters we may expect from politicians and of how much we should prefer the political manager to the politician? Even more so, was not de Robespierre's uncanny penetrating insight into the political dangers of calumny and hypocrisy, a powerful warning of what we should fear from the politician?

There is much truth in this—and though the politician may give us the best of politics, we can also expect the worst from him. Nevertheless, if I may speak here at the end of this essay for myself, I would yet prefer the politician to the political manager. For, though I am well aware of the political dangers embodied in the politician, I think we need not fear that these dangers will actually materialize in Western democracies, in which the habits of democracy are firmly rooted. More importantly, there is one advantage of the politician over the political manager that the latter will never be able to realize. Recall that the political manager has taken science as his model. We will, then, understand that the political manager will wish to make himself—and the state—just as much invisible as the scientist: the person of the scientist is absent from his findings, and wherever this is not the case, it is not to do with science but with literature, art or the humanities. Obviously, the politician has no such aims: his public visibility is his most valuable asset.

We only have to cast a look at contemporary politics to recognize the appropriateness of this observation about the difference between the political manager and the politician. For much like the scientist, the political manager will tend to withdraw from public visibility; he has become an exponent of his bureaucracies no less than that the scientist has found his destination in his laboratory. As a result, the house of politics has become like those palaces of our former kings where nobody lives anymore, though they may still sometimes be visited by the historian or the tourist wishing to relive some of the glories of the past. Nobody is there anymore in the political realm and what is still misleadingly called 'politics', no longer bears traces of the human hand. This has instilled in us, in the electorate, the eerie feeling that we are no longer ruled by anybody—neither by our representatives nor by ourselves. Moreover, nobody seems to be willing anymore to assume responsibility for our collective fate. The electorate still looks for someone or something to hang political responsibility on to; but the political manager fends this responsibility off by hiding behind the impassive image of a technocratic and apolitical truth. To put it all into one formula, *with the political manager we have moved from democracy to nemocracy, that is, to the government by nobody.* And this is not a good thing. For, what could the future be of a society that has radically eliminated both the discourse and the political platform for discussing its future?

The politician, in opposition to the political manager, knows that it is not truth but political creativity that determines politics, that politics is not a science but an art; and he has taken to heart the lesson of the

French Revolution, according to which this art is the art of meaning- and symbol-making. He knows that political responsibility and accountability are what representative democracy has always been about. Above all, he is fully aware that the political meanings and the symbols he creates are what make him a recognizable figure in the political realm, and that these comprise his duties and responsibilities towards the public.

Notes

1. For a political interpretation of von Schiller's distinction, see also Ankersmit (2002: 133–63).
2. Thinking over Hunt's account of the French Revolution may also help us clarify Michelet's ecstatic account of it. For one may well say that Hunt's account has its anticipation in Michelet's *La Révolution Française*—though Hunt made explicit what remained merely implicit in Michelet. Most illuminating here is Gossman's (1990) analysis of Michelet in his *Between Literature and History*. Gossman argues here that for Michelet, (French) history is, essentially, a series of obstacles that had to be overcome before the Revolution could take place. The result of this peculiar narrative strategy was that the Revolution itself was now, so to say, lifted out of narratable history and that we have entered a wholly new world with the Revolution. In this way, Michelet's *La Révolution Française* can be seen as an implementation of Hunt's thesis. All the more so since no nineteenth-century historian had been more sensitive to the Revolution's symbolism than Michelet.
3. For a further discussion of Rorty's views, see Ankersmit (2002a, 2002b).
4. Suggesting, once again, that Rawls is, beyond competition, just about the worst guide that one may choose in matters of political theory. The ravages committed by Rawlsian political philosophy can best be measured by having a look at the journal *Political Theory* that in the twenty years of its existence managed to avoid almost all issues of any political urgency. In the rare cases that it actually addressed them, it did so in such a way so as to rob them of any actual relevance. Rarely has academic debate been more successful in emptying itself of any practical significance than in the contemporary Anglo-Saxon political philosophy.
5. As was recently most compellingly argued by Mark Kranenburg (2002: 7) in his column: 'Till now the majority of politicians believe in the pseudo reality of reports rather than in actual political reality. The counting-frame is holy. The Hague still debates arid figures whereas the rest of society takes its lead in experience: hence the gap between politicians and the electorate' [my translation]
6. This is also where I would disagree with Claude Lefort's (and Carl Schmitt's) well-known conception of political symbolism. Both situate political

symbolism in a quasi-theological sphere beyond political reality. But we should resist both the attempt to locate political symbolism with the foundationalist in a science of politics and the opposite attempt to discover it with the political theologist in a realm *beyond* politics itself.

References

Ankersmit, F.R. 2002a. *Political Representation*. Stanford: Stanford University Press.

———. 2002b. 'Representational Democracy: An Aesthetic Approach to Conflict and Compromise', *Common Knowledge*, 8(Winter): 24–47.

Arendt, H. 1990. *On Revolution*. Harmondsworth.

de Robespierre, M. 1965. *Discours et Rapports à la Convention*. Paris: Le Monde en 10/18.

Gossman, Lionel. 1990. *Between Literature and History*. Cambridge, Massachusetts: Harvard University Press.

Hegel, G.W.F. 1976. *Philosophie der Weltgeschichte: Band II–IV*. Hamburg: Felix Meiner Verlag.

Hunt, Lynn. 1984. *Politics, Culture, and Class in the French Revolution*. Berkeley and Los Angeles: University of California Press.

———. 1992. *The Family Romance of the French Revolution*. Berkeley and Los Angeles: University of California Press.

Kranenburg, M. 2002. 'Moord op de Politiek', *NRC-Handelsblad*, 29 March.

Michelet, J. 1952. *Histoire de la Révolution Française*. Paris: Gallimard

Rawls, J. 1972. *A Theory of Justice*. Oxford: Clarendon Press.

Rorty, R. 1991. 'The Priority of Democracy to Philosophy', in *Objectivity, Relativism and Truth: Philosophical Papers*, vol. 1. Cambridge: Cambridge University Press.

von Schiller, F. Undated. 'Über Naive und Sentimentalische Dichtung', in *Schillers Werke*. Stuttgart, s.a.

Control of Power through Freedom

An Issue in Kant's Political Philosophy

4

BINOD KUMAR AGARWALA

The liberal vision of Power as the binding element that keeps society united, and Freedom as the control of this power, is arrived at by inscription of art and morality within the perspective of modern metaphysics. Yet, liberal vision can be made actual only by overcoming and going beyond that vision to recover the Greek experience, embodied in the *humaniora* (humanities), as represented by genius of Plato and Aristotle. These two theses bring out the contradiction inherent in the liberal society. So, in a way, it is being argued that the actuality of liberal vision requires the delicate and fine balancing of contradictory elements. The aim of this study is to show how Kant balances this contradiction in his critical writings.

The state of nature

The *a priori* conditions of knowledge in the critical philosophy of Kant are such that when any member of society takes the stance of the subject, that is, conceives of himself as the subject to get knowledge of society, or in other words, conceives of society as the object of knowledge, then he must reflect himself out of the society, out of all social relations. The transcendental condition of knowledge as determined by critical philosophy requires that the duality of subject and object be maintained. To maintain the duality of subject and object, namely, of himself and society, the subject must conceive himself as a being outside society. That is to say, when any member of society conceptualizes himself as the subject of knowledge that has society as its object, he must reflect himself out of all social relations, which is to say, he must think of himself as an individual who can exist independent of society. Any member who, by taking the stance of subject, reflects himself out of all social relations, as also when he conceives each member of society as a subject, reflects them all out of all social relations and, hence, sees them all as individuals. So the transcendental logic leads inevitably to the collapse of society and society being reflected out of existence, since each member is conceptualized as an individual. This is the reason why Kant cannot admit the ontological autonomy of society and admits only the primacy of existence of individuals and, thereby, begets metaphysical individualism in philosophy. Together with society, by similar arguments, both tradition and history also get dissolved as no one belongs to tradition and history. The concept of individuals standing in no social relations to each other, and also without tradition and history, is the concept of state of nature of political philosophy.

The inscription of art and practical reason in the perspective of the subject

When art and morality is inscribed within the perspective of the subject, the distinction between acting (or doing, *agere*, πράττείν) and making (*facere*, ποιείν) gets transformed. To put it differently, the distinction between *praxis* and *poeisis* gets transformed. The *Nicomachean Ethics* of Aristotle opens with a distinction between actions, which are ends in themselves, and actions, which have ends different from these activities themselves, and the former is produced as consequences by the latter. The former kind of action is designated 'acting' or 'doing', while the latter as 'making'. For Aristotle, *phronesis* or practical reason is concerned with activities that are not the concern of arts and, hence, not concerned with activities that aim at products which go beyond these activities themselves and, hence, concerned with activities that aim at the performance of these activities themselves. Aristotle is making a distinction between acting and making in a manner that makes them mutually exclusive categories, since for him this is brought about by actions whose excellent performance is an end in itself and the actions that are performed for the sake of ends apart from them. The former is the subject matter of morality and politics while the latter is the subject matter of art. When this distinction is inscribed within the perspective of the subject due to transformation of the distinction, only 'making' (*facere*) remains as action done with free will and, hence, properly human action. But activities falling under the category of *agere* cease to be recognized as human action at all. When the distinction between making and doing is inscribed within the perspective of the subject, *making* occupies the whole space of human action. The reason for this is that the objective knowledge based on subject–object dichotomy is of the nature of power. Hence, for the Kantian subject, Bacon's dictum 'knowledge is power' holds good. Since knowledge is knowledge of causality operating in substance of the object in space and time, it gives power to the subject to manipulate the object by his own will. Although causality and will appear to belong to different realms in Kant's transcendental philosophy, in reality, they fit with each other. The subject with 'will' can manipulate the object through knowledge of causality. For Kant, action is nothing but exercise of power, that is, the initiation of a chain of causality to achieve the desired result called 'end'.

Making (*facere*) as the only schema of all human action

To attribute an act of making, in the perspective of the subject, to a person is first of all to impute the consequences of this act for the future, that is, who has made, is also he who will admit the fault, if any, in the thing made, who will repair the fault and who will bear the blame for the faulty product. In other words, he is the bearer of sanctions. He is brought into the dialectic of praise and blame for the product. That is to say, the person is responsible for the ends he chooses to bring about as a consequence of his action.

The dialectic of praise and blame associated with making is such that making does not admit to moral evaluation and, hence, it is not required that the act of making be a good act. What is required is that the result should be good and the act of making be evaluated only for its efficiency in achieving the desired results. Hence, the craftsman's art does not enable him to live well morally but it enables him only to produce a good work of art.

Since attribution of the act of making to a person is to regard him as the bearer of sanctions in case the product is faulty, it requires placing the person before the consequences of his act, that is, before the product. The person is referred back to the moment prior to his act of making, as one who not only acted, but also could have acted otherwise or who could have made otherwise or who could have given another form to the external matter or who could have chosen some other end. This conviction of something being done freely is not a matter of observation; rather, the agent is being declared after the fact as the one who could have made otherwise. He, on whom we put the consequences or the product, is declared free, and we discern this freedom as already at work in the incriminating act. This movement from the front to behind the responsibility is essential according to Ricoeur (1974: 432). It constitutes the identity of the moral subject through past, present and future. He who will bear the blame is the same as he who now takes the act upon himself and he who has acted. He posits the identity of him who accepts future responsibility of action and he who has acted, and the two dimensions—that is, future and past—are linked in the present. The future of sanctions and the past of action of production committed are tied together in the present of avowal by himself and attribution by others. That is to say, the ego remains identical throughout from initiation of action to bearing of sanctions, if any. So the maker is conscious of his own identity. He is a self-conscious person.

This awareness that one could have done otherwise is closely linked to the awareness that one should have done otherwise. It is because one recognizes his 'ought' that he recognizes his 'could'.

The shift in the schema of morality

Although originally morality was concerned with a kind of action that excluded making, with the inscription of morality in the perspective of the subject, it becomes concerned with making only. Hence, morality loses its character of knowledge, that is, knowledge as virtue; rather, it becomes a self-willed side constraint both on actions and ends. Since the only mode of human action recognized by moderns is the mode of making, the self-willed law is interpreted by them as law 'made' by human reason. Be it noted that although both art and morality relate to the same kind of action, they relate to action differently in the new schema according to Kant. That is to say, art and morality do not relate to mutually exclusive categories of action any more, but they relate differently to the same action. Art relates to action via the technically practical rules that connect the action to the end sought to be achieved through that action and, hence, gives rise to hypothetical imperatives only.

So when we perform an action for the end to be achieved as a consequence of it, we relate to action in the mode of art. Morality relates to the same action as a side constraint not to be violated and as a constraint on ends that can be achieved.

So when we determine our choice for the sake of following the law disregarding the end to be achieved by the action chosen, we relate to action in the mode of morality and it gives rise to categorical imperative. This is what morality becomes when it is inscribed in the perspective of the subject.

The liberal vision and the Kantian 'ought'

In the state of Nature, man is endowed with power of choice and practical reason. The faculty of free choice makes it necessary to have society, and the faculty of giving laws autonomously makes it possible to have society, provided the free choice is exercised according to the laws of autonomy. The vision of society, according to Kant, in the state of Nature that individuals come to have is that of many individuals pursuing their divergent ends or goals but living together under common laws. This imagery follows from the new understanding of Man as maker and the new interpretation of morality.

If the right to liberty of pursuing the goal of one's choice is admitted within the laws, only then do we have a vision of a liberal society. We will see that Kant adds this liberty subsequently. Hobbes starts with the right to this liberty to unlimited extent and later restricts it by the laws of nature. Although the extent of liberty that he finally admits to, satisfies no liberal. Hence, they have not admitted him as having a vision of a liberal society. But the structure of society is exactly the same as that of a liberal society, that is, individuals pursuing their own ends within the limits set by the sovereign who does not impose any single conception of the good but only restricts the choice.

Why has liberty become so significant? The answer is that the subject who has knowledge of objects, necessarily conceives himself as a *homo faber* endowed with a faculty of free choice, who chooses his own goals and achieves them through *techne* as argued before. Such *homo fabers* in the state of Nature necessarily encounter interference from other *homo fabers* due to their attempt to achieve their goals through *techne*. So each *homo faber* needs freedom from interference from others to achieve his goals. This is how freedom becomes the central concern of modern political philosophy. Such freedom can be enjoyed by *homo fabers* only if everyone is willing to follow the principle of right: 'Every action which by itself or by its maxim enables the freedom of each individual's will to coexist with the freedom of every one else in accordance with a universal law is *right*' (*Kant's Political Writings* 1970: 133).

So the liberal vision is what we 'ought' to realize by abandoning the state of nature. It is not in being in the state of Nature. So the status of the liberal vision of society is that it is not actual in the state of Nature; rather, because of practical reasons, we are under an obligation to bring it (this liberal society) about. It is an ideal for the establishment of which we ought to act.

Liberalism as a coercive political order

Society can be generated from the state of Nature if and only if the persons in the state of Nature have effective good will, and this in turn requires the existence of a monopoly of coercion. In other words, a society generated from the state of Nature has to be a political society, that is, a society based on power and coercion. Hence, it has to be a modern state.

According to Kant ('Idea for a Universal History with a Cosmological Purpose', in *Kant's Political Writings*.: 44), individuals in the state of Nature are unsocial.

> But he also has great tendency *to live as an individual*, to isolate himself, since he also encounters in himself the unsocial characteristic of wanting to direct everything in accordance with his own ideas. He, therefore, expects resistance all around, just as he knows of himself that he is in turn inclined to offer resistance to others.

In a Hobbesian vein Kant (ibid.) argues, 'Through the desire for honour, power or property it drives him to seek status among his fellows, whom he cannot *bear*, yet cannot *bear to leave*.' In the absence of coercive public laws by which each can be given what is due to him and secured against attack from others, the insatiable desire for possession or even power among human beings, enviously competitive vanity and social incompatibility reigns supreme. The state of Nature of Kant turns out to be the Hobbesian state of war.

It is an empirical fact that human beings act in a violent and malevolent manner, and that they tend to fight among themselves for pursuing the ends set by themselves in the absence of external coercive sanctions. But Kant is not satisfied with this contention, for in his *Critique of Practical Reason*, he argues for the obligation of respect for the moral law to determine action overcoming the impulse of empirical desires. So if individuals have effective respect for the moral law expressed in 'I ought', then how can there be conflict? Or to put it differently, hadn't Kant solved the problem already? Isn't it the case that if everyone ought to act as practical reason dictates, that is, if private ends ought to be limited by maxims that are fit to be universal laws of Nature, then the violence of Nature can be avoided?

Kant gives a transcendental argument to show why mere limiting of private ends of each by himself through moral law cannot solve the problem of violence in the state of Nature and, hence, the problem of existence of law also cannot be solved in the state of Nature.

But it is not experience or any kind of factual knowledge that makes public legal coercion necessary. On the contrary, even if we imagine men to be as benevolent and law abiding as we please, the *a priori* rational idea of a non-lawful state will tell us that before a public and legal state is established, individual men, people and states can never be secure against acts of violence from one another, since each will have his own right to do *what seems right and good to him*, independently of the opinion of others (ibid.: 137).

That is to say if everyone acts according to what he conceives as his moral duty, then no one is secure from coercion of others; hence, there is no law in existence in the state of nature. This explains why the law must remain an 'I ought' for rational beings in the state of nature and it cannot become 'I will', nor can it be translated into external action.

Both Hobbes and Locke prior to Kant also recognized this right of private judgement as the culprit in the state of nature. So it becomes a prior requirement of reason or moral duty 'to adopt the principle that one must abandon the state of nature in which everyone follows his own desires and unites with every one else ... in order to submit to external public and lawful coercion' (ibid.). This is what the moral law or the categorical imperative commands persons to accept as duty, since it is the condition of making it possible to follow one's moral duty for everyone without coming into conflict with each other so that a kingdom of ends is possible.

The principle on which a public lawful coercion is based is the Universal Principle of Right stated earlier: the principle of right states the condition of the restriction of individual freedom with the use of coercive sanctions in civil society. Even though this puts a person under an obligation to restrict his freedom, it does not require that this obligation be recognized as a motive for so restricting the freedom. This fact makes the principle of right a principle of political obligation and not a moral obligation. That is to say, Kant argued, that we have a moral duty to take upon ourselves the legal duty and the universal principle of right is only an application of the universal principle of morality as laid down in the categorical imperative to the sphere of law or external coercive relations. So the vision of a liberal society is in fact a vision of a society in which members stand in a mutually coercive external relation.

The Hobbesian sovereign

The all-important question now is how can this coercive political order be translated into an actual order? How does one abandon the state of nature to unite with every one else?

Hobbes gives one answer to this question. Kant, of course, rejects Hobbes' answer ('On the Common Saying "This May be True in Theory, but it Does Not Apply in Practice"', in ibid.).[1] According to Hobbes, subjection to a single sovereign is the ground of social unity. And as the act of authorization through the covenant makes it clear, the sovereign is above the law and not bound by law; yet, he has the supreme power to make laws, and here comes the idea of positive law. The law posited by the sovereign is the positive law of the realm.

Kant rejects the idea of this kind of contract. In his view (ibid.: 73):

> Among all the contracts by which a large group of men unite to form a society (*pactum sociale*), the contract establishing a *civil constitution* (*pactum unionis civilis*) is of an exceptional nature. For while, so far as its execution is concerned, it has much in common with all others that are likewise directed towards a chosen end to be pursued by joint effort, it is essentially different from all others in the principle of its constitution (*constitutionis civilis*). In all social contracts, we find a union of many individuals for some common end which they all *share*. But a union as an end in itself which they all *ought to share* and which is thus an absolute and primary duty in all external relationships whatsoever among human beings

(who cannot avoid mutually influencing one another), is only found in a society in so far as it constitutes a civil state, that is, a commonwealth.

According to Kant this contract establishes a *civil constitution* based on the following *a priori* principles (ibid.: 74):

1. The *freedom* of every member of society as a *human being*.
2. The *equality* of each with all the others as a *subject*.
3. The *independence* of each member of a commonwealth as a *citizen*.

Kant makes it clear that these principles are not laws given by an already established state; rather, these are 'laws by which a state can be established in accordance with pure rational principles of external human right' (ibid.).

For Kant, man's *freedom* as a human being means (ibid.), 'Each may seek his happiness in whatever way he sees fit [provided] he does not infringe upon the freedom of others to pursue a similar end which can be reconciled with the freedom of everyone else within a workable general law.'

Man's *equality* as a subject is explained thus (ibid.): 'Each member of the commonwealth has right of coercion in relation to all the others, except in relation to the head of state.' He argues (ibid.: 74–75):

For he [head of state] alone is not a member of the commonwealth, but its creator or preserver, and he alone is authorized to coerce others without being subject to any coercive law himself. But all who are subject to laws are the subjects of a state, and are thus subject to the right of coercion along with all other members of the commonwealth; the only exception is a single person (in either the physical or the moral sense of the word), the head of state, through whom alone the rightful coercion of all others can be exercised. For if he too can be coerced, he would not be the head of the state, and the hierarchy of subordination would ascend infinitely.

Although Kant is arguing against the idea of Hobbesian sovereign, the argument he gives for keeping the head of the state out of the scope of coercive laws brings in the Hobbesian sovereign in the very heart of Kant's liberal vision. Not withstanding his protestations, Kant ('The Metaphysics of Morals', in ibid.: 144) comes very close to Hobbes' position when he denies any possibility of rightful coercion of the head of the state, 'The actual constitution cannot contain any article which might make it possible for some power within the state to resist or hold in check the supreme executive in cases where he violets the constitutional laws'. So the Kantian ruler is as absolute as the Hobbesian sovereign. But Kant succeeds in evading this from the readers by claiming that the sovereign is not the head of the state. For Kant ('On the Common Saying...', in ibid.: 77):

> A public law ... is the act of a public will.... And this requires no less than the will of the entire people ... thus an individual will cannot legislate for a commonwealth. For this requires freedom, equality and *unity* of the will of *all* the members. And the prerequisite for unity, since it necessitates a general vote ... is independence. The basic law, which can come only from the general, united will of the people, is called the *original contract*.

For Kant, only the united will of the people is the *sovereign* ('The metaphysics of Morals', in ibid.: 147). By *citizen*, he (ibid.: 77) means 'anyone who has the right to vote on ... legislation.' Kant makes it clear that all members or subjects of the commonwealth are not its citizens. Only an adult male who is his own master (*sui iuris*), who has some property to support himself and who does not earn his living 'by allowing others to make use of him' (ibid.: 78) qualifies as a citizen. This is what Kant means by the independence of a member of the commonwealth as a citizen.

If we take Kant's idea of the sovereignty of the united will of the people on its face value, we see a problem. This theory presupposes the corporate existence of people in society while that is precisely what the theory of sovereignty is supposed to account for. That is to say, this theory of sovereignty begs the question immediately. Only a Hobbesian sovereign seems to serve the purpose of accounting for the corporate unity of all individuals in society within the conceptual resources of modern liberalism. Why should the Hobbesian theory of sovereignty be admitted within the liberal theory? Why not Rousseau's sovereignty of the general will or Locke's sovereignty of the majority? The reason is that all these theories presuppose the corporate existence of people in society while that is precisely what the theory of sovereignty is supposed to account for. That is to say, again, that these theories beg the question immediately.

But natural law theorists must face the question of how to make the sovereign legislate according to natural law within their scheme of things. That is to ask: how can the sovereign be limited within the conceptual apparatus of modern liberalism? As argued by Kant, there can be no higher authority in their philosophy. The right of revolution to make the sovereign conform to law of nature also cannot be accepted by Kant. The latter option is not available since revolution is a corporate act and all corporate acts have to be authorized by the sovereign, but this corporate act will dissolve the corporate unity. Kant (ibid.: 145) argues:

> The reason why it is the duty of the people to tolerate even what is apparently the most intolerable misuse of supreme power is that it is impossible ever to conceive of their resistance to the supreme legislation as being anything other than unlawful and liable to nullify the entire legal constitution. For before such resistance could be authorized, there would have to be a public law which permitted the people to offer resistance: in other words, the supreme legislation would have to contain a provision to the effect that it is not supreme, so that in one and the same judgment, the people as subjects would be made sovereign over the individual to whom they are subject. This is self-contradictory, and the contradiction is at once obvious if we ask who would act as judge in this dispute between the people and the sovereign.... It then becomes clear that the people would set themselves up as judges of their own cause.

Kant expects history to do the job. But at this stage of the argument there is no history either to pin one's hope on it to produce the natural law state. There is no custom or tradition to limit the sovereign. The original liberal Locke, whom we recognize to be father of theory of limited government no doubt, failed to limit the real sovereign, that is, the majority in his theory. And we also know how Madison in the *Federalist Papers* was worried about the tyranny of the majority when Locke inspired the founding fathers of the American Constitution.

Yet, Kant is right in noticing that Hobbesian sovereign cannot foot the theoretical bill it is supposed to pay. But reasons for this are different. To institute a sovereign by mutual contract is a moral obligation of each individual in the state of nature. Yet, reason tells the individual that in the state of Nature, it is in his own self-interest not to discharge this obligation (the Empirical Argument). Even if it is in his self-interest to discharge this obligation, what is the guarantee that others will discharge their obligation to enter the contract (the Transcendental Argument)? The condition of discharging the moral obligation will arise only if there is already a sovereign in existence. So the moral obligation to institute a sovereign through contract can be discharged only if there is already a sovereign in existence. Hence, infinite regress follows. So the sovereign cannot be established by institution. And consequently, liberal civil society cannot be established by contract. Rather, as we have already seen, Kant declares ('On the Common Saying...', in ibid.: 73):

> In all social contracts, we find a union of many individuals for some common end which they all *share*. But a union as an end in itself which they all *ought to share* and which is thus an absolute and primary duty in all external relationships whatsoever among human beings (who cannot avoid mutually influencing one another), is only found in a society in so far as it constitutes a civil state, i.e. a commonwealth.

Kantian *original contract* presupposes the existence of society but that is yet to be established. What is the way out?

The Machiavellian political actor

Remember that this argument is going on in the consciousness of the subject who has taken the stance of the subject to society and conceives of others as subjects and of them all as individuals in the state of Nature, and still grappling with the question how to create the liberal civil society. And Hobbes also supplies the answer that institution of the coercive political order is just an imaginary analytical idea to determine what its elements are. Kant also will agree with Hobbes on this point that the state of Nature is a hypothetical idea of reason and not an historical state of affairs. He writes (ibid.: 79), 'But we need by no means assume that this contract (*contractus originarius* or *pactum sociale*) ... actually exists as a *fact*, for it cannot possibly be so.... It is in fact merely an *idea* of reason.'

Actually, sovereignty is established by acquisition or conquest, according to Hobbes. He, of course, tries to analyze the acquisition of sovereign power also in terms of contract which turned out to be a failure. It was Machiavelli who really understood the dynamics of the acquisition of sovereign power. The subject who has taken the stance of the subject to society is the prince: the individual with a will to power or will to found the republican state, that is, endowed with *virtu* as conceived by Machiavelli. The person who had taken the stance of a subject towards society had merely conceived of others as individuals but they were never individuals. They (excluding himself) were in society, a mere natural mass of society. The mass of society, a natural phenomenon, was there in front of him to get knowledge of, the knowledge formed and categorized, the knowledge of causality operating in the society in space and time, the knowledge of empirical necessity.

It is only through the knowledge of empirical necessity of causality that will can operate, indeed, the prince can operate. When humanities were turned into social sciences on the model of natural sciences, they became instruments of the Machiavellian political actors.

It is interesting to note that Machiavelli is the first thinker to cast his political actor, that is, the prince in the mould of an artist or an artificer. 'Clearly *homo faber* is the role in which Machiavelli is forever casting his hero' (Singleton 1971: 431). In Machiavelli's writings, the announcement of his prescription as to what the political actor has to do is generally preceded by either the clause beginning with the pronoun *whoever* (*chi* in Italian) followed by a verb of volition or an 'If' clause with a verb of desiring writ large. So for Machiavelli these prescriptions—to use Kantian language—are hypothetical imperatives announcing technically practical rules. And then occasionally, he passes the moral judgement on the same actions prescribed for the political actor. 'Doubtless these means are cruel and destructive of all civilized life and neither Christian nor human and should be avoided by everyone'(Machiavelli's *Discourses*, 1950: Chapter 26). Before Machiavelli, no thinker took political action to be a *making (facere)*. Rather, it was taken to be a doing (*agere*).

If my argument is correct, then within the conceptual apparatus available to modern philosophers, the liberal vision can be achieved only by political action based on Machiavellian prescriptions. Yet, be it noted, that there is a great discrepancy between liberal aspiration and Machiavellian prescriptions. While liberal vision is a part of modern morality, Machiavellian prescriptions are formulated from the point of view of art only. Not only that, they contradict each other. The contradiction is due to the fact that liberal aspiration is based on the assumption that everyone is an individual while the Machiavellian prince acts by dropping this assumption and taking only the prince to be the individual subject and everyone else to be natural mass of matter belonging to nature. Hence, there is a glaring contradiction between the liberal vision and the model of political action to achieve it. No doubt, modern liberals have paid more attention to the ideal and no attention to political action to achieve it.

Staunch liberals like Kant explicitly reject Machiavellism. For Kant, establishment of a civil state is not a technical task (*Kunstaufgabe*) (*Kant's Political Writings*: 122). He wants to follow the older tradition. Since he has rejected *doing (agere)* as a category of human action, he cannot admit it as a category of political action either. So, for him, political actor is a moral politician and the establishment of the civil state is a moral task based on duty. But how can this task be performed? How does Kant answer this question?

To solve the problem of social unity to control political power, Kant in his *Religion Within the Limits of Reason Alone* (1934) brought in the idea of one true religion, on which the one universal church is based, but he landed up with faith of several kinds with a multiplicity of churches. Thus, the problem of social unity and the control of power eluded him. He had the problem of multiple organized churches at hand, which further accentuates the problem of control of power to protect the freedom of religion.

Kant's failure was nothing but the philosophical working out of the failure of medieval experience in the modern world. In the beginning of the Christian era in Europe, there was no supremacy of *raison d'etat*. The universal Christian religion setting up a universal moral command subordinated the political power and *raison d'etat* to it by implanting the moral values in the hearts of men. Then in the Middle Ages, Germanic jurisprudence combined with Christian ethics in keeping down the political power. The political power did exist in the Middle Ages but it did not rank supreme. Law was set above it; it was a means for enforcing the law. In the words of Kern (1919: 57), 'Politics and *raison d'etat* were not recognized at all in the Middle Ages.' In the later Middle Ages (Meinecke 1971: 403–4):

> the struggle between Church and Papacy fostered the conscious power politics of great rulers like the Emperor Frederick II and Philip IV of France. The Emperor Charles IV in Germany and King Louis XI in France were examples of a thoroughly unscrupulous and rational art of government, based on their own authority. Even the Church itself, by its inner transformations, by the progressive permeation of the Papacy with worldly political interests, by the often very utilitarian approach of the Church Council, and by the rational perfecting of Papal finance, paved the way for the new spirit in the art of government.

In the process the Church lost its authority over the political power in Europe. But with the emergence of the secular absolutist states with modernity, whatever little power the Church had over the secular rulers was completely lost. And with the reformation and division of Christianity into many churches, not only did the Church became completely defunct in controlling the state power, but also it made the problem of control of state power more acute by giving rise to the issue of religious liberty. This is the European experience being articulated philosophically by Kant in his book on religion.

A new beginning in the *Critique of Judgment*

The other way to turn the Machiavellian political actor into a moral politician is to block the question of the origin of the civil society. The question of origin can be blocked provided we push the prince we have deduced back into the society from which he came out, to become an individual in the state of Nature. Only by interpreting the transcendental ego as a social being can the question of origin be blocked and space for authentic political action be opened.

If my argument is correct, then our prior belonging to a society with customs and history sustains the liberal political order. This society is the nation. From the very beginning of the emergence of the modern era, although theoretical philosophizing went on in terms of individualism and the structure of the modern state, the real burden of the social unity and identity was born by the nation. Nation is a historical and political idea. Even modernity, individualism and liberalism succeeded in establishing and controlling the sovereign or the state by becoming national mores and ethos. Hence, it was not accident that the idea of the nation-state emerged with modernity. Theoretically modernity has no theoretical tools to understand what it means to belong to a nation or a tradition or a history; yet, it cannot do without it unless modernity wants to degenerate into fascism. It must be kept in mind that Fascism's appeal to nationalism (even this was not genuine) is not the same thing as the sovereign or state being sustained and controlled by the nation. Fascism, by equating nation with state—even while advocating nationalism—was advocating pure statism, and leadership principle became supreme.

So, we must face the question as to what it means to belong to nation, tradition and ethos, or even to the world? This is the question that has become paramount in the post-modern era after the holocaust in Europe. This was the question that became uppermost in Kant's mind when French Revolution began for achieving liberty, equality and fraternity, the liberal ideals, even before he witnessed the reign of terror in France.[2]

In his *Critique of Judgment*, Kant (1952: 59) made it clear that 'a monarchical state is represented as a living body when it is governed by constitutional laws, but as a mere machine (like a handmill) when it is governed by an individual absolute will.' But from this it should not be concluded that he is advocating any organic theory of constitutional state. For he (ibid.) clarifies, 'but in both cases the representation is merely *symbolic*. For there is certainly no likeness between a despotic state and a handmill, whereas there surely is between the rules of reflection upon both and their causality'. And no doubt there can be 'no likeness' between a constitutional state and a living body either for Kant. There is likeness only 'between the rules of reflection upon both and their causality.' But Kant (ibid.) laments, 'Hitherto this function has been but little analyzed worthy as it is of a deeper study.' His *Critique of Judgment* is a preparation for that study. Here he was inspired by Greek experience, as he (ibid.: 60) says.

> There was an age and there were nations in which the active impulse towards a social life regulated by laws—what converts a people into a permanent community—grappled with the huge difficulties presented by the trying problem of bringing freedom (and therefore equality also) into union with constraining force (more that of respect and dutiful submission than of fear).

How did they achieve the limit of union of the two: force and freedom?

> And such must have been the age, and such the nation, that first discovered the art of reciprocal communication of ideas between the more cultured and ruder sections of the community, and how to bridge the difference between the amplitude and refinement of the former and the natural simplicity and originality of the latter—in this way hitting upon that mean between higher culture and the modest worth of nature, that forms for taste also, as a sense common to all mankind, that true standard which no universal rules can supply.
>
> —(ibid.)

What Kant has in mind is that the happy harmony of freedom and force was possible in the nation, which had strengthened its channels of mutual communication and education. Kant is here referring to the Greek experience embodied in the genius of Plato and Aristotle. Not only that he is arguing for the recognition of the political significance of the authority based on knowledge—knowledge as virtue, not power—which is the real element that keeps society together in harmony. Political authority cannot be legitimately instituted without prior recognition of authority based on knowledge in society. Genius is such authority.

Unless we follow the Greek experience as a model, no civil state can be achieved—

> Hardly will a later age dispense with those models. For Nature will ever recede farther into the background, so that eventually, with no permanent example retained from the past, a future age would scarce be in a position to form a concept of the happy union, in one and the same people, of the law-directed constraint belonging to the highest culture, with the force and truth of a free nature sensible of its proper worth.
>
> —(ibid.)

Hence, for Kant *humaniora* (humanities) as represented by the Greek model is the sociability embodied in nation that is appropriate and necessary to sustain a civil state.

Notes

1. The second section of this essay titled, 'On the Relationship of Theory to Practice in Political Right', (pp. 73–87), is an attempt to refute Hobbes' political theory.
2. His *Critique of Judgment* (1952) is an attempt to answer this question. Especially the second part of *The Third Critique* refers to French revolution.

References

Kant, I. 1934. *Religion Within the Limits of Reason Alone* [trans. Theodore M. Green and Hoyt H. Hudson]. Chicago: The Open Court Publishing Company.

———. 1952. 'The Critique of Judgment' [trans. James Creed Meredith], in *The Critique of Pure Reason, The Critique of Practical Reason And Other Ethical Treatises*, in *Great Books of the Western World, Vol-XLII*. Chicago: The University of Chicago, Encyclopaedia Britanica Inc.

———. 1970. *Kant's Political Writings* (trans. Hans Reiss and H.B. Nibset). Cambridge: Cambridge University Press.

Kern, F. 1919. 'Recht und Verfassung im Mittelalter', *Historische Zeitschrift*, 120: 57.

Machiavelli, Niccolo. 1950. *Discourse on the First Ten Books of Titus Livy* [trans. Christian E. Detmold]. New York: The Modern Library.

Meinecke, Frederich. 1971. 'Machiavelli', in James V. Down, Jr and David K. Hart (eds), *Perspectives on Political Philosophy, Volume I—Thucydides through Machiavelli*. Holt, Rinehart and Winston, Inc.

Ricoeur, P. 1974. *The Conflict of Interpretations*. Evanston: Northwestern University Press.

Singleton, Charles S. 1971. 'The Perspective of Art', in James V. Down, Jr. and David K. Hart (eds), *Perspectives on Political Philosophy, Volume I—Thucydides through Machiavelli*. New York: Holt, Rinehart and Winston, Inc.

Power of Modernity and the Tail of the Devil

5

PHILIP QUARLES VAN UFFORD

'His last word—to live with', she insisted. 'Don't you understand I loved him—I loved him—I loved him.'
I pulled myself together and spoke slowly.
'The last word he pronounced was—your name.'
—Joseph Conrad, in *Heart of Darkness* (1973: 121)

Introduction

This chapter is about two themes in their coherence. The first is everyday evil contemplated rather reflectively. I would advocate that we make use (again) of concepts such as 'evil' and use them also in the social sciences. Such concepts refer us to matters we no longer seem to notice. Because of this, we understand some things less; and we let ourselves be fooled by conventional platitudes. With Stephen Toulmin (1990: 32), I would say: 'Don't believe a word of them.' I hold that our modern view of the world is impaired because we have tossed concepts such as 'evil' or 'the devil' overboard. We pay a price for it. We must learn to do better. But how?

In this essay, I suggest we problematize the dynamics of evil as a dimension of normal everyday life. It is better not to focus our search for an understanding of evil on extreme events or diabolic persons. We must resist the temptation to regard evil as a special category which can clearly be distinguished from 'normal' everyday life. As Annemarie Mol (2000: 10–13) has suggested for the study of ethics, we must not focus on dramatic events or extraordinary evil persons. It is better to try to learn to improve our 'drawn-out descriptions' and analyzes of the commonplace. While Mol makes this suggestion for the study of ethics, I would follow her in our quest for understanding evil.

Fest, one of the great biographers of Hitler, made some pertinent remarks in his biography of Albert Speer in this respect. Speer was one of Hitler's main helpers, minister, architect and companion. In this biography, Fest (2000) remarks that for our understanding of evil, it may be more important not to focus too much on Hitler himself. It may be better to try and understand why so many highly professional and talented people such as Albert Speer, apparently 'normal' and competent, came to provide a man like Hitler with the space and tools for carrying out his agenda. Why and how was the 'diabolical' constituted in the enactment of the 'normal'? We may benefit more from this line of questioning. The two dynamics—of evil and of normalization—must be distinguished to be sure. But the two cannot be separated from one another. How may we start to grasp the interactions between the two? How was evil domesticated, how was professionalism—in the case of Speer—perverted? Fest asks our attention to a specific aspect of this. He asks how important concepts and words were being robbed of their substance. He gives an unexpected example of this: after the War, Fest refuses to believe Speer when he shows remorse about his subservience to Hitler. Speer seems again to conform himself, saying all the right morally and politically correct things. Are we well prepared for detecting the truth from a lie when words of remorse are spoken? Is Speer too normal again, too well adapted to a new regime? It is along the edges of language that we must learn to make important distinctions again and improve sensitivities that we have lost. We must learn to recognize the devil again, learn to grasp him by the tail when he runs along. Baudrillard (1993) reserves his description of evil to this reversal in the language we speak. He calls it a 'metastasis' of meaning. He takes the view that evil has become part and parcel of everyday life in our modern world. It has now become the routine of the day, Baudrillard tells us, a normal condition in modern society.

We must link the dynamics of evil and processes of normalization. While dramatic events and extraordinarily evil people may continue to call for our attention, we had better focus on everyday life. How is one to engage in such a task?

I submit that we may discern the tail of the devil in everyday life in the form of exaggerated forms of optimism and overly facile promises of social order. The content of such promises may vary and even contradict, but what is invariable is the *exaggerated* preoccupation with 'order' which we must note, and the perception that, essentially, the process of imposing order is no problem. Order, then, becomes mostly a technical matter. In the domestication of evil, therefore, the issue is not a specific social phenomenon as deviant or violent behaviour. Evil and normalizing are linked. We must not focus on the extraordinary. On the contrary, more interesting are the various characteristics of evil as giving form to the various kinds of normality.

The devil can take on many a form. At times, he will present himself as his own opponent. If convenient, he will enthusiastically denounce the promises he made yesterday. You recognize him by deproblemat-ization of his promises: he will see you through. This can lead to various forms of utopistically shored-up thinking, but people can also succumb to the other side, losing themselves in exaggerated anti-utopian preoccupations and a post-modern, apolitical pragmatism (Kolakowski 1998). *Prima facie*, the current wave of depoliticizing seems a break with modernist quests for the ideal order. But it only seems that way. In its one-sided mirroring, post-modern development is most of all a continuation of modernity, be it as a criticism of it. It is a nihilistic negation of modernity rather than something new. Polish–British philosopher Kolakowski emphasizes these aspects of both continuity and blind alley. Recently, before he began his lecture, he whispered a secret to his audience: 'God exists, but almost nobody knows about it.' I'll come back to this. You do find an obsession with order in post-modern thinking, too; no longer on the political level but in the lifestyle of individuals (Sardar 1997) and the aesthetic order.

Mine is an 'essay' in the literal sense of an attempt. Beyond mod-ernity, beyond the last variant of post-modern thinking, within the empirical I look for transcendent dimensions. For this, we need words like the 'devil' and 'domestication of evil'. Immanence is not the polar opposite of transcendence; it is interwoven with it. In the social sciences, J. van Baal (1991) pleaded for this and, in recent years, studies are ap-pearing with increasing frequency, advocating a 'turn to religion'. I restrict myself to literature that seeks to join in with the scientific debate. Specifically, philosophers reflect on the exigency of a turn to religion. Calvin Schrag (1997, 2000), a student of Ricoeur, for example, investigates how we can trace the dimension of transcendence in im-manent empirical reality and then poses the question as to how to deal with it. Schrag, who builds on a new French tradition, and George Marsden (1996), who makes a plea for reconsidering the option of Christian science, though differing in many respects, are pioneers in this respect. They pose new questions and evoke in me the candour to simply go ahead and write about the devil. It seems pertinent to ask where we can find the devil, if God has re-entered the stage and is being reflected upon in French philosophy, for example, by Ricoeur and Derrida (for an overview, see Jonkers and Welten 2003).

The second theme has a more conventional social–scientific background. I will get an empirical hold on the devil's tail. But what is the route from a different perspective to a new way of studying the empirical? It makes little sense to revisit the devil with dogmatic or classical philosophical/ontological reflections. As a social scientist, I stand closer to a phenomenological tradition (de Boer 2003: 43–67) which is closer to a questioning of his manifestations, not asking who or what the devil 'is'. We must trace him as a dynamic force or a specific dimension of everyday life. It is important to question his 'deeds'. And by asking so, we forestall fruitless abstraction and quarrels of religious doctrine. The question is: how can we use the domestication of evil as a 'sensitizing concept' in our cultural and social analyses? If the devil is doing his thing, just how does he do it? Did you really see the tip of his tail? Why didn't you arrest it on video? We have to present proof.

The devil's disappearing act

In the eighteenth century, the devil successfully performed a vanishing act (*cf* Kittsteiner 1993). We were left with the débris. All that remained were 'social' problems and these were increasingly considered solvable. The disappearance act led to exaggerated optimism. The hypothesis of human cultural autonomy and the idea that culture is a human 'construct' became virtually universally accepted. This belief in the autonomy and limitation of human culture led us—as true children of the Enlightenment—to make rather facile use of words like culture and society, to see the object of our study as more or less rounded out and to hold the limits of empirical reality as non-problematic.

Toulmin (1990, 2001) suggests that this faith emerged when, towards the end of the sixteenth century, the world proved literally 'round'. One could circumnavigate it. This changed the concept of 'world' and made room for the notion of the empirical as an autonomous social reality. Ignorance increasingly lost its transcendent idea of 'unknowable'. In this way, a gradual rift was introduced between the essentially knowable empirical and transcendence, which had best be left to specialists.

In the Vasco da Gama era of the seafarers, mysteries thus became matters that we 'did not yet' comprehend but were, in principle, to be grasped and known. We unveiled the mysteries and gradually charted the gaps in our knowledge. The metaphor of 'charting' implied optimism. Well-executed charts were the most cherished secret in the seafaring world. And in this 'rounding out' of the world, there was outside collaboration. And—as again Toulmin tells us—the Enlightenment must also be seen as an effort to cope with catastrophe, as an effort to save the world from the immense destruction brought about by warring religions in Europe in the early seventeenth century. New definitions of a humane world were badly needed. It was clear that these definitions of the human condition avoided any mentioning of God or the devil. Any notion of transcendence had proven to be a mortal danger. The various forms of Christian religious doctrine had become utterly destructive and violent. The War of Thirty Years had almost destroyed Central Europe. A new era emerged when in 1648 peace was made in Westphalia, with the state as a source of progress and the world as a bounded whole which should be defended against any transcendent imposition. And as we know, states in this modern sense had clear boundaries and well-defined notions of sovereignty. And as Norbert Elias (1998) has taught us, the core of processes of state formation is the effort constraining and monopolizing violence. Indeed, havoc was what religion had brought about before the peace of Westphalia in 1648. Nothing was more dangerous than transcendence set free in human interactions. Or so it seemed at the time.

Yet, some of the greatest proponents of the new 'progress' made a reservation. In his *Faust*—summit of the Enlightenment—Goethe devotes two lines to basic doubt regarding all tales about the liberation of the emancipated, rational human being. Perhaps, we err in our optimism. Did we truly wrest free of the galling bonds of the old belief in transcendent powers? He writes:

Den Bosen sind sie los [You are rid of the devil]
Die Bosen sind geblieben [Evil men remained]

At first sight, these words fit in with the sketch above. *Prima facie*, Goethe writes that we are delivered from the devil—*den Bosen*. Evil as transcendent power does not exist. The old belief in the devil rests on an illusion, an obsolete pattern of thought. It is not the devil, but people who do evil things. Evil is the work of man. That is why we have to learn to understand how people achieve the wrong things and we no longer need metaphysical or religious notions. To this extent, Goethe confirms the new conventions of his day, the Enlightenment.

But there's a viper—yes, a snake!—in the grass. The tenor of Goethe's lines is not to affirm but to relativize the notion that evil does not exist. These words are, namely, uttered by Mephistopheles, the devil himself, and addressed to Faust and a witch. The devil has directed his own disappearance. The idea of human autonomy, the domestication and socialization of evil is a phantom called to life by the devil himself. The *Abschaffung des Bosen* (abolition of evil), that is, the idea that evil does not exist comes from the devil himself and he fools everybody. Goethe, a pioneer of Enlightenment, thus looks beyond the conventional wisdoms of his day. In disappearing, the devil creates room for himself. If no one still believes that he really exists, well, who is to spy him out? Our task is rather to seek a solution for people who do evil things—*die Bosen*. These are criminal, deviant, underdeveloped or sometimes just plain evil. For them we build prisons, provide the police with appropriate means, build schools and offer development aid. We can get a grip on evil people by way of proper organization or by mobilizing sufficient political will. Goethe, however, suggests that we should take a critical second look at the idea of evil understood as a social and human problem.

God as history's rationality

Another important step was the transformation of hope and faith into the notion of 'policy'. After the abolition of evil, came the domestication of hope and faith. Transcendence had to be given serious empirical footage. Confidence in the self-sufficiency of empirical reality also marginalized the notions of transcendence in its virtuous dimensions. Next to having the devil disappear from the scene and having to cope with concrete problems, enlightened man needed a new and secure sense of direction, rounding up culture or society as a social whole. The marginalization of evil and the defining of hope and faith as part of an immanent whole become part of totalization of the world as empirical object. Various processes of social closure go hand in hand. What remains is the evil people, that is, we must confront 'social problems'. Evil people seem to disturb the peace all the time in various ways. That means now that the state must take care of this, or some experts or 'civil' society. It will hardly do to appeal to transcendent notions. We must look for a benchmark in the 'here and now' when dealing with '*die Bosen*' evil people who have remained with us, as Mephistopheles in Goethe's *Faust* remarked. The benchmark of hope, of the good life, has to be in the here and now, too. We need a new foothold that will permit us to identify a 'detrimental' social problem. Any! The vanishing act of the devil as 'perpetrator' of evil could not remain an isolated affair. Disappearance of transcendence had to be completed with a well-staked-out claim: the socially 'good'. Order became a preoccupation. Only when the domestication of hope and faith—those practices which may lead us beyond the here and the now and, therefore, must be seen as potentially dangerous indeed—is paired to the domestication of evil can we have a new foothold, a new standard for our judgements. It is then that people, vectors of culture, can take up their work: as architects, designers and maintenance engineers of society. It is, then, that to give meaning is possible again.

In the nineteenth century, the socialization of hope and faith was given strong stimulation. The question as to when is something good and valuable beyond doubt became answerable. New forms of historical awareness led to new definitions of socially relevant hope and faith. The idea that the empirical world can be understood as a *history of civilization* offers a solution to the problem of judging when nothing but an empirical world is left. The idea of a history of civilization allows us to attribute purpose and meaning to our acts and makes possible immanent empirical judgements concerning the meaning of human existence.

Safranski (1997: 31) offers a number of notable comments on this modern idea of a history of civilization. He views the nineteenth-century optimism to which it gave birth not as a process of emancipation from the restricting bonds of the transcendent world. On the contrary, that optimism is a fierce but misdirected response to a crisis, a reaction to a major loss: 'History, then, begins when the best is lost. All that remains for mankind is to glorify work and reproduction. Humanity must take flight in civilization' (ibid.).

As Safranski sees it, the idea of a history of civilization is a flight, a non-adequate response to an enormous political crisis or disaster. The idea of a history of civilization as development, as progress, has to be recognized as a mode of coping with crisis first of all, and next we ought to assess its adequacy as response to crisis. Toulmin (1990: 28–41), too, reminds us that we should not swallow the standard tales that 'explain' modern developments; they are rife with pseudo-religious legitimations and fancy talk. The abolition of 'evil', then, is dubious. This is why an understanding of history as process of civilization must provide a new hold; the 'good' has to be ensconced in human time. 'Historified' myths about a desired social order are given a hallmark as it were, be it as prophecy, utopia or glorification of the 'now' in post-modernism. They constitute the sheet anchor for definitions of modernity, providing a new grip on good and evil.

The primacy of order—however defined—is the core moment of the modern world. The abolition of evil as a transcendent concept and the introduction of a point of reference in time are tied together. The reformulation of both good and evil makes self-containment in the empirical possible. These matters are not separate. And it was in this mould that the great nineteenth-century social sciences cast their ideas. The concept of order is the core of modern theories of social history, however mutually different they may be.

Dostojewski's grand inquisitor

Much as Goethe allowed for some doubt and scepticism about the project of domesticating the devil as 'social problem', the effort to domesticate hope and faith in the nineteenth century was put into doubt, too, in a paradigmatic way. Precisely at a time, the nineteenth century, when the notion of history as a human project with an end and meaning was coined, F.M. Dostojewski, the famous Russian novelist, wrote a remarkable comment on these turns. In the 'Grand Inquisitor', a special chapter in his famous novel *The Brothers Karamazov*, he presents us with a very telling parable that on the surface again seems to underpin the need to stress the overall importance of the problem of order and responsibility. Now, as Dostojewski writes, it is not just the secular man who emancipates from the constraints of faith. The parable informs us how ecclesiastical and religious views elaborate and 'round up' our quest for reason and social responsibility. Ecclesiastical authorities, that is, religion, provide us with the rationale to give primacy to social order over and against faith. The clerics make this absolutely clear. Yet, Dostojewski puts this preoccupation with order between brackets and suggests that by this process of social closure, religion must become violent and paradoxically a source of disorder. The preoccupation with order in his story indeed is a murderous affair. Dostojewski takes us to Spain, at the end of the fifteenth century, to the year 1492, when the wars there seemed over and the orderly issues of social responsibility became increasingly important.

At the end of the fifteenth century in Sevilla, Spain, the Catholic authorities note a sudden major unrest. They speedily launch an investigation. The Inquisition, experienced as that it is, soon uncovers the cause of unrest. They uncover a most unsettling event: Jesus has returned to earth. He wanders around in the alleys and streets of the city, causing considerable agitation among the people. Immediately, the Grand Inquisitor orders His imprisonment. He does not need much time to take this decision. Being a civilized man, however, the cardinal is aware of the fact that some may find this a curious step. Moreover, he is aware that Jesus Himself, the son of God, may be surprised, too, that the Church puts Him in prison after His return to the world. The Grand Inquisitor is a responsible and reasonable man. He does not wait long to contact the incarcerated Jesus and explain to Him why he had to take these measures and why this heavy-handed incarceration is for the good of all. Why?

During his first visit on earth, 2,000 years ago, Jesus had made rather a mess of things. So much has become clear to the modern Church authorities. The Church cannot afford to take this risk a second time. The Grand Inquisitor feels obliged to explain this attitude to Jesus in prison. Surely He will understand now. In his exposition, the Grand Inquisitor reminds Jesus of the three temptations in the desert, fifteen centuries earlier (Luke 4: 1–13). The cardinal explains to Jesus the reasonableness of the devil's request at that time that Jesus perform a miracle. The devil meant to conclude an altogether reasonable deal with the Lord. At issue were some 'strategic' miracles like flying through the air for all to be seen and being carried up by angels. Such a singular intervention from transcendence would have solved the problem of the maintenance of order. These problems would no longer have posed a problem. The miracle would have prevented much trouble and devastation. Its return would have had an enormous multiplier effect. And look at all the suffering and devastation that had come about. All that killing and violence could have been prevented if only Jesus had behaved in a more responsible way. He had made the tasks of all people who had been responsible afterwards much more difficult.

The thread in the parable is the insight that 'reasonable' care and responsibility implies that in the end the world has to be defended against God Himself, if need be with the use of force. Reasonableness and rationality require that the Christian religious authorities must be willing to imprison Christ himself. A Christian church, to be responsible and diligent, must be willing to do away with God himself. Otherwise the result will be chaos. And as Grand Inquisitor, the cardinal knew better than anyone else how much he had suffered when he had to burn thousands of people, Muslims, Jews, Protestants. The discourse of reasonableness of God's removal is the crux in the story that he tells his Lord. By reason of his responsibility as administrator, the cardinal is forced to take God, the Son into custody.

Interesting here is that Dostojewski—like Goethe—has the devil (now in the desert) advance arguments for the reasonableness of social responsibility. The devil is not done away with; he is the reasonable custodian of the desired social order. The Grand Inquisitor confronts Jesus with this rationality, which had been grasped at such great cost and which had to be, indeed, defended vigorously. The cardinal proudly explains to Jesus the rationality of the three questions the devil had posed to Jesus in the desert. They were so much to the point, not 'temptations' at all.

These very questions, the miracle that they could be asked, demonstrate that here we are not dealing with mere human comprehension; rather, we are dealing with the understanding of an eternal, absolute mind.

The world had an alternative now, an eternal, absolute mind, standing guard over good and evil domesticated, and responsible for the political production of serenity and order. Even God would understand the rationality of his removal from the world.

In *Darkness at Noon* (1969), Arthur Koestler, almost a century later, tells us of a comparable encounter in prison during the political purges in the 1930s. The authorities are now communist; the prisoner a faithful follower of the party. Again, faith and 'reasonable religion' are on a full collision course. Koestler sets the encounter in the Lubyanka prison. The interrogator comes to the cell to explain why the prisoner has received a death sentence. A lot of effort and time is invested to make the prisoner accept the verdict. He is pressured to acknowledge the rationality of his own execution. The officer of the KGB represents the greater good as defined by the party, the vanguard of Progress. Evidently, Koestler re-enacts the Grand Inquisitor's visit and mission to Jesus in prison as told by Dostojewski.

The parable is re-enacted again. Again the choices are clear and a lot is at stake. The political situation must be 'rounded up'. In *Darkness at Noon*, the KGB officer almost begs the condemned prisoner to submit voluntarily to the *coupe de grace* he is about to receive. His very faith in the good cause is represented by the executioner, which makes this submission imperative. The party needs his sacrifice. His faith and political responsibility now must generate an eager willingness for being executed.

Koestler makes it clear that any church or party that takes the problem of social order seriously must do its bit of killing. This cannot be avoided. There is no alternative, however hard this task may be for the executioners. There is an intrinsic relation between the Catholic faith and *auto-da-fé*, between the communist utopia and the Lubyanka prison. Violence becomes indispensable if you 'really' want to act responsibly and abolish evil from this world.

While the problem of order came to the fore as a rational response to mass murder and killing in 1648, this could not avoid a repetition of the very evil that it had tried to domesticate. On the contrary, the effort to establish a new order on a global scale became an affair as lethal. In 1898, another parable of the continuation of onslaught was written; again, to tell the story of the intricate interrelationships between the quest for order and the mission of civilization and the constitution of evil. This story rounded up, too, as it were: the killing did not stop in prison. Now, those engaged in the mission of civilization itself became victims too. The onslaught now started to become a rounding up of all. The killing was brought home.

Conrad's *Heart of Darkness*

More or less contemporaneous with the rather chauvinistic belief in progress in Europe, the days of a new 'proud tower of Babel', as Barbara Tuchman (1996) characterizes the close of the nineteenth century, Joseph Conrad's *Heart of Darkness* appears. Again the project of civilization and the onslaught that this brings about are portrayed as two sides of the same coin, now on a global scale. Conrad's novel is a scathing criticism of the modern project let loose globally. He gives a concise account of what it brings about in its very implementation. The author goes on a journey to one of the black spots on the world map at the end of the nineteenth century. He goes to the inlands of Congo and does his fieldwork. The scene moves beyond Europe. Notable about this novel is that it describes the awesome consequences of colonization and globalization for all. Not just for the Africans but also for the Belgian colonizers, merchants and agents of the king. Although the devastation in Congo is unspeakable, Conrad indicates that the seeds of destruction are sown in Brussels as well. The forces of destruction cannot be localized in the Congo: these will come home, too. This global aspect of destruction of the colonizers through the very process of colonizing, indeed, civilizing, must be noted in the novel, too. Conrad indicates to us that both the agents of civilization and their victims are paying the price, though in varying ways and at different times. Along with the message and dynamism of the mission of modernity, the author shows in great detail the lethal effects of that mission. Destruction, as Conrad writes, at the end of the nineteenth century had become a force in world affairs. Destruction works in two directions now. A word about each.

The novel relates the western idea of civilization and the use of violence in Africa

The novel describes a journey from light to dark, from the civilized world to 'nowhere', the wasteland, a large blind spot on the European world atlas. Towards the end of the nineteenth century, unchecked optimism reaches its peak in London. The journey to the blind area, the Belgian Congo, is its counterpoint. The story is told on the banks near the estuary of the Thames river. The storyteller looks towards the West and sees London in the far distance. The rays of the setting sun and reflections in the water light up the city and so focus our view on the centre of the world, the wellspring of civilization, commerce and imperial greatness.

Thus, the contrast is defined: the dynamism is a movement from light to darkness; from city to wasteland, from civilization to ignorance. This is the normal atlas of a world that believes in itself, an empire that looks upon itself as source of civilization for others. The larger part of the novel describes a journey by boat from the Atlantic coast to the heart of Africa.

At a 'lonely' trading post in Congo, lives a successful merchant, Kurtz. Commissioned by the king, he buys and collects rubber and ivory. Here and there he is praised for his spiritual gifts and ideals, although less complimentary comments as well circulate. After a long journey, the boat reaches Kurtz's house at last. Upon arrival, the travellers note that the rumours were true; a great store of trade goods has been amassed but because of that the region is all but depopulated and despoiled. The heart of Africa is in truth a black hole of destruction and ruin, in sharp contrast with the light of London. The link is there, however. The light and the black hole are now intimately related: the darkness is the effect of the light.

After a few days the fully loaded vessel sails back. The journey is successful. Kurtz is aboard but dies before they reach the coast. According to the storyteller, it is shortly before his death that Kurtz utters a few now famous words: 'the horror, the horror'. Commentaries on the novel suggest that these words stand for three distinct dimensions of the horrible destruction and ruin. The first is that Kurtz realizes what he has brought about in Congo. According to the second, he confronts the black hole in his own soul, the unconscious violence driving his deeds. It is suggested that, here, Conrad leans on Freud's ideas about the 'wild' unconscious in every civilized human being. The third dimension refers neither to Africa nor to Kurtz, but to civilized Europe.

Conrad suggests that the European ideal of civilization may call disaster upon its advocates

The closing pages of the novel are a coda, an almost unexpected but essential extra, in which the story circle closes upon itself and the explorer's journey to the *modus operandi* of evil is finished. The *Heart of Darkness*, the destruction in Congo, can only be understood if the story of the civilizers, too, is told. It is only when Brussels and Congo are seen as complementary to each other that both light and dark come into view. In the coda (Conrad op cit.: 149), the storyteller, the 'I' figure, is in Brussels. Stopping at the office of the 'company' for which Kurtz worked, he delivers the report 'On the Suppression of Savage Customs'. Next he goes in search of a woman somewhere in Brussels. She is Kurtz's fiancé. He finds her at home and is admitted by a servant:

> I had to wait in a lofty drawing room…. The tall marble fireplace had a cold and monumental whiteness. A grand piano stood massively in a corner; with dark gleams on the flat surfaces like a sombre and polished sarcophagus. A door opened—closed. I rose … I noticed that she was not very young … she had a mature capacity for fidelity, for belief, for suffering. The room seemed to have grown darker.

Conrad here relates light and darkness in a manner quite differently than he did in the opening pages of the book. There, light and dark seemed clearly situated—here and there. Good and evil were separate domains. Light above London reflected in the Thames, followed by a journey to darkness, moving up the Congo river. In this odd coda in Brussels, light and darkness can no longer be distinguished, they coalesce. In the room, the dark piano is like a sarcophagus. A woman enters who reflects the good: hope, faith, the 'capacity for fidelity, for suffering'. Once again the good is linked to evil; without light no darkness. The fiancé tells her visitor of all the wonderful civilizing activities they and Kurtz had planned in Congo, and to which his death had now put an end. She asks: "'His last word—to live with'…. "Don't you understand I loved him—I loved him—I loved him." I pulled myself together and spoke slowly. "The last word he pronounced was—your name.'"

The story has come full circle. The ideals of civilization not only destroy the 'barbarians' at whom these were directed, they put their perpetrators into prison, too, in the end. The grand piano in the fiancée's room is a sarcophagus: her life has come to full circle, from Brussels to the Congo and now back home again. Death has entered her room. The image of a truly global metastasis comes forward. The distinction which was so clear at the beginning of the novel, between light and dark, between Congo and Brussels, between there and here, is done away with. There is no future for the two of them together, for a marriage. And much as Kurtz comes to an awesome end, now even the kind lie about his very words puts his designated (intended) into prison. The core words of the novel, 'the horror, the horror', and 'your name' flow together. Love and murder cannot be separated anymore. Civilization and destruction go hand in hand. Such is the order of things.

Crisis management and contingency

After the devil's vanishing act we are confronted with a new problem. We had to fill the void. The domestication of evil, and of hope and faith was its consequence. If it is true that we can no longer believe in the closure of the empirical, the 'rounding off' of our world, then how should we go on? Let me end with two remarks.

'History' is not a time-path from or to a social order

As a core term, the concept of 'coping with crisis', or crisis management, seems more adequate as the notion of history as civilizing process proves problematic. Safranski speaks of civilization as a 'flight path'; Dostojewski related civilization, rationality and the application of violence; Conrad linked the civilization offensive with destruction and death on a global scale, truly global as the terror and hecatomb which the process indicates are exported and come home again. We can only concur with Goethe when he indicates that the devil fools us with his disappearing act. We must not believe him when he says that he is not there anymore, has disappeared. Is there an alternative?

Let us give the concept of *coping with crisis* the central place in our study of history. This is how Toulmin and Safranski understand the origin of the notion of the history of civilization. They interpret the core moment of the Enlightenment, that is, the body of thought regarding an ideal order here and now, as a reaction to mass killings and to all serious social problems that come with this. In this way, Enlightenment takes on a specific dimension of crisis management, whereby hope and optimism struggle forward, moving away from despair. Thus, the belief in progress is seen as answer to a way out of the awesome slaughter of the Thirty-Year War in Middle Europe. The idea of civil humanity, the emancipation of man and history as a process of unfolding order became—as Toulmin suggests—stronger as a flight forward away from the mass slaughter of religious wars in Europe. The optimism that exploded, as it were, out of despair must be understood as a particular form of crisis management. New forms of order and 'normality' were born out of great suffering. People badly wanted to believe the devil when he declared that he existed no more. That willingness was quite rational after the peace of Westphalia in 1648. Habermas (1996: 11–25) speaks of extreme situations. He states that these are the only contexts in which man seems to be able to really change his view of the world. Habermas advocates a 'return to historicism', that is, a notion of history that is not linear nor dialectic. We must understand history as a succession of modes of coping with extreme contingencies, each giving rise to a new ideal order where the devil has disappeared.

Conrad's *Heart of Darkness* tells us the story that the civilizing process was enacted by Europe in other continents. He shows not only the great suffering there; he indicates that the devastation comes home, to Brussels. Conrad wrote the novel in 1898, at the end of the nineteenth century, that is, fifteen years before another Great War would destroy Europe's landscape. Recently, some German historians have started to speak of a second War of Thirty Years, starting in August 1914 and coming to an end in May 1945. The mass killing and the war against ordinary people—as much as against armies—started almost immediately, with mass executions of Belgian hostages along the river Meuse taking place already after two or three days. Terror and violence came home in totally new ways, much as Conrad had indicated. Thus, history started to repeat itself. The order of Westphalia, the new beginning of an era with the great optimism that it engendered totally collapsed in the years after 1914. The European states in which so much hope was invested in 1648 now turned out to be the very agents of destruction of a continental, indeed, of a global order. The notion that we have lived through a second Thirty-Year War between 1914 and 1945 opens our minds to a line of questioning that is parallel to Toulmin's and Habermas'. If Enlightenment received great impetus from the need to cope with extreme destruction, how did we try to overcome the disasters of a second Thirty-Year War? What new modes of legitimacy were constituted, now that both organized religion, and the state, too, had proven to be a spring of great disaster? Does the devil enact a second disappearing? What kind of promises of order now emerge? What new forms of legitimacy come about?

A recent, penetrating example of a thought-up ideal as form of coping with crisis is given by Canadian intellectual Michael Ignatieff (1999). He discusses a number of studies on the historical origin of the Universal Declaration of Human Rights, signed by the United Nations in 1947. He wonders how that declaration came to be signed by all countries and how it was possible that there was a political consensus regarding universal human rights. In his analysis, he discusses specific elements of the historical constellation of the day. One of these is that the 'universal' declaration could be signed by all countries, East and West, North and South, because nothing was stipulated about observance. The declaration could be universal because the factual power relations did not change on its account, at least not within the immediate future. Ideal and observance did not coalesce; they remained separate. Order and chaos did in a sense flow together, and well they might. The declaration was of signal importance as a form of crisis management in response to the holocaust. In 1947, the first photographs appeared of the slaughter of naked men and women from whom all was taken, who had not a single right left, not even a right to live. These images filled the minds of the delegates. Humanity had to be 'clothed' again; the primacy had to be placed with the moral agenda; hope and perspective had to be offered again, and the political reality could wait a while. Restoration of hope came first; implementation of it was secondary. In due time, the universal declaration could be appealed to. The declaration clearly was a response to an extreme situation, it was a practice of vigorous hope against the background of great despair. Practical concerns came in the second place again.

We must wonder whether we are making the same kind of mistakes as before, in new contexts and practical daily concerns. Do we believe that the devil has disappeared again?

On contingency

At the start of this essay, I said that we can recognize the devil in the exaggerated preoccupation with the concept of order in which system and coherence dominate. The devil 'thrives' in such exaggeration. How and why?

When faced with extreme situations, we have shown that images of order and coherence enter our hopes. When faced with a bleak past, we make an effort to get the devil out of the way. Each time, images of an ideal order emerge; each time, new agents of unambiguously possible progress come about; and each time, new images of historical process come about that are unhampered by incoherence and contradictions. In this sense, our post-modern views are not different. It is but the latest of a longer series of reinvention of a sense of history, now by flattening our sense of historical process into short cycles. Now that a sense of utopian purpose and direction has been lost, order must be enacted in increasingly shorter time-frames. With the loss of a sense of purpose in the various subsequent violent applications, we now witness another enacting of the devil disappearing from the scene: it now becomes vital to be playful, to emphasize the richness of multiple lifestyles and to celebrate the loss of meaning and purpose in a preoccupation not with goals, but with means, that is, with 'management' and promises of a nihilistic view of the world. The cult of the here-and-now and of a history that has no meaning, is not so different from its modernistic predecessors. Earlier on, we have witnessed a devil unleashed by utopian—extreme—inclinations, emerging from earlier devastation. Now we try and find a way out by abolishing any sense of meaning and purpose, and declaring that the means, the management of our interactions, is the best way to move forward. If a sense of 'history' and civilization has led us into a *cul de sac* in the past in various Thirty-Year Wars, our post-modern response is not very much different. It begs us to believe that the answer lies not in a new purpose but in the means. It tells us that it is possible to 'pursue and grasp happiness' in ways we organize ourselves, turning the means into a goal. Again, we are inclined to believe the devil when he informs us that 'really' he is not there any more, that managed order here and now is the answer to it all. The devil has learned from past experiences; his is a pragmatic mind now. So we tend to miss his workings again. We must again sharpen our sensitivities to discern his doings. And, perhaps, from time to time we may grasp him by his tail and learn to cope better. However, we can again discern the unleashing of new violence. It is not the religious fundamentalist movements that cause it now. Rather, the core of it may well be our own latest orthodoxy of hyper-modernity. It again confronts the others at the fringes of the modern society, and at the same time comes home in the West, starting to eat its own folk, too. We call this 'globalization'. The coffin, of which Conrad spoke, stands again in the living room of the house of hyper-modernity. The devil is awaiting. Again.

But, perhaps, we can learn again. It may be by allowing notions of contingency as well as giving the notions of transcendence and faith their place in our views of history. Perhaps, an opening of our minds to transcendence as well as an acute sense that the devil is there to stay, may enable us to find a better, and more responsible and realistic ways to cope. Perhaps, we can avoid being confronted with extreme situations when we start to understand our routine transactions in everyday life also as mysterious and ambiguous, by becoming open to discerning mystery in its various manifestations. Let us heed Goethe's insight and not believe the devil as he whispers to us that now he has 'really' disappeared. The dividing lines between the agents and the patients have blurred.

References

Baal, J van. 1991. *Boodschap uit de Stilte/Mysterie als Openbaring* ['Message from the Still/Mystery as Revelation', my translation]. Baarn: Ten Have.

Baudrillard, Jean. 1993. *The Transparency of Evil: Essays on Extreme Phenomena.* London and New York: Verso.

de Boer, Theo. 2003. 'De Bijbel Denken: Paul Ricoeur', in Peter Jonkers and Ruud Welten (eds), *God In Frankrijk: Zes Hedendaagse Filosofen over God*, pp. 43–67. Budel: Damon.

Conrad, Joseph. 1973. *Heart of Darkness.* London: Penguin Books.

Dostojewski, F.M. 1978. *Verzamelde Werken: De Gebroeders Karamazow.* Amsterdam: Van Oorschot.

Elias, N. 1998. 'On Violence, Power and Knowledge', in Stephen Mennell and Johan Goudsblom (eds) and Introduction), *Selected Writings*. London and Chicago: University of Chicago Press.

Fest, Joachim. 2000. *Speer, Eine Biographie.* Alexander Fest Verlag.

Goethe. 1998. *Faust: Der Tragodie Erster und Zweiter Teil.* Frankfurt am Main: Insel Verlag.

Habermas, Jurgen. 1996. 'Coping with Contingencies: The Return of Historicism', in Josef Niznik and J.T. Sandes (eds), *Debating the State of Philosophy: Habermas, Rorty and Kolakowski*, pp. 11–25. Westport, CT: Praeger.

Ignatieff, Michael. 1999. 'Human Rights: The Midlife Crisis', *New York Review of Books*, 46(9): 58–62.

Jonkers, Peter and Ruud Welten (eds). 2003. *God In Frankrijk: Zes Hedendaagse Filosofen over God*. Budel: Damon.

Kittsteiner, Hans Dieter. 1993. 'Die Abschaffung des Teufels in 18. Jahrhundert. Ein Kulturhistorisches Ereignis und seine Folgen', in Alexander Schuler and Wolfert von Rahden (eds), *Die Andere Kraft: zur Renaissance des Boesen*, pp. 55–95. Berlin: Akademie Verlag.

Koestler, A. 1969. *Darkness at Noon*. London: Penguin.

Kolakowski, Leslek. 1998. 'Afgoderij na de Dood van God', *Nexus*, 21: 101–10.

Marsden, George M. 1996. *The Outrageous Idea of a Christian Scholarship*. New York and Oxford: Oxford University Press.

Mol, Annemarie. 2000. 'Dit is Geen Programma: Over Empirische Filosofie', *Krisis*, 1: 6–26.

Safranski, Ruediger. 1997. *Das Bose oder Das Drama der Freiheit*. Munchen: Carl Hanser Verlag.

Sardar, Ziauddin. 1997. *Post Modernism and the Other*. London: Pluto Press.

Schrag, Calvin. 1997. *The Self After Post Modernity*. New Haven and London: Yale University Press.

———. 2002. *God as Otherwise Than Being*. Evanston: Northwestern University Press.

Toulmin, Stephen E. 1990. *Kosmopolis: Verborgen Agenda van de Moderne Tijd*. Kampen: Kok Agora.

———. 2001. *Return to Reason*. Cambridge: Harvard University Press.

Tuchman, Barbara. 1996. *The Proud Tower*. New York: Ballantine Books.

Rethinking Power

Aesthetics, Dialogue, Hegemony

6

KANCHANA MAHADEVAN

> Our modern identity crisis could be resolved only by never being alone.
>
> —Arendt (1977: 187)

The twenty-first century continues to witness large-scale violence in the public sphere. The subsequent disenchantment with political activity is grounded in the belief that political power is identical with violence. This depoliticization of human life, reflecting a disempowerment of people, is accompanied by a tendency to replace political identity with communal, ethnic, religious or familial identity. However, such a renunciation of politics is troubling because political identity differs from religious, ethnic and other forms of identity in crucial ways. Political identity, whose public character makes it inexhaustible, entails inhabiting with strangers; whereas communal identities are restricted to bonds such as kinship. The loss of public political identity is correlated to the naturalization of relationships that is largely responsible for the prevalent climate of xenophobia. Since the end of the Cold War there has been an increase in hostilities in many parts of the developing world. Indeed, the global consolidation of capital's logic of profit is opposed by innumerable versions of fundamentalisms. Yet, global capitalism and fundamentalism are not antithetical to one another; instead, a market that is blind to everything but profit encourages all forms of chauvinism to proliferate. Neither of these phenomena is political in the sense of encouraging deliberation, debate and decision making in public over issues that concern all those who are affected by them. On the contrary, global capital and the resurgence of diverse ethnic identities are both equally responsible for the ongoing loss of the public domain: a loss that is emblematized in exclusions as well as physical injury in human life today. However, to revive politics one has to move beyond its equation with violence and comprehend it as the very antithesis of domination. Moreover, one has to link its regeneration to an empowerment that surfaces from democratic processes. Hence, the standard identification of power and violence has to be questioned only because without power one cannot work towards the ideal of a peaceful political life.

This essay explores the political promise contained in accounts of power offered by Michel Foucault and Hannah Arendt, both of who see it as a productive force. The first section evaluates Foucault's criticisms of the Archimedean model of power as control and his own positive version of will-to-power. The essay argues that in spite of offering a positive account of power, Foucault is saddled with the sovereign subject because he tends to use power as a catch-all term. The second section interrogates Arendt's non-foundational and pluralistic conception of power. Despite offering a significant approach for denaturalizing communal identities with her notion of power, Arendt also exhibits certain residues of subjectivism in ignoring strategy and advocating personal interaction. The third section concludes by discussing the prospects for rethinking the notion of power in the context of public life. The essay argues that by combining the notion of strategy found in Foucault and Arendt's normative dimension, one might be able to draw out a notion of power that could address the problem of depoliticization in present day life. But this also evokes the concept of hegemony, along with the human ability to communicate through distances.

Foucault's advances and retreats

Foucault has critiqued and reversed the standard notion of power. He maintains that instrumental rationality homogenizes the effects of power by centrally locating it in the motivations of a sovereign agent. According to this standard view, of which Hobbes's *Leviathan* is a good example, power is a tool that executes the thoughts of a self-sufficient subject. Typically, power is understood through a negative lens as dominating, homogeneous and repressive. By sharply demarcating the mental sphere and that of external action, this approach confronts an untenable dualism. Furthermore, power is located in an unjustifiable foundational premise of a sovereign subject. In order to eschew such aporias, Foucault understands power to be a productive and external array of heterogeneous and micro-level forces.

Foucault (1997: 544–46) externalizes power in an anonymous network of standardized practices and comprehends subjects as products of the same.[1] He (1982: 219) argues that power exists only when it is put into action, as a set of actions upon other actions (ibid.: 220). Power is a form of conduct or government wherein one structures the field of actions by directing, stabilizing, modifying and even calculating the effect of one's actions on others (ibid.: 221). Subjects are produced through actions and do not exist prior to power, so that 'individuals are vehicles of power, not its points of application' (Foucault 1997: 546). Thus, power does not function in a repressive manner because there is no human nature prior to power that is productive.

Foucault maintains that power is not concentrated but diffused in concrete relationships. It can neither be located in a natural proclivity nor in an institutional right, such as, say, the political. An identifiable visible subject such as a tyrant does not execute complex, decentralized anonymous relations of power (Foucault 1980: 94), which have a capillary effect, permeating throughout the innumerable formal and informal organizational conduits of society. A person or group's actions can criss-cross, impose, reinforce or cancel the actions of others (Foucault 1982: 224). Yet, in modern times, power can be regarded as 'governmentalized', not in the sense of being derived from the state but in the sense of coming under state control. State power gains access to the bodies of people, to mould their attitudes and behaviour. The state governs by rationalizing actions under the aegis of pedagogy, family, judiciary or economy. Foucault reverses the strategy of Hobbes's *Leviathan* with a non-metaphysical notion of power that is anonymous, complex and polymorphous in its effects (Foucault 1997: 545, 548). Power is a network of dynamic forces where each force tries to overcome the impediments of contemporaneous forces and adjust to the same. Such non-teleological forces make and remake nature, art, institutions; in short, the world and subjects who inhabit the world, neither of which have a pre-given character. Power also functions as a circulating chain: 'Power ... comes from everywhere' (Foucault 1980: 93, 1997: 546–47). It does not have a single rationality that homogenizes the whole of society but has several of these (Foucault 1980: 94, 1982: 210). Foucault (1997: 548) has devoted much attention to the micro-level particularities of power in psychiatric, penal and sexual practices among others. He claims that the various shades of power can be garnered only through a thoroughgoing empirical documentation.

Foucault argues that power relations are not homogeneous, since any application of power is always accompanied by a counter-action. Hence, instead of investigating power through its internal rationality, he studies its oppositional relations. For instance, sanity is studied through insanity or obedience through disobedience (Foucault 1982: 211). According to Foucault, these transnational resistances are immediate reactions to the effects of power. They affirm the importance of being different from the calculative demands of power relations. They also oppose themselves to the circulation of knowledge that supports dominant power relations. The struggle between the forces of imposition and opposition, which constitute a power relation, becomes apparent when resistance to power is taken seriously. According to Foucault (1980: 95), 'Where there is power, there is resistance, and yet, or rather consequently, this resistance is never in a position of exteriority in relation to power.'

Foucault's reconstruction of power is significant in that its worldly turn displaces the foundational subject to repudiate possessive individualism and authoritarianism. In comprehending subjectivities as a product of power operating through historically located practices, capillary power grasps the complexity of social life. Hence, power does not remain confined to a singular unit such as the state but permeates throughout the practices of everyday life. An increasingly globalized world can be comprehended through such a decentred analysis of power relations. Although the normalizing practices of power, namely, the determinate and set patterns of legal, rational, pedagogic and sexual behaviour, do not emerge from an easily recognizable source; there are many forms of oppositions to them. Thus, one is not inexorably trapped within the mechanisms of power. Instead of dismissing power as bad, Foucault sees it as an antidote to social domination. He makes it very clear that there can be no power-play without an 'other', excluded by the uniformity of forces; an 'other' who inevitably rejects and rebels against the demands of power with counter-power. Society rests on the contingent foundations of dominance/resistance that constitute power relations. Subordinate groups can re-establish human practices and institutions from their own perspective, given that they resist the power relations of the dominant groups. Further, if there is no natural order governing the universe, there is ample scope for invention in an artistic vein to challenge quantitative rationality.

However, there is a fundamental ambiguity in Foucault's analysis in that he uses the term power in an indiscriminate manner to apply to both disciplining techniques and resistances to them. Given that productive, pluralistic and capillary power is present in both, there is no qualitative distinction between them. Further, the so-called victims of domination do not have a normative right to resist; they do so as a matter of a mechanical routine. Foucault dismisses all commitments to norms as attempts at absolutism.[2] However, he does subtly commit himself to the perspective of the oppressed, since the whole point of documenting the operation of the controlling practices of micro-power is their indictment. Yet, Foucault does not make his denunciation explicit but, on the contrary, maintains a neutral posture vis-à-vis the equations of power. Given that power and its opposite are eternally locked in battle, there is no 'just' point of view; each point to a certain extent strives to 'win' against the other in the war.[3] The dominant groups of society construct all norms such as 'justice', and one cannot appeal to any transcendental ground to justify one's normative claims. Each side of the power opposition would claim to be right from its own standpoint and neither can see the point of view of the other. There is a positivist residue in this analysis of power. Positivists construe atomic facts as given and normatively neutral, and dismiss values as superfluous. Consequently, emotivists are unable to transcend the prevailing ethical conventions. This tacit support to conventional morality, inherent in the legacy of Hume, is intact in the Nietzschean heritage as well. In Foucault's case, considerations of right as well as domination are reducible to strategies of power endorsing the prevailing *status quo*. This value-neutral stance makes it difficult to use Foucauldian power to critique social domination.

It could be objected that Foucault (1982: 220) does distinguish between power and violence. Unlike power, violence does not leave any room for activity and resistance; violence annihilates and silences the 'other' completely and is in this sense a negative activity. It is, thus, unproductive. In contrast, power produces otherness and resistance. It may employ violence in its normalizing strategies but very often it also makes use of consent for the same. Given its constructive dimension, power cannot be equated with violence. However, Foucault overlooks that although anonymous disciplinary techniques may not result in a brutal annihilation of their targets, there is still a certain amount of violence in these techniques. This violence consists in imposing a point of view upon the subjects (even and especially if they consent to it) and extracting obedience in a seemingly non-coercive fashion. The uniformity of behaviour or particularity of interests in these techniques betrays the homogeneity of dominant power. Clearly, disciplining techniques, which aim at producing obedient subjects, are cases of violence. The opposition of such subjects to the strategies of power cannot be equated with normalizing strategies because they do not anticipate them. Thus, Foucault's distinction between violence and power is not very adequate for differentiating between disciplinary power and resistance; he uses the term 'power' ambivalently to depict both phenomena.

Foucault's analysis of power inscribes resistance as a permanent reactionary shadow of domination. Since power consolidates itself through prohibition and regulation; it is always antagonistic to forces that resist it. Consequently, resistance is always caught up with the demands of dominant power, without ever being in a position to independently shape its identity. Further, instead of subverting domination, such a confrontation ends up strengthening it! Slavoj Žižek (1999: 215–16) cites the example of global capitalism where it does not conduct its activities of colonizing remote corners of the world from a centre such as the nation-state. Multinational corporations, multilateral credit institutions and military alliances such as the NATO that are the prime agents of economic globalization do not have a stable location. They are spread out in many different parts of the globe. However, economically privileged representatives from the G-8 group of nations carry out the decision-making processes at such global conglomerates. These decisions are primarily oriented towards profit. Despite these unilateral aspects of multinationals, their operations are diffuse and pluralistic. Thus, they locate offices for investment purposes in the central areas of major metropolitan cities in all parts of the world and transfer the manufacturing units to the non-central areas of the developing world (Sassen 1998). They also function by adjusting to the cultural differences in a given milieu. For example, the multinational food chain McDonald's does not serve beef in India and has variations of Indian cuisine on its menu. There is a paradox at work in this process. On one hand, globalization contains the logic of sameness; and yet, on the other hand, it is committed to multiculturalism. In this situation, those who attempt to resist globalization from the point of view of indigenousness and diversity of their own cultures only reinforce it. Even though capital is not centred in any tyrant, it has a global reach, so that local opposition to it would be quite inefficacious. Further, an emphasis on local organization does not necessarily make it immune to domination—a quick glance at the innumerable feminist critiques of the family goes to show that the local is susceptible to despotism. Foucault (1980: 39–40) does realize the futility of this type of resistance at times; for example, he claims the language of deviance and the like, characteristic of mainstream sexuality, can colour homosexuality (Wolin 1992: 188). However, he does betray an unstated sympathy for the 'others' who have been victimized by dominant power—a sympathy that he is unable to anchor. From Foucault's point of view, one can never move beyond the frame prescribed by dominant power, in which case the violence of domination is an eternal reference point! Resistance, instead of being a mere local reaction to dominant power, has to work towards reconfiguration of the field of power relations in an alternate ways. But Foucault does not even hint at prospects for changing the situation.

Although he does try to propose a 'solution' to the mechanics of disciplinary techniques in the form of art, it is quite problematic. He argues that from the fact that the self is not given, one can only conclude that it is made just like works of art. Art has the ability to transcend the stultifying uniformity of quantitative rationality; in which case one has to extend the artistic idiom from objects to subjects, where art is not an endeavour of experts. Foucault (1984: 350) urges everyone to treat his or her life as a work of art so that one can constantly invent at the everyday level. A person who is sensitive to the contingent dimension of subjectivity and who constantly remakes it is the exact opposite of a normalized person. Foucault dissociates art from the discovery of the true self, a position he associates with Sartre, to construe art as the creation of the self (ibid.: 351). Denaturalizing the reifying practices induced by dominant power by stressing on the invented character of everything is, indeed, very important. But Foucault does not explore the avenue of art through a social lens. He acknowledges the productive dimension of art at the cost of the receptive dimension of its appreciation. Thus, for him the subject who is invented is of prime importance. Most philosophers who have written on art highlight its productive dimension. However, in order to move out of the aporias of subjectivity, one has to acknowledge that artistic invention is possible because art locates itself in the visible lived body instead of the domain of pure thought. Kant's (1987: 157–62) third critique breaks out of the inventive mould of art by turning to the aspect of art appreciation. The latter invokes a shared feeling, as opposed to personal pleasure. This feeling, termed as *sensus communis* or common sense, relates understanding and imagination without subsuming them under determinate laws as scientific knowledge tends to do. In the latter case, art would merely be a logical formula! However, the relation between understanding and imagination is not unruly either, as this would make art incoherent and impossible. The relation between understanding and imagination produces a feeling that can be communicated—the *sensus communis*. However, given Foucault's indifference to the receptive dimension of art, critics such as Wolin (1992) have rightly noticed the resurgence of the foundationalist sovereign subject in his turn to art. Foucault does attempt to transcend the sovereignty of the self by connecting the artist with intimate others such as friends and lovers (Huijer 1999: 71–73). Such a tenuous and private togetherness can hardly ruffle the logic of normalization. Despite his or her intimate relations, the aesthete remains isolated from politics by escaping all norms and leaving intact all types of heterogeneous micro-power. As Foucault himself realizes, such options are open only to a select few. He cites Stoic ethics as an example of the aesthetics of existence, since it does not involve normalization techniques. Further, Stoics confined their practices to a small section of society without prescribing a pattern of behaviour for everybody. According to Foucault (1984: 341), Stoic ethics was an antidote to the normalization of mass behaviour and universality considering that 'it was a personal choice for a small elite' (Wolin 1992: 193). However, as Hegel (1979: 121) reminds us, 'Stoicism is the freedom which always comes directly out of bondage and returns to the pure universality of thought.' Thus, Stoic ethics is a turn to the interiority of the subject and does not offer much by way of changing the *status quo* of domination. Paradoxically, Foucault adopts an elitist attitude, despite decrying exclusions in mainstream society.

The productive concept of relations of power, which Foucault offers, is unable to provide an alternative to the current canvas of violence. Violence betrays a loss of sharing and interacting in public, which is indeed the domain of politics. In the context of the current globalized scenario, irreconcilable affiliations to naturalized definitions of the community mar human interaction, as so many examples of extremism portray. There is a widespread tendency to ally with either global capital or homogeneous ethnic/religious identity, both of which are produced by the normalizing logic that Foucault indicts. Thus, both alternatives are violent in that they involve manipulation and control of what lies outside their purview. Ironically, despite his very promising start with the notion of productive power, Foucault does not provide resources for the revitalization of public life. On the contrary, he retreats from public life either by condemning it to a futile and eternal battle between the forces of oppression and opposition, or by individualistically escaping from it through private aesthetic creation. If power has to be explored for its positive potential to revive public life, one would have to move beyond resignation and retreat. In this respect, Arendt's analysis of power advances over Foucault's. The following section explores to what degree Arendt's contribution to power and politics is an improvement over Foucault's.

Arendt: Between solidarity and subjectivity

Foucault does not clearly distinguish between power and violence, and reduces resistance to a reaction to the dominating power structure. Further, he reintroduces the sovereign subject as a solution to quantitative rationality in the guise of the individual who chooses to fashion his/her life as a work of art. In contrast, Arendt remarks that the modern period has obscured the distinction between power and violence by reducing politics to governmentality—a phenomenon of violence. She connects power with solidarity to invigorate politics because the sovereign subject is at the root of all forms of violence.

At the outset, Arendt considers violence to consist in the eradication publicity, plurality and natality (Disch 1994: 24). Thus, the making paradigm, a form of teleological action, is an epitome of violence. Teleological action grounds itself in instrumental rationality while competently working towards a set goal. Instrumental reason is the capacity to quantify and efficiently arrive at some pre-given end, assumed to be certain (Arendt 1969: 51). This logic is based upon the sovereign subject's capacity to reflect upon objects in isolation: the greater the distance between the subject and object, the greater the control exercised by the subject. The subject commands in order to materialize his or her reflections while the object obeys for the same reason: a sovereign subject first thinks of an idea in isolation and calculates an effective way of materializing it (Arendt 1958: 225). The dichotomy between thought and action is, thereby, built into an unencumbered self, paradigmatic of traditional philosophy. Modern politics and science stress on distance and sovereignty; indeed, the government's or the technologist's separation from their object of study, such as needs or natural processes, makes it possible for them to execute their functions efficiently. Thus, politics is reduced to leadership where the ruler exercises governance over the ruled who merely obey. This applies to the ancient approaches to politics upheld by Plato and Aristotle for whom it is a soul craft as well as the modern Hobbesian approach, which sees politics as a means of self-preservation (ibid.: 195, 221–30).

Arendt (1969: 35–40) observes that political theory has for most part ignored the phenomenon of violence by glibly equating it with power, an equation that persists even in the writings of Foucault. However, to disentangle violence from power, it has to be understood in its own right. Violence consists in imposing a single subject's or a small group's point of view upon all others, causing injury and domination (ibid.: 46). Moreover, violence is dumb, since those who employ it do not discuss with those upon whom they inflict it. This dumbness where the subject or the group refuses to share his or her perspective with those who are affected, gives it an element of secrecy. The subject does not openly admit the urge to impose or the inability to take the point of view of others seriously, since the subject assumes his or her point of view to be absolutely correct. Further, the subject often requires the strength of instruments to execute decisions in an efficient manner, so that violence is a commodity that can be owned (ibid.: 42, 43). Moreover, violence is also a threat to plurality and dialogue, since it imposes a uniform point of view upon everybody. For instance, the homogeneity of assimilation under a profit-oriented global economy underlies the diversity of cultures. Totalitarian states, policies of imperialist nations, communal groups and patriarchal structures routinely depend upon violence for their existence. Arendt concisely sums up modern politics, with its administrative emphasis on rule and command, as a substitution of violence for power.

Power, according to Arendt, can provide an alternative to the cycle of violence. Violence enters to fill the gap left by the absence of power and can, therefore, never be a substitute for power (Arendt 1969: 49, 56). Arendt maintains that all attempts at reducing violence to power ignore that violence presupposes power, since even secret service agents have to, to some degree, interact with one another (ibid.: 49–51). Despite the various attempts to drive out power, it does show up in many ways as an inevitable feature of human life—a feature that has been cut-off once too often! Thus, Arendt is quite unlike Foucault who assimilates administration and power. She upholds power to be the capacity to act in the company of others,[4] which cannot be exercised by a sovereign subject (ibid.: 44). Action is not determined by any prior motivations nor is it geared towards any future achievements; it is confined to the intrinsic value of its performance (Arendt 1958: 206). Hence, power can be legitimized whereas violence can only be justified (Arendt 1969: 52).

Arendt (1958: 201) maintains 'human power corresponds to the condition of plurality to begin with.' Power enables human beings to act through their plurality, whereby they are both equal and distinct. It is precisely because of their equality that persons can relate to one another. On the other hand, their unique distinctness, their quantitative and qualitative differences provide the impulse for human subjects to communicate with one another. Plurality is possible only in the context of their mutual coexistence. Human beings are inspired by the presence of others to make their unique distinctness visible through their public deeds. Action, as Arendt characterizes it, does not belong to a predictable cause–effect scheme that governs the necessity of needs or utility underlying labour or work. She sees the latter as natural and rejects naturalistic bonds such as the family or a racially knit community as the basis of action. Arendt (ibid.: 179) contrasts action with natural givens as free; it discloses 'who' the actor is to others without merely referring to 'what' the person is. Thus, the disclosure through action is possible despite the flaws of the person (ibid.: 242).

Like Foucault, Arendt argues against the Archimedean conception of power. The phenomenon of power spontaneously gives rise to new forms of solidarity amongst people, transcending the ties of family, race, caste and so forth. Thus, people who are total strangers to one another can unite in unprecedented ways by exercising their capacity for action. Arendt (1958: 191) upholds that this is because to act is to take an initiative to begin something *new*.[5] Distinguishing qualities among people are not naturally given but are invented through action. At the same time, action also brings people together in new ways by revealing their distinct aspects to them. The capacity to invent and experiment is missing in the phenomenon of violence, which grounds itself in the predictability of calculative rationality. Action in a creative vein initiates new relationships by cutting across all existing boundaries (ibid.: 190–91). Thus, action is both creative and boundless, whose outcome cannot be predicted. When diverse human beings recognize one another as equals, they initiate something new without being determined by pre-given intentions or circumstances. Freedom is experienced while acting in concert. According to Arendt, the power of doing what one wills, 'I can', without internal or external constraint, can only be found in political communities.[6]

Power also gives rise to publicity, which Kant (1983: 135) defines as the 'publicly announced aim' that concerns the rights of other people in a common place—all just actions would have to be constituted through this principle.[7] Arendt's doctrine of power also appeals to this principle in the political sphere. Publicity would have to be postulated insofar as human beings are with one another; the actor, who is always in the company of others, establishes a togetherness, whereby he/she is not just a 'doer' but is also a 'sufferer' (Arendt 1958: 190). Action starts a story whose consequences and reactions are indeterminate and diverse. Hence, one cannot point to its exact origin or specific patterns of responses to it: action is never a closed circle but is illimitable in both initiation and response. No single individual can be said to hold the centre of the network generated by action. Hence, action is anonymous, an anonymity made possible by its public character. Those who act together do not keep any secrets from one another nor do they make pompous proclamations. Since secrecy is necessary only when an individual or group tries to manipulate others, it embodies violence. The latter leaves no room for the public space of reciprocity and sharing. Public appearance and declaration makes the revelation of persons possible, since they are not opposed to each other (ibid.: 180). Power cannot be owned like a commodity. Being a quality of a plurality of individuals acting and speaking together, it can only exist in collective action. Hence, politics is 'that public part of it where everything and everybody are seen and heard by others' (ibid.: 77). People who exercise power are citizens who neither rule nor obey but share their distinct points of view with one another. They also exercise the capacity for judgement, namely, of thinking from the point of view of others. Yet, this togetherness introduced by power is elusive in that it can never be fully materialized, even though it can be fleetingly actualized. The power to act generates respect, which is a 'friendship' without intimacy or closeness. In this relationship, distinct persons who are distant, in that they do not necessarily like or admire one another's qualities, exhibit regard for one another exclusively on grounds of being persons (ibid.: 243).

The contingent facet of power lies in 'man's inability to rely upon himself or to have complete faith in himself' (Arendt 1958: 244). According to Arendt, sovereignty is an 'ideal of uncompromising self-sufficiency and mastership' and a contradiction of plurality (ibid.: 234). Politics is possible because human beings inhabit the world together creating a 'web of human relationships' (ibid.: 184). Thus power is the very opposite of violence that presumes the self-sufficiency of the subject (ibid. 1969: 56). The dimension of relationships, which is opened up by power, is denied wholeheartedly by violence, whether that of an individual or a group. If a group exercises violence, it acts in the place of a self-sufficient unified subject; imposes its directive on other groups; and denies its 'web of relationships' with them. Davidson (1986) adequately brings out the problems with group solipsism when he says that the claim that there exists a plurality of groups unrelated to one another is as dogmatic as the claim that there is only one absolute group. Interrelations enable reciprocal give-and-take between pluralities and have the power of originality. If plurality, publicity, natality and contingency are the ingredients of power, violence is based on predictability, uniformity and secrecy. Although it cannot produce power, violence can annihilate it. As Arendt (1969: 42) puts it, 'The extreme form of power is All against One, the extreme form of violence is One against All.'[8]

The public space that comes into being when human beings act together is quite fragile. This space, held together by their actions, disappears when they depart. The public that comes into existence only when people gather together, is neither eternal nor necessary (ibid. 1958: 199). Power cannot be owned and stored like a commodity and used whenever required. This is a feature of violence, which requires armies and weapons. In contrast, power, which can never be measured or fully materialized, exists only insofar as it is actualized. Power can be generated, maintained, renewed and reconfigured only when people from diverse cultures, histories, nations, families, and so on, organize themselves to form collectivities. Thus, political awareness requires human plurality and the subsequent power emerging from human beings acting and speaking together.

Arendt's notion of power promises to be a constructive endeavour towards evolving new forms of solidarity. It eschews organic unity around a fully given metaphysical principle that can be realized in the future. Nor does it endorse homogenizing a group of persons by distinguishing them from an external 'other'. Rather, power is possible only when there is an internal absence of telos, togetherness and action. This becomes possible when the process of disavowing that upon which one depends is called into question by publicly acknowledging it. Thus, new forms of solidarity are possible only when existing groups engage in an exercise of self-criticism: when they comprehend the limits posed by a naturalistic understanding of themselves. Consequently, the specific content and shape created by power is always unpredictable; after all politics is the *art* of public dwelling.

In striving towards new forms of solidarity, one moves beyond existing group identities to create something new. Natality as the capacity to make a new beginning veers from the routine mechanization that rules modern society. Arendt's improvement over Foucault lies in connecting natality with otherness. She also draws upon Kant's aesthetics for connecting the dimensions of creation and appreciation (Arendt 1982).[9] Foucault detours the morass of instrumental reason via an aesthetic of existence. However, natality can be productive only if it initiates a way of life that is sensitive to others. The audience perspective inaugurated by Kantian aesthetics plays a key role here. In creating something novel, one is sensitive to the other and similarly the other is also sensitive to oneself. Invention matters because there are people to appreciate it. One does not do it only for oneself, one invents in the company of others. Significantly, theatre is 'the political art par excellence; only there is the political sphere of human life transposed into art. It is the only art whose sole subject is man in his relationship to others'(Arendt 1958: 188).

The notion of solidarity among strangers, found in Arendt's conception of public power, can play a crucial role in reviving contemporary politics by interrogating group loyalties and creating solidarity in unexpected ways. The public consists of a heterogeneous array of persons from diverse strata who act to initiate new beginnings. Moreover, Arendt does not locate politics in a separate institution such as the state that merely performs the task of administering pre-given needs. She highlights the need for politicizing the whole of society, associating politics with the deliberations of an enlightened public. In a period marked by a profusion of identity politics and fundamentalism, politics as a deliberative and public capacity of ordinary persons can go a long way to reconstruct the democratic impulse. However, to pursue these strengths contained in Arendt's analysis of power some of its limitations would have to be remedied.

Struggle and anonymity in times of globalization

Arendt's notion of power would have to be modified to take into account both struggle and distances in a globalized scenario. She tends to neglect the importance of struggle for maintaining relations of solidarity in the context of the prevailing dangers of parochialism. Further, with her proclivity towards personal associations, Arendt also ends up by subscribing to the sovereign subject. This section discusses how her concept of power can be remedied in light of these difficulties.

The role of struggle

As Habermas (1994) argues, Arendt underplays the role of strategy by equating it with violence.[10] If power has to be materialized, one would have to consider strategy to resist the numerous threats of violence. To be sure, as Habermas points out, strategy involves acting in such a way as to achieve success. However, this is not necessarily the prerogative of instrumental action employed by a solitary subject. Collective networks too can resort to strategy while opposing violence. Arendt's associated public would require strategy to institutionalize their deliberations as well as to resist organic notions of community. Institutionalization would enable these associations to move beyond being mere vehicles of public opinion to decision making. Arendt's public networks are informal and unregulated (in not being institutionalized); they form the basis of debate and opinion formation, which influence parliamentary processes and the like in a democracy (Habermas 1996: 307). This public, termed by Habermas as 'weak', forms the 'context of discovery' that initiates new problems and perspectives. He contrasts this public with the 'arranged' public found in parliamentary bodies, which forms the 'context of justification', whereby competing ways of looking at a problem are taken into account and justified.[11] Arendt does demonstrate the importance of a 'weak public' for democratic politics. Such a public has the capacity to initiate unpredictable dimensions and expand discussions covering a wide arena of people due to its open-ended character. As Habermas rightly observes, an incipient and even marginal presence of such a public has generated awareness of complex issues. The latter includes environmental safety, pacifism, women's rights and, one might add here, workers' and migrants' rights among many others. The state or corporate agencies have hardly been active proponents of such topics. Politics has been reduced to administration due to its separation from the 'weak public'. Hence, it can be revitalized only through critical public debates. There is a dearth of such publics today, considering the disposition towards brainwashing the population by corporate houses, political parties and media. But although public debates and opinions can be influential, they cannot be equated with political power per se. Public opinions would have to first reflect a democratization in which all sections of society have participated. Subsequently, such opinions would have to struggle to acquire credence at the institutional level. This entails more than just negotiation of demands: it involves the right to be an equal partner in decision-making processes. As Žižek (1998) remarks, such a struggle aspires for what is impossible within the current *status quo*. Subsequently, one would have to transform the existing hierarchical equations between institutions and publics through the coincidence of weak and strong publics. Strong publics such as parliaments or the United Nations would have to be accountable to weak publics, especially because matters such as taxation, welfare or declarations of war affect them. In such an eventuality, the United Nations would change character in not being controlled by a small group of influential nations but by transnational publics who have the power to make decisions. The various military, economic and other alliances amongst nations, responsible for a hierarchical world, would give way to a more egalitarian universe. Eschewing the weak public would revert to a sharp bifurcation between the weak and strong public, or the civil society and state, characteristic of liberalism. Such a separation reduces politics to state administration where citizens are peripheral. As Fraser (1997: 89–92) notes, an overlap between weak and strong publics implies blurring the line between civil society and state, and, one might add here, the global and the local. But such an overlap is not spontaneous; it is the outcome of ongoing struggles waged by ordinary people from diverse locations.

The struggle for institutionalization also involves the struggle for politicization, or making public topics that have been considered trivial or obvious. Arendt's (1958: 58–73) politics is based on exclusion, not so much of people, but of 'private' topics that pertain to family and society. The social realm, according to Arendt, is made of relations based on economics, race, caste and gender, and is governed by instrumental reason. She identifies all striving for social equality as the quest for conformism that is characteristic of the social (ibid.: 41). For Arendt, social equality aspires for the lowest common denominator and is opposed to human distinctness. This is clear from her approach to race relations. Even though she concedes that racism is an ideological system, she excludes it as a topic of public discussion. According to her, desegregation measures in American cities did not attain racial equality because of the conflicting interests between ghettoized African-Americans and lower-income whites for housing in urban areas (Arendt 1969: 76). However, these interests are neither irreconcilable nor are they the outcome of natural difference of race.[12] Many differences like race and caste are based on unequal and exploitative relations. Thus, the term 'African-American' is not merely descriptive but betrays a history of being victimized.[13] Consequently, one has to strive for a social order where race or caste stratifications are eliminated. But this need not imply the abolition of cultural diversity. For instance, the economic condition of both African-Americans and lower-income whites can be improved by creating job opportunities, so that they do not scramble for basic necessities. (This is a common feature in Indian cities.) Paradoxically, Arendt (1969: 18–19) seems to look at affirmative action measures for racial parity as instances of counter-racism, the lowering of academic standards and bowing down to the violence of the racially disadvantaged. She overlooks that the African-American movement in the 1960s was a struggle for their right to enter public places such as the university and not a form of counter-racism against whites. Indeed, Arendt is clearly oblivious to the role played by unequal race relations in defining the criteria of 'standards' in education and jobs. Debates on race and caste have shown that notions such as 'standard', 'merit' and so forth are neither innocuous nor natural. Predictably, they violate the principle of publicity because they are often used to support privilege and exploitation through race, caste and even gender. The political sphere has to be widened so that terms like 'standard' and merit that are used to maintain social hierarchy are called into question. Political equality is linked with social equality (Bohman 1996: 66–69, 74). Further, American universities did not accommodate the demands of African-American students because of their tendency to bend to violence (Arendt 1969: 19)! Rather, the power of the African-Americans, namely, their capacity to act in concert effected change in the system of racial segregation. The latter need not and did not adopt the path of 'violent' overthrow suggested by Fanon or Sartre. As Arendt rightly observes, this is tantamount to revenge (ibid.: 20).[14] The movement for empowerment of African-Americans was not obsessed with 'counter-racism', as Arendt suggests. Rather, like many other subaltern groups facing the obstacle of severe injustice, the African-American movement was often forced to adopt violence. Certainly, force is not the answer to racism. Though over thirty years have passed since the student power movement (that adopted force) and the civil rights movement (that adopted civil disobedience), racism remains a persistent problem in America, albeit in subtle forms. In order to erase racism, African-Americans should show how the system depends upon their exclusion. They cannot merely work towards cultural recognition or toleration of differences (Žižek 1999: 218). This would also require active participation of other racial groups, migrants, women and so forth. As Žižek observes, such an activity is political because it moves beyond nativism, identity politics and multiculturalism to universalize the predicament of the African-American. It also gives rise to the power of solidarity of plural persons envisaged by Arendt.

Collective associations would have to struggle to politicize topics that have been earlier considered apolitical in their struggle for institutionalization. Arendt's exclusion of labour and work from the sphere of politics is rightly criticized for its tacit support to patriarchy.[15] She subscribes to an old philosophical prejudice with her sanitized version of politics as a domain of power and action that extricates itself from the realm of necessity; a prejudice that is predominant from Plato to modern liberalism. Empowerment in the areas of labour and work is necessary for an egalitarian world. This is because they have served as the supplement of activities in the public realm, despite being renounced as trivial. As Habermas (1996: 313) observes, topics cannot be automatically excluded in a democratic milieu, although one can restrain the manner in which debates take place. Thus, the restraint is on the kind of attitude that one should adopt. One should, for example, acknowledge the contingency of private group identity. In replacing group identity with a public identity, one moves beyond the premise that one's race, gender, nation or community automatically determines subjectivity. On the contrary, public identity consists in accepting differences as factual givens and subsequently subjecting them to debate to identify the role of hierarchical institutions as well as socio-political practices in casting them. Thus, public capacity entails denaturalizing what one takes for granted. Since publicity is politicization of identity, there has to be an openness to expand and include in the political sphere topics previously considered taboo. In this context, Arendt's concern with the political does not seem to fit very comfortably with her treating the social as antithetical to the political. A cursory glance at aspects of the social dimension reveals that iron laws of necessity do not govern them. The conditions and identity of workers and women have changed over history. Workers and women, having worked for interest of others rather than their own self-interest, have been victims of violence. It is precisely in this context that they need to enter into the public space and acquire the power of association. Thus, in order to consistently develop Arendt's notion of power, the zones of labour and work, traditionally perceived as natural, would have to be politicized.

Further, in order to form unlimited publics,[16] one would have to struggle to dismantle dogmatic conceptions of community and rigid worldviews (Habermas 1996: 308). Heterogeneous publics once formed would also be susceptible to the various exclusions and violence that prevails in society (ibid.: 307–8), considering their unregulated character. Consequently, to maintain, renew and expand the public sphere, it becomes necessary to 'struggle' against competing alternative 'organic' notions of community that denounce pluralism or solidarity amongst strangers (ibid.: 314).

The struggle towards institutionalization and inclusion or the resistance against dogmatic worldviews consists in the 'right to remain strangers' while engaging in political action, forming opinions and so forth (Habermas 1996: 308). Administrative politics and naturalistic communities violate this right with their indifference and, often control, over public opinion.[17] The term 'struggle' indicates that society, given its unfettered character, is not a harmonious whole where all persons are alike. As Habermas points out, although Arendt does successfully show how publics can come into existence, she overlooks the issue of how they can be maintained. To quote Habermas (1994: 221), 'The *acquisition* and *maintenance* of political power must be distinguished from both the *employment* of political power—that is, rule—and the *generation* of political power.' However, even at the stage of forming such publics, one has to proceed through a prolonged process of critique of the violent limits that underlie the naturalistic claims of existing groups. Thus, even at their incipient stage, publics are formed through a process of struggle. As Arendt reminds us, such publics once formed tend to be elusive. But one should also not treat them as completely sporadic and arbitrary. Hence, it is important to work towards their maintenance, which is an arduous task considering that heterogeneous publics do not exist in a vacuum but in a dogmatic, stratified and, perhaps, even an apathetic world. The public as a counterfoil to inertia and fundamentalism has a two-fold role to play, as Habermas (1996: 370–73) observes, the 'defensive' role of protecting themselves from the perils of violent forms of association, they also have an 'offensive' role of re-establishing institutions on the basis of heterogeneous solidarity. It is in attempting to fulfil these roles that they transcend the danger of being sporadic or marginal. Hence, once public associations are formed, there is a crucial need to plan out ways of maintaining them, expanding them and renewing them by taking the numerous threats to their existence seriously. This requires the notion of resistance and even strategy, which Foucault's model of power emphasizes but which Arendt neglects. Surely the revitalization of politics cannot just rest on a spontaneous coming together of persons; it has to generate mechanisms of solidarity at the institutional level.

Interestingly, Foucault (1982: 224–26) discusses the notion of strategy, an expression he uses in three different ways: a means required to arrive at a certain end, anticipating the other person's movement and acting to have an advantage over the person and, finally, chalking out procedures in a confrontation so as to make the other person give up struggle. Power can thus be implemented and maintained through effective means or by calculating the actions of others. Perhaps, one can reject these two senses of strategy as violent, since they involve a significant amount of reckoning and imposition of one's own point of view upon others. They do not synchronize with the principle of publicity, which is inherent in Arendt's notion of power. However, the most important dimension of power introduced by Foucault is that of struggle. He rightly maintains that there can be no power without struggle, since power entails tak-ing its opposite point of view seriously. But Foucault pessimistically argues that the power struggle renders its other passive when one party becomes victorious or violent. But it is also possible that if the opponent succeeds in continuing to struggle, each side of the battle continues permanently within the limits of power. Thus, the choice is between a violent victory or a ceaseless power struggle. The problem with Foucault is that he adopts an atomistic approach, wherein each power point has its own distinct identity that is ultimately irreconcilable. His choice of the expression 'agonism' demonstrates this well enough; the options are either losing to the other or maintaining a permanent struggle. Clearly, Arendt's notion of associative power cannot encompass struggle in either of these senses: dogmatic communities cannot be violently suppressed, for power cannot employ violence. Further, violence cannot succeed in removing dogmatic beliefs; it may only stifle the latter for a temporary period. Alternatively, heterogeneous communities and their dogmatic others cannot be construed as having a permanent strife with one another, as associative power would become a futile exercise. Thus, Foucault's notion of struggle is important but not adequate in renewing and maintaining power. Žižek (1998) aptly reminds us that a major bulk of Western political thought negates politics by reducing it to particu-lars such as community, competing interests, economy or militarism.[18] Whether one adopts a harmonizing attitude where one tries to resolve disputes through rules of affirmative action or whether one sees it as an insurmountable dispute of communities, one ignores the traumatic dimension of the political, namely, the struggle on the part of the excluded for being heard and recognized as equal partners in public debate. For this the excluded should be able to show the universal breath of their predicament, namely, that the entire system thrives on their exclusion and thus speak on behalf of the whole of humanity that is undoubtedly diverse (ibid.: 1002). Thus, the excluded cannot get justice by merely negotiating with the existing authorities, without changing the state of affairs. Fulfilling momentary demands by lobbying is a form of self-interest and not politics. Violent forms of militarism, or non-violent preservations of traditional community, are also extensions of the logic of self-interest. Regardless of the specificity of demands made, politics is struggle for public discourse. Arendt's dismissal of the naturalism of the economic and social sphere—while advocating the contingent dimension of the public sphere—would have to be read in this sense. Allen (1999) suggests that we treat Arendt's distinction between the private/social and the public as a distinction in 'attitudes', where the former represents the attitude of self-interest while the latter is one of common interest (Žižek 1998: 111). Public attitude would not take interests for granted, but would see them as products of interpretation. Thus, struggle in a broad sense is a struggle for politicization tout court.

The notion of struggle can be extended in a more constructive direction with Gramsci's notion of hegemony.[19] Gramsci has distinguished between hegemony and rule (*dominio*), whereby hegemony literally means consensual influence while rule is tantamount to violence (Williams 1977: 108). He maintains that the ruling class controls through non-coercive influence rather than overt violence. Hegemony, as persuasive influence, operates in civil society that is located between the economy and the state. Hence, to oppose the prevailing hegemony of the dominant forces, marginalized or subaltern groups have to struggle for establishing their own counter-hegemonic point of view. It is in this sense that the pluralistic/dialogical aspects of Arendt's associations of power would have to struggle for influence in persuasive and non-coercive ways. This notion of resistance is important because associations of solidarity cannot merely coexist with, say, fundamentalist associations, since the latter would always work to negate the former. Further, a pluralistic scheme that keeps violence alive is hardly conducive to the rejuvenation of politics. Public solidarity would have to oppose fundamentalism in order to open the prospects for a non-repressive diversity. Negotiation with extremism or parochialism entails giving it credence; hence, counter-hegemonic power should critique naturalistic conceptions of community. Such a process of struggle and critique would aim at consensually winning over people to the side of associative power, where they are not reduced to passivity but are finally able to act in the company of others. Associative power would have to work out strategies for resisting regressive forces and cultivating wider spheres of influence. Hence, hegemony is not based on the violent principle of command and obedience but of securing confidence of people at large. This kind of transformation of people at the level of civil society would be the first gesture in the direction of a politics that is more that just administration. Hegemony is never a once-and-for-all matter; it has to be continuously 'renewed, recreated, defended and modified' (ibid.: 112). Arendt's notion of power acquires its material and public dimension where one struggles against dogmatism to maintain power, with the help of hegemony.

Power is not maintained through personal decisions and contracts as the natural rights tradition upholds. On the contrary, it is retained by exercising its influence consensually, through public processes of struggle for institutionalization of its point of view and resistance to dogmatism. The diverse people who form the collective unit or publics[20] are involved in the activity of maintenance and renewal of power. Thus, power does not rest on decisions of a sovereign agent. As Williams (ibid.: 113) puts it, 'We have then to add to the concept of hegemony the concepts of counter-hegemony and alternative hegemony, which are real and persistent elements of practice.'

Impersonal networks of dialogue

Arendt's (1958: 244) power is 'generated when people gather together ... which disappears the moment they depart.' Thus, the presence of proximate human beings generates power. According to Arendt, violence exercises its control through distance over the persons, upon whom it is exercised, producing a depersonalization of human relations. Administration, scientific experimentation and the like retain their hold over objects across wide distances. As an alternative, Arendt suggests that distinct individuals appear in a common place, deliberate and reveal their unique personalities to one another. Thus, power is consolidated through face-to-face contact of human beings. Contrary to Habermas's (1996: 147–48, 296–98) claim, Arendt does not uphold the Rousseauian position of treating the group as a coordinated collective subject, since the individual, a unique person, emerges in the company of others. This is also apparent in her contention that actors can maintain their togetherness only on the basis of a promise or contract to one another. 'The force that keeps them together ... is the force of mutual promise or contract' (Arendt 1958: 244–45). There is a combination of both difference and unity in her concept of power but it can only be materialized through direct contact with other human beings. As many commentators observe, Arendt does combine distance and nearness, for the distance of differences among subjects is possible only by being near one another (Disch 1994: 42–43); solidarity emerges through commitment (Allen 1999: 113). As Habermas (1994: 225) rightly observes, she 'retreats' to the social contract theory. Despite her critique of sovereignty, Arendt tacitly introduces the subject of natural law, whose decision is the foundation of the political association. However, there are various problems with such a focus on physical presence.

First and foremost, there is a foundational undertone, where the ahistorical subject of philosophy reappears in the form of unique individuals.[21] The equation between distance and violence can be disputed, since proximity does not always yield political solidarity that respects plurality and questions stratification. Face-to-face contact appeals to the notion of intimate bonding that Arendt herself would wish to transcend. The personal has a seemingly 'natural' quality about it, where one gives priority to one's own family, group or those who are immediately present. Arendt's identification of violence with distance overlooks that violence, as insensitivity to otherness, can occur even when people are proximate.[22] There are innumerable instances of violence in the family or in close-knit associations; hence, one cannot equate violence with depersonalization. A predilection towards personal contact introduces many of the problems connected with foundational subjectivity.

Further, any form of immediate interface between actors who are situated in close range is possible only through mediation. By taking the dyadic relation of the actors, namely, the self and its alter, as its point of departure, the observer is neglected (Strydom 1999). However, even those who interact directly have to appeal to the intervention of language, culture, society—in short, distance.[23] Derrida's (1982: 316–17, 318) discussion of language makes it very clear that there is no such thing as pure presence. He argues that words have to be severed from the so-called pure presence of both sovereign subjects and context for communication to take place. The latter depends upon repetition, which is possible only because they are not tied to mental intentions or promises, allowing words to be read against their purported intentions. As Derrida contends, in using words one reiterates what is inherited by extricating oneself from subjective intentions and group contexts. Thus, diverse people are held together, regardless of the mental wishes, through processes of culture and life bequeathed to them and over which they do not have any subjective control. The observer and the situation constitute the public sphere in which interaction between the actors takes place. The demands of the situation, the need to reinterpret it and so forth, provide the web of relations within which the observer also participates with the actors by commenting, evaluating, and so on. These complex arrays of public forces coordinate the interplay of the participants, independently of their sovereign mental intentions. The observing public do not necessarily form a unified category; they may sympathize with the actors, criticize them or even be indifferent to them (Strydom 1999: 17), but with these variegated stances they have an impact on the actors who do not interact in a vacuum.[24] Shared practices, representations and so forth provide non-subjective rules forging bonds between individuals. Thus, in addition to the two interacting subjects, there is the perspective of 'observers' made up of the numerous other parties who are directly in the situation or related to the situation, those who have contributed to language, culture and history throughout the ages in direct and indirect ways. The so-called 'observer' perspective coordinates the dynamism between actors who act within the framework of history.[25]

To avert the decisionism of contract, the individual would have to be seen as a product of socialization, rather than as a sovereign agent. Power in this case only appeals to this inter-subjective fabric, since even violence presupposes power. Hence, promises have to be fastened to a larger canvas of language, society, history, and so on. As a language user, one moves beyond the naturalism of immediate loyalty to a given group, or immersion in one's own mental intentions. Although language is inherited, it is employed in an open-ended fashion. Language transgresses subjects and communities, and cannot be said to belong to any person or group. At a very rudimentary level then, even the direct relation between two actors is mediated through the third perspective of language.[26]

Since the advent of modernity, phenomena such as the development of commerce and the rise of the mass media have spiralled the growth of globalization, connecting economies, polities and cultures from diverse and distant regions. Consequently, the personal presence of human beings through episodic, spontaneous and direct interaction of talks and gatherings (Strydom 1999) is becoming increasingly remote. The prime player in the late twentieth- and twenty-first-century globalization is the capitalist economy whose effects on all parts of the world are decentralized.

To quote Habermas (1999: 48), 'The *international* economic system, in which states draw the borderline between the domestic economy and foreign trade relations, is being metamorphosed into a *transnational* economy in the wake of the globalization of markets.' This change is leading to a 'post-national constellation' of alliances between diverse nations in the developed world as the European Union shows (ibid.; Habermas 2001).[27] But despite disturbing territorial homogeneity and producing cultural heterogeneity through immigration and commerce, this development is not particularly harmonious, especially with respect to the developing world. As Appiah (1998: XI–XII) opines, globalization is, indeed, as old as history. Yet, there is something unique in the recent version of this phenomenon, which has seen the emergence of global cities such as New York or Mumbai. These cities have an unbounded character in connecting remote regions of the world through production, consumption and finance. The activities of investment, management and finance are often concentrated in the central regions of these cities, whereas production is fluidly spread out in overpopulated, polluted suburban areas at the outskirts. All of this has gone to create the 'outside' aspect, of migrants, geographically distant, far-flung cultures as permanent features of what is inside the various global cities around the world. Transnational corporations stretched out in the developed world make decisions about global capital. Consequently, one witnesses a uniformity in the economic activities across the world, in the form of an emphasis on profit, cuts on welfare and stress on structural adjustment programmes. The weakening of the nation-state is a process of making a conducive environment for corporate profit by abdicating its role in the democratic welfare of its citizens.[28] Thus, decisions of multinationals, often complicit with the political powers of the developing world, affect workers, tribals and professionals, both in the developed and developing world. The relocation of production companies from the US to, say, India reduces the prospects for jobs in the US or increases insecurities in India. There is a heightened interaction amongst geographically distant parts of the world, whose basis remains non-egalitarian. Indeed, the logic of globalization is such that decisions taken in a specific business corporation, in, say, Houston, Texas, affect the lives of villagers of Dabhol in Maharashtra. The exclusions of globalization are not unleashed by any tyrant or a single imperialist state but by decentralized apparatuses. The violence in this phenomenon of global capital does not lie in distance but in the failure to take the point of view of all those affected by it. It is quite obvious that it is the latter. In stark contrast to the principle of publicity, global markets create exclusions such as migrants, unemployed persons or exploitation of women that are not acknowledged (Habermas 1999: 51). Thus, it is in the sense of upholding the 'secret' of depending upon the underprivileged without admitting it that globalization exhibits violence. Given that market forces depend upon the logic of instrumental reason, 'markets, unlike polities, cannot be democratized' (ibid.: 54).[29]

Violence is not necessarily dehumanizing in the sense of impinging upon personal interaction by introducing a geographic distance between people. Rather, it is an indifference to the point of view of the other: it consists in imposing the interests of a particular section upon all others by disavowing the web of dependency on the others. Thus, groups of agents who affect the lives of masses without consulting them operate impersonally. However, violence would have to be counteracted by an equally diffuse and impersonal notion of collective power. Thus, processes of interaction that take the point of view of the other into account would have to be set into motion. Consequently, human beings and their impact on one another, despite distances, would have to be taken into consideration. In politicizing the plight of migrants or women, one would struggle for publicly declaring how the system depends upon them, subsequently moving to alternate associations. Globalization has the promise of bringing together actors across vast distances. This promise would have to be explored by those who are excluded from decision making to inculcate a culture of open-mindedness, justice and assimilation. The governments of existing nation-states are not in a position to actively resist the force of global markets with which they are complicit. Hegel (1967: 208–10) accurately remarks that sovereign nation-states have individuality and are, therefore, prone to war. For, 'individuality is an awareness of one's existence as a unit in sharp distinction from others' (ibid.: 208). But against Hegel, the catastrophes of the last two centuries have taught us that wars are not necessary. Instead of making people aware of their ethical moorings and reducing corruption, as Hegel envisaged (ibid.: 210), wars have only resulted in a decline of ethics and an increase in corruption. Further, the context of globalization demonstrates the need for a sublation of the individual nation-state and its contradictions to explore new levels of politics. The latter requires expanding the notion of 'social solidarity' hitherto confined to people within the borders of the nation-states (Habermas 1999: 57).[30] It is unlikely that the numerous transnational economic bodies, like the IMF, governed by the logic of quantitative rationality, would take any initiative in this direction. It is, therefore, left to the common people linked by a cosmopolitan solidarity that cuts across national borders to critique existing inequalities and exclusions as it struggles to articulate the point of view of those who are left out (Habermas 2001: 57–58). Local personal meetings alone cannot accomplish this. Organizations, of ordinary citizens, migrants and the like, would have to be established on a global level, which would nevertheless also be rooted in the local terrain. Globalization is a process with negative as well as positive consequences. It brings together diverse players from different cultures and economic groups in a historically unprecedented manner. There is plenty of violence in the hierarchical interaction amongst these players. Yet, there is also room for engaging in self-criticism or criticism of one's own group to work out the promise of interaction brought into effect by globalization. By developing communicative associations with strangers, which honour the notion of public and publicity, pressure can be put on belligerent states and organizations to withhold their urge to violence as the first step towards peace. Habermas remarks that national consciousness took shape gradually by rising above local, dynastic consciousness. A similar process, however gradual, could lead beyond national consciousness (Habermas 1999: 58) to an international awareness, so that Americans and Afghanis or Indians and Pakistanis could stand by one another.[31] What is important is that divisiveness and exploitation be removed, while at the same time preserving and enriching cultural specificity and diversity (ibid.: 59). Violence thrives on secrecy while power emerges from a critical public debate bringing together people across distant geographies, cultures, religions and genders. Moreover, forging such associations[32] is not a very easy task considering the various challenges of pluralistic cultures. Yet, giving up the possibility of dialogue is itself a sign of dogmatism. After all, dialogues have taken place in the most unsuspecting corners of history, geography, art or philosophy.

Global capital can be characterized as violent because the actors ignore the observing public on which they have an impact in operating through exclusionary mechanisms. It is in this sense that violence can be understood as antithetical to publicity. The personal dimension, insofar as it is confined to those who are immediately present, is antithetical to Arendt's concept of action. She (1958: 220) observes that 'the threefold frustration of action—the unpredictability of its outcome, the irreversibility of the process, and the anonymity of its authors—are as old as history'.[33] This frustration has often given way to the making paradigm (ibid.: 229). In consistency with her own account of action,

Arendt's power would have to be anchored in what Habermas (1996: 301) calls 'subject-less' institutional networks. Anonymous institutions would have to embody the procedures for communication, so that even if individuals do not have contact through physical presence there is still the possibility of acting in concert. These institutions can be developed through populations that stretch across national frontiers, social movements, genuine non-governmental organizations and the like. Such an endeavour would certainly require some amount of effort on the part of citizens and immigrants across the world. Perhaps, it would be the outcome of a prolonged hegemony. It is through such networks that the villagers of Maharashtra will be in a position to effectively and impersonally articulate their point of view, so that it can be taken into account while making decisions about their lives.

To conclude, faceless global violence cannot be overcome either through Foucault's localized resistances or Arendt's personalized associations. Both localization and proximity have to be transcended in a struggle for communication through distance, extending the principle of publicity through anonymous networks of communication across the globe. Even national boundaries have to be crossed to become sensitive to differences that might even be quite far-fetched and not visible. Politics is indeed a constructive activity where pluralities of people dwell in public, which is constantly expanding. It does not bargain for self-interest or group interest, since the latter cannot transform the *status quo*. Further, politics is not a form of militarism where one sets out to defend one's nation or group against the other. As it is quite obvious in the contemporary world, this mindset has only caused unparalleled destruction. In the current scenario, charged with militarism and fundamentalism, politics consists in a prolonged struggle for anonymous networks of power. There are glimpses of this notion of politics in the failures of fundamentalism and globalization that have ravaged the world. Thus, there is no blueprint of a perfect political order à la Plato's *Republic* available; indeed, the very idea of a perfect order is rife with dogmatism shorn of political sensitivity. The increasing failures in political life are, perhaps, an indication of its impending revitalization. Political struggle would take place within these failures by resisting naturalism, an endeavour that demands self-criticism of oneself, one's religion, one's community, one's nation and even one's gender. The latter would go a long way towards openness to the distant other, who one has probably not even seen. In short, political activity involves striving for a solidarity that is yet to come.

Notes

1. Foucault (1982: 208–9) contends that he did not initially have interest in power. He was led to power relations through his study of the formation of subjects.
2. Habermas (1987), Wolin (1992) and Fraser (1989), among many others, have commented on this ambivalence in Foucault. Fraser appropriately sums up Foucault's power as 'an admixture of neutrality and engagement' (ibid.: 31).
3. Despite claiming to steer clear of Hobbes's notion of sovereignty, centrality, mental intentions and contracts, Foucault's writings betray a strong Hobbesian tenor. Wolin (1992: 185–87) rightly describes Foucault as a 'neo-Hobbesian', since his model of social action and terminology emulates Hobbes's dictum that human beings are naturally inclined to war. Even though Foucault replaces the vocabulary of norms with that of war, he is akin to Hobbes in ignoring, that even in war, or for that matter in strategy, there is commitment (Fraser 1989: 28–29).
4. The term 'power' is derived from its Greek equivalent *dynamis* and its Latin root *potentia*, both of which mean potential. The German word for power is *macht*, derived from *mogen* and *moglich*, which mean possibilities (Arendt 1958: 200).
5. Arendt traces the term 'action' to its Greek roots in *archein* and *prattein*. *Archein* means to begin, to lead or to rule, while *prattein* means to pass through, to achieve or to finish. The term 'act' also has Latin origins in the words *agere* and *gerere*. The word *agere* means to set into motion or lead, while the term *gerere* means to bear (Arendt 1958: 189). Arendt observes that there has been a certain reductionism in the usage of the term *act*, which stresses achievement. Moreover, both *archein* and *agere* are understood as leadership or rulership. Thus, by under-emphasizing its connotation of initiating a beginning, 'action', too, has not remained immune to administration.
6. Strength is the capacity of power that is possessed by an individual, and force consists in various physiological and human relations (Arendt 1969: 44).
7. As Žižek (1999: 235) notes, Kant accords the supreme status to the principle of publicity in the field of politics, comparable to that of the categorical imperative in morality.
8. Power can overrule violence, since the moral superiority of masses without weapons can passively resist the material strength of armed violence. Many instances from history such as the French and Russian Revolutions, and national liberation movements can be cited in this context. Surprisingly, Arendt undermines the power of the Indian population through non-violent resistance. She claims that the Indian public would not have succeeded with its strategy if the enemy had been the Nazis (Arendt 1969: 53–54). The British, Arendt argues, did not rule by the sheer terror in their colonies but had constitutional governments. The British recognized that they could

not hold on to their colonies without provoking a cycle of violence to which they would also be subjected. Arendt concludes that 'the shrinking power of European imperialism' led to the process of decolonization (ibid.: 53). She seems to believe that the British were more benign than the Nazis to confer the gift of independence to Indians! However, Arendt is unaware that British rule in India was filled with violence and exploitation, in which the so-called constitutional government was a mere instrument. Her underestimation of the Indian masses (and others in similar colonized situation) overlooks that power need not rely upon sophisticated weapons. All that it needs is mass participation in the public sphere, without self-interest, which the Indian public did exhibit during the anti-colonial movement. Indeed, during this period a new form of solidarity evolved consisting of people from diverse walks of life. It helped the masses transcend hierarchical relations of caste and religion, made it possible to raise the woman's question. In short, the process of nationalist struggle ushered the era of modernity in India, spawning a mass movement that resisted the forces of British colonialism (Habib 1997). The context of nationalist movements all over Asia and Africa, and the deteriorating economies of the imperialist powers did enable the Indian movement to be effective. As Arendt herself rightly remarks, violence is a phenomenon of exclusion that can be stored. The British rule and administration in India was no exception to violence understood in these terms and the Indian resistance to the same relied upon the moral superiority of power. This was the case with many anti-colonial struggles in the developing world during the twentieth century. These struggles were quite consistent with Arendt's (1958: 200–01) notion of passive resistance that 'popular revolt against materially strong rulers, on the other hand, may engender an almost irresistible power even if it forgoes the use of violence in the face of materially vast superior forces.'

9. As Barnouw (1990: 23) points out, art's significance emerges from its ability to hold together invention and appreciation. It is for this reason that Arendt considers theatre as a crucial form of political art.

10. Habermas himself underplays the notion of strategy and power in his theory of communication (Hansen 1993: 120–21). He has for most part defined power as a steering medium.

11. Although the context of discovery is as important as that of justification in politics and science, it has been largely jettisoned in the quest for value neutrality. Consequently, both spheres face what Husserl (1965) calls as crisis in being cut-off from all relevance to life, while perfecting the craft of technical expertise. Feminists in their critique of administration and science also argue for maintaining the context of discovery (Harding 1986).

12. Critics such as Deveaux (1999) have, against Honig, indicted Arendt for not making room for pluralism by severing the social domain from the political. This is based on the assumption that identities, such as woman, worker, and

so on, can only be demarcated socially. Arendt does, indeed, tend to hold the social in disdain as well as reify it as 'natural'. Both Deveaux and Arendt subscribe to the view that the social is the domain of purely descriptive and diverse identities—they merely differ in that Deveaux upholds such an identity to be a construct, while Arendt views it as natural.

13. Honig (1992) and Villa (1996) are among those who propose a pluralistic reading of Arendt. To be sure, plurality is an antidote to a universe governed by the monotony of instrumental reason. Further, there should be scope for dissent, debate and disagreement in the political sphere, as Villa remarks. However, plurality is not an absolute virtue. Indeed, absolutization of plurality could reduce the public sphere into dissenting subject positions, which are totally indifferent to the point of view of others. Lyotard's dictum, namely, 'to speak is to fight' is a good example of such an impasse. Moreover, there could for instance be a fundamental inequality that is conducive to plurality as the phenomenon of globalization depicts. Global capital is concentrated in the hands of a privileged few (which is a substitute for the sovereign subject) who carry out decisions on their 'others' without taking their point of view into account. Yet, this state of affairs contains plenty of scope for variety: the advance of capital into the developing world through structural adjustment programmes is quite sensitive to cultural differences. An example from India can illustrate this. Multinationals that deal with computer software have packages for the Devnagari script by adapting themselves to Indian cultural specificities. Yet, these very same companies manufacture their software through free-trading zones where there is a great amount of exploitation and so forth. In the words of Žižek (1999: 216) then, a blind adherence to pluralism could endorse diversity from an 'empty' vantage point only because this does not disturb the *status quo*. Thus, there could be a disavowed dimension concealed beneath a re-generating plurality of cultures, lifestyles and attitudes that is violent in the sense of producing an exclusionary system. Abstract plurality is not a virtue in itself; it would have to be situated within democratic processes of solidarity for peace.

14. Sartre (1967) and Fanon (1967) do not confine violence to the logic of instrumental reasoning. They tend to employ the expression 'violence' in ambivalent ways to characterize a diverse array of phenomena: the exploitation of colonial regimes, armed resistance of the colonized and the dismantling of exploitative institutions. They urge the colonized to be violent, that is, engage in an armed resistance because their colonizers are not susceptible to cooperative discussions in goodwill. In recommending violence to the colonized, Sartre and Fanon equate it with force, which they perceive as the only alternative to extreme forms of disadvantage experienced in racism and imperialism. Arendt herself would agree that the oppressor's brutality could not be underestimated, as Nazism shows (though she herself tends to underplay colonial cruelty). Further, she would

also agree that under conditions of extreme injury inflicted by human beings, force could be the only way out. The major problem with Fanon and Sartre is that they do not offer much by way of an alternative forms of political organization once decolonization is set into effect. They recommend recovering an original age of innocence prior to colonization (Sartre 1967: 18)! If power in the sense of an association in public life by a plurality of persons becomes possible amongst the colonized, then armed resistance would perhaps be unnecessary for removing the colonial force. However, other forms of resistance and struggle embodying 'critical-revolutionary activity' (Habermas 1994: 218) grounded in such power would be very crucial for the same reason. This activity is seen 'when revolutionaries seize the power that lies in the streets; when a populace committed to passive resistance confronts alien tanks with their bare hands; when convinced minorities contest the legitimacy of existing laws and organize civil disobedience; when the "pure desire for action" manifests itself in the student movement' (ibid.). The national liberation movements were all illustrations of such power.

15. Arendt has, however, not been too sensitive towards issues such as race, gender or imperialism (Bohman 1996; Hansen 1993: 103). Many feminists have critiqued Arendt's exclusion of labour and work. See, for example, O'Brien (1981) and Hansen (1993: 80–88).

16. Fraser (1997: 80–85) suggests that to avoid homogenizing public space, one can construe it as consisting of multiple publics where there is room for cultural diversity.

17. Chomsky (1996) has documented the specific ways in which liberal societies and their foreign policies control public opinion.

18. Žižek (1998: 991–93) has termed these as arche-politics of communitarianism, parapolitics of liberalism, metapolitics of class struggle and ultra-politics of warfare, respectively. Arche and ultra form two versions of the traditional attitude to the community as self-enclosed, while para and meta are modern in their outlook. Whether these approaches advocate harmony or struggle, they are ridden with the problem of accepting the framework of the given *status quo*. As Žižek observes, politics strives for the impossible.

19. This discussion of Gramsci's notion of hegemony relies upon Raymond Williams' (1977: 108–14) exposition.

20. Against post-structuralist critics of solidarity, Allen (1999: 101–02) remarks that solidarity need not be grounded in rigid and determinate identity. As a collective endeavour, solidarity evokes the notion of a bonding among diverse human beings that is not already there but is yet to come. Both diversity and togetherness are equally important. Interestingly, coalition politics, proposed by post-structuralists as a replacement to solidarity, presupposes determinate groups that have a superficial link only for the sake of affirmative action and so forth. In this sense, they reflect what Žižek (1999: 218) calls the multicultural or even the post-modern celebration of

differences but only those that exist within existing stratified coordinates. Subsequently, coalitions make it difficult to question or transform the framework within which differences are articulated. Precisely because of the stress on group identities, post-modern narratives also confront the danger of falling into the trap of fundamentalism. India provides an example of this syndrome. What was, in the early days of nation building, perceived as unity in diversity has now been reduced to the hegemony of the Hindu right, which routinely violates minorities. There is a similar dogmatism emerging amongst minorities in India as well. Thus, when one stresses on elaborate group identities with fixed boundaries and so forth, one also gives rise to the other. Otherness can be as easily tolerated as it can be violated. The way out is, perhaps, working towards more fluid and cosmopolitan versions of collectivity which solidarity attempts to do. The latter differs from coalition in that it denaturalizes existing identities and works towards new forms of collectivities. Neither post-modernism nor multiculturalism allow for creating new forms of associations, especially along global lines.

21. Derrida's (1994: 166) observations with respect to Rousseau apply to Arendt: 'Conversation is … a communication between two absolute origins.' Like Rousseau, Arendt also suggests an 'ideology of the "neighborhood", of a "small community where everybody knew everybody else" and where nobody went beyond earshot … the golden age of the present and full speech' (ibid.: 168).

22. Feminist literature that celebrates the intimate personal dimension as especially pertinent to women. For example, cultural feminism and its ethics of care ignores that women are ideologically socialized into the intimate sphere. Thus, they are neither born as caregivers nor do they adopt caring patterns as a matter of personal decision.

23. Arendt's claim that violence needs instruments reflects a certain bias towards technology, administration and mediation. Both technology and administration were, no doubt, concentrated in the hands of experts, excluding the masses, during the modern period. Yet, one cannot approach these phenomena in an ahistorical way as value-neutral and condemned to experts (Sitton 1994: 321). Arendt (1990: 91) does seem to imply that such issues can be 'put into the hands of experts, rather than be considered issues which could be settled by the twofold process of decision and persuasion.' The evolution of technology and administration as instances of instrumental rationality has to be comprehended in a historically sensitive light. Neither technology nor administration can be reduced to instrumental reason. On the contrary, to mitigate their existing violence, one would have to explore their contacts with solidarity. Power's unmediated dimension, which Arendt finds fruitful, also reflects a foundationalist bias found in her privileging direct gatherings in a republican vein. All instruments need not be reduced to weapons and armies! Arendt overlooks that instruments have also made means of communication possible.

24. Fraser (1997: 82) has termed these competing observers as counter-publics.

25. Young (1990: 314) also analogously argues that alienation and mediation are not the same, 'for both face-to-face and non face-to-face relations are mediated relations and in both there is as much the possibility of separation and violence as there is communication and consensus.' However, Young seems to uphold urban life as a paramount instance of mediated relations conducive to 'solidarity among strangers'. As the example of Dabhol, Maharashtra, shows, even village life is mediated by far-flung decisions and interaction. Hence, solidarity cannot be restricted either to urban or village regions, but would have to even cut across national boundaries. Further, it would have to abidingly retain its open-endedness.

26. Larry May (1996: 96) contends that one can make moral judgements and acquire responsibility on the basis of personal intuitions derived from particular experiences. He argues that anonymous networks of communication are too general, abstract and even hierarchical to permit accuracy of judgements and responsibility. Yet, May overlooks that personal interaction is never immediate and direct but always mediated. Specificity does not hang in the air but is a product of mediation as well. Further, anonymity is not the same as abstraction but consists of sedimentations of social practices that all individuals have to presuppose in their social dynamism. With respect to the notion of hierarchy, it need not be equated with distance, since there is plenty of scope for hierarchy even at local gatherings. Anonymity replaces the sovereign ahistorical subject with a subject who is located within a concrete, culturally shared range of meanings and practices. Therefore, it does not stand opposed to particularity. Further, in a composite and globalized universe, one has to form judgements and be responsible despite being far away from the scene of exploitation. These judgements are not abstract but are very much particular. Anonymity is not the absence of contact amongst people, but is interaction through distance.

27. Although the paradox of the increasing obsolescence of nation-state and the rise in regional loyalties is quite stark, one cannot completely over-look the role played by existing governments in spiralling the global market. The latter is the product of active government connivance through neo-liberal policies of deregulation, rather than regulation and welfare (Habermas 1999). Thus, companies are very dependent on the governments for their activities of relocating in the developing world and so forth. National borders also significantly allow for the supply of cheap labour through migration, if it is not abundantly available in the major regions of the developed world, such as the Silicon Valley. Sassen (1998) discusses this issue in detail.

28. The Dabhol Power Company's (DPC) interlude in Maharashtra demonstrates this. The DPC, an auxiliary to the Houston-based Enron Company,

was set up to give electricity to Maharashtra (The Enron Corporation 1999). An agreement was ratified in 1992 between Enron and the Maharashtra government. The Dabhol region in Maharashtra was subject to severe environmental damages and farmers were forced to part with their land. Opposition was crushed through active intervention of the state of Maharashtra. The DPC continued with its activities till almost 2001, when bankruptcy forced the company to leave after bitter disputes with the Maharashtra government. This unfortunate example demonstrates many points: (*a*) that governments enthusiastically assist the growth of globalization, often against the wishes of the population; and (*b*) that violence is never publicly proclaimed. The DPC and the government of Maharashtra proclaimed that the project was for the larger good of electric supply and progress of the nation through disinvestments policies. However, a detailed analysis of the situation revealed the contrary. This example also illustrates how people's lives are tied together across wide geographic distances. A more extreme example is that of Afghanistan. The rise of the Taliban can be traced to the role played by the vested interests of transnationals like Unocal (Rashid 2001).

29. There is a general tendency to focus on 'the politics of the lived world' by talking about the empowerment through social movements, NGOs and civil society (Suzuki 2000). All three terms are treated as apolitical due to their severance from the state through processes of globalization. However, the degree to which these transnational associations are independent of the state is debatable, since the state actively assists globalization and encourages the growth of informal associations. Thus, the degree to which these associations are critical of the state, its abdication of welfare, its complicity with business is very important. Further, this shift to transnational societies does not imply a renunciation of material struggle over food, drinking water, shelter and employment for a struggle over the symbolic domain. As Suzuki observes, such a premise reproduces the dualism between the material and symbolic in underestimating their inextricable bonds. In Mumbai, the municipal authorities launched a drive for demolition of slum homes by calling them encroachments. In struggling against this oppressive measure, slum-dwellers would have to define themselves as inhabitants of homes rather than encroachers. Their material well-being is, thus, tied to the choice of terms used to define them.

30. The limits of national sovereignty are apparent in the claim made by Lubbers (2002), the United Nations High Commissioner for Refugees, vis-à-vis the victims of the communal riots in Gujarat, India. He maintains that these victims, many of whom are Muslims, cannot be recognized as refugees to extend humanitarian aid to them. This is because the Indian government has not made a request to this effect, so that the gross human rights violations are termed an internal affair. The riots, which started on 28 February 2002, continued for a few months. Many have lost life, limb,

family and possession. The victims are confined to refugee camps that are in subhuman conditions. There is an urgent need for rehabilitation, which is not coming through due to the complicity and deliberate indifference of the government. The importance of a vocal public that cuts across national lines is highlighted in this negligence.

31. Habermas (1999: 57) himself, using an example from the European Union, says, 'Social solidarity has hitherto been limited to the nation-state; it must be widened to embrace all citizens of the Union, so that, for example, Swedes and Portuguese will be ready to *stand by one another*.' As this essay argues, solidarity cannot be limited to the Swedes and Portuguese who might end up being against, say, the Myanmarese! If stratification has to be eradicated, then the modes of solidarity between the people of the developed and developing world need to be strengthened. Even Habermas's writings on globalization remain silent on the relation between corporate markets and emerging fundamentalisms in the developing world.

32. As Allen (1999: 114) puts it, 'solidarity is achieved, not assumed in advance.'

33. Beiner (1982) has distinguished between Arendt's (1958) early writings on participatory action and her (1982) later writings on judgement. He argues that Arendt shifts from the perspective of the actor to that of the spectator. Yet, the two need not be dichotomous if one attends to the observer perspective that mediates the interaction between actors. Further, while judging, one takes the point of view of the other into account with the help of language, history and so forth. Judging is not a solipsistic ahistorical activity. Arendt herself in her analysis of action as well as judgement attempts to overcome the dichotomy between thought and action. This is quite clear from the fact that she quotes Cato in her early work on action, and in her later work on thinking: 'Never am I less alone than when I am by myself, never am I more active than when I do nothing' (Arendt 1958: 325, 1982: 5).

References

Allen, Amy. 1999. 'Solidarity After Identity Politics: Hannah Arendt and the Power of Feminist Theory', *Philosophy and Social Criticism*, 25(1): 97–118.

Appiah, Anthony. 1998. Foreword. In Saskia Sassen, *Globalization and its Discontents*, xi–xv. New York: The New Press.

Arendt, Hannah. 1958. *The Human Condition*. Chicago: University of Chicago Press.

———. 1969. *On Violence*. Allen Lane: Penguin Press.

———. 1977. *Life of Mind: Thinking*, vol. 1. New York: Harcourt Brace Jovanovich.

———. 1982. 'Lectures on Kant's Political Philosophy', in Ronald Beiner (ed.), *Lectures on Kant's Political Philosophy*, pp. 7–77. Sussex: Harvester Press.

Arendt, Hannah. 1990. *On Revolution*. London: Penguin Books.

Barnouw, Dagmar. 1990. *Visible Spaces: Hannah Arendt and the German-Jewish Experience*. Baltimore: Johns Hopkins University Press.

Beiner, Ronald. 1982. 'Interpretive Essay: Hannah Arendt on Judging', in Ronald Beiner (ed.), *Lectures on Kant's Political Philosophy*, pp. 89–155. Sussex: Harvester Press.

Bohman, James. 1996. 'The Moral Costs of Political Pluralism: The Dilemmas of Difference and Equality in Arendt's "Reflections on Little Rock"', in Larry May and Jerome Kohn (eds), *Hannah Arendt: Twenty Years Later*, pp. 53–80. Cambridge, MA: MIT Press.

Chomsky, Noam. 1996. *Powers and Prospects: Reflections on Human Nature and the Social Order*. New Delhi: Madhyam Books.

Davidson, Donald. 1986. 'On the Very Idea of a Conceptual Scheme', in *Inquiries into Truth and Interpretation*, pp. 183–98. Oxford: Clarendon Press.

Derrida, Jacques. 1982. 'Signature Event Context', in *Margins of Philosophy*, 307–30. Sussex: Harvester Press.

———. 1994. *Of Grammatology*. New Delhi: Motilal Banarasidass.

Deveaux, Monique. 1999. 'Agonism and Pluralism', *Philosophy and Social Criticism*, 25(4): 1–22.

Disch, Lisa Jane. 1994. *Hannah Arendt and the Limits of Philosophy*. Ithaca: Cornell University Press.

Fanon, Frantz. 1967. *The Wretched of the Earth*. Harmondsworth: Penguin Books.

Fraser, Nancy. 1989. 'Foucault on Modern Power: Empirical Insights and Normative Confusions', in *Unruly Practices*, pp. 17–34. Minneapolis: University of Minnesota Press.

———. 1997. *Justice Interruptus: Critical Reflections on the Postsocialist Condition*. New York and London: Routledge.

Foucault, Michel. 1980. *The History of Sexuality*, vol. I. New York: Vintage Books.

———. 1982. 'The Subject and Power', in Hubert L. Dreyfus and Paul Rabinow (eds), *Michel Foucault: Beyond Structuralism and Hermeneutics*, pp. 208–26. Sussex: Harvester Press.

———. 1984. 'On the Genealogy of an Ethics: An Overview of Work in Progress', in Paul Rabinow (ed.), *The Foucault Reader*. New York: Pantheon.

———. 1997. 'Power, Right, Truth', in Robert E.Goodin and Philip Pettit (eds), *Contemporary Political Philosophy: An Anthology*, 543–50. Oxford: Blackwell Publishers.

Habermas, Jürgen. 1987. 'Some Questions Concerning the Theory of Power: Foucault Again', in *The Philosophical Discourse on Modernity*, 266–93. Cambridge, MA: MIT Press.

Habermas, Jürgen. 1994. 'Hannah Arendt's Communications Concept of Power', in Lewis P. Hinchmann and Sandra K. Hinchmann (eds), *Hannah Arendt: Critical Essays*, 211–29. Albany: Suny Press.

Habermas, Jürgen. 1996. *Between Facts and Norms: Contributions to a Discourse Theory of Law and Democracy*. Cambridge: Polity Press.

———. 1999. 'The European Nation-State and the Pressures of Globalization', *New Left Review*, 235: 46–59.

———. 2001. *Postnational Constellation: Political Essays*. Cambridge, MA: MIT Press.

Habib, Irfan. 1997. 'The Formation of India: Notes on the History of an Idea', *Social Scientist*, 25(7–8): 3–10.

Hansen Phillip. 1993. *Hannah Arendt: Politics, History and Citizenship*. Cambridge: Polity Press.

Harding, Sandra.1986. *The Science Question in Feminism*. Milton Keynes: Open University Press.

Hegel, G.W.F. 1967. *The Philosophy of Right*. Oxford: Oxford University Press.

———. 1979. *The Phenomenology of Spirit*. Oxford: Clarendon Press.

Honig, B.1992. 'Toward an Agonistic Feminism: Hannah Arendt and the Politics of Identity', in Judith Butler and Joan Scott (eds), *Feminists Theorize the Political*, 215–35. New York and London: Routledge.

Huijer Marli. 1999. 'The Aesthetics of Existence in the work of Michel Foucault', *Philosophy and Social Criticism*, 25(2): 61–85.

Husserl, Edmund. 1965. *Phenomenology and the Crisis of Philosophy*. New York: Harper Torchbooks.

Kant, Immanuel. 1983 [First Pub. 1795]. 'To Perpetual Peace: A Philosophical Sketch', in Ted Humphrey (ed.), *Perpetual Peace and Other Essays*, pp. 107–43. Indianapolis: Hackett.

———. 1987. *Critique of Judgment*. Indianapolis: Hackett.

Lubbers, Ruud. 2002. 'No Place for Displaced', (Interview by Siddharth Vardarajan). *The Times of India*, 20 June.

May, Larry. 1996. 'Socialization and Institutional Evil', in Larry May and Jerome Kohn (eds), *Hannah Arendt: Twenty Years Later*, pp. 83–106. Cambridge, MA: MIT Press.

O'Brien, Mary. 1981. *The Politics of Reproduction*. Boston: Routledge and Kegan Paul.

Rashid, Ahmad. 2001. *Taliban: The Story of the Afghan Warlords*. London: Pan Books.

Sartre, Jean-Sartre. 1967. Preface. In Frantz Fanon (ed.), *The Wretched of the Earth*, pp. 7–26. Harmondsworth: Penguin Books.

Sassen, Saskia. 1998. *Globalization and its Discontents*. New York: The New Press.

Sitton, John F. 1994. 'Hannah Arendt's Argument for Council Democracy', in Lewis P. Hinchman and Sandra K. Hinchman (eds), *Hannah Arendt: Critical Essays*, 307–29. Albany: State University of New York Press.

Strydom, Piet. 1999. 'Triple Contingency: The Theoretical Problem of the Public in Communication Societies', *Philosophy and Social Criticism*, 25(1): 1–25.

Suzuki, Tessa Morris. 2000. 'For and Against NGOs: The Politics of the Lived World', *New Left Review*, 2(2): 63–84.

The Enron Corporation. 1999. 'Corporate Complicity in Human Rights Violations'. http://www.hrw.org/reports/1999/enron/, accessed 20 June 2002.

Villa, Dana. 1996. *Arendt and Heidegger: The Fate of the Political*. Princeton: Princeton University Press.

Williams, Raymond. 1977. *Marxism and Literature*. Oxford: Oxford University Press.

Wolin, Richard. 1992. *The Terms of Cultural Criticism*. New York: Columbia University Press.

Young, Iris Marion. 1990. 'The Ideal of Community and the Politics of Difference', in Linda Nicholson (ed.), *Feminism/Postmodernism*, pp. 300–23. London: Routledge.

Žižek, Slavoj. 1998. 'A Leftist Plea for "Eurocentrism"', *Critical Inquiry*, 24(4): 988–1009.

———. 1999. *The Ticklish Subject: The Absent Centre of Political Ontology*. London: Verso.

Metamorphoses of Power

From Coercion to Cooperation?

7

JAN NEDERVEEN PIETERSE

Power is a complex metaphor. As the philosopher Bertrand Russell (1938: 11) notes, 'Of the infinite desires of man, the chief are the desires for power and glory.' In sociology, for instance, according to Parsons, power is viewed as a generalized means for attaining whatever goals or in Michael Mann's (1986: 6) words, 'an efficient organizational means of fulfilling other drives.' Since power fulfils every desire, it is the desire of desires. As the supreme means, power is also sought as an end in itself, as in Nietzsche's will to power.

Power is a formidable and profound subject. Yet, the relevant literature explicitly concerned with power is fairly limited. There is, of course, a large literature concerned with forms of power—the state, political systems, international relations, and so on. Several approaches in sociology deal with forms of power: Hobbes on the state and the sovereign, Pareto on the circulation of elites, Robert Michels on the 'iron law of oligarchy'. Marxist approaches usually think not in terms of power but of capital; the central notion is exploitation rather than domination or repression. If power is referred to, it concerns the state, which in the last instance derives from capital (with the state as 'the executive committee of the bourgeoisie'). The emphasis changed with Max Weber, who defined power as the chance of A to change the behaviour of B, even against the latter's will. Weber identified three modes of power: party (state), class (position in the labour market) and prestige (position in the status hierarchy); and three sources of power: tradition, bureaucracy and charisma. Modernization in Weber's view meant the retreat of tradition and the shift to bureaucracy as a source of power, and modern bureaucracy was viewed as a vehicle of rationalization. This is a multidimensional and historicist approach to power—forms of power are multiple and change over time—and a correction on the conventional statist view of power. Yet, the angle through which Weber looks at power and his definition of power essentially refer to a form of control.

For some time power as a terminology and a problematic has been prominent in cultural, media and gender studies, discourse analysis, anthropology, geography (as in Zukin's *Landscapes of Power*, 1991) and development studies (with notions such as *the power of development*). It has also been prominent in everyday discourse—as in power tie, power dress, power breakfast, power talk, and so on. But Roseberry (1992) notes that with all this ubiquity of power talk, we learn little about actual relations of power, about the state, colonialism, and so on. And according to Jean Baudrillard (1987: 60): 'When one talks so much about power, it's because it can no longer be found anywhere. The same goes for God: the stage in which he was everywhere, came just before the one in which he was dead.'

This reflection is concerned with transformations and changing understandings of power over time. Is there a general trend over time in the exercise of power from coercive towards cooperative and consensual forms of power? A related question is how changing forms and understandings of power affect forms and understandings of empowerment.[1]

How has the exercise of power changed over time? Specifically, has there been a trend for the use of power over time to change from coercion to persuasion and cooperation? What leads me to this question is an argument by Galbraith (1983) that over time coercive power has become archaic. One of his examples is that in World War I many American army deserters were executed but in World War II only one American soldier was executed for desertion. Galbraith notes an overall decline in the use of the death penalty, torture, flogging and starvation, and a shift towards the use of rewards or incentives (such as government fiscal policies, wage, labour, subsidies) and persuasion. In other words, in this view political systems have become relatively more democratic over time, at least in a limited sense.

Has the character and exercise of power changed over time from coercive towards consensual power, from domination to authority (or legitimate power)? This is a profound thesis, for it concerns the question whether—or not—there is an overall democratic or emancipatory trend to history. It is also a very difficult hypothesis to examine and this brief treatment is sketchy and incomplete. A general trend that would confirm this idea is that the exercise of power increasingly tends to be normatively regulated. Another general indication is the 'Gramscian turn' in thinking about power in the course of the twentieth century.

A related assumption is that this metamorphosis would parallel broad changes in the politics of empowerment: when the exercise of power becomes more democratic and consensual, so does the politics of empowerment. Thus, in recent decades a trend in many societies is that progressive social forces turn from armed struggle for the control of state power to democratic struggle, from the bullet to the ballot, for example, El Salvador, Guatemala, Nicaragua, Bolivia, Argentina, the Philippines, Burma, Thailand, and many others. But clearly this is not a uniform trend. Ethnic and religious strife in many societies continues to take violent forms and armed struggle persists or has been taken up in, among others, Palestine, Peru, Indonesia, Sri Lanka, Kashmir, the Philippines and Nepal.

As an optimistic reading of historical trends, this kind of argument may now have few takers. The more one thinks it through, the more problematic it seems. The first problem is the conjectural nature of this reasoning. We would not argue this at the time of the Vietnam War or during the bloody struggles for decolonization. The open-ended war on terrorism and the American policy of preventive war, and the unilateral and coercive turn in American foreign policy in the wake of 9/11 have radically changed the political horizon.[2] In addition, to what extent is this optimistic assessment a provincial reasoning and one that looks valid only from the point of view of one context, region or class? Clearly, what Galbraith has in mind is developments in Western countries and the international domain hardly figures in his treatment. To what extent does this resemble the shallow proclamations of Fukuyama on 'the end of history' and Mandelbaum's argument on the obsolescence of war among the major powers (discussed in Pieterse 2004)? It would be more challenging to extend this argument to the international domain and to try to overcome the 'two worlds' thesis that characterizes most depictions of world politics (see O'Hagan and Fry 2000).

Another problem is that power itself is such a complex metaphor that sweeping generalizations are apt to be problematic. For a deeper understanding, we must take into account the different dimensions or the biodiversity of power. What if the exercise of political power becomes more democratic in form but real power shifts to economic forces which are unaccountable? A general argument such as this would make sense only across the board, across all manifestations of power; but does power exist 'across the board' or is it in the nature of power to be segmented, diverse and flexible, and thus inherently oblivious to generalization? Yet, if this is the case, then what warrants the current generalizing about power in so many fields?

Hence, this treatment becomes a complex probing of power and the metamorphoses of power over time that seeks to raise questions rather than to settle them. By way of analytical preliminaries, I first consider the diversity of power—the dimensions of power. Next, I turn to changing understandings of power and in particular, Gramsci's hegemony and Foucault's power/knowledge. Then we turn to metamorphoses of power over time.

Unlocking power

Discussions of the 'faces of power' by Galbraith, Boulding, Mann and others place different emphases.[3] All distinguish between political, economic and ideological power. Mann (1986) distinguishes four dimensions of power: ideological, economic, military and political. Mann's neo-Weberian approach is trans-historical, cross-cultural and multi-dimensional. Ideological power refers to meaning, knowledge and norms; influencing or monopolizing norms is a route to power. Ideological power further includes aesthetic and ritual practices. Ideology 'surpasses experience'. As Bloch remarked, 'You cannot argue with a song.' Economic power comprises circuits of production, distribution, exchange and consumption. It is latent, extensive and symmetrical, and refers to political class structures. Class is an economic grouping; social stratification is a distribution of power. Military power is effective for the exercise of concentrated, intensive and authoritative power. It has limited reach, a concentrated core and an extensive penumbra. Political power centres on state power, is centralized, territorial and heightens boundaries.

Galbraith (1983) distinguishes coercive power (which he calls threat power), economic power (which he calls reward power) and ideological power (or conditioning power). In his view economic power can be a form of coercion or a positive sanction or a form of persuasion or engineering consent. Economic power and ideological power are interrelated, for economic power can buy propaganda, advertising, public relations (PR), media time, political campaigns, and so on. Hence, in this view there would be ultimately two forms of power: one based on coercion and the other on consent (carrot-and-stick, persuasion/reward or punishment). This is reminiscent of Wrong's (1979) distinction between three forms of power, that is, force, manipulation and persuasion, that essentially breakdown into force and fraud. However, fraud and manipulation can be regarded as forms of covert persuasion.

Boulding's (1989, 1998) approach is phrased in normative terms and his key contrast runs between threat power (or destructive power) and the integrative power of legitimacy, respect, community, identity or love.

Political and military power differ in nature but both are forms of state power and since states have the monopoly over the legitimate means of coercion, they may be grouped together. In combination with subsequent understandings of power this generates a schema of forms of power (Table 7.1).

Table 7.1   Forms of power

Source	Political	Economic	Ideological/cultural
Weber	Party	Class	Status (prestige); charisma
Mann	State & military	Class	Norms, knowledge, aesthetics, rituals
Gramsci	State	Class	Civil society; hegemony
Galbraith	Threat power	Reward power	Conditioning power
Wrong	Force		Fraud, manipulation
Boulding	Threat power	Economic	Integrative (legitimacy, identity)
Freud			Repression
Foucault	Discipline		Power/ knowledge, discourse
Said			Representation
Feminism	Patriarchy, masculinism, phallocentrism		
General	Domination, control	Capital	Persuasion, propaganda, consent, stereotypes

Source: Author.

This schema is only a boxy approximation. It does not represent the full register of political power, which includes the role of law, legislature and judiciary, bureaucracy, surveillance and standard setting. The distinction between political and economic power glosses over their intermingling as in 'money politics' (a standard term in the Philippines and Thailand), rent seeking, corruption, corporate power, and so on. Power structure research (for example, Domhoff 1979/1980) is concerned with mapping these connections.

Clearly, these various classifications follow diverse principles. Some are conceived in terms of intentions (threat, reward, conditioning) and others in terms of outcomes (destructive, integrative). Some understandings aim to apply throughout history, while others focus on a particular period (such as Foucault's focus on the modern times). Some aim to be comprehensive, while others focus on a particular domain of power (such as Said's concern with representation).

Several understandings of power just do not follow the conventional boxes of political, economic and ideological power, but run across them. Thus, Foucault's disciplinary power is not merely a matter of state agencies, but epistemic and discursive in nature and internalized by modern subjects. Feminist understandings of power such as phallocentricism and masculinism run across the political-economic-ideological spectrum and into the sphere of the family. We might add culture as an arena of power, where power takes the form of 'race', ethnicity, language or 'civilization'.

Said (1986) criticized Foucault for an imagination of power that is 'with power' rather than 'against power'. With the exception of feminism, most classifications view power from the point of view of the powerful. In addition, this schema is inadequate in dealing with power in civil society. Thus, understandings of power such as Scott's (1991) 'infrastructure of power' and hidden texts of power cannot find a place in this schema.

The lengthiest and least obvious category in this schema is under the column ideology; ideology, however, is a limited nineteenth-century notion. Repression in psychoanalysis, Freud and Marcuse is not simply an ideological extension of political oppression and domination but a matter of cultural ethos and guilt. As a term, ideology may be too cerebral and too rationalistic to convey the range of games of power-play, and the emotional and non-rational resources that are deployed. The cultures and aesthetics of power involve the aura of power, the uses of glamour, theatre, ritual, the general wizardry and snake-charming of the powerful—from divine kingship to voodoo politics and voodoo economics, and the 'magic of the marketplace'.[4] Rituals serve both elite cohesion and to intimidate and exclude outsiders, and serve to cultivate and enhance the gap between the powerful and the powerless. The relationship between power and the sacred involves claims to divine sanction, the various ways this can be negotiated and the emperor's clothes when he is naked. The aesthetics (or the pornography) of power, range from the Nazi Party celebrations at the Nuremburg stadium to Imelda Marcos' 1,700 pairs of shoes. Excesses expose the vacuity of power and the dream-like character of the will to power.

Familiar discussions in political science concern the way different political systems rely on particular forms of power (Table 7.2). These discussions are easily schematic and ideological. Totalitarianism, then, makes use of all the forms of power including heavy doses of propaganda (as in *1984* and *Brave New World*), authoritarianism relies mainly on coercion (as in General Pinochet's Chile) and the selective application

Table 7.2   Forms of power and political systems

Forms of power	Totalitarian	Authoritarian	Democratic
Coercion	+	+	(+)
Reward	+	(+)	+
Persuasion	+	−	+

Source: Author.

of rewards (for cronies, as in the regimes of Mobutu and Ferdinand Marcos). Democracy is based primarily on persuasion (hence, the manufacture of consent) and possibly on reward (social democracy), with coercion as an instrument of law and order, and in external relations. Social stability is one of the rewards of democracy. Contemporary democracy, however, faces a crisis of legitimacy, for instance, due to 'money politics' (as in campaign financing).

. The following observation by Tarschys (1987: 175) on communist policies illustrates that the exercise of power is multidimensional:

> In their efforts to mould public opinion, communist parties did not choose between cognition and imagination, intellectual and emotional communication, between *credenda* and *miranda*, between reformist continuity and revolutionary breaks, or between traditional, charismatic and rational authority; they cover the whole spectrum. Their style of political legitimation is *cumulative* rather than selective; they hammer at the whole keyboard.

Using the full register of power has become increasingly common in all forms of governance, so that the neat distinctions between totalitarian, authoritarian and democratic politics now seem old fashioned. More precisely, these distinctions belong to the ideological apparatus of the Cold War era and, arguably, actual power has been a cumulative mix of all forms of power all along.

All these considerations are only variations on the theme of *power over*. Another part of the story is *power to*, that is, capability, competence and skill. *Power to* is a key variable affecting *power over*; *power over* is embedded in *power to* or capacity: domination cannot exceed the capacity to dominate and control. Second, it is relational, for it is a function of the capability of others to outflank control. Domination is embedded in capability, in the capabilities of both the dominant and the dominated. Moreover, both *power over* and *power to* are, in turn, a function of power in the fundamental sense of *energy* (as in *shakti*, horse power, power company). This yields a further representation of dimensions of power (Table 7.3).

Table 7.3   Dimensions of power

Dimension	Keywords
Power	Energy, strength
Power to	Capability, capacity, ability, skill; mandate (authorization)
Power over	Rule, domination (*Herrschaft*), control, authority

Source: Author.

Michael Mann (1986) defines power as the *ability to organize collective action* through ideological, economic, military or political means. Organization is a central category of *power to* and itself a form or dimension of power. It has been termed the ultimate source of all power. Galbraith considers organization as one of the sources of power, along with personality and property. He argues that organization as a source of power involves three features: bimodal symmetry (external power is a function of internal power), access to the other sources of power (personality and property) and diversity of purposes (the more diverse, the weaker the impact; the exception to this logic is the state).[5] In this light, this discussion is all about capacities and strategies of organization.

Technology illustrates the fundamental importance of capability or *power to*. A familiar saying of Marx is that the windmill gave us feudalism and the steam engine gives us industrial capitalism. Here, technology is a stand-in for human capability and capability is the key variable that affects the capacity to organize. Mulgan (1994) makes the point that since the nineteenth century there has been a change from heavy to light power technologies—from the steam engine and the locomotive to contemporary light, touch-button technologies—and that the exercise of social and political power changes in accordance with technological capabilities. Party systems and organizational bureaucracies that are run from the top are increasingly old fashioned. The bullying mode of power is making place for lighter modes of power centred on persuasion, talk, and the flow and circulation of information. The premises of physics itself, a 'heavy science' and the foundation of engineering and technology, have changed from the nineteenth-century 'laws of nature', the bedrock of positivism, to more open-ended perspectives—as in quantum physics, relativity theory, new science and chaos theory. The 'butterfly effect' is an instance of light power in action.[6]

Hegemony and knowledge

These reflections on forms of power and broad changes in the exercise of power have been paralleled by profound changes in the sociological and political understandings of power. Gramsci and Foucault are major turning points in this regard.

With Gramsci, hegemony is a concept both of power and empowerment rolled into one: moral leadership. The notion of hegemony originally emerged in Russia in the 1880s. For Plekhanov, it referred to a strategy for overthrowing the Tsarist police state by means of the hegemonic leadership which the proletariat and its political representatives should provide in alliance with other groups, including the bourgeoisie, peasants and intellectuals (Bocock 1986: 25). In *What is to Be Done* (1902), Lenin proposed an alliance of all the groups seeking change, including the petit bourgeoisie, teachers, peasants and industrial workers. In Russia, this led to the strategy of the vanguard party and a direct assault on the state and then the use of the state apparatus to outflank other sectors.

According to Gramsci, this was possible because civil society in Russia was weak. Gramsci's famous observation in *Prison Notebooks* (1971: 44) runs as follows:

> In Russia, the state was everything, civil society was primordial and gelatinous; in the West, there was a proper relation between state and civil society; and when the state trembled, a sturdy structure of civil society was at once revealed. The state was only an outer ditch, behind which there stood a powerful system of fortresses and earthworks.

Insurgency, or in Gramsci's terms, war of manoeuvre, is not possible in Western Europe. For Western Europe he developed a different strategy, that is, the war of position. The proletariat is to exercise hegemonic leadership and develop a historic bloc, which would be a system of alliances. This move involves a critique of economism: to exercise hegemony, the interest of the whole bloc or the whole society should prevail over the narrow class interests of the leading group, whether bourgeois or proletarian. This approach is not Machiavellian and it is not a matter of machinations or manipulations; it seeks active consent. Hegemony is an ethical-political, moral and philosophical leadership. Gramsci attributes a key role to intellectuals, especially the 'organic intellectuals', in forging the historic bloc. He also recognizes the importance of the 'popular', of addressing the people, of passion, feeling, emotional communication and popular religion.

When Gramsci's *Prison Notebooks* was translated into English in the 1950s, it brought about a revolution in Marxism and became the keynote of 'Western Marxism'. It breaks away from Marxist determinism, materialism and reductionism. It breaks away from the sole preoccupation with the state: now there is a central concern with the civil society. Previously, all the emphasis was on the party, the trade union and the state; now schools, media, the church, cultural industries and the arts also came into view. This has been a founding inspiration of 'Cultural Marxism' and it has been influential in cultural studies (as in the Birmingham school). Gramsci's approach has been historically significant in the communist parties of Italy (in the 'Compromesso Storico'), Spain (Euro-communism) and Britain (in the journals *Marxism Today* and *New Times*); and in *Subaltern Studies* outside the Communist Party in India. The Gramscian approach has been criticized by orthodox Marxists for departing from economism and thus for lapsing into idealism, and for departing from determinism towards historicism. At the other end of the spectrum, it has been criticized for serving as a 'messiah of Marxism in crisis', for traces of Leninism and for attributing a self-congratulatory role to intellectuals (Femia 1981). For an overview of Gramsci's perspective, see Table 7.4.

Table 7.4 Gramsci and hegemony

	Target	*Methods*	*Objective*
War of manoeuver	State	Insurgence, Blanquism, vanguardism, political revolution	State power
War of position	State and civil society	Ideological, cultural, political struggle; historical bloc	Active consent

Source: Author.

Laclau and Mouffe (1985) developed the Gramscian approach in their work on hegemonic politics. In their politics of articulation, identities are not given or fixed but are constructed in the process of articulation and coalition. Another difference with Gramsci is that in their view there is no longer a single centre of hegemony. Gramsci had overcome statism to some extent, and also determinism and economism but remained Leninist in his view of a centre of hegemony that was occupied either by the ruling or subaltern forces, and this was practically the state. Thus, implicitly, hegemony theory remained a theory for the slow and indirect capture of state power in those societies where the civil society is strong.

Gramscian strategies can be used in right-wing as well as left-wing politics. In fact, Gramsci's approach is patterned on the model of dominant right-wing strategies in his time, especially on the part of the Catholic Church. Since the nineteenth-century culture wars, there has been a merry-go-round of influences across the political spectrum.

By the 1920s, the Church had stopped resisting 'modernism' and opted for active political strategies to use its popular cultural influence for political gain by sponsoring a political party, the Centre Party, in Italy (and eventually in Germany and Austria). In the *Prison Notebooks*, there are extensive sections on the Church and on popular religion. Facing the task of forging a worker–peasant alliance, Gramsci in effect recommended that the left imitate these popular strategies (discussed in Pieterse 1992).

Later, we find the right deliberately using Gramscian strategies; for instance, the extreme right in France (such as Groupement de recherche et d'étude pour la civilisation européenne [GRECE], which was the principal organization of the French New Right in the 1960s; and the Front National). The politics of Thatcherism and Reaganism may be interpreted as Gramscian in an implicit sense: seize the central symbols of the nation, identify your project in national terms and drape yourself in the national flag; as in Reagan's 'Good morning America' and Thatcher's appeals to the British character (Hall 1988). There has been a race among the centrist and right forces as to who can best appeal to the collective popular fantasies, as in Francois le Pen's claims to represent the nation, *France for the Frenchmen*, and starting a demonstration with a ceremony at the statue of Jeanne d'Arc in Orleans, as a procession that claims the 'national' religion and claims to be more Catholic than the Church. The Front National also claims the heritage of socialism, to provide jobs and welfare for the French, and thus tries to forge a historic bloc. Strategies for capturing the popular/national imagination are now standard fare on the part of virtually all political forces—from dictators to insurgents.

In international relations, hegemony originally refers to a state influencing the foreign policy (but not the domestic policy) of another. Hence, the American hegemony during the Cold War. But similar dynamics in domestic society now increasingly apply in international affairs: questions of international legitimacy, persuasion and the manufacture of consent, and coalition building. Cox (1991) extended Gramsci's hegemony to international relations. As recent developments such as the build-up to the Iraq war and the international debates surrounding the WTO and the IMF show, this is a far more difficult terrain in which to achieve active consent than domestic arenas.

Foucault's power/knowledge (1980) views power as an epistemological discourse and a regime of truth. This locates power in the dimension of knowledge, cognition and language, and implies a post-Enlightenment distrust of truth-claims. A schema that places Foucault's views on contemporary power in the context of his (conventional) views on power in previous historical settings is given in Table 7.5.

Table 7.5   Foucault and power/knowledge

Historical formation	Forms of power	Forms of struggle
Feudalism	Domination	Ethnic, religious
Capitalism	Exploitation	Class struggle
Modern	Subjection	Identity struggle,
	Disciplinary power in asylum, prison,	local resistance
	hospital, orphanage, army; docile bodies,	
	society of normalization	

Source: Author.

There are stark differences between power conceived as sovereign or state power *à la* Hobbes, conceived as hegemony *à la* Gramsci, or viewed as disciplinary power and discourse *à la* Foucault. Gramsci's hegemony also locates power in civil society and culture, and as active consent, it has a democratic content.

The trajectory from Hobbes to Foucault runs across pre-modern, modern and post-modern views on power. According to standard views, a key difference is that sovereign power, unlike hegemonic and discursive power, does not reach the soul of the subjects. But is that true? Doesn't power in any guise always tend to include symbolic resources and projects, and seek to encompass and penetrate people's souls? (See, for example, Wilentz 1985.)

Trends over time

We now turn to metamorphoses of power over time and the hypothesis that over time power has become less coercive and more cooperative and consensual.

Addressing this question involves several methodological assumptions. The argument concerns not fragments or episodes, but the overall pattern. It concerns the trend or overall direction of change over the *longue durée* and not merely the current outcomes. It does not concern conditions in 2004 but conditions in 2004 in relation to 1904, 1804, 1004, and so on. It does not concern a regional or provincial assessment of conditions in the West or in particular countries but overall human conditions. Since it concerns not only *power over* but also *power to*, it concerns the capacity for organization and the factors affecting organization over time, including values and ethics that shape organization. This means that we should observe these trends not merely in politics but also in civil society. Although some changes are changes in rhetoric, there is no sharp distinction between rhetoric and reality, for rhetoric is part of reality; so changes in rhetoric also count and need to be measured.

The main arguments should concern domestic politics and civil society and next, international affairs. Since a detailed account would easily be a book-length treatment, this is only a sketchy treatment that briefly considers the pros and cons of the thesis.

1. Over time the exercise of power is increasingly *normatively regulated*. Political and military power, generally, since the era of the French Revolution and the 'age of the democratic revolution' have been increasingly subject to constitutional and legal strictures. A case in point is the formation of standing armies, the professionalization of armed forces and the establishment of political control over armed forces virtually throughout the world.

    According to Zygmunt Bauman, with the routinization of power in the form of bureaucratic authority, the role of intellectuals shrinks from legislators to interpreters and critics, and power shifts to managers and administrators (Bauman 1992, in a variation on Weber's rationalization process leading to an 'iron cage'). In addition, with constitutionalism comes a legal and procedural turn in social intercourse; legalism is particularly pronounced in the United States. Nevertheless, normative regulation has been on the increase worldwide. That this also prompts non-compliance, simulation and a search for loopholes does not cancel out the trend itself but rather confirms it. The salience of counter-trends does not necessarily disconfirm the trend itself. Thus, human history has witnessed thousands of years of warlords but in the contemporary landscape, warlords stand out and promptly give rise to prophecies of doom (such as 'Kaplanism').

2. In most countries there is a shift from government to governance and towards interactive decision making and decentralization in public administration (discussed in detail as in Pieterse 2001).

    This trend clashes with the existing institutions of representative democracy. It also clashes with the trend towards greater international cooperation and the pooling of sovereignty, as in regional forms of cooperation such as the European Union, which comes with growing democratic deficits. Nevertheless, even if in many places they are ideals only, decentralization and greater citizen consultation are worldwide trends. A counter-trend is the growing global and domestic economic inequality and concentration of incomes and power at the top, which in the United States, increasingly takes the form of plutocracy (see Pieterse 2004).

3. Since the early twentieth century, there has been growing interest in forms of persuasion by the state and corporate actors: propaganda, the manufacture of consent, mind control, PR, impression management, advertising, corporate image building, and so on. This trend can be interpreted in several ways. It contrasts with ideology as 'false consciousness' as a nineteenth-century preoccupation. It indicates a Gramscian turn in that, apparently, consent is increasingly more important than coercion. This affirms the overall thesis. By the same token, it follows that control becomes more knowledge-intensive. As consent becomes central, so does the manufacture of consent, which is one of the main theses of Chomsky. With the character of power shifting from coercion to consent, new technologies for the manufacture of consent emerge (Chomsky 1990, 2001). The media and representation become major domains of exercise of power.

    The gradual shift from coercion to consent (and manufacture of consent) should be observed not only in relation to political and state power but also in civil society. New terrains of contestation are culture and consumption (Lasn 1999; Seabrook 2000).

4. In studies of organization, the emphasis has shifted from vertical, top-down leadership to horizontal, network structures of organization, as in the 'learning organization'. In studies of management and leadership, the discourse shifts from dictatorial styles of leadership to coordination of information flows and facilitation of collective decision making.

    While this has been the rhetoric of management gurus for some time, actual trends in corporate governance indicate several sets of variations. First, management under conditions of economic growth tends to be more democratic than under conditions of economic contraction. Second, in the United States, the predominance of Wall Street financial engineering since the 1980s leading to an emphasis on short-term gains, in combination with a general profit squeeze for companies in the late 1990s, have led to a return to authoritarian management styles in many firms. The General

Electric style of management popularized by Jack Welch has come to dominate many companies as soon as profits became weak. Third, the legal status of labour in relation to management in the United States has been much weaker all along than in continental European—and to some extent East Asian—forms of capitalism. Fourth, the talk of participatory management clashed all along with the widespread cult of the CEO and the ever-widening disparities between the CEO remuneration (and power) and the employee wages. The rollercoaster experience of turn-of-the-millennium capitalism has led to a general fascination with power in boardrooms, from the preoccupation with 'leadership' to corporate war games. Fifth, to the extent that these trends apply, they apply in advanced capitalism and in countries with a social tradition. They do not apply in emerging markets where labour conditions are much harsher.

Over time according to the democratization hypothesis, political parties and trade unions tend to function less as centralized organizations and more as coalitions and networks of power. This is only partially and regionally true.

Emancipation movements should be part of the democratization process. There is a parallel shift in progressive strategies of social transformation—from strategies aimed at seizing state power or the means of coercion (the monopoly of legitimate violence) to strategies of forging consent. Political revolution, *coup d'état*, Jacobinism, insurgency, Blanquism, Leninism and focismo are all methods of acquiring state power. Since the 1980s, armed struggle organizations in many arenas have re-tooled to take part in democratic processes (Rocamora 1992).

In penal systems, there is an overall change from containment, punishment and collective revenge towards an ethos of improvement and social reintegration. But here also the United States is an outlier. Galbraith's (1983) observation on the decline in the use of the death penalty does not hold for the United States where the use of the death penalty, while declining worldwide, has remained steady. With five per cent of the world's population, the United States has twenty five per cent of the world's prisoners. The privatization of prisons in the United States makes incarceration a profit-making business.

In pedagogy, there is a change from punishment to reward, from the nineteenth-century 'black pedagogy' to Benjamin Spock.

In education, there is a gradual change from learning as drill-and-rote learning to learning-as-understanding, and more recently from teacher-centred to learner-centred methods of education. But with illiteracy still prevalent in many developing countries and the growing neglect of education in advanced countries such as the United States, this cannot be considered a leading trend.

In therapy and treatments of mental illness, there is growing concern with difference and the problematization of 'normality'. Again, this is by no means a general trend.

5. International affairs have been conventionally viewed as more Hobbesian and anarchic than domestic politics. That they should be considered as a terrain of the increasing normative regulation is itself a trend-break and a sign of changing times. International cooperation and normative regulation have been increasing markedly in the course of the twentieth century. The Geneva Conventions regulating the conduct of war are a case in point. The twentieth century has witnessed a gradual strengthening of international law, with the Nuremburg trial, the founding of the United Nations, the United Nation's Universal Declaration of Human Rights and the International Court, among the major landmarks. Recent developments include the International Criminal Court (ICC), the ban on anti-personnel landmines and a wide range of treaties and covenants. In international relations, bullying and gunboat diplomacy have gradually made place for 'talk softly and carry a big stick', and more recently for humanitarian intervention. Thus, arguably, over time coercive power is increasingly deployed in the name of humanitarian interests. Humanitarian intervention as a justification for third-party armed intervention is a case in point. In the face of mounting global problems (ecological problems, international crime, terrorism, nuclear arms, migration, poverty and development), there is an overall gradual change from 'national interest' to international public good, from unilateralism to multilateralism, although asymmetric power-relations continue to prevail. Cases in point are the Kyoto Agreement, and nuclear arms and non-proliferation agreements.

Although these trends represent major ruptures with previous patterns, the counterpoints are momentous. The United States refuses to sign many international treaties and laws. That the United States is out of step with the worldwide trend towards growing international cooperation and regulation is not merely a matter of a single administration but a long-term trend in which the leading hegemon prefers to 'keep its options open' and maintain maximum manoeuverability. Meanwhile, through its international influence, the United States exports 'international legal nihilism'. Thus, United States foreign aid now comes with the clause that recipient countries should exempt United States citizens from ICC jurisdiction (and accept genetically modified food). Second, humanitarian intervention or 'humanitarian militarism' is profoundly controversial and selective, and hypocritical in application (see, for example, Pieterse 1998).

Trend break or momentum?

Just in case we could concur that there is a trend towards a gradual democratization of the exercise of power, how would we explain and interpret this trend? This affects how we would interpret exceptions and counter-trends.

This trend overlaps with several general perspectives in social science. According to Elias's (1994), configuration sociology, that is, the lengthening chain of inter-dependencies over time involves greater interactive regulation and internal self-control, somewhat infelicitously termed the 'civilizing process'. This broadly parallels Teilhard de Chardin's (1955) thesis of demographic compression and complexification (which would eventually result in a 'noösphere'). Beck (1992) argues that there is a trend towards growing reflexivity in 'new modernity', not merely of the self but also collective reflexivity. More momentous still is Skolimowski's (1994) view that 'we are evolution conscious of itself.' In this view, we would have collectively entered a moral space, which is being inhabited inconsistently and hypocritically but by historical standards, it is nevertheless a collective moral space. This trend is loosely confirmed by the emergence of global ethics as a theme (Küng, Kohl, Dallmayr, Falk), which however tenuous and contentious, is a historical novelty.

The circumstances of greater demographic densities and growing extensive inter-dependencies are undeniable. This planetary condition is usually referred to under the shorthand 'globalization'. The notion of growing reflexivity is contentious but plausible. Another undeniable empirical circumstance is the growing human capabilities reflected in technological change. This might suggest that new technologies decrease the gap between the powerful and the powerless (as in arguments about the internet and democracy). However, rather than referring to a direct nexus between growing capabilities and democratization, this refers to both—greater capabilities for control and for emancipation. By this logic, the dialectics of power and empowerment intensify and increasingly take on global scope (see Pieterse 1989).

It is difficult, of course, to affirm or deny a general trend towards democratization. The evidence is patchy, uneven and contradictory (and this treatment has been sketchy and incomplete; it does not address, for instance, questions of human rights, the role of media, the debate on international public good, and so on.). Whatever democratizing trends exist are regional (they do not apply worldwide), sectoral (they do not apply in all the spheres of social life), partial (they do not represent a complete change) and contradictory (they are often offset by counter-trends in other social spheres). Besides, whatever democratic trends exist are reversible and, historically, have often been reversed.

The two major hurdles that stand in the way of a general democratizing trend are the steep and growing global inequality, and the contemporary United States as a global bottleneck. With regard to the United States, there are two general possibilities. One is to negate the thesis because of the United States trends and to consider American politics as a trend-breaker. The second is that we accept the thesis and consider the United States as an outlier and a temporary anomaly (in view of the burdens of hegemony), which will eventually catch up with the global trends. Is the American imperial turn a harbinger of the future or a holdover of the past? Elsewhere I argue (Pieterse 2004) that the American imperial turn is an expression of the growing economic, political and social decline, so that this in itself is not likely to turn the global tide. Far more profound is the problem of economic and political global inequality, which is fundamentally incompatible with global democratization and outruns democratizing trends.

Nevertheless, the empirical circumstances that underlie these trends—growing demographic densities, global inter-dependence and growing human capabilities—are structurally significant. This makes greater cooperation likely. However, this may easily be the elite—domestic and international—forms of cooperation. This is why considering the politics of empowerment is as important as contemplating the changing politics of power.

Notes

1. This paper was originally presented at a conference on 'The Modern Prince and the Modern Rishi' in Kottayam and at a seminar in History at Jawarharlal Nehru University in New Delhi, 1999. An early version was published in the journal *Vision* (Nederveen Pieterse 2000). This treatment focusses on power; the politics of empowerment are dealt with in Nederveen Pieterse (2001, 2003).
2. This is taken up in Pieterse (2004).
3. See also Canetti (1973), Lukes (1974), Parenti (1978), McNeill (1982), Poggi (2001).
4. On cultures of power see, for example, Elder and Cobb (1983), Kertzer (1988), Mosse (1975), Pieterse (1993) and Taussig (1997).
5. On organization as a form of power, see Clegg (1989), and Perrucci and Potter (1989).
6. On technology and power, see Allen and Hecht (2001), and Pieterse (2004).

References

Allen, Michael Thad and Gabrielle Hecht (eds). 2001. *Technologies of Power*. Cambridge, MA: MIT Press

Baudrillard, J. (1987). *Forget Foucault*. New York: Semiotext(e).

Bauman, Z. 1992. *Intimations of Postmodernity*. London: Routledge.

Beck, U. 1992. *Risk Society: Towards a New Modernity*. London: Sage Publications.

Bocock, R. 1986. *Hegemony*. London: Tavistock.

Boulding, K.E. 1989. *Three Faces of Power*. London: Sage Publications.

———. 1998. 'The Place of Non-violence in the General Theory of Power', in Chaiwat Satha-Anand and Michael True (eds), *The Frontiers of Nonviolence*, pp. 15–17. Bangkok: Thammasat University.

Canetti, Elias 1973. *Crowds and Power*. Harmondsworth: Penguin.

Chomsky, Noam. 1990. *Necessary Illusions: Thought Control in Democratic Societies*. London: Pluto.

———. 2001. *Propaganda and the Public Mind*. Cambridge, MA: South End Press.

Clegg, Stuart. 1989. *Frameworks of Power*. London: Sage Publications.

Cox, R.W. 1991. 'Gramsci, Hegemony and International Relations: An Essay in Method', *Millennium*, 12(2): 162–75.

Domhoff, W. (ed.). 1979/1980. 'Power Structure Research, II', *Insurgent Sociologist*, 9(2–3).

Elder, Charles and Roger Cobb. 1983. *The Political Uses of Symbols*. New York: Longman.

Elias, N. 1994. *The Civilising Process* (translated by E. Jephcott). Oxford: Blackwell.

Femia, Joseph V. 1981. *Gramsci's Political Thought*. Oxford: Clarendon.

Foucault, Michel. 1980. *Power/Knowledge* (ed. C. Gordon). New York: Pantheon.

Galbraith, J.K. 1983. *The Anatomy of Power*. Boston: Houghton Mifflin.

Gramsci, Antonio. 1971. *Selections from the Prison Notebooks*. New York: International Publishers.

Hall, Stuart. 1988. *The Hard Road to Renewal*. London: Verso.

Kertzer, David. 1988. *Ritual, Politics and Power*. New Haven, CT: Yale UP.

Laclau, E. and C. Mouffe. 1985. *Hegemony and Socialist Strategy*. London: Verso.

Lasn, Kalle. 1999. *Culture Jam: How to Reverse America's Suicidal Consumer Binge—And Why We Must*. New York: Quill/HarperCollins.

Lenin, V.I. 1902[1963]. *What is to be Done?* Oxford University Press.

Lukes, Steven. 1974. *Power: A Radical View*. London: Macmillan.

Mann, Michael. 1986. *The Sources of Social Power*. Cambridge: Cambridge University Press.

McNeill, W.H. 1982. *The Pursuit of Power*. Chicago: University of Chicago Press.

Mosse, G.L. 1975. *The Nationalization of the Masses*. Ithaca, NY: Cornell University Press.

Mulgan, Geoff. 1994. *Politics in an Antipolitical Age*. Cambridge: Polity.

O'Hagan, Jacinta and Greg Fry. 2000. 'The Future of World Politics', in G. Fry and J. O'Hagan (eds), *Contending Images of World Politics*, pp. 245–61. London: Macmillan.

Parenti, Michael. 1978. *Power and the Powerless*. New York: St Martin's.

Perrucci, R. and H.R. Potter (eds). 1989. *Networks of Power: Organizational Actors at the National, Corporate, and Community Levels*. New York: De Gruyter.

Pieterse, J. Nederveen. 1989. *Empire and Emancipation: Power and Liberation on a World Scale*. New York: Praeger.

———. 1992. 'Christianity, Politics and Gramscism of the Right', in J. Nederveen Pieterse (ed.), *Christianity and Gegemony: Religion and Politics on the Frontiers of Social Change*, pp. 1–31. Oxford: Berg.

———. 1993. 'Aesthetics of Power: Time and Body Politics', *Third Text*, 22: 33–43.

———. (ed.). 1998. *World Orders in the Making: Humanitarian Intervention and Beyond*. London and New York: Macmillan and St Martin's Press.

———. 2000. 'Power and Empowerment Over Time: From Coercion to Consent', in *Vision*, pp. 5–27. Kottayam, Kerala: TMAM Research and Orientation Centre.

———. 2001. 'Participatory Democracy Reconceived', *Futures*, 33(5): 407–22.

———. 2002. 'Globalization, Kitsch and Conflict: Technologies of Work, War and Politics', *Review of International Political Economy*, 9(1): 1–36.

———. 2003. 'Empowerment: Snakes and Ladders', in K.K. Bhavnani, J. Foran and P. Kurian (eds), *Feminist Futures: Reimagining Women, Culture, and Development*, pp. 112–16. London: Zed.

———. 2004. *Globalization or Empire?* New York: Routledge.

Poggi, Gianfranco. 2001. *Forms of Power*. Cambridge: Polity.

Rocamora, Joel. 1992. 'Third World Revolutionary Projects and the End of the Cold War', in C. Hartman and P. Villanova (eds), *Paradigms Lost: The Post-Cold War Era*, pp. 75–86. London: Pluto.

Roseberry, W. 1992. 'Multiculturalism and the Challenge of Anthropology', *Social Research*, 59(4): 841–58.

Russell, Bertrand. 1938. *Power*. New York: Norton.

Said, Edward W. 1986. 'Foucault and the Imagination of Power', in David C. Hoy (ed.), *Foucault: A Critical Reader*, pp. 149–56. Oxford: Blackwell.

Scott, James C. 1991. *Domination and the Arts of Resistance: Hidden Transcripts*. New Haven: Yale University Press.

Seabrook, J. 2000. *Nobrow: The Culture of Marketing, the Marketing of Culture*. New York: Knopf.

Skolimowski, H. 1994. *The Participatory Mind*. London: Penguin/Arkana.

Tarschys, Daniel. 1987. 'Symbols, Rituals, and Political Legitimation: Some Concluding Remarks', in Claes Arvidsson and Lars Erik Blomqvist (eds), *Symbols of Power: The Aesthetics of Political Legitimation in the Soviet Union and Eastern Europe*, pp. 173–77. Stockholm: Almqvist & Wiksell International.

Taussig, Michael. 1997. *The Magic of the State*. New York: Routledge.

Teilhard de Chardin, P. 1955. *Le phénomène humain*. Paris: du Seuil.

Wilentz, Sean (ed.). 1985. *Rites of Power: Symbolism, Ritual and Politics Since the Middle Ages*. Philadelphia: University of Pennsylvania Press.

Wrong, Dennis. 1979. *Power: Its Forms, Bases and Uses*. Oxford: Blackwell.

Zukin, Sharon. 1991. *Landscapes of Power: From Detroit to Disney World*. Berkeley: University of California Press.

PART II

Beyond the Modern Prince: Varieties of Struggles and New Intimations

Non-violent Movements and the Transformation of Power*

8

STELLAN VINTHAGEN

The 'Prince' is the classic ruler who directs state power and wages war. Until today, state politics, as a scientific discipline as well as a political profession, is dominated by the so-called 'realist' thinking, pre-scribing self-help through superior military power in the interests of the state. This long-standing almost naturalized view on the management of power assumes a top-down hierarchy in which superior force and coercion is what matters. In this chapter, such a taken-for-granted view is challenged in a fundamental way. In a reinterpretation of the Gandhian 'non-violent war', it is argued that the subjects of the Prince might turn realist power upside down.

Thus, this chapter relate 'power' to a special kind of resistance; *non-violent action* (sometimes also called non-violent direct action, civil disobedience, or civil resistance). A non-violent movement is here under-stood to be a movement where people in their action repertoire let their non-violent means express their (non-violent) goals. In a non-violent movement, activists contest 'violence' or 'oppression/injustice', while they themselves avoid using such means (Vinthagen 2005). Non-violent movements relate to a tradition formulated by Mohandas K. Gandhi, the person who created the concept of 'non-violent resistance' or 'satyagraha'

* This text is a summary of chapter 6 in my dissertation in Swedish: *Non-violent Action—A Social Practice of Resistance and Construction* (Vinthagen 2005). A preliminary version has appeared as a conference paper at the IPRA (Inter-national Peace Research Association) conference at Tampere, Finland, August 2000, and in *Gandhi Marg*, Vol. 22, No. 2, July-September 2000, New Delhi, India. I am especially thankful for the comments given by the IPRA Nonviolence Commission, Sean Chabot and Senthil Ram.

(Gandhi 1999: Vol. 8:31, p. 80). My interest lies in political non-violent movements which make claims to contest a dominant or hegemonic power, and act within a society where organized violence and oppression is legitimised, normalized or *de facto* accepted by a vast population. In the anti-colonial liberation movement in India, non-violent resistance was given both a practical and a theoretical content within a certain context and dynamic relations, which furthered a development and diffusion of the non-violent repertoire (Chabot 2003).

Social movements using non-violence in their efforts to obtain changes in society are not a rare phenomenon in the world. Such movements sometimes made progress even against brutal regimes (Ackerman and Kruegler 1994; Sharp 2004; Zunes et al. 1999: 302–22). Movements that have followed and developed the Gandhian repertoire are, for example:

1. the civil rights movement in the USA;
2. the international anti-apartheid movement;
3. the 'tree-huggers' in the Indian Chipko movement;
4. the movement against nuclear weapons in Great Britain during the 1960s and the peace camps near nuclear weapon bases in western Europe during the 1980s, among them the famous Greenham Common women's peace camp in England; and
5. the ongoing struggle of hundreds of thousands of farm-workers in Brazil, who are occupying land.

To political science, non-violent movements should be of interest since they contradict established assumptions of the power of the repressive state. First, non-violent movements aim to undermine wars, injustice and dictatorships by employing peaceful means. As such they display an unconventional way of dealing with state power and violence, their approach, as we will see, is not state-centric, but regards power as multiple, relational and fluid. Second, if and when they succeed they point to a possibility of peaceful social change even under difficult conditions. The more 'non-violent war' is succeeding, the less realistic realism becomes.

Since *power* arguably is the key concept of political science and simultaneously one of the main difficulties determining the success and failure of a non-violent action, this investigation focuses on the *fundamental possibilities* available to non-violent resistance in transforming power in conflicts.

Other research needs to investigate the specific dynamics, meanings and typologies of power emanating from concrete contexts and interactions of non-violent movements, in internal and external relations, during and after the social changes for which these movements strive (Vinthagen and Chabot 2002). Expressions of power may depend on what kind of conflict, resistance or relationship one is investigating. Here, the discussion will only deal with power and (non-violent) resistance in general.

Resistance to power

In order to clarify the logic of my analysis, I will summarize the main argument. Since my aim is to discuss the possibility for non-violent resistance to affect the foundations of power, evaluating theories on *what resistance to power means* will be central.

Since Gandhi and the liberation movement in India, non-violent resistance builds on an innovative consent theory of power. Here, as we will see, 'power' is understood to be the *'chosen subordination'* by subjects who are seen to be 'dominated', thus, opening up possibilities of resistance by disobedience. Neither the force of 'coercion' nor that of 'violence' is seen as power in itself; they are only methods, which may sometimes facilitate power, and sometimes, resistance.

Existing research on non-violent movements focuses on centralized state power and does not consider the (less obvious) power that moulds, disciplines and constitutes perception and behaviour (*cf* Ackerman and Kruegler 1994; Randle 1994; Sharp 1973; 2004; Zunes 1999).[1] In this investigation, I use Foucault's power theory, which contradict the simplified analyses of non-violent 'consent theory', in order to reconstruct the non-violent theory of power, and in the process, I attempt to reinterpret Foucault. The power-producing rules of both behavioural schemata (techniques) and patterns of speech-acts (discourse) do need to be actively and constantly *applied* in order to dominate, even when the applications themselves are moulded by power. Rule-application involves the *de facto* cooperation of the actor, irrespective of a free will or knowledge. An actor, per definition, is acting and *making* a choice—and a 'rule' is not an actor. Even if power is everywhere, it is not everything. Power is not total.

Accordingly, my conclusion is that power is *participatory subordination*, and resistance is not, as is often assumed, simply another form of power fighting domination ('counter-power'), but *the undermining of subordination*, or 'anti-power' (Holloway 2002). Resistance is concerned with breaking up the power relations where humans are made into 'tools' for external interests or servants in oppressive hierarchies. Non-violent movements' use of disobedience and non-cooperation thus attacks the very foundations of power.

Let us now take the argument step by step. I shall start by clarifying what 'power as consent' means and in next section initiate a necessary theoretical development with the help of Foucault, who is arguably still the most influential power researcher in social science.

Power as consent

If the state is to exist, the dominated must obey the authority claimed by the powers that be.

—Max Weber (Sharp 1980: 212)

Concepts like 'coercion' and 'dominance' imply the existence of a force from 'above' in a hierarchy and are usually understood as 'power' (*cf* Waters 1994). Sometimes violence or war is also seen as power. The non-violent tradition, however, does not treat coercion, dominance, or violence as characteristics of the social phenomenon 'power'. Non-violent activists, as I will argue, handle power as cooperative *subordination* ('obedience'). Power does not primarily emanate from above, on the contrary, it originates from below, through subordinate behaviour. Power 'over' someone does not exist; it is a produced illusion resulting from normalized subordination. Basically subordination is seen as (*de facto*) accepted by the subordinates, even when it is involuntarily accepted in the shape of obedience, since all obedience (like all human acts) implies choice (Sharp 1973: 7–62). 'Therefore, *all government is based upon consent*' (Sharp 1973: 28). 'Power as consent' seems to be a common perception of different non-violent movements, at least implicitly (Ackerman and Kruegler 1994; Sharp 1973: 6; Zunes 1999: 2). Power relations are created, according to the non-violent movement, by subordination; expressed as obedience, and by voluntary or involuntary cooperation.

The work of the United States (US) political scientist Gene Sharp (for example, 1973, 1979, 1980) is classic, in both non-violent research and activism, and his latest work (2004)—*Waging Non-violent Struggle: 20th Century Practice and 21st Century Potential*—probably will be in the same regard. Sharp, 'the foremost writer in the world today on the subject of non-violent action', essentially claims that 'people in society may be divided into rulers and subjects; the power of rulers derives from consent by the subjects; non-violent action is a process of withdrawing consent' (Martin 1989: 213). Sharp gives historical examples and shows the effective use of hundreds of action forms and defines *social power* as the ability to control the behaviour of others, directly or indirectly, by handling groups of people, whose actions affect other groups of people (Sharp 1973: 7–8). This is expressed in the strategic struggle between actors of different 'loci of power'. Political power is social power relating to political questions. Political power is about the authority and influence leaders can use to enforce their will upon others, and, on the other hand, the means people use to influence persons in positions of power. What is unique in Sharp's contribution lies in his development of theories from Hanna Arendt and Gandhi. Gandhi stresses the force of disobedience in power relations (Gandhi 1970), and Arendt claims that 'the extreme form of power is All against One, the extreme form of violence is One against All' (Arendt 1972: 141). As Arendt sees it, power is built upon some form of organized cooperation between people, while violence is basically an act by the individual. Sharp argues that violence is not only an expression of irrational wrath, but also as a working method to attain certain political goals (Sharp 1980: 158). Violence, not power, is the moral problem and this is what could and should be abolished (Sharp 1980: 190). Sharp agrees with Arendt's reasoning on power as a creative human ability to act collectively in consent, but emphasizes non-violent sanction-techniques as alternatives to violence in the transformation of power/cooperation (Sharp 1980: 23–24). To Sharp, in agreement with Gandhi, the counter-power of resistance becomes a form of *non-cooperation* with power systems.

Sharp's starting point, when referring to the dominant understanding of power at that time, is a criticism of what he calls the established '*Monolith theory*'. This amounts to people being dependent on government, and assumes that political power is massive and uniform, that power really can emanate from leaders and that power is an entity (Sharp 1973: 7–10). This is an over-simplified theory of power or a popular perspective which can nevertheless describe reality correctly, if and only if, both the opposition and the general public within an existing power structure are made to believe in it and, therefore, act *as if* it were true (Sharp 1973: 9). The normalized monolith perspective has created the absurd phenomenon of a whole country with millions of inhabitants considering themselves 'occupied' simply because their house of parliament has been taken over and the government is incapacitated. Furthermore, the monolith theory is the basis of a belief in political violence, especially in military struggle and war. By physically capturing 'the place' of power, one gains power, as if it were a thing or position that generates power from within itself.

On the contrary, resistance, in the form of non-violent actions, assumes that governments are dependent on people; that power is manifold and vulnerable, because the control of power sources depends on many groups (Sharp 1980: 23-24). Non-violent resistance is built upon the idea that *political power is easiest controlled at its origin* (Sharp 1973: 10). The ruler's power 'depend *intimately* upon the obedience and cooperation by the subjects' (Sharp 1973: 12). It is from the (re)production of the economy, social institutions, ideology and population that the power of the leaders derives its nourishment. That nourishment comes from the subordinated inhabitants, who may choose to disobey. 'Obedience is at the heart of policial power' (Sharp 1973: 16).

Sharp differentiates the social roots of power as authority, human resources, knowledge and ability, psychological and ideological factors, material resources and sanctions (Sharp 1973: 1112). The strength of power is completely dependent upon how much of these various re-sources the power-holder can access, which ultimately depends on the degree of cooperation from the subordinates. The main point is that all sources of power lie *outside* the formal executor of power (a leader or government). Using his charismatic personality, a skilful leader plays on the feelings and traditions of the subordinates, but this does not change the fact that the sources of power lie outside him.[2] Charisma is especially important because a power-holder gains access to power through the enthusiasm of his people. The only judges who decide on what behaviour counts as 'charisma' are the people themselves.

The power-holder himself does not create power, instead, it is *given* to him by others in their daily cooperation and support.[3] It is actually in the power-holder's dependency that the necessary act of choice by the subordinate, the leader's weakness and the possibilities of resistance are manifested.

The cooperation that generates power consists of active support, passive acceptance, or unwilling obedience to demands or rules from the power-holder. He depends directly on cooperation from a significant section of the citizens to maintain the economic and administrative sys-tem and its supportive sanctions system in practice. Yet, he is clearly dependent on the vast majority actually paying their taxes and following the rules of the society and not putting up collective resistance. When only 0.01 per cent of the Indian population ended up in prison, it became a political and practical problem for the British colonial system. 60,000 people in jail and scandals of brutal violence forced the Empire to make concessions and engage in negotiations.

While power's dependency on its subordinates might be fundamental, Sharp pays no attention to the fact that there are groups that power can do without, groups that are excluded and still subordinated (Burrowes 1996: 1112). At the same time, one group of leaders may be in alliance with other power systems, thus, compensating for a lack of internal power with external support, for example, an international finance agreement. But this kind of critique does not overthrow the theory as such. It only indicates that the non-violent struggle must influence or be organized within the very groups that power *de facto* is depending upon (Burrowes 1996: 96). Therefore, a strategic struggle needs to be based on a relevant analysis of the targeted power.

Sharp argues that power systems are built upon hierarchies, chains of *obedience*, where the leaders stand or fall by the level of *cooperation* within the power pyramid. According to Sharp, people are obedient for many reasons, for example, habit, fear of punishment, sense of duty, secondary advantages, psychological identification with the leading group, acceptance or lack of confidence and resources. For the purpose of this analysis, it is enough to accept that in *de facto* behaviour people do subordinate themselves, whatever the reasons.

Sharp claims that even unwilling obedience is a choice (Sharp 1973: 25–30). Obedience is not automatic since there is always a choice; resistance is an option. Sharp considers the subordinate's *obedience a kind of voluntary cooperation*, even when violence is used as a threat. This gives resistance new and unthought of possibilities of changing power relations, possibilities that Sharp regards as his task to investigate.

Violence is a central part of the punishment for rule-breakers, and it is assumed that it will make people obedient even when they do not want to be obedient. Key groups, such as the police and military, support political and financial elites by the threat of organized violence. Since one cannot force anyone to do something unless they fear the punishment (Sharp 1973: 28), it suggests that the key to successful resistance lies in finding ways of changing the relationship to punishment or other harmful consequences of disobedience. Accordingly, Gandhi stressed fearlessness and voluntary acceptance of suffering as central for non-violent resistance. How this ability is fostered then becomes the difficult problem to solve. To Gandhi, it is through spiritual purification, to Sharp, through informed and disciplined strategy, to feminist non-violent activists, through the empowerment of communities of support—'affinity groups'—(Vinthagen 2005).

From Sharp's 'consent theory' of power, we can anticipate that possibilities of resistance to power are created by the organized and strategic use of different techniques of disobedience. Sharp maps a way for non-violent resistance and indicates a number of basic techniques and dynamics based on historical research. Many examples of how non-violent resistance can be expressed in different societies and situations are given (Sharp 1973: Part ll). Since power depends on cooperation, resistance becomes possible as non-cooperation, and the disobedience of non-violent action becomes a means for change in society. Organized non-violent resistance in the form of disobedience can be powerful by being a way of action which challenges the very foundation of power, that is, if this concept of power is correct.

Using Sharp's theory, one can actually maintain—in an analytical sense—that the citizens or the people in a society have the power in their own hands. It may be true and still be impossible in real life. Whether the citizens are aware and able to change the relations of power is a completely different question. The capacity of resistance depends, according to Sharp, on knowledge and strategic understanding. I maintain, however, that the citizens' capacity for resistance, in a profound sense, depends on whether or not power has the ability to shape people. If power is able to shape our ways of thinking, behaving and acting, resistance becomes much harder. In such a case, power is incorporated within us as individuals and in our culture. Then even thinking and speaking of resistance may be marked by features of power. The problem is that Sharp simplifies the ability of power to influence the conditions of resistance.

To Sharp, non-violence is something you will consciously choose in order to correct an unjust situation once you have learned the techniques of non-violence and realized the force of organized and strategic resistance. It is all a matter of cognitive knowledge and strategic thinking in applying the effective techniques of non-violent struggle. Sharp's view of both power and resistance is pragmatic and technical. To be sure, his perspective is fruitful and he develops our understanding of non-violence beyond earlier mostly religious, ethical and personality-based interpretations (Vinthagen 2005: Chapter 2), but at the same time it is rather one-dimensional (Burrowes 1996: 83–96; Holm 1978; McGuinness 1994), becoming a kind of antithesis of idealism and spiritual pacifism. With a simplified concept of power comes a simplified concept of resistance.

Sharp is presented as the foremost interpreter of the concept of power as it is understood today, even by critics. In my view, though a non-violent movement expresses a more nuanced understanding of power, it adopts a more realistic application of resistance (Vinthagen 2005). Sharp's theory is a reaction to the simplified theories of that time (for example, classic realism), and is but one step in a direction that was independently developed in a much more sophisticated way by others (for example, Lukes 1974; Foucault 1974). Such power theories are not incorporated within the later Sharpian 'technique approach' (*cf* Ackerman and Kruegler 1994; McCarthy and Sharp 1997; Sharp 2004), or by researchers slightly critical of the approach (Burrowes 1996; Martin 1989: Note 3).

Although Sharp's reasoning assumes the existence of a conscious and free will not formed by power (Sharp 1973: 25–32), I assert that the autonomous mind is not necessary for the survival of the basic theory. The power theory is ultimately built upon *the fact* that subordination is created or changing, not on how this is done (Sharp 1980: 98, 212, 341). Even if power forms people's consciousness and actions, I claim that the perspective remains sensible: power arises from the *participation* of the subordinate. In fact, Sharp asks for research about how the will of a person is formed by institutions and how it could be liberated (Sharp 1980: 20), indicating the need to incorporate such an understanding into the consent theory.

Power as productive discipline

In a sense, both Sharp and Foucault complement each other. Using the metaphor of 'war', both of them investigate strategies and techniques to describe political struggles. A slight difference is that Sharp emphasizes resistance, and Foucault, power. Still, the theoretical differences are considerable. It is true that they are unanimous in their opinion that power is unstable, changeable and spreading, but Sharp perceives power as a zero-sum-game (McGuinness 1994). There is a certain amount of power given to share and fight over. When one group gains power, another group loses it. Foucault, on the other hand, thinks power can increase without diminishing it somewhere else. Sharp's concept of power is characterized by the Anglo-Saxon philosophy of the subject, where individuals with a free will try to govern others against their will. Coming from a European continental tradition, Foucault is more interested in how different techniques of power form our consciousness and actions. Power is not only *prohibiting*—using laws that you may annul through substantial disobedience—but is also *producing* society and is partly *incorporated* in people's minds, language and behaviour. Foucault understands power as unstable and dynamic, yet as something that is constantly reproduced.

Different behaviour-forming techniques and discourses reconstruct social life irrespective of what the participants want or do not want. Power is 'not built up out of "wills" (individual or collective), nor ... derivable from interests' (Foucault 1980: 180), 'neither given, nor exchanged, nor recovered, but rather exercised ... in action' (1980: 89) within 'an unequal and relatively stable relation of forces' (1980: 200). Power is about how actions, independent of the actor's intentions, can actually structure the space of other actions (Beronius 1986: 25). According to Foucault, power is a productive act of dominance. The acting individual does not control the activity, rather it is the activity that controls the individual and forms her personality. A set of techniques dominates those who exercise these techniques, irrespective of whether they are 'leaders' or 'subordinates'. The individual does not exercise power, the power expresses itself *through* the individual (Foucault 1974: 36–37).

Foucault actually maintains the opposite of Sharp. The non-violent activist cannot be outside power, make a decision to resist, and then act against the power. Resistance exists as a possibility to be sure, but the fibre threads of power have infiltrated the thinking, language, methods and culture of the non-violent activist. To Sharp, the struggle for power goes on between participants, while, to Foucault, it creates the participants. Since the standpoints do not seem to be mutually exclusive, the question is whether this necessarily leads to the eradication of the non-violent understanding of power as subordination.

Here, it is important that we do not get power and the techniques of power mixed up. With Foucault, power has a tendency to appear as a virtual force without individuals or actors (Foucault 1980: 117). This is probably not a correct understanding of Foucault, but some of his followers tend to abolish the actor and her choice (Cheater 1999: Chapter 1), making the jagged intentions and consciousness of people solidify into pure power. This creates a risk of mythologizing power as being *self-acting* techniques and discursive structures. Power techniques (of behaviour) or discourses (of speaking) have to be applied and, therefore, also followed by people, otherwise they will not be effective in creating power. Techniques and discourses are social performances, not performing objects. When we subdue our behaviour to fit a routine or scheme of techniques, we become part of the power shaping. If this happens to be what we want to do, or we do it without thinking, is of no importance (for power production). The only thing that matters is what we do, not what we think about it. Power will be at work anyway as our acting forms subordination.

Foucault has wrongly been criticized for reducing everything to power (Foucault 1994: 133). But knowledge, truth, discourse, or resistance are not the same as power. If they were, there would be no need to talk about how power forms these other phenomena. Despite everything, there are, according to Foucault, 'no relations of power without resistance ... [and it] exists all the more by being in the same place as the power' (1980: 142). After all, spaces free from power always exist somewhere. The choice, will, desire, decision, or personality of the actor are not completely determined by power. If they were, people would not act, they and their behaviour would simply be 'power effects'. Foucault speaks of 'plebs', 'a feature in the social body, in classes, groups and individuals themselves which in some sense escapes relations of power' (Foucault 1980: 137-38). It is not a social entity, but a plebeian *quality or aspect* of different entities. This plebeian quality evades power by existing on its borders or under it, and interestingly enough by disengagement, by *not* resisting. When unmanageable resistance is stabilized after some time, the risk of power creeping into and configuring the resistance arises. Then, resistance may become normalized, disciplined and shaped by power. I maintain that this plebeian quality of evasion from power opens up possibilities of resistance which involve not just counter-power, but Foucault does not help us to understand the resistance that confronts power. Even though Foucault claims that resistance is where power is, plebeian avoidance or resistance is not explored, since power itself is what interests Foucault. While no person or group as a whole can exist outside power relations, they cannot either exist totally within power.

Power as subordination

The scientific discourse on power is preoccupied by the argumentation on different *aspects* of power, often with exclusive theories naming one or other form of power as the only ultimate one (Vinthagen 1998, 2001). This leads to a conceptual inflation, which makes it difficult to identify what is *characteristic* of the power phenomenon or anything that is not power. Some authors, like Foucault, are completely focused on *how* power works, what techniques are used and how powers manifest themselves in different ways. In fact, Foucault consciously avoids the question of what the common factor of 'power' is (Foucault 1994: 128–29). An understanding of what constitutes power cannot be based upon certain individual expressions of power. From Sharp, we have seen that within the non-violent tradition, power is coupled to cooperation or obedience. Foucault uses the term 'subjugation' which implies someone who has been defeated by overwhelming force, or even 'manufactured' (Foucault 2003: 45). My central concept continues to be 'subordination' implying participation by the subordinate: 'As doers separated from our own doing [through power], we re-create our own subordination. As workers, we produce the capital that subordinates us. As university teachers, we play an active part in the identification of society, in the transformation of doing into being' (Holloway 2002). The social phenomenon of 'power' is characterized by *one actor who subordinates herself, partly or entirely, by relinquishing the practical responsibility or intention of her own behaviour* (Vinthagen 2005). The actor behaves like a 'non-actor', as an instrument to be used. The crucial point is that a transfer of the control of behaviour does happen through the actor relinquishing control, whether it is wished for or not, done consciously or not. What matters is the existence of obedience or, rather, the active and participatory transfer of responsibility, which produces subordination, the *de facto behaviour*, no matter what motive, reason, or cause underlies the act of subordination.

Subordination is essentially an activity that is expressed in relationships and interactions. It does not have to be a person to whom the actor is subordinate. That which we obey is that which we let rule our activity. It can be a person, a group, or an imagined nation, but equally it may be an idea, a principle, a place, a machine, an ideology, a tradition, a god, or a part of nature. The person who gives up her control over her actions does not have to feel forced to do so and may not even be aware of the power that is given away. Subordination may, for example, take the form of an obvious yet unquestioned way of structuring our lives according to the 'laws' of a watch chained to the wrist. Or subordination may mean a subconscious obedience to a dead yet internalized and 'active' father.

Subordination may even be like sticky glue, something that stays the more you try to rub it out, refusing to go away, similar to the situation of poor Brian in the Monty Python movie *Life of Brian*. Brian, who is mistakenly believed to be the Messiah, succeeds in fleeing from his fans through the labyrinthine streets of Jerusalem. He wakes up the next morning in his house, opens the window shutters and is startled by the sight of hundreds of his devotees patiently sitting outside waiting for their Saviour. They greet him with a solemn 'God Morning Master!'

Frustrated he shouts: 'I am not the Messiah! Stop following me. You have to think for yourselves!' With one voice they all answer: 'Yes Master, teach us more!'[4]

In this way, power becomes a very special form of relationship, a subject's inferior positioning in relation to socialized objects, or a social interaction in which someone repeatedly subordinates herself, thus, giving someone else power to master the subordinated one. This signifies that power is only a possibility; it is something we can do, or stop doing. Subordination is not a state. To subordinate yourself is an action. It also indicates that power is reproduced through repeated subordination. Power may be produced everyday as a routine, reluctant and slow, or with growing intensity and willingness. It can always change. The power-holder is a power-holder only for as long as subordinated people keep reproducing the power. The more people refuse, the less power a leader is given. If the very groups who give a leader access to the sources of power refuse to obey, the leader loses his power. The better a group can withstand the sanctions of a leader and reject his temptations, the less power he has over the group. The very existence of incitements—'the carrot and the stick'—implies that power is dependent on a certain co-operation from those who are subjugated.

It is a fact that there are almost always people who, despite everything, choose to resist by not subordinating themselves. The dependence of power is brought out by the fact that dictatorships react with massive sanctions and retaliation upon even small numbers of people who resist them. Still, it is a common belief that non-cooperation only works within a liberal democracy. Perhaps, the power-holders are more aware of their vulnerability and dependence on massive cooperation from the inhabitants who provide the power with strength, than are their subordinates?

But when the oppressed people realize this and are given the means to break off their cooperation, the men in power do not sit tight any more. In a society of minority rule, this is more visible. As early as 1920, Gandhi claimed that India would be able to liberate itself as soon as its people realized the injustice and fragility of the colonisation of a vast country by a few thousand colonisers (Sharp 1979: 44–6, 54). The British Empire could not build all the prisons required to keep in order millions of Indians on the day they decided to disobey the regime and follow their own 'laws', that is, decisions made by the parallel government, the All-India Congress, constituted by the Indian liberation movement. Furthermore, the Empire would not profit from keeping its colony if the administration and economy collapsed. After a few decades, Gandhi's revolutionary ideas were victorious. India became independent through a struggle in the form of massive non-cooperation and civil disobedience, despite repeated massacres, brutality, mass-imprisonment and torture.

At the other end of the spectrum—where power is normalised and accepted, not seen as colonial occupation or oppression, but as natural or even a holy blessing—subordination is less visible. As power seems to be able to exist even when the actors act mainly in their own interests, consciously and of their own free will—the importance of power can be difficult to display. Power is simply at hand if you can establish that the actor abandons her individual and practical responsibility for her actions. It is harder, though, to establish the significance of a certain power relationship, since this depends on whose interest we emphasize and the importance given to it. A typical example of renouncement of responsibility is the worker who acts through her union to improve her working conditions, but lets the professional union leaders decide what should be improved. Or the citizen, who obeys the laws of a society, even when some laws are seen as unjust, in order to be able to lead a quiet life.

Power as 'relinquishing of responsibility' concerns practical responsibility, the initiative, decision and control of our own activity. Ethical responsibility is something different. It would be naive to claim that the participant should blame herself when things start going bad. Personal blame should rather refer to the person who profits from the relationship, not to the one being exploited. That the subordinated actually do participate signifies that there is hope of resistance against power abuse. Any ethical judgement must consider how subordination is created—usually by a combination of threats and temptations, but mainly through a lifelong moulding process—and what is reasonable for a human being to accomplish in a certain situation or position. Such an ethical judgement is beyond this investigation. What concerns us here is to gain an understanding of systems of subordination and the potential of resistance.

Resistance as fighting subordination

If we understand power as subordination, resistance becomes the attempt to hinder or break relations where humans are made into tools for others or servants in a hierarchy. Thus, *resistance means a hindrance of subordination.*

Resistance might be directed towards the structure, process, relations, or techniques of subordination.

Foucault has shown that power might form several different global and local strategies (Foucault 1980: 142). Similarily, the hindrance of subordination is formed dependent on what specific power being fought and in what situation.

On a utopian level, non-violent movements are about *dissolving* all subordination, creating space for a social order that all involved in free agreement have agreed on. But in reality, non-violent resistance is about hindering the present and serious subordination that certain activists consider wrong.

Hindrance of subordination might happen in diverse ways. Since subordination does not arise through effective coercion, but through the subservient's own subordination, violence seems not necessary or even central for resistance. Still, violence might compensate a weak mobilization of people. Through an armed resistance movement, the violence apparatus of the state might be destroyed and thus the threat of violence which supports state power. To avoid confusion, it is important that we make an analytical difference between the *goal* to make resistance to power and the *tool* violence, which clearly might be used to make resistance, but which is only one of several possible tools. Gandhian non-violence then is another possibility. For Gandhi, non-violence is a struggle against both violence and power, in an attempt to reach both reconciliation and truth (Gandhi 1999).

Thus, resistance does not demand the use of violence. But if power is supported by the threat of violence, it seems, on the other hand, to be necessary for the success of a resistance movement that the struggle continues despite opposing parties or power holders' threat of, or use of violence. Otherwise, non-violent resistance would have to be cancelled every time activists were threatened with violence.

A number of resistance types are possible to distinguish (Vinthagen 2005).[5] Lets now discuss each of them, before making conclusions of this chapter. Resistance might involve *communicative* attempts of convincing, for example, appeals, witness, reinterpretations, information, good arguments, symbolic counteracts, or the undermining of emotional impediments. Oppositional parties, those who subordinate themselves or temporary non-engaged groups, might be persuaded to change their understanding and behaviour through dialogues or negotiations. Understood as resistance, communication is a matter of arguing against and deconstruct the propaganda and ideology of power, to break the rules of hegemonic discourse.

But in power-loaded conflicts, it is not likely that dialogue is enough. The creation of *competing* and alternative patterns of relations and inter-action, through the production of parallel cultural, economic or political institutions, might be necessary. A social space for a new order is thus created. While the announcement of a 'parallel government' is virtually a 'war declaration', the effective work of such a governing body makes the resistance self-sufficient. Through the 'constructive program', Gandhi emphasized the social integration of the new society and the creation of alternatives to the oppressive institutions that the movement tried to overthrow. The dismantling of oppression is not non-violence in it-self or enough for social change, according to Gandhi. The new society does not arise with ease from the ashes of the old. The development of the new society should be initiated during the resistance struggle in order to sincerely show what is wanted instead of the present situation, and in order to make success possible (Sharp 1979: 81).

In stark contrast to violent resistance strategies, the Gandhian non-violence involves simultaneous *non-cooperation* with the oppressive system role-behaviour of the opponent, as well as *cooperation* with every human being as part of the unity of humanity (Burrowes 1996: 108; Galtung and Naess 1990: 147–53, 199ff, 243). To Gandhi, it was decisive that the non-violent activist both protected the legitimate needs of the opponent and came to assistance when the personal security of anyone was threatend. Even a readiness to die during the protection of the life of your 'enemy' was advised. The movement should also try to find allied sub-groups within the 'enemy camp' that might want to take part in some cooperative project benefiting the creation of a more just society; for example, Muslim and Hindu groups doing relief work together and reconstruction after communal riots between them. When there is something both parties agree on, the non-violent activists, according to Gandhi, should even try to develop cooperation directly with their opponent. Emotional ties and the constructive change of society might be facilitated thus, and enemy images and the power base of the oppressors might be undermined. This flexible and complex approach which differentiates between the aspects of others might then both strengthen the non-violent aspects of exisiting society and give a base of mutual cooperation in social change.

The creation of competing institutions that can replace what the non-violent movement resist is complemented with the strengthening of specific existing institutions that are *not* part of what they fight. Thus, resistance is targeted on the real enemy: oppressive power and organized violence. In connection with the West German non-violent movement's blockades of the nuclear weapon base in Mutlangen during the 1980s, some of the organizers considered it to be important to invite the soldiers to dinner in their homes, while others considered drinking beer in the local pub with them. The peace activists and the military did perhaps have divergent goals, but despite the goals, they could unite around a genuine human need: eating and drinking. In a non-violent resistance, the opponent is understood as a human being despite the conflict situation and is supposed to share at least some values and wishes with the resistance movement.

Non-cooperation in existing power relations is at the same time central in order not to naively being used and manipulated. The combination of focused cooperation and non-cooperation with the opponent is but one expression of the consensus-oriented dialectical action-approach which constitutes the core of non-violent conflict transformation (Vinthagen 2005). It is this combination that makes it part of the Gandhian form of non-violent resistance. Despite it creating an unusual contradictory repertoire of resistance, it seems reasonable. Every functional society demands some sort of social order or integration, which means that an effective hindrance of cooperation risks collapsing the present social order. The parallel creations of new forms of order exist in order to diminish this risk arising from the powerful force of non-violent resistance. Gandhian non-violence intends to strengthen social integration while doing resistance—indeed a profound and unique approach to revolutionary resistance.

When power prevails, non-violent resistance might have to involve the avoidance of subordination; in the plebeian sense, an *evasion* of power relations where liberated geographical or social zones are established. Mass emigration was proposed as a resistance act by Gandhi. Sometimes, it is difficult to categorize a technique, since it has several aspects and is part of a context. Emigration is possible to understand partly as refusal—to partake in the activities or identification as citizens of a specific country or place—and partly as avoidance from repression, to find a new life somewhere else. During their non-violent resistance to the communist regime of 1989, thousands of East Germans fled through Hungary which proved to be instrumental in forcing the opening of the Berlin Wall.

Avoidance of power might be perceived as the opposite to 'resistance', but it is part of the non-violent movement's combinatory repertoire of resistance techniques and strategy. Through avoidance of power, *space* is created which facilitate reflection, initiative, mobilization and action—at the same time *absence* arises for the power holder (of potential subservants). Sometimes, avoidance or the choice to 'not express resistance' to a hegemony is necessary for the success of a subordinate group (Cheater 1999: 5), or even a prerequisite for power not being able to dominate (Foucault 1980: 138).

But even when many are persuaded and refuse to subordinate, there exists perhaps an effective group of people who do subordinate themselves. It is then also necessary with a *direct hindrance* which blockades the processes of power systems. It might happen through action forms like collective, organized and peaceful sabotage, or civil disobedience.

Last, it is as well possible to imagine the *redefinitions creating chock, humour and irony*, or other playful forms turning normal perceptions, social prejudice, or conventional concepts upside down (Johansen 1991). During the 1970s, the Swedish homosexuals fought the World Health Organization (WHO) medical definition of homosexuality as being a sickness, through numerous persons who claimed sick-leave at work (Dielemans and Quistbergh 2000). 'Hi love, I feel slightly homosexual today and unfortunately I can't go to work, since it might be infectious. Let's hope I recover until tomorrow. Bye dear!' Or, when Norwegian conscription objectors, in protest against their friends present in prison, escaped into (sic) prison. When they refused to leave if not their comrades where released, the police carried them out of prison while the cameras of the media were flashing bright. In both of these actions, the definitions and methods of power were dramatically rendered non-frightening. The homosexual activists made a stigmatizing label of 'sickness' ridiculous, while the army objectors made the punishment of prison meaningless, since what sentence could any court give these criminals? Certainly not prison. In a similar fashion, it is possible to understand the queer group Outrage! and their carnevalesque treatment of the British society's prejudice of homosexuals during the 1990s, as the conscious undermining of power relations built on fear, avoidance, misrepresentation and silence. They performed a 'kiss-in' involving hundreds of gays and lesbians openly exposing their love, in an epoch where the government tried to forbid information on homosexuality in school books. Once some activists dressed in costumes performed 'The Exorcism of Lambeth Palace' outside the home of the Archbishop of Canterbury. The exorcists commemorated the historical tradition of Christian persecution of homosexuals, and through rituals and prayers, they tried to drive out 'The Demon of Homophobia' and compel God to forgive the church.

These non-violent resistance techniques can together shape the space for mobilization and alliances (through communication, redefinitions and cooperation), alternative social systems (constructive work and competition), removal of supportive involvement from the existing system of oppression (refusal and evasion), and make existing system's processes difficult to run or even impossible (hindrance). As a result, both the dismantling of the present social system and the creation of new ones become possible.

When applied effectively, it becomes the self-interest of elites to enter negotiations, since when non-violent resistance is escalated, oppressive power will sooner or later dissolve. If fully applied, these techniques might together lead to a 'living revolution' (Lakey 1987); the power-breaking resistance by a strong non-violent movement making negotiation with different power groups and a new and more accepted social order is made possible. Such power groups do not only consist of elite fractions. In a non-violent perspective of power and resistance, it becomes more important to enter into dialogue with those who subordinate themselves, as negotiating with 'power holders'. After all, it is the subordinates who produce power.

Subordination is created in advanced and complex social systems. Thus, it becomes reasonable that even resistance should be manifold and organized. Further resistance techniques than those that I have described might exist, but it is difficult to envision any successful non-violent struggle without at least these methods.

Non-violent resistance can therefore be generally understood as a behaviour that includes endurance of violence and oppression, while creating alternatives and hindrances, as well as new definitions and evasion of both subordination and violence—in an attempt to undermine power and the legitimacy of violence, and create conditions of reconciliation and dialogue.

This would imply that non-violent movements in principal are well equipped of resistance against power. Non-violent resistance seems to have possibilities to function as a form of peaceful conflict handling in power loaded conflicts (Vinthagen 2005).

Other investigations have to answer whether non-violent techniques are effective in practice or not. Some preliminary investigations within the underdeveloped discourse of non-violent studies seem to imply such a possibility (Randle 1994; Zunes 1999). Movements have struggled successfully against brutal regimes without major use of violence, in, for example, Philippines, South Africa and Poland during the 1980s.

By the way of conclusion

This chapter, with the help of Sharp and Foucault, shows that the power of the state ruler—the Prince—is challenged by his own subjects, the subordinated citizens. Through my preoccupation with similarities and differences between the theories of Sharp and Foucault, I have tried to do two things. First, to undermine the scientific hegemony of realism, the idea that power emanates from above, primarily through violence. Second, to move beyond Sharp and Foucault, suggesting a *decentred* understanding of (non-violent) resistance.

Like Sharp, I have argued that one can understand power as a form of obedience or active subordination, where cooperation from the subordinate is crucial. Unlike Sharp, I have, with the help of Foucault, argued that power is many-faceted and an all-too-common-element in social activity and, thereby, also a silent and often hidden force shaping people. Accordingly, not even the will, body and mind of the resistance fighter is free from power.

Opposing the common interpretation of Foucault, I have argued that incorporated techniques of power that effects subjectification, discourse-formation and body behaviour are possible to combine with a view of 'power as subordination', therefore, with choice and active cooperation. Power does not create subjects in automatic processes, but through the constant participation and modification by the very subjects themselves. Power as subordination is integrally linked to resistance as disobedience. Thus, non-violent movements are significant examples of resistance to power as well as transformation of it.

Notes

1. Martin 1984 and 1989 are in their approach on general power supportive institutions generally exceptions, but without using Foucault.
2. In this text, I call the leader 'he' and the subordinated 'she', as men have traditionally been the power-leaders over subjugated 'others': women, slaves, children, and so on.
3. This suggests that the more the extensive and detailed the power of a leader and his control is, the more dependent he is upon the cooperation of the subordinates. Accordingly, a late-modern, complexly organized, and highly technological society is, in some aspects, more dependent on cooperation and obedience from different groups to continue to function. Power relations

may be more diffuse and mobile, that is, where power resources are replaced, if necessary, and where networks of linked power relations are difficult to detect. At the same time, this should mean that resistance in key nodes of a power system involves more possibilities for obstruction than ever before in history. Today, a single individual may seriously affect the computerized world economy by unleashing a virus that disturbs the communicative IT-network on which global cooperation is built.

4. The quotes are not literal, only grasping the message of this scene in *Life of Brian*.

5. The literature gives different proposals of categorizations of non-violent techniques (Bondurant 1988; Naess 1974; Sharp 1973). These lists are all very different in structure and purpose. Naess is constructing a norm system with a logic hierarchy of proposals which taken together tries to capture the Gandhian non-violent philosophy and practical guidelines of non-violent struggle. Sharp distinguish 198 different methods from a rich historical case material of more or less peaceful actions where the manifest behaviour of participants is divided into three broad categories: protest, non-cooperation and interventions. Galtung propose yet another type of categorization, one differentiating non-violent techniques of (positive and negative) influence, structuring of action space, physical dimension, sanctions, amplification, and role-playing (Galtung 1965: 251). There are also, in books on training and education in non-violent action, other proposals of categorizations of non-violent methods. There is a need for a systematic comparison between different types of categorizations.

References

Ackerman, Peter and Christopher Kruegler. 1994. *Strategic Non-violent Conflict—The Dynamics of People Power in the Twentieth Century*. New York: Praeger Publishers.

Arendt, Hannah. 1972. *Crisis of the Republic*. San Diego: A Harvest Book, Harcourt Brace & Company.

Beronius, Mats. 1986. *Den disciplinära maktens organisering: Om makt och arbetsorganisation*. Lund: Arkiv Studentlitteratur.

Burrowes, Robert J. 1996. *The Strategy of Nonviolent Defence: A Gandhian Approach*. Albany: State University of New York Press.

Bondurant, Joan V. 1988 [1958]. *Conquest of Violence: The Gandhian Philosophy of Conflict*. Princeton: Princeton University Press.

Chabot, Sean Taudin. 2003. *Crossing the Great Devide: The Gandhian Repertoire's Transnational Diffusion to the American Civil Rights Movement*, PhD dissertation, University of Amsterdam, Amsterdam.

Cheater, Angela. 1999. *The Anthropology of Power—Empowerment and Disempowerment in Changing Structures*. London: Routledge.

Dielemans, Jennie and Fredrik Quistbergh. 2000. *Motstånd*. Stockholm: Bokförlaget DN.

Foucault, Michel. 1974. *Övervakning och straff*. Lund: Arkiv Studentlitteratur.

———. 1980. *Power/Knowledge—Selected Interviews and Other Writings 1972–1977*, in Colin Gordon (ed.). New York: Pantheon Books.

———. 1994. 'Critical Theory/Intellectual History', in Kelly (ed.), *Critique and Power—Recasting the Foucault/Habermas Debate*, pp. 109–37. Massachusetts: Massachusetts Institute of Technology (MIT).

———. 2003. *Society Must Be Defended: Lectures at the Collège De France 1975–1976*. New York: Picador.

Galtung, Johan. 1965. *On the Meaning of Nonviolence*, pp. 20–2. Oslo: PRIO-publication nr.

Galtung, Johan and Arne Naess. 1990. *Gandhis politiske etikk*. Oslo: Pax Forlag A/S.

Gandhi, Mohandas K. 1970. *Essential Writings*. Ahmedabad: Navajivan Publishing House.

———. 1999. *The Collected Works of Mahatma Gandhi*, CD-Rom version, Patiala House, Tilak Marg, New Delhi: Ministry of Information and Broadcasting Publications Divisions.

Holloway, John. 2002. 'Twelve Theses on Changing the World without Taking Power', Available on http://www.commoner.org.uk/previous_issues. htm#n4 (050131). Accessed on 31 January 2005.

Holm, Berit G. 1978. *Teknisk moralisme i teori for ikkevoldsaksjon og "civilian defence": Kritisk analyse av Gene Sharps ikkevoldsteori*, PhD dissertation, Institute of Philosophy, Oslo University.

Johansen, Jörgen. 1991. 'Humor as a Political Force, or How to Open the Eyes of Ordinary People in Social Democratic Countries', *Philosophy and Social Action*, 17(July–December): 23–29.

Lakey, George. 1987. *Powerful Peacemaking: A Strategy for a Living Revolution*. Philadelphia: Library Company of Philadelphia.

Lukes, Steven. 1974. *Power*. London: MacMillan Press Ltd.

Martin, Brian. 1984. *Uprooting War*. London: Freedom Press.

———. 1989. 'Gene Sharp's Theory of Power', *Journal of Peace Research*, 26(2): 213–22.

McCarthy, Ronald M. and Gene Sharp. 1997. *Nonviolent Action: A Research Guide*. New York: Garland Publishing, Inc.

McGuinness, Kate. 1994. 'Some Thoughts on Power and Change, Seminar Synopses, Program on Nonviolent Sanctions and Cultural Survival', Harvard University. Available on http://data.fas.harvard.edu/cfia/pnscs/ DOCS/s94mcgui.htm (000724). Accessed on 24 July, 2000.

Naess, Arne. 1974. *Gandhi and Group Conflict*. Oslo: Universitetsforlaget.

Randle, Michael. 1994. *Civil Resistance*. London: Fontana Movements and Ideas.

Sharp, Gene. 1973. *The Politics of Nonviolent Action*, Parts 1–3. Boston: Extending Horizons Books, Porter Sargent Publishers.

———. 1979. *Gandhi as a Political Strategist*. Boston: Extending Horizons Books, Porter Sargent Publishers.

———. 1980. *Social Power and Political Freedom*. Boston: Extending Horizons Books, Porter Sargent Publishers.

———. 2004. *Waging Nonviolent Struggle: 20th Century Practice and 21st Century Potential*. Manchester, NH: Porter Sargent Publishers.

Waters, Malcolm. 1994. *Modern Sociological Theory*. London: Sage Publications Ltd.

Vinthagen, Stellan. 1998. 'Power and Nonviolent Movements', Research Paper, Department of Peace and Development Research (Padrigu), Göteborg University.

———. 2001. 'Makt och Motstånd', in Leif Eriksson and Björn Hettne (eds), *Makt och internationella relationer*, pp. 179–235. Lund: Studentlitteratur.

———. 2005. *Ickevåldets sociologi* [*The Sociology of Nonviolent Action*], PhD dissertation, Department of Peace and Development Research (Padrigu), Göteborg University.

Vinthagen, Stellan and Sean Taudin Chabot. 2002. 'The Relational and Constructionist Dynamics of Non-violent Action', Conference Paper, Tromsö University, November.

Zunes, Stephen, Lester R. Kurtz and Sarah Beth Asher. 1999. *Nonviolent Social Movements—A Geographical Perspective*. Malden, Massachusetts: Blackwell Publishers.

Origins and Sources of Power

Indonesian Paradigms and Beyond

9

BERNARD ADENEY-RISAKOTTA

I ndonesians are preoccupied with power. Power is a problem. It is often associated with violence and domination. Competitions for power, even among well-meaning leaders and groups, are too often the prelude to violence. Most people and groups sincerely believe that their group, religion, or ideology is the best way to bring peace, justice and prosperity to the people. But the only way they can bring such happiness is for them to gain, keep and wield power. Unfortunately, the struggle for power often leads to the very opposite of what is hoped for by all the groups involved.

In 1997, right after yet another landslide victory of long time President Soeharto, Indonesia began to unravel. The government's naked use of violence, obvious corruption and increasingly colossal lies, broke down the fragile legitimacy of the Soeharto 'New Order' regime. After massive protests and an unprecedented economic collapse, the 32 year rule of Soeharto came to an ignoble end. At first the monetary crisis (KRISMON, that is, Krisis Moneter) led to calls for political and economic reorganization, decentralization and democratization to end 'KKN', that is, Korups, Kolusi and Neopotisme (Corruption, Colusion and Neopotism). But soon, it was recognized as more than an economic crisis. It was a Total Crisis that affected every area of life (KRISTAL or KRISis toTAL) and called for Total Reformation of social, cultural, religious and moral structures, as well as political and economic change. Of course, once the common enemy, President Soeharto, was gone, there were many different opinions on what kind of total reformation would be adequate to the immensity of the problems. Different groups struggled for the right to determine the future and this uncovered conflicts that had been suppressed for decades under a militaristic government. Without a strong, centralized government, power struggles broke out all over the country. The end of an authoritarian regime, the delegitimization of the military and the euphoria of Reformation did not usher in a golden age of freedom and prosperity rather it brought about a period of serious conflicts between races, tribes, religions, political groups, regions and naked economic interests that seemed impossible to quench. Fortunately, Indonesia has now moved past the instability of the early transition and displays signs of an increasingly mature democracy. However, the future is still contested by many groups who hold different paradigms of the origins and sources of power.

The dominant paradigm of power, in Indonesia as well as in the rest of the world, views power as a 'top-down' phenomenon. Power flows from the powerful people at the top to the weak masses below. Power belongs to the elite who are more or less able to force their will on the rest of society. According to this almost universal dogma, the most basic form of power is violence and domination. In this chapter, I question this dominant paradigm of power as unrealistic and out of touch with empirical realities. I argue that true power is extremely diverse and comes from many different sources. Within Indonesian society, it is helpful to analyze power in relation to the interactions between Modernity, Primordial Culture and Religion. Power can be defined as the capability to transform the world. In contrast, power as domination and violence is incapable of producing fundamental change.[1]

Power in Java and the West

In a celebrated article, Benedict O'G. Anderson created an ideal type analysis of ancient Javanese concepts of power that are fundamentally different from Western concepts. Anderson believed that ancient Javanese practices are still influential in the political behaviour of Indonesians. Anderson's theory explains Javanese power in relation to four basic differences with Western concepts of power:

1. 'Power' in the West, is an abstract name that describes a relationship of domination or influence between people, whereas in Java, *Kekuasaan* (power) is something concrete and substantial. A Javanese can own power, independently from his relationship

with other people. Power 'is not a theoretical postulate but an existential reality. Power is that intangible, mysterious, and divine energy which animates the universe' (Anderson 1990: 22).

2. According to Western thinking, the sources of power are extremely diverse. Power can derive from technology, wealth, social status, knowledge, organization, charisma, formal office and many other sources. In contrast, Javanese power is homogenous and derives from only one source. According to Anderson, Javanese believe power is located in all of nature, but ultimately derives from God alone. Power emanates from God and is ultimately a single, unified reality.

3. Anderson argues that Westerners believe power is continually created anew and is without any inherent limits. Therefore, there is no limit to the accumulation of power. For example, with the creation of the nuclear bomb, destructive power is now much greater than it ever was before. Good organization can increase everyone's power. In contrast, the Javanese believe that the sum total of power in the universe is fixed and unchanging. Power does not increase or decrease except with regard to its division between people (or places). That means that if power increases in one place, it must decrease in some other place. In other words, power is a zero sum game.' For political theory, this has the important corollary that concentration of power in one place or in one person requires a proportional diminution elsewhere' (Anderson 1990: 23).

4. Anderson also suggests that Western concepts of power include a moral dimension such that power is subject to ethical judgements. Power is morally ambiguous. Power can be used for good or evil. It can be legitimate or illegitimate, right or wrong and true or false. The goodness or evil of power is an overriding Western concern. But Anderson says Javanese power has no relation to morality. Javanese power is a kind of energy that exists throughout the cosmos. Power is like the strength of wind or the eruption of a volcano that cannot be evaluated in moral terms. We may or may not like the effects of power, but like the effects of the sun they are not subject to ethical judgements. 'Power is neither legitimate nor illegitimate. Power is' (Anderson 1990: 23).

Every theory is built upon a framework of particular assumptions. Anderson's theory of power in Java was not constructed just from empirical observation or the study of ancient texts, although his mastery of ancient Javanese sources is impressive. Anderson wrote this well-known article for the benefit of Western students based on Western assumptions about the meaning of power. Anderson's theory does not emerge like Venus from the half shell of Javanese culture. Rather, his ideas are shaped by concepts of power and social evolution that are derived from Max Weber. Anderson thought Javanese culture was evolving from a traditional Eastern culture towards a modern Western culture. Furthermore, his view of Javanese culture was influenced by his preference for the more Hindu aspects of Java in contrast with the more Islamic elements.

Anderson's ideal type of Javanese power is defined in relation to Western concepts of power. Javanese power is the opposite of Western power everywhere. Anderson framed his definitions explicitly to shock Western students and force them to think about the meaning of power in a new way. In a footnote to the Indonesian translation of his article, Anderson wrote:

> My previous effort (in 1970, when I wrote this essay), was intended to show Western students how different their assumptions were from those of the Javanese and that Javanese assumptions are just as fundamental and just as logical as those of Western political science. In other words, I intended to shake up the assumptions of those Western students. (Anderson 1984: 52)[2]

Ideal type analysis creates a polarity or dichotomy for the purpose of contrast and clarification, not empirical description. We may doubt whether there is anyone who really thinks in just a 'Western' way about power, let alone anyone who holds a purely 'Javanese' view of power. Anderson's article clarifies two extremes that help us understand two different ways of thinking about power. Ironically, many Indonesian students, under the influence of developmentalism (*pengbangunan, kemajuan*) and positivism, seem to hold very 'Western' views of power, while their Western counterparts are fascinated by mystical and occult concepts that are more in line with the ideal type of 'Javanese power'.

It is inappropriate to criticize Anderson's theory on the basis of its descriptive accuracy. It is a heuristic model to help us think, not an empirical description. The real question is whether this model helps us understand the actual behaviour and convictions of Javanese today. In my opinion, Anderson's brilliant typology illuminates many things about Javanese political behaviour, including many aspects of Sukarno and

Soeharto's style of leadership. However, the theory is very misleading if taken as a master, explanatory model rather than a heuristic device. The theory's most basic flaw lies in its hidden, Weberian assumptions about social evolution. The real contrast in this theory of power is not between Java and the West, but rather between traditional and modern societies.

In reality, there is no such thing as single Javanese or Western concept of power. Nor is there a unified traditional or modern view of power. Indonesian political behaviour, both in present and in ancient times, is and was, far more complex than either of these types. The Indonesian anthropologist Koentjaraningrat shared Anderson's evolutionary assumptions, but pointed out that Anderson exaggerated the mystic and supernatural elements in ancient Javanese literature (Koentjaraningrat 1984).[3] According to Koentjaraningrat, even in ancient times Javanese people could distinguish fact from fiction in a good story. Unlike many people in the secularized West, almost all Indonesians believe in substantive, supernatural aspects of power, without denying the more mundane, abstract, relational and rational realities of power politics. Thus, the first pair of contrasting types (abstract, relational power vs. concrete, substantive power), is misleading, both for understanding the difference between either traditional and modern or Javanese and Western practices of power. Most Javanese do not see any conflict between these conceptions and would probably feel confused if asked to choose which conception was 'true'.

Similarly, with the second set of types, most Indonesians would agree that all power is ultimately from God and many might acknowledge that in some sense power is One. But it would be hard to find anyone who thinks that all power is homogenous. Even Javanese mystics, who are closest to Anderson's Javanese type, do not think all power is alike, let alone the same. For example, a Javanese shaman (*dukun*) explained in detail to me why I must go to different graveyards to get different kinds of power. He said each of the ancient sages (*Wali Sanga*) was powerful in a different way. One had mystical power to do supernatural things (*sakti*). Another was extremely rich but had no supernatural powers. A third lived simply and had no powers but had great moral presence and authority (*berwibawa*). The shaman explained to me that if I wanted to get rich it was no good meditating and praying at the graveyard of a sage who had great wisdom but no wealth. Similarly, if I sought supernatural power, I should not meditate at the grave of a wise or wealthy sage. Each of the nine traditional saints of Java had a different kind of power and each could provide help, only in their area of power.

Anderson's third set of polarities, between Javanese power as being limited and Western power as unlimited, seems a little closer to some Javanese practices, but is also far too simplistic. Many Indonesians (and Westerners), seem to view power as a zero sum game ('I win means you lose'). But that does not mean that they really think power is limited. It is true that a Javanese mystic may hesitate to tell his deepest esoteric secrets to his disciples until he is on his deathbed, because he fears losing power. But this is a rather special case. In fact, everyday, the mystic may teach his students and give them various kinds of power, without losing his own. In fact, the more followers s/he attracts, who practice his wisdom, the more powerful the guru becomes. Sometimes, power politics is a zero-sum game, but Indonesians are aware of all kinds of ways to increase different kinds of power. Anderson's conception of Javanese power is much simpler than Western power, even if it is more exotic. This may reflect Anderson's evolutionary assumptions and open him to the charge of orientalism. The simplicity of Anderson's Javanese conception of power as one, homogenous, limited substance, in contrast with the relatively complex Western notions of power as extremely varied, unlimited and complex relationships, makes me suspicious. Is Javanese thinking and practice really that much more simple than Western ideas and practice? I think not.

The fourth set of contrasts, in which Anderson distinguishes Western power as morally ambiguous and subject to good or evil use, in contrast with amoral Javanese views of power as simply a natural force, is very misleading. It is the least useful part of Anderson's typology. I do not think there are any Indonesians, ancient or modern, who would deny that there is a relationship between power and morality. In fact, Indonesians are among the most moralistic people on the planet. In contrast, Western political science, which often claims Machiavelli as its founding father, seems much closer to an amoral conception of power than Javanese or Indonesian conceptions. Western social science is only recently struggling free from a long dominant myth about 'value free analysis' of power based on presuppositions of individual self-interest as a law governing all human behaviour. The Western tradition has tried and failed to account for power as simply a natural force without moral content.

There is a breathtaking oversimplification implied in the terms 'Western' and 'Javanese'. After the war in Iraq, the French would not like to have their political morality grouped with the Americans as 'Western'. In Java alone (let alone in all of Indonesia), there are widely divergent views and practices of political morality. Nevertheless, if we accept the simplifications, we may acknowledge that ancient Javanese morality and modern Western morality are different. In ancient times, there was no concept of political legitimacy similar to the concept in modern Western (and Indonesian) discourse. The power of ancient kings did not need formalized legitimacy from the people. According to the concept of fate, God (or the gods) legitimated power and allowed or even determined who became king. This was a very convenient doctrine for colonial powers and was just as much believed in the West as in the East.

Nevertheless, ancient Javanese always connected power with morality. Anderson himself relates how religious leaders who were not connected with the court, functioned as moral critics, or prophets, who were admired just because of their courage in morally criticizing those in power. According to most accounts of Javanese morality, both ancient and modern, anyone who wishes to have power must act without self-interest (*tanpa pamrih*). Anyone who rules according to selfish ambition will lose his power. Self interest is seen as fundamentally in contradiction with power. Power without justice is also believed to be a route to ruination. Both natural and social disasters are a sign that God (or the gods), are displeased with the ruler. Even today, disruptions in the cosmos are linked with disruptions in the political order. For example, a few years ago, after a major eruption of Mount Merapi (an active volcano near Yogyakarta), I joined a serious discussion with leading Indonesian intellectuals, including Abdurrahman Wahid (Gus Dur, later president), Romo Mangunwijaya and Th. Sumarthana, about the relation between the volcanic eruption the political situation. They had no doubt that the eruption was somehow connected with the leadership crisis. Shortly afterwards, Soeharto was forced out of office and their cosmic speculations seemed justified. The Javanese world has not yet and may never be 'disenchanted'.

Almost all the ancient stories related in shadow puppet plays or other art forms are tales about power and morality. Anderson often quotes these sources, but evidently has a different understanding of morality or ethics than the Javanese. Perhaps, he imagines morality as limited to universal, abstract ethical principles, *a la* Kant, rather than the confusing mix of traditions (*adat*), religion, mysticism and pragmatism that are so evident in Javanese life (Magnis-Suseno 1984). According to Koentjaraningrat, moral authority (*kewibawaan*) is a basic requirement in ancient human conceptions of power, including in Java (Koentjaraningrat 1984: 135). Authority (*Wibawa*) implies moral presence and moral virtue. In Java, someone who is shamed (*dipermal·ukan*) by having their sins exposed to public view loses his/her authority and ability to lead or rule. In fact, Indonesians like to think of their culture as a culture of shame (*budaya malu*), and frequently lament the lack of shame in the current batch of corrupt, political leaders. They think leadership without morality is a sign of cultural decadence brought on by the materialistic West, not a manifestation of Javanese culture.

Even though we may criticize all the individual elements in Anderson's theory of Javanese concepts of power, his ideal type theory remains very valuable because it stimulates so many interesting ideas. Political practices in Indonesia exist within a dialectic between ancient substantive, cosmic and integralistic perceptions of power and modern, legal, utilitarian, democratic, relational and legal practices. Many people assume that Indonesian is undergoing a process of evolution from the former more 'primitive' conceptions to the latter more progressive (*lebih maju*), rational practices. In this view, the ancient, substantive views of power are feudal and authoritarian (like the ancient Javanese Sultans), and are gradually being replaced with rational, democratic conceptions of power that are more appropriate for the modern world. I find such views over simplistic and condescending. Undeniably, Indonesia is experiencing very rapid social change, including changes in its practices of power. But rapid social change should not be equated with 'progress'. Nor should it be assumed that the changes follow a supposedly Western pattern of increasing secularization (or demythologization). The past is not just being left behind in favour of something better or more 'rational'. Sometimes social change is more like devolution than evolution. In any case, the past is not left behind, rather it is transformed by its unique interaction with the present.

Anderson's paradigm with two ideal types—Western and Java—is an attempt to simplify and rationalize Max Weber's typology of power. Weber created a model with three types of power: traditional, charismatic and legal/rational. Anderson wanted to prove that Weber is mistaken and there are actually only two types: traditional and modern. Anderson sees charismatic power as one of the elements in traditional concepts of power. It is part of the traditional view of power and not a separate type. In other words, Anderson argues that charisma is an ancient social construct and not a phenomenon separate from ancient worldviews. According to Anderson:

> One could then argue that when Weber contrasted charismatic with traditional or rational-legal domination, he was the victim of a sort

of optical illusion. In reality, there were only two general forms of domination, one linked to substantive and the other to instrumental/ relational concepts of power ... all traditional authority was charismatic, and all charismatic authority traditional. (Anderson 1990: 79)

In contrast, Weber felt that *maybe* the phenomenon of charismatic power was really independent from both ancient and modern social constructs. Weber wrote, 'Charisma shall be understood to refer to an *extraordinary* quality of a person, regardless of whether this quality is actual, alleged or presumed' (Hughes 1958: 289; also see Anderson 1990: 80). It appears that Weber is wistful about the possibility that the power of charisma, such as was seen in the ancient prophets was a real power that somehow escaped the iron cage of rationality. Anderson suggests that Weber's threefold typology is still popular with sociologists, not because they share Weber's hope that the charisma that gave birth to religion might somehow save humankind, but because they think that the category of charisma might be helpful in explaining the extraordinary power of irrational demagogues such as Hitler. Indeed the extraordinary, irrational power of evil confuses and confounds Western social scientists, especially those with a functionalist bias. Social scientists use 'charisma' as a convenient 'black hole' into which they can throw all kinds of power phenomena that they cannot explain rationally.

In the final analysis, neither Weber, nor Anderson, nor the dominant stream of Western social scientists believed there is any power that is bigger than human beings and their social constructions. Both Weber and Anderson are attracted to mystical and charismatic manifestations of power, but they both remain stubborn secularist-materialists who are sceptical of any kind of power that cannot be researched through rational and empirical methods.

In contrast, almost all Indonesians believe that the power of God and the power of the unseen, spiritual world (*gaib*) are both real and mysterious. Authority (*kewibawaan*) and competence/legitimacy (*kewenangan*) in the exercise of power is a gift from God and includes a spiritual element that can be distinguished from both 'traditional' forms of power and from 'modern/legal/rational' forms of power. Of course 'value free' social science is free to define such conceptions of power as 'traditional' or 'charismatic' in contrast with 'modern' conceptions. However, I am free to doubt the 'objectivity' of such judgements. Most Indonesians believe that power is not just from the sovereignty of the people, but also from God. The mysterious aspects of power cannot be caged within a vague category such as charisma that is either part of or separate from traditional conceptions. Power that exceeds human understanding is a common phenomenon in the modern world as well, even if dogmatic secularists deny it.

The mystery of power haunts the ancient world of the *culture of our ancestors*. Power also infuses the symbol systems of our *religions*. And power 'possesses' the social, economic and political structures of *the modern world*. The amazing wonders of power are evident everywhere, but we use different languages to describe them. The most fundamental moral and political question facing the Indonesian people is not how we may 'advance' (*maju*) from a traditional society to become truly modern, but rather, how we may survive the avalanche of social, economic and political changes without losing our soul. In other words, how can we preserve a healthy balance between the different powers available through culture, religion and modernity? The symbol systems of culture root the meaning of power in the stories and practices of our ancestor. The great religions mediate a transcendent understanding and response to power. At the same time, modern scientific knowledge creates 'miraculous' powers to dominate and transform the natural world.

In the Cartesian West, it is considered rational to divide the world into two categories. Empirical or scientific knowledge is in contrast with religious or emotional experience based on faith and imaginative symbols. However, the Indonesians are more likely to distinguish between the external, evident world (*lahir*) and the inner, invisible world (*batin*). The inner and outer worlds are linked but distinguishable. Both display various kinds of power, but the inner world is more decisive. Most Indonesians, including intellectuals, believe in God (Allah), and in human fate or destiny. Power is ultimately in the hands of God. This does not mean that most Indonesians discount the rational negotiation of power in relation to structures that regulate abstract relations between human beings. Indonesians are known as excellent chess players. They know how to play all kinds of rational power games. However, most believe that the final outcomes are not just the product of human manipulation or cultural production, but are also determined by the will of God and human destiny. God gives strength, power, authority and supernatural gifts (*kesaktian*) to certain people. In fact many Indonesians also believe that such gifts are mediated through the ancestors and influenced by unseen spiritual powers.

In my research on power, I am trying to break loose from Western social scientific assumptions about the material world in order to consider the meaning of power in Indonesia. That does not mean that

I am uncritical or that I naively consider all kinds of cultural concepts of power equally meaningful. On the contrary, in the following section, I will suggest a reconception of power that is not only in tension with dominant Western conceptions, but also with dominant Indonesian ideas of power, both ancient and modern. My approach is dialectic. I do not think we can or need to forge a unified theory of power that covers all possible cases. In particular, I think that most Indonesians are adept at using at least three different 'languages' and symbol systems to talk about power, that is, the discourses of religion, modernity and the culture of our ancestors (*adat*). Modern, cultural and religious discourses of power are sometimes complementary rather than contradictory. But that does not mean they can be unified. They are competing symbol systems that not only give different names to the same things, but just as often name different things that find no place in each others conceptions. They use different webs of symbolic meanings to discuss both the same and different things.

Theories of power

Power as domination and violence

The most common Indonesian and Western concepts of power hold one thing in common: they both regard power as domination. Both assume that leaders, kings, sultans, or presidents, possess power in order to dominate the people. According to Anderson's theory, neither Javanese nor Western concepts distinguish between power and force or violence. A powerful leader in the West, just like a powerful Javanese Sultan (or Colonial 'Resident'), imposes their will on the people by force. Power is domination by the strong people who are on top, against the weak who are below.

It would be convenient if we could claim that the theory of power as domination was a Western concept in contrast with a more peaceful concept originating from the wisdom of the East. Unfortunately, power as domination and violence is a fundamental assumption in both the West and the East. Since ancient times thinkers and politicians from China, Japan, India, Indonesia, Greece, Italy, England, Germany and Mexico (among others), whether they speak with the language of supernatural, spiritual and God-given power, or the language of modern institutions, technology and economic might, speak of power as domination.

In the discourse about power, it is common to speak of power as violence. For example, C. Wright Mills wrote that, 'All politics is a struggle for power; the ultimate kind of power is violence' (Mills 1956: 171; also see Arendt 1963). Similarly, Max Weber wrote, 'The state is a relation of men dominating men, a relation supported by means of legitimate (i.e. considered to be legitimate) violence.' Weber defines the modern nation state as, 'a human community that (successfully) claims the monopoly of the legitimate use of physical force within a given territory' (Weber 1946a [1919]). From this viewpoint, it appears that power means the ability to force the people to obey the will of the powerful, if necessary, by using violence. Power is the same as domination. The supreme form of power is violence, because violence enforces absolute obedience.[4]

Thomas Hobbes argued that the essence of the state is founded on fear (Hobbes 1952). Fear is the dominating condition of human beings in the 'state of nature'. According to Hobbes, the state of nature is the natural condition of human beings before the creation of government. In the state of nature there is no law, no morality, and no community. Human beings are in a state of war against everyone. No one is safe because without law and order, anyone, even the weakest, can kill the strongest, for example when he or she is asleep. Therefore, in Hobbes' famous sentence, life in the state of nature is 'mean, nasty, brutish and short'. The natural condition of humanity is therefore the 'law of the jungle': kill or be killed. Because of fear prompted by this condition, human beings created a powerful giant ('leviathan' or whale), which was given a monopoly on the right to use violence. Human beings gave up their freedom to use violence individually and agreed to abide by laws, backed up by the institution of the state or government (leviathan), which alone had the right to use violence to enforce law. In other words, humans gave up freedom in exchange for safety. According to Hobbes, government must be as strong as a whale and must not hesitate to use violence to enforce law. Without state violence there is no law, no obedience, no order, and no safety.

Jean Jacques Rousseau developed Hobbes' theory of the state by explaining the state as the result of a 'social contract' between those who wished to escape the state of nature. In his youth, Rousseau did not agree with Hobbes that the state of nature was a horrible condition of violence and fear. On the contrary, Rousseau thought the state of nature was a kind of paradise in which people lived simply, in peace and freedom, without the oppression of government and society. Why then did they create government? Rousseau suggests that the people were tricked into accepting a social contract that was really a means by which the rich and powerful could guard their possessions and secure their power in an unjust society. As a result, the people (that is, the many) were enslaved by the elite (the few), who controlled the institutions of state and government. The rich were protected from the jealousy of the many poor because they gained a monopoly over the use of violence; they controlled the state.

In his later writings, Rousseau developed a theory of an ideal, just, social contract, which was rooted in the idea of the 'Common Good'. The common good is not the good of the majority, nor is it what is good for everyone. Rather the common good is what is good for the society considered as a whole. For example, cheap housing for poor people may not be popular with the majority, if the majority is not poor. It is not good for everyone, since it implies taxes on the rich. But it may be considered part of the common good since it helps create a society that is more peaceful and harmonious. An ideal social contract, according to Rousseau, would guarantee the freedom and prosperity of everyone, including the poor. Rousseau's philosophy of individual freedom based on a social contract laid the groundwork for the dominant political philosophy of our time, that is, liberalism. Nevertheless, Rousseau never escaped the basic assumption of his teacher, Hobbes, that government must be based on violence. Governments must use violence to enforce order, maintain stability and protect the common good. Thinkers as diverse as Voltaire, Machiavelli, Hegel, Marx, von Clausewitz, Mao Tse Tung, Sultan Agung and Soeharto are all in agreement that power is based on violence.

Varieties of Power in Society

In my opinion, this dominant paradigm of power needs to be questioned. Is power really the same as domination? What do we mean by power? Is there only one kind of power, or should we rather think of many kinds of power? I would like to suggest a simple definition of power: *power is the ability of a people to act together and achieve their goals.* According to this definition, the meaning of power depends on what goals the people have and the context and difficulties they face in reaching their goals. For example, the power of a Balinese farmer, who wants to reap a good harvest, depends on his ability to work together with other farmers to manage the irrigation system for his terraced fields. He/she must be wise in knowing many things, including where he fits within the social organization that determines the flow of water, when to plant, how to read the weather, how to control pests, how to conserve the condition of the soil, what technology is cost effective and so on.

In contrast, the power of an artist depends on things like inspiration, technical skill, concentration and participation in an artistic community of discourse in which his art contributes something unique. The power of a pilot, an engineer, a religious leader, a neighbourhood organizer, a soldier, a king, a husband or wife, a doctor, a pedicab driver, a business executive, a street food seller, an anthropologist, a mystic, a teacher, a carpenter and so on, are all different. All have different goals and different abilities to reach their goals in diverse conditions.[5] Every kind of power is socially constructed, at least at the level of our ideas about it. Every kind of power depends ultimately on the relationship of humans with one another. Therefore, acting together to achieve a goal is an intrinsic element in all kinds of power. Society values and rewards different kinds of power differently. There is a hierarchy of power. But that does not mean that power that dominates with violence is the highest level of power. In some contexts, power based on violence is a reality. According to our definition, a soldier in a war, or a police chief investigating a crime, may have to master and mobilize violence in order to reach some collective aims.

During the years of transition and chaos in Indonesia, violence sometimes seemed like an effective tool for establishing power. If the government, or the military, monopolize the technologies of violence and is willing to use horrific violence, they will indeed dominate the people. The US apparently believed this implicitly in their attack against Iraq. They used overwhelming violence and dominated a whole country. But we may rightly ask whether power is the same as domination? The US military dominated Iraq with violence, but it is increasingly clear that the goals of the invasion were not achieved.

Hannah Arendt questions the predominant tradition that does not distinguish *power* from *violence*. Most writers also do not clearly distinguish the meanings of: *strength, force* and *authority* (Arendt 1970: 44–45). The confusion of meanings, according to Arendt, stems from the belief that there is only one political question that is ultimately important, that is, 'who rules over whom?' If this is the only question that really matters, then words like power, strength, force, authority and violence, are all seen as just means or tools for determining who becomes the ruler and who has to follow. The difference between these concepts is not important because they all have the same function. They are all just tools for domination. However, if the goal of politics is not reduced to the question of who gets to dominate all the rest, then the difference between these words becomes very important.

Power as the People's Ability to Reach Their Goals

If we discuss the concept of power in the field of politics, without assuming that politics is primarily about who dominates whom, we may ask, what is the purpose of political power? Politics is indeed about political power. But power is not the possession of one person or a small elite. It is focused on the question, 'how may we organize and regulate the people for the sake of the common good?' From this standpoint, the question of who dominates whom is subsidiary to the question of how the people in a society can reach their goals. For example, we may say that a society is powerful if they are able to reach their goals of living together in peace, justice, prosperity and harmony. Or in Indonesia we might say that Indonesia is powerful if together the country can really live up to the ideals of *Pancasila* rather than just using them as a convenient ideology to mask oppression and corruption.[6] Conversely, a society is not powerful if the people cannot reach goals that are for the common good. A powerful government is one that can lead the people to reach their goals. Government is a tool of the people to reach their goals. In other words, a government is not powerful by virtue of domination, but rather by virtue of its ability to achieve the goals of government. Government is not powerful in and of itself. Rather, it is meant to be a means for empowering the people.

Hannah Arendt suggests that power should be defined as the ability of society to act together in concert. Arendt argues that power is not possessed by the leader, but is rather owned by the people. Power may be delegated from the people to a leader to act in their name. But power still originates in the people and is dependent on the people. If a leader is not authorized by the people, then the leader's authority is open to question. Their power will decrease. Such a leader will find difficulty getting the people to act together. Therefore, power is different from strength or force.

Arendt's theory is an improvement over the traditional conceptions of power as domination or violence, however in my opinion, the ability of a people to act together is insufficient as a definition of power. Many societies, or groups of people, act together, but have no power to achieve their goals. In fact corporate action may lead to the destruction of a society. Social movements may be powerful or weak, creative or destructive. Sometimes the people act and the result is disastrous, far from the ideals and hopes with which they started. People who act together but do not reach their goals cannot be said to be powerful. It might be better to call them impotent. Power is the ability to reach your goals. Sometimes power calls for concerted action together in a certain direction. But at other times, power may call for quietness and stillness—the ability not to act, but the patience to wait for the right time. Powerful people are able to wait in quietness rather than panic. They are able to control themselves and be patient in a time of trial. But they also are able to act decisively when the time is right.

Good leaders, have power along with the people. They guide the actions of society and regulate social movements so that the people (and the government) reach their goals. This definition of power should not be mistaken as a normative definition based on ethical values rather than political reality. Sometimes governments and societies act together and reach their goals. They are very powerful, but the goals they reach are morally despicable, or at best, short sighted. Perhaps Bush succeeded in convincing the American people to act in concert to bring down Saddam Hussein. America and its government acted together and reached their goal, but the broader long-term results were disastrous. Similarly, the Soeharto regime may be termed extremely powerful, not because of their skill in dominating the people, or staying in 'in power' for 32 years, but because for many years they received popular legitimacy from the people because of the apparent success of their economic policies. The majority of the people of Indonesia were willing to accept an authoritarian government as long as their goals of economic growth, increasing prosperity and basic safety were fulfilled.

However, in the long run, the people were increasingly distressed by government policies that disregarded their will and resorted to violence and domination to solve every problem. In my opinion the economic collapse, including the collapse of the currency, was triggered by the political crisis of legitimacy after Soeharto forced one term of office too many on the long suffering people. At last, the people acted together with one goal that was very clear: to remove Soeharto from power. Some will say that Soeharto fell because the military withdrew its support. True, but the military withdrew its support because the whole nation had already risen up in revolt. Even the military could not risk the bloodbath that was looming if Soeharto refused to step down. In the end, the power of the people in Indonesia was much stronger than the power of the 'New Order' government.

A theory of power as located in the people is not necessarily in tension with the idea that power comes from God. From a theological standpoint, the power of the people to achieve their goals may well be viewed as coming from God. At the time of Soeharto's fall, I remember my surprise at seeing some Latin graffiti scrawled on a wall in Yogyakarta: 'Vox populi, vox Dei' ('The voice of the people is the voice of God'). Perhaps only in the university town of Yogya could you see Latin graffiti scrawled on the walls. While I do not necessarily agree with this ancient formula, it at least illustrates that there is no inherent conflict between locating power in the people and saying that power comes from God. In fact, locating power in the people may be more theologically respectable than equating power with violence. Only God can help the people achieve their legitimate goals. Domination and oppression, on the other hand, are not from God but rather from greed and human evil. The power that originates in God is located in the people. In contrast, God does not give power to governments except through the people.[7] Theological language is different from political language, but is not necessarily in conflict.

Some critics will reject the idea of power located in the people because it appears to mix realistic description with moral values. Niccolo Machiavelli is sometimes described as the first political scientist because he describes political behaviour as it really is, rather than continuing the ancient tradition of expounding a philosophy or theology of ideal politics.[8] Social analysis needs to describe the empirical realities of politics, and not just theoretical ideals. In my opinion, this is a misleading, Cartesian dichotomy. All description is value laden. Machiavelli describes the pathology of bad politics in sixteenth-century Italy, as if it were normative, rather than describing supposedly general 'laws' of politics. Machiavelli's analysis is also informed by moral judgements, but they are mistaken moral judgements. He assumes that the people are always evil and that the only goal of the King should be to increase his domination through violence and deceit. As a result, Machiavelli, and the Duke that he advised, ended up a failure, hated by his people.

Empirical descriptions of politics cannot be divorced from moral values about the goals and means of political power. Nevertheless, it must be admitted that there is a lot of political behaviour, in Indonesia and elsewhere, which seems closer to Machiavelli's description of power than mine. A paradigm of power from below does not claim that people do not use violence and deceit to protect or extend their spheres of domination. Rather, I argue that violence and domination are not the same as power and do not really change the world in which we live. Real power is creative rather than destructive. The question is not about which definition of power is 'true' or 'realistic', but rather which definition leads to a more profound understanding of power in the context of Indonesian politics in the 21st century.

Individual and Corporate Strength as Elements of Power

According to Arendt's theory, *strength* is different from power. An individual possesses strength, while power is social. A person's strength may be proved in relation to someone else, but does not depend on anyone else. Arendt defines *force* as a kind of energy that may be released by a social movement (for example, a revolution) or by nature (for example, an earthquake). *Authority* is the most difficult concept to define, according to Arendt. Authority may be either connected to a structural position or office (for example, the office of president), or it may be connected with the character of a particular individual (for example, Mahatma Gandhi). In some cases authority is linked to both character and position (for example, President Nelson Mandela). A person with authority is honoured and obeyed by other people, just because of their authority. Force, coercion, or even persuasion is unnecessary. If a person of authority tries to coerce or persuade his/her followers to obey, she will probably lose some of her authority. *Violence* is different from power, strength, force, or authority. Arendt says that violence magnifies the strength of a person by using weapons or tools intended to cause pain and suffering. Violence is closely connected with domination. Modern nation-states monopolize the tools of violence through the police and military. Therefore, the state is expert in using violence to force the people into submission. Nevertheless, Arendt argues that violence is not the same as power.

Arendt's explanation of the differences between power, strength, force, authority and violence is very helpful. However, her definitions are open to criticism, especially if compared with similar terms in Indonesian that have different nuances. For example, I agree that strength (*kekuatan*), is different from power (*kekuasaan*), but strength need not be thought of as just the possession of an individual. In Indonesian, *kekuatan* (strength) may be either individual or social. For example, a hunter may be physically strong, but he will become even stronger as a hunter if he can convince others to cooperate in a hunting expedition. As a group, their strength is multiplied. But they may still not be powerful if they lack one or more of the essential skills necessary to reach their goals. Unfortunately, Arendt's theory does not discuss supernatural power such as *kesaktian* that assumes that there are unseen spiritual elements in power. Most Indonesians assume that any major struggle involves unseen forces that are beyond human control. Discussion of spiritual elements in power is still a taboo in Western social science and philosophy, but that is no reason why we must assume they do not exist.

Indonesian anthropologist, Koentjaraningrat, assumes both an individual and a corporate meaning for the idea of strength. Koentjaraningrat distinguishes between 'special powers' (similar to Arendt's definition of strength) and 'power with a broad meaning' (Koentjaraningrat 1984: 140). Special powers or strength may include just an individual's strength or may include his/her ability to organize many people and motivate them through a system of sanctions. Koentjaraningrat argues that strength (both individual and social), is just one of the factors that contributes to a leader's power. Other elements of power include authority (*wibawa*), responsibility/legitimacy (*wewenang*), magical powers (*kesaktian*) and charisma (*karisma*). Koentjaraningrat's approach to the social evolution of power is interesting. It is more comprehensive and convincing than Anderson's ideal types that dichotomize supernatural or spiritual conceptions from 'rational', material conceptions. It is helpful to conceptualize power as supported by various 'gifts' such as strength. Unfortunately, Koentjaraningrat, like most writers, only pays attention to the kind of power wielded by leaders and shows little awareness of the power that is located in the people.

If power is located in the people, then the people may delegate power to leaders. Power flows from the society to its leaders, and not vice versa. Good leaders can and should empower their people. But it is easier for a powerful people to produce good leaders than it is for powerful leaders to produce a good society. In Indonesia, most people believe in the converse. Indonesian society is thought to be in crisis because there are no great leaders. People are waiting for the Just Ruler (*Ratu Adil*), who will come and restore the people to virtue and prosperity. The Just Ruler will ensure the well-being of the whole cosmos by mediating God's power to the people. In fact just the opposite needs to happen. God gives power to the people who then channel that power to the leaders of their choice. The power of the leaders comes from the power of the people.

A weak society allows a corrupt leader to flourish. In some sense, the people deserve the leader they have.[9] To wait passively for a good leader to fix everything is futile.

A good leader can inspire people to work together effectively to reach their common goals. Part of the wild hope that accompanied the election of Barak Obama in the USA, might be a completely unrealistic expectation that one new leader can overcome all the ills of the world. However, it may also stem from his remarkable ability to unify different people to work for the same goals. If Obama succeeds, it may not be because of the wisdom of his policies, but because he inspired new and unprecedented kinds of cooperation, not just within the USA, but also between nations.

This viewpoint on power contradicts ancient theories of power, both in the West and in Indonesia, namely, that power comes directly from God to the king, who is God's Viceroy or *Kalifah*. According to democratic theory, the ruler is not the viceroy or *Kalifah* of God, but the representative of the people. According to the Al Qur'an, all the people are God's *Kalifah* on earth. The Sultan may claim to be the supreme *Kalifah*, but if that is so, it is because he is given that responsibility from the people. Unfortunately this idea contradicts the assumption of many Indonesians who believe that the people are powerless to change anything unless a Just Ruler shows them the way. There are many people capable of being just rulers in Indonesia. It is up to the people to choose them and reject the many scoundrels that continually jockey for power. However, even choosing a good leader is not enough. The people also have to empower the leader. Fortunately, the Constitution of the Republic of Indonesia (UUD 1945 RI), supports the idea that power lies within the people. The foundation of national law is that sovereignty belongs to the people. Sovereignty means power. The people of Indonesia are responsible for creating a just government that will exercise the power of the people on behalf of the common good.

Violence Destroys Power

Power, strength and violence are often interwoven with each other in the actions of political leaders. They are difficult to separate from each other. Because of this, we are tempted to think that power is measured by the government's ability to enforce obedience through strength, force and violence. However, in reality, violence destroys power. Violence diminishes both the authority of the leaders and the unity of the people.

Violence may indeed strengthen the domination of a tyrant. But domination is not power. Violence can subjugate, hurt and even destroy the people's power. But violence cannot empower either the people or their leaders. The more the leaders use violence, the more powerless the people feel. Arendt explains that, 'Violence can always destroy power; out of the barrel of a gun grows the most effective command, resulting in the most instant and perfect obedience. What never can grow out of it is power' (Arendt 1970: 53. Cf Mao Tse Tung's famous dictum: 'power grows out of the barrel of a gun').

Hannah Arendt's reflections on the destructive effects of violence are a good antidote to the common equation of violence with power. However, it is equally true that violence may stimulate the growth of power in the people. State sponsored violence often provokes resistance. Resistance multiplies the strength of the people to oppose their rulers. At the very moment when the people feel most dominated and powerless before their government's use of violence, there may come a dramatic decrease in the government's power and an increase in the people's power. From a superficial standpoint it seems like the government is all powerful because the people are afraid of the government's monopoly on violence. However, at that very moment unseen forces are unleashed by the violence that may lead to the failure of the government. From the standpoint of strength and ability to use violence, the government is always much stronger than the people. But the power of the government is still dependent upon the people. Violence weakens the power of both the people and the state. Violence creates fear and hatred. A spiral of violence and revenge increasingly destroys the ability of the government and the people to reach their goals.

Before Soeharto was forced out of office in May 1998, the people of Indonesia experienced more and more incidents of state-sponsored violence, apparently designed to defend the New Order government against its opponents. Ironically, the more the government used violence against the people, including kidnapping, torture and extra judicial executions, the more the people rebelled and the weaker the government became. Violence was met with violence and both the government and the people seemed powerless to stop the spiral of bloodshed. The country seemed headed for either a one sided slaughter or a civil war. Be that as it may, in the end it was not violence or bloodshed that forced Soeharto out of office. Rather, it was the unified action of the people, including the students, the 'little people' (*rakyat kecil*), the political elite and even the military, who finally withdrew their support for the unpopular president. On 20 May 1998, students occupied the Parliament building in Jakarta. Meanwhile, in Yogyakarta, we joined about half a million people in a peaceful demonstration demanding that Soeharto step down. The military forbade the demonstration and we did not know if a bloodbath would ensue. However, the 500,000 people on the streets of Yogyakarta that day felt their power and did not care if the soldiers came and opened fire. Soeharto could not survive this massive and peaceful rejection, even though he controlled a vast and powerful military while his opponents were unarmed. If, on the other hand, he had faced a violent coup attempt, it is quite likely that the military would have come to his defence.

A similar process can be seen in the events that led to East Timor's independence. For decades the Indonesian government used violence to pacify the people of East Timor. Thousands died, and the military dominated the lives of the people. Both sides used horrific violence, but no side was safe and neither the government nor the people could reach their goals. Both sides seemed powerless. The UN sponsored Referendum process opened up a peaceful path for the people of East Timor and the pro-independence side laid down their arms. They no longer responded to violence with violence. The anti-independence (pro-integration), East Timorese militias increased their use of violence and intimidation, with support from the military. However, the more the militias used violence, the less power they had. As the people suffered, they grew in power. If they had continued to respond to violence with violence, the Indonesian military would have probably invaded to bring 'law and order', cancelling the Referendum in the process and East Timor would still be part of Indonesia. The power to create a new nation was born in the people's willingness to suffer violence without retaliation.

I do not mean to oversimplify complex situations or imply that peaceful resistance always creates power, or that violence always fails to achieve its purpose. Every case is different and violence often appears to be an effective way to meet certain ends. However, the effectiveness of violence is certainly overrated. Life is not like a Hollywood action film where killing the bad guys ends all the problems. The American experience in Iraq is a prime example of how the use of violence often creates many more problems than it solves. In Indonesia, the government is weakest in precisely the areas of the country where the military has used the most violence. There is a direct correlation between state-sponsored violence in East Timor, Aceh, the Moluccas and West Papua and the powerlessness of the government in those same areas. Whether the powerlessness of the government caused the use of violence, or the violence caused the powerlessness, is beyond the scope of this chapter. In my opinion, both are probably true. There is a vicious circle in the dynamic between powerlessness and violence.

Bertrand de Jouvenel suggests that power may be rooted in the people, not only in democratic societies, but even more so in monarchies. He writes, 'The King, who is but one solitary individual, stands far more in need of the general support of Society than any other form of government' (de Jouvenel 1948: 98; also see Arendt 1970: 41). As early as the fourth century BC, Mencius (*Meng-tse*) asserted that the voice of the people should be considered the voice of God. Therefore, according to Mencius, if the people will not acknowledge and support the king, then he is no longer a king (Weber 1946b: 249). The idea that power lies in the people is not a modern theory dependent on democratic ideology. Nevertheless, democracy is the political system most consistent with a theory that sovereign power lies in the society. If the people are sovereign, they are also free to approve and legitimate a non-democratic government. In Yogyakarta, a rather interesting phenomenon is the popular movement to have the Sultan appointed Governor rather than elected. The Sultan is already Governor of the Special Province of Yogyakarta and no one doubts that he can easily be re-elected, since he is very popular. But both he and the institution of hereditary Sultans are so popular that the people think the governorship of this province should not be elected, but inherited by all successive Sultans. A powerful people may even legitimize a tyranny, if they so choose.

The power of a government may be legitimized through the agreement and support of the society. However, the same power is justified (or not justified), by its results in the society. A legitimate government must still pass the test of whether or not its policies empower the people, or conversely deceive and cheat them. For example, if a given society agrees together that the king should lead them to war against another society, we may say that the war was legitimized by the agreement and blessing of the people. However, after the war is over, the people may well argue that the war was not justified because its negative costs far outweighed its positive results. The people were led astray and did not achieve the results for which they hoped. The 'New Order' government of President Soeharto was legitimized, not only by the rituals of elections every five years, but also by the people's tacit acceptance of the philosophy and practices of the regime. However, ultimately, the New Order was not justified. The people just got tired of the lies, corruption and violence, and said enough is enough. Soeharto had to go.

The division and limitation of power

So far we have been speaking of power abstractly, as a single entity that is located in the people. However, power is not whole or monolithic. Rather it is divided into many different kinds of power held by different groups for different purposes. These groups are rarely unified, or united with each other, except when facing some large outside threat to them all. Even then they may not unite because they hold different goals and have different interests. They are just as likely to compete with each other as to cooperate. Each group believes that they hold the key to unlock the gate leading to the right path, for the welfare and salvation of all. Similarly, each group also seeks the welfare and prosperity of its own primordial group based on ethnicity, religion, tribe, or ideology. Each is afraid of being subjugated by another group. The basic goals of each group may be idealist and universal or egoistic and narrow. However, as often as not, they are both.

For example, one group wants to build an Indonesia that is more democratic and safe from the abuse of basic human rights. Another group believes that Indonesia should become more Islamic and obedient to the commandments of Allah in the *Syari'ah*. A third group is concerned that power is too centralized in Java and wants to overcome the tendency for wealth to flow from the outer provinces into Jakarta where it serves the interests of a small elite. They want decentralization. Another group feels that foreign investment is the key to Indonesia's economic prosperity. Therefore, they press for legislation that will liberalize trade and support the interests of big businesses. Another group represents a particular ethnic group or tribe who feel that the government has discriminated against them for too long. They want to gain access and power in the government for the sake of their tribe or province. Meanwhile, another group, representing the interests of the military, are very concerned at the erosion of their authority and honour. Above all, they want to defend the unitary integrity of the Republic of Indonesia. At the same time they want to protect the considerable economic interests of the military that provide the funds needed to carry out their job, even though the national budget for the military is so small. Another group of civil servants feel very undervalued because of their miniscule salaries. Since corruption is the only way they can get the funds necessary to meet their basic needs, they want to deflect attention from the fight against corruption while at the same time strengthening their position in the bureaucracy. Another group feels that, on the contrary, corruption is the worst problem facing Indonesia and that the elimination of corruption should be the first priority of government. This hypothetical list of competing interests could go on and on.

Even if all the people in Indonesia agreed on *Pancasila* as the national ideology (and they do not), there would still remain sharp differences between different groups based on different ideologies, goals and interests. These differences are not caused by a conflict between good and evil. They are not the result of particular evil groups (terrorists, Central Intelligence Agency—CIA—, capitalists, fanatics and so on). Every group has its own legitimate interests and goals. But each group finds it very difficult to understand the legitimate interests and goals of other groups. Each group has a particular kind of power, but is limited by the power and interests of competing groups. Power within the society is divided. In my opinion, this reality will never go away. In fact, it *should* never disappear. True democracy is not a means to eliminate differences. Rather, it is a process for the negotiation of differences in order to find a tolerable balance between different, competing interests. The unity of the nation does not require uniformity.

Under the New Order government, differences were suppressed and democracy by consensus was equated with uniformity under a single, permanent commander, Soeharto. All government structures, and many non-government structures, were used as the means for pressing the people into uniformity under the guidance of the state. Whoever or whatever stood out as different was chopped off. For example, every department in every university was forced to use the same curriculum as approved by Jakarta (Mendikbud). Similarly, every institution must agree to the same fundamental ideology of *Pancasila* (*asas tunggal*). Every religion must be tolerant, agree that Deity was One (*Ketuhanan yang Maha Esa*) and cooperate with government programmes. Every village and every tribe must support 'development' (*Pembangunan*), progress (*Kemajuan*), mutual cooperation (*Gotong Royong*) and family planning (*KB*).

In spite of the apparent success of these efforts, the uniformity achieved in the society was very shallow. After Soeharto was forced out of office, the whole society broke apart into competing factions based on tribal, religious, ethnic and ideological identities (*SARA, Suku, Agama, Ras dan Antara Golongan*). The people want a governmental structure that is more democratic, but after thirty-two years of authoritarian, patriarchal rule, find it very difficult to negotiate power between different groups that represent different values, goals and interests. The people are too used to obeying a single Commando.

Actually, the people of Indonesia are very skilled at bargaining, both as individuals and among groups. But in a nation-state as large and diverse as Indonesia, there must be very strong structures, institutions and laws that enable the people to negotiate power in safety. Since the fall of Soeharto, it has been very difficult for anyone to negotiate in safety, without the pressure of money (corruption or KKN), or the pressure of violence (either from other groups or from the military). A society that was pressured into apparent uniformity by an authoritarian government for over 30 years, is finding it difficult to negotiate differences or act on common interests. In other words, the people lack power.

Reinhold Niebuhr emphasizes the ambiguity of power and the necessity of negotiating our fundamental differences and finding a meeting place between our different prejudices. A democratic society somehow manages to, 'extract a measure of truth from our contrasting errors' (Niebuhr: 1953 14). According to Niebuhr, democracy does not only protect individual freedom, 'It provides for checks and balances upon the pretensions of men as well as upon their lust for power; it thereby prevents truth from turning into falsehood when the modicum of error in truth is not challenged and the modicum of truth in error is not rescued and cherished' (Niebuhr: 1944: 2). The assumption here is that we are all limited in our understanding of truth. We need to be confronted with contrasting perceptions. The power that exists within a society is not grounded in some natural harmony of interests, rather, in the ability to negotiate differences. Every group has great difficulty in understanding the legitimate interests of another group. In negotiation we are confronted with a will that is different from our own.

Niebuhr writes that, 'Man's capacity for justice makes democracy possible; but man's inclination to injustice makes democracy necessary' (Niebuhr 1944: xiii). The problem is not that some groups are inclined to justice, while other groups are unjust. Rather, all groups may be inclined to injustice if they have unchecked power for domination. The true power for change that exists in society lies not with any one ideal group of enlightened people, but rather in the balance between different perceptions, convictions and interests. Every group has a part of the truth and none is without error. Together, they are powerful, that is, they are capable of reaching common goals, *if* institutions that protect all of their most fundamental needs aid them. From this perspective, the most serious limitation on the power of the people in Indonesia is the lack of a strong and fair legal system. The greatest treasure in Indonesia is not the oil in Kalimantan or the gold in West Papua, but the glorious diversity of the people.

According to Reinhold Niebuhr, power must be divided because there is no one 'good enough or wise enough to be completely entrusted with the destiny of his fellow men' (Niebuhr 1953: 10). The most dangerous person, according to this strand of thought, is the idealist leader who thinks that he is the chosen one, destined to lead the people to paradise without opposition from anyone. Many a leader has started with great ideals and intentions, but as he/she becomes more and more powerful, he/she becomes more and more intolerant of any opposition. In Indonesia, this tendency is easy to see in both President Sukarno and President Soeharto. Niebuhr felt that one of the most important (and rare) qualities of a good leader is humility. According to Niebuhr, both Hitler and Stalin were idealists who believed they were capable of achieving a new level of perfection in society. Because of their idealism they did not hesitate to sacrifice millions of lives of people who seemed to stand in the way of their dream. They thought that they were the saviours of the world.

In contrast, Mahatma Gandhi is one of the best examples of a humble leader who knew his limitations. There is a story that the disciples of Gandhi once asked him what he would do, if he were given the power to change anything he wanted to change in the world; what would he choose to change? Gandhi was quiet for a very long time while his disciples waited impatiently for his answer. At last he raised his head and said simply, 'I would pray for the strength to reject that power'. Whether or not this story is apocryphal, it illustrates Gandhi's humility. Perhaps he knew that even he was not 'good enough or wise enough to be completely entrusted with the destiny of his fellow men'.

From this perspective, the division of power in society is not a difficulty to be overcome, rather it is a reality to be welcomed. The division of power prevents any particular group from achieving absolute power over another group. Lord Acton is famous for his statement 'Power corrupts and absolute power corrupts absolutely'. The truth in this cliché is generally acknowledged (at least in the modern world), because of long and bitter experience. The history of the world is full of examples of leaders, who began well, but the longer they held power, the more corrupt they became. Plato believed that the most ideal form of government was the rule of a philosopher-king. Perhaps Plato was right, at least in an ideal, abstract sense. In comparison with the rule of a just and righteous philosopher-king, democracy is a messy and inefficient political process with no guarantee of a wise policies or good governance. In fact, the rulers chosen by the people are often very disappointing.[10] Nevertheless, in democracy, bad leaders can at least be removed without bloodshed. Unfortunately, there are very few wise and just philosopher-kings in the history of the world. The few that might have been, were probably assassinated before they had time to do much. At least in a democratic division of powers, the leaders never have the chance to claim absolute power.

Some religious groups in Indonesia reject democracy and the division of powers as a Western system that is in conflict with the rule of God. According to a small minority of religious radicals, the ideal government must be based on the direct commands of God. All religions include groups of radicals or fundamentalists who believe in the unmediated revelation of God's will through their prophet. Some fundamentalists are quietist, puritanical and reject all involvement in politics. But others wish to establish a theocratic state based on *Syari'ah*, the Bible, or some other version of absolute truth. The danger of this form of thinking is not just that it ignores the diversities of interpretations that arise in all readings of scripture. What is even more serious is the tendency to use the scriptures to legitimize the absolute political power of their own group. Religion then becomes a tool for absolutizing the power of a single group in a pluralistic society. The interests and prejudices of the group are then confused with the will of God. Both religion and politics are hurt by the resulting confusion.

Political power that is based on the 'absolute will and command of God' is dangerous from two directions. First, the sacred meanings in the scriptures are transformed into a political tool to promote the interests of only a small portion of the people. Second, in the name of God, the group may justify violence to force the obedience of those who disagree. The primary victims of such an approach are often people within the same religion who follow a different method of interpretation.[11] The problem is not over whether or not religious values and convictions may enter politics. Even in the West, secularism is under increasing attack since it seems to elevate the convictions of non-religious people as somehow more rational and neutral than the convictions of religious people. We are all products of religious and philosophical traditions of thought and practice. However, one religion or one interpretation of religion should not be imposed on all, as if one group has privileged access to the one absolute truth.

The challenge we face is to find a middle path between unrealistic secularism that ignores the deep religious convictions of most of the people in the world, and the domination of politics by only one set of religious convictions in a pluralistic society. Indonesia has so far avoided either of these extremes by promoting a polyvalent commitment to the 'Great Unity of Deity' (*Ketuhanan yang Maha Esa*), that is broad enough to include the great majority of religious people in Indonesia. However, the unity promoted by this national ideology is now under severe doubt as different groups jockey to assert their more particular visions of an ideal society.

Modern, religious and cultural power in Indonesia

There are three major sets of symbol systems, institutions and practices in Indonesia that interpenetrate each other and form the conscious and unconscious identity of all Indonesians. All three symbol systems are so powerful and all pervasive that none of them can overthrow the other two or claim the exclusive allegiance of any particular group. These three networks of meaning are not necessarily incompatible with each other, but they contain many elements of incommensurability such as to generate distinctive and competing worlds of discourse. Virtually, all Indonesians live, think, feel and participate in three different conceptual worlds, which are often synthesized or integrated with each other, but just as often separated and dichotomized. Each of these frameworks of meaning has generated their own institutions, practices and structures of power. I define these three Indonesian worlds as: *Modernity, Religion* and *the Culture of the Ancestors*.

Indonesians cannot be divided into three groups: those who are modern, religious, or traditional. All Indonesians are *modern* in the sense that they are shaped by modern institutions, ideas and practices. The remotest farmer knows the exchange rate on the dollar and depends on globally determined prices, modern transportation and modern ideals of progress, education and rights. Similarly, all Indonesians are *religious*. Religious institutions, ideas and practices shape the identities and practices of all, not least of which includes those who resist the dominant trends in religion. And all Indonesians are shaped by the *culture of their ancestors*. Culture is not a static, ancient set of ideas, practices and institutions, but rather, it is an evolving, dynamic power that determines the lifestyle and perspective of all Indonesians. For example, of the three main institutions of law in Indonesia, secular, religious and *adat* (traditional law), at least in some places, the most powerful of the three is *adat*. A general definition of culture includes religion and modernity: they are part of the Indonesian culture. However, I use the term 'culture of the ancestors' to designate the language and patterns of thought that have local and ethnic continuity with the past. The relationship between these three distinct webs of meaning is a useful key for understanding how power operates in the Indonesian society.

Modernity, religion and the culture of the ancestors are centred in different definitions of community. For everyone, power is located in a community. These communities are different but overlapping. *Modernity* creates communities that may be extremely broad or extremely narrow. For example, the global marketplace creates a dominant modern community. Poor farmers in Halmahera are linked with people who wear expensive perfume in New York.[12] Modernity has tied the whole world together, not only through trade, mass media and the internet, but also through many multinational organizations that cover the whole range of human interests and needs. For example, there are sports networks like the FIFA and the IOC. There are humanitarian and social organizations like the International Red Cross, the Young Men's Christian Association (YMCA), United Nations Educational, Scientific and Cultural Organization (UNESCO), World Vision and so on. Modernity links people together for common purposes. Not all modern communities are global, like the International Monetary Fund (IMF), the World Bank, or the UN. Some are extremely local, like a small labour union or a high school chess club.

From the gigantic global to the tiny local communities, all modern communities are tied together by common interests and goals. Modern institutions are ordered more or less rationally in line with their goals. The most important modern community is the nation state. Gathered together as a nation state, Indonesian society did not exist before the twentieth century. The modern nation-state made possible new forms of power, which surpassed the powers available in feudal times. Modern power is distributed among the people, not only through governments, but also through thousands of voluntary associations that operate locally, nationally and internationally. These 'intermediate organizations' give structure to civil society and enable the people to act together not only under the guidance or coercion of the state, but also in opposition to the state. If a civil society is strong, the people will be powerful.

Religion creates a different kind of global and local community that is defined by networks of fellow believers. The community (*umat*) of a particular religion is organized in formal organizations and institutions, but also in numerous informal networks. Religions define power differently, and usually include a significant supernatural and spiritual element in their understanding of power. But religions are also very involved with mundane, modern manifestations of power. Whether its source is supernatural or natural, in either case, the power of a religious community is located in its community of believers. The congregation (*umat*) can act together with remarkable consequences. Perhaps the most dramatic recent manifestation of religious power was the Islamic revolution in Iran. Religion also played a major role in the downfall of President Marcos in the Philippines and the fall of communist regimes throughout Eastern Europe, for example, in Poland.

Usually, a single religious community is the locus of power for changes, both large and small. But religion also plays a part in forming communities of communities where different religions come together for a common purpose. The World Parliament of Religions is a prominent example, but in thousands of smaller ways, religions band together to struggle for common goals. For example, not long ago, a coalition of mostly religious non-government organizations (NGO) achieved a remarkable success in persuading the US Congress to support a movement to forgive the national debts of some of the poorest countries of the world. In Yogyakarta, where I live, there are many small interreligious groups that share their experiences and struggle together for common goals. For example, Tikar Pandan started as a gathering of political activists from different religions who where working to remove President Soeharto from office. From there it evolved into a more general group that held discussions around religious issues. Soon it became involved in staging ambitious theatrical and artistic events that drew from various religious traditions. Finally, this group held almost weekly retreats for sharing spiritual resources from the members various religious background.

From the all-encompassing perspective of modernity, religions are just one of many kinds of 'voluntary associations' that makes up civil society. But in Indonesia, religions are not considered voluntary associations that are freely chosen based on personal interests. In the language of religion, the community does not do the choosing, but considers itself chosen by God. Everyone in Indonesia is born into a religion and most of them consider their religion a major part of their personal identity.

It takes a very big crisis to induce someone to choose a religion other than the religion of their family, ethnic group and tribe. From the perspective of the ethnic cultures of Indonesia, religion is a part of culture. But the major religions in Indonesia transcend particular localities, tribes, ethnic groups and cultures. For example, on a small and remote island in Indonesia, I was once surprised to be addressed by a simple farmer whose first question to me was about my religion. Although we were very different in race, nationality, culture, economic class and education, he seemed to think I was his brother if we were of the same religion. The great religions consider themselves universal and transcendent of time and place. The movements of a religious community are not limited by rational, pragmatic goals, but are often motivated by obedience to the will of God. Power in religion is not rooted in the ties of blood (as in the culture of our ancestors) or in a social contract (as in modernity), but in practices that conform to a certain conception of the will of God.

Cultures of the ancestors are plural in Indonesia. With over 300 completely different languages and racial characteristics that cover all the colours of the human rainbow, there are many cultures of the ancestors. Indonesians may consider all Westerners (*bule*) culturally similar to each other, but they know that Indonesians are very different from one another. The culture of the ancestors of the Bataks is different from the culture of the ancestors of the Javanese, Timorese, Minangkabau, Moluccans and so on. Each group is distinguished by the ancient traditions of the ancestors. Nevertheless, there is also a national culture of the ancestors in Indonesia that springs from sharing a particular history together. Indonesians, consciously or unconsciously, are defined by a single grand narrative about their struggle for identity before, during and since the colonial era.

Most communities of ancestral culture are local. However, modernity has led to so much mobility that some ethnic or tribal groups are spread out throughout Indonesia and even around the world. The most prominent and far-flung ethnic group that still maintains its ancestral culture is the Chinese.[13] However, many other ethnic groups in Indonesia are also widespread, especially the Javanese, the Bataks and the people of South Sulawesi (especially the Bugis, Makasarese and Torajans). The solidarity and power of a cultural community is enhanced when located in a limited territory with a relatively homogenized population. However, a particular cultural and ethnic community may flourish and grow very strong when surrounded by a 'foreign' culture.

Cultures of the ancestors are primarily linked by land and blood. The living are connected with the dead. They are one family. I saw a vivid illustration of this in North Sumatra, where Christian Batak families gather together on Christmas day and share a picnic on top of the graves of their ancestors. They have Christmas dinner with their dead grandparents and parents. The community of culture is not limited to the living, but also includes all that went before.

The community of power in the language of Indonesian ancestral culture, is not the civil society (as in modernity), nor is it the *umat* of the faithful (as in religion), rather it is the family. The family transcends death. It is extended to the clan, the village and the tribe who are all tied to the land of their common ancestors. Not only land and blood create obligations. The community of the ancestors is also tied together by generations of gift exchange. Rituals of exchange between families within a particular tribe create obligations to one another (*hutang budi*), which are so complex, they can never be unravelled. The cultures of Indonesia believe that their ancestors are powerful. The community of culture will also be powerful if they remain true to their traditions (*adat*). Power comes from faithfulness to the culture of the ancestors.

The following chart abstracts the three major sources of power in Indonesia according to how each conceptualizes: (*a*) the location of power; (*b*) the meaning of power; (*c*) the generation of power through practices; (*d*) the structures and institutions of power; (*e*) the tools or technology of power. In table 9.1, the key words are underlined. Of course this is a model, or typology, that is not meant as a literal description. Power in modernity, religion and the culture of the ancestors is much more complex and overlapping than this table suggests. Nevertheless, the simplicity of a model/table helps conceptualize the meaning of power in Indonesia today. The conceptions in the chart are weighted towards Islam and Christianity because they are the communities I am most familiar within Indonesia.

Conclusion

The table summarizes what I have tried to outline in this chapter. First, I have argued that the polarization of Javanese and Western (or traditional and modern) conceptions of power, is untenable and misleading. Nevertheless, the dichotomy between Java and the West is helpful insofar as it clarifies elements in Indonesian concepts of power that

Table 9.1 Power in modernity, religion and culture of the ancestors

	Ancestral culture	Religion	Modernity
1. Power is located in:			
a. Community	a. Family, clan, neighbourhood, tribe, village, ethnic group, common land	a. Umat Allah (the religious community, local, national, global) Religious institutions	a. Society, nation-state, civil society, cities, local, national and international organizations
b. Its leaders	b. Head of adat, shaman (dukun), ancestors, spirits, tribal leaders	b. God, Prophet, Ulama, Kiyai, priest, minister, spiritual leaders, theologians	b. Politicians, executives, generals, professionals, intellectuals, students
2. Meaning of power:			
a. Goals of power	a. Harmony, peace, safety, balance, tranquility	a. Will and glory of God, salvation, liberation, submission, love	a. Happiness, freedom, progress, success, riches, knowledge
b. Basis of solidarity	b. Blood, ancestors, relatedness, adat, obligations, language	b. Faith, calling, fate, worship together, tradition	b. Social contract, individual human rights, nationalism
c. Ethics	c. Cooperation, adat, rules, sincerity, honour, without self-interest, hierarchy	c. Submission, love, ministry/service to God, Umat and world, piety, faithfulness	c. Human rights, hard work, justice, efficiency, honesty, freedom, democracy, nationalism
d. Epistemology (source of knowledge)	d. Adat rules, spirits, stories, intuition, rituals, dreams	d. Scripture, preaching, ritual, interpretation, revelation, tradition	d. Scientific knowledge, empiricism, rationality, interpretation, aesthetics
3. Generation of power through practices	Rituals, gift exchange, ascetic disciplines (tapa), art, meditation, magic, consensus, war, cooperation	Sholat/worship, prayer, fasting, preaching, social ministry, pilgrimages, struggle against evil (jihad)	Rational methods bureaucracy, plans, organization, research, elections, technology, media, information
4. Structures of power			
a. Institutions	a. Adat law, Shaman, Communal consultation, council of elders, gurus, artistic associations	a. Mass organizations (NU/Muhammadiyah), churches, mosques, educational institutions, NGOs, political parties, national and International organizations (MUI)	a. Government, Bureaucracy, Military Courts, Voluntary Associations, MNC's Media, Universities, Political Parties
b. Legitimacy	b. Consensus, patriarchal honour, magic, charisma	b. Scripture, tradition, religious hierarchy Kiyai/Pastor/Pendeta	b. Law, money, elections, ideology, international organizations
c. Justification	c. Appropriateness (Cocok), consensus	c. Truth, authorization	c. Pragmatic, legal, legitimate, scientific
5. Tools and technologies of strength and power	Ritual, ascetics (tapa), magical/holy objects or places, mantras, grave yards, trance, visions	Scripture, fatwa, mission/dakwa, moral movements education, social criticism, Miracles, international network	Computer, information and communication technology, money, institutions, military technology, media scientific methods

are often neglected or ignored in Western social science. Second, the classic, almost universal paradigm of power as domination based on violence generates more misunderstanding than clarity. Power is very diverse and distributed in different ways among the people. Power is not primarily the possession of a small elite, but is located in the people. Power is the ability of the people to act together to achieve their aims. Powerlessness is the inability to initiate real change in human social reality. Third, power that is located in the people is described differently in different contexts in Indonesia. The culture of the ancestors, religion and modernity use different languages and symbols to conceptualize different practices of power. There is a dialectical interaction between each of these networks of meaning and the practices, institutions and stories of which they partake. These three different networks of power in Indonesia are overlapping and complimentary, but also competing and contradictory. All Indonesians are modern, religious people, who are formed by the cultures of their ancestors.

Social change in Indonesia is all pervasive and bewildering. But social change should not be mistaken for progress, nor equated with an evolution from a 'primitive' traditional society to a modern, rational society. Modernity, as we have described, is neither new nor 'higher' than religion or the culture of the ancestors. Indonesia has been influenced by all three of these forces for a very long time, and none of them are going to disappear in the near future. Each of them provides unique resources, both for generating power and for describing it. Many of the conflicts in Indonesia are related to different, conflicting accounts about how to live with and affirm all three. Or conversely, how to limit and prevent the domination of any one of them. Indonesia is on an exciting and dangerous journey, the outcome of which is still wide open.

A few years ago I was travelling on the island of Sumba in Eastern Indonesia. We were travelling by motorbike, far from paved roads or signs of modernity. For eight hours, I never saw an automobile and only one other motorcycle. Suddenly, I saw an amazing grave by the side of the path. The bottom of the grave was erected from huge monolithic stones, like a scaled down Stonehenge. This was a familiar sight, since Sumba graveyards that follow the tribal religion (Marapu), are famous for their ancient stone monoliths. What was surprising was that on top of the cross stone, someone had fashioned an airplane out of cement. Most amazing of all was that on top of the airplane stood a statue of the

Virgin Mary! Perhaps the people in this remote village were confused about the alternative sources of power now being offered. They wanted to be sure that their dead ancestor would truly be able to reach heaven. In keeping with the culture and religion of their ancestors, they erected a traditional stone grave and performed all the necessary rituals. In keeping with modernity, they used a new material to construct a symbol of flight to the heavens. In keeping with the religion of Catholicism, they erected a statue of the Virgin Mary. With so many different symbols of power, let us hope that their departed relative reached his final destination in safety.

Notes

1. This is an over generalization. Power as domination and violence may indeed change the world, but not necessarily in the ways intended by the powerful. Former United States (US) President, George W. Bush, seemed to think that domination and violence could be used to secure the safety of the USA. Instead it led to increasing insecurity and renewed terror all over the world. In contrast, current President Barak Obama appears to hold a much stronger paradigm of power through cooperation.
2. My translation of his footnote in Indonesian. This is an Indonesian translation of his article by someone else, but he wrote the footnote quoted.
3. Koentjaraningrat gives a description of concepts of power during a period of transition between ancient and modern cultures. His description is much more accurate and balanced than Anderson's theory. But Anderson's theory is much more interesting. Anderson's article is classic because it stimulates so many ideas and provides a new way of looking at the phenomenon of power in Indonesia.
4. In the movie *Schindler's List*, the Head of one of the Nazi death camps takes pleasure in randomly shooting Jews because it makes him feel powerful. In the story, Schindler tried to moderate the Commandant's brutality by convincing him that making a decision to forgive a Jew and not execute him, is a sign of much greater power. Unfortunately, the Nazi officer had limited success with his attempts to be powerful in forgiveness. In a telling scene, the brutal Nazi attempts to forgive the image of himself in a mirror. Unable to forgive himself, he goes back to killing Jews. In the context of this movie (and the true story it relates), Schindler is right. The power to save a life is far more meaningful than the power to kill. Killing ends all the power of life, whereas saving creates the power of life. At the end of the film, hundreds of survivors, their children and grandchildren, all pay tribute to Schindler, the powerful man who changed the world by creating a future for them all.

5. This conception of power is similar to Aristotle's idea of *excellence*. See Aristotle (1952).

6. *Pancasila* (literally 'five principles') is the national ideology and the basis for the Constitution. The five principles are: The Great Unity of Deity, The Unity of the Nation, Social Justice, Democracy by Consensus, and Civilized Humanitarianism.

7. Compare Max Weber who wrote, 'The genuinely charismatic ruler is responsible precisely to those whom he rules. He is responsible for but one thing, that he personally and actually be the God-willed master.' See Weber (1946b: 249).

8. Prof. Kenneth Waltz, my professor during my doctoral program at the University of California, Berkeley, said this in a lecture on political realism in about 1980. See Niccolo Machiavelli (1952). Machiavelli was an advisor to Duke Lorenzo, from Urbino who became the king of Firenza (Florence), in the early sixteenth century. Although Machiavelli advised Lorenzo, he was remembered as an extremely bad king who had very little success or power because the people hated him. Perhaps he followed Machiavelli's advice too closely.

9. This is overstated for emphasis. 'Deserve' is a very normative term. Nobody deserves a bad leader, just like nobody deserves a bad mother or father. But unlike a bad parent, a leader can be changed if there is sufficient will in the people. Of course no one can change a bad leader by themselves.

10. I find it completely mystifying how the people of America could have chosen George W. Bush as their president.

11. *cf* the rule of *Syari'ah* in the Sudan. Many Muslims were either killed, imprisoned, or fled the country because they did not agree with the rulers who equated their interpretation of *Syari'ah* with the law of God.

12. A major product of Halmahera is copra, which is made from coconuts and exported for use in making perfume.

13. Most Chinese-Indonesians are far more like other ethnic groups in Indonesia, than they are like other Chinese in South-East Asia or China, let alone in Europe, America, or Africa. Chinese-Indonesians in America, for example, feel more solidarity with other Indonesians than they feel with Chinese-Americans or Chinese from China. Nevertheless, ethnic and cultural solidarity among all Chinese, spread out throughout the whole world is still remarkably strong. It may account for part of the discrimination they experience, since they resist total assimilation in any local culture. Chinese-Indonesians are remarkably integrated into Indonesian culture, no doubt due to their long history of living in Indonesia and Soeharto regime's strenuous policy of forced assimilation through repressing Chinese Culture.

References

Anderson, Benedict R. O'G. 1984. 'Gagasan Tentang Kekuasaan dalam Kebudayaan Jawa',(The Idea of Power in Javanese Culture) in Dalam Miriam Budiardjo (ed.), *Aneka Pemikiran Tentang Kuasa dan Wibawa*, p. 52. Jakarta: Penerbit Sinar Harapan.

———. 1990. *Language and Power: Exploring Political Cultures in Indonesia*. Ithaca: Cornell University Press.

Arendt, Hannah. 1963. *On Revolution*. New York: Viking Press.

———. 1970. *On Violence*. London: Allen Lane The Penguin Press.

Aristotle, Nicomachean. 1952. *Ethics*, translated by W.D. Ross. Chicago: Encyclopaedia Britannica.

de Jouvenel, Bertrand. 1948. *Power: The Natural History of Its Growth*. London: Hutchinson.

Hobbes, Thomas. 1952. *Leviathan*, edited by Nelle Fuller. Chicago: Encyclopaedia Britannica.

Hughes, H. Stuart. 1958. *Consciousness and Society: The Reorientation of European Social Thought, 1890–1930*. New York: Vintage Books.

Koentjaraningrat. 1984. 'Kepemimpinan dan Kekuasaan: Tradisional, Masa Kini, Resmi dan Tak Resmi', in Miriam Budiardjo (ed.), *Aneka Pemikiran Tentang Kuasa dan Wibawa*(Various Ideas about Power and Authority), Jakarta: Penerbit Sinar Harapan.

Machiavelli, Niccolo. 1952. *The Prince*, translated by W.K. Marriott. Chicago: Encyclopaedia Britannica.

Magnis-Suseno, Franz. 1984. *Etika Jawa*. Jakarta: Gramedia.

Mills, C. Wright. 1956. *The Power Elite*. New York. Quoted in Hannah Arendt. 1970. *On Violence*, p. 35. London: Allen Lane The Penguin Press.

Niebuhr, Reinhold. 1944. *The Children of Light and the Children of Darkness*. New York: Charles Scribner's Sons.

———. 1953. *Christian Realism and Political Problems*. New York: Charles Scribner's Sons.

Weber, Max. 1946 a [1919]. 'Politics as a Vocation', in H.H. Gerth and C. Wright Mills (trans. and ed.), *From Max Weber: Essays in Sociology*, p. 78. New York: Oxford University Press.

———. 1946 b. 'The Sociology of Charismatic Authority', in H.H.Gerth and C.Wright Mills (eds), *From Max Weber: Essays in Sociology*, New York: Oxford University Press, p. 249.

Social Transformation in Contemporary Korea

10

Three Prime Movers in a Contested Civil Society[1]

HAN SANG-JIN

What do we mean by social transformation?

Social transformation could mean many different things at various levels. Yet, I would like to see it largely in terms of the conflict-ridden sequential processes of democratization. For this reason, I shall begin by referring to three distinctive issues of transformation related to democratic transition. I shall then try to clarify what I mean by 'contested' civil society relying on the recent Korean experience (Sang-Jin 2005a, 2005b). This will be followed by a discussion on three prime movers, that is, the socio-structural, technological and cultural factors of transformation.

The first issue of transformation is concerned with procedural democracy. The key problem here is the extent to which procedural democracy has been consolidated in the forms of free and equal competition and election. Transformation means political transition from authoritarianism of some kinds to democracy. The evidence of this transformation can be sought by examining whether and how, as basic human rights, the freedom of expression, religion, conscience, and so on, are respected and guaranteed. The same question can be raised as to the right to free press, media and assembly as well as fair justice. We also need to take care to see carefully such representative institutions as the political party, election and Congress to make sure whether free and fair competition for power continues to be well institutionalized. The transformation towards procedural democracy is significant when we confront the harsh reality of authoritarianism repressing human rights and representative institutions.

The second issue of transformation is concerned with the economic aspect of democratization. The key problem here is not merely the political consequence of economic development but primarily the economic consequence of democratization. Here we tend to face two kinds of problem. One is how to get rid of unaccountable privileges accorded to big economic powers, like conglomerates (for instance, Jaebeol), in order to make the market function properly. This is part of a historical transformation from the authoritarian legacy. Another is the distributive aspect of democratic reform. Democracy can last long only when it can offer benefits to the people at large, particularly to those discriminated against under the authoritarian rule. A broad democratic alliance and solidarity can be formed on this basis. Yet, many countries in the world seem to have been moving in the opposite direction. In Argentina, for example, democratic regimes have suffered a great deal from foreign debts and economic disparity deeply hit by the negative consequences of globalization. This leads us to take up the points of view of social justice and economic equity in the context of globalization.

The third issue of transformation is concerned with the democratization of civil society. The key problem here is no longer the political reform of the authoritarian state but active participation by the citizens in such discursive institutions as public sphere, civic organizations and NGOs, moral and cultural traditions, ideological formations, and so on. It is an open question how to assess the role of civil society after the transition. Insofar as the civil society continued to supply huge energy for change in terms of mobilization and protest against the authoritarian rule, it was relatively easy to form democratic consensus among active citizens and the consensus proved to be very strong. After political transition, however, in other words, when political democracy regained its strength, civil society tended to become a contested space among various orientations and ideologies, including the reactionary ones. The effect of the taken-for-granted habits, customs, conventions and norms cuts deep into human subjectivity, serving as the symbolic basis of an invisible micro-power in everyday life. It is, thus, of crucial importance to examine the patterns of social conflicts and cleavages manifested in this process together with the question of whether—or not—and if so, to what extent is the civil society able to maintain a stable order and thereby foster further democratization through rational discourse and consultation. Seen in this way, there is no doubt that the ability of the civil society to present open communication and discourse is important for the advancement of democratization.

Civil society as a contested space: The Korean experience

The relationship between the state and the civil society tends to vary, depending on the phase of democratization. When bureaucratic authoritarianism prevails, it is likely that the state reigns over the civil society with its repressive apparatus. During democratic transition, however, the civil society brings forth its resistant energy through various social movements. When authoritarian rule is on the skids and political democracy is restored, the relationship between the state and the civil society becomes fluid. By 'fluid' I mean that the civil society can be seen as a bulwark of the Establishment, as Gramsci sensitized us, or as a 'sluice' through which the pressure of change is passed to the political system as Habermas showed. This actually means that the civil society tends to become a contested space after the period of political transition.

In retrospect, many experts sought the energy of change in the civil society when democratization started in South Europe in the mid-1970s and later spread over to Latin America, East Europe and Asia. All the repressions against the freedom of expression, speech, assembly, and so on, were seen as deeply associated with the authoritarian state. Accordingly, the civil society was deemed as a reserve of energy for democracy.

However, this chapter aims to analyze the changing nature of the civil society. As implied by Gramsci's concept of 'war of position', democratic transfer of the political power is not enough. Particularly noteworthy in this connection is that the civil society, which embraces class structure, mass media, ideology and public sentiment, can constitute serious obstacles to substantive democracy. This appears more likely in countries where a radical rupture with the past seems to be impractical since those who have rejoiced in their vested interests as beneficiaries of modernization still exercise strong influence in the civil society. Moreover, after political transition, various elements hidden behind the repressive state apparatus such as power-oriented private connections, collective egotism and conservative mentalities begin to come forth. The civil society then becomes more heterogeneous than pro-democratic movements. Rather, it shows self-conflicting aspects in terms of ideologies, emotion and social movements. In other words, uncertainty and fluidity increase, increasingly making the civil society a contested space.

This is well documented by Korean experiences. Korea may represent a sequentially progressive model of democratic transition backed by the large middle class which has been formed as a consequence of the rapid economic development (Sang-Jin 2001a). The continually ongoing transition can be easily confirmed when we examine the results of the last four presidential elections (1987, 1992, 1997 and 2002). In the first elections in 1987, the candidate with the military background won mainly due to the rivalry of the two civilian leaders. But the election in 1992 gave rise to a civilian president after 32 years of military rule and this was followed by the first peaceful transfer of power from the ruling to the opposition party in 1997, thereby firmly rooting procedural democracy in the soil of Korean politics. Furthermore, in the election of 2002, citizens' power manifested itself in an impressive way never imagined before, that is, through the massive voluntary campaign and mobilization by young people through the internet, thereby facilitating the transfer of power from the older to the younger generation. The general elections in April 2004 further accelerated this trend by giving majority seats to the reform-oriented ruling party. This generational shift of power has been made possible largely by the sweeping IT-revolution and internet communication for which Korea has earned the reputation of a forerunner in the world.

More specifically, the Korean experience can be examined by the historical turning point in 1987. The preceding fifteen years had witnessed the typical bureaucratic authoritarian regime whose historic origins might be traced back to the Japanese colonial rule during the first half of the twentieth century. But the authoritarian state had its rise in the military coup in 1961 and was consolidated by President Park Chung-Hee within the institutional framework of *Yushin* in October 1972. This regime had two seemingly conflicting pursuits: maintaining a highly repressive system and building a strong and prosperous nation through a growth- and export-oriented economy. Consequently, presidential and general elections were disrupted, and public opinion was distorted. In short, procedural political democracy was destroyed. The Congress and political parties were driven into the political margin and the intelligence agencies dominated by the military exercised tight control over the civil society. Dissidents had to suffer from brutal persecution and punishment. National security and anti-communist ideology were placed before anything else. Citizens were forced to be silent. Yet, it must be noted that in collaboration with security/military officers as well as economic conglomerates that grew under the protection of the government, economic planners and bureaucrats also played an important role for the sustained economic growth.

For another fifteen years or so after 1987, Korea went through a period of democratization, during which there were four presidential elections. Perhaps, the most significant of those was that of 1997 since the political power was transferred from the ruling to the opposition party for the first time in history, giving rise to the Kim Dae-Jung government. The political development since then seems to assure the firm establishment of procedural democracy. Civic organizations and various NGOs have also made impressive advancements.

In the past, however, the state power and the establishment have long colluded to serve the vested interests of the powerful. Only as democratization proceeded did a few signs of change began to be felt among the people and political circles. A good case in point is President Kim's effort to redress social and political cleavages together with his reform policies aimed at the basic rights to life for the poor, women's participation in the labour market and the politics of engagement for inter-Korean reconciliation and cooperation. It is well known that President Kim had to put in all his energies to the imminent task of managing the economic crisis even before he took office. Yet, ironically, this crisis unexpectedly opened-up a broad road towards socio-economic structural reforms in Korea. Otherwise, this reform might have turned out as difficult as in Japan. Consequently, global standards were introduced with almost negligible resistance and applied to economic conglomerates and banks, among others, to remove unaccountable privileges accorded to them. In this way, the problematic fusion between the authoritarian government and corporates began to be dismantled. At the same time, the democratic regime faced the urgent need to improve the legal institutions of social security and welfare to tackle the burning issues of unemployment and the urban poor.

Despite this differentiation between the state power and the establishment, however, due to the fact that the former represented only a minority government, the reforms faced intransigent resistance by the powerful complexes of the establishment which mobilized various resources. This raises an important question of how to see, on one hand, the relationship between the formal and official circuit of power working at the level of the government and on the other hand, the informal and substantive circuit of power working through various connections to regional and ideological cleavages in support of the establishment (Sang-Jin 2005c).

Seen in this historical context, the presidential elections in 2002 were profoundly meaningful since the younger generation launched massive campaigns to support political reforms. It was the first time that they emerged as a decisively important political force which was well unified and with a common identity. They were capable of struggling against the conservative media, culture and society because they possessed a new technology of communication, namely, the internet. They supported Rho Mu-Hyun who represented nothing more than a small minority but strongly advocated political reform. Rho aligned with Chung Mong-Joon a symbol of the wealthy Hyundai family. When Chung announced his intention to withdraw his support to Rho late in the night just before the polling day, Rho seemed to have no hope. However, a surprisingly intensive, massive and voluntary communication and mobilization of young people by means of the internet and mobile phones took place on the polling day across the country and finally, Rho won the elections.

Furthermore, things evolved through the general elections in April 2004. Profoundly shocked by the impeachment of the president by the conservative opposition parties that occupied more than two-thirds of the seats in the Congress, the younger generation united again to protest against the power of the Congress. They saw the imminent danger of democracy in the parliamentary decision against the popular will and were thus deeply mobilized as in the presidential elections in 2002. This turned out to be consequential since the ruling party finally got more than half the seats in the national assembly. This meant that the conservative opposition parties lost not only the presidential elections twice but also the controlling power in the national assembly.

This steady advancement in political democratization as well as the socio-structural change to which I shall soon refer to, seem to have given rise to a sharp balance of power today between the conservatives and the progressives, and between the national orientation and global orientation in Korea. Figure 10.1 shows the normal pattern of the distribution of the conservative–progressive orientations in terms of subjective identification, whereas Figure 10.2 demonstrates the same pattern of the national–global orientations.[2] Furthermore, the cross-analysis

Figure 10.1 Distribution of ideological orientations

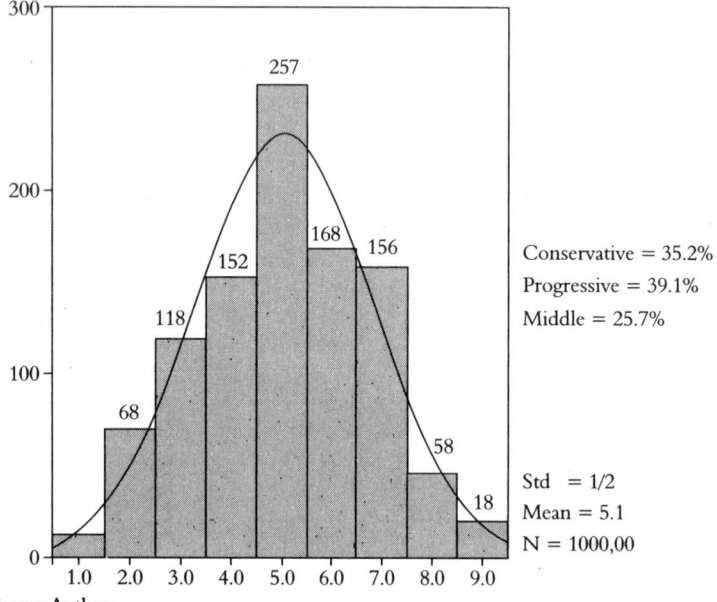

Conservative = 35.2%
Progressive = 39.1%
Middle = 25.7%

Std = 1/2
Mean = 5.1
N = 1000,00

Source: Author.

Figure 10.2 Nationalism versus globalism

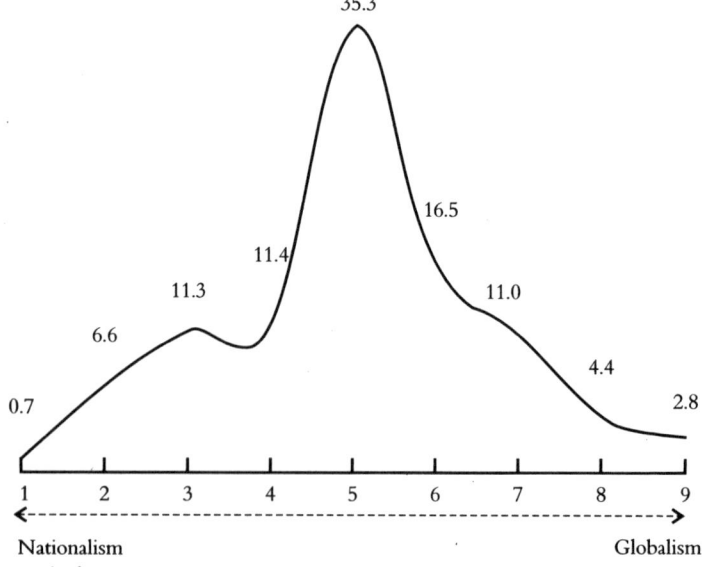

Nationalism   Globalism

Source: Author.

of these two axes of development (Figures 10.3 and 10.4) reveals the surprising fact that the more one sees himself/herself as progressively oriented, the more one prefers the global orientation to the nationalist one, independent of basic variables such as age, education, income, residence, and so on. This is the very opposite of the taken-for-granted assumption in the past, since the progressive has long been seen as deeply inclined to nationalist, not global, orientations. It becomes unmistakably evident as to how deeply and speedily the Korean civil society has been changing up to a point, where we can talk about a sharply contesting, yet structurally balanced civil society.

Sociological mover

Having said so, I would like to identify three prime movers in the contested civil society, which are influential in shaping the pattern of social transformation. They are:

(*i*) the expanded role of the reform-oriented middle class as the major actor of social transformation,
(*ii*) the internet as an alternative communication tool, and
(*iii*) the post-conventional logic of cultural change.

Figure 10.3 Conservative/progressive and nationalism/globalism

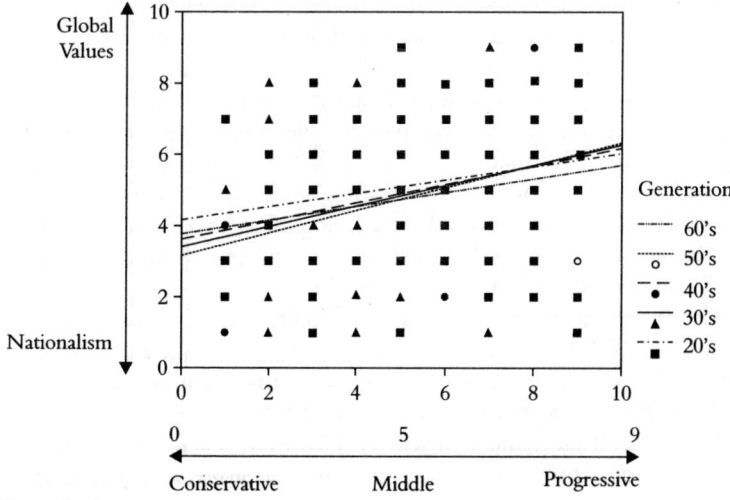

Source: Author.

Figure 10.4 Two axes of value orientation by education

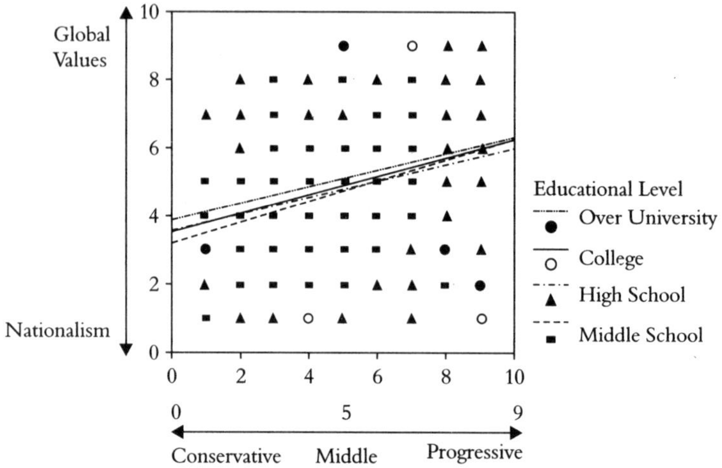

Source: Author.

The first refers to the sociological or socio-structural mover operating in the contested civil society. Social transformation may then be explained by identifying the major actor in support of reform, which means that a certain segment of the middle class is capable of challenging and changing the establishment. The second refers to the technological mover, which is important with respect to the mode of social communication. The synergy effect will be great, particularly when these sociological and technological conditions are combined. The third refers to the cultural mover demanding a discursive testing of the taken-for-granted assumptions and attitudes. The globalization of communication and information tends to intrinsically foster this process of discursive testing. If we consider these three movers operating in the civil society, it will become clear that the recent candlelight marches in Korea, for example, are not simply a display of anti-American sentiment but a new moral development supported by sociological as well as technological conditions. This implies that there is a rational and systematic ground for social transformation underway in Korea.

Of the three prime movers mentioned, let me first examine the sociological one. The key question is about the major actors leading the civil society. To make it simple, one may say that during the authoritarian rule, with economic prosperity, the conservative middle class was most influential in leading the civil society. However, this is no longer evident today as before. On the contrary, one can argue quite reasonably that the reform-oriented middle class has grown significantly in number and it is, at least, as influential as the conservative one today. In this respect, I would like to pay attention to the characteristics of those who led the nation's democratization movement in the 1980s.[3] Now in their thirties and early forties, they have become the mainstay of society, leading the IT-related industries as well as many other areas. With their devotion and struggle, they have upheld the nation's democracy in the 1980s and the 1990s, and laid a solid foundation for the tradition of civil participation (Sang-Jin 1997). Many of Korea's largest NGOs have been formed and led by them. Moreover, they have spearheaded the nation's booming venture industry related to the information technology revolution. They have also been actively involved in the politically significant net activism.

In-depth analyses show plenty of interesting phenomena (Sang-Jin 2001b). First, as they grew up and reached maturity in the midst of a culture of political protest in the 1980s, they maintained and shared a collective identity as a reform-oriented social force. Second, they understood themselves as part of the 'people' or 'grassroots', rather than as part of the establishment. Third, they tended to see history and society in their keen attention to the rights and welfare of the common people, rather than merely propping up the interests of a handful of the power elite. Fourth, they were able to better understand—through their broad social vision—the situation facing such social minorities as women, foreign labourers, the handicapped, the poor, prisoners, the homosexuals, the North Korean defectors and the socialists. They tried to embrace those minorities instead of excluding them. Fifth, they were able to maintain a sense of their national sovereignty in contrast to adopting subservient attitudes towards powerful states. Sixth, they showed their support and respect to leaders who would rather live up to principles than surrender to unjustifiable and unacceptable compromises. Seventh, they were in favour of structural reforms in accordance with global standards rather than clinging to parochialism and national preoccupation.

An interesting hypothesis in this regard concerns the formation of a distinctive middle class, which I have called the 'middling grassroots', which in Korean is *Joongmin*. Simply put, the middling grassroots are those who are part of the middle classes objectively, yet distinctive in that they hold their identity as part of the 'people', not the 'power bloc'. As professionals, for example, they are inclined to be involved in articulating the issues worthy to be discussed publicly in a way that challenges the given power constellations. They differ significantly from those middle classes that are contained within the establishment without developing a popular identity. All the available national survey data in Korea clearly point to the strong correlation between this identity and the social groups' attitudes, outlooks, action orientations, and so on. In short, it is these middling grassroots that have been most active in leading and supporting democratic movements as well as social reforms.

The middling grassroots may be seen as a specific combination of the student movements and the formation of the middle class. In other words, the middling grassroots is the concept which captures the agency of practice by linking the concept of generation and that of social class. Important in this context is the cultural history or deep mentality in which the category of people remains as opposed to that of the power bloc. It is within this context that the middling grassroots emerged significantly during the 1980s, transforming the middle class in support of a democratic transition. By and large, the middle class found itself in an embarrassing situation because they benefited economically but were disillusioned politically. In particular, the way in which the regime manipulated the mass media put it in anger and despair. Thus, it felt that the students' demand for democratization reflected its own dissatisfaction. The middle class also became sympathetic to the pains and sacrifices accrued to the students. Thus, it began to believe that reforms must be made promptly to reduce these unnecessary costs and burdens on the students.

We should keep it in mind that the students were not only active in political protests but also formed a distinctive culture in the campus, that is, the *Min-Joong* culture whose effect was profound. As a counter-culture, this provided the students with fresh imaginations, sensitivities, perspectives, and so on, which were sharply contrasted to those of the older generations. Once established, this culture also made possible all kinds of subaltern discourses, activities, performances, and so on. Constitutive of this culture was the self-reflection of one's identity, namely, 'who I am' or 'who we are'. This led the students to experience the collapse of the conventional understanding of the self and so many taken-for-granted values transmitted from the family and the school. Instead, they found themselves in painful strains and agony, searching for a new identity characterized by an increased concern for openness, solidarity, discursive justification and social justice. The students were driven to get rid of the long-held elitist conceptions and the familiarized self, projecting a new community in opposition to the injustice of the authoritarian capitalist development.

In Korea where families and the Confucian hierarchy in value orientations are particularly strong and capitalist competition is intricately interwoven in educational institutions, this new experiment turned fruitful because the students rediscovered a national and popular culture deeply sedimented in the ordinary people's way of life. So they made a great number of attempts to revitalize these cultures and identities, interpreting histories from the perspective of ordinary men, that is, *Min-Joong* and not the elite. They were also deeply motivated to understand those social groups that remain excluded from the mainstream of national development.

We can, thus, say that the student movements were essentially driven by the desire to rediscover the 'others', whether they be workers, peasants or the nation. To the extent to which they devoted themselves to understanding and defending the suppressed others, we can see a paradigmatic case in which the politics of the new identity demonstrated itself in sharp contrast to the traditional ones. The identity in question was neither traditional nor egocentric but highly reflexive in that it was directed towards reconciliation with the suppressed others by means of open discourse. The student movements were able, therefore, to get wide moral support from society even when the regime was madly repressive.

The counter-culture was, of course, very complex and multidimensional. Nothing is further from the truth than viewing it as a unified system of ideological dogma. Nor was it monopolized by the militant movement circles. Rather, its core lay in discursive testing whether—or not—and if so, to what extent can conventional selves, values, stereotypes, authorities and taboos, and so on, be made their own. Clashing with the harsh reality of authoritarianism and deeply stimulated by the avantgarde movements and protests, the majority of the students went through these processes of cultural awakening. To be sure, what was at stake was not merely about the political but included all aspects of the individual life as well. Let me list some of its dominant value orientations in a simplified manner. I do not claim that all of these were equally visible and important during the 1980s. Some were obviously more conspicuous than others but I am convinced that all began to emerge to a greater or lesser extent during the 1980s:

- Challenge to all conventional authorities (anti-authoritarianism);
- Respect for individual liberty and decision (individualism);
- Breaking down taboos (avant-gardism);
- Women's participation (gender equality);
- Solidarity with workers and peasants (social justice);
- Pursuit of convenience in life (materialism);

- Commitment to principle rather than vertical hierarchy (value commitment);
- Horizontal communication rather than vertical hierarchy (communitarianism);
- Reflexive identity and cultural reinterpretation (radical hermeneutics); and
- National reunification (nationalism).

The formation of the middling grassroots can be traced back in two ways. The first is the horizontal expansion of the movement's circles from the campus to such grassroots organizations as the labour unions, churches and educational institutions. What came out of these activities was the subaltern discourse in defence of workers' rights. Immense efforts were made to clarify the labour situations of the day and to improve the methods of labour strikes. They continued in this way a comprehensive effort at enlightenment and education, aimed at bringing the workers to the point where they could articulate their discontents.

The second is characterized by the massive vertical entry into social organizations amounting to as many as 40,000 college graduates in a year. In this respect, an empirical question is whether they continued to keep their grassroots identity even when they got jobs of their own. Data shows that they tended to preserve it, though without being as much directly involved in activism as before. They found themselves more disposed to resisting the inertia of organizations than simply assimilating into it. This means that they were not only critical of the military dictatorship but also wanted more participatory, open and transparent organizations and the decision-making processes in society.

Based on these observations, we can say that the Korean middle class is composed of two equally important segments; one is conservative and another reform-oriented. By and large, the former is now in its fifties and sixties, as the generation which had experienced absolute poverty in its childhood, and thus emphatically driven to get out of this by any means. Thanks to its desire and efforts, it became the major carrier of modernization, making its own upward vertical mobility. In contrast, the latter is a fruit of modernization: self-reflexive and critical. Largely born after 1960, they remained relatively free from poverty and thus became more concerned with such values as self-expression and participation. These values finally burst out in their campuses during the 1980s, though largely in the form of anti-authoritarian movements. Broadly speaking, nevertheless, the middling grassroots came close to 'postmaterialistic' values in the sense that they put emphasis on participation, reciprocity, solidarity, clean environment, and so on. The world value survey conducted by Ronald Inglehart (1995: 30), for example, clearly demonstrates that the generational gap, measured by the average difference between material and post-material value orientations among age groups, is the greatest in Korea, as Figure 10.5 shows.

Furthermore, there is a constructive relationship between the middling grassroots and NGO activities in Korea. The NGO activities differ from the traditional interest groups in that they pursue general and public interests, going beyond particular group interests. By focussing

Figure 10.5   Values by birth cohort in Europe, East Asia and Africa

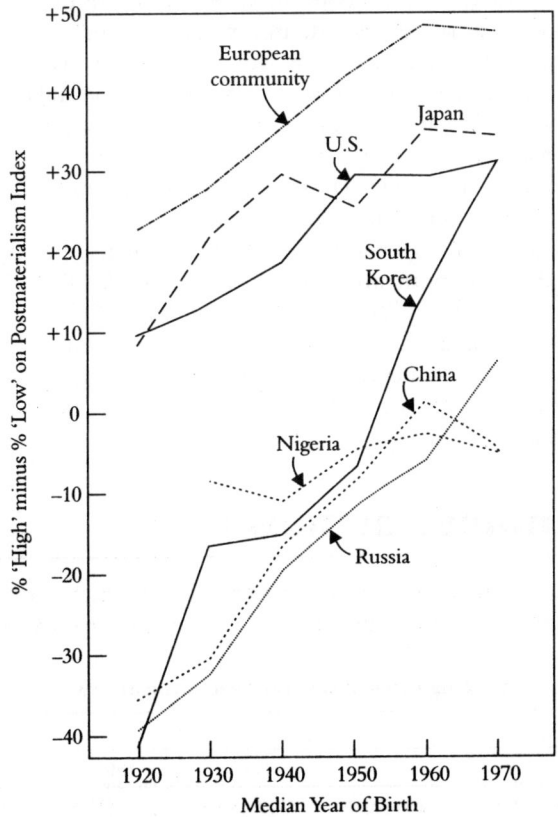

Source: World values survey (1990–91), conducted by Inglehart (1995: 30).

Note: Respondents are classified as 'high' on the twelve-item materialist/post-materialist values index used here if they gave high priority to at least three of the five post-materialist goals (ranking them among the two most important in each group of four goals). They are classified as 'low' if they gave high priority to none of the five post-materialist goals.

on concrete life issues, they are also distinguished from ideological radicalism. They share certain common attributes: they attempt to transcend class boundaries, defining themselves as speaking to wider regional or national audience. They generally advocate policies that are reformist in nature and supportive of wider and deeper democratic change.

The leadership of the NGOs has also something crucial to do with the middling grassroots (Sang-Jin 1996). Many of these leaders were former activists and have years of experience in social movements either for democracy or social justice or ecological concerns. They are almost all in their thirties and early forties, eager to construct the domestic and international networks of cooperation. According to one document, the civil society today covers wide areas ranging from economic justice, environmental protection, welfare, women's rights, consumer protection, risks prevention, state reform for decentralization and even development, electoral monitoring, producer–consumer cooperatives, foreign workers' rights, educational reform, disabled rights, and so on. All these NGO activities have been led by the reform-oriented middle class constituting the backbone of the active civil society.

It is also very interesting to note the steady increase of those who acquired the identity of middling grassroots (Table 10.1). The term 'identity' represents a subjective or cultural sense of belonging rather than objective variables.[4] According to the researches done so far, the middle class consciousness has been drastically weakened following the 1997 IMF crisis but the sense of belonging to the middling grassroots has been constantly rising.

Technological mover

There may be pros and cons of the role of the internet in politics and the civil society. Some say that the two-way stream, rapidity, openness,

Table 10.1 Changing rates of subjective identifications

Cases (%)				Unit
Classification	1987	1995	1999	2001
Middling grassroots	260 (20.8)	322 (26.0)	310 (25.9)	436 (36.0)
Middle class	418 (33.4)	468 (37.8)	106 (8.8)	98 (8.1)
People	213 (17.0)	163 (13.2)	479 (39.9)	409 (33.8)
Others	359 (28.7)	284 (23.0)	304 (25.4)	268 (22.1)
Total	1,250 (100.0)	1,237 (100.0)	1,199 (100.0)	1,211 (100.0)

accessibility and data-processing capability of digital communications are very contributive to democratization. Others are of the opinion that the internet will only aggravate social inequality. More specifically, the mobilization theory suggests that the internet will strengthen democracy by expanding political participation. Some believe that new technologies promote social capital by facilitating the exchange of opinions among people and letting them change their thinking (Rheingold 1993). In this view, the internet is essentially of democratic nature by making two-way debates possible. Budge (1995) thus asserts that the internet creates a new form of direct democracy. Negroponte (1995) and Dertouzos (1997) claim that electronic democracy will increase variety and participation by decentralizing policy-making power in the digital world. The power balance is shifting between the government and the people. Citizens are capable of collecting information more easily, spreading their ideas freely and participating in each policy-making process through electronic balloting.

On the contrary, the reinforcement theory predicts that the existing patterns of political participation will not drastically change even with the increase in internet use. To put it concretely, the digital divide between the haves and the have-nots will widen or strengthen the participation gap. Even though the internet is surely a new source of information, the possible imbalance in internet connections makes the expectation of increasing political participation skeptical (Davis and Owen 1998). In other words, the effect of socio-economic inequality and distortion will never decrease or disappear at all in the network. Some express a negative view that the new media might further widen the gap between the information haves and have-nots (Murdock and Golding 1989). Despite the wide use of the internet, people are not expected to change too much because in cyberspace, they will reflect their interests and preferences in the real world (Hill and Hughes 1998).

Each of the two conflicting views is, however, somewhat one-sided. What is important in my opinion is to see the relationship between technology and social forces. Neither technology nor social structure alone determines, but the concrete interplay between these two brings about significant consequences. Seen from this perspective, there seems to be good reason to think about the significant relationship between the use of the internet and democratic participation in Korea. This has nothing to do with technological determinism. Instead, this is largely because the sociological mover referred to earlier is ahead of other groups in making use of the internet in support of social transformation.

Needless to say, the internet can be used in many different ways depending on the social context. In this connection, Korea's experience is interesting and inspires the imagination (Sang-Jin 2000). The first interesting point is the sharp increase in the number of subscribers. Korea is a forerunner in the world in supplying the super-highway IT facilities all over the country at cheap prices. Based on this, the internet has become an indispensable equipment of everyday life for an increasing number of people. Its impact on society at large seems to be enormous. In 1999, the number of internet subscribers was merely 3.7 million; however, the numbers soared up to some 4 million in 2000, 7.8 million in 2001 and 10 million by October 2002. At the end of 2001, Korea stood at the top of the world with an internet subscription rate of 17.2 per cent, followed by Canada (8.4 per cent) and Sweden (5.0 per cent). At present, Korean users spend more time on the internet than in any other nation. Besides stock trading, shopping or chatting, the internet has tremendous influence upon politics, public opinion and civil campaigns.

Having said so, I would like to pay attention to a particular socio-political context of the internet culture in Korea. Maximum internet users are in their teens, but those in their twenties may be most active in using the internet in everyday life. However, the leadership in politically significant net activism has been taken on by people in their thirties whom I called the middling grassroots. As the major actors for democratization in the 1980s, they have spearheaded IT industries, exploring a new form of net-mediated activism. To sum up, Korea's net activism has been led and expanded by those with strong participatory orientation and experience. This may explain why the use of the internet has great socio-political effect in Korea, sometimes escalating online debate to offline mass mobilization in a remarkable way.

At the same time, it should be mentioned that due to the mounting distrust in the mass media, particularly major newspapers, young people tend to see the internet as an alternative public sphere. These newspapers supported the military regime for a long time. During the 1980s, when the nation was struggling to get out of the long tunnel of military dictatorship, these newspapers, however, opportunistically sided with the historical tide of democratization. When the military rule came to an end later on, the newspapers appeared highly power oriented, brandishing their omnipotence by manufacturing conservative opinions and moods in every sector of the society (Sang-Jin 2001b). Since democratization promotes social pluralism and a variety of values and topics, the opinions of minority groups should be duly respected.

But the powerful media failed to pay proper attention to the needs of the needy, only reinforcing the mainstream conservative stereotypes. This motivated civil organizations to launch massive campaigns to check the monopolized power of the family owner, promote transparency in management and institutionalize the division between the management and the editorial.

Of most significance in this respect is the question as to who is leading net activism. At this point, we need to carefully examine the relationship between agency and technology. As already stated, those who led the nation's democratization in the 1980s are at the centre, while younger generations in their teens or twenties are at the forefront of the online movements. This means that the internet and the value orientations of the young generation are closely interwoven, not because of any reason of the internet itself but because of the social conditions of its use.

As of the end of 2001, some 93.3 per cent of the age group 7–19, 84.6 per cent of those in their twenties and 61.6 per cent of people in their thirties were using the internet. On the other hand, 35.6 per cent of people in their forties and 8.7 per cent of those in their forties were internet users (Table 10.2). It is surprising to see how fast the rate of internet use increased from October 1999 to December 2001. The rates soared from 33.6 to 93.3 per cent in the age group 7–19, from 41.9 to 84.6 per cent among people in their twenties and from 18.5 to 61.6 per cent among people in their thirties. As of December 2001, 88.4 per cent of elementary pupils, 99.8 per cent of middle school students, 99.0 per cent of high school students and 99.3 per cent of college students were using the internet.

The internet can be a powerful political weapon for those who have been struggling to get out of the established norms and customs tainted by hierarchical authoritarianism. The following excerpt (Yoon 2001: 255) seems to grasp the motive and the cultural context of the enthusiasm among the younger generation of Koreans over the use of the internet:

Table 10.2 Increasing rates of internet use by age group

Age	Oct. 1999	Dec. 2000	Dec. 2001
7–19	33.6	74.1	93.3
20s	41.9	74.6	84.6
30s	18.5	43.6	61.6
40s	12.8	22.7	35.6
Over 50	2.9	5.7	8.7

Source: Korea internet white paper (2002).

The hierarchical system of ordinary social reality turns upside down as soon as Korean students enter cyberspace.... This is not only because the internet has exciting information but also because it provides them with a new experience and an alternative hierarchy. It is something of an experience of deconstructing power in reality, especially in Korean society, which is strongly hierarchical and repressive for young students.... Using the internet is a strategy of the new generation: a habitus which affects peoples minds and living patterns through its symbolic power, and at the same time it allows for diverse strategies of resistance. Relying on the cultural power of new technology, young Korean students attempt to break-up the hierarchy of old authority and experience their new identities in the cyberspace.

At this point, the relationship between the reform-oriented middle class in thirties and early forties, and the digital generation in its twenties needs to be reviewed. One may define the former as a 'politicized, social-movement generation' and the latter as 'relatively conservative depoliticized generation' (Park 2002: 27). One may put more emphasis on the difference between the two. The former can be viewed as a generation that 'experienced political eruption through the June uprising' (ibid.), while the latter is a generation that 'created cultural eruption in the 2002 World Cup, reddening the entire Korean peninsula' (ibid.). One (Cho 2002: 147) sociologist goes further to mention the possibility of the greatest generation conflict between the two.

But we should not overlook the common nature of the two generations. Despite so many empirical differences, they have one thing in common, that is to say, their underlying motivation to escape the taken-for-granted stereotypes and customs. In other words, the former spearheaded the struggle against the military dictatorship, while the latter attempts to verify a variety of issues in its daily living. On the surface, the former seems to be collectivistic and ideology-oriented, and the latter individualized. But both of them seem to share a post-conventional logic of testing and, hence, are strongly motivated to question the taken-for-granted conventions such as the Cold War mentality, and the authoritarian and hierarchical ways of life. In this respect, it can be said that in this age of digitalization, the challenging spirit of the post-conventional testing is further spread by the younger generation in a more diverse and individualized way.

Finally, the possibility of combining the online with the offline attracts our keen interest. Probably, Korea may be the best place to observe this peculiar phenomenon. As shown in many exemplars like the street cheering during the World Cup, the political campaigns during the period 2002–04, including the presidential and general elections, the anti-Chosun campaign and the protests against the construction of Dong-gang Dam, there have been many successful stories by individuals of constructing websites that later turned out to be explosive in linking online and offline activities by expediting the flow of information. Numerous times, certain argument or information has been copied or carried over free of charge from one website to another.

Thus, we can say that the internet can play an important role in the democratization of the civil society as it can raise a wide range of issues that are often neglected in the course of arbitrary selection of agenda by the established mass media. By finding the way around or getting over the gatekeeper that controls the selection and exclusion of relevant information, the internet can be an efficient means of launching various human rights campaigns for, say, children, women or homosexuals, as well as consumers' movements. In other words, the new medium can dismantle 'the iron triangle of the exclusively powerful apparatuses such as the government, mass media and political circles' and further streamline 'the process of identifying and mobilizing diverse issues and groups through political activities outside the socio-economic boundaries' (Koh 2002: 12).

Cultural mover

The cultural landscape of Korea has many common traits with Japan and China, while at the same time displaying numerous distinctive qualities. Historically, Koreans have been as much network-oriented as the Japanese and the Chinese, albeit major foci were somewhat different. This can be exemplified by many sorts of lineage networks that have played an important role in the Korean history. Korea has also been successful in preserving its unique identity while actively engaging in inter-cultural learning. Although it may be true that the question of national identity was more desperate among the Koreans than the Japanese due to the colonial legacy imposed upon Korea, the former have proved themselves able at absorbing many foreign cultures, without losing their national identity.

One of the unique potentials of Korea seems to have been emerging from an active civil society backed by the tradition of various social movements and bottoms-up popular cultures. Historically speaking, the origin of the Korean civil society may be traced back to the sixteenth century, when private academies began to be formed as moral centres where intellectuals and students studied Confucian teachings. Originally, the separation between scholarship and politics was presupposed. As academies increased in number from the seventeenth century 'a procedure evolved and a network developed among private academy students that allowed them to address matters they thought required attention' (Choe 1999: 44). In the memorandums to be sent to the throne, they dealt with not only political issues, but also 'a wide variety of topics pertaining to local affairs, social issues and scholarly concerns' (ibid.). In particular, the year 1666 marked the beginning of 'private academics' participation in the national political discourse' (ibid.).

Needless to day, this intellectual participatory tradition was limited to the upper classes and only to men. But we can say that it has had great influences on the Korean history, giving rise to a strong civil society, together with a contesting middle class, not to mention a strong tradition of student movements. As I have argued, a key to understanding the dynamism of Korea's civil society is to grasp the characteristics of those who led the van in the nation's democratization movement in the 1980s. Similar to the sixteenth century when the reform-oriented Confucian intellectuals were formed on the basis of private academies' education, this distinctive social force has been formed today as part of the middle classes on the basis of the economic development and the student movement (Sang-Jin 1997).

The cultural mover in a contesting civil society is deeply interconnected to globalization and the logic of post-conventional testing it fosters. According to this logic, traditions can never be simply taken for granted but persist only 'in so far as they are made available to discursive justification and are prepared to enter into open dialogue not only with other traditions but with alternative modes of doing things' (Giddens 1995: 105). In this context, Giddens speaks of the 'post-traditional society' as 'the first global society' (ibid.: 83):

> A post-traditional society is not a national society—we are speaking here of a global cosmopolitan order. Nor is it a society in which traditions cease to exist; in many respects there are impulses, or pressures, towards the sustaining or the recovery of traditions. It is a society, however, in which tradition changes its status. In the context of a globalizing, cosmopolitan order, traditions are constantly brought into contact with one another and forced to 'declare themselves'.

One pertinent issue of post-traditional testing is concerned about national identity. Historically speaking, Korean intellectuals became sensitive to the issue of national identity, especially during Japanese colonialism. Unlike in Japan where the *kukhak* movement acted as a spiritual support for their modernization, Choson had lost its national will with the onslaught of the Western powers and Japanese imperialism at the end of the nineteenth century. An endogenous development was prevented, while any modernization effort connected to an outside power failed. Naturally, this increased disillusion with—and criticism of—the lack of leadership, internal degradation, factionalism and a perceived outmoded traditional culture, not to mention the imperialist interests and interference of foreign countries. Furthermore, Japan propagated a colonial mentality that belittled or denied the Korean national character. In such a context, special attempts were made by intellectuals to discover the national spirit through a study of religion, philosophy, art, folklore, history, literature and so on.

Since then, the quest for an independent and legitimate subjectivity manifested itself in various forms, depending on historical conjunctures. During the Japanese colonial rule, it provided the underlying force behind the liberation movements of various kinds and after World War II, it became embedded in differing efforts in support of 'One Unified Korea' against territorial division. In the age of the Cold War, the quest for national identity became imbued with a severe ideological polarization between North and South Korea over the issue of political legitimacy and orthodoxy.

This long-standing legacy of ideological polarization seems to break down quite visibly these days. Accordingly, a significant socio-cultural transformation has begun to manifest itself, as could be felt through the cheering in the streets during the World Cup in June 2002. Cultural sensitivities, ideas, dreams and aspirations that had been cultivated in the process of democratization and that had accumulated under the surface began to burst through finally in the form of a massive festival celebrating national pride and dignity. It was through this collective experience of self-pride and dignity that Koreans became aware of their new potentialities. It was a historical moment of self-awakening, comparable to the popular democratic uprising of June 1987. This new stream manifested itself again in the recent candlelight marches against American military globalism.

Of particular significance in this regard is the 'Be the Reds' campaign by the Red Devils, the official Korean soccer supporters, which prepared for the massive cheering through online discussions about the proper way of cheering, costumes, roosters' songs and slogans, and so on. The campaign meant the end of the Cold War mentality. Koreans have been deeply obsessed with the colour red, which evokes the memories of the Korean War and communism. Against such a backdrop, the conservative media and the elder generations, haunted by the red complex, were worried about young people who wore red shirts and called themselves 'Red Devils'. For the past several decades, the colour red was regarded as taboo, symbolic of communism or North Korea. Under such circumstances, the 'Be the Reds' campaign reflected the young people's ardent desire to escape the existing Cold War mentalities as well as to leave behind authoritarian and hierarchical relations and forms of social control. Young people say that they simply like red, which they believe symbolizes passion, determination, wealth and glory. Not by accident, the majority of the population followed the Red Devils in the World Cup street cheering, in the process subconsciously escaping from the red complex.

Here we can sense the profound impact of the street cheering during the World Cup on the Korean society beyond its merely athletic implications. On the face of it, the Red Devils was nothing more than a voluntary group of soccer lovers. Upon deeper inspection, however, we can see a strong cultural challenge against the established order and an appeal for a new order embracing humanity and upgrading national pride and dignity. In this way, the people projected their dreams through slogans like 'Asian Pride' and 'Dream Realized'. By shouting *Dae-hanminguk*, they expressed their willingness and aspirations to make a new Korea, of which all could feel proud. This was a decisive turning point from the self-humiliating legacy originating from Japanese colonial subjection towards a new self-respecting sensitivity. What came out of this experience was by no means the revival of the old paradigm of nationalism or collectivism. On the contrary, all kinds of liberal experiments such as body painting, fashion with the national flag, dances, songs, modes of cheering and greetings, and so on, were nicely fused with the communitarian culture emphasizing national solidarity. All these experiments were led by those in their thirties and followed by the succeeding digital generations, who, instead of surrendering themselves to hierarchical and authoritarian relationships, held up to more flexible and pluralistic voluntary organizations and value orientations.

Thanks to these experiences and concurrent socio-cultural transformations, the quest for national identity seems to be significantly liberated from the ideological burden of the past. This has created the room to see the United States not simply as a big brother but as an equal partner. In the past, it was taken for granted that what the United States does is automatically good for the Koreans (Sang-Jin 2004). Only a few with exceptional bravery could wage an anti-American rally, as well documented by the seizure of the USA Information Center in Pusan by the students of Seoul National University in 1982. But today ordinary citizens can freely ask whether the relationship between Korea and the United States is fair and equal. In other words, it is profound that Koreans have begun to ask whether Americans are respecting Koreans in the terms of a reciprocal relationship.

Yet, it must be stressed that the gap between the normative expectation and the reality still remains considerably large, which indicates a source of frustration. It may also be true that the quest for national identity involves ambiguities and uncertainties because Koreans are still far from completely overcoming the legacies of Japanese colonialism, national division, the Korean War, past authoritarian rule, and so on. Nevertheless, Koreans may be expected to become increasingly more capable than in the past of explicitly saying 'No' when they feel that their sovereignty has been severely damaged or degraded by external powers.

This cultural transformation is significant given the fact that the United States has wielded an overwhelming influence on the destiny of the Korean people since the end of World War II. First of all, the United States and the USSR made the decision to divide the Korean peninsula and the American army came to Korea as the liberator from Japanese colonialism and, hence, could act as the 'big brother'. Yet, the United States saw Korea largely from their own geopolitical interests and perspective and, with the outburst of the Korean War, Korea became a symbol and a victim of the Cold War, suffering much from territorial division, war, poverty, dictatorial military regimes, ideological confrontation, and so on.

Yet, Koreans have proved to be capable of growing fast economically (as one of the four small dragons in East Asia after Japan). In addition, they have successfully joined the global wave of democratization. The Korean development would then have to be understood as a combination of such multiple trends as aggressive economic growth, political transition towards democracy and cultural awakening in two directions: first, increasing sensitivity to the question of national identity and second, a 'post-conventional' tendency towards a discursive critical re-evaluation of taken-for-granted assumptions and worldviews. These two tracks seem to be deeply interrelated and the changing reality is thrown sharply into relief when we examine the role of the United States on the Korean peninsula.

Consequently, problems tend to arise and become serious insofar as the normative presupposition of equal respect remains damaged. It will be difficult to simply close one's eyes diplomatically if one party treats the other not as an equal partner but as a second-rank participant. As a concrete example, if and insofar as the American policy towards Korea continues to be dictated by its own ideological understanding of Korea as a reflection of the Cold War, without fully taking into account the implications of the post-conventional cultural awakening in Korea, the majority of Koreans will probably find it difficult to go along with the American war drive. What is in fact involved here is not a simple display of anti-American sentiment but the presence of a profound conflict of moral judgement. Whereas peace in the Korean peninsula is of fundamental importance for Koreans, the American foreign policy appears preoccupied with its own geopolitical security concerns while treating Korea as a piece or instrument to be moved in a greater game.

Notes

1. This chapter is a slightly revised version of a paper first presented on 9 July 2004 as a keynote speech on social transformations at the thirty-sixth IIS World Congress of Sociology held in Beijing, 7–11 July 2004. The original version has appeared in Sang-Jin (2006: 215–41).
2. The figures are based on the data collected from a nationwide interview survey conducted in November, 2002.
3. The following descriptions of the middling grassroots are taken from my previous work (Sang-Jin 2001a).
4. The category of the middling grassroots refers to those who have developed a clear-cut double identity as middle class and people. In contrast, the category of the middle class or people refers to those who have only one of these identities. Others are those who refuse both.

References

Budge, Ian. 1995. *The New Challenge of Direct Democracy*. Oxford: Political Press.
Cho, Dae-Yup. 2002. '386: Social Movement Generation in Korea', *Sasang*, (Autumn).
Choe, Yong-Ho. 1999. 'Private Academies and the State in Late Chosen Korea', in J. Kim Haboush and M. Deuchler (eds), *Culture and the State in Late Chosen Korea*, pp. 15–45. Cambridge, MA: Harvard University Press.

Davis, Richard and Dianna Owen. 1998. *New Media and American Politics*. New York: Oxford University Press.

Dertouzos, Michael. 1997. *What Will Be: How the New Information Marketplace will Change our Lives*. San Francisco: Harper.

Giddens, Anthony. 1995. 'Living in a Post-Traditional Society', in U. Beck, A. Giddens and S. Lash (eds), *Reflexive Modernization*, pp. 56–109. Cambridge: Polity Press.

Hill, Kevin A. and John E. Hughes. 1998. *Cyberpolitics: Citizen Activism in the Age of the Internet*. Lanham, M.D.: Rowan & Littlefield.

Inglehart, Ronald. 1995. 'Modernization and Post-Modernization: Changing Korean Society in Global Perspective', Paper presented in the Symposium on Korean Culture in Global Perspective, Seoul National University, Seoul, South Korea.

Koh, Dong-Hyun. 2002. 'The Patterns and the Types of the On-line Social Movement', Paper presented at the Bi-annual Meeting of the Korean Sociological Association.

Murdock, Graham and Peter Golding. 1989. 'Information Poverty and Political Inequality: Citizenship in the Age of Privatized Communications', *Journal of Communication*, 39: 180–93.

Negroponte, Nicholas. 1995. *Being Digital*. New York: Knopf.

Park, Gil-Sung. 2002. 'Why Generation?', *Sasang*, Autumn.

Rheingold, Howard. 1993. *The Virtual Community: Homesteading on the Electronic Frontier*. M.A.: Addison-Wesley.

Sang-Jin, Han. 1996. 'The NGO Grassroots Movement and Civil Society in Korea', Proceedings of the Asian Foundation Workshop on Civil Society, Good Governance and the Role of Foreign Assistance, Taipei.

———. 1997. 'The Political Economy and Moral Institutions: The Formation of the Middling Grassroots in Korea', *Humboldt Journal of Social Relations*, 23(1–2): 71–89.

———. 2000. 'Internet Revolution and Asian Values: Where does Korea Stand and Why?', *Journal of American Studies*, 32(2): 235–53.

———. 2001a. 'Modernization and the Rise of Civil Society: The Role of the Middling Grassroots for Democratization in Korea', *Human Studies*, 24(1–2): 113–32.

———. 2001b. 'The Transformation of the Public Sphere and the Media Reform', Peace and Democracy in the Korean Peninsular. Proceedings of the International Conference in Commemoration of Three Years of the Kim Dae Jung Government.

———. 2004. 'Korea and US Culture: Cultural Interaction from a Korean Perspective'. In *Pacific Partner*, pp. 163–76. University of Hawaii.

———. 2005a. 'Democratic Transformation and Non-Traditional Security: Challenges of Republic of Korea', in Zhang Yunling (ed.), *State and Civil Society in the Context of Transition*, pp. 69–118. World Affair Press.

Sang-Jin, Han. 2005b. 'People-Based Politics: The Korean Experience of Dual Democratization and Three Unresolved Issues'. A Keynote Speech at the KPI Congress VII on People-Based Politics, Bangkok, Thailand, 4–6 November.

———. 2005c. 'Democratic Transformation and Conflict Management in Korea', Background Paper for the Global Conference on Reinventing Governance held in Seoul, Korea, 24–27 May.

———. 2006. 'Three Prime Movers in Contested Civil Society: Why and How Social Transformation Occurs in Korea', *Annals of the International Institute of Sociology*, 10: 215–41.

Yoon, Sunny. 2001. 'Internet Discourse and the Habitus of Korea's New Generation', in Charles Ess and Fay Sudweeks (eds), *Culture, Technology and Communication*, pp. 241–60. New York: State University of New York Press.

Beyond Powerlessness

11

Celebrating the Power of the Displaced

JOSE JOWEL CANUDAY

Proposing a celebration of flight and even claiming that persons in flight are in possession of power may be viewed as naïve, romanticized and even presumptuous. I invite you, however, to a reflection on the discourse of the internally displaced persons (IDP) as I describe the persistence of a group of displaced people in creating and recreating their communities through years of armed conflicts in a southern Philippine island called Mindanao. In the process, we will take a critical assessment of the pervasive and destructive character of armed conflicts and their resulting displacements without losing sight of the historical capacity of the displaced communities in dealing with their condition.

To start with, this chapter will tackle the discourse of the *bakwit*, the Mindanao idiom closely resembling the IDP category. I will comment on some views that project the *bakwit* as a people without history by following their thirty-five-year experience of repeated evacuations, return and rebuilding in the village of Buliok in Central Mindanao. Buliok is located right at the heart of the continuing armed confrontations that involved the Philippine government's army and its network of paramilitary forces against rival secessionist revolutionary movements known as the Moro National Liberation Front (MNLF) and the Moro Islamic Liberation Front (MILF). These movements, though locked rivals, defined their struggle as a war of national liberation for the estimated six million largely muslim-oriented *Bangsamoro* ethno-linguistic groups of people from the Philippines.[1]

The chapter will also take a glimpse of new movements of displaced persons emerging in Central Mindanao as manifested by mass mobilizations that unleashed the *bakwit* power and the *bakwit*'s involvement in the monitoring of ceasefire agreements signed by armed groups. Finally, the chapter argues for a re-understanding of the dominant image of the *bakwit*, suggests the idea of solidarity over aid and the possibilities of harnessing the power of the displaced into peace advocacy.

I highlight the long-held capacities of the displaced in fixing their lives as an integral component in understanding the patterns of displacements and in the discussion of security issues. These capacities are often undermined, ignored and forgotten from the time aid groups start with the distribution of the first bags of relief goods to the design and construction of houses and community facilities.

The *bakwit*

Imaging powerlessness: As if a people without history

In many areas of Mindanao, the IDP takes the idiom *bakwit*, a category for persons displaced by calamities and armed conflicts dating back to the Japanese army's occupation and battles against the United States' colonial forces and homegrown guerrillas in World War II.[2] The *bakwit*, as pronounced by different linguistic background, appropriated the English verb 'evacuate'. The dictionaries of Philippine dialects note that the term (with spelling variations *bakwet* and *bakuit*) refers to 'evacuees, refugees' (Almario et al. 2001: 81; Sullivan 1986: 76) and is being used both as a verb and a noun. As a noun, *bakwit* is also used in plural and singular forms. The term does not distinguish an IDP from the refugees defined in the 1951 Refugee Convention[3] and the United Nations Guiding Principles on Internal Displacements (UNGPID). For this chapter, I take *bakwit* as referring to persons displaced by calamities and armed conflicts in Mindanao.

Following massive displacement during the Philippine government's 'all-out war' campaign against the MILF in the year 2000, civil society groups and the government's welfare agency appended to the *bakwit* the description 'internally displaced persons' (IDP) and linked such a condition to a category of forced migrants stipulated under the United Nations' guiding principles (Balay, Tabang Mindanaw).[4] The category of the IDP as people denied of their rights is emphasized in a brochure produced by the Mindanao People's Caucus, an alliance of civil society groups advocating for peace and an end to displacement in Mindanao. They are so referred to in government and civil society literature.

Some studies conclude that the displaced are 'poor and uneducated' and that their 'living conditions had further worsened and rendered dim their prospects of achieving better futures or, at least, regaining the kind of life, and the pride and self-respect they used to have' (Notre Dame University Research Center with the Commission on Population Region XII 2004: 54).

To address the *bakwit* situation, calls were issued for 'human rights defenders, service providers, peace advocates and the stakeholders themselves to take the main role in reclaiming the rights and dignity of the IDPs' (Balay Advocacy Program, undated), by empowering communities through capacity building initiatives.[5]

Descriptions of the patterns of displacement in Mindanao tend to focus on displacement events surrounding the wars in 2000 and 2003. The descriptions are limited to the implications that the displacement of women and children needs assessments, governance, conducting aid, rehabilitation efforts, and peace and development programs (Accion Contra El Hambre 2004; Daguino et. al. 2003: 3; Notre Dame University Research Center with the Commission on Population Region XII 2004; OXFAM 2000).

Further, OXFAM (2000: 28) argued that the IDP's worsening situation will continue 'with ever increasing negative impact on people's food and livelihood security ties in the evacuation centres, especially stretching their coping strategies to complete exhaustion.' These assessments offer generalized descriptions of displacement patterns that highlight the helplessness and powerlessness of the displaced, and the necessity of continued assistance as they cross the threshold of food insecurity to an even bleaker future.

Re-understanding of powerlessness

Appending 'power' to the supposedly transfixed *bakwit* opens us to other realities of forced migrants beyond perceptions of helplessness and powerlessness that appear to embody the Philippine government and civil society's framing of the IDP. This work will follow the dynamics and creative power of the human agency in displacement events and through its prism appreciate the actions of the displaced beyond coping from continuing armed conflicts and repeated displacement. I am drawing my description from a seven month fieldwork for an ethnographic study of the *bakwit* at evacuation sites and villages in the town of Pikit and Pagulungan in Central Mindanao.

Evacuations, returns and rebuilding

Movements and persistence

In the context of the thirty-five-year armed conflicts, I believe that it is meaningful to view the patterns of displacements within this time-frame and extend the assessment of *bakwits*' situation and movements beyond the wars of 2000 and 2003. I also take note of the cultural diversity and complexities of Mindanao's eighteen million people who are organized—but not exclusively—along ethno-linguistic, political and even class lines.

In understanding displacement patterns, I keep track of the events when communities evacuate and the sites which they evacuate, the period when they start the process of returning and rebuilding their villages, to the time they are displaced again. Experiences of evacuations, return and rebuilding are not limited to stories of helplessness and sufferings but are also about persistence and capabilities.

Evacuations

For this chapter, evacuations mean the time when the communities were displaced and migrated elsewhere to avoid being caught in the war. Being 'caught in the war' has two meanings for some of the *bakwit* in Central Mindanao. First is exposing oneself or family to danger, and the second is the mobilization of an individual, family and clan to join the fighting. During the evacuation period, not all displaced families run far away from their villages and farms. Some stay and hide along river banks, forest areas, behind tall grass or in dry portions of the swamps, as is the case in the experiences of the villagers across the Liguasan Marsh.[6] In recent armed confrontations, particularly in 1997, 2000 and 2003, most displaced residents would flee to evacuation centres or camps.[7]

Returns

I also distinguish return from rebuilding because the *bakwit* go through distinct experiences in both events. They keep watch, especially of patrolling soldiers, and take the first opportunity of returning to their farms or fishing grounds in the marshes and rivers once the soldiers withdraw. After working in their farms, fishing or scouring food from the field, they return to their refuge. The *bakwit* in the evacuation camps, at times, venture to their farms for a day or more. In the process of return, they do not immediately reoccupy the lands where their houses and farms used to be.

Returning families group together in certain areas where they build temporary shelters even as they work in their farms, either collectively or individually. In other cases, only the men return to the village to farm while the women, children and the elderly stay in the evacuation sites. The reason for these arrangements is their sense of insecurity, primarily during the first few months of return when government soldiers continue to conduct patrol operations and are deployed near or within their farmlands. They know that after every battle, rebel forces would simply break into smaller groups but often stay near the village. These villages are also the homes of some of the rebels the government have been fighting. Some of these rebels are the sons, husbands, brothers, in-laws and cousins of the displaced. With such a situation, civilians think that chances of getting caught in the crossfire are high because the warring forces are in their village.

Rebuilding

Rebuilding refers to the period when displaced communities start re-establishing or have already completed reconstruction of structures, materials resources, common and individual facilities, houses, farms and their sense of confidence. Rebuilding, however, does not necessarily mean the return of all the *bakwit* as some stay away from their original villages for some time. Others return home periodically to farm and tend other properties like farm animals and tools.

I associate rebuilding to that period when the communities start the designing and reconstruction of community resources and facilities like schools, houses, places of worship, traditional communal and multipurpose halls, health centres, continuation of planting cycles and abundance of harvest, purchase of farm tools, holding of elections, observance of rituals, the practice of worship, gathering of families and of the community, holding weddings, celebration of births, beautification of abandoned and bombed out burial ground and the functioning of everyday life.

I think these criteria that I set forth echo suggestions in setting the 'bare minimum' of human capabilities so that we can clearly say as to 'what would be a humanly good way of countering limitation' (Nussbaum 1995: 80).

Nussbaum offered a working list that can be made a 'basic sort of evaluating human capabilities' that includes perceiving, imagining, thinking, humour, sex, having intimate family, personal and social relations, being imaginative, emotional and intellectual (ibid.: 76–80).

I checked these capabilities from the experience of the evacuees from the village of Buliok and I find them amazingly alive. The narratives I am presenting here were told to me by those Buliok residents in the evacuation centres, who have already returned to their village or have gone elsewhere. Some of those evacuated not far away from their places of origin continue to tend their farms.

The Buliok experience

In police and military parlance, Buliok is known as 'Buliok Complex', apparently aimed at highlighting the area's strategic value as a military target. The late MILF chair Salamat Hashim established a base in this sprawling village after their main base in the hinterlands of Matanog town in Maguindanao fell during government offensives in 2000. For Buliok residents, their village is a *barangay*, the smallest political and territorial unit of the Philippine government. Before the war in 2000 and subsequently in 2003, Buliok had schools, farms, mosques, government village halls, health centres, and a population of 4,260 persons who thrived on farming and fishing. Both attacks were not the only time Buliok was under siege. The community and other residents from adjacent areas have gone through terrifying experiences of repeated armed conflicts since 1972.

Based on the narratives of the village leaders, women and the elderly from Buliok, I trace the process of displacement, return and rebuilding. Buliok villagers went through at least two long-term displacements in 1972 and late 1974. When they began returning in early 1974, fresh fighting ensued, triggering a six-year displacement from 1975 to 1981. Buliok *bakwit* started returning in the second half of 1981 and rebuilt their community until they were displaced again eight years later, in 1989. With persistence, they started returning in 1991 and went on rebuilding their community until getting displaced again around the summer of 1997. They returned at the end of 1997 but were again displaced during the 2000 war. By the third quarter of 2000, a stream of evacuees had gradually returned to Buliok only to be displaced in February 2003. At the time of writing, the *bakwit* started returning.

The persistence of the Buliok community in returning and rebuilding is worth highlighting because their experience signifies the capabilities and persistence of a community that refuses to remain victims or be broken by displacements.

Buliok before the displacements

Menandang Mamolindas, fifty-six years old, an elected village officer in the predominantly Muslim community of Buliok and the chair of the *bakwit* association called *Suara Kalilintad* in Pikit and Pagalungan towns, recalls that before the 1972 displacement, Buliok was a thriving, self-sustaining community, complete with three rice mills, several corn milling equipment, a large *okkir* and high-roofed houses on stilts, a *madrasah*, three mosques, wide swaths of tobacco, coconut, rice and corn farms, a fleet of motorized and non-motorized boats for fishing and transporting of farm produce to urban trade centres, fertile farmlands and rows of stores. 'A Story of *Barangay* Buliok', which Mamolindas (2004) wrote in long hand, described their place in the decade between 1960 and 1970 as *masagana* (abundant) because they had 'several sources of income'.

Evacuations, 1972

Mamolindas wrote, however, that along with the occurrence of communal violence in many parts of Cotabato in the early 1970s, cases of criminality in their community had gone up and that their village was embroiled in turmoil following the formation of the fanatical, armed anti-Muslim group called Ilaga.[8] In another conversation, Mamolindas says the family and other clans in Buliok and the surrounding communities actually prepared for the attack by organizing and arming their men. Clans called for contributions of arms and men in defence of the community. To him, they were defending their land as members of the community and of their clans. Armed members of the community and clans later reorganized and transformed into nationalist revolutionaries with the formation of the MNLF (Jubair 1999: 148–49).[9] As the MNLF gathered strength, the government responded by deploying massive troops and equipment, and launching artillery and aerial attacks. These combinations of military firepower proved lethal and destructive, and a prime factor of the large-scale displacements in the 1970s and in subsequent decades.

Mamolindas's neighbours[10] say that Buliok, its surrounding villages and the marshes were pounded by artilleries from army bases and the government's assault aircrafts. The bombs and operations from ground troops destroyed their village. They fled to various parts of the vast Liguasan marsh. During their evacuation to the marsh, they would fish and cook at night to ensure that the soldiers and the planes would not see the smoke from their fire and attack them. They heard that in some areas of the marsh, whole families were bombed and wiped out for making the mistake of cooking during daytime. There were no aid agencies or civil society extending help. They relied on each other and the clan structures while in the marsh.

Trading and feasting in evacuations

When the military aerial and pursuit operations stopped after a few months, the *bakwit*s tried farming the dry fertile lands of the marsh or fishing in its waterways and swamps. A few members of the family would slip past the soldiers and paramilitary forces covering the exit points from the marsh and sell their catch and harvest to the markets in Pikit or Cotabato City, an urban area about 100 km away.

Eventually, a few months after the displacements, traders, several of whom are Christians and ethnic Chinese from Cotabato City, Pikit and other areas, sailed to the marshlands peddling merchandise like biscuits, canned goods, clothes, veils, kerosene gas, kitchen wares, blades for farming and other basic household amenities. The traders in turn purchased the *bakwit* farm products and fish catch, and sold it back to Pikit or Cotabato City. Life was not as easy compared to their life in Buliok before the war, but they managed to hold *kanduli* or rites for weddings, births, remembering the dead, Islamic rituals and other cultural events. They even managed to wear their best clothes in special rites while in the marsh. Clothes are among the priority items they carried during the evacuation.

Return, 1974 and displacement, 1976

As the conflicts subsided, a few *bakwit* returned to their village around 1974 to work on their farms. Two years later, they fled again.[11] Military ground assaults and aerial bombings continued, forcing families to break up and scatter across the Liguasan marsh. Evacuees I interviewed claimed significant level of civilian casualties in the aftermath of massive air raids in 1978 and 1979. The *bakwit* thought the marsh was impenetrable from ground attacks but that belief was shattered with the landing of hundreds of soldiers in an area called Dalgan and its surroundings in 1979. The *bakwit* abandoned the marsh and sought refuge in town centres.

Mamolindas slipped out of the Liguasan marsh before the air strikes. He said some MNLF guerrilla leaders who were his relatives but who defected to the government warned him and other clan members of a planned massive air attack. He heeded the warning but other clan members and neighbours did not. They remained in the marsh for fear of a harsher life in the town centre. Mamolindas and his family fled to Pikit where he kept a low profile doing menial jobs because some of his relatives who were former local MNLF-commanders-turned-government-military-field-officers suspected him of allying with the rebels.

Return, 1981

As the guns fell silent in late 1981, a few displaced families took the initiative of returning to Buliok and were followed by more families. They, however, returned with guarded optimism by building huts close to each other. In each hut, two or three families lived together to ensure that everybody was within reach and could easily be warned in case they had to run. After a few more months without ground attacks and bombardments, the families started dispersing and rebuilding sturdier homes. Around 1983 the community was again teeming with life. They built two mosques and gradually acquired farm animals, tools, fishing equipment and later on rebuilt one of the three rice mills destroyed in the 1970s.

Evacuations, 1990

All these, however, were destroyed six years later in 1990 when another war engulfed their village. Buliok villagers kept themselves away until they began returning around 1991. They started rebuilding about two years later in 1993 when they managed to set up more stable houses, re-cultivated their abandoned tobacco, corn and rice fields, installed corn mills, and purchased motorboats. As a *barangay*, the community managed to press the government to construct public elementary and high schools, village halls and other facilities.

All these, however, came to naught in 1997 when military attacks targeted a village called Rajah Muda in the town of Pikit, just three kilometres from Buliok. Government soldiers announced that the attack was meant to flush out the kidnap-for-ransom gangs and criminal groups reported to have slipped into Rajah Muda. Artillery and aerial bombings as well as fighting extended towards the Liguasan marsh, forcing Buliok residents and other villages in Pikit and Pagalungan to flee.

Evacuation shift: From swamps to camps

Significantly, the 1997 displacements marked a shift in the destinations of the *bakwit*. By this time, more evacuees sought refuge in elementary schools, the *madrasah*, *mahad*, gymnasium, warehouses, plaza, old cinema house and other parts of central Pikit. At least 30,000 families were evacuated to Pikit town centre at that time, prompting the flow of aid from the government, humanitarian institutions, churches, Islamic associations and civil society groups. To access aid, however, the *bakwit* signed survey sheets prepared by aid agencies and waited for the process of verification attesting that they were, indeed, evacuees. Upon verification, they were given coupons required to be shown to aid workers distributing relief goods. These goods usually included, among others, five to ten kilograms of rice, cans of sardines, noodles, soap, detergent bars and other household items.

Samira Usman, a twenty-seven year old evacuee from Kudal, a village near Buliok, said never had she felt so humiliated when she lined up for food from aid agencies. Though life has been more difficult in their evacuation sites in the Liguasan marsh and other safer fields in Pikit and Pagalungan towns, they had not needed to fall in line for food.

Imaging the 'helpless' *bakwit*

The image of the *bakwit* helplessly lining for aid with hands stretching out for food, tears in their eyes, staring aimlessly at nothingness and children wearing torn clothes holding empty tin plates are beamed on television and splashed across the newspapers. I think these images of helplessness set the discourse of the *bakwit* as people who do not know their rights, as poor, uneducated, powerless, and in need of continuing assistance and lectures on livelihood and empowerment.

When the tensions in Raja Muda eased, residents started returning around 1998 and went back to farming and producing goods far from the image frozen by television and newspaper photographs at one point of their lives as *bakwit*. Two years later, the chance of rebuilding dissipated because Buliok residents fled again when the Philippine government launched an 'all-out war' against the MILF in the summer of 2000.

The MILF's main base in another part of Mindanao fell following massive air strikes and military assaults. Mosques, houses, stores, schools and communities also fell in the aftermath of air strikes and ground attacks that extended to several other provinces in Mindanao. The government placed the number of displaced persons between 7,00,000 to a million (Notre Dame University Research Center with the Commission on Population Region XII 2004: 9).

The problem with aid

Aid agencies, civil society members, churches and other groups poured relief goods into Pikit, Pagalungan and other conflict-affected areas, but sometimes relief distribution itself created conflicts. Evacuees queuing would spark tension as some aid agencies claimed that non-*bakwit*, or people who were not displaced, took advantage of relief goods by signing up as the displaced.

They said that some evacuees also took advantage of other evacuees by listing their children's names so they could get more food aid. Other aid workers complained of evacuees who sold their supplies and of traditional community leaders stealing the relief goods.

Usman says that the aid agencies do not know the whole story. She says while some of those who had their names listed for relief were not evacuees of the 2000 war, they were *bakwit* of earlier wars who failed to return home and had had economic difficulties. Evacuees listed the names of their children and even long-dead relatives because they were not certain when the next supplies would be coming. Some sold their aid goods because they found the items less needed. They used the money to purchase what they felt was more needed or what they preferred. For instance, a relief agency distributed mongo beans thinking that it is a good source of protein but some evacuees, especially those suffering from arthritis, would not eat them believing that these have high acid content and could trigger chemical reactions that could cause more pain. The money they earned from selling the beans were used to buy fish, still a source of protein that better suits their taste and health. Certain traditional leaders in host communities demanded a share of relief goods because that has been the practice in the area.

The problem with aid in the context of Usman's story is that it does not match the displaced community's expectations, thinking and preference.

Aid agencies rise above the 'helpless *bakwit*' who are at the receiving end of 'humanitarian assistance'. Aid agencies take the vantage position of power as they tend to set the ethics and morality of receiving aid. They frown on people who list more names to get more aid, scoff at traditional leaders demanding share from relief goods and decide who qualifies to be a *bakwit* and can access entitlements on the basis of the year they were displaced. In certain situations, like in Usman's story, the issue is not the ethics and morality of claiming aid but an understanding and appreciation of the complexities and problems of life in refugee camps or the evacuation centres as they are known in Mindanao.

Evacuation centres: Fields of suffering and capacity

Drawing lessons from Usman's story of camp life brings us to points raised against the idea of refugee camps (Black 1998: 4–7). The evacuation camp environment in the 2000 war brought out the best and the worst among the evacuees. Most of them lived in cramped blue plastic tents that bristled as the sun went up late in the morning to mid-afternoon. The poor layout and facilities of the camp added to the desperation of the evacuees and made them look, feel and think as suffering helplessly. The camps are also fields of contestations and of power centres. Since they are set up in lands claimed by traditional clan and community leaders of host communities, evacuees have to bow to the rules that the leader set, like the practice of sharing goods, be it relief, trade products or government resources.

Other evacuees, however, refused to be overwhelmed by desperation. Usman and her husband purchased a parcel of the land they had been occupying, using the money saved from their last harvest. Some fifty other families also brought parcels of lands adjacent to the lot bought by Usman and her husband. They raised the money using savings from the harvest, loans and support sent by children working as domestic helps abroad. Others set up cooling stations near the town hall selling snacks, drinks and lunch to police personnel and town hall employees. There were evacuees who worked as hired hands and did other menial jobs. Still, many of the evacuees returned to their farms, braving the dangers of getting caught of possible cross-fire between warring government and rebel forces.

Displaced persons in other evacuation centres also had more to share than stories of sufferings and deprivations. To celebrate the breaking of the fast during the holy month of Ramadan in November 2001, a family of Muslim *bakwit* in one of Pikit's evacuation centres managed to share probably the last of what they had with a Catholic priest who had been their friend and provider of food aid in the endless cycle of war and peace. The priest, Roberto Layson of the Pikit parish, was humbled by the gesture and thought of the action as an expression of 'human greatness' and 'capability' despite having been caught in an extremely difficult situation. Layson (2004) writes in his reflection: 'I thought that because the evacuees were starving they would keep everything for themselves, and be no longer capable of showing generosity to fellow human beings like me. I was terribly wrong. I underestimated the evacuees because I overestimated myself.'

The continuing saga of evacuations and returns

In 2001, both the government and the MILF called for a bilateral cease-fire, paving the way for the resumption of peace negotiations and talks of rehabilitating war-affected areas.[12] Buliok residents started the process of return in late 2000. This time, however, the MILF chair Salamat Hashim transferred his base to Buliok. Residents claimed they were aware of MILF presence but they continued to go about with their everyday life knowing that some of their relatives were also members of the MILF. Three years after the 2000 conflicts, another war cast away the residents of Buliok. The defence department claimed that the campaign targeted 'terrorists' who had reportedly slipped to Buliok.[13]

Interestingly, several residents started fleeing Buliok few days before the attack, keeping themselves out of harm's way. They read the signs of an impending war with the continued arrival of military troops and equipment in Pikit. They left heeding calls by Pikit's government officials, most of them also their relatives. Yet, others did not.

On 11 February 2003, a sacred day of the *Eid'l Adha*, one of the holiest religious rites in the Islamic world, a few civilians, including women and children, remained in Buliok thinking that government soldiers would spare them the attacks, given the sanctity of the occasion. Mike Luay, a Buliok resident, tells me that a few civilians, MILF and fighters were gathered in and around a mosque reciting the *Al Fatiha*, the opening words in the Holy Qur'an, when the first volley of artillery fires hit parts of Buliok. The community fell and houses were levelled. Soldiers captured and took over the MILF's base but as the military scored points, the social cost of the war was staggering. Records from the government's Department of Social Welfare and Development noted that the number of the *bakwit* reached 4,00,004. Those in Pikit were scattered in sixty-five evacuation centres (Notre Dame University Research Center with the Commission on Population Region XII 2004: 9).

The first of the *bakwit* would not return until about four months later in June 2003. In October 2004, more evacuees returned to Buliok following the pull-out of military forces from the village continuing the saga of evacuations, return and rebuilding.

New *bakwit* movements

Since the war in 2000, the evacuees in Buliok as well as in other parts of Central Mindanao adopted new strategies and explored other fields of movements rather than confining their places of refuge in the Liguasan marsh and its surrounding areas. These included networking with peace advocacy groups who could lobby for ceasefire orders with ranking government officials and before the Central Committee of the MILF.

Peace constituents: Harnessing the power of the *bakwit*

In late May 2003, several evacuees met with a civil society group called the Mindanao People's Caucus (MPC). The evacuees and the MPC representatives gathered in a school in Pagalungan not to line up for food but to discuss what they could do about the war. Agitated, the evacuees wanted to organize a rally and block a strategically busy road near the evacuation site until the government and the MILF heeded their demands for a ceasefire.[14] Some members of the MPC agreed to mass action but opposed the blocking of the highway, fearing that such a move would provoke government authorities and that the situation could turn even more bloody and untenable. The plan was debated on until they agreed not to block the highway but continue with two days of mass action.

Unleashing *bakwit* power

On 24 June 2003, an estimated 7,000 evacuees formed a kilometre-long line stretching from the Pikit town centre to Pagalungan along the national highway. They carried signboards and streamers proclaiming

'Ceasefire Now!' and the symbolic name for the mass action: *Bakwit* Power.

The *bakwit*, joined by civil society groups unleashed their power as they attracted government and rebel attention and commitment to observe a ceasefire. President Macapagal Arroyo sent Secretary Teresita Deles, a member of her cabinet, to Pagalungan and spoke before the gathering of *bakwit* and civil society groups at the town plaza. Deles read aloud the *Bakwit* Power manifesto and assured the government would work on their demands.

Following *Bakwit* Power, the *bakwit* and some civil society staff met again and reflected on their next move. They decided to organize an association that would continue the spirit of the *Bakwit* Power. They named the group *Suara Kalilintad* or Voice of Peace. *Suara Kalilintad* is steered by a board of directors and an executive committee they themselves composed. They partnered with civil society groups working in Pikit and Pagalungan for the construction of houses for the returning evacuees.

Bantay ceasefire: Winning the peace

The *bakwit* also learned to work with the civil society in a formation called the *Bantay* (Guard) Ceasefire, a community-based ceasefire monitoring network of peace advocates, the media, the academia, churches and the evacuees. Evacuees affiliated with the *Bantay* Ceasefire network played critical roles in galvanizing immediate public attention before an armed conflict escalated. In March 2004, the returning evacuees in Buliok were alarmed by the movements of the MILF and government troopers. An evacuee who is also a *Bantay* Ceasefire member sent an SMS (short messaging service) from a mobile phone describing government and MILF troop movements and the fresh wave of evacuations in early March. The evacuee noted in the message that the government soldiers and MILF guerrillas were within shooting range of each other and that a slightest provocation could lead to a gun battle and ultimately into a war.

The *Bantay* Ceasefire coordinator, who is a member of the civil society, received the *bakwit*'s message and immediately alerted the government–MILF ceasefire committees, the Philippine government, Office of the Presidential Adviser on the Peace Process, military commanders and the *Bantay* Ceasefire network about the situation unfolding on the ground. The information went through and down the military and MILF chain of command that eventually restrained the action of their forces on the field. Here, we see the capacity and ability of the *bakwit* in harnessing the mobile phone technology in keeping the ceasefire in check, nipping conflicts in the bud and consequently avoiding new displacement events. Using mobile phones, the *bakwit* effectively alerted and galvanized public attention to guerrilla and government troop movements. This prevented the unfolding of military movements that could have provoked a war and another case of displacement.

Re-understanding the *bakwit* image: The power of the displaced

When seen in a time continuum, the experiences of the *bakwit* in Buliok and other parts of Pikit is not all about desperation, helplessness and victimization. A good part of it is about persistence. They carry themselves with dignity as they struggle and initiate ways to survive and recover through their continuing experiences of evacuations. They engaged in other movements like *Bantay* Ceasefire and *Bakwit* Power mass action, and linking with aid groups and government welfare agencies. I think these are significant indications of human agency, unlike generalized description of the displaced as people who go through a 'transition from independence to being dependent on government, NGOs or individuals' and of being overwhelmed with feelings of 'fear, hopelessness, lack of power, and anger' (CFSI 2003: 5).

The power of the displaced lies in their ability to deal with and transform difficult situations into new social conditions through the years of continuing armed conflicts. With a transformed social condition, they were able to expand the options for survival, recovery and rebuilding their lives and communities. *Bakwit* actions, however, are not exactly unique to themselves. What they do and have done testifies to the capacity and the ability of humanity—whoever, wherever and of whatever group they are—in confronting and changing the most challenging social conditions into one that they can live with. The power of the displaced is the power of the human will and action, an agentive exercise which in my view is worth celebrating.

Solidarity beyond aid

Viewing the *bakwit* from a narrow frame of displaced people fleeing from wars with heavy loads on their way to cramped evacuation centres may have shaped the assessment of the 'helpless *bakwit*'. Because of the discourse of the *bakwit* as weak and vulnerable, some aid agencies asked them about their needs through needs assessment studies, facilitated their return to their communities, provided them the 'foundation for peace building and sustainable development' and offered them training to increase individual capability and community capacity to address different concerns (CFSI 2003: 10).[15]

It is quite absurd to empower and lecture on capacity and capability building to a group of people who carried themselves with remarkable capabilities and capacities in the course of evacuations, return and rebuilding in the past thirty years. The policy of teaching empowerment or lecturing capacity building are, in all likelihood, not congruent with such a group of people. On the contrary, the long but persistent efforts of the displaced peoples in evacuating and continuously rebuilding their communities should serve as the guide for aid, government welfare and civil society groups working in war-affected communities.

The government and civil society's efforts of rebuilding communities in the context of rehabilitation do not match with community-initiated rebuilding efforts. As narrated by Menandang Mamolindas, the village of Buliok was a relatively affluent and productive area before its destruction during the wars of the 1970s. Buliok residents, however, painstakingly re-cultivated their farms, rebuilt their sturdy houses, built a fleet of motorboats and set up farming and community facilities during the relatively longer reign of peace in the mid-1980s to mid-1990s. These socio-economic gains came to naught following the successive three-year cycle of wars in 1997, 2000 and 2003. Redeveloped farms, finely crafted houses and community facilities were all destroyed by the wars. The repeated wars in Buliok destroyed the material achievements of the community but not the dynamism, initiatives and persistence of its people. This is illustrated by the fact that despite the recurring character of the Buliok wars, the villagers gradually rebuilt their homes, farms and community during the years without massive displacements—a clear display of capacity, resilience and productivity. Fresh waves of displacements in the late 1990s and the early 2000s may have reversed the villagers' rebuilding efforts but their achievement indicates that before the war and during the intervening years of relative peace, Buliok was simply not an impoverished community but has become so because of repeated wars.

Establishing a distinction between an impoverished community and a community impoverished by repeated wars is of critical necessity in the crafting of intervention policies. A recognition of the remarkable level of community achievements before the war and during the absence of displacements presupposes an empowered, capable and creative community which can autonomously chart and achieve development.

Beyond aid: The displaced as a force for peace advocacy

At this point, the real challenge for all concerned is to stop treating the displaced as being at the receiving end of aid and interventions. Ethics and decency demand that we learn from the displaced and how they managed to persist in difficult circumstances, as this wisdom and capacity could be the basis of relationships in addressing situations of evacuations, and the return and rebuilding of war-affected communities. On that note, the displaced are also among the critical and significant force in preventing the cycle of conflicts, violence and displacements.

To echo a *Bantay* Ceasefire (2003: 7) report:

> If Peace in Mindanao is going to be forged, then it should not only be by two dozen or more people who compose the official peace panels and their technical committees, advisers and working groups, but by the millions of stakeholders living in what we hope would be former battlegrounds in the future

I think the *bakwit* are also an enormous force that springs from the heart of war-ravaged areas. If the power of the *bakwit* is tapped in peace advocacy, they can unleash the energy, force and network that could nip conflicts before they can escalate. The *bakwit* in Buliok did just that, and I am confident that it can be done elsewhere and in the future.

Notes

1. The MNLF is an armed group asserting a role as the representative of a protracted *Bangsamoro* people's struggle for self-rule in Mindanao. The group was founded by young intellectuals in 1969 but its existence was made public in 1973 when it started claiming credit for a series of encounters with the government forces. Soon after the founding of the MNLF, however, the leadership broke into factions (Jubair 1999: 149–57). The MILF is one of the stronger groups that came out of those that split from the MNLF.
2. Elderly residents in Pikit and Pagalungan towns of Central Mindanao recalled that their use of *bakwit* as a term for referring to forcibly displaced persons

dates back to World War II when the Japanese Imperial Army invaded the Philippines, then a United States colony.

3. Paragraph 2 of the 1951 Convention Relating to the Status of Refugees defined that the term 'refugee' applies to 'any person owing to well founded fear of being persecuted for reasons of race, religion, nationality, membership of a particular social group or political opinion, is outside the country of his nationality.' The definition, however, has been challenged and discoursed upon in various literatures (Camilleri 2003: 23; Castles 2003: 11–20; Hathaway 1997: 79–88; Turton 2003).

4. The UN Guiding Principle category of IDP are articulated and popularized in literatures produced by civil society groups like Balay, Incorporated and Tabang Mindanao. Balay, in December 2000, printed and distributed *A Primer on Internal Displacement in the Philippines.* Tabang Mindanaw, one of the major aid groups during the wars in 2000 and 2003, produced and distributed the finely crafted *Building Sanctuaries for Peace brochure*, highlighting the IDP as a category of persons who would be the subject of their assistance.

5. Views advocating for capacity-building as a way of rebuilding conflict-affected villages were espoused in literatures produced by the civil society group Tabang Mindanaw or Help Mindanao, government agencies like National Anti-Poverty Commission (2003: 19–26), and jointly by the Mindanao Economic Development Council (2004), Autonomous Region in Muslim Mindanao, United Nations Development Programme and the European Commission, in the month of September.

6. Liguasan Marsh, one of the largest swamp lands in the Philippines, stretches to 2,80,000 hectares, cutting across the provinces of Cotabato, Sultan Kudarat and Maguindanao. The government plans to develop the marsh as a leading eco-tourism destination, with an internationally known sanctuary of birds and rare animal species, as a showcase of preservation and sustainable development , in accordance to the Liguasan Marsh Development Master Plan 1999–2025 of the National Economic Development Authority, in Region 12.

7. Some of the displaced families who evacuated to the swamps eventually moved to evacuation centres. Upon reaching the camps, however, the movement of the *bakwit* continued as they transferred from one camp to another, according to a January 2004 study of the University Research Center of Notre Dame University in cooperation with the government's Commission on Population. The study noted that some of the displaced families moved up to five times while in the evacuation camps. (Notre Dame University Research Center with the Commission on Population 2004: 34).

8. Ilaga was founded by a group of Christian politicians in Cotabato, who claimed that their initiative was in response to attacks by the Moro bands in some parts of their towns. Its formation shortly followed the founding of the Mindanao Independent Movement (MIM) by powerful and well-armed

Moro politicians. MIM was formed in the aftermath of the massacre of Moro military trainees on 18 March 1968 in a government military camp. These initiatives of Christian and Moro politicians were 'easily connected with the popular sentiments of their respective constituencies' and that 'soon Moro raids were answered with Christian raids, Christian killings with Moro killings' (Rodil 2003: 132–37). Christian refers to the descendants and families of non-Muslim settlers who migrated from Luzon and Visayas, which are the two other major groups of islands in Mindanao.

9. As already mentioned in Note 1, MNLF was founded in 1969 but its existence was made public only in 1973, when it started claiming credit for series of encounters with government forces. Soon after the founding of the MNLF, the leadership broke into factions (Jubair 1999: 149–57). The MILF, chaired by Salamat Hashim, is one of the stronger organizations that emerged out of the MNLF splits. The MNLF signed a peace accord with the government on 2 September 1996. The MILF also entered into peace negotiations and signed a ceasefire agreement with the government but talks went on and off and the accord remained untenable due to periodic fighting.

10. These accounts were based on a focus group discussion among Buliok residents. The activity was initiated by the staff of the Bakwit Information Center of the Mindanao People's Caucus, the group where I served as a volunteer during my fieldwork in Buliok in May 2004.

11. In 1976, some surrendered MNLF members associated with the traditional Moro leaders who broke ties with the MNLF's central leadership in the early 1970s, joined the government forces in fighting against their former comrades, relatives and friends who remained with the MNLF. The conflict destroyed government houses, entertainment facilities, shops and inns, and drove away traders, landowners and other residents of what used to be a vibrant Pagalungan town. The historic Pagalungan was the provincial capital of the undivided Cotabato in 1966–68 (McKenna 1998: 146, 321) and the base of guerrillas and United States forces who fought the Japanese Imperial Army during World War II. Presently, Pagalungan is considered as one of the poorest and conflict-prone areas in Mindanao.

12. On 7 August 2001, a joint communiqué signed by Jesus Dureza, the then chair of the government peace panel and Al Haj Murad Ebrahim, the then chair of the MILF panel, announced the signing of a set of guidelines in Kuala Lumpur, Malaysia, to normalize the situation in the conflict areas in Mindanao and pave the way for the successful conduct of relief rehabilitation and development programmes.

13. In the *bakwit* video documentary, *Sana Wala Nang Gyera, Sana Wala Nang Bakwit* (Wishing No More War, Wishing No More IDPs) by the Mindanao-based Mindanao News and Information Cooperative Center, a clip, taken in May 2003 or about three months after the Buliok attack, shows the then Defence Secretary Angelo Reyes linking the attack to the war on terrorism.

'Well, the fight against terrorism is going to be a long drawn out war. That will last as long as there are terrorists,' Reyes said when asked by journalists how long the Buliok military campaign will last.

14. The MILF declared a ten-day unilateral ceasefire from 2–12 June 2003 and extended it by ten more days but the government did not reciprocate the declaration (Bacongco 2003).

15. This point is among the programmes highlighted by Tabang Mindanaw in its brochure, 'Tabang Mindanaw—Integrated Return and Rehabilitation Program, Building Sanctuaries of Peace'.

References

Accion Contra El Hambre. 2004. *Philippine Mission* (Liguasan Marsh Vulnerability Survey). Funded by European Commission Humanitarian Aid Office, Makati City and Cotabato City, Action Contra El Hambre Philippine Mission.

Almario, Virgilio S. (ed.). 2001. *Diksyunaryong Filipino*. Quezon City: Sentro ng Wikang Filipino and Anvil Publishing Inc.

Bantay Ceasefire. 2003. *Reports of the Grassroots-led Missions Monitoring the Ceasefire Between the Philippine Government and the Moro Islamic Liberation Front*. Davao City: Initiatives for International Dialogue and the Mindanao People's Caucus.

Bacongco, Keith. 2003. 'Bakwit power: Day 2 Along the National Highway', Davao City: MindaNews. Available on http//:www.mindanews.com\ "Bakwitpower"Day2alongthenationalhighway.htm. Accessed on 5 October 2004.

Balay Advocacy Program. Undated. *A Primer on Internal Displacement in the Philippines*. Quezon City: Balay Rehabilitation Center.

Black, Richard. 1998. *Putting Refugees in Camp in Forced Migration Review 2*. Oxford and Geneva: Refugee Studies Programme of the University of Oxford with the Global IDP of the Norwegian Refugee Council.

Camilleri, Maria. 2003. 'Refugees in All but Name? Should UNCHR's Mandate Offer Protection to IDPs?', in 'Researching Internal Displacement: State of the Art', Conference Report, 7–8 February. Trondeheim: Norwegian University of Science and Technology and Forced Migration Review.

Castles, Stephen. 2003. 'The International Politics of Forced Migration', *Society for International Development*, 46(3): 11–20.

Community and Family Services International (CFSI). 2003. *'You Listen': Internally Displaced Persons Speak About a Pilot Project in Conflict-affected Central Mindanao*. Pasay City: CFSI.

Daguino, Dolly, Jamail Kamlian, Rosalia Dagaerag, Ofelia Durante, Noram Gomez, Alano Kadil, Darwin Manubag, Marilou Siton-Nanamn and Donna Doane. 2003. 'Transition Interventions with Internally Displaced

Persons: From Conflict toward Peace and Development in the Southern Philippines', A collaborative research effort of Community and Family Services International (CFSI), Mindanao State University-Iligan Institute of Technology and Notre Dame University Research Center; funded by the World Bank Post-Conflict Fund. Makati and Cotabato City: CFSI.

Hathaway, J.C. 1997. 'Is Refugee Status Really Elitist? An Answer to the Ethical Challenge', in J.Y. Carlier and D. Vahuele (eds), *Europe and Refugees: A Challenge?* The Hague: Kluwer Law International.

Jubair, Salah. 1999. *Bangsamoro: A Nation Under Endless Tyranny*. Kuala Lumpur: IQ Marin SDN BHD.

Layson, Roberto. 2004. 'Reflections of a Peace Advocate'. Available on http://www.mindanews.com/2004/02/07fea-layson2.html

Mamolindas, Menandang. 2004. *Kuwento ng Barangay Buliok* (A Story of Barangay Buliok). Unpublished.

McKenna, Thomas. 1998. *Muslim Rulers and Rebels: Everyday Politics and Armed Separatism in the Southern Philippines*. Quezon City: Anvil Publishing, Inc., with the Regents of the University of California.

Mindanao Economic Development Council, Autonomous Region in Muslim Mindanao, United Nations Development Programme and the European Commission. 2004. 'Programme on Rehabilitating Internally Displaced Persons and Communities in Southern Philippines', Briefing Paper, 21 September.

Mindanao People's Caucus (MPC). 'Brochure on the Bakwit Information Center. Promoting Humanitarian Protection in Central Mindanao', MPC, Kabacan, North Cotabato.

National Anti-Poverty Commission. 2003. 'Focused, Accelerated, Convergent and Expanded Anti-Poverty Strategy', National Anti Poverty Commission Report.

Notre Dame University Research Center with the Commission on Population Region XII. 2004. *Migration in Conflict Situation and its Implication on Local Governance*. Cotabato City: Notre Dame University Research Center with the Commission on Population Region XII.

Nussbaum, Martha C. 1995. 'Human Capabilities, Female Human Beings', in Martha Nussbaum and Jonathan Glover (eds), *Women, Culture and Development: A Study of Human Capabilities*. Oxford: Clarendon Press.

OXFAM. 2000. *Anthropometric and Household Food Insecurity Survey among Displaced Families in Central Mindanao*. Great Britain: OXFAM.

Rodil, B.R. 2003. *A Story of Mindanao and Sulu in Question and Answer*. Davao City: Mincode.

Sullivan, Robert E. 1986. *Maguindanaon Dictionary: Maguindanaon–English, English–Maguindanaon*. Cotabato City: Institute of Cotabato Cultures, Notre Dame University.

Turton, David. 2003. 'Conceptualizing Forced Migration', RSC Working Paper No. 12, Refugee Studies Centre, University of Oxford.

Ecological Ontology and Landscapes of Democratic Struggles in Globalization Politics

12

Residual, Emergent and Transformative Dimensions

HERBERT REID AND BETSY TAYLOR

Place and landscapes of democratic space and global justice

Canuday's chapter in this volume bravely emphasizes humanity as opposed to the powerlessness of the displaced peoples. To understand or appreciate the remarkably creative capacities of people in situations of displacement, we need a deeper grasp of the ways emplacement itself underlies and guides human development. It is in these deeply formative processes of the life-world that we find the origins of the struggle for access to the commons. Resistance to displacement from familiar pathways of the commons, expropriated by absentee power structures, is found worldwide.[1] This resistance aims, initially, at preserving the very roots of the humanity of affected groups.

Naomi Klein's discussion of New Orleans in the wake of Hurricane Katrina and the 'shock doctrine' applied by a neo-liberal corporatist coalition orchestrated by the Bush–Cheney administration is instructive. 'Most people who survive a devastating disaster want the opposite of a clean slate; they want to salvage whatever they can and begin repairing what was not destroyed; they want to reaffirm *their relatedness to the places that formed them*' (Klein 2007: 8, emphasis added). Klein continues, quoting a Lower Ninth Ward resident named Cassandra Andrews clearing away debris and commenting, '[w]hen I rebuild the city I feel like I'm rebuilding myself' (Klein 2007: 8). While Klein's point is to contrast the approach of the 'disaster capitalists' put into perspective by her book, her discussion also exemplifies the role of place in any politics concerned with building more democratic spaces.

Democratic development, when posed as an alternative for resistance groups, must begin with the debts to place(s) that people register in their very humanity reflecting as it does the biodiversity of which it is (usually) a grateful part. Such an approach has many obstacles and one is that globalization talk, especially in the United States of America (USA), typically veils the commons in its various levels. Appeals to 'the global economy' frequently suggest that beneath the cybernetic fog, there is nothing but endless, flat, commodified space, the artificial turf produced by an economic machine that has dispensed with all the great questions of responsibility and justice (for critiques of this, see Escobar 2008; McMurtry 1998, especially Chapters 2 and 6, 1999; Nonini 2007; Reid and Taylor forthcoming, especially Chapters 2 and 6).

In reality, besieged democratic publics struggle to maintain and cultivate a political terrain that permits raising plausible versions of such questions. They do so amidst actually existing power arrangements that include a state turned into a legitimation machine for concealing its captive and predatory aspects. One of the most certain products of this system is increasing inequality that undercuts the political participation also needed for popular legitimacy. What has come to be called 'disaster capitalism' both promotes and then justifies massive de-localization. But much of the globalization talk tries to smooth this over with mobility as progress imagery. Simultaneously, the extent of globalized mobility as chaos is often occluded by global corporate media.

Sometimes academic discourse is complicit to this process. For example, this happens when the 'subjects' constructed by academic discourse are stuck in postmodern networks of desire and consumption devoid of political imagination. Social theory may reinforce cultural amnesia by neglecting the historicizing tasks that help lift the fog of power from the landscape. Underneath all the chatter about an 'information economy' operating at high speeds, there remains a land-based economy too often missed by academics enamoured with a linguistic approach to history. Around the world, the explosive emergence of groups concerned with community-supported farmers markets, 'organic food', a 'slow food movement', and a reliable food system not based on ecologically harmful forms of agriculture suggests the importance of another spectrum of social time (*Cf* Berry 1996 [1977]; Shiva 2000; Wirzba 2003). This alternative future expands the communing endeavours of communities as democratic publics seek a generative and more sustainable world. This work needs stronger support from public policies that take place making and re-making seriously—not only in precautionary planning but also in the wake of disaster. The bailouts of the initial response to the United States (US) version of the global economic crisis reflect a pampering of the financial sectors engaged in exactly the wrong kind of social engineering. When an economics masks the lack of conjunction between power and the public goods of social life, it is time for a new economics.

However, one of our main concerns is probing the deeper *auspices* of the critique of the destruction of place. Democratic theorists would do well to examine how the new movement sensibility often discloses ways in which *place experience* nestles both ecological and historical horizons that open towards what the late Raymond Williams called 'resources of hope' (Williams 1989). Williams' great interest in what he calls 'the complicated relationships between class and place' points in the right direction (Eagleton 1989: 180). Terry Eagleton once noted Williams's 'confident trust in human capacities' (182). At the epigraph to Eagleton's edited collection on Williams (after the latter's death in 1988), he quotes Williams referring to 'ways of thinking, with the seeds of life in them—. (Eagleton 1989). Our own probe is enhanced further by Williams's interest in 'the changing embodiment of the possibilities of common life' (183). At the front of his edited collection on Williams (after the latter's death in 1988), Eagleton quotes him referring to 'ways of thinking, with the seeds of life in them ...' (Eagleton 1989: 180–83).

Our own probe is enhanced further by Williams's interest in 'the changing embodiment of the possibilities of common life' (Eagleton 1989: 180–83).

We live in a time of world history when the idea and reality of the Atmospheric Commons has asserted itself. Our world is beginning to be torn asunder by increasingly chaotic climate change and by globalizing forms of socio-economic inequality. These trends are intertwined and both carry what Williams called the 'seeds of a general death'. If the Western hope for 'Progress' sometimes tracks domination and destruction, where are the seeds of life that could generate a new politics of hope? Jan Nederveen Pieterse points us in this volume towards 'a politics of empowerment' and that is where we seek to illuminate residual, emergent and transformative dimensions and their interplay. The fixation on global resource extraction of the politics of power to which he refers entails as well the exploitation of the places and commons involved.

As Stephen Marglin has argued, there is something drastically wrong with Western programmes for 'development' or 'modernization' that 'make political disempowerment and cultural impoverishment the price of material abundance' (Marglin 1990b: 27). The problem is an approach to growth and change that permits only the subordination if not the denigration of indigenous cultures and local knowledge. Marglin also averred that USA workers have paid a heavy price of political subordination including workers' knowledge (Marglin 1990a: 277) that helps explain, since his 1990 account, so many scenes of increasing economic insecurity and cultural degradation amidst deepening public squalor.

What should now be clear is the way in which globalizing and glorifying economic space distorts the forms of time and place vital to linking work, consumption and democratic control. The Bhopal disaster in India and a 'chemical valley' in West Virginia are linked by issues of control, resistance and class that include cultural self-determination.[2] With this, we move back into the complex relationship of class and place of such interest for Raymond Williams; we move towards John Dewey's theory of democratic publics (1927) with their roots in the local and its regenerative potencies of place and time (Dewey 1991 [1927]).

Dewey's 1925 Paul Carus lectures published as *Experience and Nature* did a remarkable job of identifying the cultural and philosophic dualisms interfering with a stronger understanding of new place-based forms of democratic inquiry and development and their political potential (Dewey 1929 [1925]). He explains that we will not get very far if our interpretation is based on a familiar modern western dualism between emotion and reason, feeling and knowledge, body and mind and nature and culture. Social scientists who allow nature only 'emotional salience' for human growth would monopolize what they regard as a 'scientific tradition' but one that has roots they seldom take into account. This historical configuration of an isolated, incorporeal intellect protected from the alleged dangers of its sensorial landscape is a long story of many chapters to which we can only allude here.

We would do much better to begin with the anthropologist's observation that 'a society's place-names schematically image a people's intentional transformation of their habitat from an unobjectified deposition of lived spaces into a pattern of historically experienced and constituted place and time' (Weiner 2001: 16). To do so, it exposes what we have called the body-place-commons triadic configuration of everyday worlds. We understand human being to be 'Subjectivity as intersubjectivity arising in embodied practices in concrete places within heterogeneous temporalities of the ecological commons. *To be a creature—human or non-human—is to be hinged between one's own embodiment and the particularity of places which accrue the grounds for life from unruly and ruly cycles of interdependence, mortality and natality of the ecological commons.'* (Reid and Taylor forthcoming: 6).

But there is, so to speak, a toll road between places and persons that the capitalist gurus of global economic space help maintain. They assert the conceptual and practical priorities of commodified space and facilitate the important processes for making invisible these integral dimensions for healthy life. The negative health impacts of socio-economic inequality and instability are chronicled in multiplying research studies. An emergent public concern for missing vitalities in the geography of childhood threatens to revive popular memories of the commons (Louv 2005; Reid and Taylor forthcoming, Chapter 7). Nevertheless, electronic mobilization remains the watchword of the corporate consumer regime of everyday life while the reality and values of virtual space continue to be prioritized. The ontological legacy of mechanistic nature remains useful for such techno-capitalist abuses of technology and human creativity perpetrated in the name of Progress (Reid and Taylor forthcoming, Chapters 4, 5, 6).

On separate paths, Merleau-Ponty and Dewey developed independent critiques of this ontological demise of nature suggesting more holistic understandings of the self-organizing forms of energy in the physical world. Dewey, calling 'every existence … an event' (Dewey 1929 [1925]: 61), went on to view 'the organism *in* nature … as events are in history, in a moving, growing never finished process' (Dewey 1929 [1925]: 241). When we talk of place, we mean more than a mere intersection of nature and culture rather their chiasmic co-envelopment and ongoing temporalization, including both sedimentation and re-activation. This is why we may speak of our placed embodiment in terms of where/when temporalization of experience works as a kind of reincarnation that *finds its political ecology* by consciously reopening to and within both 'commons' and 'world'.

An ecological hermeneutics moving between earth–ground and world–horizon illuminates and depends on landscapes co-enveloping nature and culture and their mutual reciprocities. By attending to the 'articulations of the aesthesiological body [flowing] along the contours of the sensible things … [marking] the junctures of the visible world,' Merleau-Ponty (1968: 152) returns to the soil of social and political theory, those 'seeds of life' about which we mentioned earlier. Social scientists, admitting intersubjectivity to their self-understanding, are seldom prepared to acknowledge its intimate life with intercorporeity and what Drew Leder, following Merleau-Ponty, describes as the ecstatic–recessive structure of embodiment (Leder 1990).[3] Leder, in fact, illuminates the longstanding problems of dualism and the incorporeal intellect referred to earlier. He works to show how the self-effacement of the ecstatic body contributes to the philosophic dualism that 'reifies the absences and divergences that always haunt our embodied being' (Leder 1990: 69, 108).

Leder is not wrong when he states: 'Body-based vectors are operative in shaping even the highest intellectual achievements of a culture' (Leder 1990: 151–52). However, we would go on, following his suggestions, about the ecological consequences of the modern western death of nature, to put focus on Merleau-Ponty's flesh of the world as a durable matrix of co-being with others that enables the intercultural possibilities of democratic space (*cf* Reid and Taylor forthcoming: Chapter 5). The democratic portals that might give our earth its due are here, where there is a hinging of the matrixical and the emergently particular. Globalizing capital, however, prefers policies based on the doctrines of power and knowledge that facilitate dominance for elites and worldless frills and meaningless labour when needed for many. This massive short-changing of human experience and creative potential, meanwhile, continues to manifest a shrinking range of historical choices as the neurotic quest for profit extends even to the melting Arctic.

Dewey and Merleau-Ponty bring social theory to the ecological ontology and post-dualist sensibility that begins in the intercorporeal field where place and self are co-ingredient in a never finished process. This is where the chiasmatic ecology of nature and culture can foster, without guarantee, experiments of democratic discovery and action in search of more sustainable forms of life. While we do not share his one-sided view of Dewey, we agree with Roberto Mangabeira Unger (2007: 48) that it 'does not follow from our envelopment within nature that we can map out this envelopment and describe our situation from the outside as if we were not who we in fact are'. We propose not a 'naturalistic superscience', but the reconstructive projects of a politics of empowerment informed by a deeper place-based conception of democratic inquiry.

With such a move, social theory can engage the technocorporate triad of Globalization/Subjectivization/Worldlessness that undercuts the ability of potentially democratic publics to discover and identify themselves.[4] When post-democratic plutocracies deploy information technologies in ways that help dematerialize the earth's horizon, and when consumption is structured to rob the cultural present of its traces of history, the public chances of time, memory and place serving democratic discourse and action are minimized. When an increasingly globalized inequality smothers a commodity-saturated pluralism, it becomes farcical for intellectuals to come along and proclaim 'Diversity-in-Itself' as the new democratic 'Totality' that can do without the traditional concerns with equality. This may simply demonstrate that at least some of them have yet to think through the dark side of the real comforts of junior membership in the new 'Global Investor Class'.

Beyond cages of intellectual cynicism and transnational elitism: Rethinking power, freedom and ecological transformation

The intertwining of place and human development, the child's need for non-human nature and the unfinished reciprocity of place and person in experience are important themes in a vast and growing body of interdisciplinary literature [(*Cf* Malpas 1999; Taylor and Reid 2000). Yet, it could be that the contemporary possibility of understanding better than ever before the matrix or nexus of body-place-commons is directly related to the degree to which it is threatened. Nevertheless, we contend that there is an emerging transnational politics for a world-in-common that finds its life-ground, however remnantal, here. Alas, we further think it is all too clear from serious or critical studies of economic globalization that the dark side of this corporate-dominated process is societies marked by increasing socio-economic inequalities, stripped down places and one with growing numbers of ecological refugees. These intertwined problems involve more than economic policies such as privatization, for example, of people's water around the world. Even more insidious is the way that the dominant form of globalization (including Naomi Klein's 'disaster capitalism' and its 'shock doctrine') promotes *subjectivization*, a process undermining popular access to modes of collective, public action, as we have argued (Klein 2007; Reid and Taylor forthcoming, Chapters 3, 5, 7).

We already have numerous studies of our world's politics of grass roots resistance to this 'globalization from above' and the mantra of 'free trade' dictated by a market machine-God. A central aim of 'globalization from below' based on the premise that another world is possible in reclaiming the environmental commons and restoring its various local forms under public control. While sustainability projects must aim at both ecology and equity, we need also to recognize that today, the very idea of 'publics' is in jeopardy. Here, again, we would attempt a broader view by enlisting the 'civic commons' or the challenge of reorganizing and restructuring public spheres for local-regional transformation that, from their diverse ecological grounding, reach towards new forms of global civil society. Engaging current forms or policies of corporate state elitism and nationalism fuelled primarily by transnational corporate power requires increasingly coordinated efforts on all these fronts. One claim of this essay is that in the last century Depression era works by John Dewey such as *The Public and its Problems, Individualism Old and New* and *Art as Experience* provide at least some ideas suggestive for a relevant model of cooperative inquiry and action (Dewey 1934, 1962, 1991 [1927]). Instead of proposing a universal model, our intention is a propaedeutic contribution towards a variety of democratic approaches aiming at a more sustainable world.

Climate change as a political issue may be starting to expose or reveal elite divisions providing opportunities for a democratic left trying to replace notions of 'clean coal' and such with ideas of 'green jobs' and renewable energy.[5] But in the American context, there are many obstacles to more participatory opportunities for the general public and not least among them is a problem of intellectual elitism that takes both conservative and liberal forms. The devastating years of the Bush–Cheney administration brought very little from those quarters in the way of constructive engagement with the problem of climate change. Most of the time denial seemed to be in the saddle. In the following section, we discuss ways in which these structures of denial, intertwined with public policy, got various forms of intellectual reinforcement—including certain ideas of power and freedom of a band of intellectuals connected in one way or another with political philosopher Leo Strauss (1899–1973).

One of the most informative, sympathetic, but critical studies is by political theorist Anne Norton who studied with two of the most highly regarded scholars who studied with Strauss. While Norton takes pains to distinguish Strauss from the 'Straussians' (for example, neo-conservatives Paul Wolfowitz and William Kristol), she is clear about writing a chapter in the latest American trends from republic to empire. We have every reason to stay away from this complex thicket or network of ideas, politics and personalities. However, Norton usefully renders a key theme of Strauss's magnum opus *Natural Right and History* (Strauss 1953) with its extremely rarefied conception of the 'philosophic quest for the first things ...' (Norton 2004: 89). Strauss begins, political theorists will recall, with the Declaration of Independence in 1776, which expresses faith that 'all men are created equal' with natural rights to 'life, liberty, and the pursuit of happiness'. Governments are expected to proceed with the consent of the governed, keeping these rights in view. Norton argues that unlike the 'rights made to grow' of the Declaration of Independence, 'natural rights' in the Chicago political philosopher's view, largely derived by the cognoscenti as a single standard from the ancient wisdom of Plato and Aristotle, 'present an alternative to the consent of the governed' (Norton 2004: 118–20). Yet, she also claims that his student Allan Bloom, 'far more than Strauss, has shaped the Straussians who govern in America' (Norton 2004: 58). Perhaps what deserves more attention is that while both had a big problem with 'democratic mass society', neither spent much if any time connecting its context to corporate power. Within their frame of mind which presumes a virtuous intellectual elite, such a diversion would have been petty and, perhaps, dangerous.

Whatever the case, the Straussian alternative pivots on a doctrine of intellectual elitism that is subjected to a scathing critique by Sheldon Wolin (Wolin 2008: 159–83). Quoting Strauss several times, Wolin leaves no doubt as to the special role of the 'few' presuming their unusual intellect and virtue and the context from which their grandiose and imperial ambitions arose. It would be a mistake to think that the problem of intellectual elitism has disappeared with the fading of the Straussians from public view so important to the Bush–Cheney administration. Sheldon Wolin hits the nail on the head: 'Education that is civic and populist is not a formula that accords with the requirements of American hegemony as elites conceive it' (Wolin 2008: 161). The issues of the educational implications of democratic principles of equality and shared power have been clearly drawn at least since the 1920s debate between Walter Lippmann and John Dewey.

Political or ideological labels are rife in writings on US politics and especially with regard to the so-called mainstream where the terminology seems to thicken when the overlaps become more conspicuous. In other words, there is not as much political diversity or substantive competition as one might assume. American mainstream political culture is burdened by the historical weight of a bourgeois–liberal tradition of capitalist ideology. One is reminded of the recent influence of Chicago economist Milton Friedman over the last three decades. His popularity, very likely soon to fade in the midst of horrible economic crisis, is one more clue to the common capitalist basis of much of the political mainstream. The so-called 'conservative' US circles could better be called 'reactionary liberals'. Their favourite target—what they call 'liberals'—may be better understood as 'reform liberals' in order to mark a more flexible and amelioratist, but still capitalist, approach to government and market.

The American Right knows well what holds up 'mainstream' boundaries and their 'anti-capitalism' detectors which frequently intimidate some dubbed 'liberals' who might better be called 'reform liberals' to signal their more flexible or 'pragmatic' dispositions regarding 'government'. We would underline our view that this discussion puts focus on the chief players in the elite-dominated games of the liberal–democratic polity. US history has had its conservative and radical versions of republicanism (the civic republic), but the liberal–democratic polity has prevailed and never without historic tendencies towards novel forms of empire. The main reason why elitism is of such little concern and populism so often a derogatory term is because one of this polity's mainstream functions is obscuring corporate capitalism's persistent threats to democracy.

The Lippmann-Dewey debate and the challenge of keeping democratic politics alive in the corporate state

Our key contention is that the mainstream politics of the liberal–democratic polity more often than not have had their practical basis in one or more versions of an elite-mass dichotomy. John Dewey did not go along with that and neither do we. But we want to stay on liberal–democratic terrain a little longer. Reform liberals seldom employ the reasons of the Leo Strauss school of political thought. Some are more inclined to Lippmannesque assumptions and arguments about 'leadership' and the properly limited role of publics in a complex world. In the 1950s, the prominent, veteran journalist Walter Lippmann had become extremely concerned to help remake the US political system in order to provide more room for 'a governing class', and especially for executive authority and power. As early as 1914, when his *Drift and Mastery* appeared, his brilliant political analyses and insights combined concerns for the methods of a self-governing people and the necessity for a governing class (Blum 1985: xx-xxi; Lippmann 1985 [1914]: 141, 174). While this book was still being acclaimed by liberal historians in the 1980s, it was his 1922 book called *Public Opinion* that made its way into the textbooks of political science.

While this form of renewed attention to Lippmann focussed on the role of stereotypes and political symbolism, his own interest in opinion management and possible roles for experts was blended with scepticism about majority rule and public participation. Some thirty years later, his last major work argued the necessity of a public philosophy, grounded in a conception of secular natural law, a sort of myth for maintaining a political order that would make room for governance by an elite of intelligence and character. John Dewey detected and engaged

Lippmann's challenge to democratic governance with his 1927 book *The Public and its Problems*. It explained how democratic publics might be rehabilitated that pivoted on reopening and expanding realms of local experience and cooperative inquiry. As Frank Fischer (and others) recognized on the brink of the twenty-first century, Dewey's democratic approach to reformulating the relationship of citizens and experts has been bypassed more often than not. Not the least among the reasons is that bureaucratic institutions of state, market and university have been more likely to reward work based on objectivist decision methods (Fischer 2000: 6–8, 66, 259).

Our argument is that Dewey was right about the negative historical recordof elites and the folly of top-down approaches. At a time when the global ecological crisis persistently asserts issues of the carbon taxes, atmospheric commons, the deterioration of oceans, and so on, the need for ecological actions striving for equitable solutions is the 'elephant in the room'. Are we going to get there led by people who move back and forth between Washington and Citigroup or Peabody Energy and state departments of 'environmental protection'? Is the best academic response more post-modern sophistication, cynicism and moral indifference? Reform liberal nostalgia for systems based on the right to rule and the duty to obey is best left to the Straussians.

The growing problem of transnational elitism already has been aggravated by indulgence in post-communal forms of professionalism that include the function of concealing the contributions of the Global Investor Class to interlocked crises of economy and ecology.

The problem of elitism is not confined to those circles that identify themselves as 'conservative'. Statist projects, whether of the conservative Right or the social-democratic Left, lacking legitimacy, have vacillated between aristocratic restorationism and pseudo-populism. Our proposal is that a seriously democratic transition to a 'green' economy in the US and elsewhere has much to learn from Dewey's extension of the community of investigators to include the democratic public itself.

Historian James Livingston has revisited the Lippmann–Dewey debate of the 1920s and made the interesting argument that Dewey 'understood the new scope and significance of cultural politics better than Lippmann' (Livingston 2001: 53). However, Livingston's point is made in the context of an analysis claiming, as Westbrook puts it, 'pragmatists forecast a post-modern self … located in time rather than space …' (Westbrook 2005: 60). Drawing on a particular version of feminist theory that concedes too many issues in spatial politics, Livingston weakens his own enlistment of a Gramscian 'war of position' (in cultural politics) that would have been served better by the deep reading of Dewey and Merleau-Ponty we have outlined. We think, on the contrary, that Dewey overthrew the philosophic dualism of subject/ object, thematizing dimensions of the Local reset in an 'aesthetic ecology' for public intelligence—a radically democratic approach to the problem of agency and a politics of public sphere projects (emphasize plural).

The post-modern subjectivization of Dewey's approach to culture and democratic action is not the way to find a concrete universal for the politics of diversity and *justice* in a global or any other context. Strangely, instead of Raymond Williams's neo-Gramscian cultural materialist approach, Livingston turns to a post-modernist view of cultural politics entailed by his favourable labour-endorsing Judith Butler's post-structuralist-feminism. He expects this elastic culturalism to help us be 'at home in the divisions of historical time' (Livingston 2001: 185). The metaphysical pathos of this Augustinian reference to time confirms his attempt to rely more on William James than on Antonio Gramsci. Whatever the problems with his historical rendering of James, we would question Livingston's Marxist–progressivist concept of the 'socializing imperatives of the new corporate order' (Livingston 2001: 82). It seems a back-handed way of providing historical sense to the democratic promise of pragmatism. Livingston suggests that understanding Dewey is one way that the US Left can find in our history 'a tattered but still legible map of a transnational, post-imperialist future' (Livingston 2001: 114). But Dewey's ecological ontology for the theory and practice of democratic action did not wait for corporate capitalism to enable or authorize concepts of knowledge, power and justice for the reconstruction of civil society.

Livingston's effort to put James and Dewey to work for a cultural politics supposedly configured in Gramscian terms falters early on when he misconstrues a statement on culture, class and language by Raymond Williams. Livingston quotes out of context when he argues that Williams is making a linguistic turn in cultural history. In fact, Williams was not proposing a linguistic approach to culture, one that in fact has become all too familiar in American cultural studies. His intention was reconstructing a certain Marxist concept of a 'dominant class' in order to show that a selective tradition (illustrated by the American term 'mainstream') is neither simply 'the product of a single class' nor one exhausting the alternatives of a 'transitional society' (Williams 1966 [1958]: 319–21). For a much fuller presentation of this cultural theory, Livingston could have consulted the 1977 book by Williams entitled *Marxism and Literature* (Williams 1977). Four years earlier, Williams had offered a profound interpretation of Gramsci's theory of hegemony in *New Left Review* (Williams 1973) that challenged de-materialized notions of culture in both cultural studies and Old Left circles. His non-dualistic treatment of the material dimension in the social process of culture, instead of discarding the concept of class, sketched a stronger and more flexible one just as global capital was ushering in a new era of cultural fragmentation. Livingston's warning about certain forms of abstract totalization can be applied to his own Archimedean thinking about the future presuming historical stages that oversimplify alternatives. Williams's understanding of structures of feeling and creative practice in the interplay of dominant, residual and emergent elements offers an approach to culture and politics that does not reify or value language and difference or allow 'diversity' to marginalize issues of justice, equality and ecology.

This brings us back to the US transnational corporate state's consumer culture. It is one of the crucial borders often blocking cultural (not just 'intellectual') contributions to public life, a vital public sphere where ecological action for sustainability might materialize appeals to 'community' and 'self-realization' that too often tend to be moralistic and vacuous. A democratic left must stay on this border, working against temptations to cynicism, withdrawal and symbolic violence to transform it on all sides towards a more democratic culture. We should have learned from the 1960s that technocratic scientism or corporate power cannot be fought with liberal subjectivism repackaged in a 'radical' rhetoric of 'liberation' from the 'System'.[6] And in the 1990s, we might have learned from the Zapatistas that if we are going to 'open a crack in history', our political words must become 'bridge and stone and maize and tree and the hope of tomorrow' (Marcos 2002 [2001]: 216, 283).

As Dewey came to realize, the liberal–democratic polity was not only an emerging site of corporate state hegemony but also part of a democratic heritage facilitating the pragmatic replenishment of a pluralistic civil society.[7] For several decades since Dewey's death, evidence has mounted of the extent to which a globalizing corporate state, oriented towards the cheapest labour and resource markets, continues to raze civil society leaving in its wake privatized consumer malls and escalating waves of political cynicism and passivity. Blue-collar workers, with questions about trade policy, wonder if political institutions are rigged, as even middle-class professionals worry anxiously about the limits of outsourcing. Livingston's view of pragmatism as a 'post-republican alternative' hinges on the questionable assumption of the ongoing socialization of markets and a problematic stance towards what is called globalization Livingston (1994: 275–79).[8] Questioning the wisdom of such a historical leap, we take the more pedestrian view that Dewey not only confronted corporate power in the industrialization process but increasingly recognized that the dispersal of power from the state to society (detected by Tocqueville) was more importantly a democratic opportunity than mega-corporate destiny.

When Dewey wrote in 1927, 'the prime condition of a democratically organized public is a kind of knowledge and insight which does not yet exist', (Dewey 1927: 166), he laid down the political challenge to the professions that we have underlined. As for the academic gatekeepers to the professions, their universities by and large are moving in a direction opposite to where democratic action lies. Blinded by technocratic ideologies that regularly privilege corporate spatial planning over place-based forms of life and their multi-scalar possibilities, more thoughtful scholars grow increasingly uneasy with the anti-democratic uses of certain types of research. New funding possibilities offered by 'homeland security' programmes are unable to conceal the loss of more than 50 per cent tenure track jobs. 'Terrorism' as ideological justification for at least some forms of the US military/industrial/Congressional complex increasingly sags even in a political mainstream reeking with corporate money. The widespread repression of dissenting expressions of alternative approaches to 'globalization' is not going to be swept under the rug of 'counter-terrorism'. The World Social Forum (WSF) of recent years remains a shining example of a Deweyan public sphere as a project of democratic projects. As Jackie Smith and her co-authors observe, 'WSF participants have been modelling new forms of political action for democratic empowerment within local, national, and global contexts' (Smith et al. 2008: 130).

Nevertheless, we have to bear in mind reasons for the tardiness of many US academicians in recognizing this challenge. Very often institutions of higher education are organized and administered in ways that discourage faculty from getting experience with grassroots organizations.

Academic culture could be more hospitable to participatory inquiry that, as Frank Fischer has suggested, would treat citizens as local experts and academic experts as specialized citizens (Fischer 2000). Chances are, participatory inquiry might then seem more possible and the elite appropriation of certain types of knowledge less acceptable. Academic culture is not as exempt from mainstream political language and assumptions as some would like to think. As legal scholar Richard D. Parker indicates, there is a strong 'Anti-Populist sensibility' (Fischer 2000: 65ff.) in American intellectual circles directly related, we might add, to what the late Christopher Lasch described as 'the politics of the civilized minority' (Lasch 1991: 412–75). However, as Parker puts it: 'Our attitudes towards the political energy of ordinary people shape our sense of what are the constitutive problems of our democracy' (Parker 1994: 4).

The political energy of democratic publics and John Dewey's aesthetic ecology of public intelligence

John Dewey was not afraid to harness the 'political energy of ordinary people'. We have highlighted reasons why in social and political theory, place and landscape have a key role in the search for more democratic and humane forms of space and speed. This will include an environmental discourse, especially in modern research universities, that elucidates the reasons why and how an all too 'fast capitalism' and instrumentalist technoscience usually go together. This will help penetrate the din of corporate propaganda about 'clean coal', 'energy independence' and other corruptions of the sustainability idea. It will give more room for the questions about the compatibility of democracy and corporate-dominated globalization that continue to be heard even amidst multi-cultural triumphs that threaten to end in the *cul de sac* of identity politics that has become another residual façade for post-democratic plutocracy. The 2008 US presidential election did not exactly open up to a vigorous debate on available policy proposals for changing trade regimes such as North American Free Trade Agreement (NAFTA) or public subsidies to the Fossil Fuel Sector much involved in global warming or climate destabilization.

Environmental stewardship neither begins nor ends in the realm of 'active government'. Dewey was clear about not defining democracy as confined to political institutions. As Thomas Alexander has shown, Dewey's concept of the self is situated within a theory of democratic culture as one that organizes 'stable horizons of care' nourishing forms of social imagination vital for generative (generational) participation in public intelligence (Alexander 1995: 153–54). The temporal structure of this participatory, communicative process fundamentally enables the meanings of selfhood and social action. Dewey's political philosophy should not be nearly as hard to understand as some have made it. Discussing 'Creative Democracy—the Task before Us' in 1939 Dewey identified democracy as 'belief in the ability of human experience to generate the aims and methods by which further experience will grow in ordered richness'. He concluded by saying that 'the task of democracy is forever that of creation of a freer and more humane experience in which all share to which all contribute' (Dewey 1993: 244–45).

When you go back to his thoughts roughly twenty years earlier, you find him proposing roles for philosophers and others in 'the use of intelligence to liberate and liberalize action' (Dewey 1993: 6, 37, 46–7). Picking up on John J. McDermott's reading several years ago, we think John Dewey went on to outline an 'aesthetic ecology of public intelligence' (Reid and Taylor 2003). We further think that the democratic movement for socio-ecological justice emerging in contexts such as the WSF reflects an ongoing struggle to move beyond environmental violence and ecological deprivation to the celebration not only of place-based forms of life but also of 'genuine care for common experience', to use McDermott's Deweyan language (McDermott 1976: 91). We hope to illuminate the emerging forms of politics such as those at the WSF that most certainly in the confrontation of transnational corporate power is encouraging a more holistic understanding of the local.

In 1927, Dewey stated unequivocally that the 'outstanding problem of the public is discovery and identification of itself' while also commenting that in 'no two ages or places is there the same public' (Dewey 1991 [1927]: 125). He saw the challenge as one of merging 'free social inquiry' with the 'art of full and moving communication' (Dewey 1991 [1927]: 184). Those who would make the mistake of identifying Dewey's political aims and values with the liberal–democratic politics of the

New Deal miss or ignore key points elaborated in such works as *The Public and its Problems* and *Art as Experience*. In the former, he writes: 'The prime condition of a democratically organized public is a kind of knowledge and insight which does not yet exist' (Dewey 1991 [1927]: 166). Dewey's essay of November, 1935 on 'Liberty and Social Control' makes clear he did not ignore or slight the problem of the unequal distribution of power (Dewey 1993).

Conceptualizing liberty as 'effective power to do specific things', he highlights the question of power's distribution and the connection between the system of liberties and existing systems of restraint or control. There are always varying systems of social control but the trouble in 1935, he observed, is that 'it is exercised by the few who have economic power, at the expense of the liberties of the many and at the cost of increasing disorder ...' (Dewey 1993: 158–60). Seventy years later, in the US, we think this is an accurate and fair statement of the basic problem although we have to emphasize that new dimensions of power are raising the challenge of finding new or alternative forms of a democratic public. To repeat what we hope is obvious to most readers: we need various forms of democratic publics including what we have called global regional publics (Reid and Taylor 2002).

Dewey's critique of the corporate capitalist process of industrialization was relentless and this included the way in which the sciences were being institutionalized and misused. His examination of art as experience is an attempt to bridge the 'chasm between ordinary and esthetic experience' by illuminating the aesthetic as a key infrastructural modality in the logic of practical judgement. He is not at all content with depicting a traditional utopian function for art but re-situates the aesthetic dimension of experience in work and the everyday understood as tensional landscapes. The threat or problem of the corporate mentality is never lost from view. Consequently, it is ludicrous for C.A. Bowers to claim that 'Dewey's view of democracy requires a process of colonization ...' because, for example, the 'rapid merging of scientific research and corporate values is only the latest manifestation that the method of experimental inquiry that Dewey placed so much faith in can be used in destructive ways' (Bowers 2003: 36). As James Campbell's book *Understanding John Dewey: Nature and Cooperative Intelligence* demonstrates, this is a gross misreading of his approach to democracy as cooperative, experimental inquiry (Campbell 1995). Oddly, when Bowers calls for 'radical educational reforms that replace the current emphasis on promoting forms of education that expand the economy with regenerating the capacity of cultural groups to live in more self-sufficient and interdependent ways' (Campbell 1995), he reflects precisely Dewey's concerns. For Bowers, Dewey's philosophy and politics seem to be collapsed or merged with the ideas of certain alleged followers of Dewey including Richard Rorty (Bowers 2003: 26, 28).

Our reading of Dewey's philosophy and politics has been enhanced by several astute and penetrating recent studies, especially those by Alexander, Campbell and Westbrook. Thomas Alexander, for example, confirms our reading of Dewey's efforts to formulate an ecological ontology and with it an ecological view of experience in which the aesthetic context of inquiry is acknowledged and, we might add, reconceptualized (Alexander 2002: 22). We have to shed our intellectualized and dualized notions of the knower and the known if we are to grasp our knowledge—and logic—existing or active 'within a non-cognitive temporal framework, arising from experiences which are non-cognitive and passing into experiences that also are non-cognitive' (Alexander 2002: 19). Alexander shows how Dewey worked to situate knowing in a 'creative ecosystem' distinguished by 'change, plurality, possibility and mutual interdependence ...' (Alexander 2002: 21).

This and the earlier work of scholars such as John McDermott lends support to our approach or what we call Dewey's aesthetic ecology of public intelligence. Dewey's notion of public intelligence should help us understand the matrixical conditions of public life that provoke and sustain non-reified ecological consciousness. Following Dewey, Alexander has claimed that the democratic community 'realizes that it is ever in danger of losing itself, of becoming hidden from the possibilities of the present or from its own inherently unfinished and problematic nature' (Alexander 1987: 273). Our claim is that today, confronting both the threat and challenge of economic globalization, various forms of democracy must be re-imagined in ways facilitated (though not at all completed) by Dewey's aesthetic ecology. We are especially concerned to encourage a rethinking of the role of the professions insofar as they operate in the dialectic of space and place (Harvey 1996: 29–30, 324) to promote anti-democratic aspects of transnational corporate power. We are painfully aware that Dewey, in trying to restate his theory of inquiry, sometimes capitulated to the reigning scientism (Kaufman-Osborn 1991: xii–xiii; Stuhr 2002: 282–84). Nevertheless, we find in his arguments for recasting the relationship of art and science and in the thrust of his work towards what Alexander calls an 'an ontology of environed or ecologically situated being' (Alexander 2002: 5), some vital considerations for the social theory of intellectual roles in struggles for democratic globalization including a politics of climate equity.

Democratic space, participatory reason, and a new professionalism

Raymond Williams and John Dewey wanted theory to work in what we call conflictual–constructive ecologies of emergent democratic space. As Williams put it in 1982, all that is involved with the 'the fact of material limits ... should now force our societies to the most important kind of rethinking we have had to do' (Williams 1995 [1982]: 52). We have tried to show how he cleared away misconceptions of the cultural terrain for this endeavour. Critical political theory can resituate itself in experiences of the creative interplay of residual, emergent and transformative modalities of democratic movements and events. The self-understanding of movements and the interpretive reconstruction of events are challenges always present.

When the ontological *auspices* of critique are attuned to praxeomorphic modes of practical reasoning entwined with the self-organizing capacities of other forms of natural life, it knows where to look and what some of the conditions of participation are. Theoretical vision is all about imagining democratic happenings of place that are not based on the expendability of landscapes and their communities. Merleau-Ponty has taught the foolishness of learning geography in order to forget the countryside. A democratic professionalism cultivates a cultural memory of an experimental knowledge that hones itself in the living landscapes where participatory reason serves sustainable life. A key question is whether the mode of engagement between the knower and the known is one that allows the knower to hold fast to a particular being in its manifestation as an existent in the fullness and career of time. For years we have heard Appalachians complain about 'hit and run research', so, you might say participatory reason is an antidote. The ecological restoration of places and landscapes wasted by myopic triumphs of corporate spatialization can provide models for mitigating 'the dependence of change on calamity' (Unger 2007: 206). But such lessons need a new professionalism that has its core configuration in participatory reason.

In a forthcoming book, we offer a detailed explanation of how we understand participatory reason as forms of knowledge emergent from, and embedded in body place commons (Reid and Taylor forthcoming Chapter 6). Dewey's understanding of the infrastructure to this way of knowing as an aesthetic ecology anticipates transversal enfleshments of knowledge and action that enable global solidarities without displacing the generative counter-publics catalyzing alternative worlds of democratic expression. These emergent publics often are distinguished by communal or intergroup particularities garnering complex causalities and proactive initiatives. Around the world, the search of such publics for free spaces opposing enclosure within oppressive logics of fungibility is not assisted by professional fatalists of alienated reason whatever their role in technocorporate power.

As counter-publics, their active search is one of de-essentializing economic logics, cultivating diversity and reclaiming and enlarging the commons. The scaling up of so-called local knowledge can make the difference in mobilizing against technocorporate dominance. The participatory reason in such collective endeavours works with the powers of life articulated by a formative praxeomorphic logic definitive of sensible, visible worlds. The Zapatista dream of a world of many democratic worlds comes to mind.

There are many sites where struggle is important. At the level of macro-structural political economy, John McMurtry is right that it is crucial for global financial markets to be recaptured by nation states and democratically reconstituted international bodies (McMurtry 1998: 304–18, 1999). Also, crucial is collective action to undo the legal status of corporations as persons. In many countries, but particularly in the US, it is crucial to weaken the hold of corporate money on the electoral system. But along with these efforts at structural change, this chapter has argued that there is very important philosophic and ideological labour to be done to reclaim democratic public spaces that have been thinned out and weakened. We only have space here to take a cursory look at some of the specifics of what might be possible. The most important reality to keep focus on here, is the new forms of grass-roots mobilization for socio-ecological justice, that have been experimenting with new forms of participatory knowledge, participatory planning, decentralized civic organization and new forms of subjectivity and inter-subjective solidarity that are fluid, dialogical, but (unlike much post-modern scholarship) based on particularity and are place-based, but not place-bound.

The new professionalism we advocate would transform a crucial, and weak link, in the historic bloc enabling economic globalization—the hegemonic connection between professionalism and the corporate state (Reid 2001; Reid and Taylor forthcoming, Chapter 6). Technocracy is crucial in providing the veil of legitimacy to corporate extraction. However, it is a very thin veil, based on spectacular displays of the fungibility of particularity of persons, ecosystems, habitats, places and so on, which is less and less persuasive to the public with any sort of criticality. For instance, the massive strip mining of Appalachian coal through the process called 'mountaintop removal' has been legitimated for two decades by positivist 'scientific' methodologies used by various state and national regulatory agencies—which has reduced complex ecosystems and historic human communities to mere standing reserves of energy and labour markets. However, the assault on the reproductive capacities of the land (shattered watersheds, uncontrollable toxicities, dangerous air and so on) and of humans (communities become ecological refugees without places for gainful migration) is going so deep into the ecological and civil commons that it becomes increasingly hard to maintain the illusion of infinite productivity able to exceed its externalized violence. This drama of lethal assault on the life commons is being repeated in so many parts of the world that it is creating the conditions for global empathy among those displaced from their life grounds. The hegemonic link between professionalism of the corporate state is also made weak by the reality of the global job crisis within middle-class professions. For a while, the job insecurity of symbolic analysts downsizing labour markets might reinforce quiescence and timidity. But, when job crises deepen, they can also lead to new activism and class consciousness creating possible new coalitions between working and middle classes.

There has been a burgeoning of experimentation world-wide in new forms of participatory action research that could be the basis for new regimes of knowledge. For instance, faced with environmental and social injustice, various kinds of civic environmentalists have been forced to research their own problems, because professional and governmental agents were indifferent or afraid to take on such research. Much of this research and analysis is very good, and has led to new kinds of research skills. This can be described as a kind of professionalization of civil society that needs more critical analysis. At the same time, on the hybrid edges between academe, non-government organizations (NGOs), transnational 'development' entities, grassroots mobilization there has emerged a wealth of materials and training protocols for teaching and conducting participatory action research. This has led to much experimentation in academic/community partnership in research that can be analyzed to understand effective organizational forms for these kinds of inquiry. These hybrid spaces of public reflection could be very powerful sites from which to consider new institutional forms and bases for the kind of public intelligence that Dewey and Williams were trying to imagine.

Notes

1. We describe the commons as '... the substantive grounds of collective life' which includes both 'the ecological commons as the web of interdependencies within non-human life and between human and nonhuman life' and the civic commons as 'those social webs of practices through which people tend the ecological commons and reproduce their own ability to tend the commons' in the Introduction to our forthcoming book *Recovering the Commons: Democracy, Place, and Global Justice*. There is a growing literature on the commons as the grounds for democratic political being and for political resistance to neo-liberal capitalism, including discussion of the ways in which enclosure of the commons is constitutive of capitalist (Bollier 2003; Hufford 1997, 2000; Linebaugh 2008; McMurtry 1999; Nonini 2007) and other exploitations—especially gender (Federici 2004; Reid and Taylor Forthcoming, especially Chapters 1 and 3).
2. *Chemical Valley* is an excellent film on effects of Union Carbide plants on workers and nearby communities in Institute, West Virginia and Bhopal, India by directors Mimi Pickering and Anne Lewis of the Appalachian media group, Appalshop, which explores links between racism, class, corporate power, environmental injustice and globalization (Pickering and Lewis 1991).
3. Leder focuses on the therapeutic weaving and reweaving of dimensions of self that are recessive (hidden, sedimented or tacit) with the ecstatic dimensions. Drawing of the etymological meanings of ecstatic as 'standing outside of',this refers to the ways in which the self seeks engagement in the world and is constituted relationally and in movement in the world—in dynamic and healing tensions with the recessive.

4. Our emphasis on 'world' draws on Hannah Arendt's important development of this notion. We say, 'Arendt emphasizes that world is a strange mixture of history as residue from past action and history-in-the-making as sheer openness of new possibilities for action' (Arendt 1958), and we define world as '... that durable architectonics of engagement that creates the background which actors need to illumine future and present as coherent settings for action, and, into which acts can transmute into remembrance (or habit) that avails past for future action' (Reid and Taylor forthcoming 11).
5. 'Clean coal' is an oxymoron which has been promulgated by corporate coal interests which falsely suggest technologies to sequester carbon from burning will soon be feasible (economically and technologically). It ignores the vast environmental damages from production of coal. For more, see the 'False Solutions' section of the International Forum on Globalization publication *Manifesto on Global Economic Transitions* (International Forum on Globalization 2007).
6. Reid has been making this argument for roughly thirty years. See the 1973 *Politics and Society* article, especially 211–25 and his discussion of 'The Berkeley School Critique of the American Political Tradition' on 124–38 and 144–45 in 'Toward a Post-Modern Theory of American Political Science and Culture ...' in Reid and Yanarella (1974) and Reid (1973).
7. Of Dewey's many works, those given special consideration here are *The Public and its Problems* (1927); later editions by Alan Swallow and by Ohio University Press; *Individualism Old and New* (1962 [1929–1930]) and *Art as Experience* (1934). Many years ago, Reid was alerted to the political significance of Dewey's *Art as Experience* by Henry David Aiken (1962). As Richard Rorty has commented, in Dewey's 'ideal society, culture is no longer dominated by the ideal of objective cognition but by that of aesthetic enhancement'. See Rorty (1979: 13). For a critique of professionalism as a 'quasi-religion' that partly draws on Dewey, see Bruce Wilshire (1990), a book that should be much more familiar to academicians than it seems to be.
8. See his *Pragmatism and the Political Economy of Cultural Revolution, 1850–1940* (Chapel Hill: University of North Carolina Press, 1994), especially 275–79.

References

Aiken, Henry David. 1962. 'American Pragmatism Reconsidered: John Dewey', *Commentary*, 34(October): 334–44.

Alexander, T.M. 1987. *John Dewey's theory of art, experience and nature: the horizons of feeling*. Albany: State University of New York Press.

———. (1995). 'John Dewey and the Roots of Democratic Imagination', in L. Langsdorf and A.R. Smith (eds), *Recovering Pragmatism's Voice*, pp. 131–54. Albany: State University of New York Press.

Alexander, T.M. 2002. 'The Aesthetics of Reality: The Development of Dewey's Ecological Theory of Experience', in F.T. Burke, D.M. Hester and R.B. Talisse (eds), *Dewey's Logical Theory: New Studies and Interpretations*, pp. 3–26. Nashville: Vanderbilt University Press.

Arendt, H. 1958. *The Human Condition*. Chicago: University of Chicago Press.

Berry, W. 1996 [1977]. *The Unsettling of America: Culture and Agriculture* (3rd edition). San Francisco: Sierra Club Books.

Blum, J.M. (ed.). 1985. *Public Philosopher: Selected Letters of Walter Lippmann*. New York: Ticknor and Fields.

Bollier, D. 2003. *Silent Theft: The Private Plunder of our Commonwealth*. New York: Routledge.

Bowers, C.A. 2003. 'The Case against John Dewey as an Environmental and Eco-Justice Philosopher', *Environmental Ethics*, 25(1): 25–42.

Campbell, J. 1995. *Understanding John Dewey: Nature and Cooperative Intelligence*. Chicago and La Salle: Open Court.

Dewey, J. (1929 [1925]). *Experience and Nature* (Second edition). La Salle, Illinois: Open Court.

Dewey, J. 1927. *The Public and its Problems*. New York: Henry Holt.

Dewey, J. 1934. *Art as Experience*. New York: Minton, Balch & Co.

———. 1962 [1929–1939]. *Individualism Old and New*. New York: Capricorn Books.

———. 1991 [1927]. *The Public and its Problems*. Athens: Swallow Press.

———. (1993). *The Political Writings*. Indianapolis: Hackett Publishing Co.

Eagleton, T. (ed.). 1989. *Raymond Williams: Critical Perspectives*. Boston: Northeastern University Press.

Escobar, A. 2008. *Territories of Difference: Place, Movements, Life, Redes*. Durham: Duke University Press.

Federici, S. 2004. *Caliban and the Witch: Women, the Body and Primitive Accumulation*. Brooklyn: Autonomedia.

Fischer, F. 2000. *Citizens, Experts, and the Environment: The Politics of Local Knowledge*. Durham: Duke University Press.

Harvey, D. 1996. *Justice, Nature, and the Geography of Difference*. Cambridge, MA: Blackwell Publishers.

Hufford, M. 1997. 'American Ginseng and the Idea of the Commons', *Folklife Center News*, 19(1–2): 3–18.

———. (2000). Building the Commons: Folklore, Citizen Science, and the Ecological Imagination, *Indian Folklife*, 1(3), 15–6.

International_Forum_on_Globalization. 2007. *Manifesto on Global Economic Transitions: Powering-Down for the Future*, edited by Jerry Mander. Washington DC. Available online at http://www.ifg.org/store.htm.

Kaufman-Osborn, T.V. 1991. *Politics/Sense/Experience: A Pragmatic Inquiry into the Promise of Democracy*. Ithaca: Cornell University Press.

Klein, N. 2007. *The Shock Doctrine: The Rise of Disaster Capitalism* (1st edition). New York: Metropolitan Books/Henry Holt.

Lasch, C. 1991. *The True and Only Heaven: Progress and its Critics*. New York: W.W. Norton.

Leder, D. 1990. *The Absent Body*. Chicago: University of Chicago Press.

Linebaugh, P. 2008. *The Magna Carta Manifesto: Liberties and Commons for All*. Berkeley: University of California Press.

Lippmann, W. 1985 [1914]. *Drift and Mastery: An Attempt to Diagnose the Current Unrest*. Madison: The University of Wisconsin Press.

Livingston, J. 1994. *Pragmatism and the Political Economy of Cultural Revolution, 1850–1940*. Chapel Hill: University of North Carolina Press.

———. 2001. *Pragmatism, Feminism, and Democracy: Rethinking the Politics of American History*. New York: Routledge.

Louv, R. 2005. *Last Child in the Woods*. Chapel Hill, NC: Algonquin Books of Chapel Hill.

Malpas, J.E. 1999. *Place and Experience: A Philosophical Topography*. Cambridge, UK; New York, NY: Cambridge University Press.

Marcos, S. 2002 [2001]. *Our Word is Our Weapon: Selected Writings*. New York: Seven Stories Press.

Marglin, S.A. (1990a). 'Losing Touch: The Cultural Conditions of Worker Accommodation and Resistance', in F. Apffel-Marglin and S.A. Marglin (eds), *Dominating Knowledge: Development, Culture, and Resistance*, pp. 217–82. Oxford: Clarendon Press.

———. (1990b). 'Towards the Decolonization of the Mind', in F. Apffel-Marglin and S.A. Marglin (eds), *Dominating Knowledge: Development, Culture, and Resistance*, pp. 1–28. Oxford: Clarendon Press.

McDermott, J.J. 1976. *The Culture of Experience*. New York: New York University Press.

McMurtry, J. 1998. *Unequal Freedoms: The Global Market as an Ethical System*. West Hartford: Kumarian Press.

———. 1999. *The Cancer Stage of Capitalism*. London: Pluto Press.

Merleau-Ponty, M. 1968. *The Visible and the Invisible*, trans. by A. Lingis. Evanston: Northwestern University Press.

Nonini, D.M. (ed.). 2007. *The Global Idea of 'the Commons'*. New York: Berghahn Books.

Norton, A. 2004. *Leo Strauss and the politics of American Empire*. New Haven: Yale University Press.

Parker, R.D. 1994. *Here, the People Rule: A Constitutional Populist Manifesto*. Cambridge: Harvard University Press.

Pickering, M. and A. Lewis. 1991. Chemical Valley: Appalshop. Available online at www.appalshop.org.

Reid, H.G. 1973. 'American Social Science in the Politics of Time and the Crisis of Technocorporate Society', *Politics and Society*, 3 (Winter) : 201–43.

Reid, H.G. 2001. 'Democratic Theory and the Public Sphere Project: Rethinking Knowledge, Authority, and Identity', *New Political Science*, 23(4): 517–36.

Reid, H.G. and B. Taylor. 2002. 'Appalachia as a Global Region: Toward Critical Regionalism and Civic Professionalism', *Journal of Appalachian Studies*, 8(2): 6–28.

———. 2003. 'John Dewey's Aesthetic Ecology of Public Intelligence and the Grounding of Civic Environmentalism', *Ethics and Environment*, 8(1, Special Issue on 'Art, Nature and Social Critique') 74–92.

———. Forthcoming. *Recovering the Commons: Democracy, Place, and Global Justice*. Urbana: University of Illinois Press.

Reid, H.G. and Yanarella, E.J. 1974. 'Toward a Post-Modern Theory of American Political Science and Culture', *Cultural Hermeneutics*, 2 : 91–166.

Rorty, Richard. 1979. *Philosophy and the Mirror of Nature*. Princeton: Princeton University Press.

Shiva, V. 2000. *Stolen Harvest: The Hijacking of the Global Food Supply*. Cambridge, MA: South End Press.

Smith, J., Karides, M., Becker, M., Brunelle, D., Chase-Dunn, C., Garza, R.I., Juris, J.S., Mosca, L., Reese, E., Smith, P.(Jay) and Vazquez, R. 2008. *Global Democracy and the World Social Forums*. Boulder: Paradigm Publishers.

Strauss, L. 1953. *Natural Right and History*. Chicago: University of Chicago Press.

Stuhr, J.J. 2002. 'Power/Inquiry: The Logic of Pragmatism', in F.T. Burke, D.M. Hester and R.B. Talisse (eds), *Dewey's Logical Theory: New Studies and Interpretations*, pp. 275–85. Nashville: Vanderbilt University Press.

Taylor, B. and H.G. Reid. 2000. 'Recovering Place-Based Knowledge and Cosmogenic Agency in Struggles for a Sustainable World', *Indian Folklife*, 1(3): 10–11.

Unger, R.M. 2007. *The Self Awakened: Pragmatism Unbound*. Cambridge: Harvard University Press.

Weiner, J.F. 2001. *Tree Leaf talk: A Heideggerian Anthropology*. Oxford: Berg Publishers.

Westbrook, R.B. 2005. *Democratic Hope: Pragmatism and the Politics of Truth*. Ithaca: Cornell University Press.

Williams, R. 1966 [1958]. *Culture and Society 1780–1950*. New York: Harper and Row Publishers.

———. 1973. 'Base and Superstructure in Marxist Cultural Theory', *New Left Review*, 82: 3–16.

———. 1977. *Marxism and Literature*. Oxford: Oxford University Press.

———. 1989. *Resources of Hope: Culture, Democracy, Socialism*. London: Verso.

———. 1995 [1982]. 'Socialism and Ecology', *Capitalism, Nature, Socialism*, 6(1): 41–57.

Wilshire, Bruce. 1990. *The Moral Collapse of the University*. Albany: SUNY Press.

Wirzba, N. (ed.). 2003. *The Essential Agrarian Reader: The Future of Culture, Community, and the Land*. Washington, DC: Shoemaker & Hoard.

Wolin, S.S. 2008. *Democracy Incorporated: Managed Democracy and the Specter of Inverted Totalitarianism*. Princeton: Princeton University Press.

In Search of Structures of Cooperation

13

The Discursive Construction of Morality in the Land Reform Dispute in Post-apartheid South Africa[1]

We, the people of South Africa,
Recognize the injustices of our past;
Honour those who suffered for justice and freedom in our land;
Respect those who have worked to build and develop our country; and
Believe that South Africa belongs to all who live in it, united in our
diversity.

—Constitution of South Africa

The resolution of a social conflict requires a moral universal, a set of relevant, collectively acceptable statements or rules, which makes possible the regulation of future conduct. It allows the parties to the conflict to recognize and focus on the same object of contention, despite different interpretations of it and to enter into discourse in the medium of which their respective interpretations could be related to one another. Among the structures thus generated, they must select those which would enable them to cooperate and coordinate their respective inter-pretations and eventually their actions. Where it proves impossible to identify a common issue and to enter a discourse about it, social conflict becomes endemic, so that the only remaining avenue towards closure is force or violence.

This was the case in precolonial South Africa where land had been one of the major sources of conflict in and between tribal communities. What applied there had been equally true of the colonial and apartheid eras during which the most brutal and unjust practices of land dispossession prevailed, resulting in European conquest meeting with African opposition. That force or violence had not been the inevitable outcome of land conflicts in tribal or traditional societies, however, is demonstrated by land litigation among the inhabitants of the Trobriand Islands (Miller 1992). There the required moral universal was available in the form of an unquestioned, indeed, even unquestionably given morality. While the norm under such conditions is to confine argumentation to 'is questions' to the exclusion of 'ought questions', this option is not open to post-apartheid South Africa.

Despite the persistence of a conspicuously uneven distribution of wealth and resources, contemporary South Africa is a functionally differentiated and complex society organized according to the rule of law based on an advanced constitution. As a post-conventional moral universal, the latter disallows recourse to be an absolute, traditional morality. The land issue divides large sections of the population but the competing opinions, judgements and claims of the different sections are also related to the distinct normative codes of the different components of society. Most important are function systems such as the polity and economy as well as civil society in which they are rooted. South Africa, moreover, fits into a larger, interdependent context of global governance and a global civil society in which other countries as well as international organizations, agents and public opinion play a role. Under such conditions of inter-dependency and post-traditional morality, we typically observe a more or less long-drawn, arduous and laborious process of the construction of structures of cooperation and coordination commensurate with the guiding moral universal, which often requires painful steps of social learning on the part of those involved.

The following paragraphs report on a study of contemporary, post-apartheid South Africa dealing specifically with the process of the construction of morality within the framework of the issue of land reform and the wide-ranging debates generated by it. In addition to my own research, I am fortunate to be able to draw on the first synthetic study of the land reform issue in Zimbabwe and South Africa, the report of the International Crisis Group published in 2004.[2] To analyze this process, I shall consider the land reform discourse of the past decade and a half, including those involved in it, their representations and actions, and the outcomes of their discursive engagement. The crucial focal points, however, are the structures of cooperation and coordination sought by those involved, including both the directly involved participants and those observing, evaluating, judging and commenting on the process, under the guidance of the constitution as embodiment of the relevant moral universal. The importance of this focus turns on the fact that the resolution of the land reform issue depends not only on the emergence of such structures from the discourse but simultaneously also on the degree of reflexivity the competing and conflicting parties are able to develop in relation to those structures, their discursive availability, and their potential use in concrete situations.

I

The current land dispute has its roots in colonialism and the apartheid system, both of which had been driven by an interest in land. As in the early modern European enclosure movement, here also land expro- priation had been the most important mechanism for the creation of wealth, political and economic domination, and social control. The political significance, indeed, the explosiveness the land question retains in the twenty-first century, can be traced back directly to the extent and injustice of land dispossession of past centuries. That the level of dispossession and racial distortion of the pattern of access to land and land use is comparable to the most extreme anywhere else in the world is borne out by the situation at the start of the new South Africa. In 1994, the legacy of the apartheid era bore the starkly asymmetrical profile of more than twelve million blacks—either desperately poor, landless, rural blacks eking out an existence in infertile 'homelands' or impoverished workers living on commercial farms—over against 50,000 wealthy white commercial farmers.

In the meantime, this racially skewed structure has hardly been miti- gated. During the first decade of the new South Africa, the degree of land reform achieved was rather modest. Only approximately 2.8 per cent of all agricultural land had been transferred to blacks, whether by restitution or by redistribution measures. Despite encouraging pro- gress, made especially in the restitution category, these figures detract from the government's avowed reform targets set in 2000 and 2002, respectively: 18 per cent of agricultural land or 12.5 per cent of all territory in five years, and 30 per cent of all territory in fifteen to twenty years.

This gaping disparity between goals and their practical realization leads many to regard the land reform question as one that possesses the potential of becoming a major political issue. It is not expected that South Africa would degenerate to the level of Zimbabwe since conditions differ appreciably; yet, the possibility cannot be excluded that the currently widespread dissatisfaction over poverty and the lack of employment opportunities and housing could in the course of time get attached to the land reform issue. If this comes to pass, it is likely to be transposed into a, if not *the*, major political issue confronting South Africa in the next decade. Already for some years there are indications that land rights NGOs are not only becoming more vociferous and militant but are also preparing to mobilize the landless poor to invade and occupy land.

To grasp the emerging structures of cooperation and coordination holding out the prospect of a peaceful resolution of the land reform issue, it is necessary to consider the process in, and through, which those structures are being constructed. Philosophers consider this process in the strict terms of ethical universalization, with the focus on its outcome, namely, a moral universal. In the present case, the South African constitution can be taken to represent such a universal. By contrast, social scientists are more interested in the details of the process itself and, therefore, conceive it in terms of social or discursive construction.[3] My proposal is to conceptualize this process of the construction of morality according to a communication theoretical model,[4] which methodologically makes possible a reconstruction in terms of both action, and the discursive logic and dynamics escaping privileged disposal on the part of any one agent. Since the focal concern is with the approximation of the moral universal through implementation and learning, central importance, however, is ascribed to the cognitive dimension. The latter refers to the knowledge and more importantly the structures making possible such knowledge, developed in the course of interaction and discourse. Included among these cognitive structures are the mindsets, schemata, representations or frames of the different agents, the adjustment or alignment of those agent frames and their discursive generalization so as to approximate more closely the higher level or macro-frame communicatively shared by the different agents.

This cognitive emphasis by no means implies that the proposed stereoscopic communication approach succumbs to idealism. On the contrary, it explicitly considers agents in terms of how they present themselves and relate to others through the strategic and competitive representation of their respective frames. And in order to appreciate the type and degree of power behind such strategic action and communication, it further relates the different agents and their relations to the differentiated components of society as well as the corresponding resources they are able to mobilize thanks to the particular positions they occupy. Over and above power and material conditions, the proposed approach employs a critical perspective of a cognitive kind (Strydom 2000, 2002). Gaining access to the reality of land reform through constitutive and direction-giving cultural models and cognitive structures, it exempts no one implicated in this relational context, nor even the analyst, from having their biases, rationalizations or illusions exposed.

In opposition to the traditional practice of focussing on the directly involved participants in a social situation alone, whether of interaction, conflict or discourse, the proposed approach furthermore goes beyond the classical and neoclassical theory of social interaction or communication as being based on 'double contingency' (Habermas 1996; Luhmann 1995; Parsons 1964). It adopts the principle of 'triple contingency' (Strydom 1999) instead and therefore, takes into account the role also, and in particular, of those who observe, evaluate, judge and comment on the participants. The public embodies a distinct and essential type of power by virtue of the epistemic authority accruing to it in public discourse—an authority creating a tripartite situation in which the participants (ego and alter) are compelled to undergo learning processes under the gaze of, and hence with reference to, the public (the 'other'). Triple contingency is thus indispensable not only in the process of the construction of morality but simultaneously also for the social scientific identification and reconstruction of the emergent structures of cooperation and coordination.

II

For something to be placed on the public and political agenda, it first has to be problematized and made into an issue by being moralized and politicized. Given its historical significance, land reform was virtually a readymade issue at the very start of the new South Africa. Not much effort was required either to problemize it or to create public concern and convince the political institutions that it calls for collective attention and decision making. The issue, nevertheless, needed moral and political proponents to give voice to it in public communication. Only in this way could a public discourse be generated that would compel the implicated, yet reluctant, parties to acknowledge the issue and get all those involved to shoulder their responsibility.

An overview of the materials documenting the land reform discourse[5] reveals a long list of agents who at one point or another entered the public sphere and contributed to the debates generating the land reform discourse. Through a reconstruction of participation in the discourse, however, the multiplicity of agents and their observers can be theoretically reduced to the basic relations or communicative structure of the discourse. This is possible since the discourse by its very logic divides the participants into groups that represent different and even antagonistic perspectives, while simultaneously coordinating their views and actions by leading them with the assistance of the public to focus on one and the same issue. The participants adopting ego and alter relations belong to the three basic categories of discourse coalitions who are directly involved and, therefore, carry the different cognitive frames embroiled in the discursive competition and conflict. On one hand, there is the development coalition composed of those disposing over financial resources and sponsoring economic advancement and prosperity. It is opposed, on the other hand, by the land rights coalition composed of those advocating that justice be done to the victims of land dispossession. Located between the two is the governmental coalition that plays the central role in governance, yet finds itself in the ambivalent position of often being torn between the development and land rights coalitions. The public, both national and global, occupies the third point of view and, through opinion formation in terms of the public interest, exerts not only a context defining but also a selection function insofar as it supports a particular set of structures emerging from the discourse.

For present purposes, the participants' frames are conceived as consisting of three basic cognitive components: progress, justice and solidarity.[6] Depending on the participant and the particular situation in question, however, these components are differently prioritized and combined. For the development coalition, economic advancement always retains the top priority, whereas solidarity and justice typically follow in that order. The land rights coalition invariably prioritizes justice while the order of the remaining components depends on the circumstances. The governmental coalition's prioritization varies from situation to situation but typically tends to oscillate between progress and justice. Since it is responsible for decision making and implementation, its framing, however, is central to the collectively accepted structures constructed by means of the different frames. The public's third point of view is a normatively potent yet flexible frame which allows different contents depending on the situation.

The first phase

Prior to the fall of apartheid, organizations of the liberation movement such as the African National Congress (ANC), the South African Communist Party and the Pan African Congress (PAC) had always been animated by the question of how the injustices of the colonial and apartheid land dispossession could be redressed. The same can be said of land rights NGOs that became particularly active since the 1980s. While these organizations typically did not recoil from regarding national-ization as the normatively correct answer, it was later de-emphasized by the construction of morality in favour of quite a different frame. This occurred during the first phase of the current discourse, which started in the course of the transition period between 1989 and 1994.

From nationalization to progress and solidarity

In the search for a new democratic agrarian order between the late 1980s and the early 1990s, a constellation of discourse partners and coalitions emerged that included white farmers, the business community, and foreign governments and investors as well as exiles returning from abroad. Their contributions to the discourse emphasized deep concern about the prospect and potential consequences of the nationalization of land and disillusionment with nationalization programmes in com-munist countries, respectively. This placed a question mark over the nationalization frame in terms not only of its economic efficiency but in particular also of its normative correctness and hence, its legitimacy. While land rights NGOs such as the National Land Committee continued to present a strong moral defence of the rights of the victims of land dispossession and the PAC still insisted on nationalization, the ANC, occupying a middle position between the development and land rights coalitions, felt obliged to change track. This occurred in 1992, a time of negotiations with the National Party government when the ANC revised its position on various crucial matters. Through a significant cognitive adjustment, the ANC renounced the nationalization frame as entailing an inappropriate mechanism for restoring black property rights and ownership in land, and simultaneously, advancing economic development, national reconciliation and solidarity. From the discursive structures centring on the land reform issue, then, emerged meta-communicative markers suggesting potential structures of cooperation and coordination among those involved. As the political organization most likely to take power and thus being responsible for the public interest as a whole, the ANC perceived these structures most clearly and, through a discursively induced learning process taking place in full view of the public,[7] came to recognize the need for an alignment of its frame with those of the other discourse partners—without, of course, obliterating the characteristic differences between them.

The contributions of the different discourse partners, needless to say, were backed by resources, implying that power came into play in the discourse in definite ways. The most conspicuous resources were the funds and economic progress commanded by the development coalition consisting of international organizations, foreign governments, donors and investors, the business community and white commercial farmers. The power of this coalition obviously weighed heavily on the ANC, which anticipated taking responsibility for the prosperity of a future South Africa. But that it did not simply capitulate under the weight of money is apparent from the fact that the ANC decided to retain full ownership of its land reform policy by distancing itself from the World Bank who, in its judgement, sought to take control of the policy formation process on behalf of the development coalition. The ANC was able to do so thanks to its own power-base and public support, and its guiding thread in doing so embraced normative ideas such as justice and solidarity.

Therefore, besides money, jobs and development, other types of resources should not be overlooked. Of all the participants, the ANC had disposal over the richest political resources, including political support, potential votes and a political mandate, which allowed it to assume a strong, central position in the discourse. Then, there were the moral resources possessed in different degrees by all the participants. These involve moral indignation rooted in feelings of social exclusion and injustice, which translate into moral concern, crisis consciousness and thus potential national and international public support. One cannot meaningfully speak of social learning or even of social development if the normative moment is not given its proper place. Such a process requires more than the exertion of economic and political power. As a specifically social process, it is defined by social interaction and discourse that alone can lead to social solidarity. The black population of South Africa who had been brutally and unjustly dispossessed of their land undoubtedly command the vast stock of these resources. The ANC unquestionably enjoyed the support of this section of the population who themselves were viewed sympathetically by the world public opinion. However, once the land reform discourse took off, the economically well-resourced participants could also call on moral resources on every occasion that their potential exclusion from the future social order suggested itself. This claim of theirs was, at times, linked to a veiled threat of withdrawing financial resources; yet, it gained weight in proportion, as they commanded respect for their contribution to the development of the country. The ANC's principal cognitive adjustment, accordingly, was to acknowledge that the white business community and commercial farmers also have a rightful claim on being included in a social order of reconciliation and solidarity. The ANC was compelled to find a balance between the respective moral claims of the victims of land dispossession on one hand, and the business and farming community on the other hand. Later in government, however, the ANC would not just take the words of the development coalition at face value but would also consider their actions in particular—for example, unwillingness to cooperate in, and obstruction of, land redistribution—for this is where it ultimately becomes clear whether they actually take their own moral claims seriously.

The recognition of the fact that a complex, differentiated society calls for a type of morality that allows the coordination of irreducibly different conceptions of the good—whether economic, political or social—provided a normative reference point for the constitutional negotiations of 1993, which in turn set the scene for the ANC's accession to power in 1994. The particular collective interpretation of this moral universal may be regarded as nodal point number one in the first phase of the construction of morality in the land reform discourse. On this basis, the ANC government—at the outset—reassured landowners that redistribution would be conducted in accordance with the principles and rules established thus far: a market-led approach would be followed; yet, this would be done strictly within the framework laid down by the interim constitution and Bill of Rights.

In the process of construction of morality, then, the participants searched the situational discursive structures for those beliefs or statements that are collectively acceptable. A more or less coherent, mutually recognized set bearing on appropriate economic and political conditions and, in particular, access to land, equity and justice, and the attainment of national reconciliation and social solidarity was found.

This mutual recognition or collective acceptance did not imply the consensus or final agreement of all regarding its interpretation but as a construction of the relevant moral universal, it was sufficient to allow the coordination of dissent and hence, the cooperation of the participants. Although occupying different positions and promulgating competing interpretations, the agents were nevertheless able to align their representations and actions—at least for some time, that is, until that temporary constructive synthesis, achieved under particular situational conditions, could no longer support the implementation of policy and thus called for revision or elaboration.

From progress to justice and solidarity

On coming to power, the ANC had to face a host of application problems—problems of the application of its understanding of the moral universal established in the first phase to particular cases, each of which is characterized by its own framing of facts, norms and identity requirements and related situational conflict. These problems were exacerbated by at least three factors: first, various limits against which the government ran up (for example, excessive centralization, constrained administrative capabilities, lack of personnel and resources); second, the complexity of reality (for example, ambitious plans amid a tangled web of opaque legislation, conflict of interests between the eradication of poverty and the boosting of black commercial farming); and finally, the persistence of conflicting perspectives despite the earlier established coordination of dissent (for example, lack of cooperation of white farmers, resistance to legislation). At the same time, politicians and representatives of the land rights coalition accused the ANC of having made untenable compromises in the constitutional negotiations which now rendered it incapable of redressing the basic racial inequity in land ownership. A central prong of the criticism was that having set the Natives Land Act of 1913 as the cut-off point,[8] the settlement in effect legitimized centuries of land seizures and at the same time, allowed those very white settler elites who had benefited unjustly to continue to have a say in land reform. If the nationalization frame did not make its full reappearance, the demand that the market principle of willing-seller–willing-buyer should be surrendered in favour of the compulsory confiscation of land for redistribution purposes became increasingly amplified.

By March 1996, it became publicly clear that the government's land reform endeavours were stalling. It admitted this much when it transferred responsibility from Minister Jay Naidoo to Deputy President Thabo Mbeki and replaced the Reconstruction and Development Programme by the Growth, Employment and Redistribution Strategy. Yet, already in the previous year, it had decided to redirect the original programme by embarking on a policy development process which culminated in the 'South African Land Policy White Paper' (South Africa Government 1997). As becomes apparent from a broader perspective on the discourse, the white paper effectively opened the final stretch of the first phase of the construction of morality in the land reform discourse. The revision and elaboration of a collectively accepted set of normative structures under pressure from difficulties thrown up by its application to particular cases represents the central problematic of the construction of morality. How could the frames and actions of the participants in a public dispute or situation of social conflict be coordinated so that they could enter into meaningful cooperation? How could the structures of cooperation and coordination that they accepted until recently but have now become questionable, be regenerated, reformulated or taken in a different direction? This problem loomed larger than ever as the land reform programme ground to a halt. While the policy-making process was a way to reinvigorate the land reform discourse, the white paper was the government's means of coming to grips with this problem.

In the context of the discourse conditioned by stalling land reform, we witness another—the second and last—nodal point in the construction of morality during the first phase of the land reform dispute. Reinforced by public opinion, more credence accrued to the moral claims advanced by the land rights coalition. Against the background of a strong reiteration of the nation's commitment to land reform, the government discursively arrived at a revised interpretation of the earlier collectively constructed morality. It was led to reorder its priorities so as to meet the challenge of impediments and criticisms. Redressing the injustices of apartheid and fostering national reconciliation and social solidarity were put first and second on the agenda, respectively, and at the same time, economic advancement was relegated to the third place. Although qualified by the need for reconciliation and solidarity among the different population groups, the emphasis was shifted more towards the experience of the majority population under colonialism and apartheid, thus giving a stronger, emotively supported, moral tone—of correcting past injustices—to the land reform programme. The new constitution (South Africa Government 1996), particularly Section 25, was invoked in order to ground this reinterpretation.

This redirection of the programme proved quite fruitful. According to an independent report, delivery of land reform improved significantly in the period between 1997 and 1999. Yet, this revised moral construction called forth a reaction from the development coalition. The fact that the correction of the injustices of apartheid was prioritized explains why both the white farming press and the commercial farming lobby started to launch increasingly sharp attacks against Derek Hanekom, the then minister of both land affairs and agriculture.

The second phase

The constitutionally embedded definition of morality prioritizing justice and solidarity, dating from the mid-1990s provided the baseline from which the second phase of the land reform discourse started. This phase took off after June 1999, the date of Mbeki's succession of Mandela as president. From the outset of the Mbeki era, land reform was fraught with difficulties while a little later a historically significant event—the Zimbabwean land crisis—had the effect of changing and complicating the socio-political context and, thus, intensifying the discourse. As a result, the construction of morality took a more uncertain and abruptly changing course.

From justice and solidarity to justice and progress

Shortly after Mbeki's accession to power, the development coalition's criticism of the government, among other factors, contributed to the appointment of a new minister, Thoko Didiza, responsible for the land reform and agricultural portfolios. Upon this followed a thorough reorganization of the bureaucracy which in turn caused the exodus of senior—particularly white liberal—officials and the cooling of relations with donors as well as a marked slowdown in the redistribution of land. These factors conspired to give rise to tensions which became the hallmark of the Mbeki government's first months in office. These tensions reinvigorated the discourse and in particular gave new impetus to the process of the construction of morality. The communication and hence competition and conflict among the governmental, development and land rights coalitions increased substantially, as did the attention of the observing public. As a result, the search for a situationally appropriate construction of the moral universal intensified.

The tensions between the different agents found expression in various forms. On one hand, the development coalition continued its criticism of the government in an attempt to push its own progress frame and the concomitant claim to inclusion in the social order. On the other hand, the land rights coalition engaged in vociferous denouncements of the government's conservative approach and slow progress, and launched a strident attack against the minister's proposal to try to change the racial profile of commercial farming instead of uplifting the poor, thus serving the advancement of its justice frame. Particularly shocking, furthermore, were the increasing instances of white farmers' racist outrages against farm workers and, reciprocally, murders of farm owners. The moral indignation of both the national and international public brought pressure to bear on the discourse participants in favour of finding an equitable solution sooner rather than later. In this discursive context, the government was compelled to look for a new way to end the racial injustice associated with land ownership and use without sacrificing progress.

The discursive competition and conflict between the participants and the pressure of the public, together indicate that an intense process of the construction of morality was underway. The moral construction that emerged differed quite markedly from the previous set of structures consolidated by the white paper. It clearly presupposed a shift from an emphasis first on justice, second on solidarity and finally on economic advancement to an emphasis on justice, followed by economic advancement and only then solidarity. This latter configuration represents the first nodal point of the construction of morality in the second phase of the land reform discourse.

Fixation on justice after Zimbabwe

It is this state of the South African land reform discourse and its emergent moral universal upon which the Zimbabwean land crisis broke-in when, after having been in the making for several years, it eventually erupted in April 2000. The immediate effect of this event was to focus the attention and to thus increase immensely the relevance of—and interest in—the South African land reform issue. It was now clear to everyone that there were inherent limits to a market-led approach to land reform. A sizeable portion of the development coalition, for instance, 75 per cent of white commercial farmers, came to see land reform as inevitable while in consideration of safeguarding their own interests more than half of them indicated their support for an increase in the number of black farmers. For their part, the highly resonant land rights coalition drew strong encouragement from the crisis. At their annual conference, the

PAC membership gave the attending Zimbabwean officials a standing ovation. The National Land Committee, particularly its radical offshoot, the Landless People's Movement, now had a working example of farm seizures, which in its view, exposed the government as still out of touch with reality. Simultaneously, more than half of the inhabitants of black townships all over South Africa pledged their support to the land invasion and occupation in their neighbouring state.

As regards the construction of morality, the outbreak of the Zimbabwean crisis strongly reinforced the prioritization of justice. It, thus, introduced a shift in emphasis, which established as to what can be regarded as nodal point number two in the second phase of the land reform discourse. Through its general secretary, the ANC almost immediately endorsed the farm seizures executed by the Zimbabwean war veterans backed by the Zimbabwe African National Union–Patriotic Front (ZANU-PF) party, while some four months later Vice-President, Jacob Zuma, still assumed what was widely taken as a pro-Mugabe stance. This indicated that the governmental coalition was interpreting the priority of the moral demand for justice in such a strong way that it was willing to implement drastic measures of land redistribution. Once this meta-communicative marker was picked up by the development coalition at home and abroad, a new cycle of the construction of morality got underway.

From justice to progress and justice

The development coalition came back vigorously. It articulated its moral claim to the effect that the redressing of racial injustice, while correct as such, should not be pursued so as to preclude the principle of the inclusion of all, particularly those who developed the country. Simultaneously, it backed this claim with all the resources at its disposal. This made it clear that, more precisely, this coalition's position was that justice should not be sought in a manner that fractured profit taking and the continuity of the kind of lifestyle associated with it. The accompanying threat was highlighted by the reaction of the market to Zuma's reiteration of the government's support for Zimbabwe at a conference of the Southern African Development Community. Due to the action of investors, the South African currency, the Rand, suffered a sharp loss of value. Predictably, this called forth a swift response from the government.

In order to repair relations with the development coalition, the government was compelled to make an adjustment, modifying its framing of the structures of cooperation appropriate to the discourse at that particular moment. To bring the development coalition back into a cooperative relation, it had to communicate that in some sense or another it did recognize the rights of landowners. Mbeki immediately responded to the unfavourable market reaction with assurances that land seizures would not be tolerated in South Africa and Didiza followed suit with a rejection of the Zimbabwean strategy. She insisted that although the market principle proved incapable of bringing about the desired redistribution of land north of the border, South Africa did have a viable land reform programme which was being implemented within the framework of the constitution and the rule of law. This swift reaction convinced the development coalition, particularly Agri-SA, that the government has the right mentality on land reform. Indeed, the government's confirmation proved sufficient for the Business Trust to take out advertisements in newspapers at home and abroad proclaiming that South Africa would neither adopt the ZANU-PF policy nor allow the country to degenerate into lawlessness.

Considered from the viewpoint of the construction of morality, the change in the relation among the three major coalitions indicates a clearly visible adjustment in their joint search for structures that would allow them to cooperate and coordinate their frames and actions. This cycle, thus, culminated in what may be regarded as the third nodal point in the second phase of the land reform discourse. Rather than justice being emphatically stressed, the government was compelled to shift the emphasis so that the weight was more equally distributed across justice and progress. The principle of drastically redressing the injustice of land dispossession stressed in the wake of the radicalization of land reform in Zimbabwe had to be toned down and brought into a more equal relation with economic advancement. Cognitive adjustment was required to arrive jointly at mutually recognized structures of cooperation.

Continuing tension between progress and justice

Since the government was compelled to shrug-off the radicalizing influence of Zimbabwe, it has exhibited determination not to allow the land reform issue to get out of hand. It has kept economic advancement in focus while seeking to avoid and prevent the radical use of justice. Indeed, considering that only approximately 0.4 per cent of its overall budget was allocated to the land reform programme, it would seem as though the government has since given more weight to progress than to redressing the injustices of past land seizures. On the other hand, the pressure on the government by those defending the victims of land dispossession is being maintained and increased, resulting in a relation of tension and even moments of struggle that look like a tug-of-war between the progress and justice frames.

With more than half of the black population believing that drastic measures are required to achieve an equitable and just solution to the land reform issue, it is not surprising that there is sustained public pressure for the compulsory acquisition and even forcible expropriation of land for the purposes of redistribution. This public sentiment naturally enamours the organizations and activists, belonging to the land rights coalition, who are concerned about both the government's slow pace and the landed elite's ability to blunt land reform efforts. In the face of the government's determination supported by the current structures of cooperation, however, the land rights coalition exhibits ambivalence. Some of its members and affiliates insist that they do not promote land seizures but work within the framework of the law, even when engaging in sit-ins, marches and demonstrations. Others take a very different position. Such organizations as the Landless People's Movement, Homeless People's Federation and Anti-Evictions Forum have expressed a greater willingness to engage in action and, indeed, have begun to exhibit growing activism and even militancy. Some who want to see the elimination of the requirement of state compensation for compulsorily acquired land have been keeping up the pressure by threatening radical action if the pace of reform does not quicken. Various instances of land occupation, farm attacks and well-publicized mass actions over the past decade underscore the radical potential of the land rights coalition. Since 2003, there has been evidence that the National Land Committee and its offshoot, the Landless People's Movement, are not only refining land invasion and occupation as a mechanism to increase the tempo of the government's programme, but also actively training people for the purpose.

The government's resolve to keep the land reform conflict from spinning out of control translated into a multi-pronged approach. The latter allows it to flexibly renegotiate the different cognitive structures at play in the discourse. Although it has come to see the principle of willing-seller–willing-buyer as rather circumscribed and the market-based approach, therefore, as not wholly effective, it, on one hand, continues to proceed along these lines in the conviction that it is not entirely meaningless nor fully exhausted. It recognizes, however, that it is at times necessary to facilitate the negotiation of market transactions by backing such procedures with threats of expropriation. In order to give such threats greater credibility, it has been willing to streamline legislation; for instance, the amendment of the constitution allowing administrative rather than judicial expropriation (South Africa Government 2004).

On the other hand, the government has taken a stand against both land activists' clamour for a radical solution to the land reform issue and black public sentiment in favour of the forcible acquisition of land. As regards a radical solution, officials at all levels untiringly keep repeating the government policy that illegal land invasion and occupation will not be tolerated. In conformity with public sentiment, Section 25(2) of the South African constitution (South Africa Government 1996), indeed, admits the compulsory expropriation of land for a public purpose or in the public interest, but the government nevertheless prefers to bypass this option by instead negotiating a market transaction.[9] On the whole, it regards a programme making extensive use of the mechanism of forcible acquisition as potentially counter-productive from the viewpoint of both the predictable reaction of the development coalition and its own distaste for replicating the kind of social engineering that had been so rampant under apartheid.

Two further prongs of the government's approach that complement its dealings with the development coalition on one hand and the land rights coalition on the other, are in evidence. The one is its broader legislative strategy which is aimed at strengthening the land rights of the impoverished rural black population; for instance, the Restitution of Land Rights Amendment Act and the Communal Land Rights Act of 2003 and 2004, respectively (South Africa Government 2003/2004). These acts have been shaped—and are certain to undergo further shaping—by discursive conflict between the government on one hand and organizations such as the Commission on Gender Equality, the Congress of South African Trade Unions and various NGOs, including the ones advocating the rights of rural women, on the other. The other prong of the government's approach is made visible by the steadily increasing budget for land reform since 2002 and the strengthening of the associated bureaucracy.

After the 2004 parliamentary elections that the ANC won by 69.7 per cent, NGOs participating in the land reform discourse as well as observers are closely scrutinizing government action and the resultant pace of land reform. While the speed was clearly increased prior to the elections, some like the International Crisis Group expect that after its landslide victory the government would once again tend to slow down the tempo. Others such as the Landless People's Movement and the Anti-Evictions Forum, who also are undoubtedly suspicious, are both willing and ready to take drastic action if this turns out to be the case. But besides NGOs and movements committed to radicalism, the parliamentary and public debate that ensued in the wake of President Mbeki's State-of-the-Nation address on 11 February 2005 left no doubt about of the fact that the land reform question is potentially the major political issue, indeed, the make-or-break issue South Africa will face in the next decade.

Conclusion

A consideration of the facts on the ground allowed the identification of two distinct phases in the unfolding of the South African land reform discourse. The first phase began, approximately, in 1990 and came to an end in mid-1999 when, coinciding with a new political era, various difficulties impeding land reform inaugurated the second phase which was still underway at the end of the first decade of the new South Africa. The analysis of the discourse itself indicated that the overall moral universal guiding the process of discursive construction comprises three distinct cultural cognitive structures or models of the good: the normative idea of justice, the empirical idea of progress and the aesthetic or conative idea of solidarity or identity. This moral complex was prominently integrated into the preamble to the constitution—as indicated by the motto of this chapter—which projects a conception of South Africa as a social order of reconciliation and solidarity in which justice has been achieved, underpinned by economic advancement and prosperity. Although it is a discursive construction in the first instance, this moral universal acquires a structuring power that forms and shapes the very practices through which it is being reproduced. This it is able to do due to the fact that what initially emerges as a discursive construct, later becomes transposed into a complex of value and ideal standards possessing a cultural logic of its own.

Central to the principal argument is the process of discursive construction in and through which this moral universal structures social reality. In this respect, the view was taken that each set of structures of cooperation and coordination situationally implementing this universal is the product of the interrelation of the participants and, hence, an emergent ascribable to the discursive process. As such, it is constructed out of the participants' frames, representations or cognitive concerns with justice, progress and solidarity, that themselves depend on cultural models. The theoretically informed analysis made the participants' cognitive structures quite clear. The development coalition's frame consists of the cognitive elements of progress, solidarity and justice, and the land rights coalition's frame of justice, progress and solidarity. The former's frame elements are typically packaged in a static order, whereas in the latter case the relation between progress and solidarity can become volatile under pressure. Finally, the governmental coalition's frame tends to oscillate between progress and justice, sometimes yielding more to the development coalition's conception of the good and at other times more to the land reform coalition's.

In the land reform discourse, then, the space within which the participants are able to establish collectively acceptable structures of co-operation and coordination is delimited by the combinatory possibilities of the three cognitive devices or standards of the good comprised by the moral universal. In turn, the combination of justice, progress and solidarity depends on the actual situation in which the participants find themselves at a particular moment in time vis-à-vis one another and before the public. In the course of reconstructing the process of the discursive construction of morality, accordingly, a number of nodal points were plotted through which the two phases developed, each exhibiting its own overall configuration.

The first phase was organized by two nodal points and the second phase by three. In 1992, the rejection of the nationalization of land and hence, the overemphasis on justice, accompanied the adoption of the configuration of progress, solidarity and justice as a viable structural basis for cooperation between the different coalitions and the sections of the population they represented. However, in 1997, a new configuration made up of justice, solidarity and development followed against the background of a stalling land reform programme apparently incapable of correcting the injustices of colonialism and apartheid. By late-1999, the development coalition's criticism of the government had become so penetrating and productive of tensions that a reordering of priorities giving more weight to progress became imperative. This resulted in the readjusted combination of justice, progress and solidarity. Then, unexpectedly, the eruption of the Zimbabwean crisis led to a radical reversion to an almost exclusive emphasis on justice in early 2000, which immediately drew fire from the development coalition. Not being feasible as a structural basis for cooperation and coordination, the government had to take swift action to spearhead the construction of an alternative interpretation in discursive cooperation with the other coalitions. Thus emerged the carefully nurtured and fairly widely supported configuration of progress and justice, followed by solidarity, which was the longest surviving set of cooperation and coordination structures so far.[10]

Whether these structures of cooperation and coordination will be adequate to allow a sufficient degree of fulfilment of the land reform programme is an open question.[11] It will depend on how far the different discourse coalitions are willing and able to acknowledge the post-traditional nature of the morality constructed in, yet regulating, the land reform discourse. What must be recognized throughout is that it is a morality suited to a differentiated and inter-dependent society which is discursively mediated. The danger on all sides is that, in disregard of the relational complex to which it applies, it is treated as a concrete and substantive morality rather than as an abstract and principled one, making possible not only the moral autonomy of the self or group but also cooperation between autonomous selves or groups with reference to public interest. Were any one of the participants to advocate its own point of view and pursue its own interests too strongly, the potential of the collectively accepted configuration for the peaceful resolution of the land reform issue would be fractured. Neither should the development coalition stand in the way of justice nor should the land rights coalition pursue justice *ad absurdum*, and even less should the governmental coalition identify with progress at the expense of justice. The latter is the biggest latent danger of all.

Be that as it may, it seems as though solidarity is inevitably going to take a backseat to progress and justice, whatever the relationship between them. The land rights and development coalitions advance justice and progress, respectively, at the expense of solidarity. Both particularize solidarity, yet each in its own way. This suggests that even a peaceful resolution of the land reform question, which strikes a balance between the major contending forces, is going to be painful. To the extent that progress is pursued, the rift between the rich and the poor will be reinforced, even if the general standard of living is enhanced. To the extent that justice in land affairs is pursued, some members of the society are going to feel less included than others. Therefore, the discourse participants will have to take special care of solidarity—understood in an adequate sense of the word (Brunkhorst 2005; Habermas 1999). To reduce to a minimum the pain that will be exacted by land reform, they will have to desist from operating unreflectively either with remnants of the pre-political, ethnic, cultural or other particularistic understandings, or with the blunt functional devices in favour of consciously cultivating an association of free and equal members of a legal community enjoying the same rights. This implies that the observance of the moral good of solidarity would entail that democracy is strictly pursued in constitutional terms perceivable as such from the third point of view.

Notes

1. This chapter was essentially drafted in Stellenbosch and Durbanville during a research sojourn in Western Cape in 2005. I wish to express my gratitude to all those who helped make it either possible or fruitful or both. I must single out advocate Alan Nelson, proprietor of Nelson's Wine Estate and a passionate, innovative proponent of land reform. It also benefited from research done in the framework of a project funded by the Irish Higher Education Authority under the *auspices* of the third cycle of its Programme of Research in third-level institutions.
2. John Prendergast was the principal author of the section on South Africa.
3. I have in mind, in particular, scholars working in moral and political sociology whose application of Habermas's theory to concrete cases compelled them to emphasize the process of construction. See Note 4. Lately, Habermas (2005) himself has focussed on constructive learning processes.
4. This cognitivist communication model derives from Habermas's work but has been developed to varying degrees by authors inspired by him, including Honneth (1991), Miller (1986, 1992), Eder (1993, 1996), Eyerman and Jamison (1991), and Strydom (1999, 2000, 2002).
5. They include official and non-official websites, South African, British and Irish newspaper reports, academic studies, research reports, biographies, autobiographies, and so on. Lack of space prevents me from quoting and referring in detail to these sources.
6. This categorization corresponds to a pragmatic-cognitive interpretation of Habermas's (1987) concept of culture consisting of cognitive, normative and aesthetic dimensions. Rather than holistic as in symbolist theories, culture is regarded as componential or compositional, and linked to engagement with reality.
7. This is one of the various examples of 'learning in situations of triple contingency' (Trenz and Eder 2004) meriting independent analysis.
8. This provision was contained in Section 121(3) of the Interim Constitution (SA Government 1993).
9. In 2006, after the completion of this piece, it should be noted, the government introduced a policy change towards compulsory expropriation.

10. Considering Note 9, this requires qualification.
11. The recent shift towards justice intimated in Note 9 does not invalidate this argument.

References

Brunkhorst, Hauke. 2005. *Solidarity*. Cambridge, MA: MIT.

Eder, Klaus. 1993. *The New Politics of Class*. London: Sage Publications.

———. 1996. *The Social Construction of Nature*. London: Sage Publications.

Eyerman, Ron and Andrew Jamison. 1991. *Social Movements*. Cambridge: Polity.

Habermas, Jürgen. 1987. *The Theory of Communicative Action*, Vol. 2. Cambridge: Polity.

———. 1996. *Between Facts and Norms*. Cambridge: Polity.

———. 1999. *The Inclusion of the Other*. Cambridge: Polity.

———. 2005. *Zwischen Naturalismus und Religion*. Frankfurt: Suhrkamp.

International Crisis Group. 2004. *Blood and Soil*. Brussels: ICG Press.

Honneth, Axel. 1991. *Critique of Power*. Cambridge, MA: MIT.

Luhmann, Niklas. 1995. *Social Systems*. Stanford, CA: Stanford University Press.

Miller, Max. 1986. *Kollektive Lernprozesse*. Frankfurt: Suhrkamp.

———. 1992. 'Discourse and Morality', *Archives Européennes de Sociologie*, 33(1): 3–38.

Parsons, Talcott. 1964. *The Social System*. New York: Free Press.

South Africa Government. 1993. 'Interim Constitution'. Available on www.info.gov.za/documents/constitution/93cons.htm. Accessed on 18 May 2006.

———. 1996. 'Act No. 108 of 1996', *Government Gazette*, 378: 17678. Accessed on 18 May 2006.

———. 1997. 'South African Land Policy White Paper', Available on http://land.pwv.gov.za/White%20Paper/Whitetab.htm. Accessed on 18 May 2006.

———. 2003/2004. 'Acts', Available on http://www.info.gov.za/gazette/acts. Accessed on 18 May 2006.

———. 2004. 'Constitutional Amendments', Available on www.info.gov.za/documents/constitution/amendments.htm. Accessed on 18 May 2006.

Strydom, Piet. 1999. 'Triple Contingency', *Philosophy and Social Criticism*, 25(2): 1–25.

———. 2000. *Discourse and Knowledge*. Liverpool: University of Liverpool Press.

———. 2002. *Risk, Environment and Society*. Buckingham: Open University Press.

Trenz, Hans-Jörg and Klaus Eder. 2004. 'The Democratizing Dynamics of a European Public Sphere', *European Journal of Social Theory*, 7(1): 5–25.

The Walking Rebellion

14

The Zapatista's Struggle for Autonomy and the Difficulties of Social Change

MATEO MIERY TERÁN G.C.

The Zapatista Army for National Liberation (EZLN, in Spanish), formed mainly by self-defined indigenous people, became public in 1994 with an armed uprising in Chiapas, a southern state of Mexico. From then on, this organization has become a salient and controversial left-wing social movement, with national and international impact.[1] With their words and deeds, Zapatismo represents, for some, a legitimate proposal for pursuit of a better society and hope in a context of uncertainty, global crisis, ecological disaster and political paralysis. For others, it is a political organization plagued with internal problems and contradictions.

Zapatismo has become a usual reference for anti-capitalist and anti-neo-liberal movements as a fundamental critique of the predominant way of doing politics, as well as a point of reference for indigenous rights activism. Its impact is definitively related to the innovative and creative content of their political discourse, made famous through communiqués by its spokesperson, Subcomandante Marcos.[2] Their creative discourse has contributed and stimulated participation in the paths of construction of permanent rebellion in Mexico and other parts of the world.

Apart from its discursive presence, the EZLN has had an important influence and impact in the socio-economic, political and spiritual situation of the people, predominantly indigenous, in certain regions of Chiapas. With the surprise uprising in 1994, the military organization took hold of the city-centres of seven municipalities and captured land from big and small landowners in Chiapas. With the entrance of the Mexican government army, they retreated from the city-centres, but the taken land and the properties already owned by the Zapatista support bases[3] became the territory for the construction of Regiones Autónomas Zapatistas (Zapatista Autonomous Regions, RAZ in Spanish) with its Municipios Autonomos Rebeldes Zapatistas (Autonomous Rebel Zapatista Municipalities, MAREZ in Spanish) and Juntas de Buen Gobierno (Councils or Boards of Good Government). These spaces are now the main sphere of Zapatistas actions, where its concrete influence can be seen.

This chapter starts by recognizing that most elements in the Zapatista discourse are constructive. Furthermore, the ideas developed in this article are supported in a short revision of the historical background and in reflections around day-to-day life situations in an autonomous community of '17 de Noviembre',[4] one of the more than thirty MAREZ. This method is used in order to avoid the common type of writing that navigates only in the Zapatista discourse to legitimate its constructive potential and, rather, give a further step by studying particular results of its deeds.

In the first part, fundamental aspects of the Zapatismo are outlined. Afterwards, the discourse on autonomy is described in general terms. In the third part, a brief account of the history previous to the Zapatismo is summarized to situate the point of departure of the rebel movement. In the last section, I will take as a reference some of their phrases that have been derived into political slogans: 'Everything for everyone, nothing for us' and 'Commanding by obeying'. These are phrases that contain and represent the imaginative aspects of their discourse for a new way of making politics and using power. By contrasting these slogans with concrete aspects of life in the Zapatista territory, I expect to contribute to a debate on the possible alternative views on the use of power to foment better societies.

Zapatismo: An overview

The Zapatista movement has had different layers of action. Its discourse, which will be outlined later, as well as its deeds, should be read in relation to these theoretical layers. At a local level, with concrete consequences, it has created areas of autonomous governance in indigenous communities. Nationally, it has been a critical voice demanding and trying to foment organized change in Mexico. Finally, at an international level, it has become an important reference for those involved in anti-capitalist (anti-neo-liberal) struggles, striving for an alternative world.

The EZLN (1993: 1st Declaration) has characterized itself as a rebel group struggling for a world with democracy, liberty and justice for all. They want to be identified with humility, with the excluded, the exploited, the forgotten, the small and the 'others' who are by definition excluded from modern political societies (EZLN 1993: 1st Declaration). It is an organization formed mainly by indigenous people from Chiapas, who, just as many indigenous people from other parts of the world, have been marginalized and treated not as citizens but as obstacles (objects) for the expansion of a rapacious capitalism.[5]

This movement constitutes a response to the expansion of capitalism as the unitary system for organizing society, asserting, in opposition, that many 'globalizations' are possible and that local cultures have the potential to be the building blocks of a new type of society. A phrase, in this matter, that has represented the Zapatismo around the globe, 'a world capable of holding many worlds', is an example of the imaginative tone that has inspired other activists to visualize societal alternatives where plurality is taken as a fundamental political principle.

A fundamental aspect that has contributed to the characterized Zapatista discourse, and the movement itself, as a new alternative of action is the discursive rejection of the revolutionary logic of seizing power to change society from above. The self-defined 'rebels' seek to question and erode power, and refuse to obey authority from above' (Hernández 2004). In this sense, beyond the ambiguity that a political discourse can have, the insurgents propose to construct transformation from the bottom.

There are other important characteristics to understand Zapatismo, especially in terms of its local actions. The first is the claim, as argued through their communiqués, that their internal decision process proceeds bottoms-up.[6] Every important action and communication is supposed to be 'consensed' through assemblies of the Zapatista support bases in their villages. This aspect overlaps two discursive elements. On one hand, an identification with direct democracy and on the other hand, a defence of indigenous traditions.[7] The real expression of this political discourse and its repercussions in local communities has, nevertheless, been highly controversial.[8] The concrete political, social and economic practices have contributed to the complex socio-political dynamics that range from the reproduction of rather authoritarian practices to the purported processes of radical democracy, communitarian self-determination and self-cultivation (Mier y Terán 2004; Van der Haar 2001).

A second feature is the military character of the EZLN. The Zapatismo started with a war. It took the fighters few days to turn weapons into a political campaign of words and actions.[9] As Subcomandante Marcos has written, it is important to consider the implications of being a military organization and how this relates to the development of villages where the project for autonomy is taking place. The Zapatismo has recognized that the hierarchic order of their military organization has negatively intervened in the process of democratic construction of their civilian communities. However, the military organization continues affecting the construction of democratic practices (Estrada Saavedra 2007; Olivera 2004).

It is important to understand that Zapatismo is a movement in a constant process of construction which has meant important changes in its development. Its organizational and discourse trajectories are supposed to be based in an ongoing process of self-reflection and open discourse that reviews its contents by 'walking the talk'; in other words, a practice of listening, talking and doing.

The Zapatista's relation with the Mexican political system has consistently changed in discourse and deeds through the twelve years since the armed uprising in January 1994. In the beginning, the rebels declared war against the federal executive and the army, and asked the 'other powers of the nation' (the Congress and judiciary) to restore legality and stability deposing the federal executive (EZLN 1993: 1st Declaration). During the first few years, the EZLN and the Mexican government got involved in a process of dialogue that ended in the San Andrés Accords (see the next section of this chapter) and later in a rupture of the dialogue. In the 1998 elections, the insurgents made a tacit alliance with Mexico's main left-wing party (Democratic Revolutionary Party or PRD in Spanish) which represented the opposition to the political elite in the government. Since 2001, the Zapatistas have radicalized their position and have taken a public opposition towards all political parties, the federal government and the Congress. They have declared the present electoral process illegitimate and criticized the politicians for not representing the people.

The response of the Mexican government has been a discontinuous combination of simulated dialogue and a 'low-intensity war', which 'combines particular strategies of political, economic, psychological and military character, which can be docile and sometimes legitimate, and in other occasions can be dirty and terrorist. Its principal objective is to undermine, delegitimate and isolate revolutionary movements' (Castro Apreza 1999). During the first seven years, the presence of the federal army in the Zapatista area of influence was aggressive and pervading. In 2001, after the first democratically elected administration in Mexico took office, the amount of mobilized military personnel was notably reduced and its actions de-escalated. Despite this reduction of military public actions, different levels of government (federal, state and municipal) have continued to be involved in contra-insurgent procedures.

In June 2005, the Zapatismo launched a new initiative to organize a national movement in Mexico against the neo-liberal globalization. The rebels asked non-political party groups and left-oriented citizens to participate in the construction of a 'national program of struggle', based on peaceful political resistance. This initiative is directed at '*trying* to build, or rebuild, another way of doing politics, one which once again has the spirit of serving the Others, without material interests, with sacrifice, dedication, honesty, which keeps its word, whose only payment is the satisfaction of performed duty' (EZLN 2005: 6th Declaration).

This provocative programme aims at bringing together the plurality of the society—city workers, peasants, students, homemakers, small entrepreneurs, gays—and all those that consider themselves oppressed (marginalized, ignored) by mainstream politics. They have named the beginning of this project 'The Other Campaign', in opposition to the official party campaigns for the presidential election on 2 July 2006 and to differentiate it from what the Zapatismo declares to be a simulation exercise of the dysfunctional Mexican political elite.

A word on autonomy, a project of many

Autonomy has become important as a subject of alternative action and mobilization in many parts of the world. This political flag has been brought up as an alternative response to various problems of the complex societies in which we live today.[10] In Mexico, some themes to which autonomy is related are: struggles for indigenous and cultural rights, recognition and strengthening of plurality in societies, empowerment of indigenous people, institutionalization of spaces to preserve a group's culture, local development, direct democracy, self-determination and self-cultivation. Within these matters, and others not mentioned, the possibilities of institutionalizing autonomy are still an entangled debate (and will probably continue as such for a long while). Nevertheless, there are now, in Mexico, examples of what is built under the name 'autonomy'. Some of these are the Municipios Autonomos Rebeldes Zapatistas (Autonomous Rebel Zapatista Municipalities, MAREZ in Spanish).

The origin of the MAREZ can be traced back to the beginning of the uprising in 1994. They started as 'rebel territories', that is, the land and villages of the communities supporting the EZLN. By 1997, after an intricate process of institutionalization of a dialogue process (Ruiz and Lorena 2005), the EZLN and the government, with its respective groups of advisers from the civil society and other organizations, signed the Acuerdos de San Andrés (San Andres Accords). Indigenous peoples' self-determination and autonomy are core aspects of the accords and from the time these accords were signed, they have become the Zapatistas's fundamental demands and objectives. Then the project in the Zapatista's 'rebel territories' gained another face and strength. The government's commitment meant reforms to the Mexican constitution for the 'legal recognition of the forms in which communities, municipalities or other types of native communities govern themselves and organize their political representation, administration of justice and resource management, inside the more extensive State of Mexico' (Van der Haar 2000). It was not until 2001 that a law on indigenous rights and culture (Ley sobre Derechos y Cultura Indígenas) was passed by the Mexican president (Vicente Fox), the legislative power—with the votes of the three main political parties—and a majority of the state Congress. This happened even though, in a historical event, the Zapatista comandancia (commanders) carried out a long walk from the state of Chiapas to Mexico City and spoke against this law to the political elite in the Congress (the opposition to the reform was also backed by other Mexican indigenous groups). The reform was disqualified for not sticking to the San Andres Accords, specifically on the aspect of recognition of the indigenous towns as subjects of law, which ended as recognition of indigenous communities as sub-municipal entities of public interest. In this context, the Zapatistas have remarked that the autonomous rebel municipalities are in constant construction and development, albeit a satisfactory law was not passed.[11]

The MAREZ can be understood in the framework cited earlier, but the Zapatistas themselves have spoken about autonomy in various ways. Albeit there is not a concrete definition of it, through a simplification of the discourse autonomy implies action. In a context of state repression (low intensity war) and moving in clandestinely as a leftist opposition organization, the rebels have used their creativity and have been strategic with their words and actions. The Zapatista autonomy can be, then, understood as the main territories where the rebels are experimenting with the construction of what they believe to be a path of 'well thinking' (building with common sense).

In 2003, the Zapatismo made an important move to consolidate the process of construction of the 'rebel territories'. They decided to name and make public what has been constructed as the Regiones Autónomas Zapatistas (Zapatista Autonomous Regions, RAZ in Spanish) and give them a concrete institution, the Juntas de Buen Gobierno (Councils or Boards of Good Government).[12] These Juntas de Buen Gobierno have helped concentrate decisions and organized activities in the Zapatista territory. The members of the Juntas are representatives of each community with allegedly rotational posts,[13] and the offices from which they operate are localized in the so-called *Caracoles* (seashells, snails).[14]

Brief historical background as a reminder of structural change

Although some of the things said in this chapter may apply to all Zapatista territory, the discussion here is based on a case study. It is relevant to underline this limitation as there are important differences—within all the regions—that need to be taken into account when studying the processes of social transformation.[15]

An important difference, other than languages and traditions, is the origin of indigenous towns and communities. This feature is determinant of the transformation of indigenous society. While some villages existed before the Spanish conquered Mexico, others developed with the formation of *fincas*—a socio-economic system of land ownership—linked to the project of evangelization of the Dominican order.

The villages formed around the Dominican *fincas* are what characterized the municipality of Altamirano, where the autonomous municipality '17 de Noviembre' is located. The social structure under that socio-economic system changed with the Mexican war of independence at the beginning of the nineteenth century. A central secular government arose. So most of the land owned by the Catholic Church was expropriated.

This land ended mainly in the hands of landlords who reproduced and reinforced a socio-economic system, creating a relation of dependence in which the native people were exploited.

With the Mexican Revolution at the beginning of the twentieth century, another change started taking place: the creation of *ejidos*, which was a programme of the Mexican central government to distribute land. It was through this institution that the government structured peasants and indigenous land property, organizing it as collective ownership. In Chiapas, this process had important deviations, particularly corruption and mismanagement by the authorities and powerful local groups. Because of the balance of power, landlords kept the best land and managed to continue exploiting the indigenous people. The land for *ejidos* was mainly in the hills or too far away.

The history of the second half of the twentieth century for the indigenous people in Chiapas was strongly related to the struggle for land. With important support from the catholic church of Chiapas, Maoist groups coming from other states in Mexico commenced a new process of socio-political organization in some communities in Chiapas. In some cases, this impulse helped obtain the land needed but pressures from different groups of interest turned the distribution into a difficult process. It is in these circumstances that the first members of what is now the EZLN initiated the promotion of their Marxist-Leninist objectives (Harvey 1998; Legorreta Díaz 1998; Subcomandante Marcos 1999). It was a ten-year process of clandestine work leading to the 1994 uprising. Now their words have been public and effectively disseminated for more than a decade.

Words of hope

Creativity and other aspects of the Zapatista discourse have sparked discussions among academics, social thinkers, activists and others. With less magnitude, this has also happened in the case of the impacts it has had in Chiapas (Barabas and Bartolomé 1998; Burguete 1999; Estrada Saavedra 2007; Mattiace 1998; Nash 2001; Ruiz and Lorena 2004; Van de Haar 2000). In this chapter, there is no intention to either cover or define all the aspects of the Zapatista discourse. Also the narrations, in this section, of concrete practices in MAREZ are not an exhaustive description of the many things happening in the communities.

The 'principles' promoted by the Zapatismo could be thought as objectives for the future, but considering that the rebels boast of being a movement of deeds, I would assume that the current policies or practices in the autonomous communities should follow—relatively closely—their ideas of a better society. Also, within the Zapatista logic of 'constructing by walking', their actions of today can be understood as part of a constant process of construction with no fixed end. In their discourse, they claim to be preoccupied with the process and with how this path has to be walked by listening, learning and 'moving at the pace of the slowest'. This logic can also be interpreted as a discourse that justifies, in other words, what can be understood as strategic decisions in accordance with the circumstances. In this sense, it is not absurd to understand some decisions of the EZLN as survival measures in a context of war (even if it is fought in a discursive and symbolic arena).

In the rest of this chapter I will analyze two of the most important mottos, or slogans, of the Zapatismo by comparing them with observations of life and development in the autonomous Zapatista municipality, 17 de Noviembre. In this way, I hope to contribute to the understanding of the difficulties involved in the creation of new sociopolitic relations under a discourse of alternative paths; routes thought for replacing the predominant one we live in now (capitalism).

'Everything for everyone, nothing for us'

A phrase like 'everything for everyone, nothing for us' has an intrinsic tone of humility. In the logic of struggle for humanity, it places the rebels in a position of sacrifice and devotion to the construction of a new world.

The first half, 'everything for everyone', establishes distributive justice as a principle that should direct the rebels' actions; the second half, 'nothing for us', can be interpreted as a proposal to leave out initiatives or projects where there are only personal or group gains.

There are two words of importance to situate the Zapatismo in relation to this phrase: hope and dignity. In other words, the acceptance of this motto as a principle implies a belief in the possibility of a better world (hope), a planet where justice will be defined as equity of accessibility to 'everything'. And it also presupposes a commitment by the active agent (the rebel) to an attitude of service for humanity and the well-being of all. This devotion contributes to the dignity of the rebels' existence by introducing them to an ethical life.

The consequences of the actual practice of this principle, in the villages of Chiapas where the Zapatista live, are—precisely—not like the imaginative world described earlier. In the official municipality of Altamirano, where the MAREZ 17 de Noviembre is situated, the Zapatista uprising has meant access to considerable amounts of land from big and small landholders (Villafuerte Solis et al. 2002). These properties have been distributed since 1994 among the Zapatista support bases. One of the justifications offered is that this land belonged to the ancient indigenous people and had to be recovered. But it also corresponds to a revolutionary logic of appropriation of the means of production. In the distribution process not 'everyone' benefited. Those who participated turned into reality the long-awaited hope (and need) to obtain land for their reproduction (in terms of cultural and physical survival). But actually it also excluded those who have decided not to sympathize with the Zapatismo (people who belonged to the same communities and lived in the same circumstances have been left out).

Moreover, the Zapatismo is publicly committed to improving people's welfare. This discourse has become an element of hope for those involved in the rebel territories. This objective has been part of an impressive engagement, not only by the villagers, but also many outsiders. The flux of global resources (material, non-material and symbolic) has permitted changes, most visible in education and health. The improvements and aggravations caused vary but this is not the place to evaluate its impacts. Rather, our intention is to point out the frank need of improvement in the life of people in the communities, as well as to mention how the Zapatista movement has appropriated the resources to build rebel communities and at the same time, has allowed the exclusion of those not willing to dedicate their lives to the Zapatismo.

The social fragmentation in many communities in Chiapas is not only a failure of the Zapatismo. It also has to do with a long historical process that has caused social disintegration, as well as a consequence of the low intensity war orchestrated by the government against the Zapatistas. Other factors contribute as well; for example, the world crisis in the agricultural sector, expressed with decline in food prices paid to small-scale farmers and aggravated with continuous neo-liberal policies withdrawing state support for peasants.

With the construction of autonomous territories, the EZLN intends to create a relation of independence (autonomy) between the official government and the people in rebel territories.[16] To achieve this, they have formed parallel power structures that rival with the official structure. In a way, this has brought dignity to the Zapatistas by demonstrating their capacity to respond to their socio-economic problems by practising self-determination (though in relation to the needs, the solutions might be limited). This dignity has been a crucial factor to stimulate those individuals participating in the construction of schools, in receiving courses to become community doctors or primary school teachers, to attend collective assemblies, to become authority, and so on.

There are fundamental aspects complementing dignity in the construction of autonomous territories, human and material resources. In 17 de Noviembre, the Zapatismo has institutionalized rebellion and to sustain this process of construction, it has needed a constant flux of resources and commitment by its members.

On one side, people are required to devote themselves to the Zapatismo and even though there are personal motivations and dignity gained, restrictive (or coercive) rules play a fundamental role in holding the participation system together. For example, the Zapatista autonomous municipality 17 de Noviembre is organized into microregions. Collective activities, such as communal land cultivation, take place in each region to obtain resources for the Zapatismo. Almost all the Zapatistas should do this work; failing to fulfil this obligation results in punishments that range from having to work extra to expulsion from the organization in extreme cases, depending on how serious the fault was. This fact exemplifies that coercive rules exist in the Zapatista system that intends to create paths for construction with solidarity. Details like this can help us understand how difficult it is for a social movement to consolidate shared aims and how neither initial commitment nor rules guarantee the perpetuation of solidarity for rebel objectives.

On the other side, to sustain the rebel territories and the Zapatismo as a rebel organized social movement, there is a reliance on material resources. Opposing neo-liberal policies and pushing forward the construction of autonomy (independence) from the misused Mexican political system, the Zapatistas have rejected the social programmes of the official government.[17] To improve welfare, they have relied on their own work (for example, selling small quantities of agricultural products, either produced individually or collectively) and on support given by outsiders.

Both local and external resources are used to sustain the diverse fronts of action of the Zapatista movement: local, national and global. In this way, devotion has to be for the community as well as for the rebel movement where there is expectation to participate in national and global changes for a better world.

This being said, the Zapatista construction system has to be understood as a process based in communal commitment (in terms of political participation and work to obtain resources). In this sense, the phrase analyzed applies differently to the rebel communities in accordance with the sphere of action. On one side, locally, 'everything for everyone, nothing for us' is limited to those affiliated to the Zapatismo in the communities. It can be said that 'everyone' means the Zapatista community and 'us' means an individual inside it. On the other side, at a national and global level the principle implies conviction by the rebels that their struggle is for humanity. 'Everyone' means an abstract 'all', while 'us' means the movement as a whole that should not expect exclusive gains.

Going further on the understanding of the phrase in terms of the local actions, in the context of autonomous communities constructed by the Zapatismo, 'everything for everyone, nothing for us' implies a restriction on individual gain accompanied with a faith of collective improvement. This has been translated in various practical forms. For example, in 17 de Noviembre, the Zapatismo has decided to restrict travelling out of the community and has prohibited selling handicrafts through personal or individual channels.

To understand such decisions, we need to place them in the national context. In Mexico, migration has become the second source of national income (after petroleum). This fact is a critical element affecting communities and reflects the crisis that shadows the country. As long as the agricultural system in the villages is not able to provide enough resources for (at least decent) living, people will look for other sources of income and self-realization. One of them is emigration (mainly to the United States); others are short-term contracts in the national construction industry (mainly for the tourist complexes) or in the government petroleum company. In the case of women, they typically work as housemaids in cities.

This situation has greatly affected the socio-economic, political and cultural dynamics in the communities and the Zapatismo has responded by applying restrictive measures. People from 17 de Noviembre are allowed to leave their communities for not more than two months (this rule is some times broken; so the restriction might change in the future). This determination results in adding an extra difficulty to the decision of leaving the community. It also implies a subordination of their personal needs to those of the movement.

Another restriction in the name of the community can be found in the Zapatista handicraft making, an activity that has recently developed in 17 de Noviembre as a source of income. Person-to-person transactions, from a native to a foreigner, for example, has been prohibited. The logic behind this decision is to encourage trade that requires the participation of all the interested members of the community and not only one. The main way has been the creation of cooperatives (mainly by women) that become intermediaries between the foreigner and the artisans in the community. Besides not allowing personal transactions, the fact is that this practice is a restriction on individual income and a control over monetary resources in the name of the community.[18] The resources obtained through the cooperatives are normally invested on infrastructure, small development projects and for the social movement.

The Zapatista motto 'everything for everyone, nothing for us' has to be read carefully. It can be easily idealized as a straight-forward practice of the Zapatismo but the reality lived by the rebels is far more complex. The interpretations of this principle and the results of acting under it are diverse. Both results as well as interpretations are part of what should continually be revised in the process of construction of a better world in the Zapatistas territories of Chiapas.

'Commanding by obeying'

One of the most significant mottos of Zapatismo, 'commanding by obeying' or 'leading by obeying', is a ruling principle for politics. Under this maxim, the governor, the prince, should act at all times in accordance with what is agreed to by the rest. It implies the ruler's commitment to a life of servitude and the refusal to use power as a vehicle for personal benefit or to misuse of its privileged position. 'Commanding by obeying' also presupposes (or demands) permanent and active participation from the society, so that it can actually command those who govern. In this way, a hopeful Zapatismo attempts to dignify the purpose of governments and promote a society where politicians rule but do so under the lead of society. It is a political ideal where the prince serves the community just as the rebel serves humanity.

The practice of this principle should be understood taking into account the history in the communities, as it is closer to abusive practices by the local authorities than to governments limited with direct democracy. This has been seen, for example, with the manipulation of assemblies and with mismanagement of government resources. In this sense, it is relevant to understand that the point of departure for the MAREZ is not one of isolated communities with a democratic development, but one closer to *cacique*[19] princedoms and a relative abandonment by the state. As it has been documented (Olivera 2004), the historical roots of these authoritarian practices cohabit with the intentions of constructing a better world and at moments, its thorny creepers grow and the fruits are reaped.

Given this history, 'commanding by obeying' can be interpreted as a proposal to go further than mere cultivation of political servitude and sacrifice. It contemplates that the society, the citizens, should tell the prince what to do. Society, then, has the task of ruling through the prince's actions. There are two controversial aspects in the practice of this principle. First, there are critics who point out that it is not possible to consult for every decision and certain actions will be taken by the prince without the general consent of the community. Second, the practice of 'commanding by obeying' has not happened without complications.

The EZLN as the central actor of the Zapatismo needs its support bases to survive as a rebel movement. For this, a complex system of commitment and participation has been constructed. Depending on the theme and the action, the civil bases are asked to participate. There are clear cases of different moves taken by the Zapatismo, which can illustrate the involvement by the support bases.

This movement constantly uses the strength of massive mobilization. In this sort of actions, decisions can be seen as taken from top-down. If the conceptualization of bottoms-up means the involvement of all citizens, then it is not the case when people are only informed on what there is to do and consulted to decide who will go (perhaps for some, consulting who will go is enough to consider that the ruler is obeying).

There are other sorts of compromises by the support bases, which are closer to the situation in the autonomous communities' everyday life decisions. In these cases, the participation is more active as it has to do with immediate needs and development of the community. In the construction of autonomous territories, especially in the 17 de Noviembre, the efforts to offer the inhabitants autonomous government services (legal and organizational), autonomous education and health services have implicated strong involvement from many people. In this sense, the construction of the rebel Zapatismo could be seen as bottoms-up, and a change from the past centralized decisions by the official government. But even in these cases, there is a political structure that functions as the central planner; so 'commanding by obeying' does not work constantly and there are rules and authorities the inhabitants have to obey.

A peculiar aspect of the socio-economic organization in 17 de Noviembre, and apparently in all the MAREZ, is that a salary is not considered. Whether it is autonomous authorities or community post or collective work, in principle there is no monetary payment. Then, it is the vocational motivation that can move people to participate, or an obligation through an appointment by the authorities or the community assembly. In a situation of poverty, as is the case in 17 de Noviembre, vocational motivation might not always be the strongest source of stimulus (it has been argued that there are other sorts of compensations, such as social recognition and beneficial relations with outsiders).

The practice of working without payment is considered to be an ancient one and it is actually carried out in various indigenous villages in Mexico. In the case of the autonomous government, it is argued that the work without monetary remuneration is a traditional control over corruption.

Moving on to a concrete example of communitarian participation, we could say that the project for autonomous education has been one of the most visible activities in 17 de Noviembre. It has developed with the collaboration of groups of non-natives and the Zapatistas support bases. For the activity of the educator, as said earlier, there is also no monetary remuneration. It has been a Zapatista custom that each community agrees what sort of help (alternative remuneration) the teacher will receive so that he can work his land as well as fulfil his duties as an educator. (The most common agreement has been to work as a teacher three days a week while the rest is free for personal activities. If needed, other inhabitants can do extra work on his land to provide for the basic food.) To the point of the agreement, we could say that the process runs relatively well, though the difficulties have cropped up in actual compliance. On one hand, the educators do not always attend their lessons (neither do students). On the other hand, the members of the community do not always comply with the agreements, so the teacher has to look out for himself and find a source of income, abandoning his teaching duties. These are examples of the difficulties faced in a system that is based on service and vocational motivation. It also reflects that common practices occurring in the official government education system that go against the development of education in the community also take place in the Zapatista villages. In this sense, the participation of all the community under an agreement does not seem to be enough to maintain the commitment to the commandments of the community.

Finally, 'commanding by obeying' includes direct democracy or radical democracy, in the sense that it asks for constant political advocacy from the citizens. On one hand, it can be seen as a good way to form compromised citizens. It also creates contexts where people have to define their opinion and their choices. Clear cases are the reunions and assemblies where members of the communities interact in decision-making processes. But on the other hand, the demand for complete consensus in these spaces can become a way to push out opinions (with a loss of diversity).[20] The Zapatismo has insisted in the recognition of plurality but it might be in the practices in the communities that they have not been able to establish freedom (or in other words, personal autonomy).

Conclusions

The Zapatista discourse is broad and suggestive. It has used words to question the predominant paradigm of social construction (or destructions) and has established ethical maxims as guidance for their actions. The Zapatismo is giving concrete steps by constructing autonomous regions, boards of good government and MAREZ in Chiapas. It is in these spaces that tensions and difficulties to build a better society take place.

This movement considers that rebels have to serve humanity. This attitude will dignify their purpose of being rebels, which is to struggle for a desired better world. Hope and dignity have been fundamental elements for the participation of the Zapatistas' support bases and those sympathizers who collaborate in development projects (on education, health, gender issues, ecological prevention, and so on). Although hope mobilizes people from the MAREZ, improvements and achievements have to materialize, if the rebels have to keep on walking. The Zapatismo has established rules of behaviour; some have caused exclusion, others have defined the sort of activities in accordance with the need of the social movement and not necessarily the locality. Some questions derive from this practice: How long can a system sustained in goodwill last? What is the balance of material improvement, rules, dignity and hope needed to construct a better world? Do rebels have to devote their lives for the well-being of future generations to improve the world or their communities? Can a net of solidarity make structural changes and construct better societies?

The Zapatismo has proposed an ethical use of power in their territories. The prince has to govern as server and the community has to rule the prince. The rebels in their discourse promote direct democracy and intend to transgress the limits of representation in electoral and party systems. But some practices in the Zapatista communities are cases where obligation and commitment to participate constantly in the community affairs are not enough to eradicate either exclusion or decisions for personal benefit, but have the opposite result.

There are aspect of the life in the MAREZ that have to be seen as future development, to be evaluated later. But there are others that suggest that the curse of development is trapped in the need of sustaining the rebel movement. The inhabitants of the MAREZ take various actions decided by authorities, with devotion, obedience and commitment, and this involvement is sustained in a supposed struggle for the well-being of humanity. Other decisions have created concrete results in community life and have been fundamental in the construction of the MAREZ, as these determine the capacity of the autonomous authorities to offer services. Most of these decisions are for the welfare of all the population; so it has been a slow process. In this path, individuals of the Zapatista support bases have found limits to their personal objectives and have to either subordinate to the rebels' rules and the community authorities or leave the movement. The rules established in certain Zapatistas communities lead to ask at what point personal benefit is in conflict with community welfare and improvements. Can coercive rules bring about self-realization and community improvement?

The social changes caused by the Zapatismo in the rebel territories have to be understood without idealizing the discourse. Even though the movement's words criticize various aspects of the common political and economic systems as well as the theoretical conception of the world, the actions proposed as alternative have not managed to break with practices that the discourse criticizes.

Notes

1. Zapatismo has become more than just a guerrilla, or an army for national liberation. In strict sense, militiamen and civil groups from the communities form the organized core of the movement. Having a broader view, the sympathizers and collaborators are as well part of Zapatismo, which, then, becomes a net of global support. That is why when using the words 'Zapatismo' and 'rebels', I refer to the movement as a whole, not exclusively to the armed organization or its civilian support communities. But it is important to reject an oversimplified understanding of Zapatismo as a homogeneous movement or an organization of indistinct individuals to avoid a frivolous idealization that assumes, for example, the absolute accomplishment of their ethical and inventive socio-political principles.
2. See http://palabra.ezln.org.mx/.
3. The Zapatismo has communicated that there is a division between those who belong to the military structure, the militiamen (and women) and those who belong to the civil bases called support bases. The interaction between

the two has been a controversial aspect of the Zapatismo, as the militia is inherently hierarchical and opposed to democracy.

4. A common Zapatista practice has been the changing of names as a symbolic appropriation of spaces and as a reinforcement of the history of the Zapatismo. The names correspond to important dates, like the case of '17 of November', when the EZLN was founded, ten years before the uprising of 1994. They also use names that refer to people who have died in the Zapatista struggle, or to global icons such as Che Guevara and Mahatma Gandhi.

5. This exposition of the characteristic of marginality of most indigenous people should not be taken as a simplification of the complex reality we all live in. Making a romantic characterization of indigenous people as pure and saints that are naturally born cooperative and non-egoistic do not contribute to the intentions of building a better society.

6. See http://palabra.ezln.org.mx/.

7. There is ample debate on the definition of 'indigenous traditions' as well as on their origin and the consequences of classifying them strictly, particularly because traditions change or should be changed in accordance with social developments, such as human rights and democratic principles (Barabas and Bartolomé 1998; Mattiace et al. 2002; Viqueira 2002).

8. See Barabas and Bartolomé (1998), Burguete (1999), Estrada Saavedra (2007), Mattiace (1998), Nash (2001), Ruiz and Lorena (2004) and Van de Haar (2000) who have critically studied the different aspects of the repercussion of the Zapatismo in Chiapas.

9. The Zapatista movement has had an impressive presence through the media. Its communiqués have been the main means of communication.

10. This is not the place to write on the complexity of the old term 'autonomy' that has different meanings depending on the place it is located or the level at which it is applied. The Mexican autonomy is mainly related to indigenous rights at the village level, different from what has been developed, for example, in Spain as regional autonomy in Catalonia and the 'Bask country'. Furthermore, the debate in Mexico about autonomy does not have any reference to separatism or independence.

11. From this, it has been said that the autonomous municipalities in Mexico are *de facto* autonomies and not legal autonomies. Without legal recognition, various indigenous and peasant groups have decided to establish autonomous territories around Mexico, which can be called *de facto* autonomies (Mattiace et al. 2002).

12. The Zapatismo has not been particularly interested in revealing their decision-making process and is closed for those not belonging to the communities. The decision to create autonomous regions took many Zapatista support bases by surprise. This fact does not mean that a process of consultation among the authorities is non-existent but it does discard a process of absolute consensus.

13. The rotational character of the post has developed differently in each community. So it cannot be assured here that the rotation has been done on a constant basis.
14. The Zapatista discourse is characterized by its careful use of symbols. The figure of the *Caracoles* is related to various meanings in the Zapatistas words. One of the most important of them is to have a two-way communication, a channel to be heard outside the communities and an open conduit to hear those outside. In concrete terms, the five Zapatistas *Caracoles* are spaces where different activities take place (education, assemblies, lodging, and so on.). They represent political centres, and the relations with foreigners and nationals are mainly on these grounds.
15. Also, to understand the circumstances in which the Zapatista support bases live and work, it is important to consider the general socio-economic context of Chiapas. In this state, in 2003, around 25 per cent of its population belonged to an indigenous group, twelve different languages were spoken and it was classified in government statistics as the more backward territory of Mexico.
16. This purpose is better understood considering that the government has never had total presence in those communities.
17. The rejection has been clear in their public discourse but in practice, there are cases where communities or individuals have decided to accept some official government services and programmes. In practical terms, it is impossible to isolate absolutely from government services, for example, the use of electricity (state owned) and infrastructure such as roads. In pragmatic terms, the Zapatistas use the services available in accordance with their needs, as the MAREZ do not offer everything, for example, complex health attention.
18. This logic is not followed in the transactions of agricultural products, an activity that has been the sustainability of indigenous and peasant families for a long time.
19. A *cacique* is a common figure in Mexican villages. He is usually the leader of the community and has the functions of being a representative of the community in the national political system, and a ruler of the community. It is a classification usually associated with authoritarian practices.
20. Viqueira (2002: 95) has pointed out the particular practice of the open vote with raised hands as a way in the Chiapas communities to identify dissidence and stop its development.

References

Arias Marín, Alan. 2004. 'Acuerdos de San Andrés, ¿otros Estado'. *Milenio*, 19 February.

Barabas, Alicia M. and Miguel A. Bartolomé. 1998. *Autonomías Étnicas y Estados Nacionales*. Mexico: CONACULTA, INAH.

Burguete Cal y Mayor, Araceli (ed.). 1999. *México: Experiancias de Autonomía Indígena*. Copenhagen, Denmark: International Work Group for Indigenous Affairs (IWGIA).

Castro Apreza, Inés. 1999. 'Quitarle el Agua al Pez: La Guerra de Baja Intensidad en Chiapas (1994–98)', *Chiapas* 8. Available on www.ezln.org/revistachiapas/No8/ch8castro.html. Accessed June 2006.

Estrada Saavedra, Marco Antonio. 2007. *La comunidad Armada Rebelde y el EZLN: Un Estudio Histórico y Sociológico de los Tojolabales en las Cañadas Tojolabales de la Selva Lacandona (1933–2004)*. Mexico: El Colegio de Mexico.

EZLN. 1993–2006. 1st to 6th Declaration of the Lacandon Jungle and Various Other Documents with the Zapatistas Words. Available on http://ezln.org.mx. Accessed March 2008.

Harvey, Neil. 1998. *The Chiapas Rebellion: The Struggle for Land and Democracy*. Durham y Londres: Duke University Press.

Hernández Navarro, Luis. 2004. 'Zapatismo Today: Five Views of the Bridge', *Americas Program*. Silver City, NM: Interhemispheric Resource Center. Available on http://americas.irc-online.org/citizen-action/focus/2004/0401zap-five.html

Legorreta Díaz, María del Carmen. 1998. *Religión, Política y Guerrilla en Las Cañadas de la Selva Lacandona*. México: Cal y Arena.

Mattiace, Shanan L. 1998. 'Peasant and Indian: Political Identity and Indian Autonomy in Chiapas, Mexico, 1970–96', Ph.D. thesis, University of Texas at Austin.

Mattiace, Shanan L., Rosalva Aída Hernández and Jan Rus (eds). 2002. *Tierra, Liberta y Autonomía: Impactos Regionales del Zapatismo en Chiapas*. Mexico: Centro de Investigaciones y Estudios Superiores en Antropología Social (CIESAS), IWGIA.

Mier y Terán G.C., Mateo. 2004. 'Autonomía zapatista en Altamirano, Chiapas. Estudios de Vidas del Municipio Autónomo "17 de Noviembre"', Thesis for undergraduate degree in political science, CIDE, Mexico City.

Nash, June C. 2001. *Mayan Visions: The Quest for Autonomy in an Age of Globalization*. New York: Routledge.

Olivera, Mercedes. 2004. 'Sobre las Profundidades del Mandar Obedeciendo', in Pérez Ruiz and Maya Lorena (coords), *Tejiendo Historias: Tierra, Género y Poder en Chiapas*. México: Instituto Nacional de Antropología e Historia.

Ruiz, Pérez and Maya Lorena (coords). 2004. *Tejiendo Historias: Tierra, Género y Poder en Chiapas*. Mexico: Instituto Nacional de Antropología e Historia.

———. 2005. *¡Todos Somos Zapatistas! Alianzas y Rupturas Entre el EZLN y las Organizaciones Indígenas*. Mexico: Instituto Nacional de Antropología e Historia.

Subcomandante Marcos. 1999. *Relatos del Viejo Antonio*. México: Centró de Información y Análisis de Chiapas.

Van de Haar, Gemma. 2000. 'Del Ejido al Municipio Autónomo: La Construcción de Espacios Autónomos en una Región Indígena de Chiapas', Conference Paper, Chiapas y Guatemala: Conflictos y reconstrucción social, Toulouse, France.

———. 2001. *Gaining Ground: Land Reform and the Constitution of Community in the Tojolabal Highlands of Chiapas, Mexico*, Thela Latin American Series. Amsterdam: Rozenberg Publishers.

Villafuerte Solis, Daniel et al. 2002. *La Tierra en Chiapas: Viejos Problemas Nuevos*. Mexico: Fondo de Cultura Económica.

Viqueira, Juan Pedro. 2002. *Encrucijadas Chiapanecas: Economía, Religión e Identidades*. México: El Colegio de México, Tusquets Editores.

A Yearning of the Heart
Spirituality and Politics

15

HELENA TAGESSON

This is not an academic chapter. Rather, this text is based on my personal reflections on how social movement activism—that is, practice for realizing human liberation at an outer level and spiritual practice for realizing liberation within—might link together for people like myself: activists within the secular global justice movement or any movement of the sort. I am a member of the board of Attac Sweden; a part of the international Attac network; and the globalizing movement for justice and democracy. I am also a Buddhist practitioner, practising mindfulness in the tradition of Thich Nhat Hanh, as well as various compassion practices as taught within the tradition following Tibetan meditation master Chögyam Trungpa. It is mainly teachings out of this last tradition that have accompanied my writing of this text. It is an account of why it seems to me that in my life, these two most sensitive, troubling and inspiring areas of striving for empowerment and emancipation are actually not just supporting each other but one drives the other forward, and informs and defines it.

It may be that not much of what I say here is possible to generalize to other contexts or even other people. This is especially so since for me, reflecting on these things has been a rather lonely doing. Gothenburg, Sweden, or indeed the international networks where I work, are not swarming with activist spiritual practitioners. And even though I personally find that these areas are intimately linked, I seldom discuss these issues with my activist friends and colleagues, most of whom do not recognize themselves in a discourse of spiritual practice. These thoughts have, thus, not been shared with or scrutinized by others to the extent that I would have liked them to. The reader will have to receive them for what they are: a personal tale and some rather tentative reflections.

Attac in Sweden: A political revival

Attac Sweden is part of the international Attac movement, a dynamic part of the globalizing movement for justice and democracy. Attac was founded almost by accident in France, in 1998, after an editorial by Ignacio Ramonet in *Le Monde Diplomatique*, called 'Disarm the Markets', where he lamented the overwhelming power of financial markets vis-à-vis democratic structures and the backside of neo-liberal globalization, such as uneven development. When he rather rhetorically suggested the forming of Attac, an Association for the Taxation of Financial Transactions for the Aid of Citizens as a step in counteracting all this, thousands of people wrote to the magazine and wanted to join the non-existent organization. Thus, *Le Monde Diplomatique* and various organizations and individuals ended up founding Attac, a network and a membership organization working against neo-liberalism. Its evolution continued to baffle all involved, including its founders. No one had expected the overwhelming energy of the local committees that soon started being formed, and no one had expected Attac to spread to more than forty countries in less than five years' time. I got involved as Attac was being formed in Sweden in 2000 and have been spending most of my time and energy working with it since then. Currently, we have around 3,000 members, working with auto-educational activities and creative actions, trying to lift issues of global justice, as well as issues of justice and welfare in our own national context, higher onto the political agenda. Attac works against privatization and the dismantling of welfare systems, for the introduction of a Tobin Tax on financial transactions, for the cancellation of third world debt, and for a fair and democratic regulation of international trade, amongst other things.

The way Attac started in Sweden was mesmerizing. As the word got around, in 2000, of some people planning to start a Swedish version of the organization, interest grew and pressure built in an amazing way, seemingly almost by itself. Local committees started being formed all over the country. Every open seminar held in Gothenburg, where I live, attracted hundreds of people, even when they were hardly advertised. The heterogeneity of the people showing up was very inspiring. There were people of all ages and professional backgrounds, all with the sense that the time had come to get together to stop the dismantling of the welfare state and begin to act for justice and against marginalization, at home as well as globally. The most striking feature of these groups, and what made Attac seem different from other contexts where I had been active before, was that so many people did not have any previous experience of political work.

Around 6,000 people joined the organization during the first year which was brimming with activity. I found it striking how open-minded and attentive the atmosphere was. We had the ambition to create a non-hierarchical organization, with the local groups as the basic units, where everyone would have the right to take initiatives, to define appropriate action, to act and to articulate the organization. There was a sense that anything was possible, that even if Attac certainly would not be able to change the world on its own, it still signified that something new was happening; that a political awakening was taking place amongst people who did not use to care about society in this way. Attac was a kind of political revivalist movement for us, a nation of people that needed to remind ourselves that universal welfare did not appear from grace alone and would not remain or be extended from grace alone either.

Now, three years after Attac Sweden was formally founded, we have about one-third of the members we had during the first year. We still get new members, we are still alive and evolving. We are becoming better, more professional, at much of what we do. But apparently it was harder than many of us thought to keep the spirit of openness, of breaking new ground and making room for everyone, alive. And we have lost many of the newcomers of three years ago.

In a sense, this is the oldest story there is around, as regards revivalist movements of any kind and many are happy to point that out to me and others involved. In the beginning there is a great sense of openness, of breaking free. But that spirit does not last as movements become more institutionalized and everyday life begins to take its toll on the revolutionary spirit. All this seems true. But I believe we would do well to reflect a little bit more on what can happen to us in experiencing a political awakening and joining a movement on an existential level. I believe this is necessary in order to sustain our commitment to social change. I also believe it is important in order to better understand the premises for deepened spiritual practice in a world looking to fall apart.

A practice of awakening the heart

What draws people to a movement like Attac? There is no simple answer, obviously. If I were to interview our members, I think I would find almost as many ways of expressing it as we have members, even though their motives probably all evolve around a similar will to justice and human dignity. But one thing I find in reflecting with friends and colleagues around this is that most of us come to Attac thinking we are there to work with outer structures and not with issues that are in any way intimate. That is, the idea of one public and one private sphere is firmly anchored within most of us, in spite of the echoing of the well-known feminist slogan stating that 'the personal is political'. The issues of Attac (politics, economics, issues of what can be called structural violence) seem clearly to belong in the public sphere.

Now this has truth to it but only half the truth. I think this idea of our work dealing only with outer structures leads activists and organizers to misjudge several aspects of our own work and what it is that we are actually doing together. For coming together to affirm that 'another world is possible' is in many senses a most intimate project, touching the hearts of all involved. We may be discussing something as dry and seemingly soulless as a currency transaction tax or the statutes of the European Central Bank, but what has brought people together is a yearning for human dignity, for compassion and for meaning; what seems best described as a yearning of the heart.

There is something truly moving in people finding their way of expressing this yearning politically. We are honouring it through learning together of the state of the world which means, of the pain and fear that people are living through and of the possible alternatives. A study circle on poverty and global justice issues is not just an intellectual endeavour but in a sense, a practice in opening one's heart to the painful predicament of the world. Poverty, oppression and environmental destruction become vivid and real to us in a way they did not use to be. This affects us in slightly unexpected ways, for better and for worse.

To many, it seems profoundly healing to work with others within a movement for justice and dignity. People often gain a new kind of self-respect and sense of meaning. I believe that the principal source of this is the fact that *through what we do, we are discovering our ability to care deeply about what goes way beyond ourselves*. We are getting to know a part of ourselves that we often were not quite aware of, a part that is more aware and, therefore, more fully present in the world. We are glimpsing an inherent softness and openness towards others. We are getting a hint of our capacity for love and compassion, and there seems to be nothing as healing and empowering as that. I often felt a need for the language of Buddhism to understand and describe the processes of transformation that people do go through in finding their place within the movements. My Buddhist teachers might say that our social practice can be one of awakening the *bodhichitta*, a practice of awakening the enlightened heart of compassion.

Compassion gone astray: The near enemies

Thus, a lot of unexpected good comes with the fact that social movement activism is often more of a matter of the heart than many of us thought when we entered it. But this fact also carries with it its own set of challenges that we are not always set to meet. Social movement activism seldom has the harmonious appearance my account here might have seemed to imply.

Even though the awakening heart of compassion is an amazing force, there are so many ways that personal commitment and organizational cultures can go astray, when our hearts are being touched by the issues that we are directing our attention to, and we feel confusingly unshielded or vulnerable. We do not quite expect this vulnerability, since we have this idea that we are working with something that resides in the public sphere, at safe distance from matters of the heart. And we do not really have a language to speak about, or understand, this vulnerability or confusion; especially since, as politically radical Westerners, we often squirm at anything that sounds too 'New Age', or simply wishy-washy.

Had this not been so, quite a few of us could have benefited greatly from, for example, reflecting on the traditional Buddhist teaching on the 'near enemies' of compassion. The near enemies are states of mind that seem a lot like genuine compassion but that are in fact something much less wholesome and empowering. It is said that there are three near enemies of compassion: pity, overwhelm and what American Buddhist nun Pema Chödrön so eloquently calls idiot compassion. They are pretty easily recognizable to us when we reflect a bit on their nature. They all find their own expression in a social movement context.

'When we identify ourselves as the helper, we see the other as helpless,' says Pema Chödrön (2001a: 77) on pity as a near enemy of compassion. 'Instead of feeling the pain of the other person, we set ourselves apart.' Pity is thus connected to our wish to see ourselves as a Truly Good Person. As new activists, we easily get addicted to the honeymoon rush of feeling great about ourselves because we are the excellent, compassionate people who care about the world when no one else does. One of the problematic things about this is how we risk becoming in a strange way dependent on there being someone to play the role of the bad guy. If the International Monetary Fund (IMF), the World Trade Organization (WTO) or the Bush administration were to begin to change their ways and not play their current role any more, we might unconsciously experience this as very threatening to our own identity. We become dependent on the very thing we believe that we want to rid ourselves of. This is indeed harmful, both spiritually, as we use our political engagement to reinforce a dualistic conception of others and ourselves, and politically, as we are bound to make misjudgements about our room for manoeuvre as regards the possibilities to actually have an influence on our opponents' ways of thinking.

Overwhelm is something that all activists come up against. As we begin to open our hearts to the immense suffering that is being inflicted on the world through the working of the system, as we are making the effort to realize that there are real people behind the newspaper headlines of starvation, environmental collapse and war, we often find that it is too much. As we discover that we care what happens, that we care for distant places and people that we will never meet, feelings of fear, anger, hatred or hopelessness are bound to arise and can, indeed, get out of hand. The sense of helplessness can bring people to the verge of depression; it can make us panic and think the world unbearable. More often, it is much less dramatic: it makes us lose heart, simply feeling powerless and thinking that there is no point in trying to change things. This is one of the major reasons why people quit political work. Another way for this overwhelmed state of mind to manifest in a social movement context is as over-activity. We feel that unless we keep constantly busy in saving the world, giving absolutely all we have got all the time, we cannot stand being in it. This does help in getting a lot of practical stuff done but it also creates burnout, stops us from appreciating the present and does not particularly contribute to a happier world.

Idiot compassion, writes Chödrön (2001a: 78), is 'when we avoid conflict and protect our good image by being kind when we should say a definite "no".... In the name of not shutting our heart, we let people walk all over us.' This is also something that quite a few of us end up doing in a social movement context, as we want to affirm our idea of ourselves and of our organizations as Truly Good. This is rather in line with some of our great expectations, which most of us are only dimly aware of as we are joining a movement: that since this movement claims that 'another world is possible', the movement will be a microcosm of the new world to come. This is where we will be truly seen, heard and respected. And we do try very hard indeed, striving for the structures that we create and the work that we do within them to be respectful of all, truly inclusive and transparent, non-hierarchical and oppressive of none. Sometimes this turns into idiot compassion, where we do let others walk all over us. Often the result is simply failure.

A particular dissonance

So we find that we fail. Not always and completely, of course, but often enough for the image of ourselves as the all-embracing world saviours to fall apart pretty soon. We fail to treat each other as respectfully as we would have wanted to, as meetings drag on until late night and we begin to get on each other's nerves. We fail to make sure that everyone is included in the discussions and the decisions made, as those with a lot of experience and self-esteem take their role as informal leaders for granted, while newcomers have a hard time making themselves heard at all. We fail to encourage and appreciate each other for the extraordinary effort we are making, as we seem to think that we are simply too busy doing important things to find the time to express care and concern. In short, if the world to come is to be built on the principles that we are seemingly founding our work on, it would not be much better than the present one.

What might have struck the reader as an overly rosy picture a couple of pages ago might now seem overly grim instead. Of course, it is not like this all the time but I am sure many activists recognize it. To many, it is truly discouraging to discover that our organizations are having the same problems as the rest of society. The experience of disappointment with our organizations and ourselves can be very sharp. We cannot hide from ourselves if we are really present in our work. We can try for a while, of course, and energetically do, blaming the system, our leaders or whatever we come up with. But because we are so close to our visions of a world centred on human dignity, our own personal ways of sneakiness and cheekiness stand out very clearly.

We end up touching in with a very basic kind of disappointment, the kind that is an unavoidable part of life, of its and our basic fabric. There is not necessarily anything dramatic about it. It is just a dawning understanding sneaking up on us through our everyday experiences of things or ourselves not measuring up. Reality is not confirming us; it is not conforming to the needs we think we have of understanding what is going on, of being secure and in control of our lives. Of course, there is no need to be part of a social movement to realize any of this; life tends to point it out to us wherever we are. But if you want a crash course, by all means join us.

There is no denying the earnest heart in what we do. As we build our networks and try to carry out our projects, we are continually made to reach out and open-up to others, to listen, to reflect and all this in relation to our hearts' yearning. And there is no denying our constant failing when it comes to living up to our ideals. We are living and working within this paradox and many think it to be a rather tiring and painful one. I believe that this is one of the principal reasons why many people quit political work. *The discrepancy, the dissonance, between, on one hand, our heart's earnest yearning for justice and dignity, along with our visions of a better world; and on the other hand, the paltry contributions we are able to make to the struggle as reality sets in, can be very painful.* Again, it is not necessarily something that hits us as a dramatic realization where we resign from our organizations with the explicit goal never to return. More often, it just manifests itself as losing heart in what we are doing and dropping out step by step.

But as activists, we have to start accepting that we are not immune to what we are opposing. This is an uncomfortable realization but a most central one for anyone wishing to change society. What we are struggling to overcome is not just something out there, that resides with the others, the bad guys. The world is falling apart because of hatred, craving and ignorance; these things are within us as well and for any social change to be viable in the long run, we need to address them there also. Politically, the sooner we realize this, the better. The problem for us as activists is that most often we have no way of constructively working with disappointment, with the experience of ourselves and our organizations not measuring up to our ideals. We lack concepts for understanding it and tools for any creative use of it. And because in our minds there is such a long distance between the worldliness of our political work and the world of existential or spiritual issues, we are missing out on a whole lot of insight in these fields that could help us along.

Summit preparations and dialogue efforts

Even if most of the time disappointment comes in very banal and undramatic forms, sometimes it arrives in forms that are rather to the other side of the spectrum. During our first year as Attac Sweden, we were dealt a blow that we are still having a hard time recovering from in the form of the riots and repression in connection with the European Summit in Gothenburg of June 2001.

As a global justice movement, we naturally saw many reasons to express ourselves in connection with the summit: asking for an end to European agricultural dumping on developing country markets and for a Tobin Tax to be introduced, among other things. Once we were out of our founding meeting in January 2001, one of our first tasks was finding our place in the different networks that had been formed with the purpose of mobilizing in connection with the meeting of the European Council in June that same year, which was to be a major event for alter-globalists of all kinds. This was not an easy task for several reasons. Many of us were rather inexperienced in network politics, and the heterogeneous Gothenburg coalitions, with libertarian and mainstream trade unions, in particular from countries other than Sweden, ecologists, church organizations, anarchists, anti-racist groups, and red and green parties, were uncharted territory for us. At the same time, the media's attention was very much focussed on Attac, being described as alternately the dangerous hooligans coming to wreck the city, a popular uprising ready to storm the national parliament any day and the inventors of global justice issues and grassroots networking. The attention of the media brought with it the attention of various politicians looking for dialogue partners for practical or political purposes. To many organizations that had been working on similar issues for a long time, the stir around Attac seemed unfair and unfounded. I think that all of us agree that the attention was out of proportion but the fact remained that it put us in a special position to act as bridge builders between movements and other key actors. We were in a privileged position but it was also a risky one. The local leader of the Social Democratic Party phrased it in a way that stuck with me, saying: 'We have a common interest. We do not want this city to burn. And you must know that if it does burn, Attac will be the organization blamed.'

There was a rather large risk that something would go wrong in connection with the Summit. Not only the WTO ministerial in Seattle in 1999 and the IMF/World Bank meeting in Prague in 2000 but also the preceding meeting of the European Council in Nice in December that year had been marked by mass protest and riots. The Swedish police was expressing concern over what they saw as problematic groups' mobilizing, and the media were hungrily awaiting violent clashes. Also, on the movement side, many were expecting problems, though from the police. Amongst the few who kept holding on to the belief that things might actually work out was Attac.

We came to invest ourselves heavily in various dialogue initiatives, with the purpose of preventing violent clashes and creating an arena of serious interchange around critical global issues. With Gothenburg University generously providing a space for dialogue, we struggled to bring together representatives of the networks, of local authorities and of local police to solve practical problems, begin to build trust and find principles for interaction during the Summit as such. Those involved from all sides did solve many problems: we got to rent thirteen schools from the municipality for lodging and counter-conference activities, and we sorted out transportation and food issues. There was also a deal made between the activist networks and local police, that police in riot gear, dogs and horses would be kept at a distance from our activities as long as everything was running smoothly, with the hope of evading escalations due to fear and perceived provocations from either side.

To us, this practical dialogue was a way of facilitating a political dialogue. This was something that we also put a lot of effort into realizing and it had its own set of difficulties. Government representatives were, if not overly enthusiastic, at least open to the idea of arranging discussions with movements, as openness had been presented as a key feature of the Swedish presidency of the Union. Many activists, on the other hand, were sceptical, feeling that there was too big a risk of co-option or simply of being used as some sort of political alibi by politicians wanting to enhance their own legitimacy. This dilemma made us reflect a lot on the premises for political dialogue. How could one create a space for dialogue where participants would not feel their integrity compromised? The process was one of thorough discussion mapping our understandings and more or less well-founded fears connected to the idea of dialogue with our ideological opponents. One common idea many of us were carrying was that of dialogue as negotiation: that when we have a dialogue, the parties involved give and take, to approach each others' positions, and then hopefully arrive at a consensus regarding the matter discussed. But what if parties feel their standpoints are too far apart to be reconciled? Is there a point in speaking to each other at all in such a case? Many thought not. On the other side of the spectrum from such a consensual dialogue was the idea of dialogue as debate: communication as competition, where participants try to 'win', by scoring points with the audience. Somehow there seemed to be very little room for actual communication, for really hearing what one's counterpart says in either of these models. Out of these discussions was born the idea of a *confrontative dialogue*, a concept coined by peace researcher and activist Hans Abrahamsson—a dialogue with the purpose not of winning the debate or of reaching a consensus, but of making diverging interests visible and clarifying political alternatives. This would demand a different kind of effort by the participants: one of being pedagogues instead of debaters, which in turn would necessitate trying to go beneath the surface of the ordinary rhetoric, to understand not only what the other person says but also her motivation and where she is coming from. Many activists rethought their initial positions of not wanting any dialogue at all, seeing this concept as something workable.

In the tradition of Thich Nhat Hanh, communication is a central part of the practice: learning how to listen fully, with all one's being and without preparing one's own commentary to what is being said, but simply to open oneself to really hear the other person. Without really hearing the other, we cannot speak properly; what comes out of our mouths has more to do with ourselves than with the situation of communication and with the person we are speaking with. When I first came to Plum Village, Thich Nhat Hanh's community of practice in France, and was introduced to the practices of deep listening, it was a kind of shock to me to realize how stunningly bad we are at it in our everyday lives. The contrast was sharp and naturally brought about a strong commitment to learning about mindful communication and how to restore our ability to practise it. I guess commitment comes naturally because mindful communication is so joyous that when practised consciously, there is an almost physical sense of breaking out of one's shell, of isolation melting away. There is a sense of becoming real and of the other becoming real before one's eyes and ears.

The period around the Summit preparations was one when I was not practising very much (I was feeling too stressed and generally unstable; how ironic is that?), but I remember reciting the Five Mindfulness Trainings. Students of Thich Nhat Hanh practise the traditional lay

Buddhist vows of avoiding killing, stealing, sexual misconduct, lying and the use of intoxicants in the more comprehensive phrasing known under this name. Working so much on dialogue, it was especially the fourth training (Thich Nhat Hanh 1998) on mindful communication that came alive to me:

> I am committed to cultivating loving speech and deep listening in order to bring joy and happiness to others and relieve others of their suffering. Knowing that words can create happiness or suffering, I am determined to speak truthfully, with words that inspire self-confidence, joy and hope.... I will refrain from uttering words that can cause division or discord, or that can cause the family or community to break.

I remember reciting these words and thinking that even though I was not spending much time in formal meditation and even though my head was spinning, I felt that I was moving closer to the heart of what such a vow might mean. It seemed such a privilege to be part of a process, however limited, of restoring communication in an arena where it has been, perhaps, more maltreated than anywhere else: that of contemporary politics.

In the end, two historically innovative dialogues between movements and politicians based on this idea did happen in connection with the Summit. There was one with Swedish government representatives and movements meeting in person, and one with European government representatives and movements carried out through a satellite link between the Summit and the civil society Festival of Free Speech. Trade policy, public services and asylum rights were discussed, among other things. But these efforts were never really known to the general public. Instead, it was the riots that got all the visibility at that time and for a long time afterwards.

Four days beyond control

On Thursday, 14 June 2001, the day before the Summit started, as George W. Bush was arriving in Gothenburg, police in riot gear surrounded the school where our counter-conference was happening in the centre of the city. Hundreds of activists were locked in. We did not know why this was happening and all our attempts to retrieve information through our police contacts were in vain.

I remember our mounting panic as hundreds of lorries drove up, carrying containers that were used to build a wall around the whole conference area. I was filmed running around outside the school as this was happening and have watched myself afterwards, trying to get any of the policemen present to speak to us, losing my head completely on the telephone with one of our police contacts claiming to know nothing of what was happening, fear and rage evident from my face and voice. At the time, I was not fully aware on a conscious level of what I knew in my gut, that after this there was no securing a peaceful Summit in Gothenburg. Whatever efforts we had made were going down the drain.

I never believed, neither before nor after the Gothenburg events, in the intelligence information claiming that the so-called 'black block' work in a way similar to a professional army, showing up at alter-globalist mobilizations with the one and only purpose of fighting with the police and vandalizing. In my political work, I simply never came across these masses of people with no political will except for destruction. But, of course, there are small groups of people who do believe (however alien this idea is to the majority of alter-globalist activists) that a riot is a good political means to shake the capitalist system. And, more importantly, there is a grey zone of many militant autonomous young activists who are ready to go either way. That is, to express their political will through peaceful means, through symbolic or direct disobedience actions, or to, as they see it, defend their political space with more violent means if it is under threat. On that day, as the cranes dropped the containers onto the street and the air filled with dust and calls of rage and incredulity, it became obvious that those who wanted things to get out of hand would have what they wished for, as the people of the grey zone would turn their way.

We never got a clear answer as to why the counter-conference was shut down. Officially, the purpose was to search the school for firebombs and other weapons, none of which were found, of course. Afterwards we came to realize that some kind of pre-emptive strike against an activist convergence centre before a summit starts was becoming a basic and recurring police tactic internationally, and that we should have expected it. We hold it likely that one real purpose was getting hold of a number of activists thought to be leaders of violent groupings and securing a calm summit by keeping them off the streets. The heads of police had probably received strong political signals to ensure that under no circumstances to let the American president be politically humiliated in any way and to use whatever means available to this purpose. The siege at the school certainly kept activists off the other streets until Air Force One had once again left Gothenburg.

Before the Summit was over, the shops, restaurants and banks in the centre of the city had been thoroughly thrashed, barricades had been built and burnt, and many people had been wounded in the riots, be they activists, police or simply passers-by. Another school had been stormed by the national anti-terrorist squad under terrifying conditions. Police had fired live bullets into a fleeing crowd. Four people had been shot and one of them was hovering between life and death.

I do not know how we managed to get through those days, how we managed the three major marches that went peacefully, the rescheduling of the counter-conference, our dialogues and all other practicalities. We were in shock, just like the rest of the city and country. It is hard to explain to people who are not from here exactly how traumatic the Gothenburg events were to Sweden. Riots are not a common feature of Scandinavian protest culture. It is like what happened in Gothenburg symbolized a deep, collective fear of what is happening to our society and to the world in general: the fact that we are no longer in control, that the project of the 'people's home' is slipping out of our hands while politics seems powerless, that we are no longer living in a safe corner of the world where the harms that roam the rest of the planet cannot reach us. What has come to symbolize the degree of trauma to me is the reaction to the shooting of Hannes Westberg, the activist who nearly died.

The shooting of Hannes was filmed from a very close distance. We can see it happen in detail.

A Reclaim the City party that has been surrounded by police and things are out of hand. Police and activists surge back and forth on the street. When Hannes is shot, he is nearly on his own. There are other militants around but no one as close to the police as him. We can see the policemen in the background: one of them is down but not under immediate threat; still, it is clearly an awful situation for all present. Hannes' eyes are black with rage. He bends down and chooses between two stones lying on the ground; he picks the smaller of the two and throws it towards the police. He is not in the vicinity of hitting anyone. As he turns away, a shot is fired. Hannes is hit in the back.

This scene has been broadcast many hundreds of times on Swedish television.

The purpose of telling this story is not to place blame. There is no point in getting into a discussion of who started what in evaluating such a series of events. The situation is created collectively, and exhaustion and panic can make all commit dreadful mistakes. Yet, in watching the scene over and over, as most of us have, it should be obvious that Hannes was hit by a bullet at a point in time where he was no immediate threat to anyone. We could see how he was turning away. But when journalists or activists have tried to point this out in the debate that followed, they have met with a lot of anger from the general public. It seems that to many it does not matter what the film tells: we are having a hard time with the truth, which is that someone is in fact being shot by Swedish police, without it being self-defence in any ordinary meaning of the word. This is too uncomfortable a thought. It does not happen, not here. Thus, the majority of people will not take it in and will try to 'kill the messengers' instead. I think this collective refusal to believe one's eyes can serve as one illustration of exactly how big a trauma the Gothenburg events were in Sweden.

In spite of having lived through the pain and fear of the actual events, I think many of us underestimated the intensity of this collective trauma and the stigmatizing power of being associated with what went wrong here. If we had understood, perhaps we would have taken even greater care to be skilful in our communication with the media afterwards. Yet, it is not easy to see exactly what we should have done differently. We were extremely quick in condemning the violence of both activists and police, even though we did not condemn specific organizations. But condemning, distancing ourselves, never seemed enough to us. We wanted to discuss the dynamics of what had happened, we wanted to understand the reasons why things went wrong. Our positions might not seem that controversial. We said that the violence had come about for reasons that were in their essence political and that it required political solutions; it could not be treated like a hooligan phenomenon. We claimed that there is a distinction to be made between *understanding* violence and *accepting* it. If we want to stop political violence, we have to understand its roots and dynamics; if we do not understand, we do not know how to intervene effectively. Understanding in this sense does not mean that one accepts violence. On the contrary, understanding is a means that helps us counteract it. But at the same time, in saying that it is possible to understand violence, we are stating that violence is a human phenomenon: those who use it are in fact not fundamentally different from the rest of us. This is another uncomfortable claim and many are eager to shoot the messengers of this too.

This might sound obvious and banal but in a situation where a whole nation is on a rather desperate hunt for scapegoats, such a position is a politically risky one. The riots in Gothenburg were felt to be assaults on the most basic human decency as well as on democracy itself. As human beings, when we feel we are being assaulted at a basic level, we tend to view things in black and white. What Attac did in the debate was trying to introduce the grey scales. Perhaps, this was politically naïve but it seemed the only intellectually honest thing to do. In any case, we never got back that initial ability to reach out to people who had not been involved in politics before. In most people's minds, we are still to this day more or less dimly associated with activist violence and this has hampered our work seriously.

Those of us who had been visible in the media during and after the Summit, soon came to feel the presence of the trauma in society around us. Not only did friends and acquaintances seem to have a never-ending need to discuss what had happened but also total strangers. I found myself yelled at on the tram or on the street, when people I had never met associated my face with their own frustration and sense of having been assaulted (at this point the events were commonly referred to as the 'rape' of the city). But most people were not aggressive; rather, they seemed to simply want to get hold of someone who could symbolize what had happened here to receive thoughts and feelings in connection with the events. Friends of friends came to visit to talk. People came up in restaurants and supermarkets, some with just a short comment on what it felt like to see the parade street in flames and others with a full theory on the development of the European Union. It was like we were turning into some kind of public amateur therapists which was a role we certainly had not anticipated. In a way I found this soothing, as it seemed a way to contribute to the healing needed. In another way, it was terribly frustrating as I felt my lack of capacity to lift all these little pieces of communication beyond the dwelling on, or even indulging in, the pain of what had happened here, or when I was overwhelmed by indignation at us being blamed for what seemed so clearly beyond our control and totally contrary to the purpose of our dialogue-building efforts. Many times I found myself flooded with my own anger and bitterness, as I had to take in the fact that no matter our good intentions, our efforts here had been counterproductive: the overall result was that people distanced themselves from the global justice movements and our issues. Disappointment was very vivid with this result itself, of course, but also with these emotionally overwhelming and yet small-minded reactions of mine.

Working with disappointment

Existentialist philosopher Karl Jaspers (in Bråkenhielm et al. 1992: 126, my translation) calls the meeting one's edge—the situations making us face basic conditions of existence beyond our control—*border situations*. He writes,

> Situations such as that I cannot live without struggle and pain, that I cannot avoid guilt, that I have to die, these situations I call border situations. They do not transform in themselves, only in the way that they appear; in their relation to our lives they are final. They cannot be grasped; within our lives we see nothing else beyond them. They are like a wall that we hit and perish.

It's a bit like Trungpa Rinpoche's teachings on 'death in everyday life', that Chödrön (1997: 43) hands on to us:

> We are raised in a culture that fears death and hides it from us. Nevertheless, we experience it all the time. We experience it in the form of disappointment, in the form of things not working out. We experience it in the form of things always being in a process of change. When the day ends, when the second ends, when we breathe out, that's death in everyday life.

Rinpoche takes as the starting point for all his teachings the basic experiences of our messed-up everyday lives, and how to make us see that these are not only workable on a path of realization, but rather indispensable for treading such a path. As with much of his teachings, I find Trungpa's (1973: 25) words on disappointment unsettling and encouraging; at the same time,

> we must surrender our hopes and expectations, as well as our fears, and march directly into disappointment, go into it and make it our way of life, which is a very hard thing to do. Disappointment is a good sign of basic intelligence. It cannot be compared to anything else: it is so sharp, precise, obvious and direct. If we can open, then we suddenly begin to see that our expectations are irrelevant compared to the situations we are facing. This automatically brings a feeling of disappointment. Disappointment is the best chariot to use on the path of the dharma.

Also in Jaspers' (in Bråkenhielm 1992: 127, my translation) view, facing the border situation is of utmost importance, existential importance. He says that we have to face them very openly:

> We react meaningfully [to the border situations] not by planning and
> calculating, in order to conquer them.... By entering border situations
> with open eyes, we become ourselves.... The border enters its true
> function: being immanent, but pointing towards transcendence.

What is interesting here is the claim that border situations, facing our
finitude and experiencing disillusionment and fear, are not only something to be dealt with, a problem to be solved, but in fact something
of a resource in themselves, something without which we would not
develop fully. Facing the border situation with open hearts and minds
is the way to become fully human; Jaspers claims: 'the way to touch in
with a dimension of our being that is infinite, unchartable.' Jaspers tells of
how meeting the border situation is what can make our simple presence
(*dasein*) in the world open-up into something much fuller and completely
engaging which he calls existence. There is something immediately
recognizable in what he writes to many of us, whether we are trained in
the discourse of philosophy or not. Perhaps, we have simply noticed the
fact that it is often facing our edge that makes us open up and grow.

But how do we do this? We need to get concrete about it: how do
we actually practise this opening-up relating to our own edges? Jaspers
(in Bråkenhielm 1992: 126, my translation) is very explicit with the fact
that there is more to facing a border situation than simply intellectually
trying to grasp our own finitude:

> The border situations are ... no longer situations for the knowing con-
> sciousness, since this in its characteristic of intellectual knowing and
> purposeful action simply grasps them objectively or simply evades them,
> ignores them or forgets about them; it stays within the borders, and is
> unable to even questioningly approach its origin.

So we need tools that not only deal with these issues intellectually
but which allow us to involve ourselves fully also at heart, gut, soul, or
whatever we want to call a deeper level, in the border situation.

Precepts

After the Summit, it was again the fourth mindfulness training that
came alive to me, the reason being that I was not practising it. I found
myself wanting to lash out at people who approached me, and indeed
did when I felt that I was being wrongly accused ('And what do you

know, anyway?'). Even though I could often sense the underlying fear and pain that made people want to talk to me and that making myself available would help to relieve that suffering and probably my own as well, my disappointment and anger got the upper hand and made me shut down. I felt caged or like I was on display on a broken carousel that would not stop spinning, not knowing how to get off it. I suppose that feeling came from dreading to be still and know my own pain at what had happened.

It is strange how it takes being unable to keep a precept to begin to understand what it is about. When one makes a real effort to be mindful, generous, loving, or simply to communicate mindfully, and finds that one is unable, one can begin to ask and to see at a new level why this was a thing worth striving for in the first place. The pain caused to oneself and others by not living mindfully becomes so obvious. And at the same time, one begins to see that 'striving for an unrealistic and exaggerated perfection is a madness that produces inauthenticity. In effect, it can forge a monster of pretentiousness,' as Joan Halifax (1998: 146) writes in a commentary on the five mindfulness trainings. 'Fall down into the darkness. Where are the knees of humility touching?' (ibid.). I find that where they touch, a space opens up between one's great aspiration and one's limited ability, a space where the heart begins to move and breathe. It is a space of understanding and emerging compassion for all of us, who have the aspiration to live lives of love and beauty but who just cannot seem to tame our neurotic minds enough to really walk it like we talk it. And it takes failure for us to sense the possibilities of this space. Like, for example, aspiring to build an arena that allows for mindful and honest political communication, and having the whole thing backfiring and caving in on your head, and then wanting to punish the world for it, and then wanting to beat yourself up about wanting to punish the world. We all have our personal brands.

In fact, we are touching on one of the reasons why spiritual practice can find such a fertile ground in a social movement context. As activists, we are continually in a situation of what Chödrön has called 'the big squeeze': a situation marked by, on one hand, the big vision of our hearts' yearning, and on the other hand, the often rather dubious and small-minded contributions we are making to the building of the famous 'other world'. It is an uncomfortable situation, but it can be very enriching. In the words of Chödrön (1994: 122f), it is

> The squeeze between reality and vision that causes you to grow up to be 100 per cent decent, alive and compassionate…. Times of the big squeeze

feel like crisis periods. We have the aspiration to wake up and to help, and at the same time it doesn't seem to be working out on our terms. It feels impossible for us to buy our situation and also impossible to throw it out. Being caught in the big squeeze humbles you, and at the same time, it has great vision. This is the interesting part—it softens you and yet it has a big perspective.

A soft heart is a heart that can nourish itself, since it knows how to access humility and compassion. This is what we need to sustain our commitment to social change. We need this, and we need the big perspective, our visionary capacity. We have to start appreciating the situations that come to teach us all these things at once.

Tonglen

In the Buddhist tradition, there are many exercises that offer the possibility of relating directly to one's edges. The one I personally have found most of a challenge, and most of a grace, is called *tonglen*, which is Tibetan for 'sending and taking'. This is an exercise that I have been grappling with for years, and still I feel like I am just scraping the surface of it, in spite of its conceptual simplicity.

The formal practice of *tonglen* has a series of different stages and visualizations which others much more competent than me have described in writing elsewhere (Chödrön 2001b). For now, I just wanted to talk about the heart of it. The point of the exercise is practising opening-up our hearts to suffering, opening-up where we normally shut down. By training in making our minds steadfast where we normally try to squirm away from the present moment because we find it too unpleasant, we train in awakening our inherent capacity for loving, kindness and compassion. It is a practice that works explicitly with whatever touches our hearts naturally and it can be practised on the meditation cushion as well as 'on the spot', in whatever situation we find difficult emotions arising. On the cushion, one invokes the memory of any person, animal or situation that awakens compassion. It can be laboratory animals, someone dear to us who is sick, or victims of war or natural disasters; the most important thing is that you touch-in with a situation that is somehow real to you, that you cannot walk away indifferent from. On the spot, in everyday life, it is often other more banal kinds of suffering that one has to relate to, such as the irritation, anger or arrogance of oneself or another. *Tonglen* is daring in the sense that it involves exposing oneself to experiencing such pain:

that of another as well as one's own. I have learnt it like this: with each breath-in one moves closer to the feeling that one normally would try to push away, and opens one's heart to it. One can visualize this emotional energy as something black, hot, sticky: it often awakens some sense of claustrophobia. On each breath-out, one sends out whatever one feels would be appropriate to somehow air that claustrophobic situation. Sometimes it comes out as a wish for something concrete: food, a place to stay, a hug. Often it comes out as a wish that we all could be free from this particular kind of suffering.

It might seem a bit masochistic, like one is looking to experience pain for its own sake. However, that is not what it is about. Rather, we are trying genuinely to allow ourselves to experience the present, whatever the present is like, which is really a matter of self-respect and honouring one's experience. Practising in this way slowly makes us more and more able to keep our hearts open, to stay with difficult feelings without being overwhelmed by them. We need not shut down on others and ourselves; we can avoid retreating into familiar patterns of anger, blame or resentment in increasingly difficult situations. In beginning to slow down our habitual tendency to try to shield ourselves from pain and fear, we find that our hearts and minds begin to open-up, to ourselves, to others, to the present moment. The fear or pain that we are working with, does not become pleasant or go away, but we find that it is a lot less solid and monumental than we thought, that we are able to hold it in the surprising space of our human hearts without being swept away by it. As we gradually discover this capacity of keeping our hearts open, we find that compassion begins to extend beyond the original people or situations that we have been inviting to arouse it in our practice: we can somehow touch-in with all the other beings throughout time and space who have been in that same boat.

When people ask me how I keep going, 'thinking about misery all the time', this is certainly a key part of the answer: I have been taught the practice of breathing it in. These days, it usually happens automatically: one second I am overwhelmed with frustration at whatever situation is currently exposing my own self-centredness or incompetence, that of my colleagues, that of decision makers and journalists, and pretty much anyone. The next second training kicks in and before I know it my mind goes, 'May I take all such pain into myself,' and attention comes back to the breath and to the present. I find myself remembering how we all suffer and how we all long not to. There is something stunningly simple about recognizing this shared humanity. Somehow the situation becomes workable—I begin to see what I bring to the current situation that is of help, and what is best discarded. And when I allow frustration and pain to move me, I find that yes, I care, I still care. I do want us all to be free from suffering, and I am lifted and carried forward by that care.

Conclusion

In our social practice, there is no avoiding hitting the walls of disappointment. The question is to what extent we are able to use these walls in a creative way. Can we use the border situations to get in touch with our hearts and the hearts of others, to tap into genuine compassion? Are we able to let the experiences of pain and insecurity soften us, and thus inspire us in our work and lives? Can we see each other and ourselves messing up with some kind of ease and humour? We have to empower ourselves to do this and we can only do that by practising. It is more natural to us than we think but it takes practice to find that out.

What I find is that when I am able to let my finitude and failures show me how to tap into the well of genuine compassion, I am being led back to action, to social practice for another world. Compassion is not an abstract principle that can be contained to the meditation cushion: it wants to manifest in the everyday messiness of here and now, and it will not stand back to a system that inflicts so much suffering on sentient beings. And again, in that social practice, I find there is no way to get ahead without spiritual practice. If we are out there wanting to create a saner and happier world, sooner or later we will have to ask ourselves some rather fundamental questions about what it is that brings happiness and what brings suffering in the first place; without nourishing happiness and compassion, our commitment will fade away.

And so I cannot untangle one practice from the other, and I am grateful for that.

References

Bråkenhielm, Carl R., Carl Henric Grenholm, Lennart Koskinen and Håkan Thorsén (eds). 1992. 'Karl Jaspers: Människans Gränssituationer', in *Aktuella Livsåskådningar del 1: Existentialism, Marxism*. Nora: Nya Doxa.

Chödrön, Pema. 1994. *Start Where You Are: A Guide to Compassionate Living*. Boston and London: Shambhala Publications.

———. 1997. *When Things Fall Apart: Heart Advice for Difficult Times*. Boston and London: Shambhala Publications.

Chödrön, Pema. 2001a. *The Places That Scare You: A Guide to Fearlessness in Difficult Times*. Boston and London: Shambhala Publications.

———. 2001b. *Tonglen: The Path of Transformation*. Halifax: Vajradhatu Publications.

Halifax, Joan. 1998. 'The Road is your Footsteps', in Thich Nhat Hanh (ed.), *For a Future to be Possible: Commentaries on the Five Mindfulness Trainings*. Berkeley: Parallax Press.

Ramonet, Ignacio. 1997. 'Disarming the markets', *Le Monde Diplomatique*, December. Available on http://mondediplo.com/1997/12/leader. Accessed on 13 April 2008.

Thich Nhat Hanh. 1998. 'The Fourth Mindfulness Training: Deep Listening and Loving Speech', in Thich Nhat Hanh (ed.), *For a Future to be Possible: Commentaries on the Five Mindfulness Training*, pp. 44–61. Berkeley: Parallex Press.

Trungpa, Chögyam. 1973. *Cutting Through Spiritual Materialism*. Berkeley: Shambhala Publications.

PART III

Transforming Power and
Freedom: New Horizons

Power and Wisdom

16

Does World History Have a Moral Dimension?

Akop P. Nazaretyan

History is the progress of moral tasks. Not doings, but just the tasks, which mankind's collective might put before any certain person. The tasks were more and more difficult, almost impracticable; nonetheless, they have been fulfilled—otherwise, all should have fallen to pieces long ago.

—Pomerants (1991)

'After the notion of progress was basically discredited, no one dared to ask what mattered for the history of humankind as a whole,' said William McNeill (2002) while presenting his and his son's forthcoming book (McNeill and McNeill 2003). Still, the authors indicated and welcomed the growing interest in global retrospection among both professional historians and the interdisciplinary scientific community.

In this chapter we expound some results of cross-disciplinary research on the historical experience of anthropogenic crises carried out lately by the Russian scientists. Insights from archaeology, comparative history, social psychology, cultural anthropology, ecology and biology have been synthesized. A synergetic (chaos theory) view of society as a sustainable non-equilibrium system and of culture as a complex anti-entropy mechanism served for data integration.

The research was mainly aimed at the practical tasks of ecological and geopolitical strategy; however, its results acquired additional meaning in the context of my academic interest to Big (Universal) History (Christian 1991, 2004; Nazaretyan 1991: 222, 2004, 2005b; Spier 1996). Trying to discover common mechanisms and causal links, we noted certain regularities that may throw new light on two points thoroughly discussed in historical sociology. One is whether—or not—'pan-human history' may be reasonably construed; the other is whether—or not—there may be singled out anything like 'laws of history'.

In chaos theory terms, human history is the story of one 'self-similar' system, which exists on a scale of a million or so years and has been successively transforming itself to maintain sustainability (Christian 1991). Retrospective analytical procedures have shown at least five mainstreams of consecutive global transformations: increases of world population, of technological power, of organizational complexity and of mental information capacity, and perfection of cultural regulation mechanisms.

The first three mainstreams are inferred as 'empirical generalizations' that are easily illustrated with figures. The fourth and the fifth ones require particular arguments (Nazaretyan 2004). In the continuation, perfection of cultural regulation mechanisms in conformity with developing instrumental intelligence is argued.

The hypothesis of techno-humanitarian balance

Zoo-psychologists have gathered numerous evidence of what was called *ethological balance*: the more the powerful species' natural killing power, the stronger the inhibition of intra-species aggression. Summing up remarkable observations in his brilliant book about aggression, Lorenz (1981) noted that we ought to regret not having the 'nature of the predator'. For had humans descended from lions instead of biologically harmless *Australopithecus*, he explained, we would have a much stronger aggression-retention instinct, preventing warfare.

Meanwhile, comparative calculations have demonstrated that lions (and other strong predators), in ratio to their population number, kill each other *more frequently* than humans do (Wilson 1978).

This result looked sensational. First, it is true that lions, unlike humans, have a strong instinctive ban on killing conspecifics. Second, lions' natural population density differs tremendously from that of human communities, whereas concentration usually increases aggression among both animals and humans. Third, 'killing facilities' are incomparable: the assaulting lion's sharp teeth meet the enemy's strong pelt, while mutual killing among humans who are armed if only with stones is technically very easy, and since the Stone Age, weapons' 'progress' has been enormous.

Australian ethnographers received another interesting result having compared wars among aboriginals with World War II. Out of all participants, only the USSR lost more human lives in relation to population numbers than primitive tribes usually did (Blainey 1975).

According to our calculations, from 100 to 120 million people perished in all the international and civil wars of the twentieth century. The numbers, which also involve indirect warfare victims, are monstrous. Still, they represent about 1 per cent of the century's planet population (no less than 10.5 billion in the three generations). An approximately similar ratio occurred in the nineteenth century (about 35 million war victims to 3 billion population) and probably in the eighteenth century, while in the fourteenth to seventeenth centuries the ratio had been higher.

Contradictory data and lack of coordinate calculation procedures (Urlanis 1994; Wright 1944) make comparative inquiry rather difficult. Nonetheless, general estimates reveal a paradoxical fact. While weapons' killing power and people's concentration have been successively growing for millennia, war victims' ratio has not.

Besides wars, the total amount of victims includes people who perished in 'peaceful' political repressions and everyday violence, so that in the twenteith century up to 5 per cent of the world population seems to have died in the acts of *deliberate* violence (*Social Violence* 2005).[1] The decreasing trend is more manifest when non-war violence victims are compared. To calculate them retrospectively is even more difficult but as far as the orders of magnitude are concerned, we may resort to the indirect evidence.

Wars, repressions and everyday violence carried away approximately similar numbers of human lives in the twentieth century. Meanwhile, the proportion of non-war violence victims to the warfare ones had been different in the past. We may see the difference distinctly, having compared remote epochs of cultural history.

Thus, Diamond (1999: 277) summarized his own field observations and critically revised the information of his colleagues: 'Much more extensive long-term information about band and tribal societies reveals that murder is a leading cause of death.' This conclusion apparently considers the total sum of infanticide, geronticide, inter-tribe and inner conflicts, hunting for heads, and so on.

A contrasting combination of the long-term trends—the violent death rate irregular decrease in the context of a successively increasing potential for mutual destruction and population densities—implies an additional assumption: there should have been a certain cultural factor that compensated for the growth of instrumental capacities. The factor's dynamics are better shown as we supplement global comparisons with regional ones (discussed later). As to its essence, it is described by a hypothesis that arises from quite different empirical data; in fact, our calculations are conducted to check a corollary of the hypothesis.

Summing up diverse information from cultural anthropology, history and historical psychology concerning anthropogenic crises, we suggested that there was a regular relation between the three variables: technological potential, cultural regulation quality and social sustainability. The pattern, called *the law of techno-humanitarian balance*, states that *the higher production and war technologies' power, the more advanced the behaviour regulation means that is required for the self-preservation of society*.

The circumstances of early hominids' existence were of the kind that only a dramatic development of instrumental intelligence gave them a chance to survive (Bromley 1983). Meanwhile, having begun tool making, they dramatically interfered with the ethological balance. The power of artificial weapons rapidly exceeded the power of instinctive aggression-inhibition and the proportion of mortal conflicts within the herd grew incompatible with its further existence. This could have been the main reason for a fact demonstrated in archeology (Klix 1983): many groups seem to be on the line between animals and proto-humans but very few could cross it; those few groups managed to cope with the endogenous danger.

Indeed, individuals with normal animal motivation were doomed to mutual destruction in the new unnatural conditions, and certain psychostenic and hysterical individuals got selective privileges. Their survival required artificial (beyond biological instincts) collective regulation, which was paradoxically provided by pathological changes of the psycho-nervous system, abnormal mental ability, suggestibility and phobias. Thus, irrational fear of the deceased and posthumous revenge is supposed to strongly restrain in-group aggression and stimulate care for cripples that could play a key role at the earliest stage of anthropogenesis.

The assumption of a 'herd of crazies' who seem to be our remote ancestors has been thoroughly argued by neurologists, cultural anthropologists and psychologists (Grimak 2001; Nazaretyan 2005a; Pfeiffer 1985). Here, the relevant point is that the initial forms of proto-culture and proto-morals emerged as an outcome of the first *existential crisis* in human prehistory.

From *Homo habilis* on, hominids' unnatural intra-species killing fa-
cility seems to have been a key problem of pre-human and human history: the ways of solving this existential problem influenced essentially
the forms of social organization, and cultural and spiritual processes. As
far as the further life of the *hominidae* family (including *Homo sapiens*) has
not had a natural background any longer, it was to a great extent enabled
by the adequacy of cultural regulation with technological power. The law
of techno-humanitarian balance has controlled socio-historical selection,
discarding social organisms that could not adapt to their tools' power.
We shall demonstrate that the pattern helps explain causally both sudden
collapses of flourishing societies and breakthroughs of humanity into
new historical epochs (which often look still more mysterious).

Although the pattern is based on voluminous empirical evidence,
its universal character remains hypothetical. Besides violence victims'
comparative calculations, there are some additional non-trivial corol-
laries under verification.[2] Furthermore, a special apparatus is being constructed, which will, as we expect, allow estimating social organisms'
sustainability as much as it depends on technological potential and
cultural regulation.

For an initial and rough guide, *internal* and *external sustainability* are
distinguished. The former, *Si*, expresses the social system's capability
to keep away from endogenous catastrophes and is estimated as the
ratio of catastrophes per population number. The latter, *Se*, is society's
capability to withstand the natural and/or geopolitical environment's
fluctuations.

If we letter cultural regulation quality as *R* and technological potential as *T*, a simple equation represents the techno-humanitarian balance
pattern:

$$Si = f_1(R)/f_2(T) \qquad \qquad \ldots[1]$$

It goes without saying that $T > 0$, for in case of no technology at all
we have to do with a *herd* (not a society), where biological causalities
are effective. When technological potential is very low, primitive cultural regulation means are sufficient to prevent anthropogenic crises, as
in the case of the Paleolithic tribes. A system is highly sustainable, up
to stagnation, as cultural regulation quality considerably exceeds technological might (Confucian China is a textbook example). Finally, the
denominator growth increases the probability of anthropogenic crises,
as it is not compensated by growth of the numerator.

Actually, the indices' structure, the methods of quantitative estimation and the definition of functions f_1 and f_2 are under consideration. Thus, the magnitude of R is composed of at least three parameters: the social organization's complexity, the culture's information complexity (anthropologists work over calculation procedures for these indices [Chick 1997]) and the average individual's cognitive complexity (the parameter is investigated by experimental psycho-semantics [Petrenko and Mitina 1997]). The last component is the most dynamic one and we will show that the decline of cognitive complexity under emotional impulse is the leading reason of crisis-causing behaviour. In contrast to internal sustainability, the external one is the technological potential's positive function:

$$Se = g(T...) \qquad ...[2]$$

Thus, growing technological potential makes a social system less vulnerable to external fluctuations and more vulnerable to the internal ones, that is, mass and individual mental states (less 'foolproof').

One more conclusion is that the specific weight of anthropogenic crises versus the ones caused by outside factors (spontaneous climate fluctuations, geological and cosmic cataclysms, incoming aggressive nomads, and so on) has been historically increasing.

The consequences of techno-humanitarian imbalance

Ethnographic papers are full of sad stories about the aboriginals of Africa, Asia and America as soon as they first mastered European technologies. For instance, during the Vietnam War, a Paleolithic Mountain Khmer tribe obtained American carbines. The hunters mastered the new weapon and soon after that exterminated the fauna, shot each other down, and those who survived left the mountains and disappeared (Pegov and Puzachenko 1994).

In such cases the processes were accelerated, and causes and effects were apparent because society had skipped over several historical phases, and left a deep gap between firearm and Stone Age psychology. Similar leaps do not usually occur in authentic history; therefore, the disproportion between 'instrumental' and 'humanitarian' intelligence development (the 'force' and the 'wisdom') is not that manifest. So causal links are complex, delayed for centuries, or in early history, for millennia. To be revealed, the same causalities require a thorough analysis supplied with an appropriate working model.

To explain the model, we may first resort to a classic experiment in a Petri dish. Several bacteria impetuously propagate themselves in the closed vessel with a nutrient medium and soon the population suffocates in its own wastes. This is a graphic image of living matter's behaviour: as long as the capacity of extensive growth prevails over habitat's resistance, the population keeps on capturing available vital space and repressing as much as it can any counter-action or competition. For this reason, a natural ecosystem is full of ecological micro-crises.

In natural conditions, the aggravations are usually regulated via dynamic equilibration mechanisms that have been developed over billions of years. Strategically, the processes of breaking and restoring an inner balance lead to ecosystems' increasing variety and joint sustainability, which go together with the highly irregular conditions of each population's existence (oscillations in the 'predator–prey' circuit, and so on).

Culture, in both its material and regulative hypostases, has been always aimed at emancipation from spontaneous environmental fluctuations. Social communities, unlike animal populations, do not behave so rectilinearly as the bacteria colony in a Petri dish does, until cultural restraints substitute for the environment's resistance.[3] Meanwhile, a broken balance between grown technological opportunities and former regulation mechanisms can change the situation radically. According to formula [1], it decreases internal social sustainability but the approaching menace is not noticed right away.

On the contrary, the superiority of instrumental intelligence entails the rise of ecological and/or geopolitical aggression. Insufficiency of cultural restraints makes the society's behaviour essentially similar to that of a biological population, especially as natural expansion impulses are supplemented with a specifically human factor—needs go higher as soon as they are satisfied.

The psychological aspect is given more detailed analysis in the following section. We must just note here that sooner or later, extensive growth runs against real limits, which leads to anthropogenic crisis. Most frequently, it is followed by the catastrophic phase: the society falls victim to its own non-compensated power.

Special investigations show that most tribes, states or civilizations in the past were destroyed not so much by external factors (such cases also took place but they are less interesting for our subject), as they had subverted the natural and organizational bases of their own existence. As to military interventions, epidemics, ecological cataclysms, riots, and so on, events of that kind usually accomplished the society's self-destroying activity, like a virus or cancer cells do a similar job in a weakened biological organism.

Numerous facts gathered in relevant papers (*Global Environmental Outlook 3* 2002; Grigoriev 1991) testify to the distressing destiny of the societies that could not anticipate the delayed consequences of their economic activities. In spite of all peculiarities, a common script was simple: increasing intervention into the ecosystem → landscape destruction → social catastrophe.

As many researchers have indicated, empires' destruction frequently followed their flourishing, if increasing inner diversity did not accompany their extensive growth. Toynbee (1991) cited various examples to illustrate the inverse relationship between 'military and social progress', and was puzzled by the fact that this was surprisingly true about production tools as well as weapons. As we observe agricultural technique development in Hellenistic history, he writes, we realize that new technical achievements preceded civilization's decline. On the whole, increasing power over Nature most frequently caused 'fracture and decomposition'.

The facts of the social system's fracture conditioned by technological growth are so numerous that they serve as a pretext, on one hand, for total technological pessimism and on the other hand, for denial of a common humanity's history. The patterns of closed civilization cycles deprived of continuity started to supplant the ones of single historical process in the late nineteenth and early twentieth centuries. The discussion of those problems has resurfaced lately in relevant literature. To a considerable extent, it centres on the psychological aspect: has—or has not—human consciousness been transforming historically, and if it has, were—or were not—those transformations 'progressive'?

In particular, Kohlberg's (1984) idea of correlation between humankind's intellectual and moral development[4] is still a subject of criticism, even by the adherents of social evolutionism (Sanderson 1994).

Nowadays, the idea gets new empirical and conceptual support. The techno-humanitarian balance hypothesis highlights both the facts of a social system's self-destruction and the opposite ones, concerning the constructive solution of anthropogenic crises. The latter have been less frequent in history; however, they were world history's turning points.

To take an example, as a certain crisis involves a vast region highly saturated with diverse cultures, its inhabitants manage to find a cardinal way out of the deadlock. Each time it is conditioned by a set of irreversible social, political and psychological transformations (discussed later), which have been lined up as the consecutive evolution mainstreams. As special analysis shows, society's capacity for appropriate transformation of its economy, policy and mentality essentially depends on marginal groups, which had been formerly neglected and despised; this we called *the redundant variety rule*.

No less than seven crucial breakthroughs for all of human history and prehistory have been revealed and described. Still, most researchers have so far either confined themselves to phenomenology or left the problem of revolutionary transformation causes and premises for the future. Thus, Jaspers (1955) has adduced 'the simultaneity puzzle': how could the Axial Revolution occur simultaneously on the immense geographical area from Judea, Persia and Greece to India and China?

The techno-humanitarian balance hypothesis proves helpful for causal scrutiny of great historical turning points, each of which had been preceded by a wide-scale anthropogenic crisis. Human consciousness has progressively evolved, restoring step by step the disturbed cultural balance. So more curious is the fact we find as we make a close study of social activities foregoing crises aggravation: extensive pre-crisis growth phases are attended by psychological states, processes and mechanisms that have astonishingly reproduced themselves regardless of the population's cultural and historical peculiarities. That is why a coming crisis may be diagnosed by psychological symptoms while economic, political and other signs still indicate growing social prosperity.

Mental conditions on the threshold of crises

To begin this section, I consider selected historical episodes that belong to a kind of 'optimistic tragedies'. This will help us observe some specific psychological features of both the pre-crisis state of culture and minds, and the one after having coped with the most dangerous aggravations. I should make a reservation that only the inner logic of the processes is considered; this approach does not deny the influence of outside factors, up to cosmic ones, on social events, but abstracts from it.

Apparently, in order to describe those episodes as single separate stories, we have to single them out of the continual historical process. For this reason, the conventional beginning and end of each are being made distinct by means of dots.

...Upper Paleolithic millennia were marked with an unprecedented development of 'hunting automation' and distant projectiles. Hunters learned to dig trap holes and invented the lance, lance-thrower, darts and bow with arrows (Bromby 1983; Semionov 1964). This created good conditions for demographic growth and human expansion all over the planet and the world population reached five to seven million people (McEvedy and Jones 1978; Snooks 1996). As one hunter-gatherer's nourishment required an average territory of ten to twenty square kilometres, the planet's resources could not provide for many more people.

However, not only did demographic growth create a problem (growth by itself is usually a function of a disturbed technology–psychology balance), archaeologists reveal the Upper Paleolithic hunting bacchanalia. While natural predators first go for sick and weakened individuals, a well-armed hunter had the opportunity (and desire) to kill the strongest and the nicest ones and, besides, the amount of prey far exceeded the hunters' biological needs. Some kind of wild animals' 'anthropogenic graveyards' were discovered by the archaeologists and a great part of the meat had not been used by humans (Anikovich 1999; Budyko 1984; Burovski 1998). The dwellings made of mammoth's bones exceeded construction needs. In Siberia, thirty to forty adult mammoths' bones were spent on each dwelling, plus a lot of newly-born mammoths' skulls, which were used as props and, perhaps, for ritual aims. In north-west Russia, pit-stores of mammoths' bones (their predestination is not quite clear) have been found near some dwellings. Enclosure hunting led to annual extermination of herds.

Since it was discovered that the last mammoths lived on Wrangell Island about 4,000 years ago, until the first humans appeared there (Vartanian et al. 1995), the 'overkill' theory of mammoths' and many other big mammals' extinction hardly has an alternative. The first symptoms of mega-fauna elimination are registered nearly 50,000 years ago in Africa and the process peaked about 20,000 years ago in Eurasia and 11,000 years ago in America (Karlen 2001). Skilful hunters penetrated America, quickly spread from Alaska to Tierra del Fuego and eradicated all big animals, including elephants and camels, which had never before met hominids. Similar effects of mega-fauna extinction followed the first humans' appearance in Oceania and Australia (Budyko 1984; Diamond 1999). In total, up to 90 per cent of the big animals disappeared forever, although those species had endured twenty Pleistocene climatic cycles.

The trend of merciless extermination was intensified on the threshold of the coming Holocene, the post-glacial epoch, which could have helped foraging economies flourish. Instead, it led to a deadlock. Nature could not bear endless pressure on the part of such an unrestrained aggressor as the Upper Paleolithic hunter. Uncontrolled resource exploitation led to the ecosystem's exhaustion and destruction, and it aggravated inter-tribe competition. The Middle latitudes' population decreased several times.

The Neolithic revolution was society's creative response to the Upper Paleolithic crisis. Some tribes made the transition to settled agriculture and cattle breeding, and the new economic idea rapidly spread from several centres (in Eurasia and later in America). Humans first started 'partnership with nature' (Childe 1945); their ecological niche essentially deepened. Thanks to developing agriculture, the territories' carrying capacity increased one, then two, and then three orders of magnitude (Korotaev 1991), and the population grew rapidly.

Complex transformations in social relations and psychology attended the transition from a foraging economy to food production. One needs a relevant mental horizon of delayed causalities to throw into earth eatable grains or to feed and protect animals instead of kill and eat them. The mind's grown information volume was embodied in all vital activities. Social links and role repertory essentially broadened. Production and combat tools were first differentiated, and a new kind of relationship between agricultural and 'warrior' tribes was established. The warriors could guess that it was more profitable to protect the producers and regularly appropriate production 'surplus', than to kill or to drive them away, and the farmers understood it was better to pay-off the warriors for protection than to leave the land or to perish in hopeless battles.

Such forms of inter-tribe symbiosis and 'collective exploitation' supplanted genocide and cannibalism of the Paleolithic. As Teilhard de Chardin (1965) notes, since the Neolithic, physical extermination has been an exclusive or, anyhow, secondary factor: the cruellest warfare still included some form of assimilation. Modern anthropologists have also indicated more than once that only in the Neolithic tribe integration (the chiefdoms), people learned 'for the first time in history, how to encounter strangers regularly without attempting to kill them' (Diamond 1999: 273).

Population geneticists have recently added a bright trait to the Neolithic portrayal (Sykes 2001). Unlike previously prevalent scenarios, they showed that the substitution of foraging economy by agriculture had not occurred via swimming aside or eliminating the hunter-gatherers by an incoming tide of farmers (for instance, from the south Caucasus to the east and to the north-west) but via voluntary acceptance of the progressive technologies and organization. At least, so it was in Europe: most of modern Europeans proved to be the genetic offspring of the Cro-Magnon hunters. To all appearance, the European story was not an exception.

This is a sensational discovery. It means that first in human history a progressive idea won through change of mental matrix instead of physical removal of the old idea bearers, what had been usual for the Paleolithic. So the competition of social models was not merely a struggle of races any more—it shifted partly to the 'virtual' sphere, which imparted a new long-term mechanism to historical development....

...In the twelfth to eleventh centuries B.C., iron production appeared in the Middle East, Transcaucasia and East Mediterranean, and soon spread to India and China. This produced a steep rise in extensive (including demographic) growth opportunities.

Bronze weapons had been expensive, fragile and heavy. Small professional armies composed of physically very strong men had waged wars. It had been extremely expensive to prepare and to arm such troops, as well as to replace a killed fighter. Therefore, each commander had tried to spare his own warriors and exterminate as many enemies as possible. War captives had been usually killed and a subjugated population had been terrorized into obedience by demonstratively destroying or 'taking prisoners' the local gods' statues, and so on. (Berzin 1984; Neronova et al. 1989).

Steel weapons were considerably cheaper, more durable and lighter than the ones of bronze. This allowed arming the whole male population; something like a 'people's volunteer corps' replaced the professional armies and competition for productive soils aggravated. In the meantime, the combination of new technology with former social, political and military values made early Iron Age leaders extraordinarily bloodthirsty (Berzin 1984; Vigasin 1994).

Emperors and generals hewed on stones boastful 'accounts' to their gods about the numbers of enemies killed, and towns destroyed and burned, which presented sadistic details of their 'deeds' (a relevant collection of texts is in 'Reader on Ancient East History [see Nazaretyan 2008]). Battles became so bloody that the further life of technologically advanced states was threatened.

Culture responded to the challenge with the Axial Spiritual Revolution, the causes of which, as indicated before, has remained a puzzle so far. On vast geographical area, great prophets, philosophers, statesmen and generals set the tone for society's intensive job on the whole value system's revision. Cultures transformed unrecognizably in several centuries. The cognitive complexity of social and individual minds, humans' capacity for abstract thinking and reflection, and the scale of generic identity radically increased. Universal ideas of good and evil, and personal choice and responsibility appeared. First time in history, authoritarian mythological thinking partly made room for criticism and the new private self-control instance, the conscience, made an alternative to the traditional fear of gods. Enemies learned to see each other as human beings, to understand and to sympathize. Aeschylus's tragedy 'The Persians' was the first work of art in history that described warfare as seen by the enemies' side (Jaspers 1955; Nazaretyan 1997; Yarkho 1972).

These mental processes were distinctly reflected in political relations. Objective aim achievement, instead of the number of victims, became a matter of virtue and the combat success criterion. The role of military reconnaissance and propaganda among enemy troops and population grew. A new tradition of the conqueror's protection over local gods and priests appeared. 'Political demagogy' as a means of persuasion and pacification contrasted with the usual terror methods: in 539 B.C., the Persian king, Kir Akhemenid, having captured Babel, proclaimed a manifesto that said that his army was just going to defend Babylonians and their gods and priests from their own bad king, Nabonid. The genial trick soon spread far outside Middle East, to South Europe, India and China....

...All symptoms of the evolution's next deadlock were manifest in Europe in the second millennium A.D. Development of agricultural technologies stimulated demographic growth. Besides, the Christian Church, which had primarily called to refuse marriages and childbearing, changed its stand to the opposite one in the ninth century (Arutunian 2000). The woods area was decreasing, swamps were being formed and their water steamed down to rivers, together with all the wastes of growing cities.

The ecological crisis provoked social tension, disorders and epidemics. Wars were becoming more and more murderous. Even the disaster of the black death in the fourteenth century that took away more than a third of Europe's population only temporarily interrupted the demographic tendency (Le Goff 1977). In the sixteenth century, wooded area on the territory of the actual Moscow district was two to three times less than what we have today (Kulpin 1995; Smirnova 1994), while its population was 100 times less than the present one. Development of agricultural technologies had produced a new strategic evolutionary deadlock as hunting technologies had done long before.

The crisis of agricultural civilization was partly softened by mass emigration and, besides, introduction of the overseas plants (potato, maize) and carbon utilization (Bondarev 1996; Le Goff 1977). The 'Pre-Industrial Dash' that turned Europe from a Eurasian outsider to a world leader was forestalled and attended by impetuous development of the ideas of humanism, individualism, enlightenment and progress. The values of individual success, qualification and education increased unprecedentedly. According to the calculations of the Russian economic historian V. Meliantsev (1996), at the turn of the second millennium, West European countries fell behind the leading Asian states in literacy of the adult population by twice and more, while, being on the threshold of the Indus trial Revolution exceeded them three to three and a half times industrially.

A new legal and moral mentality was being formed, which implied equal natural rights and pan-human ethics in place of the foregoing clan mentality The humanitarian achievements enabled the new historical breakthrough and it left behind the agricultural crisis (which may, therefore, be qualified as regional by geographic extension and global by the evolutionary consequences). It also implied the superiority of the active Spirit over the passive Matter, and the Future over the Past.[5]

European nations spread the light of reason with fire and sword and their power soon enveloped the whole planet, resources of which fell under the parent states' control. European citizens' faith in moral progress and future everlasting peace was based on the indisputable superiority of the Western mind and was growing together with social and economic prosperity, needs and ambitions. While the soldiers fought in exotic lands, mother countries' inhabitants believed wars and their cruelty were a thing of the past. No wonder: in all the colonial wars of the nineteenth century, Europeans' losses were 1,06,000 people, in contrast with millions of natives who perished in the same warfare (Urlanis 1994).

In the early twentieth century, reserves of extensive growth were exhausted, while it was yet far from sobering the public. By the following events, by various official and memory documents, and by indirect testimonies, we can see that the inertia of extensive development and corresponding state of minds still dominated. Thirst for new successes and achievements produced joyful expectancies of either a 'small victorious war' or a 'revolutionary tempest' among politicians, intellectuals and the masses. The photos of August 1914, which show us happy crowds in the streets of Petrograd, Berlin, Vienna and Paris after the war had been declared, are the best illustration (*Man and Warfare* 1997).

Now, we may observe a result of those social and psychological processes. Whereas European countries' summary warfare losses during the nineteenth century were about five and a half million people (according to our calculation, about 15 per cent of all war victims in the world), in the twentieth century they rose to seventy million—no less than 60 per cent. Two World Wars, Hiroshima and many years of nuclear 'equilibrium of fear' were required for Europeans' psychological alteration. Unfortunately, it was not for a long time....

Having compared crisis episodes of the past and the present, we may sum up certain psychological observations. Once new instrumental facilities exceed former cultural restrictions and an extensive development begins, public attitudes and sentiments acquire peculiar features. A sense of omnipotence and permissiveness is intensified together with increasing needs and ambitions. Optimistic ideas of a world full of inexhaustible resources and the object of subjugation are formed. Success euphoria produces an impatient expectation of new successes and victories. The subjugation process and the search for new moderately resisting enemies become self-valuable and irrational.

The proximity of the desired aims intensifies motivational tension: this is called the 'aim-gradient phenomenon' in psychology. According to another psychological pattern, the Yerkes–Dodson law, efficiency of a simple activity is proportional to motivation force, while a complex activity's efficiency decreases by excessive motivation. This is one of the sources of danger.

As psycho-semantic experiments have shown, emotional tension decreases cognitive complexity (Petrenko 1982). So the world picture becomes lower dimensional, thinking turns primitive and the problem situations look elementary, while objectively, the task of the social system's maintenance becomes more difficult, as technological opportunities grow. In other words, the numerator index in equation [1], instead of increasing in proportion to the denominator's growth, is falling. Therefore, cultural imbalance lowers the society's internal sustainability.

Exploring the premises of revolutionary crises, Davis (1969) has shown that growing life quality usually precedes them: economic level, political freedoms, social mobility, and so on. Simultaneously, expectations grow as well. In a certain moment, increasing expectancies run against a relatively reduced possibility for their satisfaction; frequently because of demographic growth and/or unsuccessful warfare, which was expected to be 'small and victorious', whereas the expectancies go on increasing under their own momentum. The gap produces frustrations, the situation looks unbearable and humiliating, people tend to seek those guilty and the aggression that cannot find release externally gives vent inside the social system. Emotional resonance (Nazaretyan 2003) provokes mass disorders, which in many cases become the last act in a pre-crisis development tragi-comedy.

Having applied Davis's model to various countries and historical situations, we have estimated its high reliability. My own experience shows that it is applicable both to large communities, such as states or civilizations, and relatively small ones, such as political parties. Nowadays, the model may be used, with certain reservations, in global situation analysis as well.

Since some countries and regions, and planetary civilization as a whole, are experiencing typical anthropogenic crises, which are fraught with great dangers in the twenty first century, the question about the mechanisms of such crises' aggravation and overcoming them is not a purely academic one. Certain facts show that during the second half of the twentieth century, some changes for the better took place. Politicians abstained from using the most destructive weapons, new kinds of inter-state coalitions were formed which were not aimed against any outer force and effective international ecological measures became usual. These facts had no precedence in human history. A hope emerged that Western type cultures had already developed a strong rational control reserve over intrinsic rectilinear expansion impulses.

Unfortunately, what followed one side's unconditional victory in the Cold War demonstrated that maturity of political thought even in the most advanced modern cultures does not yet meet the requirements imposed by actual technological potential. Current *Homo prae-crisimos* psychological symptoms are described in Nazaretyan (2004): lowered political intelligence, a lowered decision-making quality and a lowered propaganda rhetoric level in the 1990s compared to the preceding decades.

The book (its first edition appeared in July 2001) shows how a simplified worldview and rectilinear extensive activities are provoking hostility. Meanwhile, emerging forms of sophisticated weapons and new methods of political terrorism, it says, make impossible the continuation of the practices of the previous half-century, which was the canalization of the global conflict in local wars. According to the techno-humanitarian balance hypothesis, actual challenges, including the political terrorism with its growing technical opportunities, will either destroy the planet's civilization, or play *a great educating role*, comparable to the ones of the atom bomb and other dramatic technical inventions in the past.

An outline of global anthropogenic crises and revolutionary breaks

In conclusion, I will quickly enumerate human history's turning points, when anthropogenic crises which we may qualify as global ones by their evolutionary meaning, were solved via a breakthrough into the new epoch. Though some of them have been mentioned previously, I cannot escape repeating certain details to give an overall portrayal of consecutive transformations in macro-social behaviour as it is seen from the current perspective.

All appellations of the revolutions in the following list go with quote marks, for some of the terms have not been widely accepted, though all are present in relevant literature:

1. The 'Paleolithic Revolution' (0.7–2.0 million years ago) was connected with the emergence of standard tools, regular fire usage and, eventually, transition from predominantly gathering to hunting. Mystical dread of the deceased (after-life revenge) furnished the primary super-instinctive proto-cultural regulation: intra-herd aggression was first artificially limited and an

unnatural care for the cripples appeared. So hominids' further existence and development was enabled in the condition of essential unbalance between artificial weapons and instinctive aggression-retention.

2. The 'Upper Paleolithic Revolution' or the *Cro-Magnons* Cultural Revolution (35,000–40,000 years ago) was the transition from the Middle to Upper Paleolithic, and conclusive extermination of the *Neanderthals*. Stone material productivity grew and the portion of tools made of bone and horn increased as well, which gave people relative independence from natural sources of flint. Sign communication systems, including articulate speech, were obviously perfected and two-dimensional portrayal (rock pictures) appeared. Why could not *Paleoanthropes*, who had developed a complex Mustier culture and dominated their contemporaneous *Neoanthropes* (*Proto-Cro-Magnons*) during about 1,00,000 years, resist more? We have to assume that the Mustier culture was experiencing a deep crisis, though its essence is not quite clear.

I know two hypotheses that explain this; both conform well to the techno-humanitarian balance pattern. One accents the facts of culture's high material variability and very scanty signs of 'spiritual production'. Free choice of physical actions with insufficient spiritual regulation (deficit of animistic thinking that roughly developed in the Upper Paleolithic cultures) produced the *Neanderthal*'s neurotic syndrome that was expressed in antisocial activity and splashes of uncontrolled aggressive energy (Lobok 1997). Another hypothesis (Reymers 1990) attaches the Late Mustier crisis to ecological effects: the *Neanderthals* had hit upon the idea to burn vegetation off which caused landscapes' higher productivity but this led to a fatal decrease of biological diversity.

3. The 'Neolithic Revolution' (tenth to seventh millennia B.C.) saw a transition from a highly expensive foraging economy to food production, which went along with replacing the usual genocide and cannibalism with rudimentary collective exploitation forms and was also accompanied by the original symbiosis of agricultural and 'warrior' tribes.

Those deep complex transformations were a response to the Upper Paleolithic crisis, which had been aggravated because of hunter technologies' development. This had led to the elimination of wild animals' populations and species and to severe inter-tribe competition. During the Upper Paleolithic crisis, previous demographic growth had been replaced by a population decrease and just after agricultural methods dominated, the population grew again.

4. The 'Urban Revolution' (fifth to third millennia B.C.) was when large human agglomerations were formed, irrigation channels were constructed, and written language and the first legal documents appeared, which regulated large communities' lives, with a high human concentration and complex common activities.

This revolution followed spread of bronze tools, new demographic explosion and the aggravation of competition for grasslands and fertile soil.

5. The 'Axial Revolution' (the middle of the first millennium B.C.) saw new kinds of thinkers, politicians and generals, such as Zaratushtra, the Judaic prophets, Socrates, Buddha, Confucius, Kir, Asoca, Sun-Tze and others. They appeared during a short time interval in advanced societies, which were still weakly linked among themselves, and deeply transformed the world culture. Criticism first supplanted authoritarian mythological thinking; universal ideas of good and evil, and of personality as a sovereign moral choice subject were formed. Aims and methods of warfare changed: victims' numbers ceased to serve as a combat masterpiece measure and a pretext for boasting, the value of communication considerably increased, and primitive violence and terror were partly replaced by intelligence data and 'political demagogy'.

The Axial epoch followed displacement of bronze with iron weapons, which were cheaper, lighter and more durable, and instead of professional armies, some kind of people's militia had appeared. As a result, battles became extraordinarily bloody, and former values and norms in new conditions could have destroyed advanced societies. Therefore, the Axial Revolution was culture's response to a dangerous gap between new weapons' power and former aggression-retention mechanisms.

(American cultures that developed separately passed through the same stages, though later in time. There are signs that European conquerors found advanced societies of both the Americas in a deep crisis caused by overpopulation and on the threshold of a spiritual revolution, which could have been similar to the Old World's Axial Epoch (Semionov 1995). Meanwhile, aboriginals of the other isolated continent, Australia, conserved Paleolithic life, culture and psychology without having reached the Upper Paleolithic crisis, the Neolithic Revolution, and so on).

6. The 'Industrial Revolution' (A.D. eighteenth to nineteenth centuries) brought about the introduction of relatively 'spare' technologies, which had a higher special productivity than agricultural ones. It was prepared and attended by a complex spiritual framework, the 'indust-reality', in Alvin Toffler's (*The Third Wave* 1980) terms.

The Industrial Revolution was preceded by a long crisis of agricultural civilization in Europe (twelfth to eighteenth centuries), when uncontrolled extensive growth, cutting down of forests, destruction of ecosystems and people's concentration in the cities had led to outbreaks of bloody warfare and mass mortal epidemics. The development of agricultural technologies had produced a new strategic evolutionary deadlock as, long before, hunting technologies had done.

In its turn, industrial production, having increased the power of human effort, gave a new impulse to extensive development, demographic growth, and ecological and geopolitical ambitions. So like it had been mostly before, the solution of one crisis opened the way towards the following ones.

7. The 'Information Revolution': In the middle of the twentieth century, many people felt that planetary civilization was approaching a new crisis epoch. Its circumstances may also be well described in terms of the techno-humanitarian balance pattern. In the previous 100 years, weapons' power had grown by six orders of magnitude. Human intelligence had achieved such high instrumental might that the aggression-retention means that reflected previous historical experience, could not meet the new requirements any more. The instrumental intelligence became dangerous for its own bearer's further existence again....

Techno-humanitarian balance hypothesis gives an additional dimension to White's (1975) conception, which was one of the most influential models of social development in the twenteith century. In the words of his Canadian adherent V. Smil (1994: 1): 'From the perspective of natural science, both prehistoric human evolution and the course of history may be seen as the quest for controlling greater energy stores and flows.' Now as we find out that excessive power is self-destructive for a social system unless it is internally balanced with proportional cultural regulation of behaviour, the model of development reduced to the energy aspect looks dramatically insufficient even from the point of view of natural science.

Turning back to the experience of 'optimistic tragedies', we may note that the constructive solving of each of the anthropogenic crises entailed a complex leap forward by all the five long-term mainstreams mentioned earlier. More potential technologies furnished higher specific productivity, that is, the paying load for a muscular effort and a unit of Nature's destruction. This implied higher variety of the social structure, higher information volume of the social and individual intelligence, and more advanced cultural regulation. As a result, humanity's ecological niche broadened and deepened, and the population kept growing. Over time, evolutionary success entailed increasing social needs and ambitions, and the way to the next crisis continued.

This model keeps us oriented within the palliative space of the future and helps us discriminate between the constructive forecasts, scripts and projects, and the utopian ones. At the same time, it involves definite conclusions about the past.

In the nineteenth century, Russian sociologist Danilevski (1991) argued that there had been no significant landmarks for all of human history and, therefore, no world history at all. In fact, he meant, separate civilizations' ascent, flourishing and decay had taken place successively in time but devoid of causal continuity. This 'civilization approach' was later caught up by many Western thinkers for its pessimistic portrayal conformed to the twentieth-century mass disappointments. Within the paradigm, Spengler's (1980) notion that '*humankind* is a merely zoological concept' sounded reasonable.

Meanwhile, it was just in the twentieth century that historical discoveries disavowed the argument, and its far-reaching conclusions. As far as we take those discoveries into account, we may accept at least certain statements assertively.

To make sure of the substantially global character of human history, as well as life history, the proper 'unit' of consideration is to be singled out.

Thus, biological evolution is out of sight, concentrated on populations, species or separate ecosystems: more than 99 per cent species on the planet had become extinct before the first humans appeared. So nothing but lifecycles is obvious until we look at the geo-chronological table, which represents the biosphere as a whole at successive geological epochs. Similarly, humankind, or more precisely, the global society–nature system, is the only real subject of social evolution, while countries, nations, regional civilizations and even hominid species (in the Paleolithic) repeatedly changed one another as leaders;

by themselves, all those smaller subjects cannot serve for an evolutionary portrayal.

Since hominids have once and for all turned to tool making in spite of countless divergences, migrations and isolations, culture has been a single and common planetary phenomenon, which is proved by many observations, leading off the fact that the first standard tools on all inhabited continents were surprisingly identical. As to the explosive growth of local diversities in the Middle and Upper Paleolithic, and later, it was a typical process of an evolving system's inner differentiation.

What we may call 'progress' is neither an aim nor a movement 'from the worse to the better' but a means of self-preservation, with which the complex non-equilibrium system responds to the challenges of declined sustainability. A succession of a posteriori effects of restored sustainability is retrospectively construed as a step-by-step ascent from more 'natural' (that is, wild and relative equilibrium) states of society–nature systems to less 'natural' ones. So having solved dramatic vital problems, progressive transformations produce more complicated ones and at the same time, more developed means for their solution. After all, humans are still living on thanks to their virtue to adapt self-regulation quality to their own increasing might.

Notes

1. In *Social Violence* (2005), a distinctive cross-cultural index of practical social violence—bloodshed ratio (BR), a ratio of the number of killings per unit of time to the population size—was first introduced, which was completed with equations for its calculation (see also Nazaretyan 2006).

2. One more corollary is that the population density a certain community can bear, depends on how advanced its culture is, that is, the number of anthropogenic crises that have been overcome in the past (see later). A special analysis has confirmed this suggestion on the whole; however, it discovered an attendant factor, which belongs more to population genetic than cultural development. As our colleague has demonstrated (Borinskaya 2005), explosive human concentration each time intensified natural selection: pathogenic micro-organisms got favourable conditions and increased their activities, and epidemics eliminated individuals and families with weak innate immunity from certain diseases. Thus, the human gene pool has been consecutively changing; as a result, people in complex societies differ from their ancestors or contemporaries who live in simple societies by their biological resistance (that certainly has nothing to do with their mental capacities). This fact restricts the validity of the data gathered by our group. Growth of population densities and structural complexity proved to be related

not only to the improvement of cultural aggression-retention mechanisms (which followed from the hypothesis), but also to growing organic resistance against biological aggression. At least it was so until extensive and intensive development of anti-contagion measures in the twentieth century started up an opposite trend of decreasing biological resistance.

3. Those regulators may sometimes horrify an observer who belongs to another culture but they enable the society's existence in the ecological niche. Many ethnographers reported that a typical method of demographic stability for primitive tribes was normative infanticide, regular extermination of the 'unwanted' babies, especially female, and castration. In some tribes, a man may not marry without having killed or castrated another man from a neighbouring tribe.

4. In fact, it applies to social history the classical data gathered by Piaget and his followers (Volovikova and Rebeko 1990) concerning individual development and the 'conflict-enculturation hypothesis' (Chick 1998). The downward course of aggression with increasing age has been revealed both in Western and primitive cultures (Munroe et al. 2000).

5. Some Sinologists (Lin Yufu 1995) have shown that all technological and economic premises were in place for an industrial revolution in fourteenth-century China. However, the world model and value system did not favour this radical transformation, unlike the situation of Europeans in the eighteenth to nineteenth centuries, who had met the deep crisis and developed a new progress-oriented worldview, which was a psychological compensation of the Late Middle Ages' mass alarms and phobias.

References

Anikovich, M.V. 1999. 'The East-European Mammoth Hunters as a Specific Historical and Cultural Phenomenon', in *SETI: Civilizations' Past, Present, and Future*, pp. 6–9. Moscow: AC PIAS (in Russian).

Arutunian, A. 2000. *Western Europe: From Early Christianity to Renaissance (The Highlights of Cultural-historical Evolution)*. Erevan: Nairi (in Russian).

Berzin, E.O. 1984. 'Following the Iron Revolution', *Knowledge is Power*, 8: 33–35 (in Russian).

Blainey, G.N. 1975. *Triumph of the Nomads: A History of Ancient Australia*. Melbourne and Sidney: Macmillan.

Bondarev, L. 1996. 'The Mediaeval Ecological Crisis in Western and Central Europe, and its Consequences', in *International Conference 'Humanity's Ecological Experience: Past, Present, and Future': Synopsis of the Reports*, pp. 96–98. Moscow: MAI (in Russian).

Borinskaya, S.V. 2005. 'Genetic Aspects of Social Evolution', in *Social Evolution: Interdisciplinary Analysis, and Mathematical Models*. Moscow: The Humanitarian (in Russian).

Bromley, Yu.V. (ed.). 1983. 'General Questions: The Problems of Anthropogenesis', in *History of Primitive Society*. Moscow: Nauka (in Russian).

Budyko, M.I. 1984. *Evolution of the Biosphere*. Moscow: Gidrometeoizdat (in Russian).

Burovski, A.M. 1998. 'The Paleolithic Idyllic?', *Social Sciences Today*, 1: 163–74 (in Russian).

Chick, G. 1997. 'Cultural Complexity: The Concept and its Measurement', *Cross-cultural Research: The Journal of Comparative Social Science*, 31(4): 275–307.

———. 1998. 'Games in Culture Revisited: Cross-cultural Research', *The Journal of Comparative Social Science*, 32(2): 185–206.

Childe, V.H. 1945. *Progress and Archeology*. London: Watts, Thinker's Library.

Christian, D. 1991. 'The Case for "Big History"', *Journal of World History*, 2(2): 223–38.

———. 2004. *Maps of Time: An Introduction to Big History*. Berkeley, CA: University of California Press.

Danilevski, N.Ya. 1991. *Russia and Europe*. Moscow: Kniga (in Russian).

Davis, J. 1969. 'Toward a Theory of Revolution', in *Studies in Social Movements: A Social-psychological Perspective*, pp. 85–108. New York: Free Press.

Diamond, J. 1999. *Guns, Germs, and Steel. The Fates of Human Societies*. New York and London: W.W. Norton.

Global Environmental Outlook 3. 2002. 3(August).

Grigoriev, A.A. 1991. *The Ecological Lessons of the Past and the Present*. Leningrad: Nauka (in Russian).

Grimak, L.P. 2001. 'Faith as a Component of Hypnotism', *Applied Psychology*, 6: 89–96 (in Russian).

Jaspers, K. 1955. *Vom Ursprung und Ziel der Geschichte*. Frankfurt/Main and Hamburg: Fischer Bucherei.

Karlen, A. 2001. *Plague's Progress: A Social History of Man and Disease*. New York: Phoenix.

Klix, F. 1983. *Erwachendes Denken: Eine Entwicklungsgeschichte der menschlichen Intelligenz*. Berlin: Deutscher Verlag der Wissenschaften.

Kohlberg, L. 1984. *The Psychology of Moral Development*. New York: Harper and Row.

Korotaev, A.V. 1991. 'On the Economic Premises for Class Formation and Politogenesis', in *Archaic Society: The Problems of Sociology of Development. Collection of Scientific Works I*, pp.136–91. Moscow: IH AS USSR (in Russian).

Kulpin, E. 1995. *The Way of Russia*. Moscow: Moscow Lyceum (in Russian).

Le Goff, J. 1977. *La Civilisation de l'Occident Medieval*. Paris: Arthaud.

Lin Yufu, J. 1995. 'The Needham Puzzle: Why the Industrial Revolution did not originate in China?', *Economic Development and Cultural Change*, 43(2): 269–92.

Lobok, A.N. 1997. *Anthropology of Myth*. Ekaterinburg: BKI.

Lorenz, K. 1981. *Das Sogenannte Bose (Zur Naturgechichte der Agression)*. Munchen: Dt. Taschenbuch Verlach.

Man and Warfare. 1997. 'A "Round Table" of Scientists', *Social Sciences Today*, 4: 152–67 (in Russian).

McEvedy, C. and R. Jones. 1978. *Atlas of World Population History*. London: Allen Lane.

McNeill, W.H. 2002. Interview. *Historically Speaking*, 4(2).

McNeill, J.R. and W.H. McNeill. 2003. *The Human Web: A Bird's-eye View of World History*. New York: Norton.

Meliantsev, V. 1996. *East and West in the 2nd Millennium: Economy, History, and Modernity*. Moscow: Moscow State University (in Russian).

Munroe, R.L., R. Hulefeld, J.M. Rogers, D.L. Tomeo and S.K. Yamazaki. 2000. 'Aggression Among Children in Four Cultures', *Cross-cultural Research: The Journal of Comparative Social Science*, 34(1): 3–25.

Nazaretyan, A.P. 1991. *Intelligence in the Universe: Sources, Formation, and Prospects*. Moscow: Nedra. (in Russian)

———. 1997. 'La Autoconciencia Moral Como Fenomeno Historico', in *Perspectivas Humanistas, Anuario 1996*, pp.79–89. Santiago de Chile: MHI.

———. 2003. *Aggressive Crowds, Mass Panic, and Rumors: Lectures in Social and Political Psychology*. St Petersburg and Moscow: Piter (in Russian).

———. 2004. *Civilization Crises Within the Context of Universal History: Self-organization, Psychology, and Forecasts*. Moscow: Mir (in Russian).

———. 2005a. 'Fear of the Dead as a Factor in Social Self-organization', *Journal for the Theory of Social Behaviour*, 35(2): 155–69.

———. 2005b. 'Western and Russian Traditions of Big History', *Journal for General Philosophy of Science*, 36(1): 63–80.

———. 2006. 'Evolution of Non-violence: A Historical retrospection', in A. Korotaev and S. Malkov (eds), *History and Mathematics*, pp. 16–46. Moscow: URSS (in Russian).

———. 2008. *Anthropology of Violence and Culture of Self-organization: Essays on Evolutionary Historical Psychology*. Moscow: URSS (in Russian).

Neronova, V.D., I.S. Svensiskaya and I.M. Diakonoff (eds). 1989. 'Decay of Ancient Societies', in *History of the Ancient World*. Moscow: Nauka (in Russian)

Pegov, S.A. and Yu G. Puzachenko. 1994. 'Society and Nature on the Threshold of the 21st Century', *Social Sciences Today*, 5: 146–52 (in Russian).

Petrenko, V.F. 1982. 'Experimental Psycho-semantics: The Research of Individual Consciousness', *Problems of Psychology*, 5: 23–35 (in Russian).

Petrenko, V.F. and O.V. Mitina. 1997. *A Psycho-semantic Analysis of the Dynamics of Social Consciousness*. Smolensk: Smolensk State University Press (in Russian).

Pfeiffer, J.E. 1985. *The Creative Explosion: An Inquiry into the Origins of Art and Religion*. New York: Cornell University Press.

Pomerants, G.S. 1991. 'An Essay on Philosophy of Solidarity', *Problems of Philosophy*, 3: 57–66 (in Russian).

Reymers, N.F. 1990. *The Usage of Nature: A Reference Book*. Moscow: Mysl (in Russian).

Sanderson, S.K. 1994. 'Evolutionary Materialism: A Theoretical Strategy for the Study of Social Evolution', *Sociological Perspectives*, 37(1): 47–73.

Semionov, S.A. 1964. 'Essay on Development of the Paleolithic Material Culture and Economy', in *Humankind's Sources (The Basic Problems of Anthropogenesis)*, pp.152–90. Moscow: Moscow State University Press (in Russian).

———. 1995. 'The Ideas of Gumanism in the Ibero-American Culture', *Social Sciences Today*, 4: 163–73 (in Russian).

Smil, V. 1994. *Energy in World History*. Boulder, CO: Westview Press.

Smirnova, O.V. (ed.). 1994. *The Large-leaved Forests of Eastern Europe*. Moscow: Nauka (in Russian).

Snooks, G.D. 1996. *The Dynamic Society: Exploring the Sources of Global Change*. London and New York: Routledge.

Social Violence. 2005. 'The Evolutionary Aspect: A "Round Table" of Scientists', *Social Sciences Today*, 4: 138–47 (in Russian).

Spengler, O. 1980. *Der Untergang der Abenlandes: Umrisse der Morphologie der Weltgeschichte*. Munchen: Dt. Taschenbuch Verl.

Spier, F. 1996. *The Structure of Big History: From the Big Bang until Today*. Amsterdam: Amsterdam University Press.

Sykes, B. 2001. *The Seven Daughters of Eve*. New York and London: Norton.

Teilhard de Chardin, P. 1965. *Les Phenomene Gumain*. Paris: Seul.

Toffler, Alvin. 1980. *The Third Wave*. London: Pan Books.

Toynbee, A.J. 1991. *A Study of History*. Moscow: Progress (in Russian).

Urlanis, B.Ts. 1994. *History of Warfare Losses*. St Petersburg: Polygon (in Russian).

Vartanian, S.R., Kh. A. Arslanov, T.V. Tertychnaia and S.V. Chernov. 1995. 'Radiocarbon Dating Evidence for Mammoths on Wrangell Island, Arctic Ocean, Until 2000 B.C.', *Radiocarbon*, 37(1): 1–6.

Vigasin, A.A. 1994. 'The Ancient China's Wise Men', in *Ancient World Viewed by the Contemporaries and the Historians: Part I—The Ancient East*, pp.183–207. Moscow: Interprax (in Russian).

Volovikova, M.I. and T.A. Rebeko. 1990. 'The Correlation of Cognitive and Moral Development', in *Psychology of Personality in the Socialist Society*, pp.81–87. Moscow: Nauka.

White, L.A. 1975. *The Concept of Cultural Systems: A Key to Understanding Tribes and Nations*. New York and London: Columbia University Press.

Wilson, E.O. 1978. *On Human Nature*. Cambridge, MA, and London: Harvard University Press.

Wright, Q. 1944. *Study of War, Vol. I*. Chicago: University of Chicago Press.

Yarkho, V.N. 1972. 'Did the Ancient Greeks Have A Conscience? (Towards the Representation of Humans in Antique Tragedy)', in *Antiquity and Modernity*, pp. 251–63. Moscow: Nauka (in Russian).

Towards a Critical Biography and the Legacy of the *Rishis*

17

Kautilya and the Calling of Political Ethics

GODABARISHA MISHRA

Then Krishna and Arjuna step down from their chariot, throw away their arms, walk into the fiery circle of that ultimate weapon and forcibly make Bhima obey and stop fighting. Then the weapon become quiescent and inactive. In the very midst of the discourse of violence what more eloquent testimony could there be to the power of non-resistance, or non-violent resistance, which is the quintessence of Gandhi's philosophy of non-violence.

—Mehta (1990: 255)

The ultimate aim of those who have power should be to promote social cooperation, not in one group, as against another, but in the whole human race. The chief obstacle to this end at present is the existence of feelings of unfriendliness and desire for superiority. Such feelings can be diminished either directly by religion and morality, or indirectly by removing the political and economic circumstances which at present stimulate them—notably the competition for power between states and the connected competition for wealth between large national industries. Both methods are needed: they are not alternatives, but supplement to each other.

—Russell (1983: 184)

Introduction and invitation

The Platonic ideal of a philosopher king has been a setting point of synthesizing power and wisdom, which ensures certain amount of freedom for the individual subject in a monarchical format of the government. The Machiavellian model of polity has not only discounted the individual liberty but also perceived the conflicting interplay between nobility and the common people as the basic source of the strength and vitality of Roman political life. The ancient Indian scenario of power and polity as depicted in the *Ramayana* and *Mahabharata* too convey a system of benevolent kingship, similar to the ideals of Plato, in which the monarch, hereditary or otherwise, is at the centre of power and individual freedom is subjected to the prevalent codes of conduct of that particular period legislated by the king, either by himself or with the assistance of the wise men around him. The love for power and position is a very universal phenomenon and the Indian epics are replete with such narrations of capturing power even by resorting to unethical means. The history of the epics contains numerous instances of such power-hungry royalties who instigate different varieties of battles and litigations to remain in power. The history of pre-Ashokan India records the profile of a priestly minister Kautilya, whose manoeuvring polity dethrones the Nanda dynasty and puts him at the centre of a power polity that empowers him to install Chandragupta, one of his disciples, as the king. The cases of passion for power are not a new phenomenon, as desire is an essential feature of human traits, though the *modus operandi* of accumulation of power differs from time to time and person to person.

The laws governing social dynamics are only capable of being stated in terms of power in various forms. In order to discover the inner dynamism, it is necessary to understand and review the historical examples of mechanisms of power in different ages and the persons who designed the stage for the proceedings of capturing power. The possession of power or the process of becoming powerful can be of different types. It need not be political all the times; it can be religious, spiritual and the like. Even in religions, a strong impulse of subordinating others has been clearly visible in different forms. The religious masters do not go to the forefront of the power struggle or polity but stage-manage the power process and become king makers instead of kings. As Russell (ibid.: 19) would put it, 'They attach to themselves people who combine a love of submission with an impulse to revolt.' Tolstoy, Kautilya and many others can be thought of belonging to this category of persons who in a different way control the whole power process in a particular set-up rather than taking the responsibilities involved in it and disowning the immanent disadvantages which may arise out of such a phenomenon.

Throughout the centuries, the political set-up and the religio-spiritual bodies have acted and interacted with each other like that of the Church and monarchy in mediaeval England. In ancient India, we find the *rishi*s, the saints, controlling the royalties and designing the statecrafts for them to perform duties in accordance with their specifications guaranteeing a benevolent sovereign for the subjects. This chapter aims at understanding the prince and the *rishi*s, standing for the power and the freedom in an ancient Indian set-up by examining the concept associated with the *rishi*s within the religious and philosophical framework of Hinduism.

An invitation to the world of *Rishi*s

The word *rishi* has been derived from the Sanskrit root '*ṛ*', which means to move or to perceive, and the term '*rishi*', which means a person who by his vision can transcend or go beyond the ordinary world. The term in its different connotations stands for the person showing ways and means to enlightenment, liberation and himself becoming a model of selfless service for others. An assessment of the significance of the different roles ascribed to *rishi*s shows that the *rishi* is a visionary who brings about a change or a transformation in himself and also in his surroundings. He is the one who devotes himself in rigorous ascetic pursuits in order to build up his inner resources of energy and becomes a powerhouse of potential energy that emanates from his austerities for the welfare of humankind. Because of extra-empirical attainments, he can create and recreate to expand and transform society around himself. Being content in himself, he directs his powers towards the external world with the sole purpose of maintaining righteousness, the correct order of the world. Ancient Indian history contains numerous examples of such *rishi*s who have made use of their influence by providing political and diplomatic nuances to the royalty, and nurtured kings and their subjects from the different crises that could have befallen them.

In keeping with the aforementioned paradigms of a *rishi*, an attempt has been made in this essay to show how Kautilya was successful as a centre of power polity in the Mauryan empire and though he yielded so much power, he was indifferent to execute an iota of it and preferred to take to teaching his students. A similar example is seen in the case of the Vijayanagara empire where the *madhavacharya* (Vidyaranya) played an important role in installing Bukka as the king, relegating himself to the background. The synthesis of a prince and a *rishi* is found in the Buddha who had no desire to wield any political power at all. This becomes a different question altogether as the transformation of Gautama, the prince, to the Buddha, a *Rishi*, made him to transcend the state of a prince, the political power centre. The examples of a number of social reformers in pre- and post-independent India can be cited in favour of their *rishi*-hood as they tried to engage themselves in social services without getting into the nexus of political power-centres. Gandhi, Phule, Periyar and many others were the centres of political potency that they did not make use of. Their ideas and ideals were used by others who wielded power by resorting to the ideology propagated by their masters. This chapter, using examples from ancient Indian literature, analyzes the shift from ancient *rishi*-hood to the contemporary centres of power by depicting the legacy of the ancient *rishi*s in their austerity and indifference to power.

Rishi tradition and its relevance

As has been pointed out, ancient Indian literature gives us a wide range of personalities who decided the destiny of kings and authored treatises on the science of polity for the smooth running of the kingdom. The role of Visvamitra and Vasistha in the *Ramayana*, and Sandipana, Dronacharya and many others in the *Mahabharata* endorse this point. In vedic India, the *rishi*s were the seers who envisioned the eternal vedic hymns. In other words, the hymns were revealed to them in the sense of divine revelations, which means they were the vehicles or the means whereby these 'eternal revelations' were made known to humankind. This role of a *rishi*, though an important one, had no implication on the political set-up of any period. The second important connotation of the term *rishi* is that of the sacrificer, *purohita*, and has immense importance as it underlies the fulfilment of a desire. The word *purohita* means 'a person leading from the front'. In many epic narrations, we find *rishi*s performing sacrifices for kings for the fulfilment of their desires. The famous example is of Vasistha performing sacrificial anointing for Dasaratha for offspring, rain, and so on. The third implication of the term is that of a teacher as distinct from their role as seers or sacrificers, as it emphasizes activities in passing on and handing down knowledge and revelation which they have received. This shows their control on the royalty and their loyalty towards them. For example, Visvamitra taught the sons of Dasaratha, and Vasistha took Bhisma, the son of Santanu, as his pupil and taught him the ancient lores. There are many examples in the epics and *purana*s in which a *rishi* is said to have given instructions to an enquirer or pupil, thereby emphasizing the role of the *rishi*s as teachers who give instructions on both sacred and secular matters, so that the future power centres would be well-versed in the nuances of statecraft and other allied subjects to run the state.

The performance of *tapas* might rightly be termed one of the most characteristic pursuits of the *rishi*s. The word *tapas* is derived from the Sanskrit root *tap* meaning heat. Thus, *tapas* conveys the idea of inward heating in the sense of disciplining through the performance of various religious and ascetic practices. The aim of performing *tapas* is directed to certain inward and outward transformations in the performer, giving a divine status to a gross and material form of the performer. This bestows them certain extra empirical powers that may be creative or destructive, always aiming at the welfare of the society at large. As has been noted earlier, the *rishi*s of ancient India had enough interaction with kings. With their visionary ideas, they were often successful in obtaining conquests for the kings. There are instances when a *rishi* would destroy the enemies of a king by sacrifice. For example, when King Mucukunda's army was destroyed by demons, the king appealed to his *purohita* Vasistha, who killed the demons by his austerities and then instructed the king at great length as to how a king depends on the *rishi* for success (*Mahabharata* 12.75.1 ff.). In several instances, the *rishi*s have extended shelters to exiled or cursed kings. When King Trisanku had been cursed by Vasistha, Visvamitra agreed to become his *purohita* and eventually transferred him to the sky, that is, Trisnku Svarga (*Valmiki Ramayana*, 1.56.10 ff.). In certain cases, the *rishi*s had significant influence on kings, as evident in the case of Vasistha persuading a reluctant Dasaratha to part with his sons Rama and Laksmana to go with him to kill notorious demons. Bharadvaja is said to have composed a treatise on the statecraft and the duties of the kings. Visvamitra, a *ksatriya* and a king, renounced both his kingdom and *ksatriya*-hood in order to become a *brahmarshi*, which shows that it is not proper for an *rishi* to exercise political authority.

Though the institution of *rishi*s is based on the concepts of non-violence, austerity and the like, we find many of them having continuous involvement in world affairs, at times out of sheer necessity. There is sanction in the tradition that *rishi*s should try their best for *loka-sangraha* (welfare of the people) in the state of *vyutihana*, and out of sheer compassion, *rishi*s take to such means of social services for the benefit of humankind.[1] The *rishi*s are not simply meek and humble individuals devoted only to the trans-empirical destinations. They become detached from the unreal and phenomenal aspect of the material existence, yet merge with the real, which is an integral part of the phenomenal and the material (Mitchiner 1982: 305). In other words, the *rishi*-hood consists of an attainment which transcends any material or other attainments, as the very idea of gain is attached to sense beyond the sense of 'I' and 'mine'. Their understanding of reality does not negate the world; rather, it makes a fresh reaffirmation of reality, denying the only existence of a material world and they try to bring illumination to all who come across them.

Powering politics:
The Kautilian way

In the following passages, we shall dwell upon the character of Kautilya who wielded power and became instrumental in the establishment of the Maurya empire, making Chandragupta the emperor. The contribution of Kautilya to the history of power politics is diverse, interesting and full of diplomatic sophistication. A person of extraordinary achievement, he was respected for his insight and wisdom. His ideas and insights on the statecraft and diplomacy are yet to be critically assessed in the light of modern political thinking. In spite of him being an extreme realist, he represented the abiding virtues of the ancient Indian way of life and thought. His magnum opus *Arthashastra* is an epitome of political thinking of his times and has had tremendous influence on later writings on similar themes. Kautilya clearly explains his indebtedness to earlier authors on the science of polity. This shows that the study of statecraft was not something very new as held by Western scholars and ancient India did have its ways to maintain and manage statecraft.

Arthashastra contains a mine of information on several social, religious and political issues. Kautilya stood for the materialistic aspirations of man, as he strongly felt that spiritual pursuits could not be undertaken without basic material comforts. To him, spirit and matter did not completely divorce from each other. His political ideas revolved around the king as the centre of society and state. Hence, as a minister and a king maker, his problems were those of maintaining and improving the strength of the royalty rather than the society and the state as a whole. He felt that a benevolent and secure king would be able to take care of the welfare of the state. Kautilya gave a higher meaning and purpose to Indian political thought through his extraordinary genius and understanding. Though he advocated monarchy, he wanted them to be responsible and answerable to the people. He enunciated the emancipation of slaves and women, and mitigation of judicial torture. Kautilya gave importance to the basic common sense than that of the codified laws. That is amply demonstrated in the steady rise of the Mauryan empire, as Kautilya uprooted the earlier corrupt kings when he felt that there was a desperate need for change. In this sense, he was a revolutionary in activities and ideas. This seems to be a digression from the age-old law that one should not work against the king. Kautilya was of the opinion that in case of a conflict between the sacred law and the rational interpretation of *dharma*, reason shall be authoritative. And that is what has been the touchstone of his righteousness, which has been amply demonstrated in the way he tackled the Nanda dynasty and brought Chandragupta to the throne. For him, power was justified in terms of protection and in conformity with the conception of *dharma*. The greatness of Kautilya as a *rishi* lies in his advocacy of restraint and discipline as the foundation of power. His *Arthashastra* is a collection of rules and maxims that a king would be wise to follow if he wishes to acquire and wield power. As to how a prince can maintain power and enlarge it, the ideas of Kautilya are like that of Machiavelli, but in many respects the former differs strongly from the latter.

Kautilya: A life of action

Kautilya seems to be an ordinary teacher of politics as far as his profession is concerned.[2] One legend has it that he was a Kerala *brahmin*, impoverished and lean who found himself in the court of the Nanda king at Pataliputra. Another legend relates that he was a north Indian *brahmin*, born and educated in the famous university town of Taxila, who came to Pataliputra to win laurels from the royalty in philosophic disputation. From Buddhist sources we come to know that he was known for his proficiency in three *veda*s, the *mantra*s, stratagem, dexterity in intrigue and policy, but also for his physical ugliness, disgusting complexion, deformity of legs and other limbs.[3] He was responsible for the disintegration of the Nanda dynasty, that is, the hereditary rule of the Nandas from the throne of Magadha. When it came to administration, he did not tamper with the Magadh empire; rather made Chandragupta the ruler. He says, 'In the happiness of his subjects lies the king's happiness; in their welfare his welfare. He shall not consider as good only that which pleases him but treat as beneficial to him whatever pleases his subjects' (Unni 2006: 103). We may find parallels to this in the writings of modern thinkers. Bertrand Russell (1983: 184) held such a view:

> The ultimate aim of those who have power should be to promote social cooperation, not in one group, as against another, but in the whole human race. The chief obstacle to this end at present is the existence of feelings of unfriendliness and desire for superiority. Such feelings can be diminished either directly by religion and morality, or indirectly by

removing the political and economic circumstances which at present stimulate them—notably the competition for power between states and the connected competition for wealth between large national industries. Both methods are needed: they are not alternatives but supplement to each other.

Nicolo Machiavelli (1469–1527), in his book *The Prince* (1952), argues that the state should wield all power. He discounted individual liberty and proposed his theory stating that the basic strength and vitality of the nation depends on the binary opposition between the state and its citizens.

Kautilya's *Arthashastra*, a treatise on the art of governance, is based on a similar theme. It is meant to instruct all kings about *rajadharma*. For Kautilya, the existence of the state and the king are pre-eminent. In fact, the king and his rule encapsulate all the constituents of the state (*Arthashastra*, 8.2.1). Kautilya's special contributions to the theoretical analysis of the functioning of the state are:

(*a*) analysis of aspects of internal administration in terms of the six constituent elements of the state, and

(*b*) analysis of the relations between states in terms of the theory of the circle of states.

The rest of the treatise is a manual of instruction for kings and officers of the state. It is true that many areas covered by the *Arthashastra* are also included in the *Dharmashastras*. There is, however, a crucial difference between the two. The *Dharmashastras* address themselves to the individual, teaching him his *dharma* and regard deviations from it as sins to be expiated by rituals. The *Arthashastra* is addressed to rulers and regards transgressions of law as crimes to be punished by the state. From the quotations and references in *Arthashastra*, we know that there were at least four distinct schools and thirteen individual teachers of *Arthashastra* before Kautilya.

Kautilya as depicted in *Mudraraksasa*

In discussing a critical biography of a political *rishi*, it would be worthwhile to portray how the character of Kautilya has been depicted by the eighth-century dramatist, Visakhadatta in his famous *Mudraraksasa*. The dramatic theme centres on Kautilya (here named Chanakya) who has installed Chandragupta as the king by vanquishing the Nanda dynasty. The detailed development of the drama is complicated but perspicuous; ingenious but highly interesting from a dramatic point of view. The drama is a significant historical and political play that unfolds the diplomacy of Kautilya to overthrow the Nandas and place Chandragupta on the throne and appoint Raksasa, a Nanda follower, as the minister. The drama in its last act sees the minister Raksasa cornered and compelled to accept the ministership of Chandragupta. Although sharp and relentless and having mastered the art of deception, impersonation and forgery, as depicted in the drama, Kautilya is depicted as a cool and ingenious plotter. His nobility is not spared even though he engages in all diplomatic movements to achieve his ends. The third act of the play begins with the observation of the chamberlain (Kanchuki) as he happens to visit the house of Kautilya. He says (*Mudraraksasa*, 3. 15,16):

> This is noble Chanakya's home,
> Let me enter *(entering and observing)*
> Oh, the affluence of the King of the kings,
> Thus:
> 'Here is a piece of stone for breaking the cow dung cakes,
> here is a heap of Kusa grass brought by the young disciples;
> the shed too is seen with dilapidated walls and the corners of the roof,
> bent down by putting holy sticks exposed to drying.'

> But it is proper that to him the king Chandragupta is only an idiot (Vrsala).

> 'Those person who speak the truth, indulge in words through helplessness and belaud the Lord with mouths tired even foe qualities, which he does not possess—all that is indeed the full power of the desire. Otherwise to those whose desire is gone completely a king is an object of disrespect like a straw.'

This is an example of simple living and high profile that Kautilya embodied in his thinking and action. None of his actions in the play is shown to be an outcome of doubt or apprehension; he does everything out of sheer knowledge and conviction of things, and the play proves the diplomatic capability of a person in the role of Kautilya.

Since it is a political drama, its ethical significance has to be understood from a political angle. Kautilya has been portrayed as a person who can upstage his enemies without employing any weapons. This becomes clear from a statement in *Arthashastra* (chapter 6), where he says: 'An arrow shot by an archer may or may not kill a person but intellect devised by wise men may kill even those who are in the womb.' *Mudraraksasa* shows how the proper application of political expedients prevents the danger of war and brings forth peace and stability in the state without bloodshed. The capture of Malayaketu and winning over of Raksasa to the side of Chandragupta are achieved without any war or bloodshed. Kautilya displays his mastery of the secret as against a more risky open war. He holds all power over the king who is his disciple, but like a good *brahmin*, he continues to stay in a forest hut devoting himself to the education of his disciples. Kautilya declares that his intellect, which has exhibited its prowess by uprooting the Nandas, is by itself endowed with the strength of more than a hundred armies (*Mudraraksasa*, 1.25). In the depiction of the character of Kautilya, Visakhadatta wants to stress the point that intellectual prowess (*mantra-sakti*) is superior to valour (*utsaha-sakti*) or royal power (*prabhu-sakti*).

As to the moral dimension of the play, it may be observed that it represents a curious state of public morals in which fraud and assassination are the means by which inconvenient obligations are acquitted, and troublesome friends and open enemies are removed (Wilson 1935: 92). It raises the age-old question as to what is the place of ethics in the sphere of politics. The ethics on politics appears to be different from ordinary ethics. This ideal is also relevant in case of the *Bhagavad Gita*, since Krishna talks of ethics from a different angle. The diplomacy of Kautilya makes liberal use of fraud and assassination to subserve his political end. But because of that the greater evil of mass destruction is averted (*Mudraraksasa*, 1.11). The avoidance of a greater war is not an immoral act and can be justified ethically.

A close reading of the play reveals that in the very beginning itself, it is made clear that all means are to be directed, deliberately planned and effected with great skill to secure Raksasa as the minister of Chandragupta. Kautilya watches all the movements of Raksasa and spoils his efforts, and ultimately succeeds in throwing him in a desperate condition so that he has to yield as the minister and serve his previous enemy and present king Chandragupta his accused foe. Well designed in the beginning, the play advances towards its goal through the turnings of the events showing the well-organized execution of the plans to one crowning effect. One thing that is evident in and through the play is its compromises with normal ethical modes of life. Usually a play ought to teach good morals and virtue should always succeed in the long run, and vice and cruelty be punished as they deserve. This one does it in a different way. It is not that such acts are not held in themselves as crimes or the perpetrators engaged, instigated by vulgarity or ferocity, are not condemned as culprits. But when such an enterprise is undertaken for a political end, it becomes compatible with virtue. So there is a necessity of looking at the character of Kautilya from a different angle. Fraud is no doubt used, but used for the noble purpose of winning over Raksasa to Chandragupta's side. A man of sterling virtues and great administrative talents, Kautilya knew that Raksasa was a champion of the lost cause. To allow him to have his own way would have entailed needless suffering and misery for himself, for Chandragupta and for the country. To avoid all these and to see that virtue was properly rewarded, Kautilya directed all his efforts in a particular direction. His objective was not to become the prime minister himself. Hence, to situate renunciative motivations of Kautilya with fraudulent means, we need to look at the problem from a different angle. Kautilya was driven to adopt such a course because of the exceptional circumstances of his times. The Nanda kings were unpopular and there was a political revolution spearheaded by Chandragupta to overthrow the Nanda king. Chandragupta appealed to Kautilya for help and the latter was convinced that by helping him he would not only help the right man but also the right cause. Now the task before him was to accomplish his objective with the least possible bloodshed or trouble to the people. There were two ways available to Kautilya: to be guilty of adoption of fraudulent means for the removal of a few political adversaries; or to plunge the country into general warfare and carnage. He chose the lesser of the two evils. Not that he did not know the sinful enterprises, but he could not help it in keeping with his end of bringing about a peaceful society ruled by a just king. In accomplishing this end, people like Parvataka, Sarvarthasiddhi and the five allies of Malayketu were killed. The unsuspecting Malayketu was betrayed and made a captive, but Kautilya restored him to his original possessions. Excepting the aforementioned, he was not directly responsible for any other homicide that occurs in the play. The threatened executions of Sakatadasa and Chanadanadasa were meant more as political expedience than ends to be accomplished. Thus, the noble intention of stabilizing the country redeems Kautilya of the immorality with which he might otherwise be associated. Hence, his ethics must be seen in the background of political ethics, and not ordinary or individual ethics.

Notwithstanding the love of glory and spirit of heroism, Kautilya acted with full confidence as though he knew the exact course of happenings in the state. In this regard, he can be compared to any *rishi* who wants to engage himself for the welfare of humankind. His polity is a possibility of a disciplined social order as a condition precedent for individual achievement. In this, Kautilya is nearer to Aristotle, not to Machiavelli. Machiavelli stood for force and Kautilya for perseverance (*udyama*). Like Aristotle, Kautilya appealed to a sense of honour, duty, human dignity, moral responsibility and enlightenment, in the name of *dharma*. He recognized the importance of power in politics for the acquisition and maintenance of wealth and security. He despised slavery unlike Plato and Aristotle, who felt that there were some people born to serve and others to be served. The play-sequences quoted here shed a lot of light on the lifestyle of Kautilya in spite of the enormous royal laurels he could command. It shows that though he was powerful to make and transform power centres by his visionary ideas and implementations, he cherished to remain a teacher all through, without taking up the benefits that went with posts of power. This shows the renunciative attitude of Kautilya and his legacy of a saint diplomat as the author of the *Arthashastra*.

Conclusion

In India, any thinker or reformer may be described as an *rishi* if he has significantly contributed to the welfare of the society without any selfish motives. For example, even a thinker like Carvaka, who was the proponent of materialistic hedonism, has been referred to as a *rishi* since he was the one who gave a logical base to the materialism and denied extra-empirical ethos of certain texts and beliefs. So is the case of Vatsyayana, who authored a treatise on sex and sexual practices, and has been respected as a *rishi* in this tradition. But Kautilya is a *rishi* because he perceived the pre-eminence of life and ethical living as an outcome of good governance. His period was marked by political disorder, mal-administration and anarchical form of government perpetuated by the Nanda kings. Because of his farsighted vision and implementation, he could reorganize the entire state, ensuring honest and efficient administration. In this sense, there is a complete agreement between Plato, Aristotle and Kautilya regarding ethics and politics as identical, which provides more space to normal ethics, with the aim that the happy life is virtuous life, for the fulfilment of which the whole of creation moves. Unlike Machiavelli, for Kautilya, the separation between politics and morality was unthinkable, and political power acquired legitimacy only when it promoted human happiness.

There are two aspects of a *rishi*; one who prefers to stay in solitude to practise his penance out of sheer understanding of the reality, and the other who engages in action by coming back to society out of sheer compassion to share the miseries of the humankind to develop a healthy social order, which may ultimately show the path of liberation to others. In *Advaita Vedanta*, they may be called *jivan-muktas* and various other terms in other traditions, but the fact remains that they are the ones who could serve humankind without any selfish motive, as has been the prime paradigm assigned to *rishis* in the Indian tradition. It is on that score that the Buddha, Mahavira, Jesus, and all the sages, saints and reformers down the ages are *rishis*, as they have endeavoured to salvage fallen people and pave the way towards a respectable human society.

Notes

1. The example of Sankaracharya may be cited in this context. Though as a Sannyasin, he is supposed to be engaged in tapas and meditation, he took to social service and established four monasteries in different parts of the country to spread his message of unity.
2. The name 'Kautilya' denotes that he is of the *kutila gotra*, and 'Chanakya' shows him to be the son of Chanaka, though his personal name was Vishnugupta.
3. According to Buddhist and Jain traditions, his parents noticed that Kautilya was born with a full set of teeth, a mark of a future king. They had the teeth removed (making him uglier) because neither the father nor the mother did want him to become a king. He became a king maker instead.

References

Machiavelli, Nicolo. 1952. *The Prince*. London: William Benton Publisher, Encyclopaedia Britannica Inc.

Mehta, J.L. 1990. *Philosophy and Religion*. New Delhi: Indian Council of Philosophical Research.

Mitchiner, J.E. 1982. *Tradition of Seven Rishis*. New Delhi: Motilal Banarsidas Publishers.

Russell, Bertand. 1983. *Power*. London: Unwin and Co.

Unni, N.P. (Trans.). 2006. *The Arthasastra of Kautilya*. New Delhi: New Bharatiya Book Corporation, Delhi.

Wilson, H.H. 1935. *The Theatre of the Hindus*. London: Allen Unwin and Co., London.

Meister Eckhart

The Power of Inner Liberation[1]

18

DIETMAR MIETH

Introduction

Speaking of 'inner liberation' today could be dangerously misunderstood: poverty and war, suppression and suffering everywhere call for action, for actual political and social liberation. In this context, Meister Eckhart's 'power of inner liberation' is a scandal. It is, however, a scandal that reveals the core of every religious liberation movement: *vita activa* (active life) and *vita contemplativa* (contemplative life) are intertwined. Spiritual liberation has the power to create political consequences; Christology can be understood through a radical social approach and encompasses the solidarity of human beings in Christ.

Neither this radical theology nor Meister Eckhart as a theologian are without context. Neither his person nor his theology can be adequately understood without remembering his relationship to extraordinary women like Marguerite Porete and Agnes of Hungary, and his relationship to the women of the Bible. The influence of women's religious history on this master of the Holy Bible is often forgotten. This is a kind of forgetfulness that did not end at the end of medieval times. Remembering this forgetfulness, we recognize the connection between Eckhart and Elisabeth Schüssler Fiorenza, not only in their discipline and in their trans-disciplinary approach to this discipline but, above all, in the spirit of liberation. The master of the power of inner liberation certainly would have appreciated Schüssler's power in the whole field of liberation.

Meister Eckhart: His life and works

There is considerable interest in Meister Eckhart (1260–1328) worldwide, even within the context of non-Christian approaches to religious experience. Through his connections to Jewish and Islamic philosophy and mysticism, Eckhart also lives on in such traditions. Declared atheists, too, are fascinated by his thought, at least those with a religious background, or *Religion im Erbe* (Bloch 1970). A representative example is Erich Fromm (1976). His book *Haben und Sein* is well known (see also Frederking 1994). The chapter on Eckhart is relatively brief (refer to my works for further detail). Yet, Erich Fromm, the famous humanistic psychologist, actually read Eckhart daily over a period of twenty years, more frequently than he last read Karl Marx and Sigmund Freud, his other sources in addition to the Bible. Following in-depth correspondence,[2] I had the opportunity to spend an intense working weekend with Fromm in Locarno in 1975. He impressed me greatly and we continued our correspondence on Eckhart for a while. Unfortunately, his health did not allow any further studies. Despite our consensus in reading Eckhart, we remained divided on the question of God. Fromm read Eckhart agnostically; I read him theologically, from a Christian perspective (Mieth 2002).

Meister Eckhart is, in my opinion, the communicator of a transmitted compendium of experience accessible through the Judaeo–Christian Bible with the assistance of philosophical interpretation. In accordance with his title, *magister sacrae scripturae*, he was a *meister*, an expert on the Holy Scriptures, an exegete, an interpreter of scripture. In fact, Eckhart was both exegete and philosopher, since he considered it essential to interpret the Holy Scriptures 'with the natural arguments of the philosophers' (see LW[3]: 361).[3] His approach was two-fold: to open the Bible to the highest form of scientific knowledge—in the tradition of his teacher, Albert the Great—and to interpret it with the subtlest type of philosophical thought. The reverse is also conceivable: to retranslate the subtlest form of philosophical thought and the broadest forms of human knowledge about the world into the language of faith, that is, given these intellectual possibilities, and given these possibilities in knowledge, to revert to an authentic, existentially fundamental experience. Faith and its 'virtues', hope and love, are to be taken seriously.

Meister Eckhart is, thus, the historical mediator of a philosophically established experience of belief. Beyond this he also partakes in the widespread contemporary interest in the Middle Ages. Currently, historical novels on the Middle Ages are in abundance. There are even murder mysteries intentionally set in the Middle Ages to captivate readers with the ambience of medieval life. The entire trend can be summarized in the title of a single novel, Umberto Eco's *The Name of the Rose*. This novel, also filmed very vividly, is set in northern Italy during the first decade of the fourteenth century, the time of Meister Eckhart. The Dominican was then over forty years of age and at the peak of his creativity, a recognized scholar and *magister* in Paris. Eckhart held this university position from 1301 to 1303, a great honour for a medieval scholar, the greatest conceivable at that time. Later he was awarded this Dominican chair of theology in Paris again from 1311 to 1313. The only other person to have received this honour before him was Thomas Aquinas. In *The Name of the Rose*, there are numerous quotations from Eckhart. This wealth of quotations is not at all surprising given the biographical origins of the fictitious monk, Adso of Melk (Melk is a Benedictine monastery in Austria where many mystic texts were copied).

The title *meister*, that is, *magister*, is from Eckhart's position in Paris. This was the same chair which his *confrere* and predecessor, Thomas Aquinas, held during the fifties of the preceding century. Thomas Aquinas died in 1274, on the way to the Council of Lyons. The Dominican *studium generale* in Cologne, where Albert the Great taught Thomas Aquinas, was the first German university—a Dominican university.

Eckhart's first literary texts in the German language date to the last decade of the thirteenth century. One extant text entitled *Reden der Unterweisung* (1293–94) is written in Middle High German. These *Reden der Unterweisung*, literally, talks of instruction, arising from conversations on religious questions following meals with the friars in Erfurt. Whoever has been a guest at a monastery is familiar with the custom of strolling in the garden after the midday meal.

Spirituality is a concept that I have attempted to describe as the intellectuality of the spirit and the spiritualness of the intellect (Haug and Mieth 1992). Spirituality always encompasses a certain intellectual dynamics. It is neither pure emotion nor an undertaking carried by feelings. Today it has become fashionable to polemicize against the intellectualization that purportedly plays such a central role in philosophy, theology, and other academic disciplines. The appropriate refutation of this enormously popular reproach is that the human brain is also body.

The question of intellectuality, of thought, is crucial to the study of Meister Eckhart. The *meister* radiates an undeniable intellectual fascination. Yet, it is not exclusively an intellectual fascination. Eckhart is not only capable of thinking in an adventurously abstract manner; he is equally capable of expressing himself in an extremely vivid manner. This explains his fascination as a highly figurative preacher. He can speak of fire, consuming a piece of wood, and of the human being, analogous to this piece of wood, suffering from the burning of the fire as long as he or she has not taken on the form of the fire, has not yet become light, warmth and heat. Only the surrender of that which burns us, namely, being wooden, being individual, offers the possibility of becoming uniform with the burning fire. Glowing without burning is a concrete image and, at the same time, exceedingly abstract. Expressions such as *'feuerförmig sein'*, literally, having the form of fire, belong to the discourse of philosophical thought and must be imagined as well as contemplated.

In 1302, Meister Eckhart was sent to Paris as a *magister* in theology. The chair was one of the Dominican Order reserved for non-French citizens. Teaching was limited to one academic year, during the course of which the new *magister* had the opportunity to enter the debate on the theological issues of the age. He did so with verve, and there is a second significant literary textuality in his writings, the questions (*quaestiones*) on the relationship between understanding and being in God. The quintessence of the theses under discussion was: 'God's being is his understanding' (*Deus est intelligere*). With this thesis—comparable to a German *Habilitationsschrift* today—Eckhart established his reputation as a scholar. A year later, in 1303, he was directed to leave the academic world and was entrusted with the administration of the newly created province of Saxony, the northern part of the German Dominican province. He held the office of the provincial for seven years, a very long tenure for the times. In addition, in 1307 he administered the Bohemian province as vicar-general, quasi as acting Dominican master-general, during the period, without a provincial. The activity of visitation, primarily consisting of travelling, can only be described as exhausting, given the great distances involved.

In 1311, the Dominican General Chapter in Naples did not, however, confirm Eckhart's election as the provincial for a different province (Teutonia). Eckhart had been elected by this south German province, apparently to carry out a reorganization similar to that in the north German province. Instead, the Domnican General Chapter sent him to the University of Paris for the second time (1311–13). There Eckhart attempted, ostensibly for the first time, to organize his scholarly writings. These were scholarly texts, occasional pieces and sermons written during his travels as a provincial. Surprisingly, unlike Augustine, he did not sigh over the lack of time remaining for contemplation, for a life of tranquility. Nowhere is such a lament to be found, although there is a sermon (Pr. 60 [Largier 1993: vol 1; DW: vol. 3]) on the verse from Ecclesiasticus: 'Among all these I searched for rest.'

Following this second mastership at the University of Paris from 1311 to 1313—Eckhart was already fifty four years old—he was appointed to another important but difficult position. In 1313, he went to Strasbourg as vicar for the Dominican master general, where he remained until 1322 or 1323, an entire decade. This was his longest term as *lehrmeister*, and, the concept surfaces in his writings of the period, as *lebemeister*. Within the framework of the so-called *cura monalium*, the supervision of women of orders delegated to the Dominicans, Meister Eckhart was, above all, commissioned to oversee the spiritual life in the convents on the Upper Rhine, that is, in the region surrounding Basel and Strasbourg.

What did this entail? A huge religious movement was to be integrated, that is, a movement at its peak along the Rhine river aound 1300. This was the religious movement of the Beguines. The Beguines, who played such a major role in Meister Eckhart's destiny, were free groups of women who, often following the deaths of their husbands, in times of war or in times of a surplus of women in general, or perhaps, in times of a new 'emancipation' of women, joined together to lead a simple religious life in poverty. Initially they earned a living by organizing burials and for this reason, often had their houses near cemeteries. The Beguines also undertook charitable activities related to nursing, and tried to organize themselves as houses of prayer—women among women.

Beyond the Beguines, there were innumerable other religious movements, of men or women, that cannot be totally reconstructed. The religious movements of this age were extremely diverse, perhaps comparable to the current esoteric trends. Many of these religious movements in the early fourteenth century were not in accordance with the orthodox conception of Christian belief or of the Church, at that time a colossal organization fragilely united with the state. Synods were convened in an endeavour to separate the wheat from the chaff, the teachings often being inordinately vague. At the same time, endeavours were made to generate renewal and peace on an organizational level. One measure was the attempted reorganization of the parishes. The religious movements had effected a flight from the parishes: the Beguines, and a large percentage of their sympathizers, gathered in public squares, or in the churches of the minorities, the Franciscans or the Dominicans, and listened to the travelling missionaries and preachers. Meister Eckhart did not function in this capacity on the Upper Rhine, but as an officially sanctioned preacher and as a representative of the general Magister of the Dominicans.[4] These 'independent believers' no longer attended mass at their parish churches and parishes began to disintegrate (for example, in Strasbourg). The bishops reacted with the powers invested in them by initiating a counter-movement: the decision was made to reorganize the parishes and to prohibit the alternative church services in the public squares. Order was to be restored; order was to be reinstated under the crozier.

A second, related measure was the attempted integration of as many religious women and their communities as possible—communities which existed freely and independently—into the existing orders, above all the Dominican Order, under the aegis of the advisory male friars. There were approximately one million Beguines between Amsterdam and Basel. Obviously, this was an arduous undertaking delegated to Eckhart in his mid-fifties, a relatively advanced age at the time. To all appearances, he considered it his duty to carry out these measures to restore order as humanly as possible, and to spiritually accompany and practically organize the inflow of the women's movement into the convents.

Enmity and the trial

On one hand, this was management of the highest calibre; on the other hand, a position demanding a great deal of the spirituality that characterized Eckhart so distinctly: serenity, inner release and self-detachment. Amazingly, Eckhart even had an excellent reputation among women during this time. Much of the knowledge about him is based on the legends that arose around the figure. These legends consistently portray him as modest as well as capable of listening and learning (Quint 1979: 422–88 ['Eckhart Legenden']). Moreover, the women were interested in the transcriptions of his sermons held in German. Not all but a large majority of these sermons are from this period, that is, between 1313 and 1326.

From 1323 to 1326, Eckhart was offered a chair in the Dominican *studium generale* in Cologne, once again a transition to an academic profession. The exercise of alternating between theory and praxis, undoubtedly, allowed a greater proximity between the ivory towers of the university and the practical realms of everyday life.

It is not absolutely clear whether Eckhart's transfer to Cologne by the General Chapter of the Order was not, in actuality, the 'political' relocation of a figurehead. This measure was ostensibly undertaken in conjunction with Church politics. During the course of his office in Strasbourg between 1313 and 1323, accusations surfaced for the first time. These reproaches had two different tenors. In his *Rechtfertigungsschrift* of 1326, Eckhart described the first as his 'ardour for justice'. Today it requires fantasy to imagine that it was a humanitarian concern for the persecuted who very easily landed in the clutches of the Inquisition, once this gigantic chaos of religious movements had arisen. Despite all conflicts, the Church—and the state as bailiff of the Church—strove to maintain order. To keep these powers at bay is difficult, particularly if this is seen under humanitarian aspects. Eckhart once said that heresy is a matter of the will.[5] In other words, he did not consider anyone a heretic who did not intend to be heretical. Mere erroneousness in comprehension did not, in his opinion, constitute heresy. Only insistence—unabating, deliberate insistence—on a condition in which the erroneousness had long since been evident, was heresy in his opinion and in the legal opinion of his time (Trusen 1988: 98, 106ff., 164–83).

Meister Eckhart's 'ardour for justice' was the reproach. The other, perhaps not unrelated, was his preaching in the vernacular. In the churches of the mendicant orders, of the Dominicans and the Franciscans, as well as in other orders, Eckhart had preached differently, though not in content, in another manner than earlier (as the provincial). In the years between 1304 and 1311, as the provincial, he also held sermons in German. An almost complete collection of these sermons in German is extant. Its title, *Paradisus Animae Intelligentis*, means 'The Paradise of the Intellectual', that is, the comprehending soul, the paradise of the human beings who possess insight or actively seek deeper insight. Today it is difficult to translate the title correctly because in Eckhart's day the word 'intellectual' hovered between comprehension and experience. In these sermons, however, one theme which later becomes so characteristic for Eckhart does not yet appear, namely, the theme of the *Gottesgeburt*.[6]

Of course, as the spiritual director of the Order, and the provincial, Eckhart also preached in Latin. There are fascinating Latin sermons written by him. I have edited a book on Eckhart's sermons and other texts including a number of his Latin sermons (Mieth 2002: 263–345) in order to present the unity of his thought as well as the scope of his manner of expression. The Latin sermons are sermons composed in an art form, highly literary in style, an intellectual delight for theologians who enjoyed listening to such artful works.

Beyond these Latin sermons, Eckhart also wrote commentaries on the Holy Scriptures in Latin, in accordance with the vocation and self-conception of a *magister sacrae scripturae*. The most significant was the commentary on the book of John. This may possibly have been written during his second period of residence in Paris. Late in life, Eckhart undertook the attempt to systematically organize his writings. His conception was an *opus tripartitum*, that is, collected works in three parts. The sermons and the exegetical texts were to constitute the last of these three parts. He apparently comprehended his sermons as an integral part of the third part, the *opus expositionem*, that is, the scholarly exegesis. Today only fragments of this tripartite work are extant. Many of the texts have been lost and, as his biography suggests, Eckhart had very little time to compile a scholarly edition.

As for Strasbourg, according to Eckhart, the reproaches were directed towards the 'ardour' which he had for 'justice' (see Ruh 1989: 179). This was the one aspect of the problem. The other was that he dared to preach to 'the uneducated'.[7] He exhibited virtuosity in his mastery of the Latin art form of the sermon. He also commanded the German language brilliantly, with the greatest malleability it had developed through courtly literature and religious writers, for example, Mechthild of Magdeburg, in the thirteenth century. The malleability and expressiveness of the German language that he attained assured him an esteemed position in medieval German literature. In fact, much of the research on Eckhart is carried out by scholars of medieval German literature; the figure, the innovative use of the German language, together with his thought being a exceptionally challenging and profound topic. This was the language of his sermons to the 'uneducated'.

Eckhart also preached to monks in this language as well as to scholars. His *Buch der göttlichen Tröstung* stands in the tradition of consolation through philosophy. In the sixth century, for example, Boethius wrote a famous consolation of philosophy. Eckhart's consolation is written in German, that is, the greatest intellectual consolations, which a philosopher and theologian developed in self-monologues on the divine, were thus accessible to everyone. In the conclusion to this book, he directly addresses the reproach mentioned earlier: 'I am told that I should not hold these sermons to the uneducated.' And counters: 'If one doesn't speak to the uneducated about learned things, no one would ever become educated.'[8] These sentences anticipate his magnificent speech in self-defence. Eckhart sent the *Buch der göttlichen Tröstung* with a personal dedication to Queen Agnes of Hungary, who no longer reigned and then resided between Basel and Zurich. Her father, Albrecht I of Austria, the son of Rudolf of Hapsburg, had been assassinated in 1308. However, Eckhart's book on consolation can hardly allude to this since, as Kurt Ruh (1985: 117; 1996: 308ff.) has convincingly shown, it was written during the Dominican's sojourn in Strasbourg (around 1318), and the dedication was more likely intended to explain his manner of preaching, and garner support (for sermons to the uneducated?). At this time, Lewis of Bavaria was ruling in Germany, and John XXII rectified the finances of the Church as Pope in Avignon. John XXII is also known for his rigid regulation of the dispute on ecclesiastical poverty. In resolution, all those who were of the opinion that not only the individual but the entire order should be poor were burnt at stake.

In the midst of this chaos, this wildly raging controversy over the renewal of Christianity from its very foundations, someone is preaching to the 'uneducated', who comprehend everything according to their personal intellectual capacities. Here it is important to exercise caution in the understanding of the term 'uneducated', above all, if women are meant. In medieval society, erudition was the domain of women; men carried on business, and women were literate; a long-established tradition in craftsmen's families. More precisely, women were often well-educated while men, on the average, were not. In contrast to the religious movement south of the Alps, with the Franciscans and the Dominicans, the religious movement north of the Alps was a women's movement. These women were knowledgeable about literature and well-informed about religion.

Excessive ardour for justice; excessive 'preaching to the uneducated': are these the reasons why Meister Eckhart was again sent to the *studium generale* in Cologne as a professor? This academic role was less dangerous. Did he continue to preach in the vernacular in Cologne? The philologists are undecided on this point. One so-called Cologne sermon, especially famous, is the sermon on the Annunciation, *Ave, gratia plena*. It is a text discussing the birth of God in the soul. Did Eckhart preach such sermons in Cologne, which can be analyzed for passages possibly responsible for creating misunderstandings and for incurring the displeasure of the archbishop of Cologne, Henry II of Virneburg? The archbishop had instituted the reorganization of his diocese on two levels: religious proclamation was prohibited in public squares and the women were whisked into convents. Whoever did not comply risked trial and condemnation. One known case is the condemnation of a priest named Walter on the grounds of espousing the Free Spirit. There were, however, many so-called Brethren of the Free Spirit who were able to avoid persecution. Yet, it was a situation in which it was extremely dangerous to insist on humanity, to demonstrate 'ardour for justice', and to continue to preach to the 'uneducated'. Moreover, those who avoided persecution probably invoked Eckhart. Esoteric enthusiasts invoke him in a similar sense today, when they assert that theologians essentially mean the same thing that they do, namely, authentic experience, the difference being that theologians are neither as advanced nor as free and thus cannot be recognized as being on the same side until they have freed themselves from the institution of the Church.

Eckhart remained true to the Church. It is crucial to fully comprehend what that signified: on one hand, to seek a highly personal form of faith in the self, undistortable, undeniably individual, to say 'I' as a religious person, unusual for the times that preceded; and on the other hand, to understand oneself as an ecclesiastical person, as a member of the Church community, even in the face of the fierce confrontation to come.

Eckhart was charged with heresy by the archbishop. For Archbishop Henry II of Virneburg it was a matter of pastoral care and ecclesiastical politics, and not theological or scholarly issues, as debated at the University of Paris or academic conflicts, even discussed by synods at that time. Academic disputes were confined to the ivory tower. Their danger was not as imminent if a professor of theology made an erroneous statement. This is still the case: only the concern about the salvation of the believers leads to an extraordinary procedure without adequate possibilities for defence in the Vatican today (examples: Stefan Pfürtner 1973; I. Ballasuryia 1997). When churchgoers are moved by theological statements, it seems that the pastoral mission of a bishop is seriously affected. With Henry II of Virneburg, it was presumably a pastoral concern that led him to initiate a trial, on the basis of several complaints and denunciations (two friars from the same order diligently collected and reported information and made accusations). It was *a trial for heresy before the Inquisition*, an improper and abnormal act towards a *magister*.

Not a single theologian—let alone such a renowned theologian—had been tried for heresy before the Inquisition in the entire Middle Ages. In contrast to an academic process, a trial for heresy before the Inquisitorial commission had the disadvantage that the presentation of evidence was not limited to the academic discussion, and that, since it was a penal process, could also be carried out with punitive measures.

Eckhart could only defend himself by invoking the exempt status of his order, that is, the Dominican Order was as such not subordinate to the bishop but to its own leadership, the master general of the Order in Rome, and ultimately to the Pope in Avignon. The Franciscan scholar, William of Ockham, a possible historical model for the friar in *The Name of the Rose*, also sojourned in Avignon at the time. Incidentally, he thought little of Eckhart's philosophy; they differed substantially on the theory of knowledge. Eckhart was a realist; for him names correspond to a thing to be described (in being) and effectively refer from this to that which is described. Ockham, conversely, was a nominalist; for him names are conceptual conventions. Eckhart's only recourse was the appeal to Rome. His friend Nicholas of Strasbourg, nominally his superior as visitor of the province in Cologne, had initiated a separate investigation within the Dominican Order to preclude action by the archbishop, an internal investigation that ended a total acquittal. The archbishop was not appeased, however, and the appeal to Rome remained the only possibility.

The appeal to Rome took two forms: that to a higher instance, the papal court in Avignon, where Nicholas of Strasbourg, the superior of the Order, travelled together with Eckhart; and the latter's public speech in self-defence at the Dominican Church in Cologne. This was again unusual because the public audience was also comprised of laypersons, both male and female citizens. Eckhart explained his position on his writings; he explained what had been misunderstood, and attempted to argue against the charges. But in this public statement he also announced his retraction of all passages in his writings that proved to be heretical. He revoked everything—the Latin phrase was *inquantam*—to the degree that it contradicted orthodox Church doctrine. Eckhart did not think that he had actually said anything heretical. Yet, he had an exceedingly high opinion of theological argumentation in this process and was willing to recant should he be disproved.

Such confrontations easily escalate into matters of ecclesiastical politics; more specifically, it is probable that the Franciscans approved of Eckhart's condemnation (perhaps as a compensation for their loss of face in the trial against the spirituals). The Dominicans, of course, opposed it; they did not wish to have 'their' professor withdrawn from circulation. At the same time, it was a dispute over the future of the Order with respect to its spiritual orientation. A resolution of this conflict, a compromise, was not found, as is frequently the case, until after Eckhart's death. He died in Avignon. A compromise proved to be necessary after Henry II of Virneburg had once again urged the Pope to make a decision in order to subdue his believers; apparently, there was still considerable uproar in 1328. Consequently, in 1329, the bull *In agro dominico* was issued, a bull which was only intended for the archdiocese of Cologne and not for the rest of the world. It was to be publicly posted only in Cologne, and only there was it to be valid. Thus, in the diocese of

Cologne Eckhart was not declared a heretic, but a man who 'wanted to know more than is necessary', as the bull reads, and who, for this reason, has strewn 'tares (weeds) among the wheat', and 'thorns' in God's field. In this overblown and maliciously ritualized language, some of his sentences are dismissed in classifications typical of the times and ranging from heretical to evil-sounding (*male sonans*).

These sentences were taken out of context. Today it is not difficult to refute the judgement, and there is a group of Dominicans actively committed to Eckhart's rehabilitation (Stirnimann and Imbach 1992: Dokimion [vol. 11]).

In a good interpretation, it is possible to demonstrate that the sentences taken out of context are reconcilable with the orthodox Church doctrine (Denzinger-Schönmetzer 1965: 950–80), but this is not what interests me in this context. It did, however, constitute a serious problem for the Dominicans. During the fourteenth century, the chapters of the Dominican Order were compelled to deal with the case retrospectively and repeatedly. Ultimately, Eckhart was deleted from the annals of the famous personages of the Order, which meant that his writings were withdrawn and their transmission curtailed over time. Curtailment, and not prohibition, is the correct description. Further veneration was offered, for example, by several Dominican spirituals, who are equally as famous as Eckhart: John Tauler, Henry Suso and Henry Seuse Denifle, all of whom, together with other Dominicans, continued to preach sermons in Eckhart's spirit. Seuse Denifle declared his solidarity with Eckhart in his books and held this tradition upright. And annals of certain convents from the seventeenth century even exist that list Eckhart as a saint! Today it may be less important to see him justified in one way or another in that time than to encounter his teachings, his wisdom and his deeply spiritual personality in his writings.

The influence of women's religious power

The power of inner liberation in Meister Eckhart cannot be understood without remembering his relationship to extraordinary women. The first of them is Marguerite Porete. A contemporary of Eckhart's, she is believed to have come from Valenciennes. The place of her death is certain: she was burned by the French Inquisition in Paris on the Place de Grève on 11 June 1310. At the same time, the Inquisition was persecuting the Templar; their last grand master would be burned at the stake at the same place three years later. Porete had been in prison since 1307, under the jurisdiction of the Great Inquisitor, Guillaume Humbert de Paris (*inquisiror hereticae pravitatis in regno Franciae auctoritate sedis apostolicae deputatus*). Her famous work 'Le Miroir des Simples Ames' (*Mirror of Simple Souls*, 1993) was burned by the Bishop of Cambrai about ten years ago (in 1297). Maybe she was condemned because she refused to obey the order not to distribute her book, one of the most successful publications in the Middle Ages. The work was translated into Latin, Italian and English. At the council of Basle (1439), a Pope was accused of possessing twenty-six copies!

The reason of the condemnation, which was not unanimously accepted by all the theologians involved, was the assertion that the soul annihilated (that is, the soul which is reduced to pure passivity and susceptibility) is no longer under an obligation to the virtues but is dominating the virtues by her own perfection. This was later also condemned in the Council of Vienna (1312) as an error of the Beguines and Beghards. It is a topos of contemplative experience which can also be found in Eckhart, who also asserted that the perfect soul or the just person has all virtues in its status of being. The question is, whether this topos in a pious book on the intimacy of the soul with God, the 'Loingprés', was sufficient for such a persecution. In my opinion, the main reason was that Porete presented her book as a 'doctrine' and not as a compendium of mystical visions and prophetical pictures. This corresponded to her teaching on the freedom of the soul annihilated. The hierarchy of the Church and world understood very well that the services demanded of women, even of religious women, was in danger, when Beguines began to insist on their right to contemplative life as individuals without the control of the Church.

When Eckhart was sent to Strasbourg by the master of the Dominicans after his second round of teaching in Paris at the Sorbonne as *magister sacrae scripturae* during 1311–13, he was certainly well informed about the trial of Porete and about the judgements of the Council of Vienna. During his visitations at monasteries and convents, it was one of Eckhart's main tasks to educate the nuns and Beguines, and integrate them into the Dominican Order. He stayed in Strasbourg for a long time (1313–23), and many of his sermons were given in this region. In his teaching, he stressed the natural nobility of the soul, freedom and justice, and the power of inner liberation. Among those most praised in his sermons was the biblical figure Maria from Magdala (who was identified by the legend with Maria from Bethania) and the history of the saints Elisabeth from Thüringen. In both the cases, he insisted on the power of inner liberation, but he also insisted on practical service. In his sermon about Elisabeth, he gives an explanation of the theological virtues, how these virtues transform the person, and enable the unity of religious being and charitable action. In his sermon about Maria and Martha, he tries to develop the figure of Martha as an example of the unity of active life and contemplative life. The unity leads to the apostolic teaching of both the sisters. The legend tells us that they were missionaries in the south of France. As Ignatius of Loyola later says: *contemplativus in actione*. This figure is presented as a shining example for Maria (of Magdala and Bethania), which would also come later-on in the status of a life as '*apostola*'. His respect for the figure of Maria Magdalena is also made clear in another sermon, in which he praises her as the first witness of the resurrection. For him, this is a reflection of the high status of her inner liberation. This dialectic approach to the annihilated and 'separated' (*abgeschiedene*) soul maintains the unity of practical, charitable and apostolic service. In my opinion, this is an attempt to reconcile the ideal of the annihilated soul with the necessity of active life (which at least was not denied by Porete).

There is no difference in the ranking of men and women in the treatment of biblical and holy figures in Eckhart, who was always well accepted by the sisters. Many legends grew around their meetings with him, in which he himself, a famous magister, learns from the 'simple souls'.

In 1326, when Eckhart himself was accused in Cologne in an unusual and unique trial of the Inquisition against a theologian, he needed help and sought support from a woman. He turned to the female leader of the house of Habsburg, in the homeland of this aristocratic family, in Königsfelden, Switzerland, not far from Winterthur, next to a convent of Franciscan nuns (Klarissinnen). It was Agnes of Hungary (1280–1364), daughter of the German King Albrecht I (murdered in 1308), wife of King Andreas III of Hungary (1296, he died in 1301), sister of the dukes of Austria, one of whom was elected king but was replaced by Ludwig the Bavarian. Agnes had a close relationship with her brothers and to their resistance against the king. She later lost her younger brother Leopold, the successful military leader of the house of Habsburg, in Strasbourg in 1327. She is remarkable in this context for two reasons: as a woman promoting the convents with a very good relationship with Pope John XXII in Avignon (also for political reasons) and as a leading figure in the Habsburg faction, to which both Dominicans and the Archbishop of Cologne, Henry II of Virneburg, belonged.

Eckhart sent his 'book on divine consolation' and his sermon 'on the noble human' to Agnes of Hungary. Researchers disagree about the date when he sent it. Early research suggests it was on the occasion of the death of her father (1308). But a leading researcher on medieval mysticism, Kurt Ruh, has proved that it must have been at a later date, when Eckhart was in Strasbourg. I have now an absolutely new proposal: that the book was not written for the consolation of a former queen, but was written for Eckhart himself in the tradition of the *consolatio philosophiae* (consolation of philosophy) of Boethius. This must have been before the false brothers of his Order collected sentences of his sermons and this treatise on divine consolation. I suppose, however, that the denunciation had begun earlier, because at the end of the treatise (see later), Eckhart defends himself against objections. Nothing contradicts the idea that Eckhart sent his book to gain protection from a queen who had great influence in both religion and in politics. We do not know her reaction, but it is a fact that Eckhart made an appeal to the Holy See and that he had the chance to look after his cause in Avignon. When the book of divine consolation, including the self-apology of the master, was sent from Cologne in 1326, it is plausible that Eckhart was searching for support for himself and the Dominican Order from an influential person that he had known since his days of work in Strasbourg.

Christ: The social in the human being

Fundamental to Meister Eckhart's thought is the mutual revelation of God and human being, theology and anthropology through the incarnation of Jesus Christ. Christ reveals both the compassion of God as the inner structure of the world, and solidarity as the inner structure of the human being. Christ is not a stage in the history of salvation but rather the salvational inner structure of history. This inner structure is at the same time dynamic and perpetually present: *creatio* and *incarnatio continua*. Incarnation is the epitome of historicity. The traditional differentiation between the vertical—God's work for the human being and the human being's work for God—and the horizontal—the human being's work for the human being—is no longer appropriate here.

The direction of God's work and the direction of human work are revealed as parallels through Christ; the incarnation of the human being is working in functional unity with God. God's work is not an end in itself but an impetus for human working. Naturally, this impetus is not to be forgotten over the commitment of the human being for the human being, and a lasting zone of thankfulness, contemplation and accountability secures the motivational power of belief. Parallelism between the working of God and that of the human being, by no means, signifies an equation of belief with humanness, but the revelation of belief towards humanness and the reverse.

The revelation of the human being in the openness of his or her understanding, striving and willing, is faith, hope and love; the revelation of God through Jesus Christ is incarnation as presupposition and realization. Given the solidarity of all human beings in the human nature of Christ, this incarnation is a social incarnation as well, not only a self-realization of the individual human being. Christ justifies the priority of the social as the inner structure of the human being. The discovery of the social dimension has a Christological foundation. The offer of a Christocentric anthropology in Eckhart's thought has structures that could theologically stimulate the approach of a contemporary socially oriented anthropology.

Such an approach would be distinguished by four characteristics. The first is a specifically theological justification of the autonomy of the human being. This is so in its distinction from a superficial conception of autonomy leading to an ideology of individual self-determination as well as in its Christological derivation. What is generally understood under the normal conception of autonomy is the self-determination of the human being, who, on the basis of personal insight and achievement, shapes his or her life, and the self-determination of humankind, which, on the basis of progress in knowledge and productivity, can create a better future. This private and collective self-determination has been exposed as pure illusion by the humanities. Nonetheless, a scapegoat is often sought and found for the inherited and acquired limitations to human freedom. Some see it in human nature, others in cultural and social development. In these views, either the establishment of the right social institutions or the breakthrough of original human nature is all that is necessary to allow autonomy to become a real possibility of human existence. The theological distinction lies in the fact that this possibility, too, remains an illusion as long as it is comprehended as self-determination. The human being does not actually have power over himself or herself; that which he or she thinks is under his or her power, in reality has power over him or her. The common conception of autonomy does not signify a true emancipation of the human being but limits him or her in his or her own personal limitedness. The opening of this limitedness is the offer of a Christologically justified autonomy. Not until Christ has replaced private and collective limitedness is the human being autonomously revealed, since he or she is first revealed to himself or herself in the incarnate Christ. Jesus reveals the human being; this is the meaning of a Christologically derived autonomy. In the Gospel of John, this is described through the opening of the eyes of the blind (see John 9: 1–41) with its paradoxical interpretation: 'I am come into this world, so those without sight may see and those [ostensibly] with sight become blind.' Jesus reveals the chance to attain sight by seeing one's own blindness. This is also Eckhart's teaching: only in the openness, inaccessibility, undirectedness and detachment, in the relinquishment of access to the self, is the human being revealed, as Christ reveals him or her. Only through distance to the common conception of autonomy does the human being become truly autonomous. This autonomy is neither inherited nor acquired; it is a gift of grace. The statement that Nature assumes grace corresponds to the statement that autonomy assumes incarnation. Christian autonomy is founded on the assumptions immanent in revelation. This both limits and fosters the possibility of human autonomy. In actuality, the endeavours for the liberation of the human being under Christian or non-Christian assumptions are often indistinguishable: the idea of the incarnation of the human being as gift and challenge does not require the recourse to Christ to be accepted today. Consequently, the Christological derivation of autonomy does not signify the apologetic valorization of the Christian. On the basis of faith, there is no resignation over human inadequacy because precisely this is the basis of hope. The Christian autonomy of the human being also means, of course, that the human being can freely determine his or her incarnation. However, this power to determine should stand up to the incarnation of Christ and not be misconstrued as a lasting ownership structure. For this reason, the specifically theological justification of human autonomy is categorized with the second characteristic, the permanent breaking through of the economic structures of actual human existence.

Eckhart clarified the characteristic of the permanent breaking through from several perspectives: freedom, poverty, detachment. It corresponds to the utopia of the expropriated existence, that is, of a mode of existence that does not accept economic structures as valid and needs structures as definitive. It is not a matter of the abolition of physical conditions (see Pr. 28 [Largier 1993: vol. 1; DW: vol. 2]), nor of the ascetic life, but of the incompleteness of human striving, like a wound that remains open until a true, and not a supposed, healing process ensues. This striving or permanent breaking through is stimulated by Christian hope. Possessions, necessity or *genügen*, as Eckhart writes, are first revealed when Christ replaces them, thus infinitely extending the perspectives of incarnation. The reference to Christ reveals the expropriated or propertyless existence as fulfilled existence. The infinite extension of the human way, which is announced in the conception of the permanent breaking through, is not ground for resignation, but for hope and commitment. The reference to Christ reveals the expropriated existence as a social and action-oriented existence.

A Christocentric anthropology logically encompasses as a third characteristic, that is, the solidarity and socialization of human beings in Christ. Through the exposure of human self-realization—at the expense of or under the forensic inclusion of the moral responsibility of other human beings—the social existence replaces the ownership and personal structure of the person of individual means and the individualist. Eckhart exposes self-realization in the sublime forms of piety and the *Do et des* ('I give that you may give') relationship between human beings. The trend towards sexual permissiveness with calculation of the consequences for the partner is one such form of private self-fulfilment, an equation with two unknowns, both being assumed as known in the blindness of supposed self-determination: the inaccessible self and the self of the other. The social is not simply the cumulation of self-determining, self-reliant individuals, but an indeterminate system of relationships between and in human beings. Eckhart's thesis is that this system of relationships first attains its ultimate perspective in Christ, because Christ is the foundation of the solidarity of the human race. Christ is the social in the human being, both from the perspective of his permanent expropriatedness, as well as from the perspective of his human solidarity. He reveals the breakthrough character of human existence together with its meaning and its purpose.

The fourth characteristic, the orientation towards action in the Christian anthropological approach, is already evident in the dynamism that this approach produces with regard to autonomy, the breaking through of economic structures and sociality. The dynamics of structure become a postulate of action for Eckhart. This does not make the case for a rhetorical activism; an alienation of the human in over-activity would not fulfil this orientation towards action as human 'inwardness'. The orientation towards action is the incarnation itself because it offers orientation and constitutes action, to the point that, for Eckhart, 'incarnation' encompasses all the actions of Christ. Action on the basis of an autonomous faculty of reason impelled by the motivational power of faith is 'inward', and is not an outward drivenness induced by needs. Eckhart has illustrated this clearly in the figures of Martha and Elizabeth. The inwardness of acting is not, on the other hand, a quietistic category. It simply distinguishes rational social 'action' from mere 'behaviour', in that the human being acts not on the basis of inner distance ('*bei den Dingen, nicht in den Dingen*') but 'as if possessed', driven by short-term goals and expectations which he or she does not control but which control him or her.

Conspicuous is Eckhart's exclusive naming of love as the orientation for action. Love is more closely specified, however; it is neither a category of the needs structure nor a category of the just balance between giving and receiving. Love is essentially 'social' love, that is, 'expropriated' or unpossessing love, a motivation-less love, not a category of acquisition or entitlement, not a category of eros as a sophisticated form of the extension of the individual identity through the other. In this love, Christ replaces the individuality of the human being; it is the love of the human being who has become truly incarnate, truly human, who already exists as a social being and, therefore, unquestionably acts socially. The question is naturally justified whether this love of the truly incarnate human being is not a utopia, just as the expropriated existence is a utopia. But for Eckhart, it is unimportant whether Christocentric autonomy, expropriated and social existence, and true human incarnation are actually existent. All of these have a critical and stimulating function as well as the function of broadening perspectives. The existing reality is not the orienting standard but rather the promised hope, the motivational power of faith, and the ultimate form of love, which is revealed in Christ. Not that which it serves as orientation for acting but that which is to be. On the other hand, that which is to be is a reality already anticipated in Christ. Thus, the utopia is not illusion; the future has already been imparted to the human being. What is to be is *within* the human being. Eckhart's comprehension of Christ as the social in the human being appears to be an interpretation of Paul's words that the human being no longer lives as 'I' but as Christ (Galatians 2: 20). This is how God reveals the process of becoming human in Christ.

Greek mythology tells the story of Prometheus, who stole fire from God, and in so doing, revealed and obtained 'divine' possibilities for humankind. Human autonomy emancipated itself from God violently; consequently, the myth of Prometheus is often considered the myth of our times. Fire is the first symbol of the economic structure of actual human existence. The apostle Paul interprets Christ's actions quite differently: Christ does not cling to his possession, divinity, like 'booty', but relinquishes that which he possesses in order to receive it from God through exaltation (see Philippians 2: 6–11). The incarnation is the first symbol of the breaking through of the economic structures, the utopia of the expropriated existence. If humankind's image of God were as similar to this symbol as Eckhart's conceived image of God, then human autonomy would not have to be wrested from God in a Promethean manner. On the contrary, it would be received as gift and challenge, for the sake of the human being himself or herself, because incarnation is the will and the glorification of God.

Greek mythology also tells the story of Sisyphus, whose endless lack of success also demonstrates the perspective of the expropriatedness of human existence. This myth, too, has often been seen as the myth of our times. And it takes the inaccessibility of human existence as seriously as Eckhart does in his Christocentric anthropology. Yet, the biblical teaching incessantly repeats that infinite loss is actually infinite gain. This is the tenor of the hymn to Christ in the letter to the Philippians. The only alternative to hope on the basis of faith is essentially abbreviated hope on the basis of ideology, resignation or despair. For Eckhart, as exegete of the incarnation, the most significant adversary is the abbreviated hope on the basis of ideology. This is why he breaks through all the perspectives of abbreviated hope in his time and discloses the abyss of nothingness behind them. Only over this abyss does it appear possible to him to offer *the* hope, which Christ has brought; a hope without a structure of entitlement or acquisition that in detached and dynamic commitment knows that the unknown house, to which human beings carry the building blocks, is being built by another builder outside of the realm of human existence.

Naturally, it is important to be conscious of the difference between the times. Eckhart may have offered some approaches that today acquire a concreteness not conceivable to him at that time. It would be wrong to develop a programme—other than cautious suggestions—from the radical social approach inherent in Eckhart's Christology. In a concrete agenda for social change, the critical symbolic nature of the presented perspectives is lost. Consequently, this programme, if it is not to lose its own critical authority, is not a concern of theology. It can, however, be the concern of theology to disclose that what human beings today conceive as meaningful is in accordance with the motivational power of faith, and in so doing, encourage their active commitment without specifying an agenda.

In conclusion, I would like to mention several limitations that affect any attempted actualizations of Meister Eckhart's thought. In his sermons, Eckhart rarely mentions the historical Jesus. Prevalent are references to the Christ of faith. The historical Jesus, 'as he ate and drank with us', hardly interests him at all. The incarnation as Jesus's 'message' is much more important to him than the 'person' Jesus. Yet, if Jesus's 'message' is separated from the person Jesus, as Eckhart does, to focus on his topic, it quickly becomes a series of philosophemes. What is, then, interesting about the incarnation of Christ is the possibility of deriving phenomena of the human from the 'idea of incarnation' as an ontologically structured occurrence; for example, how 'Jesus's message' as a socially structured occurrence can today serve to reveal phenomena of social change. In both cases, the possible application is the impetus of the process. This is justifiable through the fact that faith must be expressed in time, and in a manner that it effects something. This, of course, has limitations because the question about Jesus extends farther than the question about the realization of his message today.

A second limitation exists in Eckhart's system of relationships of 'world', 'human being' and 'morality'. Eckhart comprehends the world as Nature, not as history; the human being in the cosmos, not in society. Accordingly, his radical social conception of human morality does not have a 'political' component. If this limitation is taken seriously, the curious phenomenon arises that the communication of faith becomes 'political' when it transforms the *status quo*, that is, when it is oriented towards action and thus cannot remain without consequences. Religious belief provokes political action when it is oriented towards acting, often even against itself, and precisely then is it legitimate in orientation. For Meister Eckhart's trial reveals and exposes the position of those *beati possidentes* (happy possessors), the refutation of which was the goal of his theology as the breaking through of the economic structures of actual human existence. A faith that exposes the ambiguity of the *status quo* has, whether it will or not, political consequences, and in the future, those who pass judgement on it will be called to judge themselves.

Notes

1. The text was first published in the 'Festschrift' for Elisabeth Schussler Fiorenza. See Segovia (2003: Chapter 17). The english translation is by Jo Ann Van Vliet.
2. The correspondence is published in International Erich Fromm Society (2001).
3. German (Deutsche) and Latin Works of Meister Eckhart (1936), cited as DW and LW, respectively.
4. Martina Wehrli-Johns even construes Eckhart as inquisitor and inventor of the useful discrimination 'heresy of the Free Spirit' (*cf* 'Mystik and Inquisition', in Haug and Schneider-Lastin 2000: 223–52). In my opinion, the major argument of this thesis, namely, that Eckhart is to be counted among the *doctores humanae et divinae legis* who encouraged the bishop to carry out inquisitions, is not convincing. The title *doctor* was unspecific and academically indeterminate at that time and the legal specification totally inaccurate.
5. See his self-defence published in the edition by Augustus Daniels (1923: 2).
6. In the meantime, the editor of the German works, Georg Steer, has shown that this is not necessarily the case if the sermons 101–04 (DW: Vol. 4) are attributed to an earlier period. See 'Meister Eckhart's Predigtzyklus, Von Der Ewigen Geburt' in Haug and Schneider-Lastin (2000: 253–81).
7. See his defence at the conclusion of the *Buch der göttlichen Tröstung* (DW: Vol. 5).
8. See, again, the conclusion to the *Buch der göttlichen Tröstung*.

References

Bloch, Ernst. 1970. *Religion im Erbe: eine Auswahl aus seinen religionsphilosophischen Schriften*. Second edition. Munich: Siebenstern.

Daniels, Augustinus (ed.). 1923. *Eine lateinische Rechtfertigungsschrift des Meister Eckhart*. Münster: Aschendorff.

Denzinger, Heinrich and Adolf Schönmetzer (eds). 1965. *Enchiridion symbolorum, definitionum et declarationum de rebus fidei et morum*, 33rd edition. Freiburg: Herder.

Eckhart, Meister. 1857. *Predigten Traktate*. Edited by Franz Pfeiffer. Leipzig. Reprinted as: Aalen, Scientia. 1962. *Deutsche Mystiker des vierzehnten Jahrhunderts, ed. Franz Pfeiffer, Bd. 2*. Verlag.

———. 1936. *Meister Eckhart: Die deutschen und lateinischen Werke herausgegeben im Auftragder deutschen Forschungsgemeinschaft*, German (Deutsche) and Latin Works of Meister Eckhart, cited as DW and LW, respectively, (Critical edition). Stuttgart and Berlin: Kohlhammer.

Eckhart, Meister. 1979/1981/1987 (Vol. 1, Vol 2 and Vol. 3). *Sermons and Treatises*. Translated with 'Introduction' and 'Notes' by Maurice O'Connell Walshe. London: Watkins. (Vol. 3 with the newly discovered fragment of an unknown sermon).

Fischer, Heribert. 1974. *Meister Eckhart. Einführung in sein philosophisches Denken*. Freiburg and Munich: Karl Alber.

Fromm, Erich. 1976. *Haben oder Sein*. Stuttgart: Deutsche Verlagsanstalt.

Frederking, Volker. 1994. *Durchbruch vom Haben zum Sein. Erich Fromm und die Mystik Meister Eckharts*. Paderborn: Schöningh.

Haug, Walter and Dietmar Mieth (eds). 1992. *Religiöse Erfahrung: Historische Modelle in Christlicher Tradition*. Munich: Fink.

Haug, Walter and Wolfram Schneider-Lastin (eds). 2000. *Deutsche Mystik im Abendländischen Zusammenhang*. Tübingen: Niemeyer.

Heid, Ulrich. 1988. 'Studien zu Marguerite Porete und Ihrem 'Miroir des Simples Ames', in Peter Dinzelbacher and Dieter R. Bauer (eds), *Religiöse Frauenbewegung und mystische Frömmigkeit im Mittelalter*, pp. 185–214. Cologne: Böhlau.

International Erich Fromm Society (ed.). 2001. Meister Eckhart, Karl Marx and the Question of God. *Fromm Forum*, 5: 44–49.

Jacobi, Klaus (ed.). 1997. *Meister Eckhart: Lebensstationen—Redesituationen*. Berlin: Walter de Gruyter.

Largier, Niklaus (ed.). 1993. *Meister Eckhart Werke. Kommentierte zweisprachige Ausgabe in 2 Bänden*, 2 vols. Frankfurt: Deutsche Klassiker Verlag.

Manstetten, Reiner. 1993. *Esse est Deus: Meister Eckharts christologische Versöhnung von Philosophie und Religion und ihre Ursprünge in der Tradition des Abendlandes*. Freiburg and Munich: Karl Alber.

McGinn, Bernard. 2000. 'The Four Female Evangelists of the Thirteenth Century: The Invention of Authority', in Walter Haug and Wolfram Schneider-Lastin (eds), *Deutsche Mystik im Abendländischen Zusammenhang*, pp. 175–94 (on Marguerite Porete, pp. 188–93). Tübingen: Niemeyer.

Mieth, Dietmar. 1994. 'The Model of an Ethics of Being in Meister Eckhart and in the Structural Philosophy of Heinrich Rombach', *Listening/Journal of Religion and Culture*, 29(3): 186–98.

———. 2002. 'Religiöses Erleben ohne Erlebnis, die X-Erfahrung bei Erich Fromm und die Zeichen der Gewißheit bei Meister Eckhart', *Fromm Forum*, 6: 24–29.

——— (ed. and trans.). 2002. *Meister Eckhart: Einheit mit Gott*. Dusseldorf: Patmos, (Reprint of *Meister Eckhart: Die Einheit von Sein und Wirken—Texte mit Einleitungen*, Munich: Piper, 1991; subsequent editions in 2007 and 2008).

Porete, Marguerite. 1993. *The Mirror of Simple Souls*. Translated and introduced by Ellen L. Babinsky. New York: Paulist Pr.

Quint, Josef (ed. and trans.). 1979. *Meister Eckhart: Deutsche Predigten und Traktate*. Zurich: Diogenes.

Ruh, Kurt. 1989 [1985, 1st edition]. *Meister Eckhart: Theologe, Prediger, Mystiker*, 2nd edition. Munich: C.H. Beck.

———. 1993. *Geschichte der abendländischen Mystik*, Bd. II, pp. 340–73 (on Marguerite Porete). Munich: C.H. Beck.

———. 1996. 'Die Mystik des deutschen Predigerordens und ihre Grundlegung durch die Hochscholastik', in *Geschichte der abendländischen Mystik*, vol. 3. Munich: C.H. Beck.

Segovia, Fernando, F. (ed.). 2003. *Toward a New Heaven and a New Earth: Essays in the Honour of Elisabeth Schussler Fiorenza*. New York: Orbis Books.

Steer, Georg, and Loris Sturlese (eds). 1998/2002. *Lectura Eckhardi: Predigten Meister Eckharts von Fachgelehrten gelesen und gedeutet*. (2 vols). Stuttgart, Berlin and Cologne: Kohlhammer.

Stirnimann, Heinrich and Ruedi Imbach (eds). 1992. *Eckhardus Theutonicus, homo doctus et sanctus: Nachweise und Berichte zum Prozess gegen Meister Eckhart*. Freiburg, Switzerland: Universitätsverlag.

Sturlese, Loris. 1993. 'Meister Eckhart: ein Porträt', *Eichstätter Hochschulreden*, 90. Regensburg: Pustet.

Trusen, Winfried. 1988. *Der Prozeß gegen Meister Eckhart: Vorgeschichte, Verlauf und Folgen*. Paderborn: Schöningh.

von Liebenau, Heinrich. 1868/1869. *Lebensgeschichte der Königin Agnes, 2 Bde.* Regensburg: G.J. Manz.

Wilde, Mauritius. 2000. *Das neue Bild vom Gottesbild. Bild und Theologie bei Meister Eckhart*. Freiburg, Switzerland: Universitätsverlag.

A War against the Turks?

19

Erasmus on War and Peace

Fred R. Dallmayr

Several years ago, in a well-known essay, Sheldon Wolin (1996) spoke of 'fugitive democracy'. Today democracy is joined by another fugitive: everywhere peace seems to be in retreat or on the defensive. Ominously, the sound of war drums—akin to African bush drums— reverberates through many parts of the world, from the Near East to South Asia and the Far East; nor are Africa and the Americas shielded from their noise. Thus, the horrors of the twentieth century—the sequence of world wars, genocide and ethnic cleansings—seem to clamour for emulation in the new millennium, probably on a still more destructive scale. Leading political pundits in the West speak alarmingly of looming 'clashes of civilizations', pointing to the yawning gulf between North and South, between the West and 'the rest', and particularly between Western and Islamic civilizations (Dallmayr 2001; Huntington 1993; Wolin 1996). Not to be outdone, self-styled religious experts boldly prophesy the cataclysmic end of history or the imminent approach of 'judgment day'—with some of them not only anticipating, but actively campaigning for the great Armageddon, the final battle between the forces of 'good' and 'evil'. As it appears, the advent of God's kingdom in this scenario is to be achieved through globalized malice and destructiveness.

In such grim surroundings, Erasmus (*The Praise of Folly* [*Moriae Encomium*, 1511], in Dolan 1964: 94–173) continues to offer inspiration and solace—a solace nurtured by his close familiarity with the perennial follies of humanity. Erasmus age was in many ways like our own. Warfare and preparations for warfare were, everywhere, the order of the day. The unravelling of the medieval social fabric gave impulse to bitter conflicts between feudal barons and landless peasants-serfs, or between rich and poor. At the same time, the unfolding dynamic of the Reformation carried in its wake the prospect of bloody religious wars; wars whose ferocity was further intensified by the mingling of religious fervor with national-dynastic aspirations. To compound the perils of this explosive mixture, the Ottoman Turks were perceived as a major threat to Europe or European civilization—not without reason: under the leadership of Suleiman the Magnificent, the Ottomans were extending their reach throughout northern Africa and through the Balkans towards Vienna. A careful observer of human affairs, Erasmus, in his writings, perceptively commented on all the major events of his time—always with the aim of defusing potential conflicts and of fostering goodwill in the teeth of prevailing animosities. The following discussion will explore his endeavours in three main contexts. The opening section examines his views on the brewing conflict between Europe and the Ottoman Empire (or between Western Christianity and the Muslim world). The middle section expands the scope of discussion by reviewing Erasmus more general thoughts on war and peace, especially on the festering national-dynastic struggles at the dawn of modernity; the chief reference point here is his famous adage 'war is sweet to the inexperienced'. The concluding part shifts attention to Erasmus position on interreligious belligerence—the discussion here being guided by an ulterior motive: the hope of garnering lessons for interreligious or inter-faith relations in our own globalizing age.

A war against the Turks?

One of the central concerns of European politics at the beginning of the sixteenth century was the advance of Ottoman power. European fears in this respect were not imaginary. Under successive imperial rulers, the Ottomans had been able to incorporate into their domain, major portions of the Middle East and Central Asia, while also rendering much of northern Africa subservient to their rule. In 1526, the armies of Suleiman conquered Hungary and, in 1529, they beleaguered Vienna. Throughout Europe, animosity against the Ottomans was at a fever pitch and many military leaders clamoured for an all-out war 'against the infidels'. It was in this situation, and shortly after the successful defence of Vienna, that Erasmus wrote his memorable treatise *De Bello Turcico*, translated into English as *On the War against the Turks*. In his treatise, Erasmus did not adopt an absolute pacifist stance. He readily admitted that under certain circumstances, or under extreme provocation, war may be unavoidable and justified. The Turkish assault on Vienna was such a provocation—and required a defensive response designed to halt further aggression. As Erasmus ('On the War against the Turks', in Rummel 1990: 316–19) wrote (using language uncannily familiar today):

> While we have been endlessly fighting among ourselves over some useless plot of land … the Turks have vastly extended their empire or, rather, their reign of terror: to the north, it stretches to the Black Sea; to the east, it extends to the Euphrates, and to the south, to Ethiopia. More recently, they have moved up the Danube and passed even further to the river Dnieper. In the face of these advances, total pacifism—the idea that 'the right to make war is totally denied to Christians'—is farfetched and implausible. The focus should rather be on the 'when' and 'how'; for 'sometimes war against the Turks is rightly undertaken, sometimes not.

Once the focus was thus shifted to the 'when' and 'how', and especially to the 'rightness' of military action, severe restrictions on warfare came quickly into view. For Erasmus, it was imperative that war be undertaken only for self-defence and only as a last resort, after all other avenues have been explored and proved unsuccessful. In his words: 'I think that all other expedients must be tried before war is begun between Christians; no matter how serious nor how just the cause, war must not be undertaken unless all possible remedies have been exhausted and it has become inevitable.' In emphasizing restrictions on the beginning of warfare, Erasmus modified and went beyond the medieval 'just war' doctrine—a doctrine that had been too often abused and manipulated by political rulers for their own benefit. 'My message is,' the treatise reiterates, 'that war must never be undertaken unless, as a last resort, it cannot be avoided', adding, 'War is by its nature such a plague to man that even if it is undertaken by a just prince in a totally just cause, the wickedness of captains and soldiers results in almost more evil than good.' Even a cursory glance at the behaviour of Christian princes—or European realpolitik—demonstrated that, all too frequently, the call to arms was prompted 'by ambition, anger or the hope for plunder'—motives cloaked for popular consumption in the garb of a 'just' grievance or cause. An observer familiar with Christian teachings—and, in fact, any ethically sensitive observer—could not fail to look through this subterfuge and to condemn impulsive warmongering for what it was: the unleashing of illicit violence: 'If the war is inspired by such motives as the lust for power, ambition, private grievances or the desire for revenge, it is clearly not a war but mere brigandage' (Rummel 1990: 318–19).[1]

Erasmus comments on illicit warfare must have grated on the ears of many contemporaries eager for military action, especially action against the hated 'infidels'. As mentioned before, Ottoman advances under Suleiman had unleashed in Europe a cauldron of angry passions and a clamouring for swift revenge. Erasmus was no doubt familiar with these passions. Undaunted, his treatise tried to inject some sense and good judgement into the situation. 'Whenever the ignorant mob hear the name "Turk",' he writes, 'they immediately fly into a rage and clamor for blood, calling them dogs and enemies to the name of Christian.' What this mob completely forgets is that, in the first place, 'the Turks are men' (or human beings) and, in the second place, that they are 'half-Christian' as co-heirs of the Abrahamic legacy. Carried along by their intense passions, zealots for war fail to ponder the most important questions, namely, 'whether the occasion of the war is just' and 'whether it is practical to take up arms and thereby to provoke an enemy who will strike back with redoubled fury.' In the case of the Turks, military or geopolitical considerations were overshadowed and contaminated by religious prejudices which seemed to vindicate acts of outright barbarism. Here, Erasmus issued a stern reprimand predicated on both legal and religious premises:

> The mass of Christians are wrong in thinking that anyone is allowed to kill a Turk, as one would a mad dog, for no better reason than that he is a Turk [or Muslim]. If this were true, then anyone would be allowed to kill a Jew; but if he dared to do so he would not escape punishment by the civil authorities. The Christian magistrate punishes Jews who break the state's laws, to which they are subject; but they are not put to death because of their religion. Christianity is spread by persuasion, not by force; by careful cultivation, not by destruction.

Addressing itself to religious fanatics, the treatise briskly debunked a false zeal for martyrdom (in language uncannily resonating again with contemporary events): 'Any who believe that they will fly straight up to heaven, if they happen to fall in battle against the Turks, are sadly deluding themselves' (Rummel 1990: 317, 321–22).

If the motives of warfare had to be carefully scrutinized, the same care needed to be taken in the actual conduct of war, which was circumscribed by religious and legal norms (*ius in bello*). 'If absolute necessity dictates that a war must be fought', Erasmus observes, in agreement with a long line of theological-juridical teachings, 'Christian clemency demands that every effort be made to confine the numbers involved to a minimum and to end the war with the least possible bloodshed, as quickly as may be.' The treatise at this point invokes the testimony of Bishop Ambrose who, during the reign of Emperor Theodosius, firmly upheld a code of military conduct, for he did not approve any war 'simply because it was necessary or just'; he also insisted that war must be accompanied by 'a religious spirit which places all its hopes of victory in God [not political aggrandizement] and aims only at the peace of the state.' Sentiments of this kind, to be sure, were likely to be brushed aside by warmongers animated only by the spirit of revenge, especially revenge for perceived Turkish atrocities. Referring to a media campaign spreading throughout Europe (still without the aid of television), Erasmus notes, 'Pictures are painted showing examples of Turkish cruelty'; examples designed to stir up bitter hatred. Without denying the evidence of cruelties, the Dutch humanist pens a caveat against media manipulation (which remains valid today). Although deplorable, he states, the depicted cruelties 'ought in fact to remind us how reluctant we should be to make war against anyone at all, since similar "amusements" have been common in all the wars in which, over so many years, Christian has wickedly fought Christian.' While the media accounts 'condemn their [the Turks'] cruelty, [yet] worse crimes were perpetrated at Asperen [a town sacked by the Duke of Gelders in 1517], not by Turks, but by my own country men, many of them even my friends.' For Erasmus (Rummel 1990: 318, 320), the reported atrocities—today we might call them 'war crimes'—should serve as lessons and warnings, not as incitements for revenge:

> If the subjects of these paintings truly shock us, we should curb our own impetuosity, which so easily leads us headlong into war. For however cruel the deeds of the Turks, the same deeds committed against his fellow by a Christian are still more cruel. What a sight it would be if men were confronted with paintings of the atrocities which Christians have committed in the last forty years [or four hundred years]![2]

One of Erasmus main concerns was the brutalization and dehumanization generated by war of any kind, especially war prompted by sheer revenge. Differently and more pointedly phrased, if the aim of warfare was to curb Turkish 'terror', great care needed to be taken lest Christian princes and armies turned themselves into agents of terror (or 'terrorists'). In Erasmus words, zealous to take revenge, Christian princes tend to 'assail the Turks with the selfsame eagerness with which they invade the lands of others.' In their actual conduct of war, Christian rulers come to imitate or mimic 'Turkish' behaviour: 'We are betrayed by our lust for power; we covet riches; in short, we fight the Turks like Turks.' Looking around in European lands at the time, Erasmus found little evidence of genuine piety and moral uprightness. The vaunted religious and cultural superiority of Europe—so often invoked as a justification for war against the infidels—was largely a sham and a sign of empty vanity: 'Where now is to be found a vestige of true faith, of Christian charity, of peace and harmony? What age ever saw fraud, violence, rapine, and imposture practiced so freely? And yet, all the while, like good Christians we hate the Turks!' Instead of indicting the so-called infidels, Europeans were better advised to indict themselves; instead of carrying war into foreign lands, they should first of all war against their own base impulses: 'If we wish to succeed in ridding ourselves of the Turks, we must first cast out from ourselves all our loathsome "Turkish" vices' (that is, vices often ascribed to the Turks)—such as 'avarice, ambition, power-lust, self-indulgence, luxury, anger, hatred, and envy.' If this self-correction was accomplished, war might still be required as a last resort; but it might also be avoided in favour of an another, religiously and ethically more commendable path. For, looking beyond raging enmities, we might find it to be more beneficial and religiously salutary 'if, instead of slaughtering the Turks, we manage to join them to us in a common faith and observance'—an objective not far-fetched given their status as 'half-Christian' (Rummel 1990: 317, 323–25).[3]

Turning from religious-ethical to more political or geopolitical considerations, Erasmus adds some startling comments (which again seem pertinent in our own globalizing age). Under the cloak of a war against the infidels, he notes, something else might actually be afoot, namely, an attempt by European rulers to solidify their domestic control and to squash dissent. Whatever the actual intent of rulers, their behaviour was worrisome. Complaints were heard in many places, the treatise states, 'that some of the Christian princes seem to be aiming at the sort of tyranny formerly called "Turkish"', namely, by 'oppressing their people with intolerable impositions, and adding to the burden every day.' In point of fact, if one compared present conditions with the situation only 'seventy years ago', it is staggering how 'the freedom of the people, the power of the towns, the authority of parliaments' have diminished while the powers of rulers have increased. Developments of this kind added fuel to popular apprehensions and to the fears of those who suspected:

that the princes are being very cunning in this matter; [that] under the pretext of a Turkish war, a tiny clique will seize power, after plundering towns, countryside, and people, overthrowing the rule of law, suppressing the liberties of the states, removing the authority of parliaments; and [that henceforth] government will be carried on in the Turkish fashion, by force of arms rather than by the rule of reason.

The great danger in combating despotism and tyranny was the latter's contagiousness. On this point, *De Bello Turcico* did not mince words: if war was to be waged, it 'must not be made an excuse to undermine the freedoms and laws of the various states; ... while overthrowing the tyranny of the Turks, we must not bring a new and worse tyranny upon ourselves.' (Rummel 1990: 329–30, 332).[4]

'War is sweet to the inexperienced'

Erasmus condemnation of warmongering and illicit warfare was not restricted to his treatise on the Turkish question; it can readily be seen as a *leitmotif* in all his successive writings. About a decade earlier, in response to mounting national-dynastic rivalries in Europe, he had penned his famous *Querela Pacis* or *The Complaint of Peace* whose basic message was that no Christian and, in fact, no ethically sensitive person, could possibly be indifferent to the benefits of peace and justice as compared with the pernicious ravages of war (Erasmus, *The Complaint of Peace* [*Querela Pacis*, 1517], in Dolan 1964: 177–204). For Erasmus, preference for the former benefits was not simply a matter of taste or private idiosyncrasy. As a learned humanist, he was able to garner support for this preference both from sacred scriptures and from a large host of ancient Greek and Latin writers. As is well known, one of his persistent endeavours throughout his life was to collect and reinterpret ancient proverbs and wise sayings in such a manner that they would speak again to the concerns of his time. The chief fruit of these endeavours was the *Adagiorum Opus* or *Collectanea* (*Collection of Adages*), a work—started in 1500 on a limited scale—which grew over the decades in scope and size to emerge finally as one of the most celebrated texts of Renaissance. Easily the most prominent of the collected adages, and the one eliciting Erasmus most extensive commentary, is a proverb that can be traced to Pindar and some Roman authors: 'War is sweet to the inexperienced' or 'to those who have not tried it' (*dulce bellum inexpertis*) (see Barker 2001: 317–56 [Adage IV, i, 1]).[5]

Referring to a statement by Aristotle linking youth with boldness and recklessness, and mature age with seasoned judgement, Erasmus stresses the salutary effects of mature experience—especially experience gained through misery and suffering. In this respect, the experience of war can be a great task master of humanity; for no one who has really experienced its horrors and devastations is likely to wish for their repetition. 'If there is any human activity', he writes in a stirring passage, 'which should be approached with caution, or rather which should be avoided by all possible means, resisted and shunned, that activity is war'—the reason being that 'there is nothing more wicked, more disastrous, more widely destructive, more hateful, more unworthy in every respect of man [humanity], not to say a Christian.' In depicting the horrors of war, Erasmus commentary does not limit itself to vague allusions or the polite canons of *belles lettres*. Corresponding to the depicted brutalities, his language is grim and brutal—in a manner that is likely to resonate with the experiences of later ages, especially of people familiar with the horrors of Hiroshima, Bosnia, Rwanda and Jenin. Using sharp staccato strokes, his essay speaks of 'the mad uproar, the furious clash of battle, the monstrous butchery, the merciless fate of the slain and those who kill, the slaughtered lying in heaps, the fields running with gore, the rivers dyed with human blood.' To prevent misunderstanding, Erasmus makes it clear that the evoked images do not only characterize so-called 'unjust' wars or unscrupulous terrorist campaigns. For, he adds (Barker 2001: 319, 321–22), these are the consequences of 'even the most successful and just war':

> Peasants plundered, land-owners oppressed; so many old men left desolate, more tormented by the slaughter of their children than if the enemy had killed them and erased the knowledge of their grief; so many old women left destitute, condemned to a crueller death than by the sword; so many wives left widows, children left orphans, homes filled with mourning, rich folk reduced to poverty.

As Erasmus was well aware, warmongers and devotees of realpolitik are quick to find an alibi for their misdeeds, namely, by blaming warfare on a presumed design of savage 'nature', which has placed humans and animals alike under the law of the jungle. His essay is equally quick to debunk this alibi. For one thing, the equation of humans and animals does not hold up on inspection; for another thing, even wild animals do not wage 'war' as a collective enterprise. Most animals, Erasmus writes, 'live in harmony and good order with their own kind, moving in herds and ensuring mutual protection.' Not even all wild animals are 'fighters by nature'; only a few of them like lions, wolves and tigers, and not even those 'make war on each other as we do.' For the most part, the aggressiveness of 'fighting' animals is not internecine, in the sense that 'dog does not eat dog-flesh, lions do not inflict their ferocity on each other, snake lives in peace with snake.' More importantly, the motives for fighting among animals tend to be limited and narrowly circumscribed: they do not become fierce 'for trivial reasons', but only 'when hunger drives them mad, or when they feel they are being hunted, or when they fear for their young.' Here, the contrast with human behaviour is enormous. For, 'God in heaven', Erasmus exclaims, 'we humans, what tragic wars we stir up, and for what frivolous causes! For the emptiest of territorial claims, out of childish anger, because some woman we intended to marry has been denied us, and for reasons even more ridiculous than these.' Still more importantly, ferocity among animals is always singular, not collective; always a quick outburst, rather than a festering habit; basically, combat among them tends to be 'one to one', and terminates with the wounding of one party: 'When did anyone hear of a hundred thousand animals falling dead together after tearing each other to pieces, as men do everywhere?' Anticipating an adage later invoked by Thomas Hobbes (*homo homini lupus*), Erasmus concludes that 'for man, no wild beast is more dangerous than man'.—adding that animals, when they do fight, fight with their own weapons, like teeth and claws, whereas we equip soldiers 'to destroy men with unnatural instruments devised by the art of devils' (a statement written long before the advent of ballistic missiles and long-range methods of technological mayhem) (Barker 2001: 323).[6]

While admitting the perversity of warfare—the possible descent of human behaviour into wild and seemingly beastly savagery—Erasmus is by no means ready to exculpate this perversion. As a classical humanist as well as a believing Christian, he is unwilling to blame human misconduct either on nature's design or on divine providence. Considering the charge of human beastliness as a slur on both Nature and religion, his commentary offers a different account of 'human nature' or nature's design for human beings, an account, however, that needs to be read cautiously. For Erasmus, the point is not to demonstrate the 'goodness' or 'badness' of human nature in a metaphysical or 'foundational' sense. His style of argumentation is not that of a scholastic philosopher or an Enlightenment thinker constructing a theoretical system in which conclusions can abstractly be deduced from a *priori* premises. Following in the footsteps of Aristotle and Cicero, his style of writing throughout is hortatory and educational, aiming at moral transformation. Although there may be 'good' propensities implanted in humans by Nature, these propensities mean nothing unless they are nurtured and cultivated and thus made into practical habits or virtues. It is in this sense that one should read Erasmus comments on Nature and 'Nature's God', especially the comments he places into the mouth of a personified 'Nature' addressing herself to humankind: 'There was one creature I brought forth made entirely for kindly actions—peaceful, friendly, helpful.... I made you a creature in some sense divine; what came into your head to change yourself into a brute so monstrous that no beast will be called a brute in future if compared to man?' (Barker 2001: 324–35).

In invoking Nature's design for his own purposes, Erasmus enlists the help of a kind of philosophical anthropology—though again without systematic or 'foundational' intent. In terms of his commentary, human beings are both physically and mentally ill-prepared for conflict and, hence, predisposed for fellowship and mutuality. 'If we consider just the condition and appearance of the human body', he states, 'is it not apparent at once that Nature, or rather God, created this being not for war but for friendship, not for destruction but for preservation, not for aggression but to be helpful?' While Nature endowed all species of the animal kingdom with some indigenous weapons—like claws, horns, tusks and stings—human beings enter into the world in a comparatively handicapped condition, which also dictates a longer period of maturation: 'Man alone she produced naked, weak, delicate, unarmed, with very soft flesh and a smooth skin.' Given this vulnerable condition, no part of the human body seems to be 'intended for fighting and violence'—not to mention the fact that other animals are capable of fending for themselves soon after birth, while human beings must 'long be dependent entirely on the help of others.' For Erasmus, physical handicaps of this kind, however, can also be read as social gains, that is, as subtle inducements to mutual assistance and friendship. Moreover, handicaps are compensated by the gift of other endowments pointing in the same direction—above all, the 'use of speech and reason', a gift that serves above all else to 'create and nourish [mutual] good will.' As a corollary of the use of speech and reason, humanity developed a 'dislike of solitude' and a 'love of companionship' averse to selfish aggressiveness. At this point, Erasmus adds a moving paean to the blessings of companionship and goodwill, seen as antidotes to warfare. Given the noted physical and mental features, we read (Barker 2001: 319–20), it seems clear that human beings are destined not for enmity and slaughter but for 'thankfulness and brotherly love':

> The appearance she [nature] gave humans was not hideous and terrifying, as with other creatures, but mild and gentle, bearing the signs of love and goodness. She gave them friendly eyes, revealing the soul; she gave them arms to embrace; she gave them the kiss, an experience in which souls touch and unite. Humans alone she endowed with laughter, the sign of merriment; them alone she endowed with tears, the symbol of mercy and pity.[7]

Returning to the wording of the chosen adage (*dulce bellum inexpertis*), it is important to grasp Erasmus distinct reading of its terms. In his commentary, 'experience' does not simply denote a random occurrence. Emulating Aristotle's teachings (and anticipating those of Hegel), experience for Erasmus signifies not just a factual happening, but rather a seasoning or learning process that transforms the person undergoing the experience. Given their endowment with speech and reason, human beings also are capable of reflective remembrance, especially of the re-collection of past sufferings—leading to the determination to avoid their recurrence in the future. Unfortunately, Erasmus laments, this capability is not always exercised or developed; with the result that many people grow older without apparently learning anything, especially from the horrors of past and present wars. Given this obtuseness or amnesia, he writes, war has in fact become 'such an accepted thing that people are astonished to find anyone who does not like it.' Promoted by warmongers and demagogues, warfare and the cult of violence are in many places 'such a respectable thing that it is wicked—I might almost say "heretical"—to disapprove of this which of all things is the most abominable and most wretched.' What is particularly amazing is that the cult of violence and the frenzy for war have gripped the minds not only of ignorant fools but of seemingly respectable people, not only of the young but of the old, not only of the impious but of the seemingly pious. Is it not stunning, Erasmus asks, how warfare is celebrated 'not only by pagans but by Christians, not only by laymen but by priests and bishops, not only by the young and inexperienced but by older people who have known it already so many times?' The problem is compounded by the everready armies of lawyers and theologians 'who add fuel to the fire of these outrages and, as the saying goes, sprinkle them with holy water.' Surrounded by this frenzy, defenders of peace are shunned and marginalized; in fact, their ideas are 'laughed at as the ravings of academics' by the pretended rulers of this world 'who have nothing human about them but think themselves gods' (Barker 2001: 319, 328).[8]

Towards the end of his commentary, Erasmus turns to an important political issue (one also raised in *De Bello Turcico*) that warmongering not only marginalizes intellectuals but also jeopardizes the rights and liberties of peoples. On this score, Erasmus shows himself not only as a learned humanist and classical moralist, but as a clear-headed political thinker concerned about political agency or praxis. Looking around among the princes or rulers of his day, he found ample grounds for suspicion or scepticism. 'There are some', we read, 'whose only reason for inciting war is to use it as a means to exercise their tyranny over their subjects more easily.' While in times of peace 'the authority of the assembly, the dignity of the magistrates, the force of the laws' act as obstacles to governmental licence, this quickly changes in war time. 'Once war is declared, the whole business of the state is subject to the will of a few.' The mottoes usually bandied about at such time are 'reason of state' (*raison d'état*) and public security or safety (*salus populi*). What is completely forgotten is that the safety or well-being of people cannot be secured by military bravado; in fact, there is 'no other way by which states go more quickly and completely to ruin than by war.' Again (as in *De Bello Turciro*), Erasmus plea is not for pacifism, under any and all circumstances, but for a careful restriction of warfare to the barest minimum and as a last resort employed only after all other means have been exhausted, and conducted with the goal of a speedy return to peace. To quote him (Barker 2001: 350–52):

> If, because of general perversity, there is no way of avoiding it [that is, war], when you have left nothing untried and no stone unturned in your search for peace, then the best expedient will be to ensure that, being an evil thing, it is the exclusive responsibility of evil people, and is concluded with a minimum of bloodshed.

Orthopraxis and interreligious peace

Erasmus remonstrations against war and violence were addressed, in the first instance, to the princes and dynastic rulers of his day. As a close observer of political developments, he keenly perceived the danger posed to the welfare of peoples by dynastic rivalries and by the growing competition between the emerging European nation-states. On a more recessed level—but a level which steadily gained prominence over the decades—his comments were also aimed at clerical or religious leaders: first of all at the leaders of the Catholic Church, but second also at the leaders of the Protestant movement, which gathered momentum during his life. In this respect again, his admonitions were timely and nearly prophetic, given the ravages brought about by subsequent religious wars. In addressing himself to religious leaders, Erasmus did not strike the pose of a rational secularist, claiming liberal neutrality vis-à-vis religious faith. Rather, his language was that of a faithful Christian but one inspired by a new and different reading of the gospels, a reading focussed not on rigid dogma but on pious and peaceful practical conduct (*orthopraxis*). This emphasis on practical conduct explains a feature which has baffled many interpreters: his ability to combine and reconcile classical humanist teachings with biblical instructions. For him, what linked classical and biblical texts, rendering them mutually complementary, was their joint accent on transforming or 'humanizing' human conduct. In this respect, it is well to remember his statement in *Dulce Bellum Inexpertis*: 'If we acknowledge Christ as our authority, and if he is love, if he taught nothing and handed down nothing but love and peace, well, let us declare him, not by wearing his name and badge, but in our deeds and lives' (Barker 2001: 353).[9]

The accent on religious conduct—on practising religious faith in 'deeds and lives'—was evident in one of his earliest writings titled *Enchiridion Militis Christiani* (*The Handbook of the Militant Christian* of 1503 [Dolan 1964]). The text was by no means a call for Christian 'militancy' or (what today would be called) 'fundamentalism', but rather an invitation to sincere religious engagement in opposition to dogmatic quarrelling and external ritualism.[10] In an epigram later attached to the treatise, Erasmus stated, 'May this book lead to a religious life rather than theological disputations'—a statement well in keeping with his life-long effort to rescue the gospels from scholastic encroachments and to retrieve the practical example of Jesus (*pure docere Christum* or *Christum ex fontibus praedicare*). As Dolan (1964) notes, Erasmus practical religiosity or piety was greatly indebted to the undogmatic *devotio moderna*, which he had absorbed as a student of the Brethren of the Common Life in Holland. As a result of this influence, Dolan adds, Erasmus was strongly opposed to scholastic theology which, in his view, had perverted religion into a 'prestigious intellectual gymnastic' and instilled in its devotees an 'obstinate pertinacity in their opinions, dangerous to the peace and unity of the Church.' One of the early sections of the *Handbook* ... clearly spells out the direction of its inquiry by highlighting the basic wellsprings of faith in contrast to mere accessories. If your interest in religion, Erasmus writes, 'revolves more about what is vital and dynamic rather than merely dialectical [or theoretical]', if you incline more towards 'what moves the inner man than what leads to empty arguments', then 'read the Fathers'. For, he continues, 'Their deep piety has withstood the test of time; their very thoughts constitute a prayerful meditation', penetrating into 'the very depths of the mysteries' they propound. 'I do not mean to condemn [all] modern theologians; I am merely pointing out that in view of our purpose, namely, a more practical piety, they are hardly to be recommended' (Dolan 1964: 13, 28–37).[11]

The main body of the *Handbook* ... offers a list of rules or maxims conducive to a properly Christian or religious life. From this list—too extensive to be reviewed here—one item (Rule Five) deserves to be mentioned because it captures eloquently the gist of the *devotio moderna*. In this rule, Erasmus exhorts his readers not to cling stubbornly to external or sensible phenomena but to search for their deeper significance. Without completely neglecting or shunning the sensible world, Christians are meant to free themselves from its immediate grasp, that is, to ascend from the visible world to the invisible or rather to discern the invisible sheltered in the very heart of the visible (*per visibilia ad invisibilia*). In Erasmus words, 'In getting closer to the inner spiritual meaning you will find what is really most important—a hope for the unknown.' This maxim clearly has profound implications for religious practices. On this score, Erasmus does not hesitate to use stern language: 'But to place the whole of religion in external ceremonies is sublime stupidity. This amounts to a revolt against the spirit of the gospels.' Surveying religious customs at his time, he finds them mired in superstition and much humbug. Genuine religion, he insists, does not consist 'in many visits to churches, in many prostrations before the statues of saints, in the lighting of candles, or in the repetition of a number of designated prayers'—for 'of all these things God has no need.' When St Paul spoke of religious faith, he placed the accent instead on helpfulness to one's neighbours, on the effort 'to integrate all men into one body so that all may become one in Christ'; for just as Christ 'gave himself completely for us', so also should we give ourselves to fellow human beings. As Erasmus adds, in an important caveat, the stress on inner faith does not imply a complete rejection of existing church practices or 'honorable traditions'—whose meaning can sometimes be recovered and redeemed:

'I am not condemning external works but am trying to impress upon you that such works are of little value unless they are accompanied by inner piety' (Dolan 1964: 64, 68–69).

With these comments—and other statements of a similar nature—Erasmus placed himself in the thick of a controversy brewing at the time over the issue of 'justification', a controversy pitting against each other proponents of 'good works' against defenders of 'faith alone' (*sola gratia*). In his formulation, mere works alone—as manifestations of self-important busy-ness—are surely not redemptive or justificatory; at the same time, however, if performed faithfully, works or deeds do have an important revelatory significance. How else could one make sense of Jesus's admonition that 'by their fruits you shall know them' (Matthew 7:16)? On this issue, Dolan's observations are again helpful and on the mark. The entire aim of Erasmus approach, as outlined in the *Handbook*..., was 'an interiorization, a spiritualization of religious practice, a more personal affair between the individual soul and God.' Yet, interiorization here does not simply mean privatization or a passive retreat from the world and action in the world. In Dolan's words, 'He will not preach retirement from the world but holiness in the world.' The purpose of his *Handbook* ... was to encourage neither purely private contemplation nor abstract-theological cleverness but to offer a compendium to lay people of 'what it means to live a Christian life'. Moreover, such a life for him was not to be confined to the home or personal affairs but was to radiate into the public arena (without trying to dominate doctrinally or ecclesiastically that arena). 'This is Erasmus constant effort', Dolan adds, 'to break through the narrow confinement and isolation that keep religion out of the arena of public life.' For Erasmus, *bene agere*, that is, to act well and faithfully in all domains of life, meant nothing else than 'to consider all in Christ' (*in Christum spectare*) or to permeate all actions and deeds with the spirit of love and redemptive hope (Dolan 1964: 26–27).[12]

In the decades following the writing of the *Handbook*..., Erasmus was increasingly drawn into the cauldron of religious conflicts, involving both denominational or confessional disputes among Christians, and the wider relations between Christianity and other religions or cultural traditions. In both the domains, he invariably displayed his character-istic 'irenicism' or what has sometimes been called the 'velvet softness' of his piety. Regarding wider inter-cultural relations, Erasmus was particularly troubled by the harsh missionary methods employed by the Spaniards in the Americas, that is, by the collusion of Christian faith with imperialism or colonial domination. At one point, he actually met with the son and biographer of Columbus, Ferdinard, and through him was familiar with the Spanish exploits in the New World and with the protestations of Bartolemé de las Casas against the forced conversion of American Indians. Partly in response to these events or developments, he composed, in 1526, a curious dialogue between a butcher and a fishmonger titled *Concerning the Eating of Fish* (*Ichthophagia*). Apart from remonstrating, again, against the focus on external habits—like the eating or not-eating of fish on Fridays—the dialogue contains some telling comments on Christian expansionism and on the proper way to spread the 'good news' of the gospel. Speaking in the butcher's voice, Erasmus complains bitterly about the feuds and 'deadly altercations' that afflict Christian nations, wondering what kind of example this violent behaviour was setting for non-Christian peoples. Moreover, violent aggressiveness was spilling over from Europe into other parts of the world, contaminating or poisoning the gospel message. 'The nations of the world would more readily embrace religion', the butcher notes, 'if it were accompanied by liberty' or offered non-coercively. Not to be outdone, the fishmonger pleads for gospel piety as the standard of cross-cultural relations. If such piety were practised, he holds, then non-Christian nations would more clearly perceive that they are 'not called to human servitude but to the liberty of the gospel', and that they are 'not sought after to be exploited', but are invited to 'a fellowship of happiness and holiness.' If such a policy were pursued, non-Christian peoples would 'freely offer us more than the greatest violence can now extort from them' (Dolan 1964: 273, 287–88).

Given the mounting confessional rivalries in Europe, the final decade of Erasmus life was largely overshadowed and absorbed by this conflict and his own effort to steer a conciliatory path between the battlelines. As he wrote to a friend at the time, 'It is my fate to be pelted by both parties while I endeavor to satisfy them both. In Italy and Brabant, I am considered to be a Lutheran, and in all of Germany, where I live so much, an anti-Lutheran.' Basically, his own hope was to reach a settlement within the existing Church—but, of course, a Church radically reformed and transformed. This hope found expression in one of his last writings, titled *De Sarcienda Ecclesiae Concordia* (*On Mending the Peace of the Church*, of 1533). Here again one finds a critique of purely outward ceremonies and rituals, and an exhortation to lead a genuinely Christian or pious life in accord with the gospels. As he states, with respect to one contentious issue, 'I think we can say without vexing anyone that the saints are best venerated by imitating their lives.' If the emphasis is placed on pious conduct, then there is a chance that the venom injected into Christianity by conflicting doctrines or forms of worship might be lessened or removed. Addressing himself to all the parties in the confessional strife, Erasmus (Dolan 1964: 381, 386) implores them to abandon dogmatic self-assurance and claims to infallible knowledge in favour of Christian charity and modesty:

> I take this stand, not because what I say should be taken as absolutely certain or because I wish to dictate what the church should do. It is rather that, while awaiting a general council, we must eliminate—so far as lies in us—the causes of dissension. Let us not do anything by force, and rather do unto others what we wish them to do unto us. Let us beseech heaven and earth, but in no way force anyone into a religion that repels him. It is equally important that those who do not want to be forced in the matter of religion refrain from attacking the religion of others, especially when that religion is sheltered behind ancient practices.[13]

As we know, Erasmus admonitions regarding political and religious peace went largely unheeded. This, however, does not in any way diminish their importance and continued relevance. In fact, they provide a much-needed guidepost and loadstar for the troubles of our own globalizing age—an age marked by nearly interminable warfare and clashes of civilizations. To quote Dolan again, 'Perhaps the time is ripe for this gentleness of Erasmus to bear fruit.' Certainly (he adds) those who hope for a religious humanism that can 'galvanize the disparate elements of society today', we might say, the discordant elements of our world today—can revisit his writings with 'a realization that his failure is a warning and the sincerity of his effort an inspiration' (Dolan 1964: 15–16). With specific reference to inter-religious and cross-cultural relations, it seems clear that his accent on pious or ethical conduct is the only feasible and beneficial way to proceed. For on purely doctrinal or dogmatic grounds, how could one possibly reconcile the absolute 'oneness' of God (*tawhid*) with the notion of the trinity as well as with a multiplicity of gods and the complete denial of a personal deity?[14] In moving across doctrinal boundaries, Christians can take aid and comfort from the behaviour of Jesus in his encounter with the woman of Samaria at Jacob's well. It was to this non-Jewish woman that Jesus said, 'The hour is coming, and now is, when the true worshippers will worship [God] in spirit and truth' (John 4:23). As one should note well, Jesus in this meeting did not just tolerate the Samaritan distantly and grudgingly but treated her with the same loving friendliness which he had pinpointed as the heart of divine commandments (Matthew 22: 37–39, John 15:17). As Christians will also recall, Jesus limited the command of love not just to friends and neighbours but extended it to enemies or those appearing to be enemies (Matthew 5:44). In light of these teachings and his own example, how can followers today persist in enmity and hatred towards everything alien or unfamiliar? Both religiously and ethically, what excuse do we have for engaging, with or without provocation, in rampant hostility, aggressiveness and relentless warfare?

Notes

1. Erasmus adds a further restriction on the beginning of warfare (or *ius ad bellum*), one particularly congenial to our democratic (or democratising) age: Christian princes 'must not resort to this most dangerous of expedients without the consent of their citizens and of the whole country' (Rummel 1990: 320).
2. Contemporary readers may be reminded here of genocides in Europe, of the 'dirty wars' and disappearances in Latin America, and of episodes like May Lai in Vietnam (to name just a few examples).
3. To be sure, the aim of conversion still falls far short of genuine recognition. However, Erasmus's comments on this point may have been dictated by political prudence.
4. Erasmus in this context (Rummel 1990: 332) mentions a further suspicion nurtured by some, that, under the guise of war, one or the other European ruler might aim at world domination: 'The idea of universal monarchy, at which certain princes are supposed to be aiming, frightens some.' While not fully sharing this fear, the preferred solution for Erasmus—given 'human frailty'—resided in 'a number of modest dominions, linked together by the bonds of Christianity' or ethical-religious standards.
5. According to Barker (2001), the proverb appeared as a single sentence in the collection of 1500 but expanded into the longest essay by 1515.
6. The *Adages* ... contain a very brief entry on the saying *homo homini lupus* ('man is a wolf to man') and a much longer essay on the parallel saying *homo homini deus* ('man is a god to man'). See Barker (2001: 37–41 [Adages I, i, 69 and I, i, 70]). For Thomas Hobbes' invocation and privileging of the former proverb, see Lamprecht (1949: 1 [Dedicatory Letter]). Compare also Lamprecht (1949: 21–30 [Chapter 1]) and *Leviathan* (1953: 63–66 [Part I, Chapter 13]).

7. (The citation has been corrected for gender bias.) For some recent trends in 'philosophical anthropology' pointing in a similar direction see, for example, Plessner (1964, 1965, 1970) and Dallmayr (1981: 69–93).

8. As Erasmus adds (Barker 2001: 350), 'If you examine the matter more closely, you will find that almost all wars between Christians have arisen either from stupidity or from malice. A few youths, with no experience, have been influenced by the bad example of their forbears and of stories which fools have spread from foolish books. Then they have been encouraged by the call of flatterers, goaded by lawyers and theologians, with the consent or connivance of bishops, perhaps even at their demand.' On the notion of 'experience' compare Heidegger (1970) and Gadamer (1989: 346–62).

9. For interpretations of Erasmus as basically a precursor of Enlightenment rationalism and secular liberalism, compare, for example, Bainton (1952), Smith (1923) and Huizinga (1952).

10. How far Erasmus was removed from any kind of fanatical or 'fundamentalist' militancy can be gleaned from a concluding passage in *Handbook...* where he warns readers against falling 'into the clutches of those superstitious religious who, partly for their own advantage, partly out of great fervor, but certainly not out of any definite knowledge, "wander about seas and deserts". If they ever get their hands on a man returning from vices to virtue, then by outrageous arguments, blandishments, even threats, they drag him into the monastic life.' See Dolan (1964: 92).

11. As one should note well, Erasmus aim was not to condemn theorizing or philosophizing as such—one of his basic efforts was precisely to elucidate the 'philosophy of Christ'—but rather to challenge a purely abstract speculation completely divorced from practical conduct. He valued reason and philosophy but not as a substitute for piety and praxis. This outlook is captured in his well-known motto *eruditio et pietas*: learning *and* piety, not one in place of the other.

12. On the issue of faith vs. works, one may note a recent conciliatory breakthrough in the debate between Catholic and Protestant (Lutheran) theologians—a breakthrough very much in the spirit of Erasmus's *Handbook...*: the 'Joint Declaration on Justification' signed on 31 October 1999 in Augsburg, the same city where the Peace of Augsburg between the Confessions had been signed in 1555. (Students of comparative religious studies may also note the similarity between Erasmus approach and what in the Hindu tradition is called *karmayoga*.)

13. For Erasmus letter, see Allen (1951: 76), cited in English translation in Dolan (1964: 327–28).

14. Perhaps, one way to deal with this problem might be to treat the 'oneness' of God not as a numerical oneness but in the sense that God or the divine (however defined) is 'the one', that is, more important than anything else in the world.

References

Allen, P.S. (ed.). 1951. *Opus Epistolarum Desiderii Erasmi Roterdami*, vol. VI. London: Oxford University Press.

Bainton, Roland. 1952. *The Reformation of the Sixteenth Century*. Boston: Beacon Press.

Barker, William. 2001. *The Adages of Erasmus*. Toronto: University of Toronto Press.

Dallmayr, Fred R. 1981. 'Social Role and "Human Nature": Plessner's Philosophical Anthropology', in *Beyond Dogma and Despair: Towards a Critical Phenomenology of Politics*, pp. 69–93. Notre Dame, IN: University of Notre Dame Press.

———. 2001. 'Beyond Fugitive Democracy', in *Achieving Our World: Toward a Global and Plural Democracy*, pp. 71–89. Lanham, MD: Rowman & Littlefield.

Dolan, John P. (ed.). 1964. *The Essential Erasmus*. New York: Mentor Book.

Gadamer, Hans-Georg. 1989. *Truth and Method*, 2nd revised edition (trans. Joel Weinsheimer and Donald G. Marshall). New York: Crossroad.

Heidegger, Martin. 1970. *Hegel's Concept of Experience* (trans. J. Glenn Gray and Fred D. Wieck). New York: Harper & Row.

Hobbes, Thomas. 1953 [1651]. *Leviathan*. London: Everyman's Library.

Huizinga, Johan. 1952. *Erasmus of Rotterdam*. London: Phaidon Press.

Huntington, Samuel P. 1993. 'The Clash of Civilizations?', *Foreign Affairs*, 72(Summer): 22–49.

Lamprecht, Sterling P. (ed.). 1949. *De Cive or The Citizen*. New York: Appleton-Century-Crofts.

Plessner, Helmuth. 1964. *Conditio Humana*. Pfullingen: Neske.

———. 1965. *Die Stufen des Organischen und der Mensch, Einleitung in die philosophische Anthropologie*, 2nd ed. Berlin: de Gruyter.

———. 1970. *Laughing and Crying: A Study of the Limits of Human Behavior* (trans. James S. Churchill and Marjorie Grene). Evanston, IL: Northwestern University Press.

Rummel, Erika (ed.). 1990. *The Erasmus Reader*. Toronto: University of Toronto Press.

Smith, Preserved. 1923. *Erasmus*. New York: Harper & Bros.

Wolin, Sheldon S. 1996. 'Fugitive Democracy', in Seyla Benhabib (ed.), *Democracy and Difference: Contesting the Boundaries of the Political*, pp. 31–45. Princeton: Princeton University Press.

Machiavelli, *The Prince* and Leadership Responsibility

20

Sapir Handelman

Niccolo Machiavelli, author of *The Prince*, was born in 1469 in Florence, Italy. His time is well remembered as a season of endless wars and civil strife, rending Italy into violent regional rivalry. Therefore, it is only natural that the most urgent social problem should have been how to stop the fighting and bloodshed.

The conventional wisdom in Florence, Machiavelli's hometown, was that any decent society should be directed according to moral ideals rooted in traditions such as those of the Church and of moral philosophy. The general idea, which sounds quite simple and attractive, was that a moral, decent society has the potential to diminish evils, wrongs and destruction. Accordingly, professional politics and statecraft is an ethical mission for well-educated intellectuals with special expertise in ethics and morality. Therefore, it is hardly surprising that Machiavelli, who showed excellence in humanist studies,[1] was chosen to serve as a diplomat at the age of 29.

During his public service, Machiavelli gained a great deal of experience and knowledge in politics, statecraft and diplomacy. Therefore, it seems that no one had to teach Machiavelli the vicissitude of politics, especially in times of endless wars when borders were 'flexible' and rulers changed frequently. Indeed, after thirteen years of his public service of Florence, a new regime came into power. And it is only natural that any new regime would be very suspicious of the loyalty of its predecessor's right-hand men. And the Medici family, the new rulers of Florence, was no exception. Indeed, Machiavelli lost his tenure, was tortured and condemned to live in poverty. This drastic change left him spare time to be deeply engaged in scholarly work.[2] And, among all of Machiavelli's compositions and creations, it is *The Prince*, a book of advice to the common authoritarian ruler, that the world will never forget.

Between politics and ethics

The Prince is a unique exploration into the mystery of politics, composed as a book containing advice for the common authoritarian leader who has an unlimited desire for power, rulership and authority. The horrible and shocking advice and recommendations of Machiavelli leave a strong impression that politics and morality are concepts and practices worlds apart. Indeed, it is quite acceptable among historians that *The Prince* has contributed to the principle suspicion upon any pure ethical intentions of ambitious politicians. Yet, Machiavelli, with his sharp cynicism, seems to stretch this point to the very limit.

As strange it may sound, it seems that our sophisticated author does not separate between statecraft and ethics, despite every reasonable impression to the contrary. Indeed, Machiavelli has constructed his political agenda upon a clear ethical perception. He introduces to his readers a monistic ethical worldview, that is, an ethical perception which centres around one specific core value that must be defended almost at any price.[3] And the leading value in Machiavelli's thought is the survival of the prince.

According to Machiavelli's distinctive moral perception, any means are qualified for maintaining the prince's regime. To put it another way, the worthiness of any political action is measured by its contribution, usefulness and efficiency to the survival of the prince. However, it seems that Machiavelli, the sophisticated adviser, is also a cunning author whose intentions and motivations are not always clear. To be more specific, reading *The Prince* with special attention, comparing it with Machiavelli's other works, and examining carefully his advice, leave many doubts and much confusion that can be distilled into one clear question: Is Machiavelli himself consistent with the ethical perception that he himself introduced and supported?[4]

It is quite acceptable that Machiavelli, by writing a handbook for the authoritarian leader, had turned the study of politics into an applied science. The dismissed diplomat seems to sketch a more realistic picture of politics than the conventional wisdom which identified decent statesmanship with ideals like kindness, generosity and social justice. Nevertheless, Machiavelli's version of realism may seem even somewhat bizarre.

On one hand, Machiavelli's advice, often bordering upon inhuman cruelty, gives the impression that only a manipulative brutal gangster might have the natural talents for state leadership. But, on the other hand, it is quite clear that no person has ever achieved a position of power and rulership by applying Machiavelli's advice (*cf* Silone 1938: 26). In other words, the thinker who introduces a 'special' monistic ethical perception, the survival of the prince at all costs, seems to be a bad adviser or a sinner according to his ethical perception.[5] No doubt that the peak of this very tension is that the same Machiavelli who composed *The Prince* wrote *The Discourses*, an exceptional republican book.[6] Under the assumption that Machiavelli did not suffer from split personality, it is pretty reasonable to suspect that in *The Prince*, he had a hidden agenda in promoting the authoritarian regime of a gangster (*cf* Russell 2005: 466).

In most of the chapters of *The Prince*, Machiavelli indeed speaks for the interests of the ruler to stabilize his regime. But it seems that he does so under the assumption that only a hungry leader has the potential to develop the necessary political power to unite Italy. In the closing chapter of *The Prince*, he opens his heart to reveal his prime agenda: the unification of Italy and the restoration of the corona to Rome. Moreover, if we connect all the pieces together and stretch a little bit more the republican guideline (which appears clearly in *The Discourses*), it becomes possible that Machiavelli had a larger ulterior agenda even beyond the unity of Italy. Meaning that, reading between the lines, it is possible to understand that he aspired that the unity of Italy and the restoration of glory to Rome would lead to the revival of the Roman republic.[7] In other words, according to this republican interpretation of *The Prince*, Machiavelli dresses his brutal manipulative prince with the royal clothes of the Redeemer. Therefore, there is no escape from wondering and asking: Is it necessary for a ruler to commit so many horrible crimes in order to bring salvation?

It seems that understanding Machiavelli's creative reconciliation of crime and salvation requires an overview of the bigger picture. And the bigger picture means examining the political situation of Italy in the light of the classical infinite debate over the decent conduct of society.

A signpost in strivings towards a decent social order

History shows that the struggle towards building and conducting a decent, stable society is unending. The dynamics and complexity of social life lead to infinite social problems and various unexpected crises. Accordingly, the map of the philosophical, political and social debate is constantly shifting. There is no doubt that many factors, such as changing circumstances, different levels of accessible knowledge and diverse personal ambitions, have motivated the best minds of all times to support dissimilar, and even opposing, political and social agendas. Indeed, it seems that the common denominator to the various prescriptions is that they are all located somewhere in the spectrum between complete chaos and total tyranny. However, as strange as it might sound, the wall which separates chaos and dictatorship is sometimes exceedingly thin. Indeed, according to the republican interpretation of *The Prince*, the solution, or at least the immediate solution, to chaos and civil war is an authoritarian regime of a cruel prince.

Machiavelli's age is well remembered as a period of civil wars and social strife. In that time, Italy was embroiled in endless internal and external conflicts. Contrary to the destructive reality, as already stated, the conventional wisdom was that a decent society should be conducted according to well-set moral virtues directed by the Church or moral philosophy. It was a utopian vision which blocked any possibility of developing a practical programme to lead the society to overcome the endless civil wars. Machiavelli, the dismissed diplomat, the author of *The Prince*, turned the conventional wisdom on its head.[8]

As an alternative to conducting society according to 'reasonable' moral ideals, Machiavelli proposes an authoritarian regime of a brutal criminal. According to the republican interpretation of *The Prince*, only an adroit manipulative gangster might have the 'qualifications' to unite the fighting factions and establish a republic.

Machiavelli proposes a simple cost and benefit analysis—a dictator that survives, as cruel as he might be, his evils are relatively much smaller than the intolerable damage from protracted civil wars.[9] Moreover, from Machiavelli's writings it is implicit that despite the heavy costs incurred by the authoritarian regime, holding the bridle of power remains ever contingent upon the prince's ability to act for the benefit of his society, at least in the final account.[10] And the benefit of society meant, at the first stage at least, to develop enough political power, unite Italy and restore glory to Rome (*cf* Agassi 1985: 193; Strauss 1989: 44–47).

No doubt that uniting people of vastly different priorities and dissimilar worldviews, under some acceptable agenda is extremely difficult, even in times of peace. But to reach an agreement and reasonable compromise in ages of civil war, often enough seems to be an impossible mission. Indeed, *The Prince* was considered a watershed in the beginning of a long tradition of scholarship embracing the idea that a post-civil war republic can emerge only after a strong authoritarian transitional period (see, for example, Wantchekon 2004). This tradition, which started with Machiavelli (1979) and continued with Hobbes (1985 [1651]) also encompasses contemporary thinkers such as Samuel Huntington (1968) and Friedrch A. Hayek (1981).

At first blush, it might sound astonishing to find Friedrich Hayek, the protagonist of the free market system, the scholar who has restated the ideas of classical liberalism in the twentieth century (Hayek 1944, 1960), in a list of scholars who supports the regime of a dictator. According to Hayek's view, which shares similarities with Machiavelli's position in *The Discourses*, a necessary condition for conducting a decent, stable society is the establishment of an effective constitution (ibid.). However, in societies that lack the tradition of liberty, it is sometimes necessary to have 'a strong ruler' using his dictatorial powers to establish the necessary constitutional foundations for a liberal society. But how can we guarantee that our authoritarian redeemer is indeed a liberal dictator? Is it possible to make sure that the absolute ruler is a temporary dictator who stays in power only to complete the great tasks that Hayek and Machiavelli designated for him?

It is very hard to find real-life benevolent dictators who ever re-linquished power out of a free goodwill. And it is extremely difficult to believe that a manipulative criminal, as described by Machiavelli, will devote himself to noble tasks such as establishing a republic. Nevertheless, civil strife and intractable conflict are desperate situations. In this respect, the sad history of the Arab–Israeli conflict seems to dem-onstrate many of the insights that Machiavelli proposes in his brilliant and shocking rhetoric.

Between two Machiavellian leaders and the Arab–Israeli conflict

Intractable conflict and civil strife are social crises that appear the most desperate. The impression is that almost every social element that might pertain to the conflict survives, and whatever operates against it becomes extinct. In this respect, Machiavelli's *The Prince* works as a signpost to the beginning of a long tradition of scholarship embracing the idea that any kind of solution to civil strife and intractable conflict depends upon unusual and dramatic activities of 'strong' political leaders.

The sad history of the Arab–Israeli conflict shows that concrete steps towards any kind of conflict resolution are only achieved by the drastic moves of political leaders who are not 'saints' and whose political actions do not primarily arise from 'noble' intentions, to say the least. The first such leader was Anwar Sadat, the president of Egypt, whose astonishing arrival in Israel in 1977 paved the way for a peace agreement between the two nations. The second is Ariel Sharon, the Israeli prime minister, who bravely stood against his party, leading a withdrawal from occupied territories. Ironically, Sadat, the Egyptian dictator, led the peace process through negotiation and cooperation, while Sharon, the democratic prime minister, conducted his dramatic move without any consideration and coordination with the Palestinians.

Of course, it is hard, if possible at all, to understand the 'real' motivations behind the actions of human beings. Basically, and crudely speaking, we do not have X-ray visions into Sadat's and Sharon's minds and souls to explore their way of thinking more directly. However, combining the logic of the circumstances, or more precisely the complexity of the situation, with a political theory might help us constructing a 'good' story. Such a story, or a fable, whether true, half true or completely imaginary, enfolds a lesson. Therefore, I propose to sketch a Machiavellian interpretation to Sadat's and Sharon's dramatic historical moves.

Looking back at the disconsolate financial situation of Egypt, and the immense social problems resulting from that, indicates that the country desperately needed an 'economic fuel' (see, for example, Hirst and Beeson 1981: 252–54). Therefore, it is quite reasonable to surmise that Sadat, who challenged the very existence of Israel in the 1973 war, did not abandon his old desire to return the Sinai desert back to Egyptian control. This magical desert, one of the most beautiful places on Earth, has all the potential to attract tourists from all around the world. However, it seems that the Egyptian leader felt trapped. On one hand, it was quite clear to him, from past painful experiences, that it would be extremely difficult to recover the lost asset by force and violence. On the other hand, it also appeared impossible by peaceful means. This is because Israel, which constantly worries for its existence,[11] conducted an uncompromised foreign policy. Moreover, Israel's policy compelled Sadat to understand that routine and conventional means of diplomacy and negotiation where only doomed to fail.

In short, any attempt to bridge the gap between the Israel and Egypt was inevitably to be greeted with extreme suspicion. Even the most optimistic statesmen were quite sceptical about the genuine intentions of the two bitter rivals to reach a peace agreement.[12] Therefore, in defiance of any 'rational' prediction, the Egyptian leader made an astonishing move: in 1977, Sadat, the leader of the strongest Arab country, the most rigidly entrenched of Israel's most bitter enemies, came to Jerusalem to talk peace in the Israeli parliament, the *Knesset*. No doubt that this astonishing visit was a turning point in the Israeli–Arab conflict.[13] However, it is not utterly fanciful to consider that this dramatic turning point was part of a manipulative strategy: returning the Sinai desert to Egyptian control by a peace agreement with Israel.[14] Therefore, Sadat's historical move seems to rewrite one of the basic rules of *The Prince*: not every subversive manipulation is indecent, at least in the final account.[15]

Ariel Sharon, the legendary warrior, has many dubious 'credits' in the Israeli–Palestinian conflict. For example, it is hard to forget that in 1989, not so long ago, he led aggressive political moves to block any realistic possibilities for the Israeli government to negotiate and compromise with the Palestinians.[16] Nevertheless, the same Ariel Sharon, who devoted a major part of his life to build and strengthen the settlements, also led a historical 'one-sided withdrawal' from territories in the West Bank. The irony of fate is that this one-sided disengagement which was led by Ariel Sharon, the 'father' of settlements, seems to penetrate in the Israeli mind, more than anything else, the idea that the occupation might be more harmful than beneficial to the existence of Israel. And I would like to expand and explain that.

It can scarcely escape notice how much of the Jewish experience is so devastatingly tragic and traumatic: the historical—yet still fresh and fairly recent—trauma of endless pogroms culminating in the Holocaust, along with the ancient ingrained painful memory of the destruction of the temple. Indeed, a common refrain in the Jewish prayer is: 'every generation they tried to exterminate us but we survived.'[17] And a society in which a major part of the culture and tradition is based upon traumas, naturally tends to be a fortified society and not an open one. In other words, people, who in the back of their minds, are always fearful of their very existence, will not readily compromise on issues concerning their security.[18] Indeed, a noticeable 'symptom' in the Jewish Israeli[19] experience has always been the absence of any serious public debate upon fundamental issues relating to the existence of Israel; for example: What are the borders of the country? What is the fate of Jerusalem?

The disengagement from the Palestinians, which meant withdrawal from Gaza and some territories in the West Bank, and evacuating Jewish people from their homes against their will, is not an usual event for Jewish Israelis. But Israel survived. Accordingly, it seems that a majority of the people in Israel began to seriously consider the idea that even in times of intractable conflict, when a reasonable peace negotiation seems to be an unrealistic option, Israel is strong enough to lead one-sided initiatives. Moreover, a one-sided withdrawal might be more beneficial to the survival of Israel than a continuing unnecessary occupation. However, this is only part of the picture. This is because Sharon's one-sided withdrawal seems to send a clear message to the Palestinians.

The unilateral disengagement signals to the Palestinians that they have to begin considering seriously the option of establishing an independent state. Independence and freedom also mean responsibility. And the burden of responsibility requires establishing institutions, fighting corruption, decent education, and all the heavy tasks that any modern desirable society has to take care of.

If there is an amount of truth in my interpretation of Sadat's and Sharon's way of thinking, then it is worth recalling Machiavelli's hidden insight as to how the personal ambition of a 'hungry' leader might operate for the benefit of society. In Sadat's case, Egypt gets Sinai, and both countries gain peace. However, in Sharon's situation it is too soon to predict the results, but it is pretty reasonable to assume that his personal ambitions to stay in power and retain his tenure drove him to such a drastic move.[20] It seems that Sharon very well understood that holding the bridle of power depends upon the ability to act for the benefit of society. And the benefit of society depends, first and foremost, upon stopping bloodshed and advancing a peace process.

Intractable conflict seems to be an immense social crisis. Among the characteristics of this tragic phenomenon are violence, dehumanization of the rival, almost everyone feels that it is a war for his or her existence, and, of course, it is a long, continuing conflict. Those situations are extremely severe in long-term conflicts, wherein generations in turn are born into the reality of intractable conflict. The bitter irony is that every side evades responsibility and blames their rivals with almost the same accusations—'there is no reasonable partner for any peace process'. Hence, utter deadlock. The public debate hardly exists, those who are most desperate can react very aggressively, and even the government is wrapped in the same chain of destruction.[21]

The bitter irony is that many of the main characteristics, or more precisely, symptoms, of this puzzling phenomenon demonstrate the tenacity and stupidity of entrenched closed minded worldviews. Indeed, from the standpoint of the impartial spectator, often enough, it appears that the conflict may be easily resolved. However, social life is not conducted according to the suggestions and recommendations of the impartial spectator. In this respect, it is worth reminding that it took four bloody wars for an Arab leader to come to Jerusalem to talk peace and almost sixty years of bloody strife for an Israeli leader to withdraw from some Palestinian territories. Therefore, the inevitable lesson from our two short stories of long bloody conflicts unfolds in one question: Should any responsible citizen wait until a 'hungry' leader, at long last, handily discovers an overlap between his personal narcissist ambitions to stay in power and the altruism of advancing peace for the benefit of society?

Leadership and responsibility

No doubt that there is a noticeable place for *The Prince* in the pantheon of social ideas. However, it is not always clear whether it is an honorary chair or a place of shame. But it is pretty obvious that no reasonable human being can stay apathetic to the idea that the rescuer of society is a brutal manipulative criminal.

History shows that the suggestion to support the regime of a gangster, hoping that he will bring salvation, is—to say the least—very dangerous. Moreover, it sounds naïve and even utopian to hope that Machiavelli's insight—the ambitions of a sophisticated leader will lead him to act for the benefit of his society at least in the final account—will come true. Nevertheless, it is hard to doubt that in many extreme cases, breaking the chain of destruction depends upon brave and creative initiatives of political leaders. Therefore, especially in time of essential social crisis, there is much room to ask and even demand for leadership responsibility. This means demanding from political leaders to act for the benefit of society even when it requires unpopular moves at heavy personal costs.[22] Of course, leading a society to overcome an essential crisis such as an intractable conflict, seems to be an extremely difficult mission. However, a quick glance once again at *The Prince* might yet teach us a new lesson.

There is no need for a meticulous textual scrutiny of *The Prince* to take due notice that Machiavelli's descriptions focus upon failures of kings, princes and rulers to preserve their regimes. In contrast, he guides his prince to overcome the obstacles and barriers that endanger his rule.

The essential point is that Machiavelli does so through careful analysis of the heavy ethical costs entailed in any necessary move. And it is the implications of his methodology that deserve special attention. [23]

As strange as it may sound, combining Machiavelli's methodology (analyzing failures, evils and wrongs) with the republican interpretation of *The Prince* (authoritarian regime as a desperate solution to civil war) might shed light upon the notion of leadership responsibility which means going beyond *The Prince* as we know, and embodying careful moves, minimizing damage and, of course, opening up to new ideas.

Notes

1. See, for example, Skinner (1981: 3–4): 'The concept of the *studia humanitatis*... came to exercise a powerful influence on the universities and on the conduct of Italian public life.... The humanists ... expected their students to begin with the mastery of Latin, move on to the practice of rhetoric and the imitation of the finest classical stylists and complete their studies with a close reading of ancient history and moral philosophy. They also popularized the long-standing belief that this type of training offers the best preparation for political life. As Cicero had repeatedly maintained, these disciplines nurture the values we principally need to acquire in order to serve our country well: a willingness to subordinate our private interests to the public good, a desire to fight against corruption and tyranny and an ambition to reach out for the noblest goals of all, those of honour and glory for our country as well as for ourselves.'

2. See Bondanella and Musa (1979:16): 'Although the fall of Soderini's government was a personal misfortune for Machiavelli, his enforced retirement seemed to have acted as a catalyst for his political imagination. After 1513, he composed ... all of his major literary, historical and political works ... including *The Art of War*, *The Discourses*, *The History of Florence*, *The Mandrake Root*, *Belfagor*, *The Life of Castruccio Castracani*, *Clizia*, *A Dialogue on Language* and *The Golden Ass*.'

3. In contrast to monistic ethical-political theories that centre upon one core super-value, pluralism is usually associated with the idea that there are irreducibly many prudential values. For a further discussion upon the monism-pluralism issue, see Griffin (1986: 89–92).

4. Among many scholars, it is generally agreed that Machiavelli, who was cast out by the Medici family, wrote *The Prince* in order to return to active political life. By writing this brilliant treatise, according to these interpretations, he intended to impress the prince and prove his loyalty to the regime. See, for example, Skinner (1981: 21–24).

In principle, I do not see a necessary contradiction between this view and the kind of reading I suggest—a monistic ethical-political perception (the maintenance of a rulership at all cost). However, the problem is that it is very doubtful if Machiavelli, indeed, offered such prudent advice to the prince.

5. The very inapplicability of Machiavelli's advice to realistic situations was the basis for many interpretations of *The Prince*. For example, Dietz (1986) noted that the intentions of Machiavelli, who was cast out by the Medici, were actually to trap the prince. According to this interpretation, Machiavelli hoped that Lorenzo de Medici, to whom he dedicated *The Prince*, would follow his deliberately poisonous advice that would eventually lead him to lose his regime.

6. One of the most astonishing points is that in the dedication to both *The Prince* and *The Discourses*, Machiavelli claims to present everything he knows. For a further discussion, see Mansfield (1972: 102).

7. According to Machiavelli (1979 [1531]: 175–81), an ideal city-state regime is a composite of three types of government: 'a principality, an aristocracy and a democracy'. In this context, the Roman republic government had successfully balanced between the rulers (two consuls), the aristocrats (represented by the senate) and the people (the plebeians). Therefore, Machiavelli had noted that the Roman republic was a perfect state: 'Fortune was so favorable to Rome that even though she passed from a government by kings and aristocrats to one by the people...nevertheless the kingly authority was never entirely abolished to give authority to the aristocrats, nor was the authority of the aristocrats diminished completely to give it to the people; but since these elements remained mixed, Rome was a perfect state; and this perfection was produced through the friction between the plebeians and the senate.'

   There are many interpretations of *The Prince*, indicating that Machiavelli was concerned about the fate of his society. For example, some of the well-known ones point that he saw the authoritarian regime as a desperate alternative to the devastating and nigh total chaos that was so common in his time. For a further discussion, see Baron (1961), Rigby (1977), Pocock (1975) and Dietz (1986: 778–79). However, in this chapter, I will embrace the classical republican interpretation, that is, Machiavelli, the same person who showed strong republican inclinations in *The Discourses*, aspired to the revival of the Roman republic.

8. For a further discussion upon the Machiavellian revolution in modern political philosophy, see Mannet (1996: 10–19) and Strauss (1989: 39–51).

9. See, for example, Machiavelli (1979 [1532]: 130): 'A prince must not worry about the reproach of cruelty when it is a matter of keeping his subjects united and loyal; for with a very few examples of cruelty he will be more compassionate than those who, out of excessive mercy, permit disorders to continue, from which arise murders and plundering; for these usually harm the community at large, while the executions that come from the prince harm one individual in particular.'

10. Indeed, this point arises many times in Machiavelli's text. See, for example, Machiavelli (1979: 153). Leo Strauss emphasizes (1989: 42) this issue and even stretches in a somewhat different direction. He underscores that the ultimate passion for glory is the power that drives the prince to undertake great and noble tasks for the benefit of society: 'The passion in question is the desire for glory. The highest form of the desire for glory is the desire to be a new prince in the fullest sense of the term, a wholly new prince: a discoverer of a new type of social order, a moulder of many generations of men. The founder of society has a selfish interest in the preservation of society, of his work. He has therefore a selfish interest in the members of his society being and remaining sociable, and hence good.'

Not by any means or scope to underestimate the sheer Narcissism of princes, kings and rulers, and even though I tend to agree with Strauss that the engine behind the prince's actions is his selfish ambitions, nevertheless, my emphasis lies elsewhere. While Strauss underscores the prince's desire to gain world fame, I emphasize the difficulties in leading and marshaling society, especially in times of crises. Therefore, I eschew expectations of unmitigated megalomania and instead embrace the inevitable minimum. Machiavelli's ruthlessly realistic prince mainly wants simply to survive and it is the difficulties inherent to the craft of rulership that must ultimately compel him to act in the benefit of society.

11. It seems that the fear and worry, which are fundamental to the Jewish–Israeli essence, were well known to the Egyptian president. Indeed, in his historical speech in the Israeli parliament, Sadat (1977) had repeated several times that every peace agreement would have to include guarantees to ensure security for Israel: 'What is peace for Israel? It means that Israel lives in the region with her Arab neighbors, in security and safety. To such logic, I say yes. It means that Israel lives within her borders, secure against any aggression. To such logic, I say yes. It means that Israel obtains all kinds of guarantees that ensure those two factors. To this demand, I say yes. More than that, we declare that we accept all the international guarantees you envisage and accept.'

12. Sadat describes the situation in his historical speech well in the Israeli parliament on 20 November 1977: 'I can see the point of all those who were astounded by my decision or those who had any doubts as to the sincerity of the intentions behind the declaration of my decision. No one would have ever conceived that the President of the biggest Arab State, which bears the heaviest burden and the top responsibility pertaining to the cause of war and peace in the Middle East, could declare his readiness to go to the land of the adversary while we were still in a state of war. Rather, we all are still bearing the consequences of four fierce wars waged within thirty years. The families of the 1973 October War are still moaning under the cruel pains of widowhood and bereavement of sons, fathers and brothers. As I have already declared, I have not consulted, as far as this decision is

concerned, with any of my colleagues and brothers, the Arab Heads of State or the confrontation States. Those of them who contacted me, following the declaration of this decision, expressed their objection, because the feeling of utter suspicion and absolute lack of confidence between the Arab States and the Palestinian People on one hand, and Israel on the other, still surges in us all. It is sufficient to say that many months in which peace could have been brought about had been wasted over differences and fruitless discussions on the procedure for the convocation of the Geneva Conference, all showing utter suspicion and absolute lack of confidence.'

13. For a further discussion on Sadat's trip to Jerusalem as a major turning point in the conflict, see Kelman (1985).

14. In this context, it seems important to pay attention that Sadat's historical speech is not clean of demagogic motifs. For example, he approaches the Israeli Jews and says: 'You have to give up … the belief that force is the best method for dealing with the Arabs.' Of course, such preaching does not come from a liberal ruler that respects the democratic rights of his people.

15. See, for example, Machiavelli (1979: 133): 'How praiseworthy it is for a prince to keep his word and to live by integrity and not by deceit everyone knows; nevertheless, one sees from the experience of our times that the princes who have accomplished great deeds are those who have cared little for keeping their promises and who have known how to manipulate the minds of men by shrewdness; and in the end they have surpassed those who laid their foundations upon honesty.'

16. See http://likud1.ios.st/Front/NewsNet/reports.asp?reportId=29214.

17. A good example is the Passover *Haggada* (text used on the festival meal that opens the Passover holiday).

18. This chapter is not an exploration of the Arab–Israeli conflict. Therefore, I bring here only a basic general background. For a further discussion see Bar-Tal (1998).

19. I am emphasizing 'Jewish Israeli' because not every Jew is Israeli and not every Israeli is Jewish. Indeed, many Israelis are not Jewish. For a further discussion upon this issue, see Agassi (1999).

20. The political instability of Israel led Sharon's predecessors—Benjamin Netanyahu and Ehud Barak—to lose their tenure.

21. For interesting articles and further discussion upon intractable conflict, see http://www.BeyondIntractability.org.

22. In regard to the Israeli case, Agassi (1999) had noted that leadership responsibility means opening a public debate upon a well thought strategy for Israel.

23. This last methodological implication of Machiavelli's work is actually somewhat reminiscent of Karl Popper's philosophy of science. Popper argued that science, or more precisely, natural science, is progress gained by constructing and refuting theories. Of course, there remains a significant

difference between natural and social science in general, and Popper and Machiavelli in particular. Nevertheless, the similarity lies in the knowledge dimension. Indeed, both Popper and Machiavelli emphasize the importance of 'negative knowledge'. Popper (1965) points out how science is ever developing through the method of conjectures and refutations, while, however similarly, Machiavelli guides his prince through careful analysis of evils, wrongs and failures.

References

Agassi, J. 1999. *Liberal Nationalism for Israel: Towards an Israeli National Identity.* Jerusalem and New York: Gefen Publishing House.

———. 1985. *Technology: Philosophical and Social Aspects.* Dordrecht, Holland: D. Reidel Publishing Company.

Bar-Tal, D. 1998. 'Societal Beliefs in Times of Intractable Conflict: The Israeli Case', *International Journal of Conflict Management*, 9: 22–50.

Baron, H. 1961. 'Machiavelli: The Republican Citizen and the Author of the Prince', *English Historical Review*, 299: 217–53.

Bondanella, P. and M. Musa. 1979. Introduction, in *The Portable Machiavelli.* New York: Penguin Books.

Dietz, M.G. 1986. 'Trapping The Prince: Machiavelli and the Politics of Deception', *The American Political Science Review*, 80: 777–99.

Griffin, J. 1986. *Well-being: Its Meaning, Measurement and Moral Importance.* Oxford: Clarendon Press.

Hayek, F.A. 1944. *The Road to Serfdom.* Chicago: University of Chicago Press.

———. 1960. *The Constitution of Liberty.* Chicago: University of Chicago Press.

———. 1981. *Interviews in El Mercurio.* 19 April, Santiago, Chile. Available on http://fbses.webou.net/spip.php?article425

Hirst, D. and I. Beeson. 1981. *Sadat.* London: Faber and Faber.

Hobbes, T. 1985 [1651]. *Leviathan* (ed. R. Tuck). Cambridge: Cambridge University Press.

Huntington, S. 1968. *Political Order in Changing Societies.* New Haven, CT: Yale University Press.

Kelman, H.C. 1985. 'Overcoming the Psychological Barrier: An Analysis of the Egyptian–Israeli Peace Process', *Negotiation Journal*, 1(3): 213–34.

Machiavelli, N. 1979 [1531]. 'The Discourses' and 'The Prince', in P. Bondanella and M. Musa (eds), *The Portable Machiavelli.* New York: Penguin Books.

Mannet, P. 1996. *An Intellectual History of Liberalism* (trans. by R. Balinski). Princeton: Princeton University Press.

Mansfield, H. 1972. 'Necessity in the Beginnings of Cities', in A. Parel (ed.), *The Political Calculus.* Toronto and Buffalo: University of Toronto Press.

Pocock, J.G.A. 1975. *The Machiavellian Moment*. Princeton: Princeton University Press.

Popper, K. 1965. *Conjunctures and Refutations: The Growth of Scientific Knowledge*. New York: Harper Torchbooks.

Rigby, J.H. 1977. *Florence and the Medici*. London: Thames and Hudson.

Russell, B. 2005. *History of Western Philosophy*. London and New York: Routledge.

Sadat Anwar. 1977. Statement to the Knesset by President Sadat. Forty-third meeting of the Ninth Knesset, 20 November, Jerusalem.

Silone Ignazio. 1938. *The School for Dictators*. New York and London: Harper and Brothers Publishers.

Skinner, Q. 1981. *Machiavelli*. Oxford: Oxford University Press.

Strauss, L. 1989. *An Introduction to Political Philosophy*. Detroit: Wayne State University Press.

Wantchekon, L. 2004. 'The Paradox of "Warlord", Democracy: A Theoretical Investigation', *American Political Science Review*, 98(1): 17–32.

Transforming Power and Freedom 21

From Voluntary Servitude to Non-violent Resistance

CHRISTIAN BARTOLF

Certainly, in principle, we see a contradiction between the modern prince and the modern sage. But in any case we do not any longer ignore Count Leo Tolstoy (1828–1910) and his tremendous impact on modern political science, philosophy and action. Without Tolstoy's heritage and inspiration we cannot understand and realise the meaning of Mahatma Gandhi (1869–1948) and Martin Luther King Jr (1929–68), whom I dedicate this chapter to because they are the authentic and obvious followers of the ancient sages and prophets: Socrates, Jesus, Buddha and Lao-Tzu. All of these sages and prophets pleaded for non-violent resistance and transformed their lives, thought and action into glorious and heroic examples of the living spirit—princes of the divine spirit: the Conscience.

Following the concept of Conscience as a universal challenge as it has been codified in the Universal Declaration of Human Rights, we can no longer resist the fact that all witnesses or martyrs of Conscience have been non-violent resisters. They inspired people during their lifetimes to follow their lifelines, and most of them will never be forgotten as long as humankind is searching for truth. But are we still longing and searching for truth? Or does the law of violence and greed prevail forever? This is the challenge for us today: not to give up hope and humanity. Where do we find good advice for ourselves, for our contemporaries and our followers? One example is in the writing of Tolstoy, the modern sage of Russia.

Let us take, as an example, Tolstoy's last major work, *A Calendar of Wisdom: Daily Thoughts to Nourish the Soul* (1904–07). Tolstoy's *Thoughts of Wise Men* appeared in 1904 in the first edition. Three editions followed during his lifetime—between 1904 and 1910—with different titles: *The Way of Life, Circle of Reading* and *A Wise Thought for Every Day*. *A Calendar of Wisdom* is now the first English translation of the enlarged and completely revised second edition of *Thoughts of Wise Men*, written between 1904 and 1907.

A Calendar of Wisdom is a compilation of thoughts grouped according to topics for a certain day, week and month, topics like God, Intellect, Law, Love, Divine Nature of Mankind, Faith, Temptations, Word, Self-Sacrifice, Eternity, Good, Kindness, Unification of People (with God), Prayer, Freedom, Perfection, Work, and so on, as Tolstoy wrote in his diary on 3 June 1904. He added about a hundred of his own thoughts, taken from previous diaries of his, starting each day with an opening thought of his own, followed by a quotation of another source and finishing each day with a closing thought of Tolstoy. At the end of the week, he added a short story or vignette, three to ten pages in length. All fifty-two stories, 'The Sunday Reading Stories' (adapting the writings of Plato, Buddha, Pascal and others), corresponded to each week's moral, philosophical and religious topic.

What is interesting for us now, re-reading this almost unknown *Calendar*, is that we find—among those quoted—some princes and kings. For example:

1. **Frederick II:** *If my soldiers started thinking, not a single soldier would remain in my army* (entry on 29 December [Tolstoy 1997: 376]).
2. **Marcus Aurelius:** *A small branch cut off from a big limb is separated from the whole tree. In the same way, when a person is in an argument with another person, he is separated from all humanity* (entry on 17 December [ibid.: 364]).

* * *

Why are you so afraid of change? Nothing in this world can be done without change. Only one rule should remain constant: do not do anything inhumane to others (entry on 7 December [ibid.: 354]).

* * *

A person's soul may be compared to a transparent ball which is lit from the inside with its own light. This flame is not only the source of all light and truth, but it illuminates everything around you. In this state, the soul is free and happy. Only if it becomes addicted to anything outside you, will it become troubled, darkened and impenetrable. Distractions obstruct the light which shows you the way (entry on 27 November [ibid.: 344]).

Doubtless, these quotations refer to the Conscience, to the non-violent resistance of the conscientious objectors of the past, present and future. And how does it come that these thinkers were princes and kings? This has been a good question since the life of the Buddha or King Ashoka, since the truth-related solar origin of monotheism in ancient Egypt, followed, then, by Moses and the prophetic tradition until today. Sigmund Freud taught us as much in his last great work on Moses and monotheism.

But how can we learn to follow our Conscience being neither a prince nor a sage? There is one sure remedy for all of us: not the ambitious and greedy attitude of the parvenu who imitates the prince, but to listen and follow the voice of the Conscience. But how will we be able to listen to the still, small voice from within? How can we be sure of following the voice of humanity and not the seducing one of the beast of brute force. There is one basic condition. Let us remember the lessons of those who taught us the secret mechanisms of 'voluntary servitude'. For example, Ralph Waldo Emerson's friend Henry David Thoreau (1817–62) and Michel de la Montaigne's friend Etienne de la Boétie (1530–63).

Let us first find Tolstoy's quotes of Thoreau in the *Calendar*. Thoreau's wonderful image of the non-violent grassroots revolution is given here: 'The most tender plants can push their way through the hardest rocks, and it is the same with kindness. Nothing can stop a truly kind and sincere person' (entry on 12 December [ibid.: 359]). This seems to have become a motto for Gandhi and King, and for so many others without a name. And this quote reminds us of another sage's thought, that of Lao-Tzu (entry on 30 November [ibid.: 347]):

There is nothing in this world more tender and more pliable than water, yet hard and rigid things cannot resist it. Weakness defeats strength, tenderness defeats rigidity. Everyone knows this law but no one acts upon it. The weakest in the world gain victory over the strongest; therefore, there is a great advantage in humility and silence. Only a few people in this world are truly humble.

Silence and humility enable us to listen to our voice of Conscience, the alphabet of reason and thought—a good guide for us scientists and thinkers. This guide enables us to appreciate the value of meditation and contemplation, to gain wisdom and insight in the secret mechanisms of 'voluntary servitude', which prevent us from emancipation. And Tolstoy adds in his own words: 'The more humble a person is, the freer and stronger he is' (entry on 30 November [ibid.: 347]). Freedom and strength are the outward attributes of sovereign princes, the inward attributes of true and real sages. Again, according to Lao-Tzu: 'In those countries where wise people are in power, their subjects do not notice the existence of their rulers' (entry on 13 October [ibid.: 299]). And Tolstoy added that 'people should conceive of a kind of future government in which violence will not be necessary', and as a basis, 'You should live in such a way that violence is not necessary for you' (entry 13 October [ibid.: 299]). Again, Thoreau said: 'When you feel the desire for power, you should stay in solitude for some time' (entry on 27 August [ibid.: 252]); and Lao-Tzu: 'He who is really skillful in communicating with people is usually a humble and quiet person. This is called the virtue of non-resistance. This is called harmony with Heaven' (entry on 17 July [ibid.: 211]).

This is really a good guide for scholars and scientists of the present; we could all learn from it. According to Lao-Tzu: 'In order not to pour out a vessel full of water, you should hold it evenly. In order to have a razor sharp, you should sharpen it. The same should happen with your soul if you are looking for real goodness' (entry on 27 June [ibid.: 191]).

The humility and silence of the real sage in us overcomes the pride and vanity of the idle prince in us. But how? Let us consult again Lao-Tzu in Tolstoy's *Calendar* (entry on 8 June [ibid.: 172]): 'Always respond to hatred with kindness. The most difficult enterprises are easiest at their inception, and the greatest of enterprises have humble origins. Confront difficulties while they are still easy, then, and tackle a big thing when it is still small.' And again: 'He who defeats others is strong; he who defeats himself is powerful, and he who knows when he dies that he will not be destroyed is eternal' (entry on 10 June[ibid.: 174]). Non-violence in heart and mind and the real knowledge of the immortality of the soul—these are two keys to transform power in freedom. But this real knowledge excludes pride and ambition according to Lao-Tzu, who says: 'A person who stands on his tiptoes cannot stand long and a person who is too proud of himself cannot set a good example' (entry on 2 June [ibid.: 166]). What a challenge for the academic community! Lao-Tzu explains (entry on 8 May [ibid.: 141]):

> The rivers and seas are the masters of the valleys across which they flow. This is because they are lower than the valleys. In the same way, a person

who wants to be higher than other people should be lower than they; if he wants to guide people, he should be below them.

That is why true scholars and scientists should identify with those who have been excluded and marginalized, oppressed, repressed and suppressed, with the outcasts of society, the children of God who do the dirty jobs, work of impurity everywhere, untouchables, those who remain invisible, in the shadow of the political scenery, almost not-existent, victims of false pride and cruel prejudice. Empathy for the scapegoats of society brings together the modern sage and the modern prince, because princes and kings—as representatives of the community—frequently practice immorality in the name of the community. Again, Thoreau says: 'The only way to tell the truth is to speak with kindness. Only the words of a loving man can be heard' (entry on 24 February [ibid.: 67]). And: 'The most powerful weapon known is the weapon of blessing. Therefore, a clever person relies on it. He wins with peace, not with war' (entry on 9 February [ibid.: 52]).

Humility and silence as the virtues of the real sage are complemented by renunciation and abstention according to Lao-Tzu: 'Abstention should be a habit in your life; it should support you in your virtues. For he who is resolute in goodness, there is nothing that he could not overcome' (entry on 6 January [ibid.: 18]). Renunciation and abstention from greed, desire, jealousy, hatred, prejudice and resentment give us the basis to overcome the system of fear, suspicion and distrust that cages us, because we tend to surrender to those princes without enlightenment, misusing their sovereign power and liberty. Tolstoy's opening thought in his 19 January entry is: 'Society can be improved only by self-sacrifice' (ibid.: 31). Then follows Lao-Tzu: 'Heaven and earth are eternal. They are eternal because they do not exist for themselves. In the same way, a truly holy person does not live for himself and, therefore, he can become eternal, and can achieve anything' (ibid.). And Tolstoy concludes: 'There is only one law, both in your personal and social life: if you want to improve your soul, you should be ready to sacrifice it' (ibid.).' To gain more inner freedom—this is the improvement of man and real progress.

But where do we find our role model while striving to improve ourselves, to reconcile the prince and the sage? Let us listen to the advice of Lao-Tzu (entry on 10 February [ibid.: 53]):

To be strong, you have to be like water: if there are no obstacles, it flows; if there is an obstacle it stops; if a dam is broken, then it flows further; if a vessel is square, then it has a square form; if a vessel is round, then it has a round form. Because it is so soft and flexible, it is the most necessary and the strongest thing

Tolstoy advises us to become humble and not to forget that we live for a short period of time in this world, but to live it according to the laws of eternal life: non-violence, Conscience and truth.

Let us finally remember the words of Michel de la Montaigne's friend Etienne de la Boétie (1530–62) in his *Discourse on Voluntary Servitude* (1548), an appeal to us to expand our inner freedom, to follow our voice of conscience, to emancipate society from violence, greed, hubris, hypocrisy and untruth:

Everyone knows that the fire from a little spark will increase and blaze ever higher as long as it finds wood to burn; yet without being quenched by water but merely by finding no more fuel to feed on, it consumes itself, dies down and is no longer a flame. Similarly, the more tyrants pillage, the more they crave, the more they ruin and destroy; the more one yields to them and obeys them, by that much do they become mightier and more formidable, the readier to annihilate and destroy. But if not one thing is yielded to them, if, without any violence they are simply not obeyed, they become naked and undone and as nothing, just as, when the root receives no nourishment, the branch withers and dies.

Poor, wretched, and stupid peoples, nations determined on your own misfortune and blind to your own good! You let yourselves be deprived before your own eyes of the best part of your revenues; your fields are plundered, your homes robbed, your family heirlooms taken away. You live in such a way that you cannot claim a single thing as your own; and it would seem that you consider yourselves lucky to be loaned your property, your families and your very lives. All this havoc, this misfortune, this ruin, descends upon you not from alien foes, but from the one enemy whom you yourselves render as powerful as he is, for whom you go bravely to war, for whose greatness you do not refuse to offer your own bodies unto death. He who thus domineers over you has only two eyes, only two hands, only one body, no more than is possessed by the least man among the infinite numbers dwelling in your cities; he has indeed nothing more than the power that you confer upon him to destroy you. Where has he acquired enough eyes to spy upon you, if you do not provide them yourselves? How can he have so many arms to beat you with, if he does not borrow them from you? The feet that trample down your cities, where does he get them if they are not your own? How does he have any power over you except through you? How would he dare assail you if he had no cooperation from you? What could he do to you if you yourselves did not connive with the thief who plunders you, if you were not an accomplice of the murderer who kills you, if you were not traitors to yourselves? You sow your crops in order that he may ravage them, you install and furnish your homes to give him goods to pillage; you rear your daughters that he may gratify his lust; you bring up your children in order that he may confer upon them the greatest privilege he knows—to be led into his battles, to be delivered to butchery, to be made the servants of his greed and the instruments of his vengeance; you yield your bodies unto hard labor in order that he may indulge in his delights and wallow in his filthy pleasures; you weaken yourselves in order to make him the stronger and the mightier to hold you in check. From all these indignities, such as the very beasts of the field would not endure, you can deliver yourselves if you try, not by taking action, but merely by willing to be free. Resolve to serve no more, and you are at once freed. I do not ask that you place hands upon the tyrant to topple him over, but simply that you support him no longer; then you will behold him, like a great Colossus whose pedestal has been pulled away, fall of his own weight and break in pieces.

Let us therefore learn while there is yet time, let us learn to do good. Let us raise our eyes to Heaven for the sake of our honor, for the very love of virtue, or to speak wisely, for the love and praise of God Almighty, who is the infallible witness of our deeds and the just judge of our faults. As for me, I truly believe I am right, since there is nothing so contrary to a generous and loving God as dictatorship—I believe He has reserved, in a separate spot in Hell, some very special punishment for tyrants and their accomplices.

References

de la Boétie, Etienne. 1548. *Discourse on Voluntary Servitude* (trans. Harry Kurz). New York: Columbia University Press. (Complete text available at http://www.constitution.org/la_boétie/serv_vol.htm).

Tolstoy, Leo. 1997 [1904–07]. *A Calendar of Wisdom: Daily Thoughts to Nourish the Soul. Written and Selected from the World's Sacred Texts* (trans., ed. and Introduction by Peter Serikin). New York: Scribner.

Gandhi and Empowerment 22

MRINAL MIRI

The idea of empowerment as a motivation for social/political action is a modern idea. I think it even has a post-modern tinge about it—at least a post-Marxian change of emphasis. Marx talked about the dictatorship of the proletariat and not about the empowerment or enfeeblement of the proletariat. Of course, Marx can be interpreted in such a way as to suggest that the very basis of the Marxist framework of understanding human reality is the notion of empowerment and its opposite, that is, enfeeblement. But the talk of empowerment, which has not become a part of our moral political vocabulary, really derives its spirit from a more recent popular Western ideology; and this ideology in turn derives its strength from a strand of nineteenth-century European thought that perhaps finds its most powerful expression in the writings of Nietzsche and, in a somewhat less rhetorical way, in those of Schopenhauer.

Inalienable motivations

Empowerment presumes a distinction between the powerful and the powerless. It is also connected with a central notion of the late twentieth-century ideology, namely, that power is an inalienable human motivation. A necessary constituent of this idea is that all human motivations are reducible to the basic motive of power; even motivations that are apparently as far removed from power as can be imagined. This really was the crux of Nietzschean thought. The idea that there is a basic human motivation to which all other motivations can be reduced is, of course, a familiar one. We all know that for Freud the irreducibly basic human motivation is sexuality. In his monumental work, *The Interpretation of Dreams*, Freud argued with great power and imagination that the apparent disjunction between motives other than sexuality, and sexuality, is only apparent, that in reality there is no motive that does not have an inalienable basis in sexuality. Nietzsche, coming a generation earlier, thought that he had shown with utter finality that all human motives are reducible to that of power. The contrast between this understanding of human motivation and another idea, very closely associated with a dominant Indian cultural and intellectual tradition, is quite stark, especially when we consider the belief associated with the latter idea, that the state of total desirelessness is the best possible human condition.

What I wish to suggest here is that the idea of empowerment is really a natural corollary of a whole way of thinking which has become increasingly pervasive in the contemporary West, centring round the notion that all human motivations are reducible to the motive of power. Another point that is important to note in this connection is that a central thesis of the ideology of power is not just the relationship between the obviously dominating and the obviously dominated. Power works in multifarious and invidious ways. Even those who exercise power or those who are the victims of power are frequently not aware of the fact that they are the wielders or the victims of power. So power, as it were, has autonomy and a life of its own, and it also appropriates all other human capacities in the pursuit of its own ends.

For power to be constitutive of knowledge is for it to be an essential element in the very idea of knowledge: the epistemological enterprise is, as it were, essentially an exercise in the pursuit of power.

The most important aspect of this latter phenomenon is that power co-opts knowledge. This, more than anything else, is the great contemporary innovation in our thinking about power. To say that power appropriates knowledge is the same thing as to say that power is constitutive of knowledge and this idea is obviously very different from the old idea that knowledge is an instrument of power. So it is not merely as though Western science with its incredible technical spin-off can be put to use in man's attempt to gain control and mastery over Nature. This certainly is true; but, more importantly, scientific knowledge itself is both a product, and an articulation and exercise of power.

This view of knowledge is a radical departure from the traditional conception of knowledge. Traditionally, knowledge itself was regarded as a fundamental human motivation: a motivation whose aim was to achieve truth. In the power–knowledge theory, truth—which certainly remains closely associated with the idea of knowledge—is no longer considered to be something which has a status independent of the knowledge process. Truth, like knowledge itself, is a product of power and, in turn, serves the interests of power. This completes the power–knowledge theory's undermining of the traditional philosophy of knowledge.

Another notion which may be worth mentioning in the context of empowerment is the notion that the seat of power is not just the individual. The individual, of course, in a minor, peripheral way does wield power, but the seat of power, centrally, is the community. It follows, therefore, that life is necessarily a continuous, unceasing power game between groups and communities. The best that can happen is an uneasy, ever-so-tenuous equilibrium between these groups and communities. Therefore, the battle for empowerment of *dalits*, women, subalterns and tribals is a battle for achieving such equilibrium, tenuous as it will necessarily be. The venue will be different, the actors and contestants will be different, but the game continuous. The aforementioned is the background against which much of our contemporary talk about empowerment takes place.

Gandhian perspective

The view that power is the generator of knowledge and constitutive of it makes, from a Gandhian point of view, a travesty of the concept of knowledge. Now Gandhi's thought is in stark contrast to the views about power and knowledge that I have outlined. To him, all this would have appeared utterly strange. From a Gandhian perspective, the view that power is the only human motivator, involves an incredible distortion of the idea of a human being. Similarly, the view that power is the generator of knowledge and constitutive of it makes, from this point of view, a farce of the concept of knowledge. Power cannot generate knowledge; it can only generate illusion. This, I think, is the Gandhian view of knowledge.

Power is essentially self-centred, and self-centredness has to do with selfishness. Selfishness is really the prime enemy of authentic self-knowledge. Authentic self-knowledge and authentic knowledge of the other are two sides of the same coin. You can know yourself only through genuine knowledge of the other, and your knowledge of the other must have a basis in genuine self-knowledge. It is in the constant interplay of the two that knowledge and understanding grow. For Gandhi, a central necessary condition of authentic self-knowledge is *ahimsa*, which, in a more positive mode, is love. This is certainly one reason why Gandhi said that truth and *ahimsa* are one and the same thing. Self-knowledge generated and informed by *ahimsa* is necessarily generative of self-confidence. Gandhi would, therefore, talk of self-confidence and *swaraj* rather than of power. What we must strive for is not a tenuous and uneasy equilibrium of power; an equilibrium always on the brink of being upset. Gandhi's preferred word here is 'fellowship'; fellowship between communities and individuals.

Virtues and internal goods

Power is never an internal good, that is, it is never a good that is internal to a practice; it is always external. A debate in modern philosophy, which may help us appreciate the Gandhian rejection of power as the fundamental human motive, is the debate about the place of virtues in an adequate conception of human life. We may, to begin with, make a distinction between two kinds of human goods and values. This, in fact, is a very old distinction. In recent times, it has come into focus again because of the profound monistic implications of modern science and the culture it promotes and nurtures. This is the distinction between external good and internal good. The distinction may be thought of as implicit in the concept of human practice. A general point about the notion of practice is that if there were no practices in this sense, then human life as we know it to exist would not be there at all. Perhaps, the best account of this practice is to be found in Alisdair McIntyre's book, *After Virtue* (1981: 109). The important points in McIntyre's definition of practice are:

- It is a cooperative human activity.
- It has goods internal to it; there are, therefore, also goods external to it.
- Its internal goods are inalienably associated with standards of excellence specific to it.
- These standards of excellence are not static and are sometimes transformed in the course of the history of the practice.

The important point about practice from a Gandhian perspective is that pursuit of goods internal to a practice requires an active recognition of values as inalienably associated with engagement in a practice.

Take the qualities of character such as honesty (truthfulness), fairness (justice), courage and selflessness. The power–knowledge ideology would obviously treat such virtues as instruments in the hands of power and, therefore, in a deep sense, not virtues at all. But given the idea of practice just outlined and the distinction between internal and external goods, the instrumentalist account of virtues does not any longer seem plausible. Dishonesty in the pursuit of goods internal to a practice defeats the very purpose of such a pursuit; the appreciation of internal goods, of the standards of excellence, also requires the capacity to judiciously discriminate between the better and the worse, between the higher and the lower, between a Plato and a Karl Popper. Hence, Justice—a practice—is a cooperative human activity. It can thrive only on the basis of a cooperative care for internal goods. And cooperation, in the real sense, is not possible without concern for the other, the fellow practitioner. Therefore, the need to be unselfish. This relationship between virtues and internal goods points to a moral order in the affairs of man insofar as these affairs allow for the possibility of practices in the sense that we have discussed. To deny this is, perhaps, to deny the very distinguishing character of human social life.

It is my contention that power is never an internal good, that is, it is never a good that is internal to a practice; it is always external. One mark of the externality of power is that *virtues qua virtues* need not come into play at all in the pursuit of power. So we come round to the Gandhian view that the pursuit of power, and of empowerment as such, is an essentially self-centred and, therefore, a selfish activity.

Reference

MacIntyre, A. 1981. *After Virtue*. London: Duckworth.

None is Free until All are Free

Sartre's Ontology of Freedom and His Politics

23

ROBERT BERNASCONI

Jean-Paul Sartre is widely remembered today as *the* philosopher of freedom, the one who told us in *Being and Nothingness* (1957: 441; *L'être et le néant*, 1965: 516 [henceforth BN and EN, respectively]) that we are not just free, we are totally free. The extravagance of this claim has contributed to the decline in his philosophical reputation. Indeed, it seems, retrospectively, as if the fate of Sartre's philosophy was already decided in 1945, only two years after the publication of *Being and Nothingness*, when Merleau-Ponty, in the final chapter of *Phenomenology of Perception*, is thought to have highlighted the deficiencies of this account. There are significant differences between Sartre's account of freedom and Merleau-Ponty's. In *Phenomenology of Perception*, Merleau-Ponty focusses more on action than on the decision, and he provides a stronger discussion of class identity than Sartre does in *Being and Nothingness*, which is one of the weakest points of the book because it pays too little attention to the role of material conditions in identity formation. Nevertheless, in the context of post-War French philosophy, Merleau-Ponty was properly perceived as lending support to Sartre's account, albeit with a few friendly amendments.[1] To be sure, when the two friends subsequently fell out, the seeds of their dispute were already found in these early exchanges. But who had the better of the argument? The existence of Simone de Beauvoirs spirited defence of Sartre against Merleau-Ponty in 'Sartre and Pseudo-Sartreanism' in 1955 has not succeeded in breaking the popular consensus that Sartre's account of freedom lacks merit. It is largely forgotten that many of the scholars who examined the debate concluded that Sartre won the argument.[2] If support for Sartre's early account of freedom has waned, this is perhaps because he, particularly in interviews, preferred to renounce his earlier position rather than defend it. However, one must use the evidence of the interviews with caution. Sartre was never a reliable interpreter of his own work, particularly in interviews, where he gave free reign to his passion for extravagant claims. Sartre's inability to resist a dramatic statement where a more nuanced one is what is called for, created the need for him to repudiate his earlier views in subsequent interviews, but it also made these repudiations of his earlier views on freedom themselves suspect, precisely because they are couched in the same dramatic register as the discussions of freedom that they renounce for being overstated.

My intention here is not to reopen the case of Sartre on freedom in *Being and Nothingness* with the aim of offering a new verdict. Instead, it is the more modest one of trying to show that, once one sees that Sartre's subsequent, more explicitly political, discussions of freedom leading up to the *Critique of Dialectical Reason* (1960) arise from the project already begun in *Being and Nothingness*, then it becomes apparent that his discussion of freedom was from the outset directed towards political action, and that the ambiguity of our relation to things and their resistance, which he is often said to have neglected, were his concerns from the outset. It has been observed by one commentator that the word 'freedom' has at least three different meanings in Sartre: first, the fact that man is condemned to be free; second, the goal that each should liberate him- or herself and the rest of humanity; and, third, a criterion such that choice must be free if it is to engender moral values and imply moral responsibility (Frondizi 1981: 382). These can be called ontological, political and ethical freedom, respectively. However, it is not enough to distinguish them. One must see how they are connected. Although Sartre's example of the prisoner who is free even under conditions of confinement seems to suggest that the author of *Being and Nothingness* had a deficient conception of political freedom. I will attempt to show that his account of freedom was from the outset directed to politics.

My account raises the question as to why, for the most part, both Sartre and in particular his debate with Merleau-Ponty, has come to be so badly misconstrued by non-specialists. I believe the reason for this is that the focus has fallen almost exclusively on Sartre's ontology rather than on his concrete descriptions. Indeed, Merleau-Ponty, in *The Visible and the Invisible* (1968: 89; *Le visible et l'invisible*, 1964: 122–23 [henceforth VI and VeI, respectively]), acknowledged the difference between Sartre's abstract ontological categories and the descriptions, as if he knew that the descriptions might salvage the categories, but he decided to focus on the categories in isolation anyway.[3] In 'Merleau-Ponty and Pseudo-Sartreanism', Simone de Beauvoir acknowledged the difference between the ontological account and the concrete description but without clarifying their relation. Even before Merleau-Ponty elected in *The Visible and the Invisible* to repeat his gesture of focussing on the former rather than the latter, she (de Beauvior 1955: 2121–22 [henceforth M-P]; DSM: 489) warned against his tendency to do so:

> As early as *Phenomenology of Perception*, he [Merleau-Ponty] coldly denied the entire Sartrean phenomenology of engaged freedom. Even if the conciliation of Sartre's ontology with his phenomenology raises difficulties, one does not have the right to grab from his hands one 'of the two ends of the chair', to use Merleau-Ponty's words.

What are these difficulties of reuniting the ontology with the phenomenology? How difficult would it be? If Sartre's apparently dualist ontology undoes, or perhaps, even undercuts the phenomenological description, then the account has little to recommend it. However, I shall argue here that Sartre's ontology is indispensable to his politics and that therein lies its great merit.

For Sartre, the goal of his philosophizing was always the concrete. This is as true of the *Being and Nothingness*, as it is of *Critique of Dialectical Reason*. Nevertheless, the fact that it was the goal meant that it was not the starting point. He started from the abstract. At the very beginning of *Being and Nothingness*, he quoted Jean Laporte as saying 'abstraction arises when something not capable of existing in isolation is thought of as in an isolated state' (EN: 37; BN: 3). This is true of Sartre's ontological categories. The for-itself and the in-itself are indeed abstractions (EN: 715–16; BN: 621–22). To answer the possible charge that this leads to an insurmountable dualism, Sartre observed that 'the For-Itself and the In-itself are reunited by a synthetic connection which is nothing other than the For-itself itself' (EN: 711; BN: 617). The problem is that Sartre was suspicious of employing synthesis to join the results of analysis.

Sartre was one of the most articulate opponents of analytical thinking of the last sixty years. That does not mean that he was an articulate opponent of analytical philosophy: he was largely ignorant of it, and much of what is often called analytical philosophy is not analytical in the sense he meant it. The rubric which should govern our reading of *Being and Nothingness* is found on the first page of the first chapter and it is directed specifically against Descartes. It is relevant to all those who accuse Sartre of Cartesianism: 'It is not profitable to first separate the two terms of a relation in order to try to join them together again later. The relation is a synthesis. Consequently the results of analysis cannot be covered over again by the moments of this synthesis' (EN: 37; BN: 3). Hence, Sartre presented the concrete as 'the synthetic totality of which consciousness, like the phenomenon, constitutes only moments' (ibid.). Sartre's problem was that, at the time of *Being and Nothingness*, description and a passion for paradox were his main tools for counteracting his ontological dualism. As a result, in spite of his intentions, the synthesis constantly falls apart into its dichotomies: consciousness and things, for-itself and in-itself, freedom and facticity, and so on. That is why one hears so much about Sartre's Cartesianism or his dualism, and that is why Merleau-Ponty is seen as the perfect antidote. Against Cartesianism, against a philosophy of the clear and distinct, Merleau-Ponty proposed Heidegger's notion of being-in-the-world—'I belong to myself while belonging to the world' (1970: 407; *Phénoménologie de la Perception*, 1945: 466 [henceforth PP and PdP respectively])—and at the same time embraced the notion of ambiguity. Merleau-Ponty's criticism of Sartre is ultimately that he was an analytic thinker, indeed that the dichotomy between total freedom or non-existent freedom is a product of analytical reflection (PdP: 518; PP: 454), which is why Simone de Beauvoir levels the same charge against Merleau-Ponty, at least by implication (M-P: 2019; DSM: 487). When, in 1948, Sartre turned to dialectical philosophy to address the problems of analytical rationality, his first efforts to do so showed little understanding of dialectics, and continued to rely on a crude notion of synthesis (Sartre, *Cahiers pour une morale*, 1983: 475–76; *Notebooks for an Ethics*, 1992: 459–60 [henceforth CM and NE respectively). However, by 1960, he had developed a richer notion of dialectical reason, where it is understood as the ongoing totalization of praxis. Dialectical reason was no longer opposed to analytical reason, it included it, as indeed it must do, in order to present itself as dialectical.

If the starting point of Sartre's discussion of freedom were the ontological abstractions of the for-itself and the in-itself, the goal was to understand freedom in situation. This term 'situation', which Sartre borrowed from Karl Jaspers and Martin Heidegger, is crucial for understanding Sartre's early philosophy of freedom. Sartre's claim that we are all totally free in all contexts does not mean that all situations are equal. That raises the question as to how and why the situation is sometimes not seen as an opportunity, whereas at other times it is.

The reason why Sartre insisted that no situation undermines ontological freedom is that one can conceive that situation as being otherwise. One can give it a different meaning. However, the converse is that, if one is immersed in a situation, one cannot always conceive the failures and lacks of a specific political or economic organization. He rejected the explanation that sometimes one is habituated to a situation and so comes to accept it, in favour of saying that sometimes one cannot imagine that one can exist in it otherwise. The condition of an action is the recognition of an objective lack or a *négatité*. That is to say, action arises insofar as consciousness 'leaves the level of being in order frankly to approach that of non-being' (EN: 509; BN: 434). But that condition is not always met. It is only when we can conceive of things being different that we decide that they are unbearable and so seek to change them. Otherwise we are resigned to them. Sartre gave the example of the workers at Croix-Rousse who rioted, took over Lyons, but did not know what to do with their victory. So they returned home and turned victory into defeat. Sartre in *Being and Nothingness* saw their failure as a failure to see the in-adequacies of the political and economic system, a failure to see the possibility of things being otherwise, because the workers had come to equate existence with suffering. That was why suffering alone does not motivate one's actions in politics. The workers experience their suffering as natural. Sartre wrote of such a worker, 'To suffer and to *be* are one and the same for him' (EN: 510; BN: 435). His point was that it is ultimately not the political and economic structures that motiv-ate one's actions, but the nihilating power of consciousness. It alone has the capacity to effect a rupture from the past, through which alone there is a factual state at all, let alone the capacity to apprehend what is lack-ing in the existing structures.

The example of the workers at Croix-Rousse reveals a flaw in Sartre's account that it took time for him to identify and correct. One finds a similar problem in Simone de Beauvoir's *The Ethics of Ambiguity*, albeit her examples are even more problematic in the way they are formulated, such as when she wrote of 'slaves who have raised themselves to the unconsciousness of their slavery' and of 'women in many civilizations' who 'submit to the laws, the god's, the customs, and the truths created by the males' (*Pour une morale de l'ambiguité*, 1962: 54; *The Ethics of Ambiguity*, 1976: 37 [henceforth MA and EA respectively]). However, behind de Beauvoir's polemic is an attempt to convey the difference between those who in anger, within a given situation, attack the civilization that oppresses them, and those who have at their disposal a philosophy of liberation, the possession of which makes it a fault or a form of bad faith not to exploit the possibilities of the situation (MA: 56; EA: 38). The problem with these examples is that, even though they purport to show that situations are not determinative and that the workers could have acted differently, they suggest that the oppressed lack agency. Similarly, according to Sartre, suffering does not motivate action and, indeed, is an obstacle to it as it prevents seeing the situation otherwise. This is in keeping with Sartre's earlier claim that the class consciousness of the workers arises not from hard work or low living standards, but is imposed on them by the oppressing class (EN: 492; BN: 420). It was only subsequently, when Sartre moved from a humanism of labour to a humanism of need, such that the truth of humanity and of society was revealed by the gaze of the least favoured, that he resolved the issue (Sartre, 'Les Communists et la paix', 1964: 344; *Communists and Peace*, 1968: 201 [henceforth SVI and CP, respectively]). However, although Merleau-Ponty in *Adventures of the Dialectic* correctly identified the importance of this idea to Sartre, he resolutely refused it, just as he refused, as Simone de Beauvoir recognized, the growing significance of need in Sartre's thought (M-P: 2096–98 DSM: 467–69). She complained that Merleau-Ponty ignored dire situations and that need appeared nowhere in his analyses (M-P: 2116; DSM: 484), albeit subsequently he did credit Sartre with the idea that 'in the beginning is not play but need' (*Signes*, 1960: 38; *Signs*, 1964: 28 [henceforth S and Ss, respectively]).

Sartre's philosophy of inter-subjectivity in *Being and Nothingness* is correctly seen as a philosophy of conflict with each seeking the upper hand over the other, but this was never intended to be the last word. Freedom is ultimately for Sartre not freedom over the other man or woman: the meaning of freedom for Sartre is responsibility or, more specifically, it is, for each of us, *my* responsibility. The third brief section of the chapter on freedom that appears under the title 'Freedom and Responsibility', is not an afterthought. It serves to highlight the ethico-political motivation for the preceding account. My ontological freedom is responsibility for everything except my responsibility itself, which is given (EN: 641; BN: 555). That I am condemned to be wholly responsible for myself is my facticity (EN: 642; BN: 556). Sartre is not saying that there is, on one hand, my facticity, and on the other hand, opposed to it, my freedom, such that the two are in constant negotiation, although certain formulations sometimes suggest this. Facticity is fundamentally the facticity of freedom, that is to say, the fact that I am not able not to be free, just as my contingency is the fact of not being able to exist (EN: 567; BN: 486). My freedom is my responsibility for myself and for the world (EN: 639; BN: 553).

Familiar illustrations still tell the story best. For example, I am a prisoner: perhaps, I see this as a premature death and sink into apathy and depression; or perhaps, I see my confinement as an opportunity to work to improve myself; or perhaps, I plan to escape and in that way refuse my fate. In each case, the 'same' situation presents itself to me differently. Sartre relates the differences to my original choice. But the term 'choice' can easily prove misleading. The original choice, the decision, is not the selection of one option over another. It often sounds as if Sartre is saying that my world is a matter of my choice or decision, but the fact that the prisoner is left to decide how he or she lives his confinement does not mean that the prisoner chooses the world he or she lives in without experiencing the resistance of things and their adversity. To be sure, the fact that one prisoner experiences his or her conditions in one way, whereas another might experience those same conditions entirely differently, points to the role of the original project. We are each of us free insofar as things in the world appear to us as they do in the light of our original projects. Insofar as that project is chosen by me, I choose my world. It must be understood that at the heart of Sartre's account of freedom is an understanding—or, more precisely, a misunderstanding—of Heidegger's account of human existence as a thrown project, according to which the projection of the for-the-sake-of-which as a possibility of one's own being constitutes the worldhood of the world (Heidegger 1953: 119). Sartre took from it the idea that things are not simply given to me: I am not a recipient. I am immersed in things, involved with them, but how they appear to me is determined by my project. As de Beauvoir explained, 'Faithful on this point to the Heideggerian in thesis that human reality announces what is based on the world, Sartre has always insisted on the reciprocal conditioning of the world and that of the Ego [*Moi*]' (M-P: 2074; DSM: 450). And I would argue, together with Pietro Chiodi (1976: 8–15), that Sartre became even more faithful to Heidegger on this point in the *Critique of Dialectical Reason*.

Anyone who reads Sartre's description of the prisoner, where he endeavours to show that even in prison one's ontological freedom is not compromised, is bound to be suspicious: the prisoner is not free in any ordinary sense of the word. However, the lack of concrete freedom was precisely Sartre's point. It is the contradiction between, on one hand, the ontological freedom that we share with the slaves, prisoners and sweatshop workers and, on the other hand, the freedom denied to them concretely that calls me to act. The slave has a choice but has no real choice: ontologically, freedom; concretely, an absence of freedom. Sartre's argument at this point is that ontological freedom is not only something I cannot avoid in its form as responsibility, but also something I must strive to concretize, not just for myself but for others. Hence, he argued in *Existentialism is a Humanism* that nobody is free unless all are free (*L'existentialisme est un humanisme*, 1946a: 83–84; *Existentialism and Humanism*, 1968: 52):

> Obviously, freedom as the definition of man does not depend upon others, but as soon as there is a commitment, I am obliged to will the liberty of others at the same time as mine. I cannot make liberty my aim unless I make that of others equally my aim.

Sartre found another way of arguing towards the same conclusion in *Notebooks for an Ethics*. He claimed that if one had a full intuition of one's own freedom, one would see it as requiring universal freedom and one would not be able to destroy the freedom of others. It was only bad faith, the grasping of myself as an object, while at the same time having a certain recognition of the other as a freedom, that made oppression possible (CM: 341; NE: 328). In outlining the ontological conditions of oppression, Sartre had also shown how they led directly to a politics directed against oppression. Indeed, it led so directly to politics that ethics was postponed until such time as the politics had performed its work (CM: 16, 95; NE: 9, 88).

Later, Sartre would write a politics of the oppressed that received its orientation from the gaze of the least favoured, but at this relatively early stage in the development of his political philosophy, he was writing on behalf of the oppressed, instead of listening to them. On this reconstruction of Sartre's argument, it is the contradiction between my ontological freedom and the phenomenological description, which demonstrates a lack of concrete freedom, that generates the move to politics. That is to say, one task of the ontological analysis is to establish that distance from things which allows me to negate the present circumstances. It is because the ontology as abstract always stands beyond the description of the concrete that ontology is indispensable for politics. One finds a similar claim in Simone de Beauvoir (MA: 125; EA: 86–87): 'To want existence, to want to disclose the world, and to want men to be free are one and the same will'.

Sartre's ontology does not dictate his politics but it makes it possible. Hence, he wrote in 'Materialism and Revolution' in 1946: 'If man is not originally free, but determined once and for all, we cannot even conceive what his liberation might be' (Sartre, *Situations III*, 1976: 207 [*Materialisme et revolution*]; *Literary and Philosophical Essays*, 1955: 228 [*Materialism and Revolution*] [henceforth SIII and LPE, respectively]). Sartre made the same point elsewhere in more detail. For example, in an interview in Berlin in 1948 (*Verger* 1948, quoted by Follesdal 1997: 404), he explained that metaphysical freedom plays a decisive role as a precondition of that political freedom which is—

> our concrete goal, which is highly actual and modern, is to liberate man. This had three aspects. First, metaphysical liberation: to make him conscious that he is completely free and that he must fight against everything which contributes to limiting this freedom. Secondly, artistic liberation, to further the free man's communication with other men and, aided by this, to place them [the communicates] in one and the same atmosphere of freedom. Thirdly, political and social freedom: liberation of the oppressed and other men.

We get a clue that it is appropriate to link these conceptions in 1947, when in connection with the publication of a collection of his plays, Sartre (Sartre, *Bulletin N.R.F.*, quoted by Contant and Rybalka 1974: 161) wrote:

> No matter what the circumstances, no matter what the time or place, man is free to choose himself a traitor or a hero, a coward or a conqueror. In choosing either slavery or freedom for himself, he will at the same time choose a world where man is free or enslaved—and the drama will arise from his attempts to justify this free choice. Whether we are face to face with gods, with tyranny or death, there is one thing we can be sure of: we are free.

The quotation shows clearly Sartre's attempt to associate ontological freedom with political freedom. I have tried to show that this attempt already governs the conception of freedom set out in *Being and Nothingness*, and I will show next that many of the discussions after *Being and Nothingness* were dedicated to strengthening that link. Nevertheless, Sartre made no secret of the fact that he subsequently repudiated this position. In an interview, in 1969, he (1974: 33–34 [henceforth BEM]) declared:

> The other day, I re-read a prefatory note of mine to a collection of these plays—*Les Mouches, Huis Clos* and others—and was truly scandalized.

I had written: 'Whatever the circumstances, and wherever the site, a man is always free to choose to be a traitor or not....' When I read this, I said to myself: it's incredible, I actually believed that!

Sartre explained his earlier view as a product of the German occupation of France, and in particular of resistance, which presented itself simply as a question of courage. There were risks, but one was either for the Germans or against them: 'There was no other option. The real political problems, of being "for, but" or "against, but," were not posed by this experience' (BEM: 34).

That this was Sartre's experience is confirmed by a 1944 text, 'The Republic of Silence', where he wrote, 'We were never more free than under the German occupation'(SIII: 11). Torture was on the mind of every Frenchman in the form of the question of freedom: 'If they torture me, will I hold out?' The secret of each human being lay in their ability to resist torture. Each was alone but, at the same time, in the presence of the whole Resistance Movement. 'A word was all it took for ten or a hundred arrests. Isn't that total responsibility, the revelation of our freedom in total solitude?' Sartre's recollections are not without a certain curious romanticism, but they serve to give his answer to the question he (Sartre 1946b: 9 [henceforth LC. Trans. LPE 169) posed at the beginning of his essay 'Cartesian Freedom' as a question that should be addressed to all philosophers who defend freedom: 'In connection with what exceptional *situation* have you experienced your freedom?' For Sartre, in 1943, it might have been having to face torture in his imagination where indeed it is simply a case of resistance or giving in (*cf* BEM: 34). This, then, would be what enabled him to say that he was never more free than under the Germans, even though he explained in 'Cartesian Freedom' that 'the situation of a man and his powers cannot increase or limit his freedom' (LC: 20; LPE: 173). Ontologically, there are no degrees of freedom, but phenomenologically there are, and they are revealed in the exhilaration of freedom experienced.

Sartre's account of the situation establishes that he had much more in common with Merleau-Ponty in the middle of the 1940s than subsequently appeared to be the case when their differences were read through the distorting lens of the latter's 'Sartre and Ultrabolshevism'. There is a critique of Sartre in the chapter on freedom in *Phenomenology of Perception*, but Merleau-Ponty's account of the situation, to be found there, is not part of it. He (Pd P: 517; PP: 453) wrote: 'The generality of the "role" and of the situation comes to the aid of decision, and in this exchange between the situation and the person who takes it up, it is impossible to determine precisely the "share contributed by the situation" and the "share contributed by freedom".' However, in fact, this is little more than a paraphrase of what Sartre had already written in *Being and Nothingness*. On the basis of his descriptions, Sartre (EN: 568: BN: 488) wrote: 'These observations should show us that the situation, the common product of the contingency of the in–itself and of freedom, is an ambiguous phenomenon in which it is impossible for the for–itself to distinguish the contribution of freedom from that of the brute existent.' In other words, 'ambiguity', the favoured term of Merleau-Ponty, is already at the heart of Sartre's descriptions, albeit this is not apparent if one chooses to focus on Sartre's ontological dualism.

This is not to deny that there are important differences between Sartre and Merleau-Ponty. However, they are not to be found in the latter's direct response to Sartre's idea that we are condemned to freedom, which is that we are condemned to meaning because we are in the world (PdP: xv; PP: xix). To be sure, Merleau-Ponty's idea that we are condemned to meaning is intended, as he explained in *Adventures of the Dialectic*, to correct the Sartrean claim that consciousness '*gives* meaning' (*Les aventures de la dialectique*, 1955: 156–57; *Adventures of the Dialectic*, 1973: 115 [henceforth AdD and AD, respectively]), but there are objective significations in Sartre (EN: 592; BN: 486; see also de Beauvoir, M-P: 2077; DBS: 453). Let us not forget that Sartre himself understood his account of freedom as a correction of phenomenology's failure to acknowledge adequately the resistance of things. In *Being and Nothingness*, Sartre accepted Gaston Bachelard's criticism that phenomenology had not taken into account the 'coefficient of adversity' in objects (*L'eau et les Rêves*, 1942: 213; *Water and Dreams*, 1999: 159). In the first instance, Sartre associated the phrase with the body in its being-for-us, specifically, the body as facticity; that is, the fact that as a result of my birth, certain things are more or less accessible to me, certain social realities are open to me and others closed off, and so on (EN: 392–93; BN: 328). Although Merleau-Ponty was well aware of the extent through which, by his use of the phrase 'coefficient of adversity', Sartre had acknowledged the resistance to freedom from the given, in an early response to Sartre, he employed the idea of resistance in an attempt to drive a wedge between his own account of freedom and Sartre's. In a radio interview in 1951, Merleau-Ponty (1951, cited by Whiteside 1988: 240) suggested generalizing Sartre's notion of a 'coefficient of adversity': 'It seems to me that [Sartre's] idea should be generalized. I have called "adversity"… that which opposes itself in fact to the realization … of harmony, of agreement with oneself, with others, but what opposes these things without being an adversary that one can name.' Merleau-Ponty, drawing on Bachelard, via Sartre, thus comes to formulate what he calls an 'anonymous adversity' (S: 304; Ss: 239).

Another difference that seems to separate Merleau-Ponty's account of freedom in *Phenomenology of Perception* from that of Sartre is that the former, by emphasizing history, focussed more single-mindedly on political freedom. However, in the course of directly addressing political issues after *Being and Nothingness*, Sartre showed the strong connection between his ontological conception of freedom and political action. So in *Anti-Semite and Jew*, Sartre defined the human being as 'a being having freedom within the limits of a situation' (*Réflexions sur la question juive*, 1954: 109; *Anti-Semite and Jew*, 1976: 90). Sartre then proceeded to show that this conception leads directly to political action. To be authentic is to assume the responsibilities and risks that arise from consciousness of the situation. In fact, this was already prepared for in *Being and Nothingness*, when he illustrated his fundamental conviction that actions—in principle—are intentional, by offering the example of a worker charged with dynamiting a quarry. The worker simply obeyed orders and produced the expected result but, nevertheless, he acted, 'he knew what he was doing or, if you prefer, he intentionally realized a conscious project' (EN: 508; BN: 433). What this means is that the excuses of the collaborators and of soldiers who claim only to be obeying orders is rejected. Already at the time of *Being and Nothingness*, freedom meant neither arbitrariness nor the ability to change in an instant, let alone resignation or stoic indifference to one's circumstances. It meant responsibility. There are no excuses, whatever the conditions. This is confirmed in *Truth and Existence*, a manuscript dating from 1948 (Sartre, *Vérité et existence*, 1989: 90; *Truth and Existence*, 1992: 46):

> I have shown that freedom *always* means assuming our responsibilities *afterwards* for what we have neither created nor wanted. (That car knocks me down. I couldn't avoid it. I'm missing an arm. My freedom began there: assuming that disability that I did not create.) But it cannot escape from its condition.

Here, one sees a possible passage from Sartre to Levinas, and at the very point where one would expect them to be most distant, in the conception of freedom: it comes in the passage from legal responsibility to an ethical responsibility that the tradition largely failed to recognize.

In *Communists and Peace*, Sartre highlighted his political conception of freedom. To be sure, freedom is still the power to invent, to transcend the given (SVI: 50; CP: 130), but freedom is now associated with revolutionary actions and, therefore, is associated with class, a class that exists only in acting. The worker asserts his freedom in action. This freedom is a concrete power. To be sure, one might hesitate over the specifics that his identification of the worker as the agent of history rather than giving the role to the oppressed of the Third World, as he would later. That, too, would necessitate a challenge to his claim that freedom takes place in relation to the Communist Party. Furthermore, it is because my freedom means my responsibility for the world and thus for everyone's oppression that history has direction, thereby rescuing Sartre from the idea of freedom as arbitrariness and equivocation, which is what Merleau-Ponty attributed to him (PdP: 512; PP: 448–49).

One also finds in *Communists and Peace*, Sartre's first attempt to resolve the problem posed in *Being and Nothingness* of the workers at Croix-Rousse who rioted, won a quick victory, but did not know what to do with it. Sartre wrote that it was not the task of the workers to have a concrete vision or plan: this is to be provided by the Communist Party. The Party is their freedom (SVI: 251; CP: 131). Nevertheless, this solution does not last long and, indeed, already in *Communists and Peace*, we see Sartre giving a greater centrality to the privileged insight of the oppressed, in the form of the gaze of least favoured. To be sure, in an important note to *Communists and Peace*, he explained that it does not mean that what the proletariat demands for itself, it must claim for all (SVI: 282n; CP: 154n). He warned against transforming the radical humanism of the proletarian, such that it is faithful to the human, into a particularism that is built upon the idea that a class carries a unique incommunicable message. Instead, what happens here is that Sartre incorporated a theory of need into his theory of freedom, thereby transforming the latter. As a result and contrary to the account in *Being and Nothingness* of the workers of Croix-Rousse, the impulse to demand freedom is now found in the experience of hunger. To be sure, in *Notebooks for an Ethics*, Sartre had already located the very substance of oppression in the piece of bread that constitutes someone's only food (CM: 344; NE: 331); nevertheless, it was still with some exaggeration and a disregard for the transformation that Sartre's philosophy was undergoing that Simone de Beauvoir claimed that Merleau-Ponty's entire polemic against Sartre was 'immediately discredited since it is based on the confusion of a theory of need with a theory of freedom' (M-P: 2096; DSM: 468). In other words, need establishes a relation between 'man' and 'nature' that runs counter to the dualism of subject and object associated with so-called pseudo-Sartreanism.

This integration of an ontological account of freedom into an account of a world dominated by need led Sartre, in *Communists and Peace*, to attack the widespread tendency to separate politics as the sphere of freedom from economics as the sphere of necessity (SVI: 117; CP: 30). Given that this distinction is at the heart of Hannah Arendt's still influential theory of politics, it is worth seeing how Sartre addressed it. His point was not only the methodological one, that the distinction between economics and politics conforms to the tendency of the bourgeois to compartmentalize (SVI: 117; CP: 30), that is, to practise analytic thought at the expense of the dialectic. His main point was that the distinction works to the advantage of the bourgeois and not that of the workers: it is the freedom of the rich to exploit the poor. He also made the further point that the distinction has no phenomenological basis for the worker (SVI: 119; CP: 31):

> But, while the bourgeois point of view is clear enough in itself, I cease to understand it as soon as I try to envisage things from the wage earner's point of view, where the distinction between economics and politics becomes so vague and fugitive that I have difficulty believing it exists.

Sartre took his attack on this distinction between the political and the economic a stage further, when he observed that it is indeed economic freedom that the upper middle class wants (SVI: 141–42; CP: 48):

> It's well known that the leaders of industry are quite unconcerned about democratic freedoms: what do you expect them to do with freedom of thought? … they pay fools to enjoy it in their stead. The freedom they demand, the only one, is the freedom to direct, at will, the battles of production: this is called liberalism.

Or, more precisely, they want the concrete power to take profits. It is the petit bourgeois who want 'the formal freedoms of our democracies' (ibid.). But, of course, the bourgeois makes nothing of this freedom: 'he is lost if he doesn't think as everybody else does' (SVI: 242; CP: 124). By contrast, what the worker wants is the right to live and the instrument the worker needs is the right to strike (SVI: 142–45; CP: 48–50).

In 1960, in the *Critique of Dialectical Reason*, Sartre built on this insight into the relation of freedom to need. Whereas in *Being and Nothingness* there is a lack or *négatité* at the heart of the ontological account of freedom, in the *Critique* there is 'a lack (*manqué*) within the organism' (CRD: 166; CDR: 80). What the human being lacks as an organism, for example, food, refocusses the account from desire towards need. That is to say,

Critique of Dialectical Reason completes the shift from desire—a relation without material mediation which had been the focus in *Being and Nothingness*—to need, where the organism's restoration takes place as the negation of the negation. The organism preserves itself by transcending itself. What at the abstract level is need is, in our history, scarcity. Hence, the fundamental project is transcending scarcity (CRD: 212; CDR: 137). Scarcity, not the search for recognition, is the source of tension (CRD: 202; CDR: 125). The other is a threat not, *in the first instance*, because the other wants to kill me, as in Hegel, but because the other may want what I need to survive (CRD: 205; CDR: 128). Hence, the concrete impossibility in our history of coexistence (CRD: 205; CDR: 129), even though we are ontologically, in Heidegger's terms, *Mitsein*. Reciprocity as modified by scarcity gives rise to the radically 'other', the one who threatens me with death (CRD: 208; CDR: 131–32).

Early in the *Critique of Dialectical Reason*, Sartre offered a defence of his abstract starting point under the title of a formalism. Sartre's (CRD: 179; CDR: 97) concern was that 'skipping the abstract discussion of the human relation and immediately locating ourselves in the world of productive forces ... is in danger of giving unwitting support to the atomism of liberalism and analytical rationality.' It is only by distinguishing the project, as transcendence, from circumstances, as conditions, that one is freed from the idea of the human being as a mere product of history and one understands that 'men make history to the extent that it makes them' (CRD: 180; CDR: 97). This confirms that for Sartre, ontological freedom does not merely provide the formal conditions for the possibility of action but also has a critical function. Part of its critical function is to expose the limits of concrete freedom. Sartre has a negative view of the freedoms we do have in society: '*True* bourgeois freedom, positive freedom, is a power of man over man. Society makes the decision before our birth: it defeats in advance our capacities and our obligations; in short, it situates us. It *ties* us to others' (SVI: 240; CP: 122, translation modified). Or again, 'Free? Yes: free to engage in certain very concrete activities which generally have their source in our economic power or in our social functions' (SVI: 240; CP: 122). It is because my ontological freedom implies a moral responsibility that I am unable to fulfil in the current situation that I must fight politically to change the situation. To that extent, the three conceptions of freedom in Sartre's work merge into one. His philosophy of freedom is a philosophy of responsibility that, once it is located in the context of a theory of need or scarcity, yields a radical politics in which the ontological, ethical and political conceptions of freedom can be seen to work together within the same dialectic. It might on another occasion be worth speculating as to whether it was, perhaps, because Merleau-Ponty did not have in place a specifically ontological conception of freedom as responsibility for all that it was so easy for him, after his inspirational account of responsibility in *Humanism and Terror*, to become disillusioned with the demand for radical change and, thus, be inclined to opt for a strategy of amelioration.

Notes

1. Apparently in 1949, in a text not written for publication, Merleau-Ponty did acknowledge that he wrote the chapter on freedom 'against Sartre' (Whiteside 1988: 66).
2. Perhaps the best example is Whitford (1982: esp. 56–77). See also Sheridan (1998: 36–47 [Henceforth DSM]).
3. Merleau-Ponty also denied that 'the progress of the investigation' could change the initial idea of *Being and Nothingness*, in spite of what Sartre claims at the end of the book (VeI: 99; VI: 69). The fact that Merleau-Ponty proposes instead a dialectic, as a situational thought (VeI: 126; VI: 92) should not, however, tempt one to propose that he believed a philosophical reconciliation would have been possible. They each appear to mean something very different by dialectic.

References

Bachelard, G. 1942. *L'eau et les rêves*. Paris: José Corti. (trans. Edith R. Farrell. 1999. *Water and Dreams*. Dallas: Dallas Institute of Humanities and Culture.)

Chiodi, Pietro (trans. Kate Soper). 1976. *Sartre and Marxism*. Hassocks: Harvester Press.

Contant, Michel and Michel Rybalka. 1974. *The Writings of Jean-Paul Sartre, Vol. 1*. Evanston: Northwestern University Press.

de Beauvoir, Simone. 1955. 'Merleau-Ponty et le pseudo-sartreanisme', *Les Temps Modernes*, 10(114–15 [July]): 2121–22. (trans. Venonique Zaytzeff. 1998. 'Merleau-Ponty and Pseudo-Sartreanism', in Jon Stewart (ed.), *The Debate Between Sartre and Merleau-Ponty*. Evanston: Northwestern University Press.)

——. 1962. *Pour une morale de l'ambiguité*. Paris: Gallimard. (trans. Bernard Frechtman. 1976. *The Ethics of Ambiguity*. New York: Philosophical Library.)

Follesdal, Daggfin. 1997. 'Sartre on Freedom', in Paul Arthur Schilpp (ed.), *The Philosophy of Jean-Paul Sartre*. Illinois: Open Court.

Frondizi, Risieri. 1981. 'Sartre's Early Ethics: A Critique', in Paul Arthur Schilpp (ed.), *The Philosophy of Jean-Paul Sartre*. Illinois: Open Court.

Heidegger, Martin. 1953. *Sein und Zeit*. Tübingen: Niemeyer. (trans. John Macquarrie and Edward Robinson. 1967. *Being and* Time. Oxford: Basil Blackwell.)

Merleau-Ponty, Maurice. 1945. *Phénoménologie de la perception*. Paris: Gallimard. (trans. Colin Smith. 1970. *Phenomenology of Perception*. London: Routledge.)

———. 1951. 'L' homme et l adversité', RTF broadcast, 15 September.

———. 1955. *Les aventures de la dialectique*. Paris: Gallimard. (trans. Joseph Bien. 1973. *Adventures of the Dialectic*. London: Heinemann.)

———. 1960. *Signes*. Paris: Gallimard. (trans. Richard C. McCleary. 1964. *Signs*. Evanston: Northwestern University Press.)

———. 1964. *Le visible et l'invisible*. Paris: Gallimard. (trans. Alphonso Lingis. 1968. *The Visible and the Invisible*. Evanston: Northwestern University Press.)

Sartre, Jean-Paul. 1946a. *L'existentialisme est un humanisme*. Paris: Nagel. (trans. Philip Mairet. 1968. *Existentialism and Humanism*. London: Methuen.)

———. 1946b. 'La liberté Cartésienne', in *Descartes, 1596–1650*. Genève-Paris: Traits. (trans. Annette Michelson. 1955. 'Cartesian Freedom', in *Literary and Philosophical Essays*. New York: Criterion.)

———. 1954. *Réflexions sur la question juive*. Paris: Gallimard. (trans. George J. Becker. 1976. *Anti-Semite and Jew*. New York: Schocken.)

———. 1960. *Critique de la raison dialectique*. Paris: Gallimard. (trans. Alan Sheridan-Smith. 1976. *Critique of Dialectical Reason*. London: New Left Books.)

———. 1964. 'Les communists et la paix', *Situations, VI*. Paris: Gallimard. (trans. John Kleinschmidt. 1968. *Communists and Peace*. New York: Georges Brazilier.)

———. 1965. *L'être et le néant*. Paris: Gallimard. (trans. Hazel Barnes. 1957. *Being and Nothingness*. London: Methuen.)

———. 1974. 'The Itinerary of Thought', in *Between Existentialism and Marxism*. New York: Panthem.

———. 1976. *Situations, III*. Paris: Gallimard. (trans. Annette Michelson. 1955. 'Materialism and Revolution', in *Literary and Philosophical Essays*. New York: Criterion.)

———. 1983. *Cahiers pour une morale*. Paris: Gallimard. (trans. David Pellauer. 1992. *Notebooks for an Ethics*. Chicago: University of Chicago Press.)

———. 1989. *Vérité et existence*. Paris: Gallimard. (trans. Adrian van den Hoven. 1992. *Truth and Existence*. Chicago: University of Chicago Press.)

Sheridan, James F. 1998. 'On Ontology and Politics: A Polemic', in Jon Stewart (ed.), *The Debate Between Sartre and Merleau-Ponty*. Evanston: Northwestern University Press.

Verger. 1948. 'Jean-Paul Sartre à Berlin', *Verger*, 1(5).

Whiteside, Kerry H. 1988. *Merleau-Ponty and the Foundation of an Existential Politics*. Princeton: Princeton University Press.

Whitford, Margaret. 1982. *Merleau-Ponty's Critique of Sartre's Philosophy*. Lexington: French Forum.

Rethinking Freedom in the Face of Ecological Crises

24

MARK LINDLEY

New practices are needed when big problems arise due to new circumstances. I think that the present unprecedented problem of macro-ecological degradation calls for us to reform certain aspects of some great cultural traditions—economic, religious and humanistic— that are hindering our ability to cope with the problem. This essay will describe a few examples of those aspects.

Free enterprise has bestowed the benefits of twentieth-century-style affluence on a large part of humanity. It appears (since the collapse of state capitalism in the USSR less than a century after the peasant revolution against the then Russian government) that the great tradition of free capitalist enterprise entails a degree of economic inequality enabling the rich to undertake the large-scale creative enterprises that have led, directly or indirectly, to so many splendid inventions and their diffusion. But now the freedom of the very rich to become a worldwide oligarchy and of their corporations to become more powerful than most national governments, has also led to a socially dangerous aggravation of economic inequalities and to the maintenance of enterprises that are seriously irresponsible from an ecological point of view. So the objective of prosperity needs to be counterbalanced by complementary objectives of fairness and ecological sustainability (see Figure 24.1).

Amartya Sen's (1999 and alter editions) concern for one of those other two objectives, fairness as well as prosperity, has led him to describe freedoms as being themselves subject to human development and not bestowed by any superhuman power. This seems to me a correct premise even though I was brought up (in the USA) to believe that 'all men …

Figure 24.1 Fairness and ecological sustainability

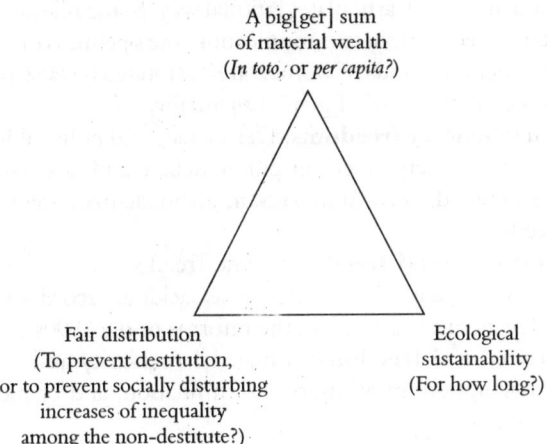

A big[ger] sum
of material wealth
(*In toto,* or *per capita?*)

Fair distribution
(To prevent destitution,
or to prevent socially disturbing
increases of inequality
among the non-destitute?)

Ecological
sustainability
(For how long?)

Source: Adapted from a similarly triangular scheme devised by Andersson (2006: 1).

are endowed by their Creator' with an inalienable right to 'liberty'.[1] I value freedoms of speech, of information, and so on, and I want more people to have them; but I see freedom and fairness in a more post-modern light than truth. A correspondence theory concept of scientific truth (using the premise that a true statement is one which corresponds to reality) supplies a rule of thumb for determining which of any two mutually contrary statements—if both are scientific in Popper's (1959 [1935]) sense of being susceptible to disproof by evidence—is truer; it is the one which fits better the evidence at hand. But we do not have such a good rule of thumb in regard to fairness and/or the relative values of different freedoms; those things are subjective. Just consider how (a) freedoms impinge upon each other (for instance, my freedoms to smoke in public and to make noise, vis-à-vis your freedoms to breathe clean air and to have peace and quiet); and (b) new circumstances, have given rise to changes in our freedoms; for instance, the development of automobiles has given rise to rules about getting a driver's licence, keeping one's vehicle in repair, being sober when driving, observing speed limits, using headlights at night, stopping at traffic lights, and so on; and most of these rules impinge upon common-sense freedoms of yesteryear.

Sen's *Development as Freedom* (1999) discusses five kinds of freedoms, which he says should be cultivated and expanded:

1. **Internal freedoms:** The freedom to be creative, to reason and to think in a lucid, articulate, rational way. Some relevant topics are literacy, education, communication, the openness of society, and whether the minds of women are beclouded by false perceptions of the 'naturalness' of gender inequality.
2. **Participatory freedoms:** Democracy and political liberty and, hence, a society based on public debate and discussion. China has attained, according to Sen, an inadequate degree of such freedom.
3. **Transactional freedoms:** The freedom to exchange and to deal with each other (such as was lacking, according to Sen, in independent India before the reforms of the 1990s).
4. **Procedural freedoms:** Financial regularity and the absence of corruption, of arbitrary discrimination, and of inequality of treatment.
5. **Protective freedoms:** Social safety nets to prevent people from falling down under. A lack of such freedom is apparent (to Sen and to me) in the dramatic rise of mortality rates in Russia after the collapse of communism.

He says that all these kinds of freedom should be expanded, for the sake of 'replacing the domination of circumstances and chance over individuals by the domination of individuals over chance and circumstances.' However, I consider it important to balance this charming latter ideal with good sense as to which circumstances one should try to dominate over, and in what sense dominate, and which, on the other hand, one should accept. The ideal of seeking always to dominate over chance and circumstance seems to me especially quaint in view of the historically unprecedented problems of macro-ecological degradation that we are now beginning to encounter: global warming, deforestation, sinking water tables, the oceans permeated with inorganic rubbish, a growing heap of radioactive waste, tough new epidemics, and so on. Problems of this kind and on this scale oblige us to acknowledge that humankind cannot change—and in that sense cannot dominate over—its basic biological and ecological circumstances. It would be mistaken, for instance, to suppose that our descendants might be able to migrate to another planet as science fiction tales suggest.

The planet we have to live on is so much bigger than we are that its geological and meteorological forces often outstrip our capacity to defend ourselves when they attack us; yet, not so big that they are only trivially affected by our economic activities. In this light, it is unfortunate that most of the humanity today belongs to a religion which in effect venerates the Biblical teaching that God, after creating humans in His image, enjoined them to 'subdue' the Earth and 'have dominion over ... every living thing' on the land and in the sea and the air.[2] Some Christian apologists say that this was supposed to be merely stewardship. (A similar idea is found in Gandhi's view that just as rich people should manage their wealth in trusteeship for the benefit of humanity, so humans should have regard for the weaker species.) But in fact the most powerful Christian societies in the nineteenth and twentieth centuries interpreted the Biblical injunction to have dominion over the Earth in an aggressive and intrusive way. I think it is now clear that the actual Christian interpretation has in reality been far too much along the lines of 'dig it up', 'burn it', 'throw it away'—that is, of freewheeling economic and technological expansion without regard for the macroecological effects (Mahatma Gandhi 1958–94: Vol. XXI, p. 248). The big Marxist governments were just as naïve.

The macro-ecological effects are more complex—and subtler—than local blights like a polluted river or the immediate after-effects of a nuclear power plant gone awry. Figure 24.2 summarizes, for example, the available data in regard to global warming since 1880. Given such data, propagandists paid and promoted by extremely wealthy vested interests can harp on distracting details (in this particular case, the zigzags in annual mean temperature) to argue that no overall trend has been demonstrated, and it thereby becomes all the more difficult to establish whether there is a risk, due to the unprecedented current pace of ecological degradation, to the survival of humanity in the foreseeable future.

Yet, the stakes are so high that no palpable risk can be acceptable to any sane person. Such a person will in certain circumstances risk his or her own life, and many people consider it perfectly sane to risk a lot of other people's lives in a war, but nearly everyone will agree that it would be insane knowingly to risk for any cause the survival of the human species.

I recall apropos 'Pascal's wager', so-called after the seventeenth-century French mathematician, experimental scientist and religious writer, Blaise Pascal. His achievements included some valuable steps in the early development of the mathematics of probability. In his religious writings he could be remarkably poetic, as when he wrote, 'The heart has its reasons, unknown to reason.' His famous 'wager' is like this:

Figure 24.2 Global temperature: Land–ocean index

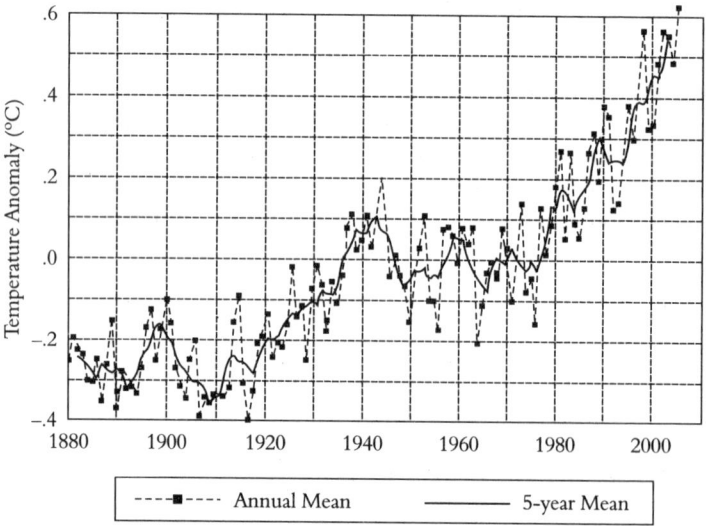

Source: http://data.giss.nasa.gov/

Suppose you can be only theist or else atheist (that is, with no possibility of agnosticism). Which should you choose? Consider the stakes in the four possible cases (Pascal 1670: 233):

1. If there is no God and you are an atheist, you win in terms of truthfulness in this life, and nothing good or bad will happen to your soul after you die (because the Western belief has been that only God could cause anything like that).

2. If there is no God and you are a theist, you lose in truthfulness during this life, but again nothing bad on that account can happen to your soul after you die.

3. If there is a God and you are a theist, you win in truthfulness in this life and also in the eternal happiness of your soul after you die.

4. If there is a God and you are an atheist, not only do you lose in truthfulness in this life, but also your soul will be eternally damned after you die. So you had better believe.

Today this has to be transformed as follows. Whereas most people no longer really believe in an afterlife, most of us sense that humankind is indulging in ecological gambling that could conceivably cause its extinction. Given such high stakes, we cannot afford to hope that any kind of divine providence will intervene to rescue us from the natural consequences of such gambling. We must instead take active responsibility for maintaining our ecological nest even if our hearts may incline us to the religious beliefs we learned as children. (I will come back later to this point.)

Is there a palpable risk? Some related indications are published in the World Conservation Union's authoritative data as to how many species of plants and animals have been found in recent field studies to be threatened or not threatened with extinction. Among the nearly 10,000 species of birds evaluated, more than a tenth have been found to be currently 'vulnerable to extinction' or even 'in danger of extinction' (meaning that only a few members of the species in question are left); and more than a fifth of the nearly 5,000 species of mammals are in such danger.[3] The findings are alarming because in a normal phase of evolution they would probably be lower by one or even two orders of magnitude. We humans are not in any such category; our numbers have been, as Figure 24.3 shows, growing at an unprecedented rate in the last few decades; and yet, one has to doubt whether *Homo sapiens* is decisively tougher biologically and decisively better-off ecologically than some of the many hundreds of mammalian species for which the future is bleak.

And there is, of course, a far greater risk of catastrophes that, though short of extinction, are nonetheless highly undesirable. Here I should mention that it is misguided to regard ecological concerns as contrary to concerns for the welfare of the poor; for it is the poor who are most vulnerable to the effects of most of the catastrophes that will be caused by the current macro-ecological degradation. They will suffer the most from the droughts, floods and storms due to weird meteorological conditions, from the higher cost of water due to lower water tables, from the crop failures, from the new or revived diseases, and so on.

In considering such problems I am humanistic in the sense of putting the welfare of humanity at the peak of my concerns, but not in the sense of regarding humanity as eternal or as central to the cosmos. The cosmos is so much bigger than we are that we cannot presume to know or alter any cosmic purpose. How long will humanity last? It is not my concern beyond a foreseeable number of generations: two, three, four … forty, something like that. Nevertheless, the ecological outlook, while not placing us at the centre of the universe, gives us a sufficiently

Figure 24.3 Human population

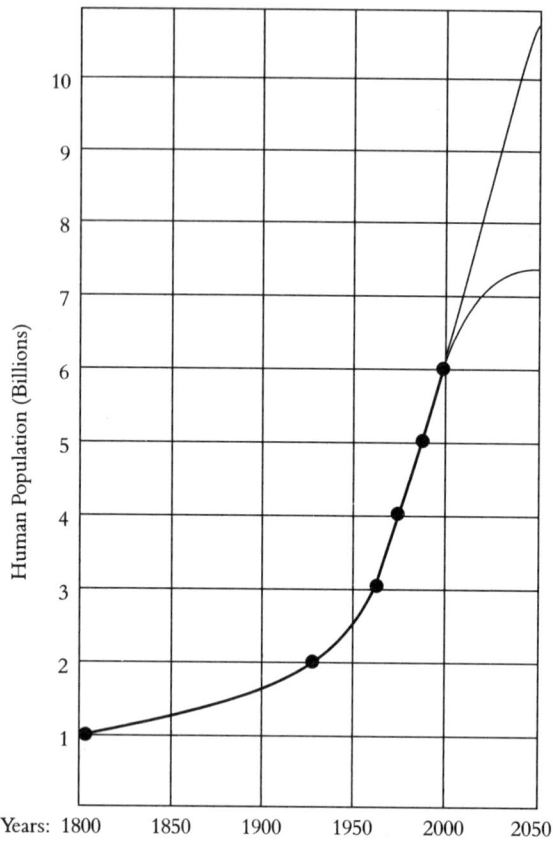

Source: Author.

satisfactory cosmic view to cope with the lingering culture shock due to the discovery, in the seventeenth century, that the Earth has no privileged cosmic status.

It seems to me that:

1. More and more people in civil society are sensing the problem of a looming macro-ecological menace. So there may be some hope of dealing with it in a sane way.
2. It is only sane to presume that the problem is not yet so grave that a proper way to confront it is to hold hands and sing, as if on the decks of the sinking Titanic, 'Nearer, my God, to Thee'.

3. However, the problem is—unlike those of war, oppression, poverty, famines, mass migration and culture shock—so unprecedented that it calls for detailed rethinking in regard to the maintenance and/or modification of freedoms. The modifications should curtail freedoms in regard to those uses of modern technological power that are evidently causing the problem.

The curtailing should consist in part of governmental threats to impose restrictions if industry does not on its own (as if voluntarily, without bureaucratic intrusion into details) meet certain national goal, such as, those negotiated at Kyoto in 1997 for carbondioxide emissions. Yet, it is a pity when freedoms are curtailed by authoritarian governments; far better is a humane preponderance of consent over coercion. And in any case, we need effective laws that become feasible only when there is a widespread consensus as to their value. That is how the freedom to pollute the air with tobacco smoke in enclosed public places (restaurants, auditoriums, aeroplanes, and so on) was curtailed in recent years in the USA: the new laws were preceded by a substantial public consensus as to the cause-and-effect relation between tobacco smoke and lung cancer.

Probably the best hedge against arbitrary or mistaken curtailing of freedoms is a free discussion amongst a well-informed public. In this regard I worry, however, about the capacity of vested interests to wield influence by dishonest propaganda and lobbying; and in regard to India, I worry as to whether it can, with it ongoing population explosion, attain in the twenty-first century a well-informed public, given that the number of illiterate citizens has already grown from less than 300 to more than 400 million in the last 60 years. I regret also that the ingenious but untrue doctrine of *karma*, according to which one's misfortunes are due to bad deeds that one has committed in a previous life on Earth, is hindering India's capacity to deal energetically with ecological as well as social problems. Pavan Varma's book, *The Great Indian Middle Class* (1998), includes a chapter on the 'inner landscape' describing some unfortunate moral consequences of the fact that the typical middle class Hindu cosmic view has 'held an individual to be a cosmos unto himself.' Dr Anil Agarwal, founder of the Centre for Science and Environment (in New Delhi), told me how his religious friends insist that asthma is always only due to an inner spiritual fault in the victim and never to particles in the air. And an experienced

Gandhian social worker, Lavanam, told me how his first effort to teach reading to rural 'untouchables' in India was frustrated by their pious belief, due to the doctrine of inherited *karma*, that they ought not to learn; they told him, 'It is written on our foreheads that we are to be poor and illiterate.'

A correct approach to the problems of ecological degradation lies between such fatalism and the Biblical precept of having dominion over the Earth.

In suggesting that to curtail some freedoms will be *necessary* if humanity is to survive, I do not mean that it would be *sufficient*. The consensus I have in mind is to involve a cultural maturation, especially among the affluent, whereby the modern Western idea of civilization, the idea that more is always better (more knowledge, more beauty, more comfort, more products), will be balanced by Gandhi's complementary idea that 'the essence of true civilization is voluntary restriction of wants'. Especially in the current stage of the history of capitalism, when manufacturers are so urgently stimulating new wants by means of glittering advertisements, people who do not to a considerable extent resist by reflecting as to their true needs—by asking themselves 'When is more really better?'—can rightly be described as consumerist barbarians.

It may be appropriate to mention that as a rationalist, I am struck by Gandhi's uses of his 'inner voice', his moral intuitions. I regard intuitions as an invaluable source of ideas, but since we never know whether a given intuition is due to valid unconscious thinking or to mere bias, I think we should in due time assess it rationally, rather than automatically taking it as correct. I do not want a shrivelled, Voltaire-style rationality, but a warm, robust and aesthetic one. We need good sensibilities as well as good ideas. Yet, even so, it seems to me that among the alluring but misleading ideas bequeathed to us by religion are that: (*a*) the fate after death of our individual souls is more important than the social, moral and ecological condition of our children and grandchildren; and (*b*) acts of piety, such as the reciting of venerated scriptures or the offering of sincere prayers beseeching God's forgiveness, can bring about a miraculous solution of the problem of macro-ecological degradation. If an act of piety is an indispensable part of some individual's or some group's way of changing their practices for the better, then I am for it. And I don't bother with trying to convert people to my religious non-beliefs because the problem of environmental degradation is so important, and maybe so urgent, that it would be foolish to let its solution depend on something as difficult and slow as a change in people's religious identities bestowed upon them in their most tender years. We all have to cooperate now, regardless of religious and philosophical differences, in meeting the problems of ecological degradation, and meanwhile urge business and government to take the steps that need to be taken for the sake of humanity.

Notes

1. Thomas Jefferson and others, *Declaration of Independence*, signed on 4 July 1776 by the founding fathers of the USA.
2. *The Book of Genesis* (in the Bible), Chapter I, Verse 28.
3. http://www.redlist.org/info/tables/

References

Andersson, Jan Otto. 2006. 'International Trade in a Full and Unequal World', paper presented at the workshop, 'Trade and Environmental Justice', Lund, Sweden, 15–16 February. Available at http://www.lucsus.lu.se/Jan_Otto_Andersson_Paper.pdf.

Mahatma Gandhi. 1958–94. *Collected Works*. New Delhi: Publications Division, Ministry of Information and Broadcasting, Government of India.

Pascal, Blaise. 1670. *Pensées*. Paris.

Popper, Karl. 1935. *Logik der Forschung*. Vienna: Julius Springer. Translated in 1959 as *The Logic of Scientific Discovery*.

Sen, Amartya. 1999. *Development as Freedom*. New York: Knopf.

Varma, Pavan. 1998. *The Great Indian Middle Class*. New Delhi and New York: Viking.

Power and Self-cultivation

25

Aesthetics, Development Ethics and the Calling of Poverty

ANANTA KUMAR GIRI

The mission of development ethics is to keep hope alive. By any purely rational calculus of future probabilities, the development enterprise of most countries is doomed to fail. Poor classes, nations and individuals can never catch up with their rich counterparts as long as they continue to consume wastefully and to devise ideological justifications for not practicing solidarity with the less developed. Only some transcultural calculus of hope, situated beyond apparent realms of possibility can elicit the creative energies and vision which authentic development for all requires.

—Goulet (1995: 28)

The quest to live as an art work, which is at the core of the Foucauldian conception of ethics, is necessarily premised on an extreme individualism to which everything is subordinated to the task of aestheticizing life. 'Being-for-oneself' is present in this project of self-stylization but not 'being-for-others'. Purely aesthetic criteria cannot give us the ability to formulate intersubjective norms in the context of practical social life; they cannot enable us to reflect productively on our status as answerable, moral agents.

—Gardiner (1996: 42–43)

Putting first the last goes further. It confronts issues of power. With altruism and generous behaviour, the first remains first; Uppers remain uppers. Putting the first last is more radical. For it means that those who are uppers and powerful step down, disempower themselves and empower others. It implies that uppers have to give up something and make themselves vulnerable.

—Chambers (1997: 234)

The problem

There is a resurgence of interest in both ethics and aesthetics at present which can enrich our contemporary effort to rethink power and freedom, especially help us come to terms with the challenge of self-cultivation (Ankersmit 1996; Foucault 1986; Giri 1998, 2002; Quarles van Ufford and Giri 2003). Contemporary ethics thinking now urges us to realize the significance of the aesthetics and ethics of self-development and self-cultivation, that is, on the need for actors to cultivate their lives as a work of art rather than just attend to the other. The aesthetic emphasis on the ethics of self-development is certainly a welcome development and it has a lot of promise for the theory and practice of development, particularly of development ethics. Development as an intervention has been aimed at ameliorating the condition of the other but the agents of development have not given much attention to developing themselves. Self-development has been a neglected theme and mode of life in development discourse and practice, and the contemporary resurgence of aestheticized ethics can help both the development discourse and development ethics to bring to the centre the challenge of self-cultivation and self-development. But self-development is also equally a challenge for the beneficiaries of development who are usually condemned and stigmatized as a target group. Tackling poverty now requires processes of generating self-development of the poor as the poor cannot come out of the vicious circle of poverty unless they become responsible for their destiny.

But while contemporary aestheticized ethics of self-cultivation helps the practice of development and development ethics to deepen itself, development ethics also can help the former not to fall into the trap of narcissism. Work on self-cultivation, or what Foucault calls 'self's work on itself', can sometimes be forgetful of the face of the other (Davidson 1994). Cultivation of self, then, becomes an end in itself where others are used as a means and not related to as ends in themselves. Development ethics (*cf* Goulet 1995; Gasper 1996, 1998, 2004) with its concern with poverty, human security, violence and the plight of the vulnerable can help aestheticized ethics to remember that ethics also depends on the quality of relationship between the self and the other. But the challenge of poverty is not just of any otherness; it is a challenge of what can be called radical alterity. Despite the celebration of otherness now, the radical alterity that poverty poses has been deliberately relegated to the background at the contemporary juncture. Poor people have now melted into the thin air of aestheticized post-modernity. In this chapter, I submit that poverty presents a deep ethical challenge for all of us concerned and the aesthetics of the care of the self must accept the imperative of responsibility of the self-development of the poor so that they have 'functioning' and 'capabilities' (*cf* Sen 1989, 1990, 1999), and beyond these, they are able to lead a spiritually meaningful life— a life based on an integration of food and freedom.

Power, self-cultivation and aesthetic ethics

Foucault is valorized for a power-model of the human condition but the challenge for self-cultivation and an aesthetics of existence for the logic of power that Foucault has presented in his later *Care of the Self* (1986) has not received adequate attention. Among contemporary interlocutors, he is probably the most influential in urging us to realize that 'the search for an ethics of existence' must involve an 'elaboration of one's own life as a personal work of art' (Foucault 1988: 49). His agenda of an aesthetic ethics is developed in the context of his discussion of ethical life and ethical ideals in antiquity. However, this is not meant only to be an archaeology of the past but to suggest a possible mode and ideal of ethical engagement for the present and future. For Foucault, in antiquity, 'the search for an ethics of existence' was 'an attempt to affirm one's liberty and to give to one's own life a certain form in which one could recognize oneself, be recognized by others, and which even posterity might take as an example' (ibid.). Taking inspiration from Plotinus, the great savant of antiquity, Foucault argues: 'The care of the self does not take the form of a pose or posture, of the fashioning of oneself into a dramatic character… It is, instead, the sculpting of oneself as a statue, the scraping away of what is superfluous and extraneous to oneself' (Davidson 1994: 130). In this preoccupation with cultivating oneself as an example who is not a dramatic superman, Foucault 'rejects the aristocratic pretensions of Nietzsche' (Gardiner 1996: 35) as he asks rhetorically: 'Art is something which is specialized or which is done by experts who are artists. But couldn't everyone's life become a work of art?' (ibid.).

For Foucault, life as a work of art involves care of the self, a conversion to self, an intense relationship with oneself. While ethics is usually conceived of as an attentiveness to the other, for Foucault, ethics at the same time must help one 'to take oneself as an object of knowledge and a field of action, so as to transform, correct and purify oneself, and find salvation' (1986: 42). For Foucault, this intensification of one's relation to oneself does not necessarily result 'in a strengthening of values of individualism or of private life', and he gives the example of the Christian ascetic movement in the first centuries. He interprets the ethical agenda of antiquity as 'the care of the self appears intrinsically linked to a "soul service", which includes the possibility of a round of exchanges with the other and a system of reciprocal obligations' (ibid.: 54). Foucault makes 'the distinction between the care of the self and knowledge of oneself, putting the emphasis on the former' (Szakolczai 1994: 311). He draws inspiration for his agenda of care of the self from Socrates. 'The project which Foucault locates in Socrates and which he claims to lie at the heart of European philosophy is to wake others up from the slumber in which they conduct their everyday existence in order to live differently: not following any precept but starting to be *concerned* with themselves' (ibid.).

Aesthetic ethics as care of the self involves cultivation of appropriate virtues in the conduct of life. The most important challenge here is not to be obsessed with exercising power over others and to be concerned with discovering and realizing 'what one is purely in relation to oneself' (ibid.: 85). For Foucault, 'It is then a matter of forming and recognizing oneself as the subject of one's actions, not through a system of signs denoting power over others, but through a relation that depends as little as possible on status and its external forms' (ibid.). Care of the self then involves discovery of one's true self beyond the illusive determination of status and power. More important, it involves cultivation of appropriate virtues vis-à-vis the use and work of power. While for the holders of power it involves cultivation of virtues of self-restraint and self-governance, for the powerless it means cultivating the courage to resist and revolt, which expresses 'Foucauldian spirituality' (Bernauer and Mahon 1994: 153).[1] For Foucault, 'it was one of the most constant themes of Greek political thought that a city could be happy and well-governed only if its leaders were virtuous' (Foucault 1986: 88). And one important virtue here is learning 'the art of governing oneself' (ibid.: 89). Foucault (ibid.) quotes Plutarch who writes in his *To an Uneducated Ruler*:

> One will not be able to rule if one is not oneself ruled. Now, who there is to govern the ruler? The law, of course; it must not however be understood as the written law but rather as reason, the *logos*, which lives in the soul of the ruler and must never abandon him.

In Foucauldian care of the self, rulers are expected to 'control their passions, which is seen as the guarantee that they will themselves be able to set a limit on the exercise of their political power' (ibid.: 89).[2] Moreover, one should not pursue power for the sake of it: 'One must prepare oneself by setting a prior limit on the ambitions that one entertains' (ibid.: 92). In case of disturbing situations that 'prevent one from attending to oneself ... it is good to withdraw' from the field of power (ibid.: 93).

Foucault's meditation on the cultivation of self-restraint on the part of the holders of power can be of enormous transformative significance in thinking about the field of development and in the practice of development ethics. The field of development has been critically thought of as constituting a nexus of power–knowledge that subjugates people. Foucauldian critics of development such as Escobar (1995) point to the subjugation to which people are subjected in the regime of modern development. But Escobar does not explore the challenge for self-transformation that holders of power and agents of modernist development face, which the Foucauldian agenda of care of the self presents. Though Foucault does not explore all the dimensions of the self,[3] especially its transformative and transcendental dimension, this is still a significant challenge for critical discourses on knowledge and power. For Foucault, though the relationship to self belongs to an ethics of control, yet in this relationship, one is able to 'delight in oneself' (Foucault 1986: 64–65), one is able to take pleasure in oneself. This pleasure in oneself is contrasted with pleasure 'whose origin is to be placed outside us and in objects whose presence we cannot be sure of' (ibid.: 66).

In presenting his outline of aesthetic ethics and the care of the self, Foucault (1986: 90) presents to us, approvingly, what Marcus Aurelius writes about one Emperor Antonius of antiquity, which can help us rethink our ethics as holders of power and destiny makers in the field of development:

> By avoiding useless outbursts, satisfactions of vanity, transports of anger and violent displays, by eschewing everything in the way of vindictiveness and suspicion, by keeping flatterers away and giving access only to wise and frank counsellors, Antonious showed how he rejected the 'Ceasarian' mode of being. Through his practice of self-restraint (whether it was a matter of food, clothes, sleep or boys), through the moderate use he made of the comforts of life, through the absence of agitation and the equanimity of his soul, and through the cultivation of friendship

without inconstancy or passion, he trained himself in the art of sufficing himself without losing his serenity.... A whole elaboration of the self by oneself was necessary for these tasks, which would be accomplished all the better because one did not identify in an ostentatious way with the trappings of power.

The calling of aesthetic ethics at present gets another creative manifestation in Charles Taylor's (1991) discussion of the contemporary quest for authenticity. While commentators such as Christopher Lasch (1979) dismiss the contemporary quest for authenticity as an expression of narcissism, Taylor urges us to understand the quest for meaning involved here. This quest embodies a close connection between 'self-discovery and artistic creation' (Taylor 1991: 61). Here, 'artistic creation becomes the paradigm mode in which people can come to self-definition' (ibid.). While this striving for the cultivation of the artist within oneself shares a long romantic tradition such as that of Herder's and its 'tendency to heroize the artist', it also carries a new understanding of art not only as mere imitation but as an original creation (ibid.: 64). Contemporary quest for authenticity stresses that the primary ethical ideal is to fulfil oneself and realize oneself as an artist. However, this urge for self-fulfilment, for Taylor, reflects the condition of a 'flattened world, where the horizons of meaning become fainter'(ibid.: 69).

The aestheticization of ethics, that is, the ideal that the primary task for ethical engagement is self-cultivation and self-fulfilment, can be better understood by a dialogue with the trajectory of self-cultivation, or *bildung* in the German tradition. And here anthropologist Louis Dumont's discussion of the German tradition of *bildung* helps us. Aesthetic ethics is an important part of the quest for *bildung* or self-cultivation. Dumont presents us the ideal of Karl Philip Moritz for whom it is through the beautiful that we constantly rejuvenate ourselves and make ourselves. For Moritz, in making life a work of art, 'man must reach beyond himself' (ibid.). Moritz tells us that in devoting ourselves to life as a work of art, there occurs a process of transformation; a transformation which is akin to the self-transformation that takes place in the Foucauldian care of the self. In the words of Moritz (ibid.: 78):

For man as an individual it is clear that the beautiful replaces God as transcendence. We subordinate ourselves or we 'sacrifice' ourselves to a higher existence in order to attain beauty.... Aesthetic unselfishness requires the same abandon towards the beautiful that pietism required toward God.

The ideal of *bildung* in the German tradition, as one of its main proponents Wilhelm von Humboldt tells us, stresses that the most useful thing a man can do for others is to work at his own improvement. According to Humboldt (ibid.: 102):

> Politics must remain subordinated to *Bildung* [and] utmost enjoyment is to be found not in contemplation but in activity.... This activist or energetic conception of man helps us understand that *bildung* is not a goal to be reached, that is, a whole that would be 'the highest and most profound formation' in an absolute sense, but rather it consists in the constant effort to increase and better proportion our forces, in short, a process directed toward the ideal.

For Humboldt, *bildung* is characterized by a normative preoccupation in which the subjective and the objective communicate (ibid.: 112). While the subjective is characterized by an attempt to know oneself and define one's originality,[4] this aspiration for originality also possesses another aspect (ibid.: 143). 'The *bildung* subject must, according to Humboldt, draw from his environment the largest number of diversities compatible with what is positive in his own particularity, that is to say, with his "originality" in order to enrich it and constitute it as a whole' (ibid.: 143).

Such visions and practices of self-cultivation are also available from many other traditions as well as contemporary movements of thought. Of particular significance here is the work of Confucian tradition in its emphasis on learning, humility and servanthood on the part of holders of power. As de Barry (1991: 4) writes: 'When Confucius talks about Heaven's Mandate he does not address a ruling house, urging fidelity to the example of its founder as a condition of its longevity and tenure. Rather, the Mandate has been reconceived as an individual mission and personal commitment to the service of mankind in the broadest sense.' Such an emphasis upon service is not totally different from the emphasis upon *kenosis* or self-emptying of the will to dominate in Christian spiritual traditions. Vattimo (1999), in this regard, proposes a pathway of weak ontology as significant to the working of self, society and the dynamics of power characterized by cultivation of humility, love and non-violence. His weak ontology is humble to learn and to serve rather than wedded to a cult of mastery, and this finds a transformative parallel in Dallmayr's (2001) pathways of 'practical ontology' and 'achieving our world', which reiterate the significance of self-cultivation, learning and practical labour. Instead of being fettered by power, Dallmayr (ibid.), building upon Heidegger, also pleads for realizing a 'power-free existence'.

This last pointer to the challenge of realizing a 'power-free existence' brings self-cultivation, aesthetic ethics and the calling of transformation of power to a new height and depth. As Dallmayr helps us understand in an original reinterpretation of the Heideggerian pathway: 'Heidegger's middle and later writings came to see the pitfalls and streamlining effects of linear power seeking and to adumbrate a realm beyond power and impotence, domination and submission under the rubric of a "power-free" (machtlos) dispensation that allows being(s) "to be"' (ibid.: 190). In his works such as *Beitrage zur Philosophie* (Contributions to Philosophy, 1936), *Besinnung* (Meditative Thinking, 1938–39) and *Die Gesischte des Seyns* (The History of Being, 1939–40), in addition to providing critique of power, Heidegger 'adumbrates and provides guideposts for something radically "other", namely, the reflective recovery of care for Being, a care completely immune to manipulation' (Dallmayr 2001: 198).

Aesthetics of self-cultivation and the face of the other

The previous section presented us glimpses of various visions and practices of self-cultivation and aesthetic ethics as it is thought about and lived in various places and times—Foucault's antiquity, Confucian horizons and Christian spiritual visions, Taylor's contemporary Euro-American world and Dumont's eighteenth- and nineteenth-century Germany. Aesthetic ethics with its emphasis on self-cultivation, self-development, self-transformation, and creation and recreation of one's own life as well as the life of community as a work of art is of enormous significance in rethinking the discourse and practice of development, as well as transforming the discourse and practice of power and freedom. So there is a need for dialogue between aesthetic ethics and ethical reflections in the field of development, which is otherwise known as development ethics. But before initiating this dialogue, we have to take note of the fact as well as the perception that the aesthetics of self-cultivation may be preoccupied only with the self-understood as an egological monad (*cf* Harvey 1996), and may not recognize the face of the other and cultivate appropriate responsibility to the other and society. In the German context, aestheticization of life and ethics degenerated into what David Harvey (1989) calls an 'aesthetics of empowerment'—an aesthetics which was devoid of any internal ground of criticism (Hanrahan 2001). The aesthetics of self-cultivation in the middle became a handmaiden of Nazism. It is no wonder then that Dumont himself hints that Humboldt's ideal of self-cultivation was limited by his aristocracy and his subservient attitude towards the existing monarchy.[5] In this context, there is a need for the ethics of self-cultivation to practise what Habermas (1996) calls 'radical democracy'.[6]

Taylor also draws our attention to the need for aesthetic ethics to be more aware of its responsibility towards the other and society along with its emphasis on authenticity. Taylor (1991: 72–73) says, 'We ought to be trying to persuade people that self-fulfilment, so far from excluding unconditional relationships and moral demands beyond the self, actually requires these in some form.' He (ibid.: 82) further argues, 'Authenticity is clearly self-referential: this has to be *my* orientations. But this does not mean that on another level the *content* must be self-referential, that my goals must express or fulfil my desires or aspirations, *as against* something that stands beyond these.' For Taylor (ibid.: 74), 'authenticity opens an age of self-responsibilization' and 'points us towards a more self-responsible form of life.'

Similar is the challenge of recognizing the face of the other for the Foucauldian care of the self. As one insightful commentator of Foucault writes (Gardiner 1996: 38):

> In Foucault's ontology of the subjects, there are only scattered and essentially gratuitous reference to our relations with others, little real acknowledgement of the centrality of non-repressive solidarity and dialogue for human existence. One must not have the care for others precede the care of the self, he [Foucault] bluntly declares at one point.

For the same commentator (ibid.):

> The irony is that, for Foucault, the overarching purpose of an aesthetics of existence does not appear to be pure self-aggrandizement for its own sake, but ultimately to secure the approval and recognition of others. However, mutual recognition is something he can envisage only as the outcome of a contest of worthy equals, which must be 'negotiated' from a position of strength.

Taking inspiration from Emmanuel Levinas and Mikhail Bakhtin, this commentator further urges us to realize (ibid.):

> Foucauldian self is sovereign and bent on self mastery, the central imperative of the Bakhtian subject is to be open to dialogical exchange with the other.... Using the language that is reminiscent of Emmanuel Levinas, Bakhtin suggests that we need to cultivate a fundamental receptivity with respect to the other, a 'feminine passivity' rather than a Nietschean activism, for only then can we fully grasp the dialogical nature of Being and be answerable to ourselves and others.

But to be fair to Foucault, the significance of his aesthetic ethics lies precisely in stressing the point that attentiveness to and responsibility for the other requires preparation in the self and appropriate cultivation of virtues. This task of self-cultivation, as the self looks-up to the face of the other, has been unfortunately totally ignored by the ethical philosophers of the other, such as Levinas (see Giri 1998). Moreover, though the Foucauldian subject is still within the Nietzchean model of self-mastery, in his reflection on the ideal and mode of being in antiquity, Foucault urges us to be aware of the limits of both power and mastery. Of course, a fuller realization of this limitation requires a spiritual transformation of aesthetic ethics that is only hinted-at in Foucault but is not fully explored. It is probably for this reason that another insightful critic of Foucault argues (Davidson 1994: 130):

> When Plotinus tells us that if we do not yet see our beauty, we should sculpt our own beautiful statue of ourselves, far from urging any aestheticization of the self; he is enjoining a purification, an exercise that returns us to our self, ultimately identified by Plotinus with the One. The beauty of this sculpting is not independent from the reality of the Good; it is not an aestheticization of morality but a spiritual transfiguration in which we scrap away at ourselves, identifying with the good beyond ourselves so that we can see our own beauty, that is, so that the 'divine glory of virtue' will shine upon us.

Thus, the Foucauldian care of the self needs to go through the 'arduous path of spiritual exercises that require nothing less than a transformation of one's way of life' (ibid.: 129).

Such spiritual strivings enable us to realize that in ethical engagement we can privilege and neglect neither the self nor the other. What is called for in ethical engagement is a dialogical and dialectical subjectivity which accords primacy to the mid-point of emergent relationship between self and the other.

The calling of development ethics

If aestheticized ethics has a problem in recognizing the face of the other despite its salutary emphasis on self-cultivation, then a dialogue with development ethics can be redeeming. Responsibility to the marginal other and the poor is an important aspect of the calling of development ethics (Gasper 1996; Goulet 1995). For example, Denis Goulet (1995: 56), one of the most influential proponents of development ethics, tells us: 'While millions suffer deficiency diseases caused by malnutrition, a favored few fall prey to hitherto unknown degenerative diseases induced by excessive food and drink.' In this context, the calling of development ethics for ethical thinking and practice is to cultivate our identification with the marginalized poor. For Goulet (ibid.: 161), 'The main ethical point is that meeting basic needs of the very poor must be given first priority.' He further argues (ibid.: 59), 'As with individuals who are undernourished, insensitive individuals are stunted human beings.... "Human quality" consists in perceiving reality as it truly is and in feeling compassion for fellow humans.' Taking inspiration from French ethicist Pierre Antoine's argument that 'an obligation rooted in justice can exist, as a consequence of our acts, even when no fault of injustice has been committed', Goulet challenges us to realize that 'because the rich are responsible for abolishing the absolute poverty of their fellow human beings, to refuse to do so is only at the price of stunting their own humanity' (ibid.: 60). It is probably for this reason that C.J. Hamelink, another proponent of development ethics, challenges us in his (1997: 11) provocative essay, 'Making Moral Choices in Development Cooperation: The Agenda for Ethics':

> Development Ethics should confront those of us who belong to the lucky billion with a moral challenge to our personal behaviour. Ethical reflection should break through our common complacency and make us feel less comfortable about our own (individual and collective) unwillingness to allow even normal threats to our prosperity and the future of our children.

Rajni Kothari also asks us to realize the ethical imperative of poverty in the field of development. For Kothari (1993: 165):

> Beyond the institutional steps needed to restructure the processes of power and root out its worst pathologies ... there is a need to enlist human sensitivity on behalf of the poor at more basic levels. There is a need to go beyond the political, the social and ecological domains and tap the moral and ethical domain.

To him, the ethical calling of poverty is part of a 'larger reawakening and restructuring of civil society', which involves concrete interventions on our part (ibid.: 166). Such an imperative is particularly urgent at present as he writes (ibid.: 171),

> we seem to have arrived at a moment in history in which positioning ourselves vis-à-vis the poor has increasingly meant that leaving them out of the purview of the state and the development process is not only considered both economically and politically necessary but also legitimate.

Thus, development ethics reiterates the need for sharing our resources and abilities with the poor. Development ethics pushes the ethics of the other further towards recognizing the face of the poor as an extremely vulnerable other. It reiterates the need for realizing the integral link between what Amartya Sen (1989) calls food and freedom. But while in Sen this connection is established only as an aspect of public action and it is a matter of establishing legal entitlement, the ethical imperative[7] vis-à-vis poverty now urges us to realize the limits of law, and while understanding its transformative significance, to supplement it with a life of voluntary poverty and sharing one's food and resources with the poor. Sharing one's food with the hungry and the poor can be a concrete act of recognizing the face of the other; in fact looking up to the face of the other as Levinas (1969, 1991 [1974], 1995) urges us to do. But what must be stressed here is that this aspired-for ethics of sharing is not one of charity where the self is not personally involved with the plight of the other. It is also not to perpetuate an eternal cycle of dependency within the poor. A life of voluntary poverty and a life of sharing with the poor is meant to hold the hands of the poor as friends and be an instrument in their self-growth and in their leading a life of autonomy, self-determination and *swaraj*.

Sharing of food has been an important part of Indian tradition, and in order to understand the challenge that a life of sharing poses to an ethics of self-cultivation, we can be enriched by a dialogue with the ideal of what is called in the Indian tradition *annam bahu kurvitha*, that is, the discipline of growing and sharing food in plenty. This imperative of sharing one's food with not only friends and relatives but also with strangers and the non-human world is stressed dramatically in the story of Svetaketu presented in the *Bhavishyapuranam* and recently recounted for us by Jitendra Bajaj and M.D. Srinivas (1996) in their evocative text, *Annam Bahu Kurvita*. King Sveta, who was a pious king, was probably engaged in the same austere ethics of self-cultivation as Foucault's

Emperor Antonious of Antiquity. For his noble deeds on earth, after his death he went to heaven. But even in heaven, he could not but feel hungry and he had no food to satisfy his hunger except to come down to the lake on earth that still contained his mortal body and eat its flesh. When he asked Brahma, the lord of the heavens, why he still felt hungry in the heaven, Brahma told him the following which has a lot of significance for an ethics of self-cultivation to recognize the face of the other (ibid.: 13–14):

> O Sveta, you indeed undertook *tapas* of high order in your earthly life. But you nurtured only your own body. Not even a morsel of food was given out of your hands. Since you did not ever give food on earth, therefore, even here in the heavens you are destined to suffer the pangs of hunger and thirst. Therefore, partake of the flesh of your body that you have nurtured so well during your life on earth.

For many, nurturing one's own body may be considered an epitome of the ethics of self-cultivation, but the story tells us that if we nurture only our own bodies and limit our ethics of care of the self only to ourselves and do not consider it our moral responsibility to be concerned about the emaciated bodies of the other, then we will be in the same plight as that of Sveta and have nothing but to devour our flesh to satisfy our hunger. Srinivas and Bajaj help us understand this:

> The mere act of living, according to Indian understanding, involves partaking of the share of other components of the Universe, which creates a debt not only towards other members of the human society but towards the Universe in general. Giving of food, before eating, is both a recognition and a partial repayment of that debt. Not recognizing and not attempting to repay that debt is a transgression ... that makes one an outcaste, a *candala*, not merely from the human society but from the Universe as it were. And then there is nothing in the universe that may be assigned for him as food....

For Srinivas and Bajaj (ibid.: 18),

> [N]o amount of giving of diverse riches in charity can substitute for the giving of food. All the righteous living of King Sveta and all his generous gifts could be of no avail in offsetting his failure to give food because, giving of food is not a matter of merely earning virtue, which may be exchanged with virtue earned otherwise. Giving of food, before sitting down to eat, is a matter of essential discipline of living.... There is no virtue to be earned from such repayment, there is only a transgression to be avoided.

On the other hand, 'only those who feed others even when they themselves have nothing to eat ... earn great virtue' (ibid.). Bajaj and Srinivas further stress that the discipline of sharing food in the Indian tradition urges us to realize that this is confined not only among friends and relatives who have been invited, but must be ever open to the knocking of any stranger or the unknown visitor. Sharing urges us to be in a state of 'permanent wakefulness', to put it in the evocative words of Levinas (1995: 195), where we are always at the service of the other.

Contemporary reconstruction of ethics as responsibility and answerability to the other, as Levinas and Bakhtin urge us to realize, gets a concrete manifestation in the calling of development ethics with its emphasis on the imperative of establishing solidarity and identification with the poor and the marginalized. This calling of development ethics has a potential for further concrete embodiment in the ethics of sharing of food as described earlier. Here, sharing of food is also a metaphor for sharing of other resources and capabilities of life with those who do not have and who are handicapped to live and realize their lives because of such a lack. Sharing of food can be a starting point of a wider ethics of sharing; indeed, an ethics of friendship (*cf* Derrida 1997).

But while development ethics can help aesthetic ethics recognize the face of the other and embody an ethics of sharing, the field of development still requires an ethics of self-cultivation for its practitioners and agents. While development ethics reminds aesthetic ethics to be responsible to the poor, aesthetics of self-cultivation challenges both the poor as well as the rich, the beneficiaries of development as well as its more powerful and resourceful executives, to be continuously engaged in self-development and self-transformation. There is the fundamental challenge of self-development on the part of the leaders and executives in the field of modern social and economic development. This challenge is a challenge of cultivating humility or 'self-emptying process' (*cf* Wilfred 1996) on the part of development professionals who have the arrogance of both knowledge and power. The challenge is also to realize that, as Robert Chambers (1997: 32) argues, 'power hinders learning.' So the 'uppers' must make themselves vulnerable.

Thus, cultivating the capacity to be vulnerable and humble in one's relationship with the poor and downtrodden is an important part of the care of the self in the field of development, in particular; and the more widespread systemic administration of life in general, which is increasingly becoming our lot under the regime of late capitalism (Habermas 1996). An ethics of self-cultivation is very much required in the field of development as well and it can help bring the personal dimension into this field of practice. As Chambers (1997: 233) argues, 'Courtesy, respect, patience, consideration, generosity, reflecting on and being sensitive to other's realities ... such virtues seem the core of personal and interpersonal well-being.' He adds (ibid.: 232), 'When personal responsibility is given primacy, authority resides not in texts, manuals or sequences of observance or procedure, but in individual judgements, choices and actions. Improving those becomes the focus.'

Notes

1. As two insightful interpreters of Foucault tell us: 'It is through revolt that subjectivity (not that of a great man but that of whomever) introduces itself into history and gives it the breath of life. This breath of life manifests the human capacity to transcend any product of history that claims necessity' (Bernauer and Mahon 1994: 153).
2. For Foucault (1986: 95), in antiquity, 'it was the practice of superiority over oneself that guaranteed the moderate and reasonable use that one could and ought to make of the two other superiorities' (that is, the superiority exercised in the context of the household and society).
3. As Eisenstadt (2002: 38) writes, 'While the term "parrhesia", as used by Foucault, goes beyond the simple emphasis on resistance as due mainly to the inconvenience of being confined within the coercive frameworks of an order, and denotes the courageous act of disrupting dominant discourses, thereby opening a new space for another truth to emerge—not a discursive truth but rather a "truth of the self", an authentication of the courageous speaker in this "eruptive truth-speaking"—it does not systematically analyze the nature of the agency through which such other truth may emerge or how the emergence of such "truth of the self" may become interwoven with process of social change and transformation.'
4. Of course, it must be noted that for Dumont (1994: 143), 'Humboldt does not insist on the uniqueness of each individual and does not—not yet?—conceive of individuality as irreplaceable, as German tradition will do from Goethe onward.... But he at least attempted to know himself and define his own originality.'
5. In the words of Dumont (1994: 105): 'Only a young aristocrat could have undertaken to make self-education the great affair of his life and to erect it at the same time as the supreme principle of modernity. Moreover, the aristocrat's traditional vocation is to serve the state. Furthermore ... the two kinds of activity are less disparate then it would seem at first: they are both oriented toward totality; the aristocracy is traditionally

devoted to the service of the social totality, while *bildung* tends to erect a single subject into a totality.'

6. Dumont (1994: 95) tells us how Humbolt used *bildung* as an implicit 'counterpoint to French Revolution'.

7. It also needs to be taken note of here that Sen's capability ethics suffers from a problem of insufficient commitment to responsibility on the part of the concerned actors. As Lera-Lee (1997: 4) argues: 'Questions of responsibility ... are a necessary condition to bridge the capabilities approach with the real worlds of practice and compromise. Thus, in order to make the transition from theory to practice, the capabilities approach must incorporate responsibility ascription in its theoretical justification.... Through principles of accountability and the framing of development questions in terms of responsibility, the capabilities approach might be re-shaped and completed as a guideline for development theory and practice.'

References

Ankersmit, F.R. 1996. *Aesthetic Politics*. Stanford: Stanford University Press.

Bajaj, J.K. and M.D. Srinivas. 1996. *Annam Bahu Kurvita: Recollecting the Indian Discipline of Growing and Sharing of Food in Plenty*. Madras: Center for Policy Research.

Bernauer, James W. and Michael Mahon. 1994. 'Michel Foucault's Ethical Imagination', in Gary Gutting (ed.), *Cambridge Companion to Michel Foucault*, pp. 141–158. Cambridge: Cambridge University Press.

Chambers, Robert. 1997. *Whose Reality Counts? Putting the First Last*. London: Intermediate Technology Publications.

Davidson, Arnold I. 1994. 'Ethics as Ascetics: Foucault, the History of Ethics and Ancient Thought', in Garry Gutting (ed.), *The Cambridge Companion to Foucault*. Cambridge: Cambridge University Press.

Dallmayr, Fred. 2001. *Achieving Our World: Towards Plural and Global Democracy*. Lanham, MD: Rowman and Littlefield.

De Barry, Wm. Theodore. 1991. *The Trouble with Confucianism*. Cambridge, MA: Harvard University Press.

Derrida, Jacques. 1997. *The Politics of Friendship*. London: Verso.

Dumont, Louis. 1994. *German Ideology: From France to Germany and Back*. Chicago: University of Chicago Press.

Eisenstadt, S.N. 2002 (Manuscript). *Political Theory In Search of the Political*. Jerusalem: Hebrew University of Jerusalem.

Escobar, E. 1995. *Encountering Development: The Making and Unmaking of the Third World*. Princeton: Princeton University Press.

Foucault, Michel. 1986. *The Care of the Self*. New York: Pantheon.

———. 1988. 'An Aesthetics of Existence', in *Politics, Philosophy, Culture: Interviews and other Writings, 1977–84*. London: Routledge.

Gardiner, Michael. 1996. 'Foucault, Ethics and Dialogue', *History of the Human Sciences*, 9(3): 27–46.

Gasper, Des. 1996. 'Culture and Development Ethics: Needs, Women's Rights and Western Theories', *Development and Change*, 27(4): 627–61.

———. 1998. 'Charity and Obligation: Ethics and Development Aid', Paper presented at the Conference on Development Ethics, Norweignian Association for Development Research, Oslo, 5–6 June.

———. 2004. *The Ethics of Development: From Economism to Human Development*. Edinburgh: Edinburgh University Press.

Giri, Ananta K. 1998. 'The Calling of an Ethics of Servanthood', *Journal of Indian Council of Philosophical Research*, XV1(3): 125–34.

———. 2002. *Conversations and Transformation: Toward a New Ethics of Self and Society*. Lanham, MD: Lexintong Books.

Goulet, Denis. 1995. *Development Ethics: A Guide to Theory and Practice*. London: Zed Books.

Habermas, Jurgen. 1996. *Between Facts and Norms: Contributions to a Discourse Theory of Law and Democracy*. Cambridge: Polity Press.

Hamelink, C.J. 1997. 'Making Moral Choices in Development Cooperation: The Agenda of Ethics', in C.J. Hamelink (ed.), *Ethics and Development*, pp. 11–24. Kampen, Netherland: Uitgerverji Kok.

Hanrahan, Nancy W. 2001. 'Social Change/Cultural Practice: Theoretical Perspectives', in Ananta Kumar Giri (ed.), *Rethinking Social Transformation: Criticism and Creativity at the Turn of the Millennium*. Jaipur: Rawat Publications.

Harvey, David. 1989. *The Condition of Postmodernity: In Inquiry into the Origins of Cultural Change*. Cambridge, MA: Basil Blackwell.

———. 1996. *Justice, Nature and the Geography of Difference*. Cambridge, MA: Basil Blackwell.

Kothari, Rajni. 1993. *The Growing Amnesia: Poverty and Human Consciousness*. Delhi: Penguin Books.

Lasch, Christopher. 1979. *Culture of Narcissism: American Life in an Age of Diminishing Expectations*. New York: W.W. Norton.

Lera-Lee, Asuncion. 1997. 'Development and Responsibility', Paper presented at the International Conference of International Development Ethics Association, Chennai, January.

Levinas, Emmanuel. 1969. *Totality and Infinity: An Essay on Exteriority*. Pittsburg, PA: Duquesne University Press.

———. 1991 [1974]. *Otherwise Than Being or Beyond Essence*. Dordrecht: Kluwer Academic Publishers.

———. 1995. 'Ethics of the Infinite', in Richard Kearney (ed.), *States of Mind: Dialogues with Contemporary Thinkers on the European Mind*. Manchester: Manchester University Press.

Sen, Amartya. 1989. 'Food and Freedom', *World Development*, 17(6): 769–81.

Sen, Amartya. 1990. 'Food, Economics and Entitlement', in Jean Dreze and Amartya Sen (eds), *The Political Economy of Hunger: Vol 1—Entitlement and Well-Being*. Oxford: Clarendon Press.

———. 1999. *Development as Freedom*. Oxford: Oxford University Press.

Szakolczai, Arpad. 1994. 'Thinking Beyond the East–West Divide: Foucault, Patocka, and the Care of the Self', *Social Research*, 61(2): 297–323.

Taylor, Charles. 1991. *The Ethics of Authenticity*. Cambridge, MA: Harvard University Press.

van Ufford, Philip Quarles and Ananta Kumar Giri (eds). 2003. *A Moral Critique of Development: In Search of Global Responsibilities*. London: Routledge.

Vattimo, Giani. 1999. *Belief*. Cambridge: Polity Press.

Wilfred, Felix. 1996. *Leave the Temple: Indian Paths to Human Liberation*. Trichy: Carmell Publications.

Reflections on Human Security

A Buddhist Contribution

26

THANH-DAM TRUONG

E ncouraged by an apparent peace dividend resulting from the demise of East–West tension at the end of the Cold War,[1] the United Nations has been trying to work towards a new approach to issues of global peace and development as inexorably linked phenomena. The emerging concept of human security encapsulates various proposals to handle security issues as inclusive of but extending beyond traditional security concerns. The concept hinges itself on the view that beyond the military defence of state interests and territory, societal conditions that pose a threat to the daily security of ordinary people constitute an equally legitimate domain for security concerns. Covering many overlapping dimensions—such as, economic security, food security, health security, environmental security, personal security, community security and political security—the concept tends to place religion as a promoting force at the margins of these concerns. Events in world affairs—prior to and following the attack on New York's World Trade Centre on 11 September 2001—express an urgency to find an approach that gives adequate analytical space to the role of culture and religion in shaping the politics of identity, representation, resource and human security claims. As any experience, human security is not immune from political, cultural and social shaping. Every dimension of human security involves a direct or indirect mediating role of cultural and religious institutions, spanning from the most local and historically specific experience of individuals and groups, to the most global level of politics over territorial and resource control.

A discussion on the relationship between religions and human security requires the recognition of three different aspects of significance which religions have:

1. An epiphenomenon, an experiential state of communion with a life-force;
2. A symbolic representation of the life-world, the norms and institutions which reproduce it; and
3. A construct adhered to by individuals and groups through socialization or deliberate choice for identity creation, protection and salvation.

As an epiphenomenon, the religious experience is not about the process of formation of the self; rather its dissolution into another state of being—in communion with God or a life-force—however defined. By contrast, as a symbolic representation of the life-world, religion lies at the core of processes of identity formation and historically constitutes a discourse of power—the power to control the morality of followers. The entry by individuals/groups and adherence to this symbolic representation—a social and historical process of identity formation—derives from the need for affinity or security regarding self-hood.

In the current context of global disorder, the security of identity and well-being has been undermined by a complex interaction between different sets of factor that arise from a greater integration of capital and production on one hand, and polarization and disintegration of the socio-cultural world on the other hand. The search for peaceful means of conflict resolution through an appropriation of the values upheld by a given spiritual tradition is also a search for ways to link them with those of other traditions. Such has been aptly described as the art of climbing down the well in one's homestead as deeply as one can, in order to find the underground water shared by the well of one's neighbour.[2] In this vein, I seek to illustrate how Buddhist thinking may contribute to the discussion on global peace and human security in the context of the twenty-first century. By adding a spiritual dimension to the debate on human security, my hope is to open the space for inter-paradigmatic learning on ethics, rights and human interaction.

Human security: A secular concept in need of a spiritual dimension

The framing of human security issues was first initiated in conjunction with concerns for ethics in resource use in development activities. Within the disarmament and development nexus, Mahbub Ul-Haq (1995) queried the ethics of governments giving budgetary allocation priority to armaments over and above providing milk for children. 'We need today a new concept of human security—reflected in the lives of the people, not in the weapons of their countries' (ibid.: 116). To him, switching spending from military to development activities constitutes an ethical action which all governments should be encouraged to pursue. In an endorsement of the neo-liberal principle of individualism, he argued that channelling resources in the direction of human development—the enhancement of human capabilities—would contribute to a level playing field, currently distorted by class, gender, ethnic and religious divisions. An improved level of human development, he suggested, would lead to better economic performance by developing nations and a more healthy competition in the global market.

Since this intervention, the concept of human security has been subject to new debates from a variety of angles. Caroline Thomas (1999) urges us to think about neo-liberal reforms worldwide in the 1980s and 1990s as a phase of transition of capitalism—from national to global—which has generated new forms of human insecurity for which collective responses are required. In her view, the human security project cannot succeed if based on neo-liberal individualism which she regards as the problem rather than solution. Thomas sees the proliferation of forms of human insecurity that has emerged since in the 1990s (such as intra-state violence, forced migration and environmental destruction) as the result of a newly polarized global social structure. Her way of resolving the human insecurity question would involve a taming of the neo-liberal ideology at the global level along with fostering collective efforts to protect and enhance the human development of vulnerable groups—the latter in combination with a rights-based approach to extant political systems.

From another perspective, Sverre Lodgaard (2001) sees the links between state security and human security as a matter of legitimacy. Failed states, he suggests, are states that no longer provide effective governance and, therefore, invariably have fallen down in respect of the provision of human security. His view on human security is based on the rule of law, public order and peaceful management of conflicts. To maintain its legitimacy, the state has to comply with an expanding body of international law that seeks to provide—from a plethora of rights platforms—protection of citizens from torture, arbitrary arrest and detention, gender-specific violence, child abuse, mishandling of refugees, organized crime and the results of armed conflict between factions within a state (ibid.: 3–7).

He places the concept of human security within the framework of governance, wherein it is defined as the daily security of groups of people vulnerable to violence during conflict situations. In other words, ensuring human security is a matter of identifying and targeting problematic states and protecting groups of people living under problematic conditions generated by the failure of governance. In his view, policies for security (state as well as human) are future oriented; hence, the objective should be prevention. The key phenomenon that needs preventing is manmade physical violence; therefore, the concept of human security should be narrowed down to direct and personal violence (ibid.: 8). The absence of human security as an outcome of a global economic disorder does not appear very prominent in his argument. He places economic security in the definitional boundaries of human development which he believes cannot be mixed with human security. His position is backed by the Human Security Partnership between Canada and Norway, and a number of other states.[3] This is a nine-point agenda covering antipersonnel landmines, International Criminal Court, the protection of children in armed conflict, the control of small arms and light weapons, the fight against transnational organized crime, human rights education, the struggle against HIV/AIDS, implementation gaps of international humanitarian and human rights law, and conflict prevention. Human development and Humans security has been recently added to this agenda. (Acharya 2001; Paris 2001).

From the perspective of societies in Asia affected by the 1997 financial crisis and subsequent economic meltdown, the concept of human security depicts a vision of interconnectedness rather than compartmentalization. A statement by the Japanese foreign ministry notes:

> In Japan's view, human security is a much broader concept. We believe that freedom from want is no less critical than freedom from fear. So long as its objectives are to ensure the survival and dignity of individuals as human beings, it is necessary to go beyond thinking of human security solely in terms of protecting human life in conflict situations.[4]

As Acharya (2001) emphasizes, this view is also echoed by Amartya Sen (1999) in an approach to development policy which he labels 'development as freedom'. Sen brings out the indivisibility of the three generations of human rights (political, socio-economic and cultural) and provides empirical illustrations on the causal relationship between freedom and human flourishing, and between the absence of freedom and human misery.

Indeed, East and South-East Asia's experience of the social and political impacts of the financial crisis reveals a reality of human security that is systemic rather than compartmentalized. In the aftermath of this crisis, societies experienced the spiral effects of economic failure on the different dimensions of human security. At one level the crisis has set back the high performance in human development achieved through previous years of growth and investment, causing new forms of poverty and re-enforcing old forms (ILO 1998; Truong 2000). The rise in communal violence, illegal migration, human trafficking and organized crime in the region—as exacerbated by the economic downturn—has brought to the fore the inter-state character of human security, when it mainly affects the least protected (and especially migrants, women and children). It is evidently not possible to approach human insecurity as a matter of the failure of individual states, but a collective failure to protect economic and social systems from adverse forces of globalization is at issue.

Against this backdrop, governments and civic groups in Asia have become more aware of the significance of economic and societal security and not just security as assured income and physical protection for particular individuals and groups. More specifically, religious and ethnic tensions, most dramatically expressed in Indonesia, reflect the ease with which religious identity can become a rallying point for oppositional politics and violence that can spread like bushfire, quickly spilling over to new issues and new states.[5] The experience of the Asian crisis shows that human insecurity in daily life can be the result of economic insecurity that intensifies inter-community competition and promotes personal insecurity. Violent responses for self-protection or self-enhancement can be deployed as the annihilation of the other and generate a process by which different identities—religious, gender, ethnic—become objects of attack one by one.

Therefore, from the given perspective, security policy (state and human) cannot but take serious notice of issues such as structural inequality, unstable economic systems and identity politics. To follow Lodgaard's definition of the objective of security policy (state or human) as prevention, the experience of the Asian crisis tells us that prevention does not rest only with problematic states or with the violation of rights of groups of people living under problematic conditions. Prevention also concerns the problematic environment in a global political economy characterized by the ease of capital mobility that can abruptly destabilize the performance of economic systems and the livelihoods of populations. The issue is not just a matter of the failure and legitimacy of individual states; the failed legitimacy of global neo-liberalism as an economic doctrine is also an issue (Stiglitz 2002).

Placed in its original context of development ethics, the equation in the human security framework for the Asian case would extend beyond the choice between armament and human development to also cover the choice between a widening of economic liberalism and social protectionism. To rephrase Mahbub Ul-Haq's equation, we need to fashion the concept of human security that is not just reflected in the fluctuation of our stock exchanges, but also in the consolidation of harmony and cooperation between different communities in society to build locally rooted social arrangements that can assure income and protection for the most vulnerable, particularly in times of economic distress.

Finally, in all the perspectives of human security discussed so far, the ontological dimension of human security—closely related to identity politics—has not been fully addressed. Coined by Anthony Giddens (1991), ontological insecurity refers to the threat to the notion of the self and the questioning of self-identity. The notion of the self as an abstract system and the notion of self-identity as a psychic process embedded in daily interaction have been under threat by forces of globalization, which Giddens defines as de-traditionalization and re-traditionalization. These are processes by which local customs are being attacked and reconstituted in different forms. New values and practices are emerging but they are bound to be experimental and have uncertain outcomes. This uncertainty is one of the major sources of anxiety that give rise to new waves of violence and cruelty.

From a cultural standpoint, since the 1960s the notion of the self as an abstract system in humanist philosophy has been destabilized by identitarian movements. These movements have adopted a socially embedded approach to ontology to serve four main purposes.[6] First is to decentralize the abstract self as a privileged self. Second is to challenge its claim to knowledge and rights. Third is to highlight the exclusionary character of the norms of legitimacy and rights that have been restricted to a specific privileged group; for example, the white middle-class male (Flax 1990). Fourth is to show how an overvaluation of masculine traits such as autonomy, competition, reason and impartiality had been put into effect at the expense of other equally valuable traits such as interdependence, care and cooperation (Gilligan 1987). In other words, the criticism directed at the abstract self in humanist ontology seeks to expose the dimension of social power in which it is embedded.

Through this approach, identitarian movements try to integrate experience, insight and struggle of particular social groups—deprived of recognition and respect by wider currents of social interaction—into alternative visions of egalitarian politics. Their aim is to promote psychic emancipation and political empowerment and to build visions of morality informed by the social histories of the disfranchized. These visions are expected to contribute to the prescription of norms and principles of action that are responsive to the needs and demands of constituencies on the margins of society (Hennessy 1993). In other words, they believe that the recognition of different insights and perspectives into the problem of legitimacy and rights may help improve the vision of a just society.

In this struggle for social recognition, identitarian movements have diverged in two directions. One direction is to work within the normative humanist approach and forge a framework of rights that is sensitive to the needs of specific groups (such as women, *dalits* and indigenous people). In other words, there is one ethic that represents all people but, at the same time, it must remain more responsive to different rights claims. The other direction is the rejection of normative humanism and the celebration of difference, which is a characteristic of the much-celebrated post-modern approach to cultural and political resistance. In this approach, a singular ethic is considered as domination and an obstruction to emancipation; it should be resisted. Instead, the idea is to support a deliberate construction of an ethic that focusses on specific groups of people whose voice, experience and knowledge have been historically under- or overwritten. Such a construction is expected to yield cultural innovation and new ethical frameworks that redefine moral responsibility for the transformation of relations of dominance (Tong 2000).

From a political standpoint, attempts to reconstruct a civil society based on the principle of non-domination and inclusion of all identities in the cultural and legal domain have not been able to resolve the tension between norms accepted as universal and the specific process of their codification. Political resistance based on the insistence of the recognition of differences has tended to overemphasize the bearings of history and culture on the subject, without offering an alternative referrent to what constitutes the human being when undressed of history and culture. The avoidance of such a referrent reflects the awareness among the elite of identity politics about the danger that underlies the logic of reductionism. Historically, variants of biological reductionism that proposed a definition of the human species based on a number of essential biological traits have justified social domination on the basis of gender and race (Sayers 1982). Regrettably, this avoidance also left the political arena in a vacuum and, therefore, vulnerable to a gradual shift towards cultural reductionism, or in other words, a line of argumentation that privileges an over-determining role of culture that eventually lapses into a neo-liberalist form of pluralism. The political arena of postmodern cultural emancipation has become increasingly characterized by a competition between different selves, loyalties and affinities, and a total neglect of broader structural issues and social forces conditioning differences (Beneria 2003; Rai 2002). As Hennessy (1993: 136) writes, identity politics 'ultimately fragments struggle by sending "groups" off in search of their sectional identities, leaving the system of relations upon which they rely unscathed.' In other words, an overemphasis on the role of culture and diversity of identity runs the risk of discontinuity in the search for sameness as an intellectual—and social—project.

A socially embedded approach to ontology for the purpose of psychic emancipation and political empowerment of disfranchised groups shows its limits when it is unable to recognize the human being (male or female, white or coloured) beyond the cultural subject. The stress on uniqueness of specific groups and difference with other groups has led to an involutionary turn among identitarian cultural movements. As illustrated by Giri (2002), indentitarian movements are displacing many of the emancipatory goals adopted earlier. He notes an absence of a self-critical and dialogical move towards others to negotiate boundaries of coexistence and collective learning. In conflict situation, the assertion of uniqueness and rights can become internally repressive—more concerned with the collective identity than individual members irrespective of any intra-group domination—or externally destructive—capable of fuelling cleansing campaigns, once identities become intertwined with issues of material power such as resource and territoriality.

Against this background, ontological insecurity may be considered at the same time a psychosocial and a historical problem. The challenge is to find ways to resolve cultural conflicts as problems that are intertwined with overt as well as discrete processes of domination. At this historical juncture, the ethical equation in human security as ontological security may be framed as the choice between the promotion of plurality of standpoints of cultural subjects and the search for a communicative subject with a heart, as depicted in the writing of Saint Exupery.[7] To put the message in another way, the choice is between an endless struggle for widening of the rights platforms beyond core rights, and a collective protection and enhancement of essential virtues such as compassion, patience, modesty and respect for others. Rights cannot function when these virtues are not present. These virtues serve to enhance communicative action in order to acknowledge the frailty and strength of all human beings behind their cultural and historical dressing.

Ontological security and Buddhism[8]

Buddhism as a body of spiritual teachings may be understood as a vehicle—a means to reach an end rather than an end in itself.[9] The Buddhist tradition, as other traditions, is neither monolithic nor devoid of tension and violence. It has undergone several moments of transformation, manifested in the three main historical vehicles—*Hinayana* or Narrow Vehicle, *Mahayana* or Great Vehicle, and *Vajrayana* or Diamond Vehicle. Since the post-World War II period, there has been an upsurge of different forms of socially engaged Buddhism, leading some scholars to propose that we may be witnessing the emergence of a fourth vehicle *Navayana*, which is also called *Lokayana* or Global Vehicle. As Christopher Queen (2000: 1) notes, socially engaged Buddhism— the contemporary application of the *dharma* (or Buddhist teachings) to the resolution of social problems—has emerged in a global conversation of human rights, distributive justice and social progress. This application requires a renewal of ancient teachings to serve the needs of a globalizing world, a world that compels us more and more to accept ethics as the indispensable interface between 'my desire' and 'your desire' (HH the Dalai Lama 2002).

In line with this interface, Buddhist thought may be apprehended through the principle of non-duality, backed by all the Buddha's deliberations (*sutras*) on issues related to knowledge and spiritual wisdom. Non-duality may be traced through the main ontological principles of Buddhism—themselves being derived from a bio-centric approach to human life, Nature and the cosmos. Buddhist thought defines human life as a micro-organism that is interlinked with other organisms. The human being differs from other organisms in nature owing to the endowment of mind,[10] the essential quality of which is formed by this interdependence and expresses itself in different forms known as empathy, also defined as 'inter-being' by Thich Nhat Hanh (1993).

As the Dalai Lama illustrates, the first level of consciousness a child develops is through experiencing the protection and compassion of others, without which survival is not possible. The flourishing of human life is nurtured by affection and care. Therefore, the constitution of humans is more inclined towards feelings of empathy/compassion (HH the Dalai Lama and Cutler 1998: 38–39). From this basic inclination, other types of constitution also arise as directed by different states of mind. These may be categorized into wholesome, neutral and unwholesome mind. A neutral mind is neither wholesome nor unwholesome; it is as a white sheet of paper on which marks can be made. A neutral mind can be shifted into becoming wholesome or unwholesome.

An unwholesome mind is guided by conceptual errors, failure or mis-direction of perception, and is unable to grasp the principle of inter-being. Such mind tends to cling to an unchanging notion of self and its craving (*tanha*). *Tanha* is created simultaneously by bodily instincts and the formation of ego. The ego (*samkhara*) acts like a bog that sucks the mind into conceptual errors. These conceptual errors may be considered as a veil (*maya*), which prevents the mind from perceiving inter-being as 'suchness' (*tathagata*). An unwholesome mind may be even considered as a form of optical illusion (*avidya*) which is capable of distorting one's self-understanding and the understanding of others, thus negatively affecting social action and relations (Truong 1998). A wholesome mind is capable of discerning errors of perception in order to remove the veil of illusion and to emerge from the state of *avidya*. To transform an unwholesome mind to a wholesome one requires meditation, or the training of mind according to specified methods on the ethics of restraint, virtue and compassion (HH the Dalai Lama 2002).

The following statement of a Tibetan nun may help illuminate the Buddhist view on the mind and consequent action (Adams 2002):

> The one who tortures me is made to believe that what he has doing is right. He must stay blind to my pain in order to carry on. At the end of the day, he returns to his family; with arms that beat me, he embraces his women, wraps loving arms around his child, protecting her with his strength.... Through my prayers, I ask that those who imprison us be free from the darkness of ignorance and that the clouds that obscure the truth give way to clarity.

A key message in this deliberation is the acknowledgement that what comes between the self and others are unwholesome minds, and not the specific biological traits of the self or the other. The 'evil' torturer is also capable of love, albeit currently limited to his family. His inability to extend this love to the nun as another being is suppressed by his social identity. The nun—through her meditation to overcome physical suffering—is capable of seeing the broader and deeper causes of her own suffering specifically, and Tibetan suffering more generally. Clarity here refers to the interconnectedness of all human beings and darkness means the ego. The identity of the torturer expresses the ego of a collective Chinese identity formed by territorial boundaries and the Han culture. The suffering Tibetan nun is an identity capable of dissolving the ego, apprehending inter-being and being aware of the karmic consequences of violent action. Meditation in this regard becomes an ethical activity and not an individual pursuit of a 'transcendental bliss'—a stereotypical label commonly assigned to this practice (Dreyfus 1995).

The notion of *karma* may be understood in ways other than its colloquial fatalistic meaning (that rebirth is determined by action in one's life). It can also be seen from an epistemological standpoint: one conceptual error, if not corrected, leads to imbalanced action, causing imbalanced responses leading to other conceptual errors, and the chains of error and imbalanced action continues. *Karma* may be understood as action (verbal, physical, thought) that has result. Actions derived from an unwholesome mind will result in harm. Actions derived from a wholesome mind perpetrate non-violent outcomes and may thus alleviate suffering. *Karma* depicts relationships and interactions, a self and other selves that mutually interpenetrate. From the principle of inter-being can be derived the notion that at the primary level, the concepts of self and not-self are not socially but organically embedded. Human beings are, thus, organically linked both together and with Nature in which they find themselves. Knowledge is what gives an awareness of the interactive nature of mind and matter, plus the ability to discern the negative dimensions of the socially embedded self.

Non-duality is also referred to as *prajna* or penetrating insight—the ability to understand the nature of the inter-being of all forms of life. This penetrating insight has the capacity to transform individual and collective memories of trauma and sufferings (caused by conceptual errors of the self) into a release of compassion. *Prajna* stands for the image of a fountain from which compassion emerger as a non-violent life-force: a fountain which requires skilful methods of mind-training to tap. Effective reflection of mind can help achieve a transformative shift of consciousness to attain what are referred to as the four abodes—caring and friendliness (*maitri*), empathy with those who suffer (*karuna*), sympathetic joy for others without envy (*mudita*), and equanimity or constitutional balance (*uppeka*). The four abodes function like a spinning wheel.

A change of perception through *prajna* (penetrating insight) leads to a change of emotional structure (from hostility to caring and friendliness), a change of attitude (from anger to empathy), a change of behaviour (from desiring to take to a willingness to give; from readiness to cause grief to willingness to bring joy), and a change of the constitution of the self (from being averted by unwholesome mind to maintaining the constitutional balance of non-duality).

From an epistemological perspective, knowledge produced by a biocentric approach to human life, Nature and the cosmos is neither anthropocentric nor egocentric. It seeks to apprehend the interconnection between human life and other organisms. Wholesome knowledge may be considered as a type that is fully capable of comprehending this interconnection. Unwholesome knowledge perceives myopically—as far as the context of its concepts enables. The following parable may help illustrate:

A turtle meets a fish in the sea. The fish greets him:

Hello Turtle, welcome back! Where have you been?
Hello Fish, I have been on earth.
Really? Is there something beyond water? What does it look like?

The Turtle hesitates, trying to find the right means to express his experience. Impatiently, the Fish asks:

Is earth like water?
No, replies the Turtle while trying to find a means to describe what he knows.
Do you feel pressure when you go deeper?
I don't know...
How far can the sun light shine down?
I don't know, says the Turtle patiently.
Can you swim in it?
No, I don't think so.

At this point, the Fish turns to swim-off in a huff, saying:

To all the essential questions I asked, you can only say no or that you do not know. As far as I am concerned, your earth does not exist!

The message attached to this parable has two aspects to it. It is important to recognize the contextual boundaries of our conceptual knowledge. Universalizing our contextual knowledge can raise barriers to other ways of knowing. Bounded by context, the human mind ceases to apprehend interconnectedness and may even deny the larger Universe. The denial or fear of the larger Universe beyond one's own can lead to ontological insecurity since one cannot understand how other creatures can come and leave our universe, seemingly sharing another universe with other creatures that one does not know and can hardly accept. Also, it is important to recognize that when the mind functions in one epistemic order, it cannot see truth in wisdom. Wisdom, as symbolized in the turtle, which has a longer biological life than the fish, is the ability to function in different epistemic orders and thereby have empathy with others who (through conditioning and habituation) cling to a singular order of the self. Wisdom would transform the will to knowledge into the will to assist others to apprehend different ways of knowing, thus preventing mutual confrontation and mutual negation.

Buddhist ontology provides us with a vision of human nature embedded in a bio-centric worldview. Organically embedded in the universe in which it exits, the mind function in a two-fold interaction: intra- and inter-species interaction. For this reason, there is a constant struggle with condition and habituation—an unfolding process of knowing. The mind is capable both of drowning itself in conceptual errors or of liberating itself from these. Liberating the mind from its conceptual errors can lead to the capacity for generosity and appreciation of other universes. The will of mind (determination) in Buddhism is not geared towards power and control but towards understanding the nature of interconnectedness, which is the key to release empathy/compassion. In this regard, ontological security is not derived from the notion of a fixed stable self (socially or morally defined). It is derived from the *ethical ideal* to perceive oneself in relation to others and, indeed, as others (Adams 2002).

Towards a compassionate human security agenda

Owing to its bio-centric approach to human nature, Buddhist social ethics begin with humankind's moral responsibility to maintain social harmony—by nurturing empathy/compassion and penetrating insight (*prajna*). For this reason, in Buddhist social ethics, respect for others tends to be primary; law is secondary. Law functions as a form of protection when respect fails. For example, in early state formation (tenth to twelfth centuries) in the lower Mekong region, rulers and their servants in public administration had to learn the techniques of meditation to ensure the role of *prajna* in decision making. Disasters, including social and ecological, were often explained by the loss of *prajna*. Pasanathamo's study (in Truong 1998) on early state formation in Thailand shows that Buddhist social ethics were translated into five realms of respect for various rights: (*a*) those of animals and other transient beings; (*b*) those of other people's spouses and loved ones; (*c*) other people's property; (*d*) that of access to true information; and (*e*) the right to 'mindful communication'.

The last of these five realms is the one that best illustrates the principle of ethical responsibility to others in both a personalized and collectivized manner. Based on the belief that reality constitutes different parts of an *interconnected whole*, 'mindful communication' refers to an attitude or a posture in a dialogue that does not seek to assert the legitimacy of one's own view over another, but instead tries to find the seed of disharmony in each other's position, to reach a wise and balanced view on a given matter as a primary goal and to restore harmony. Furthermore, given that Buddhist social ethics expect all individuals to struggle for their own moral development with support from each other and the community, the daily well-being of individuals is regarded as primary. The following scripture on governance in early state formation in the lower Mekong region testifies this point (Pasanathamo 1987: 96, cited in Truong 1998):

> Wealth can belong to a private ownership when its owner serves the basic needs of society. If this is not so, wealth is not of value, and the wealthy are worthless. The accumulation of wealth becomes unrighteous.... If private wealth does not become the wealth of society and does not bring goodness, society should attempt to manage or reorganize the ownership system of that wealth and distribute it to make it reach all members. This is the basis for individual development and moral attainment of all members in society.

The lack of concern for social power has always left Buddhist ethics vulnerable to politics and gave it a weak commanding role in economic justice, except, perhaps, in the event of disasters. As pointed out by Ghai (1998), societies based on respect for, and duty towards, others tend to be status-oriented and hierarchical. Enforcing duty before rights in non-egalitarian societies often means the preservation of the *status quo*. Under such circumstances, well-intentioned principles are vulnerable to corruption and transformation into mechanisms of power and control. A case in point is how meditation as the training of mind (and a requirement for all public officials) had been disintegrated into mechanistic rituals; formal recognition of such training has been used to provide legitimacy for access by male members of communities to the civil service and social mobility (Keyes 1997; Reynolds 1977).

Furthermore, Whitehill (1994) suggests that Buddhism provides a weak body of social ethics because it cannot propose policy-generating principles that can be institutionalized on a wide scale. Buddhist philosophy does not offer a theory of social power since it places full trust in the good nature of human beings. It gives us the techniques to uncover this optimum nature both individually and collectively, but is rather unconcerned about what is required to apply it to the polity in ways that do not reinforce social hierarchy. Because the philosophy is thoroughly mindful of the constitutive dimension of the object towards which action is directed, Buddhist principles can only effect societal transformation by a slow permeation of a collective consciousness of non-duality—also metaphorically described as the *dharma*-drizzling rain.

The Buddhist definition of 'community' is either too wide—as when referring to all sentient beings—or too narrow when used for the *sangha*: a body of monks or like-minded laity who devote themselves to the practice of Buddhist ethics. *Sangha* communities, though, do tend to replicate society's gender divisions. For the Buddha's guidance in this respect remains ambivalent, particularly regarding the division of labour in the household. On the advice of his disciple (Ananda), Buddha Gautama decided to accept women into the *sangha* while expressing his reservation—given the implications for the maintenance of households and the general domain of care should women enrol in great numbers. Thus, despite the tenet which recognizes a natural 'good'— latent in all, and activated through nurturing and caring—the social responsibility for this goodness has primarily been placed on women. The result has been a social hierarchy—doctrinally defended—within which a man's role is to develop a wholesome mind, and so become (wholesomely) cognizant of non-duality; and the women's role is to practise this non-duality in everyday life through a balancing of her multiple identities of the self (a female being), self-*for*-others (mother and wives) and self-*as*-others (suffering bodies who must comprehend the action of its torturer).

The Buddhist path of non-violence, being more concerned with preserving systemic balance in societies/communities, has often left its subjects helpless in the face of naked force and massive violation of rights. When the virtue of a disciplined mind cannot stand up to the destructive nature of socio-political power, self-destruction may be the only alternative to violent resistance. Cases in point are the suffering monks, nuns and lay people of Tibet; and the self-immolation of monks during the height of the militarized conflict in Vietnam (1963–73), when the country suffered from uninterrupted internal insurgency, the destruction by American air-war technology, ground search-and-destroy missions that wiped out entire towns and villages. A renewal of Buddhist social ethics in the service of human security must come to terms with such issues; also with the apparent fact that, in the face of industrial–military complexes, global markets and currency trading that daily involve trillions of US dollars and eruptions of violence at every group level (from localized communities to regional and global associations), it will—yet—only be modest.

Three key aspects can be singled out for their relevance to a framing of the human security agenda. First, the bio-centred approach in the Buddhist theory of human nature may serve to promote unity in human spirituality. Religious expressions of human spirituality are variant manifestations of a meta-reality in which heart and mind are integrated. Different historical backgrounds, ecological settings and forms of social organization will inevitably produce differences in the way the human spirit is ideally expressed. Collective learning shared between different religions (or sects within a religion) should, therefore, not be some competition as to whose god is more holy/the more omnipotent, or whose interpretation of holiness is more correct, but should focus on exchanging experiences as to how the integration of heart and mind is reached; how to be open for a renewal of self and others. Inter-paradigmatic exchange about the nature of human spirituality may help encourage movement away from fundamentalist positions at all levels—family, school and community—to transform duality (which is oppositional) into inter-being.

Second, Buddhist emphasis on awareness of inter-being as a characteristic of humankind would support the principle of indivisibility of rights and the function of economic justice as a deterrent against structural violence towards specific identities—of nation, religion, gender, ethnicity or age. Global human insecurity reflects the lack of awareness of humankind's interconnectedness with each other and other life forms. In this regard, inter-being as a concept may serve as a source of moral reflection to perceive the reality of the world through the consciousness of the heart; a perception that can help alter priorities in the global agenda based on a notion of the self that is inclusive of all other selves. Accepting ethics as the interface between the self and the others is the basic requirement to enhance the capability of institutions for self-reflexivity. This would require governments to acknowledge the respect for the right to 'mindful communication' of individual and groups. The locating and removing the seeds of disharmony in government policy as well as in societal relations should be a collective exercise, using and improving existing means—such as public hearing, consultations and referenda—in decision making.

Third, the notion of *prajna* as the fountain of compassion may contribute to an enrichment of the theory of the person in the field of development ethics and its affiliated human development framework. In Nussbaum's (1992, 1996) and Sen's (1987) theory of the person, the moral relevance of compassion as an emotion may be found in the choice of the right rule and direction of public action. An extended view on compassion as a penetrating insight would recognize the moral relevance of a collective shift of consciousness to transform the unethical into wholesome behaviour—spanning from an interpersonal level through the inter-group and inter-state levels. Two centuries of institution-building to nurture the principle of equality and individual freedom have created state-based parameters of rights more and more disconnected from essential virtue—empathy/compassion—which, precisely, engineers the realization of rights.

Enforcement of the right rule in the global world order requires the moral voice of empathy/compassion, not just among decision makers, but also among and between social groups. In this regard, a policy seeking to enhance human capabilities through education may consider promoting not just marketable skills, but also individual and collective skills for self-reflexivity and empathetic communication to promote more awareness on local/global issues that affect us in our their daily lives. This capability would help foster 'mindful communication' among civic groups as a political act that would seek to free communicative action from the boundaries of interests—that are grounded in specific social identities—for the promotion of a notion of *difference as different manifestation of the same processes*, which individual and groups are part of. Such a notion of difference lies at the core of the collective will to find a solution to destructive processes and to avert violence.

Conclusion

Contemporary conflicts are often caught in the dynamics of power and identity, of material interests embedded in the hierarchical nature of human societies—the byproducts of history and political economy. They show an immense difficulty in promoting the notion of a single humanity beyond the specific identities constructed through time, space and location. Yet, our socially constructed identities and sense of self are indeed fragile in the light of the global transformation of violence. The search for human security on a global scale can benefit well from an approach to social ethics that integrates notions of respect and right, or the ethics of virtue and that of justice. Justice is a vehicle driven by the energy of virtue. The virtues of a disciplined mind and of empathetic communication are apposite to proper resolution of most conflicts. An approach which acknowledges the presence of empathy in all of us may lead—through fuller understanding and awareness of the causation of suffering in human society—to a defining of a concept of human security that gives greater recognition to spirituality and the causal relationship between its absence and human misery.

Notes

1. On a global scale, military spending was cut by one quarter, or from nearly US$ 1 trillion in 1987 to US$ 767 billion in 1994, at 1991 prices (Ul-Haq 1995: 126).
2. The metaphor was suggested by Professor Kinhide Mushakoji during our discussions on inter-faith dialogue and inter-paradigmatic learning.
3. Austria, Chile, Greece, Ireland, Jordan, Mali, the Netherlands, Slovenia, Switzerland and Thailand are members of this network.
4. Statement by Director-General Yukio Takasu at the International Conference on Human Security in a Globalised World, Ulan-Bator, 8 May 2000 (http://www.mofa.go.jp).
5. Religious tension in Indonesia initially erupted between the Muslim Indonesian and Christian Chinese, initially targeting Chinese women as objects of sexual violence. Gradually, all women, including Muslim women, became the epicentre of male violence. The attack on Bali in October 2002, and threats of similar attacks in tourist resorts in Thailand allegedly linked with the Al-Qaeda reveal the weakness of a secular approach to human security that ignores issues of subjective religious identity in conditioning acts of violence.
6. A socially embedded approach to ontology is based on a definition of a self, its knowledge and action as being encumbered by historical and cultural bearings (gender, race, colonial and post-colonial experience).
7. 'It is through the heart that one can see rightly; the most essential things are invisible to the eyes' (Saint Exupery 2000).

8. This section is mainly drawn from the teachings of parents through the use of texts, parables and action over many years—from childhood through and into activist adulthood and womanhood.
9. Vietnamese monk Thich Nhat Hanh and Thai social activist Sulak Sivaraksa—both peace workers—have pointed out that a deep insight into Buddhism would speak of this spiritual tradition without the capital 'B', beyond and above the specific orientations specified as vehicle. Consciously attaching a small 'b' to this tradition conveys a renouncement of socially constructed identity and the acceptance that there can be a diversity of means to spirituality and peace that may not necessarily be mutually opposed. So long as the means share the same end, the identity ascribed to a mean is not a matter of great consequence.
10. An introduction to Buddhist theory of mind and its meeting point with the filed of psychology is best found in the conversation between the Dalai Lama and Howard Cutler (1998).

References

Adams, Vincanne. 2002. 'Suffering the Winds of Lhasa: Politicized Bodies, Human Rights, Cultural Difference and Humanism in Tibet', in *The Anthropology of Globalization: A Reader*. Oxford: Blackwell Publication.

Acharya, Amitav. 2001. 'Human Security: East versus West', *International Journal*, 56(3): 442–60.

Beneria, Lourdes. 2003. *Gender, Development and Globalization: Economics as if All People Mattered*. New York and London: Routledge.

Dreyfus, Georges. 1995. 'Meditation as Ethical Activity', *Journal of Buddhist Ethics*, 2. Available on http://www.buddhistethics.org/2/dreyfus.html. Accessed on 6 March 2008.

Flax, Jane. 1990. 'Post-modernism and Gender Relations in Feminist Theory', in Linda Nicholson (ed.), *Feminism/Post-modernism*. New York: Routledge.

Ghai, Yash. 1998. 'Rights, Duties and Responsibilities', in Josiane Cauquelin, Paul Lim and Birgit Mayer-Konig (eds), *Asian Values: Encounter with Diversity*. Richmond, Surrey: Curzon Press.

Giddens, Anthony. 1991. *Modernity and Self-identity: The Self and Society in the Late Modern Age*. Stanford University Press: Standford.

Gilligan, Carol. 1987. 'Moral Orientation and Moral Development', in Eva F. Kittay and Diana T. Meyers (eds), *Women in Moral Theory*. Cambridge MA: Harvard University Press.

Giri, Ananta. 2002. *Civil Society and the Limits of Identity Politics*. Chennai: Madras Institute of Development Studies.

Hanh, Thich Nhat. 1993. *Inter-being: Fourteen Guidelines for Engaged Buddhism*. Berkeley: Parallax Press.

Hennessy, Rose Mary. 1993. *Materialist Feminism and the Politics of Discourse*. New York and London: Routledge.

His Holiness the Dalai Lama. 2002. *Ancient Wisdom, Modern World: Ethics for the New Millennium*. London: Abacus.

His Holiness the Dalai Lama and Howard C. Cutler. 1998. *The Art of Happiness*. London: Coronet Books.

International Labour Office. 1998. 'The Social Impact of the Asian Financial Crisis', Technical Report for Discussion at the High Level Tripartite Meeting on Social Responses to the Financial Crisis in East and South East Asian Countries, Bangkok, 22–24 April.

Keyes, Charles. 1997. 'Millennialism, Therevada Buddhism and Thai Society', *Journal of Asian Studies*, 36(2): 283–302.

Lodgaard, Sverre. 2001. *Human Security: Concept and Operationalization*. Oslo: Norwegian Institute of International Affairs.

Nussbaum, Martha. 1992. 'Human Functioning and Social Justice: In Defense of Aristotelian Essentialism', *Political Theory*, 20(2): 202–46.

———. 1996. 'Compassion: The Basic Social Emotion', *Social Philosophy and Policy*, 13(1): 27–58.

Paris, Roland. 2001. 'Human Security: Paradigm Shift or Hot Air', *International Security*, 26(2): 87–102.

Queen, Christopher. 2000. 'Introduction: A New Buddhism', *Journal of Buddhist Ethics*, 7. Available on http://www.buddhistethics.org/7/queen001.html. Accessed on 6 March 2008.

Rai, Shirin. 2002. *Gender and the Political Economy of Development: From Nationalism to Globalization*. Cambridge: Polity Press.

Reynolds, Frank E. 1977. 'Civic Religion and National Community in Thailand', *Journal of Asian Studies*, 36(2): 267–82.

Saint Exupery, Antoine de. 2000. *The Little Prince* (trans. from French by Richard Howard). Fort Washington: Harvest Books.

Sayers, Janet. 1982. *Biological Politics: Feminist and Anti-Feminist Perspectives*. London: Tavistock.

Sen, Amartya. 1987. *On Ethics and Economics*. Oxford: Basil Blackwell.

———. 1999. *Development as Freedom*. New York: Alfred A. Knoff.

Stiglitz, Joseph E. 2002. *Globalization and Its Discontents*. New Delhi: Penguin Books.

Thomas, Caroline. 1999. 'Introduction', in C. Thomas and P. Wilkins (eds), *Globalization, Human Security and the African Experience*. Boulder, CO: Lynne Rienner Publishers.

Tong, Rosemary. 2000. 'Feminist Ethics. Standford Encyclopedia of Philosophy'. Available on http://plato.stanford.edu/entries/feminism-ethics/. Accessed on 6 March 2008.

Truong, Thanh-Dam. 1998. 'Asian Values and the Heart of Understanding: A Buddhist View', in Josiane Cauquelin, Paul Lim and Birgit Mayer-Konig (eds), *Asian Values: Encounter with Diversity*. Richmond, Surrey: Curzon Press.

Truong, Thanh-Dam. 2000. 'A Feminist Perspective on the Asian Miracle and Crisis: Enlarging the Conceptual Map of Human Development', *Journal of Human Development*, 1(1): 159–64.

Ul-Haq, Mahbub. 1995. *Reflections on Human Development*. Oxford and New York: Oxford University Press.

Whitehill, James. 1994. 'Buddhist Ethics in Western Context: The Virtues Approach', *Journal of Buddhist Ethics*, 1. Available on http://www.buddhistethics. org/1/white1.html. Accessed 6 March 2008.

Towards an Islamic Hermeneutics for Human Rights

27

ABDULLAHI AHMED AN-NAIM

Introduction

The central question for us here is whether the various religious views of what it means to be truly human leave room for the acknowledgment of a set of *neutrally formulated* common human rights. It is not possible, or desirable, in my view to identify a set of neutrally formulated human rights. Any normative regime that justifies a set of rights and provides or informs their content, must necessarily represent a commitment to a specific value system. This is particularly true, I believe, of a regime that claims to justify and formulate a set of human rights because of the organic relationship between the conception and implementation of such rights on one hand, and the normative regime that provides or informs perceptions of human dignity, self-identity and personal experience on the other.

Nevertheless, I will argue in this chapter that an 'internal' commitment to a normative regime from one point of view need not and should not be exclusive of the 'other' (however he or she is identified), with respect to a set of commonly agreed human rights. In my view, therefore, what is at issue is not the possibility of abstract or absolute neutrality from any religious, cultural or ideological regime. Rather the question is how to reconcile commitments to diverse normative regimes with a commitment to a concept and set of universal human rights. If this is achieved, the reasons for commitment of some to one regime or another would be, in effect, immaterial from other points of view. In other words, it would be possible to achieve the benefits of neutral formulation instead of pursuing the illusion of neutrality as such.

It may be argued that seeking to exclude the requirement of neutral formulation simply begs the question of how to achieve consensus on a set of rights accruing universally to all human beings of whatever religious persuasion or lack thereof, and irrespective of gender or race (hereinafter referred to as universal human rights). From this point of view, to allow the formulation of a set of rights to be committed to a particular value system would impose that system's criteria of entitlement to rights which might *exclude* group(s) of human beings. Judging by the experience to date, the argument goes, commitment to religious value system would almost certainly exclude those who do not adhere to that religion, or at least not accord them rights equal to those enjoyed by the adherents of the religion in question. Religious value systems also tend to deny women equality with men. This is certainly true not only of orthodox perceptions of Judaism, Christianity and Islam, it could be added, but also of other religious traditions, cultures and even ideologies. In this light, it may be concluded, the only way to achieve consensus on a set of universal human rights is through 'neutral formulation'.

As indicated earlier, however, the difficulty of achieving consensus on universal human rights is not due to commitment to a value system as such, be it religious, cultural or ideological. What is problematic is the *exclusive* nature of value systems, that is to say, their tendency to define the relationship between the 'self' and the 'other' in antagonistic or negative terms, thereby diminishing prospects for the acknowledgment of equality and non-discrimination. I would, therefore, argue that if and to the extent it is possible to overcome this particular feature of the various value systems of the world today, global consensus on universal human rights would be attainable without requiring people to abandon their religious, cultural or ideological commitments in order to subscribe to this project.

In any case, it would be counter-productive to require people to choose between their religion, culture or ideology on one hand, and a supposedly 'neutral' universal human rights project on the other, because most people would probably opt for the former over the latter. This choice is more likely for two reasons. First, to the vast majority of people, no human rights scheme can by itself serve as a substitute for religion, culture or ideology. Second, most people would maintain that some conception of human rights is integral to their specific religion, culture or ideology. To avoid undermining the legitimacy of a universal human rights project by placing it in direct competition with what people hold as their comprehensive fundamental value systems, I would strongly recommend a strategy of *internal transformation* of perceptions of the religion, culture or ideology in question in order to reconcile the former with the latter. Without minimizing the difficulties and risks of this approach, I maintain that such reconciliation is conceptually possible in general (*cf* An-Naim 1990). In view of the greater difficulties and risks of trying to establish and implement a supposedly neutral universal human rights scheme, I would recommend attempting to achieve reconciliation at least as one of the *strategies* for legitimizing and effectuating a universal human rights project.

In this chapter, I will explore the issues and prospects of such internal transformation in relation to Islam and Islamic societies in the present globalized world of diverse religious and other normative systems. To this end, I will define and outline an *Islamic hermeneutics* for human rights. However, if the proposed analysis is to be useful for a universal human rights project, it should be applicable to other religions, cultures and ideologies. I will, therefore, attempt to extrapolate from the Islamic case some general guidelines on the conceptual and methodological aspects of the process of internal transformation as it may apply to any religion, culture or ideology.

The genesis of exclusion and inclusion

As suggested earlier, the problem is the exclusive nature of religion, culture or ideology rather than these normative systems as such. But it is also clear to me that some level of exclusivity is integral to the fundamental nature and function of normative systems: the basis of the claim of each system to the commitment of its adherents and the sanction for compliance with its precepts. That is to say, people's commitment to a given normative system is usually premised on the belief that conformity with the precepts of the system in question would bring them specific moral and/or material benefits. Part of this rationale, it seems, is the belief that other normative systems will not achieve those benefits, at least not to the same degree or quality. Thus, the advantage of adhering to one system is appreciated on its own terms as well as in contrast to the disadvantage of adhering to other systems.

However, the process of achieving the perceived benefits of adherence to a normative system is normally protracted, diffused and difficult to evaluate in daily life. In the case of some religious normative systems in particular, the most significant benefits, such as becoming a moral person in this life or achieving salvation/going to heaven in the next life, cannot be verified in concrete or immediate terms. Consequently, people need to find ways of sustaining their faith in the ability of their chosen normative system to deliver promised benefits, especially during periods of mounting frustration and helplessness.

One way in which people tend to reinforce their faith in their own normative system is to exaggerate the quality or quantity of the benefits they have or will have, and the loss of those who do not adhere to the same system. In this way, many people come to have a territorial or proprietary interest in their own system and an adverse view of other systems. This self-vindicating defence mechanism often leads to a 'them' and 'us' syndrome, which can easily degenerate into hostility and antagonism towards the 'them' and solidarity with the 'us' under any circumstances.

Despite the unavoidability of some level of exclusivity in all normative systems and its tendency to degenerate into hostility and antagonism towards the 'other', I would still argue that commitment to a system can be compatible with a degree of inclusion of the 'other' at another level. More specifically, I suggest that one can be fully committed to a certain normative system and identify with his or her co-believers for that purpose, while also being fully committed to another normative system and identifying with co-adherents of that system for its purposes as well. In other words, people can and do have *multiple or overlapping identities*, and can and do cooperate with the 'us' of each of their identities without being hostile to the 'them' of one level of identity because the latter can be part of the 'us' of another level of identity.

For example, I am a Muslim and do identify with other Muslims for the purposes of my religion. I am also a Sudanese who belongs to a certain profession and have a variety of interests and concerns that I share with other Sudanese, and with people from all parts of the world. Ultimately, and most importantly, I am a human being who is committed to protecting and promoting the values and qualities of being human. The fact that there is a variety of 'them' and 'us' at the various levels of my overlapping identities indicates to me that my relationship to the 'them' of one identify should not frustrate or diminish the prospects of relating to the same people when I need them to be part of the 'us' for me at other levels of identity.

I see the possibility and utility of overlapping identities and cooperation as integral to my faith as a Muslim, in accordance with verse 13 of

Chapter 49 of the Qur'an (that is, 49:13 as the Qur'an will be quoted in this chapter henceforth) which may be translated as follows:

> We [God] have created you [human beings] into [different] peoples and tribes so that you may [all] get to know [understand and cooperate with] each other; the most honorable among you in the sight of God are the pious [righteous] ones.

As I understand it, this verse means that human diversity or pluralism (be it ethnic, religious or otherwise) is not only inherent in the divine scheme of things, but also deliberately designed to promote understanding and cooperation among various peoples. The last part of the verse emphasizes to me that the quality of morality and human worth is to be judged by the person's moral conduct rather than by his or her membership in a particular ethnic, religious or other group.

However, I must admit that my choice of this particular verse of the Qur'an and interpreting it as supporting the principle of overlapping identities and cooperation with the 'non-Muslim other' reflects one perspective on the matter. Those who oppose this perspective may choose to emphasize other, clearly exclusive, verses of the Qur'an such as 3:28, 4:139, 144, 8: 72–73,[1] and/or interpret the quoted verse as referring to diversity and pluralism *within* the global Islamic community (*Umma*) rather than among the totality of humanity at large. A Muslim of the latter orientation may also see the last part of the verse as restricting piety/righteousness to Muslims, so that only a Muslim may qualify for honour in the sight of God in accordance with the quality of his or her personal conduct, as judged by Islamic criteria.

It should be emphasized, however, that choice and/or interpretation of verses of the Qur'an (or any other text for that matter) in relation to human experience and relationships is necessarily informed by the orientation of the person in question. Muslims, for example, have always differed, and will always differ, in their choice of verses to cite in support of their views and also in their understanding of the verses they quote. That is one of the reasons why there are so many schools of Islamic theology and jurisprudence, with a wide variety of views within each school. This feature of Islamic discourse is often cited by Muslims with great pride as conclusive evidence of the flexibility and adaptability of Islam to the different circumstances of time and place.

By 'orientation' I mean the *conditioning of the existential or material circumstances* of the person reading—or hearing the Qur'an or another textual source. That is to say, every person always understands the text in question and derives its normative implications in terms of his or her knowledge and experience of the world, perceptions of self-interests in political, economic and social contexts, realities of inter-communal and/or international relations, and so forth.

People's orientation may also be influenced by their vision for change or improvement in existential or material circumstances. In other words, one need not always feel totality constrained by existing circumstances and may wish to strive to break away from the mould of prevailing political, economic and social conditions. For such vision to have realistic prospects of fulfilment, however, it must be grounded in existing sociological, political, economic and intellectual circumstances of the society in question. This is what I will refer to in the next section as the 'historical contingency' factory in the hermeneutical process.

In my view, two conclusions can be drawn from the above analysis in relation to the thesis of this chapter. First, there is no such thing as the only possible or valid understanding of the Qur'an or conception of Islam, since each is informed by the individual and the collective orientation of Muslims will contribute to a transformation of their understanding of it, and hence of their conception of Islam itself.

Before considering whether modern Muslims already have, or are likely to have, an orientation which is conducive to actively supporting a project of universal human rights, I wish to clarify the concept of hermeneutical discourse in relation to Islam. This is important because in the following sections of the chapter I deal with what might be called an Islamic hermeneutics that can be harnessed, I suggest, in promoting and applying a human rights orientation among Muslims today.

Hermeneutics in context

Hermeneutics is usually defined as the art or science of interpretation, especially of the scriptures, and commonly distinguished from exegesis or explanation and exposition. The need for interpretation as a means of understanding the purposes and normative implications of a text like the Qur'an or the Bible is beyond dispute. But the precise nature and actual practice of hermeneutics and its relationship to exegesis would, of course, vary from one religion to another, and often within the same religion over time and/or place. I would also emphasize the anthropological dimension of these processes.

For example, according to the acts of the Christian Reformed Ecumenical Council (1992), hermeneutics is an unavoidable task of the Christian Church in seeking the abiding significance of the Word of God in the constantly changing circumstances of human life and history. It (ibid.: 28–29) says,

> Hermeneutics has to do with the interpretation of the Bible as it applies to our own time, taking into account the broad historical, cultural and scientific changes that have taken place, as well as the changes in basic mentality and outlook that characterize the modern world.

This document maintains that it is necessary to take into account contextual and cultural factors in applying scriptural ethical directives to concrete life situations (ibid.: 49–51). However, it is clear from the argument and conclusion of the document as a whole that it is cast in terms of a particular tradition within Christianity as distinguished not only from that of the Roman Catholic Church, but also from earlier views within the Protestant Church. The very fact that the document was issued at this point in time indicates to me that its authors felt the need to reformulate or update the position of their own tradition on questions of hermeneutics and ethics. It is true that each religion (and specific tradition within a religion) has its own 'framework of interpretation': a set of interpretative rules, techniques and underlying assumptions that are accepted by the adherents of the religion or tradition in question as valid or authoritative. It would, therefore, seem to follow that there is a 'correct' way of understanding and applying the content of the scriptures (or the Qur'an for Muslims), that is to say, a way which is consistent with the appropriate framework of interpretation (Vroom 1993).

As can be expected, however, all participants in the hermeneutical process would claim that their understanding of the scriptures is the correct one because it is more consistent with the accepted framework of interpretation. Others may even challenge the authority of a given framework of interpretation and seek to provide an alternative. Such claims or combinations thereof underlie differences between, for example, Orthodox Catholic and Protestant Christians, Sunni and Shi'ite Muslims, Sufi and non-Sufi Muslims, as well as among various factions within each religion.

I would, therefore, emphasize the need to understand the process through which the frame of interpretation is specified, verified and revised for reformulating how and by whom is it defined and specified? According to which criteria does that process provide for reformulation or revision, and how can that be legitimately done? Ultimately, who is to arbitrate and mediate between competing claims about the frame of interpretation and/or its application?

In my view, the community—or believers as a whole—should be the living frame of interpretation, and the ultimate arbiter and mediator of interpretative rules, techniques and underlying assumptions. This seems to have been the case during the founding stages of major religions. Over time, however, a few tended to appropriate and monopolize the process of interpretation and turn it into an 'exclusive and technical science or art'. Thus, the process of religious revival and reformation is often about breaking the monopoly of the clergy or technocrats of hermeneutics and reclaiming the right of the community to be the living frame of interpretation for their own religion and its normative regime.

In the case of Islam, for example, there is no reference in the early traditions to any special requirements or qualifications for engaging in the interpretation of the Qur'an or exercising *ijtihad* (human reasoning) to derive ethical norms and legal principles. Even the founders of the major *mathahib* (schools of Islamic jurisprudence) simply stated their views for Muslims at large to accept or reject freely without claiming an exclusive right to interpretation or *ijtihad*. By the end of the third century of Islam, however, the process was rendered so technical and exclusive that the 'gate of *ijtihad*' was said to have been closed, thereby confining subsequent generations of Muslims to become blind followers of the founding 'masters' of Islamic jurisprudence (Hallaq 1984). Since Ibn Taymiyya (fourteenth century A.D.), various scholars have tried to break the deadlock of tradition (Kerr 1966).

A possible reason for this failure, it might be suggested, is that the sociological, political, economic and other circumstances of the time were not ripe for a change in the orientation of Muslims, which would have permitted acceptance of the proposed reforms. That is to say, the requirement of historical contingency of their hermeneutical argument was not satisfied at the time of these reform efforts. I would agree that this must have been the case since—or to the extent that—previous reform efforts were not successful as a matter of fact. But I would also emphasize that *historical contingency can only be accurately judged in retrospect.*

It is integral to any reform effort that its proponents should strive to demonstrate that the circumstances of the time are ripe for change. One would also expect the opponents of reform either to dispute the validity of the proposed change as such or to claim that it is premature. Whatever one may think of the hermeneutical argument or other aspects of the case for reform, the historical contingency factor cannot be categorically judged in advance. Only time will tell whether the community in question will eventually accept or reject the proposed reform. Moreover, rejection of a hermeneutical argument for reform at any point in time should not be seen as final and conclusive, or that its historical contingency will never be satisfied in the future. Subsequent generations of would-be reformers may continue to make, refine and update the argument in their own context and may well succeed when the case for reform is made in the right or appropriate way, time and place.

An anthropological approach to Islam

The foregoing analysis may be described as an 'anthropological approach' to the Qur'an and to Islam in general, in the sense that it is premised on an organic, dynamic relationship between the Qur'an and Islam on one hand, and the nature of human beings (that is, their comprehension, imagination, judgement, behaviour, experience, and so forth) on the other. Is such an approach valid from an Islamic religious point of view? If it is valid, what does it mean for the ways in which Muslims seek to understand Islam and try to conform to its precepts today?

An anthropological approach to the Qur'an and Islam in general is fully justified, indeed imperative, in my view, by virtue of the terms of the Qur'an itself and the experience of Muslim communities throughout their history. According to Muslim belief, the text of the Qur'an contains the final and conclusive message of God to the whole of humanity. This is explicitly stated in verses 21:107, 25:1; and is also clear from the many other verses (such as 2:168, 3:138 and 7:31; and 13:49 [quoted earlier]) in which the Qur'anic form of address is 'Oh, humankind' or 'Oh, Children of Adam'.

The Qur'anic form of address is also directed mostly to the individual person, or to community in some cases, without the intermediacy of clergy or officials of the state. In so doing, the Qur'an constantly emphasizes that people should reflect and consider what is being said, should think about this or that, and so forth, as in verses 2:219, 2:266, 3:191, 16:44 and 30:8. In fact, verses 12:2 and 43:3 declare human reflection and understanding to be the whole purpose of revealing the Qur'an.

Two further points can be added in support of the validity of an anthropological approach to the Qur'an and Islam in general. First, human agency is unavoidable in understanding the Qur'an, the traditions of the Prophet, and in deriving ethical norms and legal principles from those sources to regulate individual behaviour and social relations. Ali bin Abi Talib, one of the leading earliest Muslims and the Fourth Khalifa, is reported to have said, 'The Qur'an does not speak, it is people who speak on its behalf.' Second, and as noted earlier, the actual rich and complex diversity of Islamic theology and jurisprudence clearly demonstrates the dynamic relationship between the scriptural sources of Islam on one hand, and the comprehension, imagination and experience of Muslim peoples on the other.

Thus, there is nothing new about an Islamic anthropological approach to the Qur'an and Islam in general. What is at issue, in my view, is what this approach means for the ways in which Muslims seek to understand Islam and try to conform to its precepts today. Given the fact that the specific historical context has always affected the perceptions and practice of Islamic principles by Muslims of the past, how does the modern context affect those of the present day Muslims? More importantly for the purposes of this chapter, what is the orientation through which Muslims should understand the Qur'an in the modern context?

It is obvious that the orientation of modern Muslims should be different from that of earlier generations because of the radical transformation of the existential and material circumstances of their life today in contrast to those of the past. For better or for worse, Muslims now live in a globalized world of political, economic and security inter-dependence, and mutual social/cultural influence. Their conception of Islam and efforts to live by its precepts must be conditioned by modern perceptions of individual and collective self-interests in the context of this radically transformed world. Whatever vision Muslims may have for change or improvement in the present realities of the world today, must also be grounded in the circumstances and conditions of this world. That is, their perceptions of the range of options available to them must take into account the facts of inter-dependence and mutual influence.

A central issue that modern Muslims have been struggling with over the last two centuries is how to adapt their orientation and transform their conception of Islam in an authentic and legitimate manner. Whether in terms of issues of modernity, democracy, human rights, economic development or some other concern, the central issue has often been the need for legitimizing and rationalizing desired normative or material objectives in terms of the traditions of Islamic societies. It is obvious that there is more to these traditions than the Islamic dimension, but to the extent that Islam is integral to the circumstances of these societies, there seems to be a spectrum of opinion on issues of political, economic and social change.

At one end of the spectrum, there is what might be called the traditionalist or 'fundamentalist' approach, which insists on strict conformity to the *Sharia* as an essential prerequisite for accepting the proposed change. At the other end, there are those who wish to altogether avoid the question of conformity to the *Sharia*, usually out of a conviction that reconciliation between their objectives and the relevant principles of the *Sharia* is not possible. For example, some advocates of universal human rights in Islamic societies prefer to base their position on the present international standards of human rights, irrespective of the conformity of those standards with the principles of the *Sharia*. Between these two poles, there is a variety of positions which seeks to reconcile universal human rights with the *Sharia*, or with Islam in general, in one way or another.

While I agree with those who see Islamic authenticity and legitimacy as imperative for wide and effective acceptance and implementation of universal human rights, I believe that their reconciliation with the *Sharia* is neither possible nor required. Reconciliation is not possible because the *Sharia* is premised on a fundamental distinction between the rights of Muslims and non-Muslims, and those of Muslim men and women, which totally repudiates the principle of equality and non-discrimination upon which universal human rights are fundamentally premised. That is to say, it is simply impossible for the *Sharia* to acknowledge any set of rights to which all human beings are entitled by virtue of their humanity, without distinction on grounds of religion or gender. Since what is required is Islamic authenticity and legitimacy, rather than conformity with the *Sharia* as such, I believe that this requirement can be satisfied without necessarily reconciling universal human rights with the *Sharia*. In other words, I argue that it is possible to achieve Islamic authenticity and legitimacy for a set of human rights by distinguishing between Islam and the *Sharia*.

The divinity of Islam and the temporality of the *Sharia*

In my view, as a human understanding of Islam and, hence, necessarily limited by circumstances of time and place, the *Sharia* should not be identified with the totality of the religion itself. As explained earlier, any reader of the scriptural sources of Islam would always understand those texts and their normative implications in terms of his or her knowledge and experience of the world. Since that knowledge and experience, and indeed the world itself, tend to change over time, Islam should not be bound by any particular understanding of its scriptural sources. I believe that this view is not only consistent with the Muslim belief in the divinity of the Qur'an and finality of its message, but is in fact essential for maintaining the practical relevance of that divinity and finality to the lives of Muslims through the ages.

One often hears in Islamic discourse the proposition that 'Islam is suitable (valid) for all times and places.' For this maxim to be true, however, there must be flexibility and change in the understanding and implementation of Islam over time and place. More specifically, and given the radical transformation of Islamic societies and the whole world around them, it is simply impossible for the same principles of the *Sharia* formulated by Muslim jurists more than thirteen centuries ago to remain the only valid and applicable law of Islam. It would, therefore, follow that the principles of the *Sharia* must be reformed and reformulated before they can be applied today, whether in themselves or as criteria for accepting and implementing a normative system of universal human rights.

This obviously valid proposition is usually stated in modern Islamic discourse as a critique of what is known as *fiqh* (the juridical and theological opinion of early Muslim jurists, rather than of the *Sharia* itself. Moreover, advocates of reform would also call for a modern exercise in *ijtihad* in order to change those aspects of *fiqh* that they today find objectionable or problematic. Such calls for *ijtihad*, however, are rarely followed by actual application and concrete derivation of specific new principles of the *Sharia*. Space does not permit much elaboration but I wish to briefly state two objections to this sort of reasoning from the point of view of the advocacy of universal human rights in modern Islamic societies.

First, since universal human rights are untenable in view of some clear and categorical verses of the Qur'an itself, such as verse 4:34, often cited as the basis of the inequality of women to men, the problem is one of the *Sharia* and not merely *fiqh*. Second, since the traditional principle of *ijtihad* is confined to matters on which there is no clear and categorical text of the Qur'an, it cannot challenge a principle of inequality based on such a text. In other words, there is a need to reform the principle of *ijtihad* itself before it can be used to resolve incompatibility of the *Sharia* and universal human rights where conflict between the two is due to a clear and categorical text of the Qur'an rather than *fiqh* as the opinion of early jurists.

I believe that *ijtihad* should be applied even to matters governed by clear and categorical texts of the Qur'an, as suggested by the late Sudanese Muslim reformer, Ustadh Mahmoud Mohamed Taha. According to Taha's methodology of reform, the Qur'an itself should be seen as containing two messages: one intended for immediate application within the historical context of the seventh century and after, and another message for subsequent implementation as and when the circumstances of time and place permit (Taha 1987). An historical approach to the Qur'an in general can be supported by some of the rulings of U-mar ibn al-Khatab, the second Khalifa, who decided that clear and categorical verses of the Qur'an should not apply when the objective was to develope *that* approach into comprehensive methodology of Islamic reform, which would enable modern Muslim jurists to select and interpret verses of the Qur'an in order to develop a modern version of the *Sharia* (An-Naim 1990).

Taha's methodology may appear to be too radical to many Muslims today, but I am not aware of any alternative which will adequately resolve the crisis in modern Islamic reform, especially in relation to universal human rights. Those who wish to achieve Islamic authenticity and legitimacy for universal human rights must overcome theological objections, and political and sociological resistance, to an adequate reform methodology, be it that of Taha or any other viable alternative. My own preference to date is the methodology proposed by Taha and explained in the sources cited earlier. I remain open, however, to accepting any alternative methodology which will achieve what I believe to be the necessary degree of Islamic reform.

This is as far as theory is concerned. In the next section, I will offer some reflections on aspects of political and sociological resistance to approaches that seek to develop and present an Islamic rationale for universal human rights in modern Islamic societies. In my experience, much of the so-called theological or hermeneutical objections to reform methodologies, such as that of Taha, are in fact a product of political and sociological factors. Whatever may be their nature or motivation, I believe that all obstacles to genuine commitment to universal human rights must be identified and overcome by the proponents of universality, each working within his or her own context as well as in collaboration with others.

Prospects of universality in a global context

Resistance to an Islamic rationale for universal human rights in Islamic societies today may be traced to several sources, some pertaining to regional and international considerations, while others relate to local dynamics of power relations. It is also important to note that this resistance is mostly reactive to perceived threats or other concerns, whether internal or external to the region. It is not possible, of course, to discuss all aspects of this phenomenon, but it may be useful to highlight the following with a view to suggest ways of overcoming resistance to universality of human rights.

First, there is the problem of perceiving universal human rights as yet another element of a 'Western' conspiracy to undermine the integrity and independence of Islamic societies. The best defence these societies have against this neo-colonial attack, the argument goes, is a strong and uncompromising assertion of a distinctive Islamic identity and culture. Thus, while all Muslim advocates of universal human rights are seen as agents of foreign domination and Western cultural imperialism, those who seek to base their advocacy on an Islamic rationale are even more 'dangerous' because they undermine the role of distinctive Islamic identity and culture as vital defence.

Related to this factor are popular perceptions of the double standards of Western governments, media and the public at large regarding Muslim concerns, especially in relation to Palestine and, more recently, former Yugoslavia, in contrast to devastating and decisive action against Iraq. These perceptions enhance the view that the West is not interested in universal human rights except where they serve its geopolitical and economic interests.

There is also the perception that the existing international human rights standards and mechanisms for their implementation, in fact reflect a Western bias in favour of individual civil and political rights, against economic and social rights and collective human rights. Besides reinforcing apprehensions of cultural imperialism, this bias is also used to argue that the values and priorities of Islamic societies are not served by the existing international standards.

At the local or internal level, there is resistance from those who feel that their vested interests are threatened by universal human rights.

These include ruling classes and groups, men and Muslim majorities at large who would normally tend to resist any threat to their privileged position. The usual argument used by these groups is that human rights are alien to the culture and traditions of Islamic societies. Thus, the perceived threat is even more serious when it claims an Islamic rationale, thereby seeking to undermine the rationale of the defence itself.

Strategies for overcoming these and other causes of resistance must be founded on a realistic understanding of the internal logic and perceived basis of opposition to universal human rights. For example, the facts and aftermath of Westen colonialism, and present domination and exploitation must be admitted and confronted; the facts of internal power relations and perceptions of vested interested must be understood and redressed; and so on.

The key to any effort in this regard, however, is the credibility of advocates of universal human rights in the eyes of their own local constituencies. These advocates must be able to draw on the symbols of their own culture and history, speak the 'language' of their own peoples, know and respect their concerns and priorities. In so doing, advocates of universal human rights should appreciate and utilize the 'ambivalence and contestablity' of their cultures, and seek out and explore new options and rationales for advancing the cultural legitimacy of universal human rights. All of this will have to be through what might be called an internal Islamic discourse. Outsiders can assist such an internal discourse by supporting the right of all Muslim insiders to engage in it, as well as by holding their own (Christian, Hindu, Buddhist or other internal religious) discourses to resolve the conflicts and tensions between their respective religions and universal human rights. Universality of human rights can also be enhanced through a cross-cultural dialogue to promote an overlapping consensus on global moral foundations of these rights (An-Naim 1992; An-Naim and Deng 1990).

All the major religions of the world agree that there is an organic and dynamic relationship between ends and means, so that legitimate objectives can only be realized through appropriate methods and processes. I would, therefore, conclude that, in the final analysis, the acknowledgement and implementation of universal human rights should be seen as a cooperative process as well as a common objective; as a global joint venture and not an attempt to universalize a particular cultural or religious model.

Note

1. These verses speak about 'believers' as *awliya*—allies and supporters—of one another and 'non-believers' as *awliya* of one another. I will address the question of criteria and rationale of reconciling apparently conflicting verses of the Qur'an later in this chapter.

References

An-Naim, A.A. 1990. *Toward an Islamic Reformation: Civil Liberties, Human Rights and International Law*. Syracuse: Syracuse University Press.

———. (ed.). 1992. *Human Rights in Cross-cultural Perspectives*. Philadelphia: University of Pennsylvania Press.

An-Naim, A.A. and P.M. Deng (eds). 1990. *Human Rights in Africa: Cross-cultural Perspectives*. Washington, DC: Brookings Institution.

Hallaq, Wael B. 1984. 'Was the Gate of Ijtihad Closed?', *International Journal of Middle East Studies*, 16: 3–41.

Kerr, Malcolm H. 1996. *Islamic Reform: The Political and Legal Theories of Muhammad Abduh and Rashid Rida*. Berkeley and Los Angeles: University of California Press.

Reformed Ecumenical Council. 1992. *Acts of the Reformed Ecumenical Council Athens*. Grand Rapids: Reformed Ecumenical Council.

Taha, M.M. 1987. *The Second Message of Islam*. Syracuse: Syracuse University Press.

Vroom, H.M. 1993. 'Scripture Read and Interpreted: The Development of the Doctrine of Scripture and Hermeneutics in Gereformeere Theology in the Netherlands', *Calvin Theological Journal*, 28: 352–71.

Beyond Power

Alternative Conceptions of Being and the Reconstitution of Social Theory

28

John Clammer

A major preoccupation of Western social theory, certainly since Machiavelli and greatly intensified in recent times by Foucault, has been with power. Most of the figures considered central to sociological and political theory—Weber, Hannah Arendt, Habermas, Talcott Parsons, Simmel, Aron, Polantzas, to name but a few—have addressed themselves to this issue as a central part of their work (Lukes 1986). And certainly since Foucault, the alleged nexus between knowledge and power has inspired a whole host of writings in cultural studies, media sociology, political sociology and numerous other sub-areas of the social sciences. So much so that I think it is fair to say that for most mainstream Western social theory, it is now taken for granted that power is central to the constitution of human relationships, whether at the individual or collective levels.

This chapter, however, sets out to interrogate this assumption. I hope that we can agree that the notion of power is an essential place to begin an investigation of the limits and silences of Western social theory, not only because of its widely taken-for-granted acceptance, but more importantly because built into it are fundamental epistemological and ontological assumptions. These assumptions need to be revealed and deconstructed, and the possibility of alternatives put in their place. This exercise, furthermore, is not simply one of theoretical interest but takes on added salience in that here, if nowhere else, theory has practical outcomes in a vast range of fields touching on human life—political practice, development studies, medical and psychiatric treatment, criminology, to name a few. In a nutshell, this chapter will initiate a conversation suggesting that the Western preoccupation with power is the product not of universal characteristics of the human species, but of a particular philosophical anthropology rooted in an historically powerful and even hegemonic process of civilizational construction, which, despite its contemporary reach (expressed in the current jargon of globalization) and its socially and culturally transformative mechanisms (of which I would argue that capitalism is the main one), is in fact a 'local' one. And like all civilizational projects, it is contingent and so is both temporary and could have turned out very differently, had certain combinations of circumstances not conspired to launch it into the trajectory that it is now (for the time being and until the oil runs out) enjoying.

The notion of philosophical anthropology is an important one here. This notion, originally most commonly found in German-language scholarship and debate, and to a lesser extent in forms of theological anthropology emerging from within French Catholicism, never really took root in English-speaking anthropology (or philosophy, for that matter). Originally concerned with the issue of defining human nature and locating humans in relationship to Nature and the historical process, at its centre was the question of ethics (how, by the uniquely human capacity of acting ethically, does one become more truly human?) and the related issue of self-cultivation (what forms of practice, including social and cultural ones, lead one to higher levels of character and authentic humanity?). These questions, that have largely disappeared from the forefront of Western social theory despite the efforts of individuals such as Zygmunt Bauman (1995) and Barry Smart (1999) to keep them in circulation, are in fact both implicit in certain forms of sociological investigation (the sociology of development, for example, which even at its most technical, keeps alive the major moral issues of the day), and have always been central to many of the major Asian forms of social and socio-religious thought, such as Confucianism and Buddhism. It is to a great extent the preoccupation with power that has occluded these alternative approaches, since from that perspective ethics must be seen as subterfuge or as flight from reality, or as utopianism; a view, as will be argued here, that both excludes a deeper consideration of the ethical nature of human life and ethnocentrically excludes from consideration as social theory major traditions of human thought that have shaped entire civilizations and human history.

There are a number of answers as to why and how this situation has come about—that the notion of power as domination has come to be almost the only conception of power available to us—including the idea that it is a characteristic byproduct of modernity as it has developed and been conceptualized in the West. In part this is true, in the sense that the expanding economic, military and epistemological hegemony of the West, especially during the period of high colonialism, both excluded local forms of knowledge as serious contenders to this epistemological hegemony, while turning them into objects of study by Western anthropologists and comparative religionists, making its own forms of knowledge seem so powerful and attractive (and the mastery of such epistemology the main route to colonial social mobility). The result has been that much of the social thought of Asia was reclassified as 'religious' and so the ways in which it might seriously contest Western notions of social order and organization were never admitted in any central way. But here I would wish to argue that this was the outcome of certain hegemonic practices, and that the apparently universal (although now rapidly fraying) Western 'scientific' worldview was imposed by certain historical outcomes, not by its intrinsic superiority, at least as applied to the social realm. At one level, then, this chapter is an exercise in what Roberto Unger (2001) has called 'non-necessitarian' social theory, an expression of the view of Bocchi and Ceruti (2002) that, employing the insights of complexity theory, the Universe and human societies within it are contingent and non-determined. Marshall Sahlins (1996) has argued at some length that Western society is simply a culture amongst others and that it has its own particular and peculiar cosmology, as susceptible to anthropological analysis as any other, and not in any way conceptually privileged (despite its historical reach and power). Globalization should in principle relativize knowledge by making many local traditions and epistemologies accessible to a universal audience. The temporary hegemony of Western forms of knowledge, in science and economics and also about culture, humanity, society and the appropriate methodologies for discovering what are to be considered useful facts, can consequently be challenged not only philosophically but also on the basis of its contingency. This chapter will take this idea very seriously indeed.

At a second level, this chapter will argue, coming as it were from the opposite direction, that there are profound and still largely unexplored resources within Asian thinking, whether in the explicitly social or hidden more commonly in the religious, for the reconstruction of social theory. Again, this is not a mere academic exercise, fascinating as it intrinsically is. Zygmunt Bauman (1999) has argued in one of his seminal works that the outcome of modernity, and the social and political theories that informed it, proved not to be emancipation and enlightenment, but the Holocaust. So one might continue to argue that the outcome of current social theory has been to contribute little to a world in crisis, but if anything, to retreat even further from it through the flight into post-modernism and deconstruction, the aridities of structuralism and its variants, a mania for methodology over substance, the exclusion of the ethical and the 'critical' posturings of much of what passes for cultural studies. It may be and it can certainly be argued that the resources of much conventional social theory are largely exhausted and, hence, it is urgently needed to strike out in some fresh directions. It does not, in short, centrally or successfully address the perennial existential issues of human suffering, of death, of meaningful relationships with Nature, of true freedom, of the nature of ethical relationships with each other or with the deep alienation (expressed in, amongst other ways, crime, ad-dictions and suicide) that plague the very societies that have attained the 'modernity' for which we have apparently been striving at such human and ecological cost. So are there other paths than social theory, an essential reflexive activity I would argue, if human beings are to under-stand their own primary environment, which is indeed social? Amongst these other and by no means new directions (and undoubtedly there is no one universalizing path) are the alternative resources of the Asian traditions, and it is to some of these that we will now turn in our attempt to scrutinize the centrality of power and to locate the sources for other ways of being-in-the-world. There are a number of such potential dir-ections but the one that I will examine here in most detail will be that of Buddhism, both because as a civilizational force it has shaped at least half of humankind historically or in the present, and because, I will argue, it not only poses the major challenge to Western notions of reality, but contains within itself the seeds of a social theory that is potentially truly emancipatory in a way that power-based notions of social interaction can never be.

Theses on the deconstruction of power

Why Buddhism? First, because I would suggest that any social theory worth its salt must address the pressing problems of human and social suffering. Whatever its shortcomings, the field of development studies, for example, does have the virtue of holding up for constant scrutiny the major moral issues of the moment—poverty, environmental destruction, widening social and economic inequalities, abuse of human rights, and the like. It is a conceit of Western theory (especially those varieties that label themselves as 'critical') that emancipatory projects must come from within its worldview. While the concept of social suffering has only recently been given a name in social theory (Kleinman et al. 1997), the identification and overcoming of suffering is, of course, the very foundation of Buddhism where karmic theory provides a metaphysical and social mechanism, expressed in the cosmology and hierarchical ordering of caste, for addressing both individual suffering and the nature and persistence of social injustice. As Stephen Batchelor (1998) has, with some wit, suggested, Buddhism represents what he calls 'the other Enlightenment project'—a much more fundamental attempt than most conventional social theory to address the origins, nature and overcoming of suffering. How is this so?

Buddhism attempts to address the basic question of human alienation. While many will, of course, immediately classify it as a 'religion', it can equally well be interpreted in entirely humanist terms as a theory of suffering and its cessation or as a psychology—a theory of the human person (Pickering 1997). But while recent social theory has been preoccupied with questions of the self, Buddhism is a theory of the nonself, of the transcendence of the ego, and as such represents a radical critique of Western conceptions of the human individual and the nature of personality, of power, and of what 'human rights' might mean in a universe composed of non-permanent physico-psychic entities, but in which inter-dependence between people, and between people and Nature is the basis of what in Western thought would be called 'causality' (Keown et al. 1998). In such a model the idea of authority—central to Western conceptions of power and psychology—are fundamentally deconstructed (Fontana 1997), as is the idea of attachment, also foundational to Western theories of relationships and of consumerism. If attachment is the root of suffering and power is the expression of attachment, and the overcoming of attachment (rooted itself is a false conception of the self and the permanence of external 'reality') is the cure, then we see in Buddhism both a radical critique of power and a model for social practice vastly different from that promoted by Western social and political theory (Queen et al. 2003). That is, excepting perhaps those on the libertarian or religious fringes usually excluded from academic discussion or attention, yet which prove, on closer examination, to be the basis of many social movements from the 'New Age' through liberation theologies to deep ecology. Indeed, one of the characteristics of the latter is that it shares many features with Buddhism, including a critique of the extreme anthropocentrism and over-socialized conception of people that marks Western social theory as something of an aberration when viewed from, say, a Japanese perspective (Clammer 1995) in which humans are an integral part of a total ecological system and not, as in the view of Antony Giddens, for example, of an order entirely separate from Nature. As Albert Camus nicely put it, 'The sun taught me that history isn't everything.'

Buddhism is essentially a theory (or method) of liberation. That is to say, it teaches that a correct perception of reality (the essential unity and inter-being of all things) is the first step towards emancipation, and that the false consciousness that gives rise to a misrecognition of this reality gives rise to suffering. The eradication of suffering, while it must express itself in social action against injustice, poverty and other social ills, must begin from the clear perception of the root of that suffering and must transcend the grasping or clinging to a false notion of the permanence of phenomena that is at the basis of power theories of society. The recognition of inter-being must express itself as compassion, the premier Buddhist virtue, and cannot express itself as domination which radically misconceives the true basis of human relationships and of the nature of causality and agency. The 'self', as part of this unceasing and uncreated web of causality, is itself a kind of illusion if thought of as a permanent essence: rather, it must be seen as the outcome or node as it were of a dense but ever shifting set of relationships between that self and others, and between the self and Nature—the huge complex of largely unknown forces that work constantly to shape each individual. Buddhism then, far from being an anti-social doctrine, is in fact deeply sociological, since at its very basis is the foundational theory of inter-being. Transience and fragility are fundamental elements of our existential condition: power is the illusory attempt to impose control where it cannot ever succeed, to impose structure on the inherently unstable. While I am not aware that the parallel has been seriously drawn yet, in certain respects Buddhism is closer to chaos theory in its picture of the Universe that it is to the structural preoccupations of most sociological theory (Eve et al. 1997).

Buddhism in relation to sociology has been called by one of its practitioners the discovery of 'institutionalized delusion'—the exploration on the social plane of the outcome of the 'three fires' of acquisitiveness, ill-will and existential ignorance when these are no longer confined to the individual life but are expressed collectively (Jones 2003). Certain consequences flow from this—the transcendence not strengthening of the individual 'personality' or ego-centred conception of self, non-violence or, to quote Jones's summary of the great Indian Buddhist sage Nagarjuna's formulation, 'revulsion from lusts, restraint from aggressions, vanity of possessions and power' (ibid.: 47), the centrality of ethics in practice and to practice, expressed primarily in the notion of compassion, and education being devoted not mainly to the acquisition of facts, but to awakening to one's true nature. From the basic tenets of the *dharma*—summarized by Jones (ibid.: 181) as 'compassion, inter-dependence, selflessness, and the practice of morality and mindfulness'—necessarily flows a social theory, both of relationships between humans in society, and for the expansion of individual liberation into the realm of addressing social suffering, one of the main roots of which is the striving for power (*cf* Loy 2003).

Western social theory is characterized by a strong anthropocentrism that radically separates humans from Nature, and paradoxically humans from each other since there are few philosophical resources in the West for understanding people as essentially (that is, ontologically) connected. Buddhism, however, radically decentres humans from their imagined place at the centre of the Universe and relocates them as elements in a much wider and interpenetrating web of causalities, all of which work interactively on each other. The anthropocentric view of the Universe and its associated over-socialized view of humankind, its radical individualism and its essentialized notions of the self—characteristic of Western theory (Morris 1991) that has not had the benefit of fertile contact with Asian traditions of thought—leads directly to a preoccupation with power. Or, in John Kenneth Galbraith's words, 'The exercise of power, the submission of some to the will of others, is inevitable in modern society; nothing whatever is accomplished without it.' What in fact this comment reveals is not so much a statement of a social fact as the ontological poverty of Western social and political theory, and a massive failure of the imagination: that what 'seems' to be the case has to 'be' the case (Jacoby 1999). Even a progressive thinker like George Monbiot (2003) is unable to think outside of this paradigm when, in his appeal for a form of world government based on the moral authority of a world parliament (rather than on any power of physical coercion) as a way of 'taking back' or democratizing globalization, he feels it necessary to launch a frontal attack on those who feel that power itself is the problem. Thus, he feels it essential to condemn a book such as John Holloway's *Change the World Without Taking Power* (2002) for its 'unrealism', instead of seeing it as a work that is (unlike Monbiot's own work) attempting to transcend the existing paradigm rather than situate itself as a 'radical' within it. The key to understanding models of power/anti-power is a question of ontology. Anti-power that is simply a struggle against power can never succeed: what is necessary is to deconstruct the notion and necessity of power itself and the impoverished conception of humankind upon which power theories are based; one that suggests in fact that humans cannot act ethically or outside of a framework of pure self-interest.

But the struggle with this idea has, as suggested, always been foundational to Buddhism. It is obviously true that in existing Buddhist societies, the theory of the transcendence of power is by no means always translated into practice, but attempts are certainly constantly being made to do so, often in the context of social movements such as the Sri Lankan Sarvodaya Movement, the Tzu-Chi Foundation in Taiwan, and the development activities of Japanese religious movements such as Soka Gakkai. What all of these have grasped is the fundamental unreality of power, itself a profoundly liberating insight. Power is in fact a major form of human self-deception and is the antithesis of compassion, the foundational ethical value of Buddhism (Edwards 2001) with which it cannot possibly coexist.

Buddhism is not alone in stressing this point. Gandhi also grasped this and expressed it in two key elements of his model of social transformation: the principle of *ahimsa* or non-violence and his theory of truth. The two are in fact closely connected. *Ahimsa* in its negative meaning implies non-injury to living things; in its positive sense it suggests self-sacrifice, love (including of one's enemies) and charity in its widest sense. For Gandhi *ahimsa* is a positive or constructive force, superior in fact to all others since it dissolves blockages and reframes human relationships in terms of universal compassion, not power or domination. It is in fact the truth, the basic fact about the Universe and society. Relative truth, of course, operates constantly in our attempts to grasp the nature of the world (through science, for example), but absolute truth is not knowledge of a fact in an empirical sense. It is the grasping of a state of being and hence involves action. It is an ontological and not an epistemological state, an existential condition or a way of living life, of existence before essence (Rao 1990).

Gandhi's prioritizing of non-violence, then, was not merely a political strategy but a philosophical position, one that recognized explicitly the connection between power and violence. The praxis that emerged from this indeed proved to be highly effective in delegitimizing the

British Raj, and also for highlighting the corruptions of indigenous Indian politics and the stupidity of the communal tensions that wracked pre-independence India (and still do in the post-colonial era). The counter-productive nature (to humane values) of terrorism and the re-militarization of the globe that it has provided a fig-leaf for, have indeed shown the total ineffectiveness of violence as a route to any kind of posi-tive social transformation (Boulding 1999). The utopian imagination, even in the West, where significantly the genre flourishes most actively, however knows differently (and significantly, Aldous Huxley, in writ-ing a fictionalized account of his own utopia, chose a Buddhist-like model [*cf* Huxley 1994]). And as scholars, both of traditional anarchism and of contemporary social movements, have noted (Giri 2002a; Melucci 1996), altruistic behaviour, far from being exceptional, is the basis for social action, symbolic and practical transformations, and the reintroduction of spirituality or the transcendent with all its implications for the restructuring or decentring of the self and identity that it implies for very large numbers of people. Social movements indeed turn out to be very important for the study of social transformation as they represent praxis—attempts in many cases to produce new visions of possible worlds and to attempt to carry those visions into the reshaping of reality. If social reality is constructed, as many theorists would have us believe, then it can be reconstructed. Buddhism indeed, to revert to our earlier example, is both a radical method of deconstruction that goes far beyond Derrida, and a method of radical reconstruction, the move rarely undertaken in post-modern social theory that in some ways it formally resembles. Nor, as Denis Goulet (1995: 25) rightly points out, is it enough for ethicists to simply preach noble ideals. The world already has plenty of those. The urgent necessity is to find a *method*—a means of social transformation that takes us out of our present impasse. This Buddhism has always had; one which has experientially been tested by millions of people and has transformed entire civilizations. It is rather hard, however, to find any reference whatsoever to this methodology—or its parallels that might be found in Gandhi; in J. Krishnamurti; in the thought of Pandurang Shastri Athavale, the founder of the Swadhyaya movement; or of Sulak Sivaraksa, the Thai social critic and alternative development theorist; in Japanese Buddhist-inspired psychotherapeautic methods such as *naikan*; in Chinese social thought; in the rich and almost totally unmined trad-ition of radical social thought in Korea; or even in Islam, although in this latter case a large and accessible literature exists in many languages. The alternative social visions embodied in Asian cinema, literature and visual arts is likewise marginalized. The accusation of profound ethnocentrism on the part of Western social theory is indeed supported by the evidence. Major traditions of thought about the human individual, people's place in Nature and of social organization are almost totally absent from hegemonic social theory. Of course, the civilizations that have produced this thought are studied, often intensively. But significantly, they are studied as the 'other', in comparative religion or the history of religions, and in anthropology. The possibility that they might actually challenge the canons of Western theory is rarely admitted. But they do, and our role here is to show how this is the case, the implications of this for the reconstruction of social theory, and the implications of this for promoting positive social transformation worldwide.

Reconstructing social theory

In a globalized world there is plenty of room for local knowledges but no place (if one may coin a word parallel to racism or sexism) for localism. Today all knowledges (potentially at least) interpenetrate. The problems are, however, the historical and contingent hegemony of some local knowledges and the unwillingness of given civilizational traditions to acknowledge the truth-claims of other people's knowledges. In such a situation 'multiculturalism' in fact means a kind of stand-off or armed truce in which the preoccupation of constituent groups is with the establishment of *difference* rather than of common ground, common interests or shared purpose. For this reason many social movements have had little large-scale impact or transformative power, or if they have, it has been negative. It is not at all clear that the huge numbers of NGOs that currently populate the globe are really influencing the direction of history except in very local contexts. This may be not because of bad motives but, on the contrary, because of inadequate analysis. What they lack is a *deep sociology*. The methodological and theoretical assumptions of Western sociology—its preoccupation with method, especially those of a quantitative nature, its exclusion of the spiritual, its narrow conceptions of agency, its separation of humans from the rest of Nature, its extraordinary unwillingness to confront basic existential issues such as death or love (although sex, as quantifiable behaviour, is acceptable), its inability to effectively address such fundamental issues as poverty, aggression and violence—suggest that for whatever its modest achievements, it is really a failed intellectual enterprise, one skating on the surface, unwilling to confront what actually lies behind observable 'behaviour' or 'attitudes', the stuff of standard social science. Instead, it has put the least desirable of human attributes—the desire or ability to dominate—at the heart of its model of human relations and the vast attention given to Foucault in this respect must surely signal a very strange scale of values. The question then becomes: how might we build an alternative version of social theory out of other traditions of social thought other than those of the West, since the latter has certainly not yet led us to the completion of its version of the Enlightenment project (or indeed if one follows the post-modernists, has abandoned the project altogether)? While avoiding the superficial parallels between Western post-modernism and certain Asian modes of thought (especially Buddhism), our experiment must be to see where we can take the conversation, once we are willing to admit, at least provisionally, the truth-claims of those modes of thought, or at least their legitimacy, as alternative models of human being-in-the-world.

Here again we might set out a series of basic propositions that suggest alternative bases for social theory, again based on the significance that we have given to the Buddhist worldview. This worldview suggests a model of causality ('dependent arising'), of the self (or strictly speaking the 'non-self'), of history and its underlying mechanisms, and of the place of humans within Nature that undermines the extreme anthropocentrism of conventional social theory by arguing for the (at least potential) 'Buddhahood of all beings'. Coded into Western social theory are a whole set of assumptions about the self, rationality, the body, knowledge, causality and agency, which are so much part of the doxa that they are rarely made explicit. Once they are, even within the basic framework of Western social theory, claims of value–freedom immediately collapse and such forms of theory are shown to be in fact ideological, as is most apparent, perhaps, in the case of neo-liberal economics (van Staveren 2001). These assumptions are part of the local knowledge of the West and any claims to universality on their part would have to be rigorously demonstrated, rather than imposed by history as has actually and contingently happened. Not all models of the world, in other words, lead to the conclusion that power is central as either or both, a mechanism or a value.

Of course, even outside of a Buddhist framework, power can be reclaimed or redefined. Denis Goulet (1995: 25), in discussing the work of the French philosopher Gustav Thibon, suggests that for Thibon the issue was not the abolition of power as such, but its conversion into a higher ethic, or what he termed 'the union of force with wisdom.' This might be one path to take but, perhaps, a dangerous one. An alternative or modification of this is suggested by Matthew Fox (1995: 17) who argues that spirituality is not only about states of being and individual becoming, but rather:

> True spirituality, however, is about power. It is about developing the powers of creativity, justice and compassion in all persons. It is about unleashing divine powers in us all. It is about grounding persons and communities in the powers that will enable them to survive and even flourish in the midst of adversity.... Is the spirituality of non-violence not a spirituality of a kind of power that is alternative to the ways of our modern civilization?

In summarizing his overall philosophy, Fox indeed closely approaches a Buddhist position—the movement from anthropocentric to cosmological conceptions of being, to move beyond dualism, to an ecological view of the self (Fox 1995: 29–30), or towards what the Thai social activist and theorist Sulak Sivaraksa (1992) has called 'Buddhism with a small b'. The issue here, as for Gandhi, is not the abnegation of power but its transformation from a means of domination and a mechanism of violence to a force for the positive remaking of human and natural life, the harnessing of the energy (in Japanese, *ki*) that flows throughout the Universe, but which can be focussed, concentrated and utilized for healing, and never for destruction. Participation in society then becomes a creative act—the constant making and remaking of 'reality' to a pattern that suits our species' being (Harvey 2002). Such views do indeed exist in some of the marginalized varieties of Western social theory, such as anarchism. Anthropologist David Graeber (2004) has recently suggested that drawing on the ethnographic evidence of anthropology and its expertise in the study of stateless societies, it is quite possible to develop a coherent social theory around the idea of what he calls 'imaginary counter-power' in which he counterposes his notions of 'power/ignorance' and 'power/stupidity' to Michel Foucault's rather more fashionable notion of 'power/knowledge' (ibid.: 24, 71).

For, as Henryk Skolimowski (1992: 139) suggests:

> We are the most powerful civilization that ever existed. Yet we, as individuals, are amongst the least powerful people that ever existed. The roots of this paradox are part of our tragedy. By exteriorizing power, by conceiving of it as an instrument of domination of the outside world, we have deprived ourselves (as human individuals) of the power that human beings can possess.

As he suggests, of all the many possible meanings of power, we have chosen to choose only one—the exercise of force to control and dominate—to the exclusion of possible alternatives, including the possibility that the search for power is in fact part of a transcendental yearning to identify with a larger pattern or unity, the recognition that far from being alienated from the Universe, we are an extension of its powers because we share a basic unity with it. Power in the conventional sense is, to Skolimowski, in the true sense of the word, a 'myth', which in fact prevents us from fully participating in life. Alternative views already exist in ecology; in a systems view of life, as expounded by thinkers such as Gregory Bateson and Fritjof Capra; in religious traditions both Eastern and Western; in post-modernism, and even in the varieties of so-called New Age thinking. But as Skolimowski (1992: 167) suggests:

> We cannot hope to 'tame' power or use it wisely and benevolently as long as we are within the context of the ideology that has made power the instrument of physical domination and cultural suppression. We must, therefore, work out a new socio-political paradigm. We have to create a new social reality that will provide a new context for an alternative paradigm of power.

Such a view shows up the limitations of Foucault's approach to power. As John Sturrock (1998: 65) nicely puts it:

> By calmly ascribing insidious powers of control to supposedly liberal societies such as our own, Foucault became the patron saint of abnormality and deviance. And by making relations of power into the specific form underlying all personal and collective relations, he lent high intellectual authority to the political arguments that are now commonly advanced for 'empowerment', the achievement of which, for this disadvantaged group or that, society would of course confirm, not disprove, the strength of Foucault's zero-sum case, by demonstrating that a gain in power by one group can only be achieved by power being taken away from another.

Empowerment within the contemporary paradigm of power, in other words, is essentially chimerical and provisional, and the struggle for such illusory power can only add to the sum of human unhappiness from which it was intended to subtract.

One solution to this, arising from the philosophy of critical realism which has uniquely brought together elements of contemporary Western philosophy of science and Asian, and in particular, Indian, thought, are the notions of what its founder, Roy Bhaskar (2002), calls 'ontological simplicity' and 'ontological honesty'. In this view, the 'ontological extravagance' of contemporary society is fueled by the illusion generated by capitalism that we have unlimited needs and that these cannot be satisfied without competition. This is fact is not true: we actually have or can be fully satisfied with the fulfilment of quite limited needs. Turning to Hobbes or social Darwinism as a theoretical justification for sanctioned greed, rent-taking and power-seeking is an ideological move that does not in fact accord with what we know of human nature. The post-modernist rejection of this notion as some kind of essentialism (which it need not be; David Harvey, for example, following Marx, prefers to understand it as our 'species being') paradoxically has the same effect. The basis of Bhaskar's philosophy is the rejection of dualism; a rejection that is not only a theoretical move, but has profound practical consequences: '[And] the whole vedic critique of attachment and the Buddhist critique of craving, the critique of desire or its inverse form, fear, the critique of attachment as attraction and attachment as repulsion is really based on a critique of activity which is dualistically split' (ibid.: 236). Power in its conventional Western sense is profoundly dualistic: it denies the possibility of unity between myself and the other; it assumes attachment to limited resources that can only be possessed by denying them to the other, and it assumes that psychic satisfaction can only be obtained through the ability to dominate the other. These assumptions, however, are fundamentally flawed and can be shown to be so not only within the Western tradition itself (in anarchism, in Christianity, in the communitarian movements, and in the stuff of simple everyday life, particularly in relation to the word that the West has made its icon while endlessly violating its spirit: love), but also from the centuries of experience, reflection and praxis embodied in Asian traditions of thought. As Bhaskar himself, as someone straddling the Western and the Indian philosophical worlds, suggests, 'If we were not alienated from our most fundamental essential nature we would see immediately our interconnectedness with the essential nature of all other human beings and the rest of the cosmos' (ibid.: 224). Power in the conventional sense, then, is not a symptom of mastery but of alienation. The move in Bhaskar's philosophy from a philosophy of science primarily concerned with knowledge to what he (ibid.: 224) terms a 'philosophy of freedom, human emancipation and ultimately universal self-realization' should signal a parallel shift in the nature of the social sciences; for without this shift, social theory remains trapped in an instrumentalist mode, quite unable to access the deeper reservoirs of human motivation and satisfaction.

The notion of 'resistance', which has become the leitmotiv of much progressive social theory, needs, then, to be replaced or supplemented with the notion of self-realization, not undertaken as a solitary individual activity, but precisely as a collective social process and activity of mutual co-creation. In East Asian traditions (Confucian as well as Buddhist), the notion of self-cultivation is not understood as an ego-enhancing personal project but as the process of becoming more fully human, something that can only be attained, of course, in a social context. As this idea re-enters broader social theory from Asian theorists (for example, Giri 2002b), it not only presents the possibility of rediscovered patterns of social practice and of new sociological theories of agency, but establishes links with themes in Western and Judaic thought (a kind of bridge between Asian and Western modes of thought) that have themselves been recently brought back into increasing prominence—the works of Walter Benjamin, Martin Buber and, above all, Emmanuel Levinas—in which dialogic modes of being are given priority, ethics is central, and in which authentic existence is understood as relationship with the 'other', not alienation from the 'face' of the one who confronts me in every social interaction.

Power in its older sense then represents the diminution, not fulfilment, of human possibilities. Hence, its critique lies at the heart of any alternative social theory and the exposition of constructive futures in which the critical and emancipatory qualities of Western social theory are merged with the liberatory and cosmocentric ones of Asian theory. The Asian traditions indeed contain untold riches of inspiration for the construction of such alternatives and represent reservoirs of possibilities and sources of social creativity as yet hardly tapped, but sorely in need of being so, given the human, ecological and political impasse to which classical theory and its modernist variants have so far led us. The truly radical critique of culture and society, and hence the possibility of building a new kind, reside in an 'enlightenment project' very different from that conceived by the architects of Western modernity.

References

Batchelor, S. 1998. 'The Other Enlightenment Project: Buddhism, Agnosticism and Postmodernity', in U. King (ed.), *Faith and Praxis in a Postmodern Age*, pp.113–27. London: Cassell.

Bauman, Z. 1995. *Life in Fragments: Essays in Postmodern Morality*. Oxford and Cambridge MA: Blackwell.

Bauman, Z. 1999. *Modernity and the Holocaust*. Cambridge: Polity.

Bhaskar, R. 2002. *From Science to Emancipation: Alienation and the Actuality of Enlightenment*. New Delhi and London: SAGE.

Bocchi, G. and M. Ceruti. 2002. *The Narrative Universe*. Cresskill, NJ: Hampton Press.

Boulding, K. 1999. 'Nonviolence and Power in the Twentieth Century', in S. Zunes, L.R. Kurtz and S.B. Asher (eds), *Nonviolent Social Movements*, pp. 9–17. Oxford: Blackwell.

Clammer, J. 1995. *Difference and Modernity: Social Theory and Contemporary Japanese Society*. London and New York: Kegan Paul International.

Edwards, D. 2001. *The Compassionate Revolution: Radical Politics and Buddhism*. Totnes: Green Books, and New Delhi: The Viveka Foundation.

Eve, R.A., S. Horsfall and M.E. Lee (eds). 1997. *Chaos, Complexity and Sociology*. Thousand Oaks and London: SAGE.

Fontana, D. 1997. 'Authority in Buddhism and in Western Scientific Psychology', in J. Pickering (ed.), *The Authority of Experience: Essays in Buddhism and Psychology*, pp. 31–47. Richmond: Curzon Press.

Fox, M. 1995. 'A Mystical Cosmology: Toward a Postmodern Spirituality', in D.R. Griffin (ed.), *Sacred Interconnections: Postmodern Spirituality, Political Economy and Art*. Albany: State University of New York Press.

Giri, A.K. 2002a. *Building in the Margins of Shacks: The Vision and Projects of Habitat for Humanity*. New Delhi: Orient Longman.

———. 2002b. *Conversations and Transformations: Towards a New Ethics of Self and Society*. Lanham and Oxford: Lexington Books.

Goulet, D. 1995. *Development Ethics: A Guide to Theory and Practice*. London: Zed Books.

Graeber, D. 2004. *Fragments of an Anarchist Anthropology*. Chicago: Prickly Paradigm Press.

Harvey, D. 2002. *Spaces of Hope*. Edinburgh: Edinburgh University Press.

Holloway, J. 2002. *Change the World Without Taking Power: The Meaning of Revolution Today*. London: Pluto Press.

Huxley, A. 1994. *Island*. London: Flamingo.

Jacoby, R. 1999. *The End of Utopia: Politics and Culture in an Age of Apathy*. New York: Basic Books.

Jones, K. 2003. *The New Social Face of Buddhism*. Boston: Wisdom Publications.

Keown, D.V., C.S. Prebish and W.R. Husted (eds). 1998. *Buddhism and Human Rights*. Richmond: Curzon Press.

Kleinman, A., V. Das and M. Lock (eds). 1997. *Social Suffering*. Berkeley: University of California Press.

Loy, D. 2003. *The Great Awakening: A Buddhist Social Theory*. Boston: Wisdom Publications.

Lukes, S. (ed.). 1986. *Power*. New York: New York University Press.

Melucci, A. 1996. *Challenging Codes: Collective Action in the Information Age.* Cambridge: Cambridge University Press.

Monbiot, G. 2003. *The Age of Consent: A Manifesto for a New World Order.* London: Flamingo.

Morris, B. 1991. *Western Conceptions of the Individual.* Oxford: Berg.

Pickering, J. (ed.). 1997. *The Authority of Experience: Essays in Buddhism and Psychology.* Richmond: Curzon Press.

Queen, C., C. Prebish and D. Keown (eds). 2003. *Action Dharma: New Studies in Engaged Buddhism.* London: Routledge Curzon.

Rao, M. 1990. 'Gandhian Spirituality and Social Liberation', in M. Kappen (ed.), *Gandhi and Social Action Today*, pp. 26–42. New Delhi: Sterling Publishers.

Sahlins, M. 1996. 'The Sadness of Sweetness: The Native Anthropology of Western Cosmology', *Current Anthropology*, 37(3): 395–415.

Sivaraksa, Sulak. 1992. *Seeds of Peace: A Buddhist Vision for Renewing Society.* Berkeley: Parallax Press.

Skolimowski, H. 1992. *Living Philosophy: Eco-philosophy as a Tree of Life.* London: Arkana.

Smart, B. 1999. *Facing Modernity: Ambivalence, Reflexivity and Morality.* London and Thousand Oaks: SAGE.

Sturrock, J. 1998. *The Word from Paris: Essays on Modern French Thinkers.* London and New York: Verso.

Unger, R.M. 2001. *False Necessity: Anti-Necessitarian Social Theory in the Service of Radical Democracy.* London and New York: Verso.

van Staveren, I. 2001. *The Values of Economics: An Aristotelian Perspective.* London and New York: Routledge.

Afterword

CHITTA RANJAN DAS

It has been said that in the beginning whenever people of importance spoke or wrote about society, it was chiefly social philosophy, not sociology. The latter came to be in vogue much later and it came as a science. Inspirationally, it derived itself from the very conspicuous patterns of the so-called exact sciences. The physiocrats claimed that you can study society as exactly as physics and chemistry, and thus draw more certain conclusions. It has been pointed out that the expression 'social sciences' is found in a letter written by Josef Garat to Condorcet who adopted it in one of his works. It was then taken up by Auguste Comte and from him was handed down to the scholars of the twentieth century. Comte, it seems, was keenly given to the belief that 'it is possible to establish, with the help of science, the one and the only "correct" constitution, which will rapidly impose itself on all peoples, transcending national differences.' And, 'in the end, humanity will constitute a single society. The task of positivism, the only truly universal doctrine, is to help men progress along this path.' To supplement this statement, we may do well to recall the following from one of Comte's illustrated contemporaries, Henri de Saint-Simon: 'To colonize the world with the European race, superior to every other human race, to make the world accessible and habitable like Europe, such is the sort of enterprise by which the European parliament should continually keep Europe active and healthy.' Nevertheless, the incorporation of a scientific vein into man's interest to look into society was definitely a welcome—great—step forward.

And all along, there has been also non-conformity side by side with conformity. Though many times more people have conformed, there have always been those who have not succumbed to the obligations; they have thought differently, with longer tethers, and disturbed the accepted harmonies. More often than not, a few of these have also acted differently and have suffered in the hands of the existing hegemonies. New ideas have been brewed, new dimensions in thinking, and daring new values, opening up new horizons and vistas, and new indications and emphases; even new religions, movements and revolutions. These have been suppressed by the powers-that-be but the ferments have done their job and, to that extent, have served their purpose. All this has also contributed very substantially towards the growth of science and what has been called a scientific attitude. More and more people have been involved, values have changed, and there has steadily been a growing consensus all over the world to be willing to include more and yet more people in whatever have been taken as universal mappings and undertakings. Thanks, then, both to non-conformists and conformists; we of this world have become less shy of one another and more receptive; there has been a more sumptuous give-and-take. The process has always continued, whether all of us were conscious of it or not. We are growing and being drawn nearer to one another in spite of the despots; yes, really in spite of. The non-conformists have been examples of dissent, the ones who have differed, gone against the wind and, of course, against the establishments. Differing, they have helped immensely, always, in the unfolding of newer insights, unfolding and expanding and challenging all the various varieties of encapsulation.

The seats of concentrated learning in Europe started in the monasteries of yore. They were meant mainly for the initiates and catered almost exclusively to the theological preferences of the sects that ran them. They were, by necessity as it were, islands and the so-called fraternities. If we insist on naming them as universities, then our modern universities are, with greater justification, multiversities, willingly grown up into edifices having many mansions. Their very first calling is the opening-up of more and more windows. Sociology as a study of social life by its very inception, is recognizedly a part of university academics, though it can never afford to remain so in the traditional connotations. The whole world ought to be its field and it should always take care never to close itself into a fraternity. A student of society can never be rigidly a specialist in the hackneyed meaning of the term. In the words of Alfred Korzybski (1994: 427), 'To affect the organism-as-a-whole, organism-as-a-whole methods must be adopted.' Korzybski has also suggested as what he (ibid.: 310) calls 'many-valued logic.'

Methods, in whatever we study, pertains to what has come now to be known as methodology. But the importance of following a methodology should not tempt us to what may be a methodolatry. Methods are useful but they are not sacrosanct. According to Viktor Frankl, the logotherapist, science degenerates to scientism if we are almost morbidly keen about prescribed methods. In the same way, Frankl seems to warn us about psychologism, sociologism and the like. Thus, when one happens to become over-serious about methods, one does run the risk of deviating into grim sociologism. Then methods become frontal and conspire to take us away from our real footings. In the academic echelons, one's earnestness about a theme is sometimes assessed by what methods he uses. In the social sciences also, some people give greater importance to the methods employed than the theme or themes being actually dealt with. And a scientific methodology is even at times taken for having greater importance than a scientific attitude.

Once upon a time, during the Middle Ages, the geometrical method was the approved criterion. The vogue has changed in several ways till date, fortunately. Yet, some still continue to believe that only the scientific method can lead us to certainty. It is alleged that Martin Luther of the Protestant movement was greatly disturbed about Erasmus of Rotterdam because, to him, the latter was so uncertain. He (Liebrecht 1959: 204) protested once saying: 'What is more like accursedness and damnation than uncertainty, and what is more blessed than certainty?' As an antidote and decidedly more appropriate to the state of the world today, would be what Krishnamurty (Krishnamurty Foundation 1992) of India has observed, 'If you start with certainty, you end up with uncertainty.' The world is so one-dimensional and unbending today because people, especially those who are obsessed about their own fond idiosyncrasies and the methods accruing from them, would never agree to give way to other approaches and other primaries. Such people in the academics tend to take cover under a constructed understanding of unity, as India's Sri Aurobindo would characterize it. Instead, he would suggest a more wholesome way to decipher and go by a diversity in unity. The Unity is one and it has to be sought after in diverse ways. They may seem to be contrary to one another but they are complementary. This is the right scientific method and it will give us the real insights.

The foregoing introductory asides are in way of a context upon which I shall now pass on to the papers included in the collection and do some loud thinking. Quite a number of essays have followed the more familiar methods, yet some others are exceptions in an enlightening manner. A few are studded with quotations. It is, of course, not at all a crime to corroborate with supporting quotations a point one wants to emphasize upon; yet, beyond a certain frequency, it may also seem that a writer is not fully sure about what he wants to say and hence thinks he can appear more convincing to the prospective readers by re-enforcing himself with quotations. One has but to remember that on occasions as these, one has to be parsimonious enough because one cannot usually, without risk, just pick up a few lines from another source which is basically a part of another whole frame of reference.

As one goes through the essays one by one, in no time one forgets what one may call a lacuna in the compilation, and really wonders at the catholicity with which the editor planned to choose and use the individual papers. At first sight, they may seem to smack of like square pegs put together in a round hole; yet, before long one does come to realize that there are all-through hidden connections, the sure relevances, and you feel you are really on the side of the editor. So much variety and yet so reasonably threaded together as a uniting gestalt. The fields do vary, the perspectives disturb all your established notions of hypothetical foundations; nevertheless, you are drawn nearer and nearer, as it were, and are soon ready to look at things differently. And after that, almost each presentation begins to make you realize the entire scope of the study of society come of age; nay, the entire gamut of human seekings come of age.

In addition to the mainstream essays, that is, essays that one would generally expect in a compilation like this, we have exceptions like contributions on Erasmus, Meister Eckhart, Gandhi and the Zapatismo of Mexico. Erasmus of the sixteenth century wanted to convince his contemporary rulers how foolish and devastating it was for people when the kingdoms dabbled in warfare. Through his writings, he was in several ways on the side of the conscience of Europe when Martin Luther was all thunder with his new movement about the worship of God. The language of the former's protest was satire and deep wisdom as is so imaginatively brought out in his *Morie Encomium*. Meister Eckhart (1260–1328), in his time occupying a very high post in the papal empire, incurred the displeasure of the hegemony because he delivered his sermons in the vernacular as well as disrespected the sacred tradition by 'educating the uneducated'. Eckhart had submitted, explaining his position: 'If one does not speak to the uneducated about learned things, no one would ever become educated.' He was also condemned for what was described by the authorities as 'his ardour for justice'. May we say that he was brought to book for having taken the message of Christ in earnest and this was, perhaps, what worried the functionaries in the Christian institutions. Eckhart once described Christ as 'the Social in the Human Being'.

The story of all real sociology is one of breaking open the boundaries. The discipline was originally bound strictly to its specific lines and limitations and it is great that transgressions have been happening all the time. It is becoming increasingly clearer that society and people matter more than the study of society. The older definitions and contours are fast changing and there are more and more people who are less shy and hence willing to transgress the boundaries. More mature days are in the offing and the recluses so far working in the laboratories are becoming more courageous. Yes, courage, more than anything else, always helps us ask questions and rewrite our canons of inquiry. Intellectuals are rethinking and, as it were, from within; they are more ready to revise their roles. Albert Camus had once made a remark that the intellectual's role will be to say that the king is naked when he is and not to go into raptures over his imaginary trappings. And look, all around now there are hegemonies, kings all round who are visibly naked! The intellectual's laboratory has now to come down in proximity to people where they really are, move and have their beings, and suffer all the time waiting for an appropriate remedy. The academics could not as a rule do that. Shri Ramakrishna of India had once observed that 'Some people climb the seven floors of a building and cannot get down.' But some can, he did hope, really climb and then come down. They are always of greater worth.

Universities, as they happen to function as a model now, are a Western development, and their counterparts, as they have come gradually to be structured in the East, are more or less imitations. To substantially serve humankind today they ought to transform themselves into multiversities, in the fullest meaning of the term. And this multiversity now is the entire globe and the entire humankind. Bacon once ushered in a new stance in Western thought when he said that knowledge is power. No doubt knowledge is power even now, and is valid for the whole of us as regional expressions of humankind. But power for what? Power, so derived from knowledge and yet more knowledge, has become arrogant in the long run. It has fallen into the hands of the wrong persons: state power, money power, military power, power of the many shades of vested interest, agencies of exploitation and the like. There is so much of deprivation, indifference, parochial pursuits of the ego and of the local. The realm of the social sciences have mostly been won over and tamed by those in power. To come back to Erasmus again, learning must always go together with piety—*eruditio* must create more occasions for *pietas*.

Benedict Spinoza has spoken about *potestas* and *potentia*—words that in Latin mean power. They are different in their import because they point out to different connotations. The former is functionally the urge to possess by bossing it over others, and the latter reminds us about the potentials inherent in every human being, the many possibilities of flowering up and unfolding, if freedom is the climate in which it develops. According to Spinoza, love is the mediating link between knowledge and power. Love of humanity, love of the world, a deep faith in the unending possibilities of individuals as well as the collectives. This calls for a higher consciousness that all knowledge should congenially aim at. To Sri Aurobindo, a higher consciousness, as a rule, has to prove itself in the world. It never runs away and can afford to prove itself to be an asset of the world.

But the changeover is not that easy as the wonderful words and references may suggest. There will be many-a-restraint, obstacles and oppositions, both from without and within. Hence, those who have chosen love have been men of protest. The world as it is will always be ready to put hurdles on the way of those who have opted for a world as it might be. The world changers, therefore, have faced persecution all the way. Yet, they have continued undeterred. In a world of obedience and servitude of so many shades, they have gone against the stream. In this context the work of Etienne de la Boétie (1530–62) of France is quite significant. He was a contemporary of Machiavelli and pre-ceded Martin Luther by only a few years. The span of his life was only thirty-two years and he wrote his magnum opus *Psychology of Obedience: A Treatise on Voluntary Servitude* when he was studying at the university and was only eighteen. The mode of protest, he discusses as remedies, has a great relevance in our day. de la Boétie's critics have even drawn a linking line right from him to Tolstoy and Gandhi, and we can, if we want, trace him in the current movements of struggling human groups when these rise in protest against establishments all over.

And, now, a couple of things in peroration. As has become so very actual now, each discipline has appreciably developed a vocabulary of its own; and scholars, in whatever they produce, have now to put them down in a singularly specific garb. It has, of course, an advantage of its own and the vicars would wish that it should be so. The fraternities are also happier and more at home within the structural isolations. Yet, having the social sciences as our area, our aim is to percolate and reach people as wide and yet wider as possible. This becomes even more urgent if our real intention is a renovation and a change in the vantage points. To make more and more people involved in whatever we intend to offer, they must understand the language we use in our presentations. It seems that those among the very reputed who were aware that the foremost thing was to keep on a dialogue and make more and more people concerned, have shown no scruples in using a non-technical language. We have in mind the examples of C. Wright Mills, Erich Fromm, Abraham Maslow and Viktor Frankl. One wishes that more papers in the compilation were able to do that.

The next point is: all revolution and paradigmatic departures should be accompanied by a personal revolution also. Because to be and not merely to know is the real thing, the real catalyzer, as Sri Aurobindo would say. Brilliant scholars with the brilliance of giants and with no effort to live what one professes intellectually are the 'sanyasins of the intellect', as he has described them. These brilliant *sanyasins* suffer in spite of all the glory they have earned for themselves, by clinging to the idols of the caves. The light that they have been instrumental in disseminating for the sake of the world, this home of ours, ought to help us stand erect and fight the darkness around here. Only a personal revolution would give us real backbones. *Jnana*, knowledge, becomes real and mature only when it is translated to *karma*, that is, action, both individual and corporate.

I congratulate the editor and the contributors for having brought out such a worthy compilation. It does have a liberating effect and is sure to disturb the many grooves that scholarly enthusiasms have usually constructed for the traditional stalwarts.

References

Korzybski, Alfred. 1994. *Science and Sanity*. Engelwood, NJ: Institute of General Semantics.

Krishnamurty Foundation. 1992. *The Last Talks*. India: Krishnamurty Foundation.

Liebrecht, Walter (ed.). 1959. *Religion and Culture*. New York: Harper.

About the Editor and Contributors

The Editor

Ananta Kumar Giri is currently on the faculty of Madras Institute of Development Studies, Chennai, India and has worked and taught in many universities in India and abroad including Free University, Amsterdam, University of Kentucky, Aalborg University, Denmark and Albert Ludwigs Universität, Freiburg, Germany where he was a Humboldt Fellow (2006–2007). He has an abiding interest in social movements and cultural change, criticism, creativity and contemporary dialectics of transformations, theories of self, culture and society, and ethics in management and development. Dr Giri has written more than a dozen books in Oriya and English. Among his previous books are: *Global Transformations: Postmodernity and Beyond* (1998), *Sameekhya o Purodrusti* [Criticism and the Vision of the Future, 1999], *Conversations and Transformations: Toward a New Ethics of Self and Society* (2002); *Building in the Margins of Shacks: The Vision and Projects of Habitat for Humanity* (2002); *Reflections and Mobilizations: Dialogues with Movements and Voluntary Organizations* (2004); *Self-development and Social Transformations? The Vision and Practice of the Self-study Mobilization of Swadhyaya* (2008); *Mochi o Darshanika* [The Cobbler and the Philosopher, 2009] *Rethinking Social Transformation: Criticism and Creativity at the Turn of the Millennium* (editor, 2001); *A Moral Critique of Development: In Search of Global Responsibilities* (co-editor, 2003); *Creative Social Research: Rethinking Theories and Methods* (editor, 2004) and *Religion of Development, Development of Religion* (co-editor, 2004).

Address: Dr Ananta Kumar Giri, Madras Institute of Development Studies, Adyar, Chennai-600020, India.
Emails: aumkrishna@yahoo.com/ananta@mids.ac.in.
Website: www.mids.ac.in/ananta.htm

The Contributors

Binod Kumar Agarwala is Professor of Philosophy at North-Eastern Hill University, Shillong, India. Prior to this, he had been teaching for more than two decades at Lucknow University, Lucknow. He is actively engaged in research in critical philosophy of Kant while political philosophy and philosophical hermeneutics are also his major areas of interest. He has published widely in reputed journals such as *Journal of Indian Council of Philosophical Research, Sandhân,* and *Indian Philosophical Quarterly.*

Address: Department of Philosophy, North-Eastern Hill University, Shillong, India.
Email: binodagarwala@rediffmail.com

Abdullahi Ahmed An-Naim is a Professor at Emory Law School, Atlanta, GA, USA. He is the author of *African Constitutionalism and the Role of Islam* (2006); *Toward an Islamic Reformation: Civil Liberties, Human Rights* and *International Law* and editor of *Human Rights in Cross-cultural Perspectives: Quest for Consensus* (1992); *Islamic Family Law in a Changing World: A Global Resource Books* (2002). He has also published articles and chapters on human rights, constitutionalism, Islamic law and politics. An-Naim directed three major projects from Emory Law School: one on women access to, and control over, land in seven African countries (www.law.emory.edu/WAL), the second, a global study of the theory and practice of Islamic Family Law (www.law.emory.edu/ifl) and the third, a fellowship programme in Islam and Human Rights (www.law.emory.edu/IHR). His current project is a book manuscript, *The Future: Secularism from an Islamic Perspective* (www.law.emory.edu/fs).

Address: School of Law, Emory University, 1301 Clifton Road, Atlanta, GA 30322, USA.
Email: abduh46@law.emory.edu

Bernard Adeney-Risakotta was born in China of English and American parents. Bernard finished high school in Taiwan and completed his B.A. from University of Wisconsin in Asian Studies and Literature. His second degree, a B.D. (Hons.) is from University of London, specializing in Asian Religions and Ethics. His Ph.D. is from the Graduate Theological Union in cooperation with UC Berkeley, in Religion and Society. From 1982 until 1991 he taught at the GTU. Since 1991 he has lived in Indonesia, teaching at several universities, including Duta

Wacana Christian University, Gadjah Mada University and the State Islamic University. Currently, he is Director of a cooperative, inter-religious doctoral programme in religious studies between these three universities. He has been a Fellow at University of Cambridge and International Institute of Asian Studies, Amsterdam. His books include *Strange Virtues: Ethics in a Multicultural World*. Currently, he is writing on Modernity, Religion and Culture in the Social Imaginary of Southeast Asia.

Address: Pondok Tali Rasa, Jl. Dumung 100, CT VIII, Karanggayam, Yogyakarta, 55281, Indonesia.
Email: bernfar@indosat.net.id

Frank R. Ankersmit teaches intellectual history and philosophy of history at Groningen University. He has published widely in the fields of aesthetics, political philosophy and philosophy of history. His most recent book is *Sublime Historical Experience* (2005). In 2006 he published, in Dutch, a book on the refeudalization of Western democracy and its dangers.

Address: Department of History, University of Groningen, Groningen, The Netherlands.
Email: f.r.ankersmit@let.rug.nl

Christian Bartolf (born 1960 in Luebeck, Germany), political and educational scientist, counsellor for conscientious objectors, founder and director of the Gandhi Information Center (http://home.snafu. de/mkgandhi), organiser of the campaign for the Manifesto against conscription and the military system (http://www.themanifesto.info), author and editor of following English language books: *Tolstoy and Gandhi* (1996), *Letter to a Hindoo. Taraknath Das, Leo Tolstoy and Mahatma Gandhi (1997), Hermann Kallenbach, Mahatma Gandhi's friend in South Africa* (together with Isa Sarid, 1997), *The Breath of My Life. The Correspondence of Mahatma Gandhi (India) and Bart de Ligt (Holland) on War and Peace* (2000), *Manifesto against Conscription and the Military System* (2001) and several articles.

Address: Zinzendorfstr. 8, 10555 Berlin, Germany. The address of the Gandhi Information Center: Postfach (P.O. Box) 210109, 10501 Berlin, Germany.
Email: bartolf@snafu.de

Robert Bernasconi is the Moss Chair of Excellence in Philosophy at the University of Memphis. He is the author of two books on *Heidegger – The Question of Language in Heidegger's History of Being* and *Heidegger* *in Question*. Granta Press published his *How To Read Sartre* in 2006. He is the author of numerous essays on Hegel, twentieth century European philosophy, and social and political philosophy. In recent years he has worked extensively on the history of race thinking. He edited *Race* and with Kristie Dotson *Race, Hybridity and Miscegenation*.

Address: Dept of Philosophy, Clement Hall 331, University of Memphis, Memphis, TN 38152, USA.
Email: rbernscn@memphis.edu

Jose Jowel Canuday has been studying and writing about the dynamics of conflicts, displacements, violence and Muslims, Christians, indigenous peoples' and state relations in the southern Philippine island of Mindanao. He was recently a South-East Asian visiting fellow at the Refugee Studies Centre of the Department of International Development, University of Oxford in the United Kingdom. Currently, he teaches anthropology at the University of the Philippines Mindanao in Davao City, his home-base. He is also affiliated with the Mindanawon Institute for Cultural Dialogue, a centre for academics and professionals with special interest in enriching the spectrum of Mindanao studies.

Address: 11-3 Padre Gomez Street, 8000 Davao City, The Philippines.
Email: signpen_jc2@yahoo.com

John Clammer is Director of International Courses and Special Advisor to the Rector at the United Nations University. He has previously held positions at the University of Hull and the National University of Singapore and visiting positions at the Universities of Tokyo, Oxford, Kent, Essex, Buenos Aires, Weimar, the Australian National University, Murdoch University and the Institute of South-East Asian Studies, Singapore. His work has focussed geographically on South-East Asia and Japan and thematically on contemporary social theory, the sociology of development, urban sociology, the sociology of art and culture and the sociology of religion in Asia. Amongst his major interests is that of the dialogue between Western social and cultural theory and Asian societies. His more recent books include *Japan and its Others: Globalization, Difference and the Critique of Modernity* (2001); *Diaspora and Identity: The Sociology of Culture in Southeast Asia* (2002) and *Diaspora and Belief* (2008).

Email: johnclammer@gmail.com

Fred R. Dallmayr is Packey J. Dee Professor of Political Theory at University of Notre Dame, Indiana, USA and is the author of many moving works such as *Alternative Visions* (1998), *Achieving our World* (2001), *Dialogue Among Civilizations* (2002), *Peace Talks—Who Will Listen* (2004) and *Small Wonder: Global Power and its Discontents* (2005).

Address: Fred Dallmayr, Department of Government, 746 Flanner Hall, University of Notre Dame, IN 46556, USA.

Email: Dallmayr.1@nd.edu

Chitta Ranjan Das based in Bhubaneswar, Orissa, India is an educator, writer and thinker and has now written and translated more than two hundred books on different aspects of our collective human journey and strivings for transformations. Some of his books are: *Jeevana Vidyalaya* [The School of Life], *Sukara O Socrates* [Socrates and the Pig], *Purna Ekatara Yoga* [Towards A Yoga of Fuller Unity], *Sataku Sata Ma* [Truly A Mother], *Bira Yodha Kari* [Being a Heroic Warrior], *Letters from the Forest, A Glimpse into Oriya Literature, Kristen Kold: A Revolutionary in Education and A Pioneer of Danish Folk High School Movement*, and *Manaku Stiri Besa Kari* [Making Our Mind a Woman]. Now in his mid-eighties, Das continues his creative strivings in literature, education and social transformation.

Address: 83/A Bapujee Nagar, Bhubaneswar-751009, Orissa, India.

Email: sikshasandhan@gmail.com

S.N. Eisenstadt is Rose Isaacs Professor Emeritus of Sociology at the Hebrew University of Jerusalem, where he has been a faculty member since 1946 and a Senior Research Fellow at the Van Leer Jerusalem Institute. He has served as visiting professor at numerous universities, including Harvard, Stanford, M.I.T., Chicago, Michigan, Washington, Oslo, Zurich and Vienna, Hong Kong. He has received numerous honorary doctorates and awards for his outstanding contribution to social sciences and humanities. He has published more than dozen books in a life of remarkable creativity which include *The Political System of Empires* (1963), *Fundamentalism, Sectarianism and Revolutions (* 2000), *Comparative Civilizations and Multiple Modernities (*2003), and *Explorations in Jewish Historical Experience: The Civilizational Dimension (*2004).

Address: The Van Leer Jerusalem Institute, P.O. Box 4070, Jerusalem 91040, Israel.

Email: miriamb@vanleer.org.il

Johan Galtung, born 1930, founded the Peace Research Institute in 1959 in Oslo. Galtung is one of the leading pioneers of peace and conflict transformation in theory and practice. He has played an active role in preventing violence in 45 major conflicts around the world over the past four decades, and is author of the United Nation's first ever manual for trainers and participants on *Conflict Transformation by Peaceful Means: The TRANSCEND Approach* (UNDP 2000). Furthermore he has published over 100 books which have been translated into several languages. In 1987 he received the Right Livelihood Award (The Alternative Nobel Peace Prize) for his tireless work for peace, in both theory and practice. He has been awarded honorary doctorate by many universities around the world and have been visiting professors at Princeton University, Universities of Hawai'i, Witten/Herdecke, Tromso, Alicante, and Ritsumeikan University.

Address: 7 Cret de neige F-01210 VERSONNEX France.
Email: 110125.1244@compuserve.com

Han Sang-Jin is Professor of Sociology at Seoul National University (SNU), Seoul, Korea. He teaches social theory, political sociology and cultural developments while conducting various researches on historical transformations and the role of the middle classes. He has advocated a theory of the 'middling grassroots' and initiated numerous public debates in Korea. He is the author of many books on critical social theory, including Habermas and the Korean Debate (1998), and has written numerous articles. As Visiting Professor, he taught at Columbia University in New York, EHESS in Paris and Beijing University in China.

Address: Department of Sociology, Seoul National University, Seoul, Korea.
Email: hansjin@snu.ac.kr.

Sapir Handelman is a Post Doctoral Fellow at Harvard University, Cambridge, Massachusetts and a visiting scholar at the Walter Eucken Institute, Freiburg, Germany. He holds B.Sc. in engineering, M.A. in economics and a Ph.D. in philosophy from Tel-Aviv University. His dissertation, *The Ethical Limits of Manipulation from a Liberal Perspective,* concerns the phenomenon of manipulation and the challenges it raises to the liberal philosophy and its derivatives (such as methodology of the social sciences and the optimal conduct of society). Dr Handelman is currently working mainly on two research projects:

(a) 'Manipulative behavior and freedom of choice'—an interdisciplinary research project which examines manipulation as a case study of essential questions upon the decent social order;

(b) 'Between Hayek and Machiavelli'—an examination of the possible relationships between the works of Hayek and Machiavelli.

Address: Sapir Handelman, Simtat Hanegev 9A, Kiriyat Ata 28203, Israel 28203.

Emails: handelm@fas.harvard.edu/sapirhan@zahav.net.il

Mark Lindley was born in Washington DC in 1937. His writings on topics related to Mahatma Gandhi have included *Gandhiji ko yeh kaise wishwasgaya ki antarjatiya vivahse, jati pratha ka unmulan karna hoga* (National Gandhi Museum, New Delhi, 1998),*Gandhi and the World Today* (1998), *A Recent American View* (University of Kerala), 'Gandhi's', Rhetoric (in *Journal of Literature und Aesthetics*, 1999), *Gandhi and Humanism* (3rd edition, 2005), J.C. Kumarappa, *Mahatma Gandhi's Economist* (2006), 'Globalisierung' und Gewalt, (in *Aufktarung and Kritik*, 2007), and *Gandhi as We Have Known Him* (with Lavanana Gora; 2nd edition, 2008). Dr Lindley is known also as the author of a great number of papers in musicology and has taught at leading universities in England, Germany, Turkey and China as well as in the USA and India.

Address : C/o Samskar Ashram Vidyalam, Sanskar, Kotiah Camp, Varni, Nizamabad, Andhra Pradesh-503201, India.

Email: Lindley@born.edu.tr.

Dietmar Mieth is Professor of Theological Ethics and Social ethics at the Faculty of Catholic Theology, University of Tubingen. He has a special interest in religious experience in medieval mysticism, spirituality and lifestyle with specific reference to the work of Meister Eckhart, narrative ethics and bioethics. He was a Member of the Working Group of the Bioethics Committee of the European Council for the Embry Protection Report. He has published 27 books as monographs, 50 books as editors, and more than 500 articles.

Address: Faculty of Catholic Theology, University of Tubingen, Liebermeisterstr. 12, D-72076 Tubingen, Germany.

Email: dietmar.mieth@uni-tuebingen.de

Mateo Mier y Terán G.C. was a researcher at El Collegio, Mexico City, Mexico and is currently completing his doctorate in development studies at University of Sussex. He has done fieldwork in the Chiapas since 1998 and has carried out research with Autonomous Zapatista communities. He has written a theses on the process of economic and sociopolitical transformation and organization in Altamirano, Chiapas. He is also involved in fair trade organization, at the moment is starting a net of honey consumers with fair deals for the producer.

Address: Cda De la cerca 62-2, San Angel, CP 01060, Mexico City, Mexico.
Emails: matuteom@hotmail.com/mateomt@yahoo.com

Mrinal Miri is an engaging philosopher and thinker and has been the Director of Indian Institute of Advanced Studies, Shimla and Vice-Chancellor of North-Eastern Hill University, Shillong where he has taught philosophy for decades. He is also the author of *Identity and the Moral Life* (2003).

Address: A-39, South Extension, Part- I, New Delhi-110 049.
Email: mirimrinal@hotmail.com

Godabarisha Mishra is Professor of Philosophy, University of Madras and presently Member-Secretary, Indian Council of Philosophical Research, New Delhi.

Address: Member Secretary, Indian Council of Philosophical Research, 'Darshan Bhavan', 36, Tughlakabad Institutional Area (Near Batra Hospital), M.B. Road, New Delhi-110 062, India.
Email: gmisra19@hotmail.com

Jan Nederveen Pieterse is Mellichamp Professor, Global Studies and Sociology at the Global and International Studies, University of California, Santa Barbara. He specializes in transnational sociology, globalization, development studies and intercultural studies. He teaches and lectures in many countries such as Ghana, Germany, Indonesia, Japan, Pakistan, South Africa, Sweden, Sri Lanka, Thailand. He is associate editor of *Futures, European Journal of Social Theory, Ethnicities, Globalizations, Third Text* and Fellow of the World Academy of Art and Science. Recent books include *Pants for an Octopus: Ethnicities, Global Multiculturalism* (in preparation), *Globalization or Empire?* (2004), *Global Mélange: Globalization and Culture* (2003) & *Development Theory: Deconstructions/Reconstructions* (2001) & *Empire and Emancipation: Power and Liberation on a World Scale* (1989; 1990; 1990 Award of the Netherlands Society of Sciences).

Address: Jan Nederveen Pieterse, Mellichamp Professor, Global Studies and Sociology, Global and International Studies, University of California, Santa Barbara, CA 93106-7065
Email: jnp@global.ucsb.edu

Kanchana Mahadevan is currently Reader and Head of the Department of Philosophy, University of Mumbai. Her areas of specialization include continental philosophy, feminist theory, political thought and aesthetics. Dr Mahadevan's doctoral work is an examination of Jürgen Habermas's theory of communicative action in the context of Kantian ethics. She is especially interested in relating gender to both, Western and Indian, thought and culture. She is also working on issues related to the philosophy of environment in the context of environmental problems in India.

Address: Dr Kanchana Mahadevan, Department of Philosophy, University of Mumbai, Vidyanagari, Kalina, Santacruz (E) Mumbai-400098, India.
Email: kanchmaha@hotmail.com

Akop P. Nazaretyan is a Senior Researcher at the Institute for Oriental Studies, Russian Academy of Sciences and is a Full Professor at International University (Dubna), Moscow State University and Russian Academy of State Service. He has published more than 250 papers and seven books including *Intelligence in the Universe: Origins, Formation and Prospects* (1991) and *Civilization Crises within the Context of Big History: Self-Organization, Psychology & Forecasts* (2001; 2nd edition, 2004).

Address: Rossoshanskaya – 1 – 1 – 688. Moscow, Russia, 117535.
Email: anazaret@mtu-net.ru

Philip Quarles van Ufford is attached as Emeritus to the Department of Anthropology of the Vrije Universiteit Amsterdam. He has widely published on issues of religion and development; the vicissitudes of development policy practices and problems of organisation. Currently, he is preparing a book concerning the relationships between different religious communities over a longer period of time in Central Java, and a volume about the production of order and chaos in development policy processes.

Address: Minervaplein 5-1, 1077TG, Amsterdam, The Netherlands.
Email: flipq@dds.nl

Herbert Reid is Professor of Political Science at the University of Kentucky where he has also served as Director of Environmental Studies and Director of the UK Appalachian Center. He has been an active member of the Committee on Social Theory and serves on the Editorial Board for *Human Studies*. Along with Betsy Taylor and Wolfgang Natter, he served as Co-Director for the UK Rockefeller Humanities Fellowship Program, 2001–2005. As a political theorist he has contributed to such journals as *Theory and Society* and *Dialectical Anthropology*. His recent articles have appeared in *Rethinking Marxism, New Political Science* and *Ethics and the Environment*. Currently, he is at work with co-author Betsy Taylor on a book to be entitled *Body Place Commons: The Life-world Logic of Democratic Republics and the Global Justice Movement*.

Address: 3337 Wood Valley Ct., Lexington KY 40502, USA.
Email: hgreid01@uky.edu

Piet Strydom teaches Sociology at University College Cork, Ireland. Having studied and worked as journalist, social researcher and academic in South Africa, he came as exile from the Apartheid regime to Europe where he consolidated his relation with neo-Frankfurt critical theory. His most recent publications include *Discourse and Knowledge* (2000), *Risk, Environment and Society* (2002), and *Philosophies of Social Science* (2003) edited and introduced with Gerard Delanty, and articles in journals such as the *European Journal of Social Theory, Current Sociology, Sociological Theory, Social Epistemology* and *Philosophy and Social Criticism*. He is at present editing a Special Issue of the *European Journal of Social Theory* on the theme of 'Social Theory after the Cognitive Revolution: Varieties of Contemporary Cognitive Sociology', and a book provisionally entitled *Towards a New Cognitive Sociology* is in progress.

Address: Department of Sociology, University College Cork, Cork, Ireland.
Email: p.strydom@ucc.ie

Helena Tagesson is currently completing a masters degree in International Relations at Gothenburg University. She is international coordinator for Attac Sweden since 2002 and has worked extensively with the European Attac network and the European Social Forum. She is a member of green think tank Cogito and of the management body of Globalverkstan, a three-semester professional training programme for project managers in the social movement and NGO fields. She is a student of Zen master Thich Nhat Hanh, facilitates a meditation group in his tradition in Gothenburg, and is currently writing a thesis on his vision of engaged Buddhism in Vietnam. Her areas of interest include trade and development issues, and new models for political dialogue, conflict resolution and democracy in the age of globalization.

Address: Sankt Olofsgatan 38, 41728 Goteborg, Sweden.
Email: helena.tagesson@gmail.com

Betsy Taylor is a cultural anthropologist whose recent research is on emerging forms of civil society and social movements, community-based natural resource management, place-based planning, globalization and sustainability. Her scholarly writings engage questions of environmental imaginaries and identities, the construction of identity (gender, class, place, ethnicity, religious), the constitution of public space, regimes of knowledge and the articulation of local/professionalized knowledges, participatory action research and public involvement strategies. Betsy Taylor is currently Senior Research Scholar with the Alliance for Social, Political, Ethical and Cultural Theory, at the Virginia State and Polytechnic Institute. She has also served as Research Director for the Appalachian Center and on the faculty of the Social Theory program at the University of Kentucky. She has worked on projects for community-driven, integrated development and participatory action research in Appalachia and India—including health, agriculture, forestry, culture and environmental stewardship. In addition to numerous scholarly articles, she is co-author (with Herbert Reid) of *Recovering the Commons: Democracy, Place, and Global Justice* (University of Illinois Press, 2010).

Address: 3337 Wood Valley Ct, Lexington, KY 40502.
Email: betsy.taylor@gmail.com

Thanh-Dam Truong is Associate Professor in Women/Gender and Development Studies at the Institute of Social Studies. She was one of the first scholars to have provided an academic analysis of the problem of sex tourism in South-East Asia from the perspective of international political economy. Her work has been translated into several languages (Dutch, Japanese, Indonesian and Spanish). She has published widely on subjects such as human development, gender research and international migration, human trafficking and organized crime, and the gender of transition. Her current work addresses the intersection between transnationalized human security, development ethics, the ethics of care and Buddhist epistemology.

Address: Institute of Social Studies, P.O. Box 29776 2502 LT,
The Hague, The Netherlands.
Email: truong@iss.nl

Stellan Vinthagen is a Senior Lecturer at the Department of Peace and Development Research (Padrigu), Gothenburg University, Sweden, and a Visiting Lecturer in England and India. His Ph.D. research (2005) develops a sociology of non-violent action. His area of interest includes as well resistance strategies, globalization, social change, power theory and social movements. Since the 1980 he has been a movement activist and teacher in conflict transformation and civil disobedience. Stellan has written two books, published several book chapters and articles and regularly presented research papers. His latest peace activism of non-violent direct disarmament was in England against the Trident nuclear submarines.

Address: Stellan Vinthagen, Sandeslätt 11, SE 424 36 Angered, Sweden.
Email: stellan.vinthagen@padrigu.gu.se

Felix Wilfred is the Founder-Director of Asian Center for Cross-Cultural Studies, Chennai and edits the influential theological journal *Concilium*.

Address: Asian Center for Cross-Cultural Studies, 40/6A, Pnayurkuppam Road, Panayur, Chennai-600 119, India.
Email: felixwilfred@gmail.com

Index